MANAGERIAL ACCOUNTING

Tools for Business Decision Making

Jerry J. Weygandt PhD, CPA

Arthur Andersen Alumni Professor of Accounting
University of Wisconsin
Madison, Wisconsin

Donald E. Kieso PhD, CPA

KPMG Peat Marwick Emeritus Professor
  of Accountancy
Northern Illinois University
DeKalb, Illinois

Paul D. Kimmel PhD, CPA

Associate Professor of Accounting
University of Wisconsin—Milwaukee
Milwaukee, Wisconsin

John Wiley & Sons, Inc.

New York • Chichester • Weinheim
Brisbane • Singapore • Toronto

Dedication
To Enid Weygandt, Matthew, Erin and Finn Berge, and Lia

To Donna Kieso, Douglas and Jennifer Kieso, and Debra and Michael Sondgeroth Morgan, Cole, and Erin

To Merlynn Kimmel, Croix and Marais

ACQUISITIONS EDITOR   Susan Elbe
SENIOR DEVELOPMENT EDITOR   Nancy Perry
SENIOR MARKETING MANAGER   Rebecca Hope
FULL SERVICE PRODUCTION MANAGER   Jeanine Furino
SENIOR DESIGNER   Kevin Murphy
PHOTO EDITOR   Nicole Horlacher
ILLUSTRATION EDITOR   Anna Melhorn
PRODUCTION SERVICES   Elm Street Publishing Services, Inc.
COVER ART AND TEXT DESIGN   Kenny Beck
COVER PHOTO   Powerstock Photos/Index Stock Photography, Inc.

This book was set in New Aster by York Graphic Services and printed and bound by Von Hoffmann Press. The cover was printed by Phoenix Color Corp.

This book is printed on acid-free paper.

Library of Congress Cataloging-in-Publication Data
Weygandt, Jerry J.
    Managerial accounting: tools for business decision making/Jerry
Weygandt, Donald E. Kieso, Paul D. Kimmel.
        p.   cm.
    Includes index.
    ISBN 0-471-34588-1 (cloth)
    1. Managerial accounting. I. Kieso, Donald E.   II. Kimmel, Paul
D. III. Title
HF5657.4.W49   1999
658.15'11—dc21   99-11249
                                                        CIP

ISBN 0-471-34588-1

Printed in the United States of America

10 9 8 7 6 5 4 3 2 1

ABOUT THE AUTHORS

Jerry J. Weygandt, PhD, CPA, is Arthur Andersen Alumni Professor of Accounting at the University of Wisconsin—Madison. He holds a PhD in accounting from the University of Illinois. Articles by Professor Weygandt have appeared in *Accounting Review, Journal of Accounting Research,* the *Journal of Accountancy,* and other professional journals. These articles have examined such financial reporting issues as accounting for price-level adjustments, pensions, convertible securities, stock option contracts, and interim reports. He is a member of the American Accounting Association, the American Institute of Certified Public Accountants, and the Wisconsin Society of Certified Public Accountants. He has served on numerous committees of the American Accounting Association and as a member of the editorial board of the *Accounting Review*. In addition, he is actively involved with the American Institute of Certified Public Accountants and has been a member of the Accounting Standards Executive Committee (AcSEC) of that organization. He has served on the FASB task force that examined the reporting issues related to "accounting for income taxes" and is presently a trustee of the Financial Accounting Foundation, director of M & I Bank of Southern Wisconsin, and director of the Dean Foundation. Professor Weygandt has received the Chancellor's Award for Excellence in Teaching and was recognized as one of the top 50 instructors at the University of Wisconsin—Madison. He also has served as President and Secretary-Treasurer of the American Accounting Association. Recently he received the Wisconsin Institute of CPA's Outstanding Educator's Award and the Lifetime Achievement Award.

Donald E. Kieso, PhD, CPA, received his bachelor's degree from Aurora University and his doctorate in accounting from the University of Illinois. He has served as chairman of the Department of Accountancy and is currently the KPMG Peat Marwick Emeritus Professor of Accountancy at Northern Illinois University. He has public accounting experience with Price Waterhouse & Co. (San Francisco and Chicago) and Arthur Andersen & Co. (Chicago) and research experience with the Research Division of the American Institute of Certified Public Accountants (New York). He is a recipient of NIU's Teaching Excellence Award and four Golden Apple Teaching Awards. He has served as a member of the Board of Directors of the Illinois CPA Society, the Board of Governors of the American Accounting Association's Administrators of Accounting Programs Group, and AACSB's Accounting Accreditation and Visitation Committees, the State of Illinois Comptroller's Commission, as Secretary-Treasurer of the Federation of Schools of Accountancy, and as Secretary-Treasurer of the American Accounting Association. Professor Kieso is currently serving as Chairman of the Board of Trustees and Executive Committee of Aurora University, the Boards of Directors of Castle BancGroup, Inc., the Sandwich State Bank, George Williams College, and Valley West Community Hospital. From 1989 to 1993 he served as a charter member of the national Accounting Education Change Commission. In 1988 he received the Outstanding Accounting Educator Award from the Illinois CPA Society; in 1992 he received the FSA's Joseph A. Silvoso Award of Merit and the NIU Foundation's Humanitarian Award for Service to Higher Education; and in 1995 he received a Distinguished Service Award from the Illinois CPA Society.

Paul D. Kimmel, PhD, CPA, received his bachelor's degree from The University of Minnesota and his doctorate in accounting from the University of Wisconsin. He is an Associate Professor at the University of Wisconsin—Milwaukee. He has public accounting experience with Deloitte & Touche (Minneapolis). He is the recipient of the UWM School of Business Advisory Council Teaching Award, the Reggie Taite Excellence in Teaching Award, a three-time winner of the Outstanding Teaching Assistant Award at the University of Wisconsin, and a recipient of the Elijah Watts Sells Award for Honorary Distinction for his results on the CPA exam. He is a member of the American Accounting Association and has published articles in *Accounting Review, Accounting Horizons, Issues in Accounting Education,* and the *Journal of Accounting Education* as well as other journals. His research interests include accounting for financial instruments and innovation in accounting education. He has published papers and given numerous talks on incorporating critical thinking into accounting education, and helped prepare a catalog of critical thinking resources for the Federated Schools of Accountancy.

PREFACE

In recent years accounting education has seen numerous efforts to change the way accounting is taught. These efforts reflect the demands of an ever-changing business world, opportunities created by new instructional technologies, and an increased understanding of how students learn. In this book we have drawn from what we believe to be the most promising of these innovations. Our efforts were driven by a few key beliefs:

- ## "Less is more."

  Our instructional objective is to provide students with an understanding of those concepts that are fundamental to the use of managerial accounting. Most students will forget procedural details within a short period of time. On the other hand, concepts, if well taught, should be remembered for a lifetime. Concepts are especially important in a world where the details are constantly changing.

- ## "Don't just sit there—do something."

  Students learn best when they are actively engaged. The overriding pedagogical objective of this book is to provide students with continual opportunities for active learning. One of the best tools for active learning is strategically placed questions. Our discussions are framed by questions, often beginning with rhetorical questions and ending with review questions. Even our selection of analytical devices, called Decision Tools, is referenced using key questions to emphasize the purpose of each.

- ## "I'll believe it when I see it."

  Students will be most willing to commit time and energy to a topic when they believe that it is relevant to their future careers. There is no better way to demonstrate relevance than to ground discussion in the real world. Consistent with this, we use financial information and accounting practices of real companies. By using high-profile companies like Starbucks, Microsoft, Ben & Jerry's, and Intel to frame our discussion of accounting issues, we demonstrate the relevance of accounting while teaching students about companies with which they have daily contact. As they become acquainted with the financial successes and failures of these companies, many students will begin to follow business news more closely, making their learning a dynamic, ongoing process.

- ## "You need to make a decision."

  All business people must make decisions. Decision making involves critical evaluation and analysis of the information at hand, and this takes practice. We have integrated important analytical tools throughout the book. After each new decision tool is presented, we summarize the key features of that tool in a Decision Toolkit. At the end of each chapter we provide a comprehensive demonstration of an analysis of a real-world problem using the decision tools presented in the chapter.

KEY FEATURES OF EACH CHAPTER

Chapter 1, Managerial Accounting. This chapter distinguishes the features of managerial accounting in contrast to financial accounting. It identifies the three broad functions of management and defines the three classes of manufacturing costs—material, labor, and overhead. In a further examination of costs, product costs are distinguished from period costs. The chapter explains and illustrates the difference between the financial statements of a merchandising company and a manufacturer, with particular attention given to the computation and presentation of the cost of goods manufactured section. The chapter concludes with an overview of contemporary developments in managerial accounting.

Chapter 2, Job Order Cost Accounting. This chapter is an introduction to cost accounting systems in manufacturing enterprises. The primary content is an explanation and illustration of a job order cost accounting system, including the flow of costs in a job order cost system and the importance and use of a job cost sheet. The chapter explains and illustrates the relevance, computation, and application of the predetermined overhead rate in a job order cost system and the journal entries that accompany such a system. Chapter 2 concludes with a simple presentation of the nature and treatment of under- and overapplied manufacturing overhead.

Chapter 3, Process Cost Accounting. Chapter 3 begins by explaining the difference between job order and process costing systems. The flow of costs and the end-of-period accounting procedures in process cost accounting are illustrated. The chapter demonstrates the computations of physical units of production, equivalent units of production, and unit costs. Also covered in detail are the method of assigning costs to units of output and the preparation of a production cost report.

Chapter 4, Activity-Based Costing. This chapter is devoted to a relatively recent development in cost accounting—activity-based costing (ABC). It opens with an explanation of the need for ABC and then contrasts ABC systems to traditional overhead costing systems. Numerous activities, activity cost pools, and activity cost drivers are identified for different types of manufacturing operations. To simplify the coverage of ABC, the activity-based management aspects of ABC, such as value-added versus nonvalue-added activities, are integrated later in the chapter. We also discuss the benefits and limitations of ABC and the conditions under which ABC is the preferred or more accurate system of product costing. The chapter concludes with a presentation on just-in-time (JIT) processing. An appendix to the chapter demonstrates the widespread applicability of ABC and provides a third illustration of ABC through use of a small service industry firm—a public accounting firm.

Chapter 5, Cost-Volume-Profit Relationships. This chapter begins by distinguishing between variable and fixed costs and explaining the meaning and importance of the relevant range and the concept of mixed costs. Next, the chapter identifies the five components of CVP analysis and the assumptions that underlie its application, in preparation for the heart of the chapter—various analyses of cost-volume-profit (CVP) relationships. The meanings and numerical expressions of contribution margin are presented along with illustrations of three ways to determine break-even point (mathematical equation, contribution margin technique, and CVP graph). As further CVP analysis, formulas for computing the margin of safety and the sales required to earn target net income are presented in differing business environments. To facilitate managers' need for CVP information about cost behavior and contribution margin, the chapter illustrates the CVP (contribution margin) format for the income statement. An appendix to the chapter introduces variable costing and contrasts it to absorption costing.

Chapter 6, Budgetary Planning. The purpose of Chapter 6 is to justify budgeting as a sound business technique and to illustrate the essentials and methods of budget preparation. This is accomplished by presenting the benefits of budgeting and describing and illustrating the budget preparation process that assembles the components of a master budget. The preparation and value of budgeted financial statements (income statement and balance sheet) and the invaluable cash budget are presented using one company's financial data. The chapter concludes with a discussion of budgeting in merchandising, service, and not-for-profit enterprises.

Chapter 7, Budgetary Control and Responsibility Accounting. The first half of this chapter explains how budgets are used in controlling costs and operations. Static budgets are contrasted to flexible budgets. The superiority of flexible budgeting, actually a series of static budgets at different levels of activity, is meticulously demonstrated in an extended case study. The second half of Chapter 7 is devoted to responsibility accounting—the responsibility reporting system and its applicability to cost centers, profit centers, and investment centers. The computation and use of the return on investment (ROI) formula complete the chapter.

Chapter 8, Performance Evaluation through Standard Costs. This chapter is devoted to standard costs and variance analysis. First, the chapter differentiates a standard from a budget. Next, it discusses the advantages of using standard costs and methods of setting standard costs. This discussion is followed by formulas used in determining direct materials, direct labor, and manufacturing overhead variances, with variances isolated for comparisons of actual to standard. The chapter graphically illustrates the source, computation, and information value of each variance. These computed variances are then reported and analyzed. The chapter concludes with a comprehensive illustration of the journal entries necessary in a standard cost system and the financial statement presentation of standard costs and their resulting variances.

Chapter 9, Incremental Analysis. The concept and application of incremental analysis as part of management's decision-making process is the subject of Chapter 9. It applies incremental analysis to a variety of management decisions, including (1) accept an order at a special price, (2) make or buy, (3) sell or process further, (4) retain or replace equipment, (5) eliminate an unprofitable business segment, and (6) allocate limited resources. The final section of the chapter covers one additional application of CVP concepts—analyzing and adjusting the product sales mix.

Chapter 10, Capital Budgeting. This chapter explains how companies make capital budgeting decisions. It describes and illustrates four techniques or methods of evaluating capital expenditures: (1) the cash payback technique, (2) the net present value (NPV) method, (3) the internal rate of return method, and (4) the annual rate of return technique. Integrated in the presentation of these four methods is coverage of the profitability index, the benefits of performing a post-audit, and the challenges presented in evaluating intangible benefits in any capital budgeting decision.

Chapter 11, Statement of Cash Flows. This chapter begins with a discussion of the purpose and usefulness of the statement of cash flows. The chapter then splits into two sections, allowing instructors the choice of emphasizing the *indirect method* or the *direct method.* Each of these sections follows a two-year progression, with the first year addressing only the most basic items affecting cash flow, and the second year adding additional items. The chapter concludes with an analysis of Microsoft's statement of cash flows, employing free cash flow, the capital expenditure ratio, the current cash debt coverage ratio, cash debt coverage ratio, and cash return on sales ratio. Comparative numbers for Oracle are provided.

Chapter 12, Financial Statement Analysis. This chapter is a capstone, reinforcing an understanding of analytical tools and demonstrating their interrelationships. The chapter begins with a discussion of the importance of the concept of earning power, by contrasting net income resulting from operations with net income resulting from irregular items such as extraordinary items, discontinued operations, or accounting changes. The potential usefulness of comprehensive income is also discussed. Next, the chapter presents the analytical tools of horizontal and vertical analysis, and it concludes with a thorough analysis of Kellogg Company, Inc., employing the analytical tools available to accountants and financial analysts.

PROVEN PEDAGOGICAL FRAMEWORK

In this book we have used many proven pedagogical tools to help students learn accounting concepts and apply them to decision making in the business world. This pedagogical framework emphasizes the *processes* students undergo as they learn.

Learning How to Use the Text

A **Student Owner's Manual** begins the text, to help students understand the value of the pedagogical framework and how to use it. After becoming familiar with the pedagogy, students can take a **learning styles quiz** (p. xxii) to help them identify how they learn best—visually, aurally, through reading and writing, kinesthetically, or through a combination of these styles. We then offer tips on in-class and at-home learning strategies, as well as help in identifying the text pedagogy that would be most useful to them for their learning style. Finally, Chapter 1 contains notes (printed in red) that explain each pedagogical element the first time it appears.

Understanding and Using the Content

- **The Navigator** is a learning system designed to guide students through each chapter and help them succeed in learning the material. It consists of (1) a checklist at the beginning of the chapter, which outlines features of the chapter that must be covered to master the topics, and (2) a series of check boxes that prompt students to use the learning aids and set priorities as they study.

- **Study Objectives,** listed at the beginning of each chapter, form a learning framework throughout the text, with each objective repeated in the margin at the appropriate place in the main body of the chapter and again in the **Summary of Study Objectives.** Also, end-of-chapter assignment materials are linked to the Study Objectives.

- A **Chapter-Opening Feature Story** presents a scenario that relates a real-world business situation to the topic of the chapter. The story also serves as a recurrent example throughout the chapter. Each story that focuses on a well-known company ends with the company's Internet address, to encourage students to go on-line to get more information about these companies.

- A chapter **Preview** links the chapter-opening feature story to the major topics of the chapter. First, an introductory paragraph explains how the story relates to the topics to be discussed, and then a graphic outline of the chapter provides a "visual road map," useful for seeing the big picture as well as the connections between subtopics.

Learning the Material

- This book emphasizes the accounting experiences of **real companies and business situations.** Many of these real-world examples and illustrations are identified by the company logo that appears nearby.

- Continuing the real-world flavor of the book, **Business Insight** boxes in each chapter give students glimpses into how real companies make decisions using accounting information. The boxes, highlighted with striking photographs, focus on three different accounting perspectives—those of managers, investors, and international business.

- Color **illustrations** support and reinforce the concepts of the text. **Infographics** are a special type of illustration that help students visualize and apply accounting concepts to the real world. The infographics often portray important concepts in entertaining and memorable ways.

- **Before You Go On** sections occur at the end of each key topic and consist of two parts: *Review It* serves as a learning check within the chapter by asking students to stop and answer knowledge and comprehension questions about the material just covered. *Do It* is a brief demonstration problem that gives immediate practice using the material just covered. Solutions are provided to help students understand the reasoning involved in reaching an answer.

- **Helpful Hints** in the margins expand upon or help clarify concepts under discussion in the nearby text. This feature actually makes the book an Annotated *Student* Edition.

- **Alternative Terminology** notes in the margins present synonymous terms that students may come across in subsequent accounting courses and in business.

- Marginal **International Notes** provide a helpful and convenient way for instructors to begin to expose students to international issues in accounting, reporting, and decision making.

- Each chapter presents **decision tools** that are useful for analyzing and solving the business problems discussed in that chapter. At the end of the text discussion relating to the decision tool, a **Decision Toolkit** summarizes the key features of that decision tool and reinforces its purpose.

- A **Using the Decision Toolkit** exercise, which follows the final Before You Go On section in the chapter, asks students to use the decision tools presented in that chapter.

Putting It Together

- At the end of each chapter, between the body of the text and the homework materials, are several useful features for review and reference: a **Summary of Study Objectives** reviews the main points of the chapter; the **Decision Toolkit—A Summary** presents in one place the decision tools used throughout the chapter; and a **Glossary** of important terms gives definitions, with page references to the text.

- Next, a **Demonstration Problem** gives students another opportunity to refer to a detailed solution to a representative problem before they do homework assignments. **Problem-Solving Strategies** presented in the margin help establish a logic for approaching similar problems and assist students in understanding the solution.

Developing Skills through Practice

Throughout the homework material, questions, exercises, and problems make use of the decision tools presented in the chapter.

- **Self-Study Questions** comprise a practice test to enable students to check their understanding of important concepts. These questions are keyed to the Study Objectives, so students can go back and review sections of the chapter in which they find they need further work.

- **Questions** provide a full review of chapter content and help students prepare for class discussions and testing situations.

- **Brief Exercises** build students' confidence and test their basic skills. Each exercise focuses on one of the Study Objectives.

- Each of the **Exercises** focuses on one or more of the Study Objectives. These tend to take a little longer to complete, and they present more of a challenge to students than Brief Exercises. The Exercises help instructors and students make a manageable transition to more challenging problems.

- **Problems** stress the applications of the concepts presented in the chapter. Two sets of problems—Sets A and B—give instructors greater flexibility in assigning homework. Certain problems, marked with the icon ▨▨▷, help build business writing skills.

- Each Brief Exercise, Exercise, and Problem has a **description of the concept** covered and is keyed to the Study Objectives.

- **Spreadsheet Exercises and Problems,** identified by ▨, can be solved using *Solving Managerial Accounting Problems Using Lotus 1-2-3* or *Excel for Windows.*

Expanding and Applying Knowledge

Broadening Your Perspective is a unique section at the end of each chapter that offers a wealth of resources to help instructors and students pull together the learning for the chapter. This section offers problems and projects for those instructors who want to broaden the learning experience by bringing in more real-world decision making, analysis, and critical thinking activities.

- **Group Decision Cases** help students build decision-making skills by analyzing accounting information in a less structured situation. These cases require evaluation of a manager's decision, or they lead to a decision among alternative courses of action. As group activities, these cases prepare students for the business world, where they will be working with teams of people, by giving them practice in solving problems with colleagues.

- Like the decision cases, the **Managerial Analysis** assignments build analytical and decision-making skills in problematic situations encountered by business managers. They also require the application of business communication skills.

- The **Real-World Focus** problems ask students to apply techniques and concepts presented in the chapter to specific situations faced by actual companies.

- **Communication Activities** are assignments that give students practice in communicating to different audiences in varying writing modes—written letters, reports, memos, explanations, and analysis—as well as speaking and presentations. These are skills much in demand by employers.

- Since the ability to read and understand business publications is an asset over the span of one's career, **Research Assignments** direct students to annual reports or articles published in *The Wall Street Journal* and other popular business periodicals for further study and analysis of key topics.

- **Ethics Cases** contain typical ethical dilemmas and require students to analyze the situation, identify the stakeholders affected, describe the ethical issues involved, and decide on an appropriate course of action.

- **Surfing the Net** exercises guide students to the Internet and specific Web sites from which they can mine and analyze information related to chapter topics.

ACTIVE TEACHING AND LEARNING SUPPLEMENTARY MATERIAL

Managerial Accounting features a full line of teaching and learning resources developed to help you create a more dynamic and innovative learning environment.

The success of students is a major theme of the entire supplements package. Vital current topics such as communication skills, critical thinking and decision making, ethics, technology, and real-world emphasis are integrated throughout. These resources—including print, software, and Web-based materials—also take an active learning approach to help build students' skills and analytical abilities.

The *Managerial Accounting* Web Site at *http://www.wiley.com/college/weygandt.* As a resource and learning tool for instructors and students, the *Managerial Accounting* Web site serves as a launching pad to numerous activities, resources, and related sites. Available through the Web site are links to companies discussed in the text and Instructor's Manual, additional cases and problems for students, and items such as the Checklist of Key Figures and PowerPoint presentations for download. For instructors, most of the supplements listed below will be available in a password-protected portion of the site, for access as needed. The site also provides a link to the Wiley Business Extra site, discussed below. Visit the site often for updated and new materials.

Instructor's Active-Teaching Aids

For the instructor, we have designed an extensive support package to help you maximize your teaching effectiveness, including print and technology tools. We offer useful supplements for instructors with various levels of experience and different instructional circumstances.

Instructor's Resource System on CD-ROM. Responding to the changing needs of instructors and to developments in distance learning and electronic classrooms, a CD-ROM supplement provides all the instructor support material in an electronic format that is easy to navigate and use. This CD-ROM contains all the print supplements, as well as the electronic ones, for use in the classroom, for printing out material, for uploading to your own Web site, or for downloading and modifying. The CD-ROM gives you the flexibility to access and prepare instructional material based on your individual needs.

Solutions Manual. The Solutions Manual contains detailed solutions to all exercises and problems in the textbook and suggested answers to the questions and cases. Print is large and bold for easy readability in lecture settings, and instructors may duplicate any portion of the manual without paying a permissions fee. Each chapter includes an *assignment classification table* (identifies end-of-chapter items by study objectives), an *assignment characteristics table* (describes each problem and identifies difficulty level and estimated completion time), and a *Bloom's taxonomy table* (classifies end-of-chapter items by Bloom's taxonomy of learning objective and study objective). (Also available on diskette.)

Solutions Transparencies. Packaged in an organizer box with chapter file folders, these transparencies feature detailed solutions to all exercises and problems in the textbook, and suggested answers to the cases. They feature large, bold type for better projection and easy readability in large classroom settings. Accuracy is assured—all solutions were extensively checked by the authors and reviewers.

Instructor's Manual. The Instructor's Manual is a comprehensive resource guide designed to assist professors in preparing lectures and assignments, and includes sample syllabi for preparing for the course. The print is set in a size large enough for easy reading or use as transparency masters.

Included for each chapter are an *assignment classification table*; an *assignment characteristics table*; a *list of study objectives* in extra-large, boldface print for transparencies; a *chapter review* of the significant topics and points contained in the chapter; *enhanced lecture outlines* with teaching tips and

references to text material; *suggestions for integrating supplements* into the classroom; a *20-minute quiz* in the form of 10 true/false and 5 multiple-choice questions (with solutions); and illustrations, including diagrams, graphs, questions, and exercises, for use as classroom handouts, overhead transparencies, in-class quizzes, or demonstrations (solutions are provided). (Also available on diskette.)

Teaching Transparencies. A number of illustrations are available in four-color format. The authors have selected these illustrations from the text and from original exhibits outside the text as well. Designed to support and clarify concepts in the text, the Teaching Transparencies will enhance lectures. Suggestions on how to integrate the Teaching Transparencies are included in the Instructor's Manual.

Examination Book and Test Bank. *Managerial Accounting* features a comprehensive testing package designed to allow instructors to tailor examinations according to study objectives, learning skills and objectives, and selected content. This package consists of a Test Bank of over 700 examination questions and exercises accompanied by answers and solutions. Each chapter includes a *Summary of Questions by Objectives* and a *Summary of Objectives by Questions* (linking test items to study objectives), and an indication of placement among Bloom's taxonomy. Exercises are also identified by estimated completion time. In addition to the examination material provided for each chapter, a number of comprehensive examinations covering four to five chapters are also included.

The Examination Book also includes a series of preprinted Achievement Tests for easy testing of major concepts. Each test covers two chapters from the textbook. In addition, a comprehensive test for each half of the textbook is included. The tests, easy to photocopy and distribute directly to students, consist of multiple-choice, matching, and true/false questions, and problems and exercises (computation and journal entries). Solutions are included at the end of each Achievement Test.

Computerized Test Bank. The Test Bank is also available for use with IBM and IBM true-compatibles running Windows 3.1 or higher. This Computerized Test Bank offers a number of valuable options that allow instructors to create multiple versions of the same test by scrambling questions; generate a large number of test questions randomly or manually; and modify and customize test questions by changing existing problems or adding your own.

Test Preparation Service. Simply call Wiley's special number (1-800-541-5602) with the questions you want on an examination. Wiley will provide a customized master exam within 24 hours. If you prefer, random selection from a number of chapters is possible.

Checklist of Key Figures. A listing of key amounts for textbook problems, allowing students to verify the accuracy of their answers as they work through the assignments, is available on the *Managerial Accounting* Web site at http://www.wiley.com/college/weygandt.

PowerPoint Presentation Material. This PowerPoint lecture aid contains a combination of key concepts, images, and problems from the textbook for use in the classroom. Designed according to the organization of the material in the textbook, this series of electronic transparencies can be used to reinforce managerial accounting principles visually and graphically.

***Nightly Business Report* Video.** This video contains segments from the highly respected *Nightly Business Report* that have been selected for their applicability to managerial accounting and for their reinforcement of key concepts in the text. Each of the segments is approximately 3–5 minutes long and can be used to introduce topics to the students, enhance lecture material, and provide real-world context for related concepts. An Instructor's Manual with suggestions for integrating the material into the classroom accompanies the video.

Student Active-Learning Aids

Working Papers. Working Papers are partially completed accounting forms for all end-of-chapter exercises, problems, and cases. A convenient resource for organizing and completing homework assignments, they demonstrate how to correctly set up solution formats and are directly tied to textbook assignments.

Student Study Guide. The Student Study Guide is a comprehensive review of accounting and a powerful tool for students to use in the classroom, guiding students through chapter content, tied to study objectives, and providing resources for use during lectures. **This is an excellent resource when preparing for exams.**

Each chapter of the Student Study Guide includes study objectives and a chapter review consisting of 20–30 key points; a demonstration problem linked to study objectives in the textbook; and additional opportunities for students to practice their knowledge and skills through true/false, multiple-choice, and matching questions related to key terms and exercises linked to study objectives. Solutions to the exercises explain the hows and whys so students get immediate feedback.

Take Note! This handy note-taking guide includes all the PowerPoint presentations printed out three to a page, with spaces next to them for students to take notes. Take Note! allows the students to focus on the discussions at hand, instead of focusing on copying down slides projected in class.

On-Line Business Survival Guide in Accounting. The journey of 1,000 Web sites begins with one click, and this practical guide gets you on the road. The On-Line Business Survival Guide is a brief, clear introduction to using the World Wide Web as a business research tool. Starting with the basics, this manual covers everything your students need to know to become master sleuths at finding critical information on the Internet. In addition, the guide provides a hands-on guide to using *The Wall Street Journal* Interactive Edition, as well as a discount offer for a subscription to *The Wall Street Journal* Interactive on-line.

Business Extra Web Site at http://www.wiley.com/college/businessextra. To complement the On-Line Business Survival Guide in Accounting, the Business Extra Web site gives professors and students instant access to a wealth of current articles dealing with all aspects of accounting. The articles are organized by topic, and discussion questions follow each article.

Solving Managerial Accounting Problems Using Lotus 1-2-3 and Excel for Windows. These electronic spreadsheet templates (available in either Lotus or Excel) allow students to complete selected end-of-chapter exercises and problems, identified by a spreadsheet icon in the margin of the text. The manuals, which include the disks, guide students step-by-step from an introduction to computers and Lotus or Excel, to completing preprogrammed spreadsheets, to designing their own spreadsheets. Prepared for students with a range of experience in spreadsheet applications, these templates help students develop and hone their computer skills and expose them to software packages often used in real-world business environments.

Computerized Study Guide. The Computerized Study Guide is designed to provide more flexible movement through the content of the Study Guide to meet the particular needs of each student. It offers students both extensive review information and hundreds of self-testing questions from every chapter in the text. The student can select from a number of self-study options, including chapter summaries, chapter study objectives, and self-test questions. Multiple-choice questions offer students explanations of why the wrong choices are not correct. All questions can be automatically scrambled to avoid duplication of identical tests.

We have attempted to make this book accurate, interesting, and educationally sound. Our hope is that this book provides a positive experience for both teacher and student.

Jerry J. Weygandt
Madison, Wisconsin
Donald E. Kieso
DeKalb, Illinois
Paul D. Kimmel
Milwaukee, Wisconsin

ACKNOWLEDGMENTS

During the course of development of *Managerial Accounting,* the authors benefited greatly from the input of focus group participants, manuscript reviewers, ancillary authors, and proofers. The constructive suggestions and innovative ideas of the reviewers and the creativity and accuracy of the ancillary authors and checkers are greatly appreciated.

We are especially grateful to Athar Murtaza, PhD, CMA, of Seton Hall University, for his in-depth review of the manuscript.

FOCUS GROUP PARTICIPANTS AND REVIEWERS

Nancy Boyd, *Middle Tennessee State University*
Joan Cook, *Milwaukee Area Technical College*
Cecelia Fewox, *Trident Technical College*
Jeannie Folk, *College of DuPage*
Janet Grange, *Chicago State University*
Thomas Hofmeister, *Northwestern Business School*
Shirly Kleiner, *Johnson County Community College*
Robyn Lawrence, *University of Scranton*
Deanne Pannell, *Pellissippi State Technical College*
Jill Russell, *Camden County College*
Jerome Spallino, *Westmoreland County Community College*
Cynthia Tomes, *Des Moines Area Community College*
Chris Widmer, *Tidewater Community College*

ANCILLARY AUTHORS, CONTRIBUTORS, AND PROOFERS

Anne Lee Bain, *St. Cloud State University*—Working Papers author
John C. Borke, *University of Wisconsin-Platteville*—Solutions Manual proofer and Technical Advisor
Larry R. Falcetto, *Emporia State University*—Supplements Coordinator and Instructor's Manual and Test Bank author
Jessica J. Frazier, *Eastern Kentucky University*—World Wide Web Problems contributor and NBR Video advisor
Douglas W. Kieso, *University of California-Irvine*—Study Guide author

We appreciate the exemplary support and professional commitment given us by our executive editor Susan Elbe, senior development editor Nancy Perry, our senior marketing manager Rebecca Hope, vice-president of college production and manufacturing Ann Berlin, production coordinator Jeanine Furino, photo editor Hilary Newman, designer Kevin Murphy, illustration editor Anna Melhorn, our associate editor Julie Kerr, our copy editor Ann Torbert, and our word processor Mary Ann Benson. A note of gratitude to Martha Beyerlein and Ingrid Mount at Elm Street Publishing Services.

We thank Starbucks Corporation and Green Mountain Coffee for permitting us the use of their 1996 Annual Reports for our specimen financial statements and accompanying notes.

Suggestions and comments from users are encouraged and appreciated. Please feel free to e-mail any one of us at account@wiley.com.

Jerry J. Weygandt
Donald E. Kieso
Paul D. Kimmel

STUDENT OWNER'S MANUAL
How to Use the Study Aids in This Book

CHAPTER 2
Job Order Cost Accounting

STUDY OBJECTIVES

After studying this chapter, you should be able to:

❶ Explain the characteristics and purposes of cost accounting.

❷ Describe the flow of costs in a job order cost accounting system.

❸ Explain the nature and importance of a job cost sheet.

❹ Indicate how the predetermined overhead rate is determined and used.

❺ Prepare entries for jobs completed and sold.

❻ Distinguish between under- and overapplied manufacturing overhead.

FEATURE STORY

"We'd Like It in Red"

Western States Fire Apparatus, Inc., of Cornelius, Oregon, is one of the few American companies that makes fire trucks. The company builds about 25 trucks per year. Founded in 1941, the company is run by the children and grandchildren of the original founder.

"We buy the chassis, which is the cab and the frame," says Susan Scott, the company's bookkeeper. "In our computer, we set up an account into which all of the direct material that is purchased for that particular job is charged." Other direct materials include the water pump—which can cost $10,000—the lights, the siren, ladders, and hoses.

As for direct labor, the production workers fill out job sheets that tell what jobs they worked on. Usually, the company is building four trucks at any one time. On payday, the controller allocates the payroll to the appropriate job record.

Indirect materials, such as nuts and bolts, wiring, lubricants, and abrasives are allocated to each job in proportion to direct material dollars. Other costs, such as insurance and supervisors' salaries, are allocated based on direct labor hours. "We need to allocate overhead in order to know what kind of price we have to charge when we submit our bids," she says.

Western gets orders through a "blind-bidding" process; that is, Western submits its bid without knowing the bid prices made by its competitors. "If we bid too low, we won't make a profit. If we bid too high, we don't get the job."

Regardless of the final price for the truck, the quality had better be first-rate. "The fire departments let you know if they don't like what you did, and you usually end up fixing it."

44

At the beginning of each chapter, **Study Objectives** provide you with a learning framework. Each Study Objective then reappears at the point within the chapter where the concept is discussed and is also summarized at the end of the chapter.

The **Feature Story** helps you picture how the topics of the chapter relate to the real worlds of accounting and business. You will find references to the story throughout the chapter, which will help you put new ideas in context, organize them, and remember them. Many vignettes end with the Internet addresses of the companies cited in the story.

The **Navigator** is a learning system designed to guide you through each chapter and help you succeed in learning the material. It consists of (1) a checklist at the beginning of the chapter, which outlines text features and study skills you will need, and (2) a series of check boxes that prompt you to use the learning aids in the chapter and set priorities as you study.

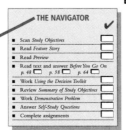

THE NAVIGATOR ✔

- Scan *Study Objectives* ☐
- Read *Feature Story* ☐
- Read *Preview* ☐
- Read text and answer *Before You Go On*
  p. 48 ☐   p. 58 ☐   p. 64 ☐
- Work *Using the Decision Toolkit* ☐
- Review *Summary of Study Objectives* ☐
- Work *Demonstration Problem* ☐
- Answer *Self-Study Questions* ☐
- Complete assignments ☐

45

The **Preview** begins by linking the feature story with the major topics of the chapter. It then gives a graphic outline of the major topics and subtopics that will be discussed. This narrative and visual preview will give you a mental framework upon which to arrange the information you are learning.

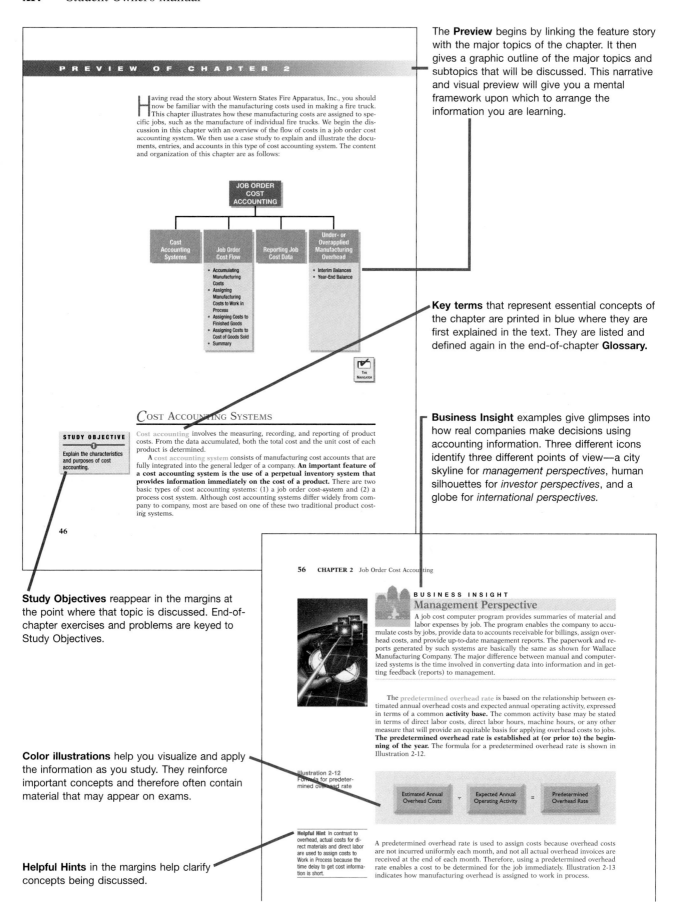

PREVIEW OF CHAPTER 2

Having read the story about Western States Fire Apparatus, Inc., you should now be familiar with the manufacturing costs used in making a fire truck. This chapter illustrates how these manufacturing costs are assigned to specific jobs, such as the manufacture of individual fire trucks. We begin the discussion in this chapter with an overview of the flow of costs in a job order cost accounting system. We then use a case study to explain and illustrate the documents, entries, and accounts in this type of cost accounting system. The content and organization of this chapter are as follows:

JOB ORDER COST ACCOUNTING

- Cost Accounting Systems
- Job Order Cost Flow
  - Accumulating Manufacturing Costs
  - Assigning Manufacturing Costs to Work in Process
  - Assigning Costs to Finished Goods
  - Assigning Costs to Cost of Goods Sold
  - Summary
- Reporting Job Cost Data
- Under- or Overapplied Manufacturing Overhead
  - Interim Balances
  - Year-End Balance

THE NAVIGATOR

Key terms that represent essential concepts of the chapter are printed in blue where they are first explained in the text. They are listed and defined again in the end-of-chapter **Glossary.**

COST ACCOUNTING SYSTEMS

STUDY OBJECTIVE
1
Explain the characteristics and purposes of cost accounting.

Cost accounting involves the measuring, recording, and reporting of product costs. From the data accumulated, both the total cost and the unit cost of each product is determined.

A cost accounting system consists of manufacturing cost accounts that are fully integrated into the general ledger of a company. **An important feature of a cost accounting system is the use of a perpetual inventory system that provides information immediately on the cost of a product.** There are two basic types of cost accounting systems: (1) a job order cost system and (2) a process cost system. Although cost accounting systems differ widely from company to company, most are based on one of these two traditional product costing systems.

46

Study Objectives reappear in the margins at the point where that topic is discussed. End-of-chapter exercises and problems are keyed to Study Objectives.

Color illustrations help you visualize and apply the information as you study. They reinforce important concepts and therefore often contain material that may appear on exams.

Helpful Hints in the margins help clarify concepts being discussed.

Business Insight examples give glimpses into how real companies make decisions using accounting information. Three different icons identify three different points of view—a city skyline for *management perspectives*, human silhouettes for *investor perspectives*, and a globe for *international perspectives.*

56   CHAPTER 2 Job Order Cost Accounting

BUSINESS INSIGHT
Management Perspective

A job cost computer program provides summaries of material and labor expenses by job. The program enables the company to accumulate costs by jobs, provide data to accounts receivable for billings, assign overhead costs, and provide up-to-date management reports. The paperwork and reports generated by such systems are basically the same as shown for Wallace Manufacturing Company. The major difference between manual and computerized systems is the time involved in converting data into information and in getting feedback (reports) to management.

The predetermined overhead rate is based on the relationship between estimated annual overhead costs and expected annual operating activity, expressed in terms of a common **activity base.** The common activity base may be stated in terms of direct labor costs, direct labor hours, machine hours, or any other measure that will provide an equitable basis for applying overhead costs to jobs. **The predetermined overhead rate is established at (or prior to) the beginning of the year.** The formula for a predetermined overhead rate is shown in Illustration 2-12.

Illustration 2-12
Formula for predetermined overhead rate

Estimated Annual Overhead Costs ÷ Expected Annual Operating Activity = Predetermined Overhead Rate

Helpful Hint In contrast to overhead, actual costs for direct materials and direct labor are used to assign costs to Work in Process because the time delay to get cost information is short.

A predetermined overhead rate is used to assign costs because overhead costs are not incurred uniformly each month, and not all actual overhead invoices are received at the end of each month. Therefore, using a predetermined overhead rate enables a cost to be determined for the job immediately. Illustration 2-13 indicates how manufacturing overhead is assigned to work in process.

Under a job order cost system, costs are assigned to each **job,** such as the manufacture of a high-speed drilling machine, or to each **batch** of goods, such as 500 wedding invitations. Jobs or batches may be completed to fill a specific customer order or to replenish inventory. An important feature of job order costing is that each job (or batch) has its own distinguishing characteristics. For example, each house is custom built, each motion picture is unique, and each printing job is different. **The objective is to compute the cost per job.** At each point in the manufacturing process, the job and its associated costs can be identified. A job order cost system measures costs for each completed job, rather than for set time periods. The recording of costs in a job order cost system is shown in Illustration 2-1.

Illustration 2-1 Job order cost system

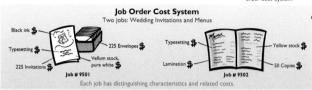

Job Order Cost System
Two jobs: Wedding Invitations and Menus

Black ink $ Typesetting $ 225 Invitations $ 225 Envelopes $ Vellum stock, pure white $ **Job # 9501**

Typesetting $ Lamination $ Yellow stock $ 50 Copies $ **Job # 9502**

Each job has distinguishing characteristics and related costs.

Infographics, a special type of illustration, pictorially link concepts to the real world.

DECISION TOOLKIT

Each chapter presents **decision tools** that help decision makers analyze and solve business problems. At the end of the text discussion, a **Decision Toolkit** summarizes the key features of a decision tool and reviews why and how you would use it.

Decision Checkpoints	Info Needed for Decision	Tool to Use for Decision	How to Evaluate Results
What is the cost of a job?	Cost of material, labor, and overhead assigned to a specific job	Job cost sheet	Compare costs to those of previous periods and to those of competitors to ensure that costs are in line. Compare costs to expected selling price to determine overall profitability.

BEFORE YOU GO ON . . .

● **Review It**

1. What source documents are used in assigning manufacturing costs to Work in Process Inventory?
2. What is a job cost sheet, and what is its primary purpose?
3. What is the formula for computing a predetermined overhead rate?

● **Do It**

Danielle Company is working on two job orders. The job cost sheets show the following: direct materials—Job 120 $6,000, Job 121 $3,600; direct labor—Job 120 $4,000, Job 121 $2,000; and manufacturing overhead—Job 120 $5,000, Job 121 $2,500. Prepare the three summary entries to record the assignment of costs to Work in Process from the data on the job cost sheets.

Reasoning: Each cost charged to a job must be accompanied by a debit to the control account, Work in Process Inventory. The credits in the summary entries are the accounts debited when the manufacturing costs were accumulated.

Solution: The three summary entries are:

Work in Process Inventory ($6,000 + $3,600)	9,600	
Raw Materials Inventory		9,600
(To assign materials to jobs)		
Work in Process Inventory ($4,000 + $2,000)	6,000	
Factory Labor		6,000
(To assign labor to jobs)		
Work in Process Inventory ($5,000 + $2,500)	7,500	
Manufacturing Overhead		7,500
(To assign overhead to jobs)		

Related exercise material: BE2-3, BE2-4, BE2-7, E2-2, E2-3, E2-7, and E2-8.

Before You Go On sections follow each key topic. *Review It* questions prompt you to stop and review the key points you have just studied. If you cannot answer these questions, you should go back and read the section again. Brief *Do It* exercises ask you to apply newly acquired knowledge. They outline the *Reasoning* necessary to complete the exercise, and the *Solution* helps you see how the exercise should be solved.

Using the Decision Toolkit   **65**

USING THE DECISION TOOLKIT

Martinez Building Products Company is one of the largest manufacturers and marketers of unique, custom-made residential garage doors in the U.S. as well as a major supplier of industrial and commercial doors, grills, and counter shutters for the new construction, repair, and remodel markets. Martinez has developed plans for continued expansion of a network of service operations that sell, install, and service manufactured fireplaces, garage doors, and related products.

Martinez uses a job cost system and applies overhead to production on the basis of direct labor cost. In computing a predetermined overhead rate for the year 1999, the company estimated manufacturing overhead to be $24 million and direct labor costs to be $20 million. In addition the following information is provided:

Actual costs incurred during 1999:

Direct materials used	$30,000,000
Direct labor cost incurred	21,000,000

Manufacturing costs incurred during 1999:

Insurance, factory	$ 500,000
Indirect labor	7,500,000
Maintenance	1,000,000
Rent on building	11,000,000
Depreciation on equipment	2,000,000

Instructions

Answer each of the following:

(a) Why is Martinez Building Products Company using a job order costing system?

(b) On what basis does Martinez allocate its manufacturing overhead? Compute the predetermined overhead for the current year.

(c) Compute the amount of the under- or overapplied overhead for 1999.

(d) Martinez had balances in the beginning and ending work in process and finished goods accounts as follows:

	1/1/99	12/31/99
Work in process	$ 5,000,000	$ 4,000,000
Finished goods	13,000,000	11,000,000

Determine the (1) cost of goods manufactured and (2) cost of [goods sold] for Martinez during 1999. Assume that any under- or overap[plied over]head should be included in the cost of goods sold.

(e) During 1999, Job G408 was started and completed. Its [job cost sheet] showed a total cost of $100,000, and the company prices its [products] 50% above its cost. What is the price to the customer if the c[ompany fol]lows this pricing strategy?

Solution

(a) The company is using a job order system because each job [product] must have its own distinguishing characteristics. For exampl[e, each type] of garage door would be different, and therefore a differe[nt cost per] garage should be assigned.

(b) The company allocates its overhead on the basis of direct labor cost. The predetermined overhead rate is 120%, computed as follows:

$$\$24,000,000 \div \$20,000,000 = 120\%$$

(c)

Actual manufacturing overhead	$22,000,000
Applied overhead cost ($21,000,000 × 120%)	25,200,000
Overapplied overhead	$ 3,200,000

(d) (1)

Work in process, 1/1/99		$ 5,000,000
Direct materials used	$30,000,000	
Direct labor	21,000,000	
Manufacturing overhead applied	25,200,000	
Total manufacturing costs		76,200,000
Total cost of work in process		81,200,000
Less: Work in process, 12/31/99		4,000,000
Cost of goods manufactured		$77,200,000
(2) Finished goods inventory, 1/1/99	$13,000,000	
Cost of goods manufactured (see above)	77,200,000	
Cost of goods available for sale	90,200,000	
Finished goods inventory, 12/31/99	11,000,000	
Cost of goods sold (unadjusted)	79,200,000	
Less: Overapplied overhead	3,200,000	
Cost of goods sold	$76,000,000	

(e)

G408 cost	$ 100,000
Markup percentage	× 50%
Profit	$ 50,000

Price to customer: $150,000 ($100,000 + $50,000)

The **Summary of Study Objectives** reviews the main points related to the Study Objectives. It provides you with another opportunity to review what you have learned as well as to see how the key topics within the chapter fit together.

SUMMARY OF STUDY OBJECTIVES

❶ **Explain the characteristics and purposes of cost accounting.** Cost accounting involves the procedures for measuring, recording, and reporting product costs. From the data accumulated, the total cost and the unit cost of each product is determined.

❷ **Describe the flow of costs in a job order accounting system.** In job order cost accounting, manufacturing costs are first accumulated in three accounts: Raw Materials Inventory, Factory Labor, and Manufacturing Overhead. The accumulated costs are then assigned to Work in Process Inventory and eventually to Finished Goods Inventory and Cost of Goods Sold.

❸ **Explain the nature and importance of a job cost sheet.** A job cost sheet is a form used to record the costs chargeable to a specific job and to determine the total and unit cost of the completed job. Job cost sheets constitute the subsidiary ledger for the Work in Process Inventory control account.

❹ **Indicate how the predetermined overhead rate is determined and used.** The predetermined overhead rate is based on the relationship between estimated annual overhead costs and expected annual operating capacity expressed in terms of a common activity base, such as direct labor cost. The rate is used in assigning overhead costs to work in process and to specific jobs.

❺ **Prepare entries for jobs completed and sold.** When jobs are completed, the cost is debited to Finished Goods Inventory and credited to Work in Process Inventory. When a job is sold the entries are: (a) debit Cash or Accounts Receivable and credit Sales for the selling price and (b) debit Cost of Goods Sold and credit Finished Goods Inventory for the cost of the goods.

❻ **Distinguish between under- and overapplied manufacturing overhead.** Underapplied manufacturing overhead means that the overhead assigned to work in process is less than the overhead incurred. Conversely, overapplied overhead means that the overhead assigned to work in process is greater than the overhead incurred.

At the end of each chapter, the **Decision Toolkit—A Summary** reviews the contexts and techniques useful for decision making that were covered in the chapter.

The **Glossary** defines all the **key terms** and **concepts** introduced in the chapter and cross-references them to the pages on which they are introduced in the chapter.

DECISION TOOLKIT—A SUMMARY

Decision Checkpoints	Info Needed for Decision	Tool to Use for Decision	How to Evaluate Results
What is the cost of a job?	Cost of material, labor, and overhead assigned to a specific job	Job cost sheet	Compare costs to those of previous periods and to those of competitors to ensure that costs are in line. Compare costs to expected selling price to determine overall profitability.
Has the company over- or underapplied overhead for the period?	Actual overhead costs and overhead applied	Manufacturing overhead account	If the account balance is a credit, overhead applied exceeded actual overhead costs. If the account balance is a debit, overhead applied was less than actual overhead costs.

GLOSSARY

Cost accounting An area of accounting that involves the measuring, recording, and reporting of product costs. (p. 46)

Cost accounting system Manufacturing cost accounts that are fully integrated into the general ledger of a company. (p. 46)

Job cost sheet A form used to record the costs chargeable to a job and to determine the total and unit cost of the completed job. (p. 52)

Job order cost system A cost accounting system in which costs are assigned to each job or batch. (p. 47)

Materials requisition slip A document authorizing the issuance of raw materials from the storeroom to production. (p. 52)

Overapplied overhead A situation in which overhead assigned to work in process is greater than the overhead incurred. (p. 63)

Predetermined overhead rate A rate based on the relationship between estimated annual overhead costs and expected annual operating activity, expressed in terms of a common activity base. (p. 56)

Process cost system A system of accounting used by companies that manufacture relatively homogeneous products through a series of continuous processes or operations. (p. 47)

Time ticket A document that indicates the employee, the hours worked, the account and job to be charged, and the total labor cost. (p. 54)

Underapplied overhead A situation in which overhead assigned to work in process is less than the overhead incurred. (p. 63)

DEMONSTRATION PROBLEM

During February, Cardella Manufacturing works on two jobs: Numbers A16 and B17. Summary data concerning these jobs are as follows:

Manufacturing Costs Incurred:

Purchased $54,000 of raw materials on account.
Factory labor $76,000 plus $4,000 employer payroll taxes.
Manufacturing overhead exclusive of indirect materials and indirect labor $59,800.

A **Demonstration Problem** is the final step before you begin homework. **Problem-Solving Strategies** in the margins give you tips about how to approach the problem, and the **Solution** demonstrates both the form and content of complete answers.

Assignment of Costs:

Direct materials:	Job A16 $27,000, Job ...
Indirect materials:	$3,000
Direct labor:	Job A16 $52,000, Job ...
Indirect labor:	$2,000

Manufacturing overhead rate 80% of direct la...

Job A16 was completed and sold on account ... completed.

Instructions

(a) Journalize the February transactions in t...
(b) What was the amount of under- or overa...

Solution to Demonstration Problem

Problem-Solving Strategies

1. In accumulating costs, three accounts are debited: Raw Materials Inventory, Factory Labor, and Manufacturing Overhead.
2. When Work in Process Inventory is debited, one of the three accounts in strategy (1), above, must be credited.
3. Finished Goods Inventory is debited for the cost of completed jobs, and Cost of Goods Sold is debited for the cost of jobs sold.
4. Overhead is underapplied when Manufacturing Overhead has a debit balance.

(a)

Feb. 28	1. Raw Materials Inventory			
	Accounts Payable			54,000
	(Purchase of raw materials on account)			
28	2. Factory Labor	80,000		
	Factory Wages Payable			76,000
	Employer Payroll Taxes Payable			4,000
	(To record factory labor costs)			
28	3. Manufacturing Overhead	59,800		
	Accounts Payable, Accumulated Depreciation, and Prepaid Insurance			59,800
	(To record overhead costs)			
28	4. Work in Process Inventory	48,000		
	Manufacturing Overhead	3,000		
	Raw Materials Inventory			51,000
	(To assign raw materials to production)			
28	5. Work in Process Inventory	78,000		
	Manufacturing Overhead	2,000		
	Factory Labor			80,000
	(To assign factory labor to production)			
28	6. Work in Process Inventory	62,400		
	Manufacturing Overhead			62,400
	(To assign overhead to jobs—80% × $78,000)			
28	7. Finished Goods Inventory	120,600		
	Work in Process Inventory			120,600
	(To record completion of Job A16: direct materials $27,000, direct labor $52,000, and manufacturing overhead $41,600)			
28	8. Accounts Receivable	150,000		
	Cost of Goods Sold	120,600		
	Sales			150,000
	Finished Goods Inventory			120,600
	(To record sale of Job A16)			

SELF-STUDY QUESTIONS

Answers are at the end of the chapter.

(SO 1)   1. Cost accounting involves the measuring, recording, and reporting of:
(a) product costs.
(b) future costs.
(c) manufacturing processes.
(d) managerial accounting decisions.

(SO 2)   2. In accumulating raw materials costs, the cost of raw materials purchased in a perpetual system is debited to:
(a) Raw Material Purchases.
(b) Raw Materials Inventory.
(c) Purchases.
(d) Work in Process.

(SO 2)   3. When incurred, factory labor costs are debited to:
(a) Work in Process.
(b) Factory Wages Expense.
(c) Factory Labor.
(d) Factory Wages Payable.

(SO 3)   4. The source documents for assigning costs to job cost sheets are:
(a) invoices, time tickets, and the predetermined overhead rate.
(b) materials requisition slips, time tickets, and the actual overhead costs.
(c) materials requisition slips, payroll register, and the predetermined overhead rate.
(d) materials requisition slips, time tickets, and the predetermined overhead rate.

(SO 3)   5. In recording the issuance of raw materials in a job order cost system, it would be *incorrect* to:
(a) debit Work in Process Inventory.
(b) debit Finished Goods Inventory.
(c) debit Manufacturing Overhead.
(d) credit Raw Materials Inventory.

(SO 3)   6. The entry when direct factory labor is assigned to jobs is a debit to:
(a) Work in Process Inventory and a credit to Factory Labor.
(b) Manufacturing Overhead a credit to Factory Labor.

(c) Factory Labor and a credit to Manufacturing Overhead.
(d) Factory Labor and a credit to Work in Process Inventory.

(SO 4)   7. The formula for computing the predetermined manufacturing overhead rate is estimated annual overhead costs divided by an expected annual operating activity, expressed as:
(a) direct labor cost.
(b) direct labor hours.
(c) machine hours.
(d) any of the above.

(SO 4)   8. In the Cleo Company, the predetermined overhead rate is 80% of direct labor cost. During the month, $210,000 of factory labor costs are incurred, of which $180,000 is direct labor and $30,000 is indirect labor. Actual overhead incurred was $200,000. The amount of overhead debited to Work in Process Inventory should be:
(a) $120,000.
(b) $144,000.
(c) $168,000.
(d) $160,000.

(SO 5)   9. In BAC Company, Job No. 26 is completed at a cost of $4,500 and later sold for $7,000 cash. A correct entry is:
(a) Debit Finished Goods Inventory $7,000 and credit Work in Process Inventory $7,000.
(b) Debit Cost of Goods Sold $7,000 and credit Finished Goods Inventory $7,000.
(c) Debit Finished Goods Inventory $4,500 and credit Work in Process Inventory $4,500.
(d) Debit Accounts Receivable $7,000 and credit Sales $7,000.

(SO 6)   10. In preparing monthly financial statements, overapplied overhead is reported in the balance sheet as a(an):
(a) prepaid expense.
(b) unearned revenue.
(c) noncurrent asset.
(d) noncurrent liability.

Self-Study Questions provide a practice test, keyed to Study Objectives, that gives you an opportunity to check your knowledge of important topics. Answers appear on the last page of the chapter.

---

70   CHAPTER 2 Job Order Cost Accounting

QUESTIONS

1. Kenna Quayle is studying for an accounting midterm examination. What should Kenna know about how management may use job cost data?

2. (a) Nels Hoadley is not sure about the differences between cost accounting and a cost accounting system. Explain the difference to Nels. (b) What is an important feature of a cost accounting system?

3. (a) Distinguish between the two types of cost accounting systems. (b) May a company use both types of cost accounting systems?

4. What type of industry is likely to use a job order cost system? Give some examples.

5. What type of industry is likely to use a process cost system? Give some examples.

6. Your roommate asks your help in understanding the major steps in the flow of costs in a job order cost system. Identify the steps for your roommate.

7. There are three inventory control accounts in a job order system. Identify the control accounts and their subsidiary ledgers.

8. What source documents are used in accumulating direct labor costs?

9. Entries to manufacturing overhead normally are only made daily. Do you agree? Explain.

10. Elaine Gould is confused about the source documents used in assigning materials and labor costs. Identify the documents and give the entry for each document.

11. What is the purpose of a job cost sheet?

12. Indicate the source documents that are used in charging costs to specific jobs.

13. Differentiate between a "materials inventory record" and a "materials requisition slip" as used in a job order cost system.

14. Phil Agler believes actual manufacturing overhead should be charged to jobs. Do you agree? Why or why not?

15. What relationships are involved in computing a predetermined overhead rate?

16. How can the agreement of Work in Process Inventory and job cost sheets be verified?

17. Judy Jansen believes that the cost of goods manufactured schedule in job order cost accounting is the same as in manufacturing accounting. Is Judy correct? Explain.

18. Ron Patten is confused about under- and overapplied manufacturing overhead. Define the terms for Ron and indicate the balance in the manufacturing overhead account applicable to each term.

19. Under- or overapplied overhead is reported in the income statement when monthly financial statements are prepared. Do you agree? If not, indicate the proper presentation.

20. At the end of the year, under- or overapplied overhead is closed to Income Summary. Is this correct? If not, indicate the customary treatment of this account.

BRIEF EXERCISES

Prepare a flowchart of a job order cost accounting system, and identify transactions.
(SO 2)

BE2-1 Redeker Tool & Die begins operations on January 1. Because all work is done to customer specifications, the company decides to use a job cost accounting system. Prepare a flow chart of a typical job order system with arrows showing the flow of costs. Identify the eight transactions.

Prepare entries in accumulating manufacturing costs.
(SO 2)

BE2-2 During the first month of operations, Redeker Tool & Die accumulated the following manufacturing costs: raw materials $8,000 on account, factory labor $4,000 of which $3,600 relates to factory wages payable and $400 relates to payroll taxes payable, and utilities payable $2,000. Prepare separate journal entries for each type of manufacturing cost.

Prepare entry for the assignment of raw materials costs.
(SO 2)

BE2-3 In January, Redeker Tool & Die requisitions raw materials for production as follows: Job 1 $1,000, Job 2 $1,200, Job 3 $1,600, and general factory use $600. Prepare a summary journal entry to record raw materials used.

Prepare entry for the assignment of factory labor costs.
(SO 2)

BE2-4 Factory labor data for Redeker Tool & Die is given in BE2-2. During January, time tickets show that the factory labor of $4,000 was used as follows: Job 1 $1,200, Job 2 $1,300, Job 3 $1,000, and general factory use $500. Prepare a summary journal entry to record factory labor used.

Prepare job cost sheets.
(SO 3)

BE2-5 Data pertaining to job cost sheets for Redeker Tool & Die are given in BE2-3 and BE2-4. Prepare the job cost sheets for each of the three jobs. (Note: You may omit the column for Manufacturing Overhead.)

Questions allow you to explain your understanding of concepts and relationships covered in the chapter. Use them to help prepare for class discussion and tests.

Brief Exercises help you focus on one Study Objective at a time and thus help you build confidence in your basic skills and knowledge. (Keyed to Study Objectives.)

EXERCISES

E2-1 The gross earnings of the factory workers for Gaetti Company during the month of January are $90,000. The employer's payroll taxes for the factory payroll are $9,000 and the fringe benefits to be paid by the employer on this payroll are $4,000. Of the total accumulated cost of factory labor, 90% is related to direct labor and 10% is attributable to indirect labor.

Prepare entries for factory labor.
(SO 2)

Instructions
(a) Prepare the entry to record the factory labor costs for the month of January.
(b) Prepare the entry to assign factory labor to production.

E2-2 Lorenzo Manufacturing uses a job order cost accounting system. On May 1, the company has a balance in Work in Process Inventory of $3,200 and two jobs in process: Job No. 429 $2,000, and Job No. 430 $1,200. During May, a summary of source documents reveals the following:

Prepare journal entries for manufacturing costs.
(SO 2, 3, 4, 5)

Job Number	Materials Requisition Slips	Labor Time Tickets
429	$2,500	$ 2,400
430	2,000	3,000
431	4,400	7,600
General use	800	1,200
	$9,700	$14,200

Lorenzo Manufacturing applies manufacturing overhead to jobs at an overhead rate of 70% of direct labor cost. Job No. 429 is completed during the month.

Instructions
(a) Prepare summary journal entries to record the requisition slips, time tickets, the assignment of manufacturing overhead to jobs, and the completion of Job No. 429.
(b) Post the entries to Work in Process Inventory and prove the agreement of the control account with the job cost sheets.

Exercises, which gradually increase in skills, understanding, and time necessary to complete them, help you continue to build your confidence as you make the transition to more challenging homework problems. (Keyed to Study Objectives.)

Certain exercises and problems, marked with a pencil icon ▉▉▉▶ help you practice **written business communication,** a skill much in demand among employers.

Instructions
(a) ▉▉▉▶ On the basis of the foregoing data answer the following questions:
(1) What was the balance in Work in Process Inventory on January 1 if this was the only unfinished job?
(2) If manufacturing overhead is applied on the basis of direct labor cost, what overhead rate was used in each year?
(b) Prepare summary entries at January 31 to record the current year's transactions pertaining to Job No. 92.

Analyze costs of manufacturing and determine missing amounts.
(SO 2, 5)

E2-4 Manufacturing cost data for Kosko Company, which uses a job order cost system, are presented below:

	Case A	Case B	Case C
Direct materials	(a)	$83,000	$ 65,000
Direct labor used	$ 50,000	90,000	(h)
Manufacturing overhead applied	42,500	(d)	(i)
Total manufacturing costs	190,650	(e)	287,000
Work in process 1/1/99	(b)	15,500	18,000
Total cost of work in process	201,500	(f)	(j)
Work in process 12/31/99	(c)	11,800	(k)
Cost of goods manufactured	192,300	(g)	262,000

Instructions
Indicate the missing amount for each letter. Assume that in all cases manufacturing overhead is applied on the basis of direct labor cost and the rate is the same.

Compute the manufacturing overhead rate and under- or overapplied overhead.
(SO 4, 6)

E2-5 Gomez Company applies manufacturing overhead to jobs on the basis of machine hours used. Overhead costs are expected to total $275,000 for the year, and machine usage is estimated at 125,000 hours.
In January, $26,000 of overhead costs are incurred and 10,000 machine hours are used. For the remainder of the year, $274,000 of overhead costs are incurred and 120,000 machine hours are worked.

Instructions
(a) Compute the manufacturing overhead rate for the year.
(b) What is the amount of under- or overapplied overhead at January 31? How should this amount be reported in the financial statements prepared on January 31?
(c) What is the amount of under- or overapplied overhead at December 31?
(d) Assuming the under- or overapplied overhead for the year is not allocated to inventory accounts, prepare the adjusting entry to assign the amount to cost of goods sold.

Spreadsheet Exercises and Problems,

identified by ⬚, can be solved using the spreadsheet software *Solving Managerial Accounting Problems Using Lotus 1-2-3 and Excel for Windows*.

PROBLEMS: SET A

Prepare entries in a job cost system and job costs sheets.
(SO 2, 3, 4, 5, 6)

P2-1A Good Manufacturing uses a job order cost system and applies overhead to production on the basis of direct labor hours. On January 1, 1999, Job No. 25 was the only job in process. The costs incurred prior to January 1 on this job were as follows: direct materials, $10,000; direct labor, $6,000; and manufacturing overhead, $10,500. In addition, Job No. 23 had been completed at a cost of $45,000 and was part of finished goods inventory, and there was a $5,000 balance in the Raw Materials inventory account.
During the month of January, Good Manufacturing began production on Jobs 26 and 27, and completed Jobs 25 and 26. Jobs 23 and 25 were also sold on account during the month for $52,000 and $58,000 respectively. The following additional events occurred during the month:
1. Purchased additional raw materials of $45,000 on account.
2. Incurred factory labor costs of $31,500. Of this amount $6,500 related to employer payroll taxes.

Two sets of **Problems—Sets A** and **B**—help you pull together and apply several of the concepts of the chapter. (Keyed to multiple Study Objectives.)

BROADENING YOUR PERSPECTIVE

The **Broadening Your Perspective** section helps you pull together various concepts covered in the chapter and apply them to real-world business situations.

GROUP DECISION CASE

BYP2-1 Costello Products Company uses a job order cost system. For a number of months there has been an ongoing rift between the sales department and the production department concerning a special-order product, TC-1. TC-1 is a seasonal product that is manufactured in batches of 1,000 units. TC-1 is sold at cost plus a markup of 40% of cost.

The sales department is unhappy because fluctuating unit production costs significantly affect selling prices. Sales personnel complain that this has caused excessive customer complaints and the loss of considerable orders for TC-1.

The production department maintains that each job order must be fully costed on the basis of the costs incurred during the period in which the goods are produced. Production personnel maintain that the only real solution to the problem is for the sales department to increase sales in the slack periods.

Linda Gurney, president of the company, asks you as the company accountant to collect quarterly data for the past year on TC-1. From the cost accounting system, you accumulate the following production quantity and cost data:

Group Decision Cases help you build decision-making skills by analyzing accounting information in a less structured situation. These cases require evaluation of a manager's decision or they lead to a decision among alternative courses of action. These group activities help you prepare for the business world, where you will work with teams of colleagues to solve problems.

Managerial Analysis assignments build analytical and decision-making skills in situations encountered by managers. They also will require you to apply and practice business communication skills.

MANAGERIAL ANALYSIS

BYP2-2 In the course of routine checking of all journal entries prior to preparing month-end reports, Li Chin discovered several strange entries. She recalled that the president's son Jeff had come in to "help out" during an especially busy time and that he had recorded some journal entries. She was relieved that there were only a few of his entries, and even more relieved that he had included rather lengthy explanations. The entries Jeff made were:

Work in Process	20,000	
Cash		20,000

(This is for materials put into process. I don't find the record that we paid for these, so I'm crediting Cash, because I know we'll have to pay for them sooner or later.)

...ring Overhead	12,000	
		12,000

...or bonuses paid to salespeople. I know they're part of overhead, and I can't ...ccount called "Non-factory Overhead" or "Other Overhead" so I'm putting ...nufacturing Overhead. I have the check stubs, so I know we paid these.)

...ense	120,000	
		120,000

...or the factory workers' wages. I have a note that payroll taxes are $8,000. ...nk that's part of wages expense, and that we'll have to pay it all in cash ...r later, so I credited Cash for the wages and the taxes.)

...rocess	3,000	
...terials Inventory		3,000

...or the glue used in the factory. I know we used this to make the products, ...ugh we don't use very much on any one of the products. I got it out of ..., so I credited an inventory account.)

...mation above, answer the following questions:
...d Jeff have recorded each of the four events?
...was not corrected, which financial statements (income statement or bal-
...would be affected? What balances would be overstated or understated?

REAL-WORLD FOCUS

PARLEX COMPANY

BYP2-3 Founded in 1970, **Parlex Corporation** is a world leader in the design and manufacture of flexible interconnect products. Parlex produces custom flexible circuits and laminated cables utilizing proprietary processes and patented technologies which are designed to satisfy the unique requirements of a wide range of customers. Its facilities are located in Methuen, Mass., Salem, N.H., Shanghai, China, and Empalmè, Mexico. Parlex provides its products and engineering services to a variety of markets including automotive, computer, telecommunications, industrial controls, medical, consumer, and military-aerospace. Parlex's common stock trades on the Nasdaq stock market under the symbol PRLX.

The following information was provided in the company's annual report:

PARLEX COMPANY
Notes to the Financial Statements

The Company's products are manufactured on a job order basis to customers' specifications. Customers submit requests for quotations on each job, and the Company prepares bids based on its own cost estimates. The Company attempts to reflect the impact of changing costs when establishing prices. However, during the past several years, the market conditions for flexible circuits and the resulting price sensitivity haven't always allowed this to transpire. Although still not satisfactory, the Company was able to reduce the cost of products sold as a percentage of sales to 85% this year versus 87% that was experienced in the two immediately preceding years. Management continues to focus on improving operational efficiency and further reducing costs.

Instructions
(a) Parlex management discusses the job order cost system employed by their company. What are several advantages of using the job order approach to costing?
(b) Contrast the products produced in a job order environment, like Parlex, to those produced when process cost systems are used.

The **Real-World Focus** problems ask you to apply concepts presented in the chapter to specific situations faced by actual companies.

COMMUNICATION ACTIVITY

BYP2-4 You are the management accountant for Modine Manufacturing. Your company does custom carpentry work and uses a job order cost accounting system. Modine sends detailed job cost sheets to its customers, along with an invoice. The job cost sheets show the date materials were used, the dollar cost of materials, and the hours and cost of labor. A predetermined overhead application rate is used, and the total overhead applied is also listed.

Cindy Ross is a customer who recently had custom cabinets installed. Along with her check in payment for the work done, she included a letter. She thanked the company for including the detailed cost information but questioned why overhead was estimated. She stated that she would be interested in knowing exactly what costs were included in overhead, and she thought that other customers would, too.

Communication Activities ask you to engage in real-world business situations using writing, speaking, or presentation skills.

84 **CHAPTER 2** Job Order Cost Accounting

Instructions

Prepare a letter to Ms. Ross (address: 123 Cedar Lane, Altoona, Kansas 66651) and tell her why you did not send her information on exact costs of overhead included in her job. Respond to her suggestion that you provide this information.

RESEARCH ASSIGNMENT

BYP2-5 The February 1994 issue of *Ohio CPA Journal* includes an article by Eun-Sup Shim and Joseph M. Larkin entitled "A Survey of Current Managerial Accounting Practices: Where Do We Stand?"

Instructions

Read the article and answer the following questions:

(a) What percent of manufacturers surveyed used job order costing?

(b) What was the smallest cost component of the three factors of production? What portion of total manufacturing costs does it represent?

(c) What percent of manufacturers surveyed operate in a single product environment— that is, what percent produce only one product?

(d) What two managerial decisions were considered most affected by overhead allocation?

Research Assignments direct you to *The Wall Street Journal,* annual reports, or articles published in other popular business periodicals for further study and analysis of key topics.

ETHICS CASE

BYP2-6 Roblez Printing provides printing services to many different corporate clients. Although Roblez bids most jobs, some jobs, particularly new ones, are often negotiated on a cost plus basis. Cost plus means that the buyer is willing to pay the actual cost plus a return (profit) on these costs to Roblez.

Kristi Peat, controller for Roblez, has recently returned from a meeting where Roblez's president stated that he wanted her to find a way to charge most costs to any project that was on a cost plus basis. The president noted that the company needed more profits to meet its stated goals this period. By charging more costs to the cost plus projects and therefore less costs to the jobs that were bid, the company should be able to increase its profits for the current year.

Kristi knew why the president wanted to take this action. Rumors were that he was looking for a new position and if the company reported strong profits the president's opportunities would be enhanced. Kristi also recognized that she could probably increase the cost of certain jobs by changing the basis used to allocate manufacturing overhead.

Instructions

(a) Who are the stakeholders in this situation?

(b) What are the ethical issues in this situation?

(c) What would you do if you were Kristi Peat?

Through the **Ethics Cases** you will reflect on typical ethical dilemmas, analyze the issues involved, and decide on an appropriate course of action.

SURFING THE NET

BYP2-7 The Institute of Management Accountants sponsors a certification for management accountants, allowing them to obtain the title of Certified Management Accountant.

Address: http://www.rutgers.edu/Accounting/raw/ima/certletter.htm

Steps:

1. Go to the site shown above.

2. Under the heading "About the Certification Programs," choose **Objectives.**

Surfing the Net exercises guide you to Internet sites where you can find and analyze information related to the chapter topic.

Answers to Self-Study Questions provide feedback on your understanding of concepts.

Answers to Self-Study Questions

1. a   2. b   3. c   4. d   5. b   6. a   7. d   8. b   9. c   10. b

After you complete your homework assignment, it's a good idea to go back to **The Navigator** checklist at the start of the chapter to see if you have used all of the chapter's study aids.

 Remember to go back to the Navigator box on the chapter-opening page and check off your completed work.

HOW DO YOU LEARN BEST?

Now that you have looked at your Owner's Manual, take time to find out how you learn best. This quiz was designed to help you find out something about your preferred learning method. Research on left brain/right brain differences and also on learning and personality differences suggests that each person has preferred ways to receive and communicate information. After you take the quiz, we will help you pinpoint the study aids in this text that will help you learn the material based on your learning style.

Circle the letter of the answer that best explains your preferences. If a single answer does not match your perception, please circle two or more choices. Leave blank any question that does not apply.

1. You are about to give directions to a person. She is staying in a hotel in town and wants to visit your house. She has a rental car. Would you
   V) draw a map on paper?
   R) write down the directions (without a map)?
   A) tell her the directions?
   K) pick her up at the hotel in your car?

2. You are staying in a hotel and have a rental car. You would like to visit friends whose address/location you do not know. Would you like them to
   V) draw you a map on paper?
   R) write down the directions (without a map)?
   A) tell you the directions by phone?
   K) pick you up at the hotel in their car?

3. You have just received a copy of your itinerary for a world trip. This is of interest to a friend. Would you
   A) call her immediately and tell her about it?
   R) send her a copy of the printed itinerary?
   V) show her on a map of the world?

4. You are going to cook a dessert as a special treat for your family. Do you
   K) cook something familiar without need for instructions?
   V) thumb through the cookbook looking for ideas from the pictures?
   R) refer to a specific cookbook where there is a good recipe?
   A) ask for advice from others?

5. A group of tourists has been assigned to you to find out about national parks. Would you
   K) drive them to a national park?
   R) give them a book on national parks?
   V) show them slides and photographs?
   A) give them a talk on national parks?

6. You are about to purchase a new stereo. Other than price, what would most influence your decision?
   A) A friend talking about it.
   K) Listening to it.
   R) Reading the details about it.
   V) Its distinctive, upscale appearance.

7. Recall a time in your life when you learned how to do something like playing a new board game. (Try to avoid choosing a very physical skill, e.g., riding a bike.) How did you learn best? By
   V) visual clues—pictures, diagrams, charts?
   A) listening to somebody explaining it?
   R) written instructions?
   K) doing it?

8. Which of these games do you prefer?
   V) *Pictionary*
   R) *Scrabble*
   K) Charades

9. You are about to learn to use a new program on a computer. Would you
   K) ask a friend to show you?
   R) read the manual that comes with the program?
   A) telephone a friend and ask questions about it?

10. You are not sure whether a word should be spelled "dependent" or "dependant." Do you
    R) look it up in the dictionary?
    V) see the word in your mind and choose the best way it looks?
    A) sound it out in your mind?
    K) write both versions down?

11. Apart from price, what would most influence your decision to buy a particular textbook?
    K) Using a friend's copy.
    R) Skimming parts of it.
    A) A friend talking about it.
    V) It looks OK.

12. A new movie has arrived in town. What would most influence your decision to go or not to go?
    A) Friends talked about it.
    R) You read a review of it.
    V) You saw a preview of it.

13. Do you prefer a lecturer/teacher who likes to use
    R) handouts and/or a textbook?
    V) flow diagrams, charts, slides?
    K) field trips, labs, practical sessions?
    A) discussion, guest speakers?

Results: To determine your learning preference, add up the number of individual Vs, As, Rs, and Ks you have circled. Take the letter you have the greatest number of and match it to the same letter in the Learning Styles Chart. Next to each letter in the chart are suggestions that will refer you to different learning aids throughout this text.

LEARNING STYLES CHART

V | VISUAL

WHAT TO DO IN CLASS	WHAT TO DO WHEN STUDYING	TEXT FEATURES THAT MAY HELP YOU THE MOST	WHAT TO DO PRIOR TO AND DURING EXAMS
Underline. Use different colors. Use symbols, charts, arrangements on the page.	Use the "In Class" strategies. Reconstruct images in different ways. Redraw pages from memory. Replace words with symbols and initials.	**The Navigator** **Feature Stories** **Previews** **Infographics/Illustrations** **Photos** **Business Insights** **Decision Toolkits** **Key Terms in blue** **Words in bold** **Questions/Exercises/ Problems** **Real-World Focus** **Research Assignment** **Surfing the Net**	Recall the "pictures of the pages." Draw, use diagrams where appropriate. Practice turning visuals back into words.

A | AURAL

WHAT TO DO IN CLASS	WHAT TO DO WHEN STUDYING	TEXT FEATURES THAT MAY HELP YOU THE MOST	WHAT TO DO PRIOR TO AND DURING EXAMS
Attend lectures and tutorials. Discuss topics with students. Explain new ideas to other people. Use a tape recorder. Describe overheads, pictures, and visuals to somebody not there. Leave space in your notes for later recall.	You may take poor notes because you prefer to listen. Therefore: Expand your notes. Put summarized notes on tape and listen. Read summarized notes out loud. Explain notes to another "aural" person.	**Infographics/Illustrations** **Business Insights** **Review It/Do It** **Summary of Study Objectives** **Glossary** **Demonstration Problem** **Self-Study Questions** **Questions/Exercises/ Problems** **Managerial Analysis** **Group Decision Case** **Communication Activity** **Ethics Case**	Listen to your "voices" and write them down. Speak your answers. Practice writing answers to old exam questions.

Source: Adapted from Neil D. Fleming and Colleen Mills, "Not Another Inventory, Rather a Catalyst for Reflections," *To Improve the Academy,* Volume II (1992), pp. 137–155. Used by permission.

READING/WRITING

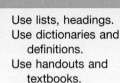

WHAT TO DO IN CLASS	WHAT TO DO WHEN STUDYING	TEXT FEATURES THAT MAY HELP YOU THE MOST	WHAT TO DO PRIOR TO AND DURING EXAMS
Use lists, headings. Use dictionaries and definitions. Use handouts and textbooks. Read. Use lecture notes.	Write out words again and again. Reread notes silently. Rewrite ideas into other words. Organize diagrams into statements.	**The Navigator** **Feature Stories** **Study Objectives** **Previews** **Review It/Do It** **Using the Decision Toolkit** **Summary of Study Objectives** **Glossary** **Self-Study Questions** **Questions/Exercises/ Problems** **Writing Problems** **Group Decision Case** **Managerial Analysis** **Real-World Focus** **Communication Activity** **Research Assignment** **Ethics Case**	Practice with multiple-choice questions. Write out lists. Write paragraphs, beginnings and endings.

KINESTHETIC

WHAT TO DO IN CLASS	WHAT TO DO WHEN STUDYING	TEXT FEATURES THAT MAY HELP YOU THE MOST	WHAT TO DO PRIOR TO AND DURING EXAMS
Use all your senses. Go to labs, take field trips. Use trial-and-error methods. Listen to real-life examples. Use hands-on approach.	You may take notes poorly because topics do not seem relevant. Therefore: Put examples in note summaries. Use pictures and photos to illustrate. Talk about notes with another "kinesthetic" person.	**The Navigator** **Feature Stories** **Previews** **Infographics/Illustrations** **Decision Toolkits** **Review It/Do It** **Using the Decision Toolkit** **Summary of Study Objectives** **Demonstration Problem** **Self-Study Questions** **Questions/Exercises/ Problems** **Group Decision Case** **Managerial Analysis** **Real-World Focus** **Communication Activity** **Research Assignment** **Surfing the Net**	Write practice answers. Role-play the exam situation.

BRIEF CONTENTS

DETAILED CONTENTS

CHAPTER 1

Managerial Accounting

Study Objectives gives you a framework for learning the specific concepts covered in the chapter.

STUDY OBJECTIVES

After studying this chapter, you should be able to:

1. Explain the distinguishing features of managerial accounting.
2. Identify the three broad functions of management.
3. Define the three classes of manufacturing costs.
4. Distinguish between product and period costs.
5. Explain the difference between a merchandising and a manufacturing income statement.
6. Indicate how cost of goods manufactured is determined.
7. Explain the difference between a merchandising and a manufacturing balance sheet.

THE NAVIGATOR

The **Feature Story** helps you picture how the chapter topic relates to the real world of accounting and business. You will find references to the story throughout the chapter. Many Feature Stories end with the Internet address of the company cited in the story, to help you connect with these real businesses.

FEATURE STORY

Spokesman Says, "Cut the Scrap"

You've heard of the Big Three automakers—that's shorthand for General Motors, Ford, and Chrysler (now Daimler-Chrysler), the three big domestic car companies. Well, there's also the Big Three U.S. bicycle makers—Huffy, Murray, and Roadmaster. Like their automotive counterparts, the bike makers have a big challenge: produce domestically a bicycle at a reasonable sticker price when there's a lot of foreign competition.

Murray (short for Murray Ohio Manufacturing Co.) has found a way to keep costs and prices down—and to make a profit. The company manufac-

tures 15,000 bicycles per day at its plant in southern Tennessee. Instead of marketing the bikes to independent bicycle stores, they sell their products to mass merchants such as Sears.

A bicycle's direct materials include steel, tires, spokes, hubs, and brakes. "We take steel and turn it into tubing which, in turn, becomes the bike frame," says Tom Appleton, product manager. "You do have some planned scrap," he says, because you might want to stamp a round sprocket out of a square piece of steel. "By taking a round part out of a square piece, you've automatically got around 25% scrap," he says, "which we sell to scrap dealers at 5 percent of its original cost. Then, there's

unplanned scrap which occurs when one of the workers—to put it bluntly—makes a mistake. We also sell this scrap, but we lose the labor cost."

The direct labor time to make a Murray bike is only about 30 minutes. That's one good reason why an American manufacturer can do well against global competition. "The key is to manage your costs better than the next guy," says Appleton. The most expensive Murray bicycle retails for around $250 and they sold approximately 3 million units to the U.S. market in a recent year.

THE NAVIGATOR

On the World Wide Web
http://www.murrayinc.com

The Navigator is a learning system designed to prompt you to use the learning aids in the chapter and to help you set priorities as you study.

THE NAVIGATOR ✔

- Scan *Study Objectives* ☐
- Read *Feature Story* ☐
- Read *Preview* ☐
- Read text and answer *Before You Go On*
  p. 7 ☐   p. 10 ☐   p. 19 ☐
- Work *Using the Decision Toolkit* ☐
- Review *Summary of Study Objectives* ☐
- Work *Demonstration Problem* ☐
- Answer *Self-Study Questions* ☐
- Complete assignments ☐

The **Preview** describes the purpose of the chapter and outlines the major topics and subtopics you will find in it.

This book focuses on issues illustrated in the feature story about Murray Ohio Manufacturing Co., such as the costs of material, labor, and overhead and the relationship between costs and profits. In a previous financial accounting course, you should have studied the form and content of **financial statements** for **external users** of financial information, such as stockholders and creditors. These financial statements represent the principal product of financial accounting. The chapters in this textbook on managerial accounting focus primarily on the preparation of **reports** for **internal users** of financial information, such as the managers and officers of a company. These reports are the principal product of managerial accounting. The content and organization of this chapter are as follows:

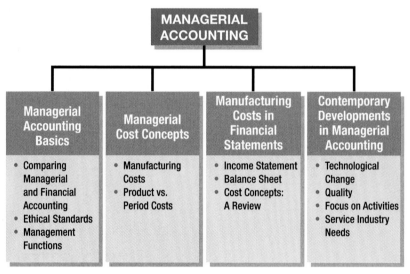

MANAGERIAL ACCOUNTING BASICS

Essential terms and concepts are printed in blue where they first appear and are defined in the end-of-chapter **Glossary**.

Managerial accounting, also called management accounting, is a field of accounting that provides economic and financial information for managers and other internal users. The activities that are part of managerial accounting (and the chapters in which they are discussed) are as follows:

1. Explaining manufacturing and nonmanufacturing costs and how they are reported in the financial statements (Chapter 1).
2. Computing the cost of rendering a service or manufacturing a product (Chapters 2, 3, and 4).
3. Determining the behavior of costs and expenses as activity levels change and analyzing cost–volume–profit relationships within a company (Chapter 5).
4. Assisting management in profit planning and formalizing the plans in the form of budgets (Chapter 6).
5. Providing a basis for controlling costs and expenses by comparing actual results with planned objectives and standard costs (Chapters 7 and 8).
6. Accumulating and using relevant data for management decision making (Chapters 9 and 10).

7. Preparing and interpreting information regarding the company's ability to generate cash (Chapter 11).

8. Analyzing financial information to evaluate performance and financial position (Chapter 12).

Managerial accounting applies to all types of businesses—service, merchandising, and manufacturing—and to all forms of business organizations—proprietorships, partnerships, and corporations. Moreover, managerial accounting is needed in not-for-profit entities as well as in profit-oriented enterprises.

COMPARING MANAGERIAL AND FINANCIAL ACCOUNTING

There are both similarities and differences between managerial and financial accounting. An important similarity is that each field of accounting deals with the economic events of an enterprise. Thus, their interests overlap. For example, determining the unit cost of manufacturing a product is part of managerial accounting. In contrast, reporting the total cost of goods manufactured and sold is part of financial accounting. In addition, both managerial and financial accounting require that the results of an entity's economic events be quantified and be communicated to interested parties. The diverse needs for economic data among parties interested in an enterprise are responsible for many of the differences between the two fields of accounting.

The principal differences between financial accounting and managerial accounting are summarized in Illustration 1-1.

STUDY OBJECTIVE

❶

Explain the distinguishing features of managerial accounting.

Illustration 1-1
Differences between financial and managerial accounting

	Financial Accounting		Managerial Accounting
Primary Users of Reports	External users, who are stockholders, creditors, and regulatory agencies.		Internal users, who are officers, department heads, managers, and supervisors in the company.
Types and Frequency of Reports	Classified financial statements. Issued quarterly and annually.		Internal reports. Issued as frequently as the need arises.
Purpose of Reports	To provide general-purpose information for all users.		To provide special-purpose information for a particular user for a specific decision.
Content of Reports	Pertains to entity as a whole and is highly aggregated (condensed). Limited to double-entry accounting system and cost data. Reporting standard is generally accepted accounting principles.		Pertains to subunits of the entity and may be very detailed. May extend beyond double-entry accounting system to any type of relevant data. Reporting standard is relevance to the decision to be made.
Verification Process	Annual independent audit by certified public accountant.		No independent audits.

ETHICAL STANDARDS FOR MANAGERIAL ACCOUNTANTS

We will emphasize throughout the textbook the importance of ethics in business and in accounting. Managerial accountants recognize that they have an ethical obligation to their companies and the public. To provide guidance for managerial accountants in the performance of their duties, the Institute of Management Accountants (IMA) has developed a code of ethical standards, entitled *Standards of Ethical Conduct for Management Accountants*. This code divides the manage-

Helpful Hints clarify concepts being discussed.

Helpful Hint The IMA code of ethical standards is provided in Appendix D.

rial accountants' responsibilities into four areas: (1) competence, (2) confidentiality, (3) integrity, and (4) objectivity. The code states that management accountants should not commit acts in violation of these standards, nor should they condone such acts by others within their organizations. You may wish to review the code to understand the importance of ethics in companies today.

MANAGEMENT FUNCTIONS

The management of an organization performs three broad functions. They are:

1. Planning.
2. Directing and motivating.
3. Controlling.

In performing these functions, management must make decisions that have a significant impact on the organization.

Planning requires management to look ahead and to establish objectives. These objectives are often as diverse as maximizing short-term profits and market share, maintaining a commitment to environmental protection, and contributing to social programs. A key objective of management is to add **value** to the business under its control. Value is usually measured by the trading price of the company's stock and by the potential selling price of the company.

Directing and motivating involve coordinating a company's diverse activities and human resources to produce a smooth-running operation. This function relates to the implementation of planned objectives. For example, in companies such as Campbell Soup Company, IBM, General Motors, and Oscar Mayer, purchasing, manufacturing, warehousing, and selling must be coordinated. Similarly, it is necessary to select executives, appoint managers and supervisors, and hire and train employees. Most companies prepare **organization charts** to show the interrelationship of activities and the delegation of authority and responsibility within the company.

Business Insight examples illustrate interesting situations in real companies and show how they make decisions using accounting information.

BUSINESS INSIGHT
Management Perspective

Business researchers have identified different organization types, or "corporate cultures." The ways in which the management function of directing and motivating are carried out differ from one organization type to another. Researcher Jeffrey Sonnenfeld has labeled four types of corporate culture:

1. Academies—For the steady climber who must thoroughly master each new job and make one company his or her career home. A classic academy is IBM because as one expert noted: "You don't move ahead until you perform where you are."

2. Clubs—For the individual who strives to fit in. What counts isn't individual achievement, but sincerity, commitment, and doing things for the good of the group. An example is United Parcel Service where one executive noted: "When decisions have to be made we get everyone's opinion, and the company feels like a family to a lot of us."

3. Baseball teams—For those who like to consider themselves free agents. In these situations, companies seek out talent of all ages and experience and reward them by what they produce. They don't care how committed you'll be tomorrow—they want cutting-edge results today. Examples are accounting firms like Arthur Andersen and consulting firms like First Boston Corp.

4. Fortresses—For those who like crisis situations. Many fortresses are companies concerned with survival. Fortresses may be academies, clubs, or base-

ball teams that have failed in the marketplace and are struggling to reverse their fortunes. Other fortresses are in a perpetual boom-and-bust cycle, such as natural resources companies.

Companies do change over time. Apple Computer started out as a baseball team but is now an academy. And with deregulation, banks—once clubs—have evolved into baseball teams.

Source: Adapted from an article by Carol Hymowitz, "Which Corporate Culture Fits You?" *The Wall Street Journal,* July 17, 1989.

The third management function, **controlling,** is the process of keeping the firm's activities on track. In controlling operations, management determines whether planned goals are being met and what changes are necessary when there are deviations from targeted objectives.

How do managers achieve control? In small organizations, a manager might use personal observation. A smart manager in a small operation should know the right questions to ask and how to evaluate the answers. But such a system in a large organization would be chaotic. Imagine the president of Ford Motor Company attempting to determine whether planned objectives are being met without some record of what has happened and what is expected to occur. Thus, a formal system of evaluation that includes such items as budgets, responsibility centers, and performance evaluation reports is typically used in large businesses.

As shown by the graphic in the margin, the three functions of management may be depicted as the spokes of a wheel that move around the axle or hub of decision making. Decision making is not a separate management function. Rather, it is the outcome of the exercise of good judgment in planning, directing and motivating, and controlling.

You are now ready to study specific applications of managerial accounting. As you study these applications, you will encounter many new terms, concepts, and reports. At the same time, you will find some new uses and interpretations of a number of familiar financial accounting terms.

Before You Go On . . . Review It questions at the end of major text sections offer an opportunity to stop and reexamine the key points you have studied.

BEFORE YOU GO ON . . .

● **Review It**
 1. Compare financial accounting and managerial accounting, identifying the principal differences.
 2. Identify and discuss the three broad functions of management.

MANAGERIAL COST CONCEPTS

To perform the three management functions effectively, management needs information. One very important type of information is related to costs. For example, questions such as the following need answering:

1. What costs are involved in making a product?
2. If production volume is decreased, will costs decrease?
3. What impact will automation have on total costs?
4. How can costs best be controlled in the organization?

To answer these questions, management needs reliable and relevant cost information. We now explain and illustrate the costs that management uses.

MANUFACTURING COSTS

Manufacturing consists of activities and processes that convert raw materials into finished goods. Contrast this type of operation with merchandising, which sells merchandise in the form in which it is purchased. Manufacturing costs are typically classified as shown in Illustration 1-2.

Illustration 1-2 Classifications of manufacturing costs

Illustrations like this one convey information in pictorial form to help you visualize and apply the ideas as you study.

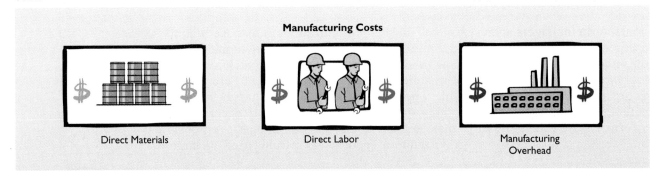

Manufacturing Costs

Direct Materials   Direct Labor   Manufacturing Overhead

Direct Materials

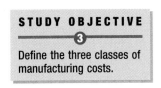

Direct Materials

To obtain the materials that will be converted into the finished product, the manufacturer purchases raw materials. **Raw materials** represent the basic materials and parts that are to be used in the manufacturing process. For example, steel, plastics, and tires are raw materials used in making automobiles.

Raw materials that can be physically and conveniently associated with the finished product during the manufacturing process are called direct materials. Examples include flour in the baking of bread, syrup in the bottling of soft drinks, and steel in the making of automobiles. In the opening story, direct materials for the bicycles included steel, tires, spokes, hubs, and brakes.

Conversely, some raw materials cannot be easily associated with the finished product; these are considered indirect materials. **Indirect materials** (1) do not physically become part of the finished product, such as lubricants, rosin, and polishing compounds used in the manufacturing process, or (2) cannot be traced because their physical association with the finished product is too small in terms of cost, such as cotter pins, lock washers, and the like. Indirect materials are accounted for as part of **manufacturing overhead.**

Helpful Hint The manufacturer of a product uses masking tape to protect certain sections of the product while other sections are painted. The tape is removed and thrown away when the paint is dry. Should the cost of tape be accounted for as direct or indirect materials? Answer: Indirect.

Direct Labor

Direct Labor

The work of factory employees that can be physically and conveniently associated with converting raw materials into finished goods is considered **direct labor.** In the story about Murray Ohio Manufacturing, it took 30 minutes of direct labor to make a bicycle. Bottlers in a soft drink plant, bakers in a bakery, and typesetters in a print shop are examples of employees whose activities are usually classified as direct labor. In contrast, the wages of maintenance people, timekeepers, and supervisors are usually identified as indirect labor because their efforts have no physical association with the finished product, or it is impractical to trace the costs to the goods produced. Like indirect materials, indirect labor is classified as **manufacturing overhead.**

BUSINESS INSIGHT
Management Perspective

The trend toward more automated and computerized factories will change the way managers and employees interact. For one thing, managers will have fewer direct labor employees to supervise because fewer will be needed on the line. Instead of standing in one spot all day, employees and managers will become more mobile, monitoring the computers that handle the production, and involving themselves in a variety of jobs.

Jobs will be more varied. As machines do more of the repetitive work, employees and managers will need to be more problem-solvers than "cogs in a machine." They will need to be more analytical, to receive more technical training, and to be more highly educated. As a result, they also will be more highly paid.

Manufacturing Overhead

Manufacturing overhead consists of costs that are indirectly associated with the manufacture of the finished product. These costs may also be defined as manufacturing costs that cannot be classified as either direct materials or direct labor. Manufacturing overhead includes indirect materials, indirect labor, depreciation on factory buildings and machinery, and insurance, taxes, and maintenance on factory facilities.

The magnitude of the three different product costs in terms of the total product cost is provided in the following chart, which covers seven industries:[1]

PRODUCT COST BY INDUSTRY Percentage of Total Manufacturing Cost			
Industry	Direct Materials	Direct Labor	Manufacturing Overhead
Aerospace	51.7%	19.3%	29.0%
Computers	69.9	7.5	22.5
Electronics	48.6	15.1	36.3
Industrial and farm equipment	46.0	12.8	41.2
Metal products	52.0	15.7	32.3
Motor vehicles and parts	63.8	7.8	28.4
Scientific and photographic equipment	52.3	11.3	36.5
Average for seven industries	54.4%	12.9%	32.6%

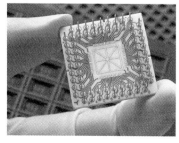

Illustration 1-3 Product cost components by industry

Alternative Terminology notes present synonymous terms that you may come across in practice.

Alternative Terminology
Terms such as *factory overhead, indirect manufacturing costs,* and *burden* are sometimes used instead of manufacturing overhead.

Note that the direct labor component is the smallest. This component of product cost is dropping substantially because of automation. In some companies, direct labor has become as little as 5% of the total cost.

BUSINESS INSIGHT
Management Perspective

In valuing inventories, accountants include three types of costs: materials, overhead, and labor. Allocating materials and labor costs to specific products is fairly straightforward. But accountants have big trouble dealing with overhead, a black hole that swallows up everything from the equipment

---

[1]James A. Hendricks, "Applying Cost Accounting to Factory Automation," *Management Accounting,* December 1988, p. 26.

used to fashion a product to the security guard who watches over the plant at night. How much of the purchasing agent's salary is attributable to the semiconductor chip, how much to the personal computer on his or her desk, how much to the hundred other products made in the same plant? What about the grease that keeps the machines humming, or the computers that make sure paychecks come out on time? Boiled down to its simplest form, the question becomes: Which products cause which costs?

PRODUCT VERSUS PERIOD COSTS

STUDY OBJECTIVE

4

Distinguish between product and period costs.

Alternative Terminology
Product costs are also called *inventoriable costs.*

Each of the manufacturing cost elements (direct materials, direct labor, and manufacturing overhead) are product costs. As the term suggests, product costs are costs that are a necessary and integral part of producing the finished product. These costs do not become expenses under the matching principle until the finished goods inventory is sold. The expense is cost of goods sold. Direct materials and direct labor are often referred to as prime costs because of their direct association with the manufacturing of the finished product. In addition, because direct labor and manufacturing overhead are incurred in converting raw materials into finished goods, these two cost elements are often referred to as conversion costs.

Period costs are costs that are identified with a specific time period rather than with a salable product. These costs relate to nonmanufacturing costs and therefore are not inventoriable costs. Period costs include selling and administrative expenses that are deducted from revenues in the period in which they are incurred.

The foregoing relationships and cost terms are summarized in Illustration 1-4. Our main concern in this chapter is with product costs.

Illustration 1-4 Product versus period costs

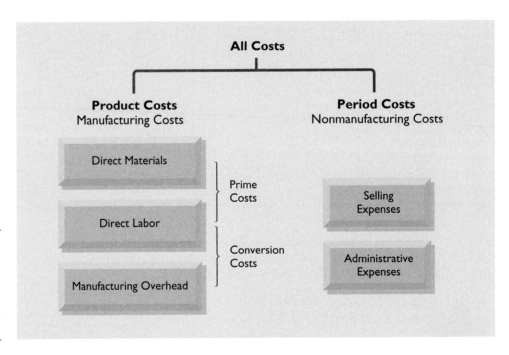

Helpful Hint An unethical manager may choose to inflate the company's earnings by absorbing period costs (such as selling and administrative expenses not pertaining to production) in the ending inventory balances.

BEFORE YOU GO ON . . .

● Review It

1. What are the major cost classifications involved in manufacturing a product?
2. What are product and period costs and their relationship to the manufacturing process?

● **Do It**

In making bicycles, a company has the following costs: tires, salaries of employees who put tires on the wheels, factory building depreciation, wheel nuts, spokes, salary of factory foreman, handle bars, and salaries of factory maintenance employees. Classify each cost as direct materials, direct labor, or manufacturing overhead.

Reasoning: Direct materials are raw materials that can be physically and conveniently associated with the finished product. Direct labor is the work of factory employees that can be physically and conveniently associated with the finished product. Manufacturing overhead are costs that are indirectly associated with the finished product.

Solution: Tires, spokes, and handle bars are direct materials. Salaries of employees who put tires on the wheels are direct labor. All of the other costs are manufacturing overhead.

THE NAVIGATOR

Related exercise material: BE1-4, BE1-5, E1-1, E1-2, and E1-3.

Before You Go On . . . Do It exercises ask you to put to work newly acquired knowledge. They outline the reasoning necessary to complete the exercise, and they show a solution.

MANUFACTURING COSTS IN FINANCIAL STATEMENTS

The financial statements of a manufacturing company are very similar to those of a merchandising company. The principal differences pertain to the cost of goods sold section of the income statement and the current assets section of the balance sheet.

INCOME STATEMENT

Under a periodic inventory system, the income statements of a merchandising company and a manufacturing company differ in the cost of goods sold section. For a merchandising company, cost of goods sold is computed by adding the beginning merchandise inventory and the **cost of goods purchased** and subtracting the ending merchandise inventory. For a manufacturing company, cost of goods sold is computed by adding the beginning finished goods inventory and **cost of goods manufactured** and subtracting the ending finished goods inventory. The different components are shown graphically in Illustration 1-5.

STUDY OBJECTIVE

5

Explain the difference between a merchandising and a manufacturing income statement.

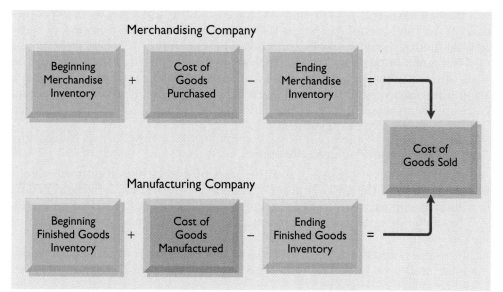

Illustration 1-5 Cost of goods sold components

Helpful Hint Note that a periodic inventory system is used here.

Illustration 1-6 Cost of goods sold sections of merchandising and manufacturing income statements

The cost of goods sold sections for merchandising and manufacturing enterprises shown in Illustration 1-6 highlight the different presentations:

MERCHANDISE COMPANY Income Statement (partial) For the Year Ended December 31, 1999		MANUFACTURING COMPANY Income Statement (partial) For the Year Ended December 31, 1999	
Cost of goods sold		Cost of goods sold	
Merchandise inventory, January 1	$ 70,000	Finished goods inventory, January 1	$ 90,000
Cost of goods purchased	650,000	Cost of goods manufactured	
		(see Illustration 1-8)	370,000
Cost of goods available for sale	720,000	Cost of goods available for sale	460,000
Merchandise inventory, December 31	400,000	Finished goods inventory, December 31	80,000
Cost of goods sold	$320,000	Cost of goods sold	$380,000

The other sections of an income statement are similar for a merchandising and a manufacturing company.

A number of accounts are involved in determining the cost of goods manufactured. To eliminate excessive detail in the income statement, it is customary to show in the income statement only the total cost of goods manufactured and to present the details in a Cost of Goods Manufactured Schedule. The form and content of this schedule are shown in Illustration 1-8 (page 13).

Determining the Cost of Goods Manufactured

STUDY OBJECTIVE

6

Indicate how cost of goods manufactured is determined.

An example may be helpful in showing how the cost of goods manufactured for a period is determined. Assume that Ford Motor Company has a number of automobiles in various stages of production on January 1. In total, these partially completed units are called **beginning work in process inventory.** The costs assigned to beginning work in process inventory are based on the **manufacturing costs incurred in the prior period.** In the current year, Ford Motor continues the production of automobiles. The manufacturing costs incurred in the current year are used first to complete the work in process on January 1 and then to start the production of other vehicles. The sum of the direct materials costs, direct labor costs, and manufacturing overhead incurred in the current year is the total manufacturing costs.

Helpful Hint Does the amount of "total manufacturing costs for the current year" include the amount of "beginning work in process inventory"? Answer: No.

We now have two cost amounts: (1) the cost of the beginning work in process and (2) the total manufacturing costs for the current period. The sum of these costs is the total cost of work in process for the year.

At the end of the year, some vehicles may be only partially completed. The costs of these units become the cost of the **ending work in process inventory.** To find the cost of goods manufactured, we subtract this cost from the total cost of work in process. The determination of the cost of goods manufactured is shown graphically in Illustration 1-7.

Cost of Goods Manufactured Schedule

An internal financial schedule called the **cost of goods manufactured schedule** shows each of the cost elements explained in Illustration 1-7. The schedule for Olsen Manufacturing Company using assumed data is shown in Illustration 1-8. Note that detailed data are presented for direct materials and manufacturing overhead.

A review of Illustration 1-7 along with an examination of the cost of goods manufactured schedule, Illustration 1-8, should help you distinguish between "total manufacturing costs" and "cost of goods manufactured." The difference is the effect of the change in work in process during the period.

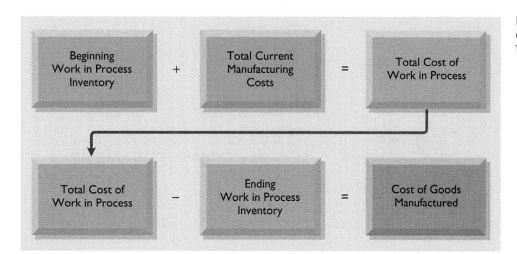

Illustration 1-7 Cost of goods manufactured formula

OLSEN MANUFACTURING COMPANY Costs of Goods Manufactured Schedule For the Year Ended December 31, 1999			
Work in process, January 1			$ 18,400
Direct materials			
Raw materials inventory, January 1	$ 16,700		
Raw materials purchases	152,500		
Total raw materials available for use	169,200		
Less: Raw materials inventory, December 31	22,800		
Direct materials used		$146,400	
Direct labor		175,600	
Manufacturing overhead			
Indirect labor	14,300		
Factory repairs	12,600		
Factory utilities	10,100		
Factory depreciation	9,440		
Factory insurance	8,360		
Total manufacturing overhead		54,800	
Total manufacturing costs			376,800
Total cost of work in process			395,200
Less: Work in process, December 31			25,200
Cost of goods manufactured			$370,000

Illustration 1-8 Cost of goods manufactured schedule

Often, numbers or categories in the financial statements are highlighted in **red type** to draw your attention to key information.

Each chapter presents useful information about how decision makers analyze and solve business problems. **Decision Toolkits** summarize the key features of a decision tool and review why and how to use it.

DECISION TOOLKIT

Decision Checkpoints	Info Needed for Decision	Tool to Use for Decision	How to Evaluate Results
Is the company maintaining control over the costs of production?	Cost of material, labor, and overhead	Cost of goods manufactured schedule	Compare the cost of goods manufactured to revenue expected from product sales.

BALANCE SHEET

STUDY OBJECTIVE

7

Explain the difference between a merchandising and a manufacturing balance sheet.

Unlike the balance sheet for a merchandising company, which shows just one category of inventory, the balance sheet for a manufacturing company may have three inventory accounts. They are:

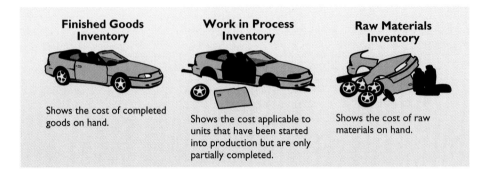

Illustration 1-9
Inventory accounts for a manufacturing company

Finished Goods Inventory is to a manufacturing enterprise what Merchandise Inventory is to a merchandising firm because it represents the goods that are available for sale.

The current assets sections presented in Illustration 1-10 contrast the presentation of inventories of a merchandising company with those of a manufacturing company. Manufacturing inventories are generally listed in the order of their liquidity—their expected realization in cash. Thus, finished goods inventory is listed first. The remainder of the balance sheet is similar for the two types of companies.

Illustration 1-10 Current assets sections of merchandising and manufacturing balance sheets

MERCHANDISING COMPANY **Balance Sheet** **December 31, 1999**		**MANUFACTURING COMPANY** **Balance Sheet** **December 31, 1999**		
Current assets		Current assets		
Cash	$100,000	Cash		$180,000
Receivables (net)	210,000	Receivables (net)		210,000
Merchandise inventory	400,000	**Inventories:**		
Prepaid expenses	22,000	Finished goods	$80,000	
Total current assets	$732,000	Work in process	25,200	
		Raw materials	22,800	128,000
		Prepaid expenses		18,000
		Total current assets		$536,000

Each step in the accounting cycle for a merchandising company is applicable to a manufacturing company. For example, prior to preparing financial statements, adjusting entries are required. The adjusting entries are essentially the same as those of a merchandising company.

The closing entries for a manufacturing company are also similar to those of a merchandising company. The use of a work sheet in the accounting cycle and the journalizing of closing entries for a manufacturing company are illustrated in the appendix at the end of this chapter.

DECISION TOOLKIT

Decision Checkpoints ✔	Info Needed for Decision	Tool to Use for Decision	How to Evaluate Results
What is the composition of a manufacturing company's inventory?	Amount of raw materials, work in process, and finished goods inventory	Balance sheet	Determine whether there is sufficient finished goods inventory, raw materials, and work in process to meet forecasted demand.

COST CONCEPTS—A REVIEW

You have learned a number of cost concepts in this chapter. Because many of these concepts are new, we believe an extended example will be helpful in illustrating how these various cost concepts are used. To illustrate, assume that Northridge Company manufactures and sells pre-hung metal doors. Recently, it decided to start selling pre-hung wood doors as well. An old warehouse that the company presently owns will be used to manufacture the new product. To manufacture and sell these pre-hung wood doors, Northridge identifies the following costs:

1. The material cost (wood) for each door is $10.

2. Labor costs involved in constructing a wood door are $8 per door.

3. Depreciation on the new equipment used to make the wood door using the straight-line method is $25,000 per year.

4. Property taxes on the old warehouse used to make the wood doors are $6,000 per year.

5. Advertising costs for the pre-hung wood doors total $2,500 per month or $30,000 per year.

6. Sales commissions related to pre-hung wood doors sold are $4 per door.

7. Maintenance salaries for the old warehouse are $28,000.

8. Salary of plant manager in charge of pre-hung wood doors is $70,000.

9. Cost of shipping pre-hung wood doors is $12 per door sold.

These manufacturing and selling costs can be assigned to the various categories shown in Illustration 1-11.

Illustration 1-11
Assignment of costs to
cost categories

	Product Costs					
Cost Item	Direct Materials	Direct Labor	Manufacturing Overhead	Period Costs	Prime Costs	Conversion Costs
1. Material cost ($10) per door	X				X	
2. Labor costs ($8) per door		X			X	X
3. Depreciation on new equipment ($25,000 per year)			X			X
4. Property taxes ($6,000 per year)			X			X
5. Advertising costs ($30,000 per year)				X		
6. Sales commission ($4 per door)				X		
7. Maintenance salaries ($28,000 per year)			X			X
8. Salary of plant manager ($70,000)			X			X
9. Cost of shipping pre-hung doors ($12 per door)				X		

Remember that total manufacturing costs are the sum of the product costs — direct materials, direct labor, and manufacturing overhead costs. For example, assume that Northridge Company produces 10,000 pre-hung wood doors the first year. The total manufacturing costs are:

Illustration 1-12
Computation of total
manufacturing cost

Cost Number and Item	Manufacturing Cost
1. Material cost ($10 × 10,000)	$ 100,000
2. Labor cost ($8 × 10,000)	80,000
3. Depreciation on new equipment	25,000
4. Property taxes	6,000
7. Maintenance salaries	28,000
8. Salary of plant manager	70,000
Total manufacturing costs	**$309,000**

If total manufacturing costs are $309,000, then the manufacturing cost per unit (cost to produce one pre-hung wood door) is $30.90 ($309,000 ÷ 10,000 units).

The cost concepts above will be used extensively in subsequent chapters. Study Illustration 1-11 carefully. If you do not understand any of these classifications, go back and reread the appropriate section in this chapter.

CONTEMPORARY DEVELOPMENTS IN MANAGERIAL ACCOUNTING

Since the early 1970s, the competitive environment for U.S. businesses has changed significantly. Within the United States, for example, the airline, financial services, telecommunication, and utility industries have been deregulated.

Globally, competition from such countries as Japan and Germany has intensified, particularly in the automotive and electronics industries. Consequently, business managers demand different and better information than they needed just a few years ago. Such factors as those discussed below contribute to the expanding role of managerial accounting as we look toward the next century.

TECHNOLOGICAL CHANGE

Through **computer-integrated manufacturing (CIM),** many companies can now manufacture products that are untouched by human hands. An example is the use of robotic equipment in the steel and automobile industries. Automation significantly reduces the importance of direct labor costs in some cases, because the worker simply monitors the manufacturing process by watching instrument panels.

Also, the widespread use of computers has greatly reduced the cost of accumulating, storing, and reporting managerial accounting information. Computers now make it possible to do more detailed costing of products, processes, and services than is possible under manual processing.

BUSINESS INSIGHT
Management Perspective

The use of computers is as important in managerial accounting as in financial accounting. As one expert on manufacturing recently noted, "I am convinced that the manufacturers that survive will be those with an unbelievable amount of automation and computerization. The winners will have true computer-integrated manufacturing (CIM). In such a scenario, computers will do everything. They will design the parts, tell you if they can be built, set up the machines on the line, inspect the products, and pop them out on the loading dock with a computerized bill of lading."

QUALITY

Many companies have installed a **total quality control (TQC) system** to reduce defects in finished products. This system requires timely data on defective products, rework costs, and the cost of honoring warranty contracts. As a result, more emphasis is now put on **nonfinancial measures** such as customer satisfaction, number of service calls, and time to generate reports. Attention to these measures, which employees can control, leads to increased profitability.

In addition, many companies have significantly lowered inventory levels and costs using **just-in-time inventory methods (JIT).** Under a just-in-time method, goods are manufactured or purchased just in time for use, which lowers costs of holding and storing inventory. More will be said about this factor in Chapter 4.

FOCUS ON ACTIVITIES

In order to obtain more accurate product costs, many companies are accounting for overhead costs by the activities used in making the product. Activities include purchasing materials, handling raw materials, and production order scheduling. This development, called **activity-based costing (ABC),** is further explained in Chapter 4.

SERVICE INDUSTRY NEEDS

Illustration 1-13 Service industries and companies

Service industries and companies include the following:

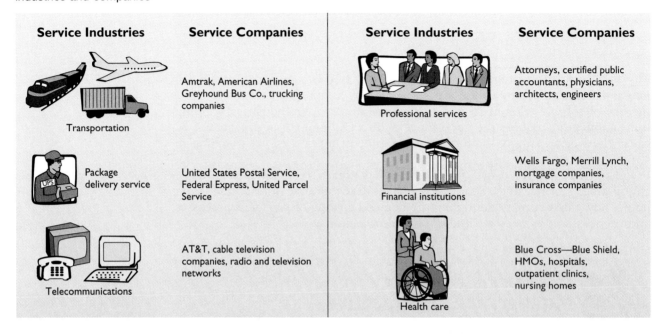

Service Industries	Service Companies	Service Industries	Service Companies
Transportation	Amtrak, American Airlines, Greyhound Bus Co., trucking companies	Professional services	Attorneys, certified public accountants, physicians, architects, engineers
Package delivery service	United States Postal Service, Federal Express, United Parcel Service	Financial institutions	Wells Fargo, Merrill Lynch, mortgage companies, insurance companies
Telecommunications	AT&T, cable television companies, radio and television networks	Health care	Blue Cross—Blue Shield, HMOs, hospitals, outpatient clinics, nursing homes

In some respects, the challenges for managerial accounting are greater in service enterprises than in manufacturing companies. How does a professional firm measure the efficiency and productivity of its professional staff? How does a brokerage firm measure the cost of serving individual customers? What measures can be used to evaluate the quality of services in a hospital or a bank?

Managers of service enterprises look to managerial accounting to answer these questions. In some companies, it may be necessary for the managerial accountant to develop new systems for measuring the cost of serving individual customers and new operating controls to improve the quality and efficiency of specific services.

BUSINESS INSIGHT

Management Perspective

At South Central Bell (Telephone), management accountants have shed their scorekeeping image. A corporate reorganization plan challenged the accountants to "show their stuff." The accountants took on the roles of interpreter, advisor, and partner. To do so, the management accountants had to understand what the numbers mean, relate the numbers to business activity, and recommend alternative courses of action. In addition, they evaluate alternatives and make decisions to maximize business efficiency.

FINAL COMMENT

Not long ago, the managerial accountant was primarily engaged in cost accounting—collecting and reporting manufacturing cost to management. Today, the managerial accountant's responsibilities extend to cost management—providing managers with data on the efficient use of company resources in both manufacturing and service industries.

BEFORE YOU GO ON . . .

● **Review It**

1. How does the content of an income statement differ between a merchandising company and a manufacturing company?
2. How are the work in process inventories reported in the cost of goods manufactured schedule?
3. How does the content of the balance sheet differ between a merchandising company and a manufacturing company?

THE NAVIGATOR

*U*SING THE DECISION TOOLKIT

Giant Company specializes in manufacturing different models of mountain bikes. Assume that a new model, the Jaguar, has been well accepted. As a result, the company has established a separate manufacturing facility to produce these bicycles. The company produces 1,000 bicycles per month. Giant's monthly manufacturing cost and other expenses data related to these bicycles are as follows:

1. Rent on manufacturing equipment (lease cost) $2,000/month
2. Insurance on manufacturing building $750/month
3. Raw materials (frames, tires, etc.) $80/bicycle
4. Utility costs for manufacturing facility $1,000/month
5. Supplies for general office $800/month
6. Wages for assembly line workers in manufacturing facility $30/bicycle
7. Depreciation on office equipment $650/month
8. Miscellaneous materials (lubricants, solders, etc.) $1.20/bicycle
9. Property taxes on manufacturing building $2,400/year
10. Manufacturing supervisor's salary $3,000/month
11. Advertising for bicycles $30,000/year
12. Sales commissions $10/bicycle
13. Depreciation on manufacturing building $1,500/month

Using the Decision Toolkit ex-ercises, which follow the final set of Review It questions in the chapter, ask you to use business information and the decision tools presented in the chapter. We encourage you to think through the questions related to the decision before you study the solution.

Instructions

(a) Prepare an answer sheet with the following column headings:

| Cost Item | Product Costs | | | Period Costs | Prime Costs | Conversion Costs |
	Direct Materials	Direct Labor	Manufacturing Overhead			

Enter each cost item on your answer sheet, placing an "X" mark under the appropriate headings.

(b) Compute total manufacturing costs for the month.

Solution

(a)

Cost Item	Direct Materials	Direct Labor	Manufacturing Overhead	Period Costs	Prime Costs	Conversion Costs
1. Rent on equipment ($2,000/month)			X			X
2. Insurance on manufacturing building ($750/month)			X			X
3. Raw materials ($80/bicycle)	X				X	
4. Manufacturing utilities ($1,000/month)			X			X
5. Office supplies ($800/month)				X		
6. Wages for workers ($30/bicycle)		X			X	X
7. Depreciation on office equipment ($650/month)				X		
8. Miscellaneous materials ($1.20/bicycle)			X			X
9. Property taxes on building ($2,400/year)			X			X
10. Manufacturing supervisor's salary ($3,000/month)			X			X
11. Advertising cost ($30,000/year)				X		
12. Sales commissions ($10/bicycle)				X		
13. Depreciation on manufacturing building ($1,500/month)			X			X

Product Costs: Direct Materials, Direct Labor, Manufacturing Overhead

(b)

Cost Item	Manufacturing Cost
Rent on equipment	$ 2,000
Insurance	750
Raw materials ($80 × 1,000)	80,000
Manufacturing utilities	1,000
Labor ($30 × 1,000)	30,000
Miscellaneous materials ($1.20 × 1,000)	1,200
Property taxes ($2,400 ÷ 12)	200
Manufacturing supervisor's salary	3,000
Depreciation on building	1,500
Total manufacturing costs	$119,650

Problem-Solving Strategies

1. Remember the definitions of: Prime costs = direct materials + direct labor. Conversion costs = Direct labor + manufacturing overhead costs incurred in converting raw materials into finished goods.
2. Make sure you are doing the computations for the appropriate period: month, year, unit, etc.
3. Period costs are not manufacturing costs and, therefore, are not inventoriable.
4. Product costs are manufacturing costs and are inventoriable.

THE NAVIGATOR

SUMMARY OF STUDY OBJECTIVES

① *Explain the distinguishing features of managerial accounting.* The distinguishing features of managerial accounting are:

Primary users of reports—internal users, who are officers, department heads, managers, and supervisors in the company.

Type and frequency of reports—internal reports that are issued as frequently as the need arises.

Purpose of reports—to provide special-purpose information for a particular user for a specific decision.

Content of reports—pertains to subunits of the entity and may be very detailed; may extend beyond double-entry accounting system; the reporting standard is relevance to the decision being made.

Verification of reports—no independent audits.

② *Identify the three broad functions of management.* The three functions are planning, directing and motivating, and controlling. Planning requires management to look ahead and to establish objectives. Directing and motivating, involves coordinating the diverse activities and human resources of a company to produce a smooth-running operation. Controlling is the process of keeping the activities on track.

③ *Define the three classes of manufacturing costs.* Manufacturing costs are typically classified as either (1) direct materials, (2) direct labor, or (3) manufacturing overhead. Raw materials that can be physically and conveniently associated with the finished product during the manufacturing process are called direct materials. The work of factory employees that can be physically and conveniently associated with converting raw materials into finished goods is considered direct labor. Manufac-

turing overhead consists of costs that are indirectly associated with the manufacture of the finished product.

④ *Distinguish between product and period costs.* Product costs are costs that are a necessary and integral part of producing the finished product. Product costs are also called inventoriable costs. These costs do not become expenses under the matching principle until the inventory to which they attach is sold. Period costs are costs that are identified with a specific time period rather than with a salable product. These costs relate to nonmanufacturing costs and therefore are not inventoriable costs.

⑤ *Explain the difference between a merchandising and a manufacturing income statement.* The difference between a merchandising and a manufacturing income statement is in the cost of goods sold section. A manufacturing cost of goods sold section shows beginning and ending finished goods inventories and the cost of goods manufactured.

⑥ *Indicate how cost of goods manufactured is determined.* The cost of the beginning work in process is added to the total manufacturing costs for the current year to arrive at the total cost of work in process for the year. The ending work in process is then subtracted from the total cost of work in process to arrive at the cost of goods manufactured.

⑦ *Explain the difference between a merchandising and a manufacturing balance sheet.* The difference between a manufacturing and a merchandising balance sheet is in the current asset section. In the current asset section of a manufacturing company's balance sheet, three inventory accounts are presented: finished goods inventory, work in process inventory, and raw materials inventory.

THE NAVIGATOR

DECISION TOOLKIT—A SUMMARY

Decision Checkpoints	Info Needed for Decision	Tool to Use for Decision	How to Evaluate Results
Is the company maintaining control over the costs of production?	Cost of material, labor, and overhead	Cost of goods manufactured schedule	Compare the cost of goods manufactured to revenue expected from product sales.
What is the composition of a manufacturing company's inventory?	Amount of raw materials, work in process, and finished goods inventory	Balance sheet	Determine whether there is sufficient finished goods inventory, raw materials, and work in process to meet forecasted demand.

ACCOUNTING CYCLE FOR A MANUFACTURING COMPANY

STUDY OBJECTIVE

⑧

Prepare a work sheet and closing entries for a manufacturing company.

The accounting cycle for a manufacturing company is the same as for a merchandising company when a periodic inventory system is used. Except for the additional manufacturing inventories and manufacturing cost accounts, the journalizing and posting of transactions is the same. Similarly, the preparation of a trial balance and the journalizing and posting of adjusting entries are the same. Some changes, however, occur in the use of a work sheet and in preparing closing entries.

To illustrate the changes in the work sheet, we will use the cost of goods manufactured schedule for Olsen Manufacturing presented in Illustration 1-8 of the chapter and other assumed data. For convenience, the cost of goods manufactured schedule is reproduced in Illustration 1A-1:

Illustration 1A-1 Cost of goods manufactured schedule

OLSEN MANUFACTURING COMPANY			
Cost of Goods Manufactured Schedule			
For the Year Ended December 31, 1999			
Work in process, January 1			$ 18,400
Direct materials			
Raw materials inventory, January 1	$ 16,700		
Raw materials purchases	152,500		
Total raw materials available for use	169,200		
Less: Raw materials inventory, December 31	22,800		
Direct materials used		$146,400	
Direct labor		175,600	
Manufacturing overhead			
Indirect labor	14,300		
Factory repairs	12,600		
Factory utilities	10,100		
Factory depreciation	9,440		
Factory insurance	8,360		
Total manufacturing overhead		54,800	
Total manufacturing costs			376,800
Total cost of work in process			395,200
Less: Work in process, December 31			25,200
Cost of goods manufactured			$370,000

WORK SHEET

When a work sheet is used in preparing financial statements, two additional columns are needed for the cost of goods manufactured schedule. As illustrated in the work sheet in Illustration 1A-2, debit and credit columns for this schedule have been inserted before the income statement columns.

In the cost of goods manufactured columns, the beginning inventories of raw materials and work in process are entered as debits. In addition, all the manufacturing costs are entered as debits. The reason is that each of these amounts

OLSEN MANUFACTURING COMPANY
Work Sheet (partial)
For the Year Ended December 31, 1999

	Adjusted Trial Balance		Cost of Goods Manufactured		Income Statement		Balance Sheet	
	Dr.	Cr.	Dr.	Cr.	Dr.	Cr.	Dr.	Cr.
Cash	42,500						42,500	
Accounts Receivable (Net)	71,900						71,900	
Finished Goods Inv.	24,600				24,600	19,500	19,500	
Work in Process Inv.	18,400		18,400	25,200			25,200	
Raw Materials Inv.	16,700		16,700	22,800			22,800	
Plant Assets	724,000						724,000	
Accumulated Depr.		278,400						278,400
Notes Payable		100,000						100,000
Accounts Payable		40,000						40,000
Income Taxes Payable		5,000						5,000
Common Stock		200,000						200,000
Retained Earnings		205,100						205,100
Sales		680,000				680,000		
Raw Materials Purchases	152,500		152,500					
Direct Labor	175,600		175,600					
Indirect Labor	14,300		14,300					
Factory Repairs	12,600		12,600					
Factory Utilities	10,100		10,100					
Factory Depreciation	9,440		9,440					
Factory Insurance	8,360		8,360					
Selling Expenses	114,900				114,900			
Administrative Exp.	92,600				92,600			
Income Tax Exp.	20,000				20,000			
Totals	1,508,500	1,508,500	418,000	48,000				
Cost of Goods Manufactured				370,000	370,000			
Totals			418,000	418,000	622,100	699,500	905,900	828,500
Net Income					77,400			77,400
Totals					699,500	699,500	905,900	905,900

increases cost of goods manufactured. Ending inventories for raw materials and work in process are entered as credits in the cost of goods manufactured columns because they have the opposite effect—they decrease cost of goods manufactured. The balancing amount for these columns is the cost of goods manufactured. Note that the amount, $370,000, agrees with the amount reported for cost of goods manufactured in Illustration 1A-1. This amount is also entered in the income statement debit column.

The income statement and balance sheet columns for a manufacturing company are basically the same as for a merchandising company. For example, the treatment of the finished goods inventories is identical with the treatment of merchandise inventory. That is, the beginning inventory is entered in the debit column, and the ending finished goods inventory is entered in the income statement credit column and the balance sheet debit column.

As in the case of a merchandising company, financial statements can be prepared from the statement columns of the work sheet. In addition, the cost of goods manufactured schedule can also be prepared directly from the work sheet.

CLOSING ENTRIES

The closing entries for a manufacturing company are different than for a merchandising company. **A Manufacturing Summary account is used to close all accounts that appear in the cost of goods manufactured schedule.** The balance of the Manufacturing Summary account is the Cost of Goods Manufactured for the period. Manufacturing Summary is then closed to Income Summary. The closing entries can be prepared from the work sheet. As illustrated below, the closing entries for the manufacturing accounts are prepared first. The closing entries for Olsen Manufacturing are as follows:

Date	Account	Debit	Credit
Dec. 31	Work in Process Inventory (Dec. 31)	25,200	
	Raw Materials Inventory (Dec. 31)	22,800	
	Manufacturing Summary		**48,000**
	(To record ending raw materials and work in process inventories)		
31	**Manufacturing Summary**	**418,000**	
	Work in Process Inventory (Jan. 1)		18,400
	Raw Materials Inventory (Jan. 1)		16,700
	Raw Materials Purchases		152,500
	Direct Labor		175,600
	Indirect Labor		14,300
	Factory Repairs		12,600
	Factory Utilities		10,100
	Factory Depreciation		9,440
	Factory Insurance		8,360
	(To close beginning raw materials and work in process inventories and manufacturing cost accounts)		
31	Finished Goods Inventory (Dec. 31)	19,500	
	Sales	680,000	
	Income Summary		699,500
	(To record ending finished goods inventory and close sales account)		
31	Income Summary	622,100	
	Finished Goods Inventory (Jan. 1)		24,600
	Manufacturing Summary		**370,000**
	Selling Expenses		114,900
	Administrative Expenses		92,600
	Income Tax Expense		20,000
	(To close beginning finished goods inventory, manufacturing summary, and expense accounts)		
31	Income Summary	77,400	
	Retained Earnings		77,400
	(To close net income to retained earnings)		

After posting, the summary accounts will show the following:

Manufacturing Summary

Dec. 31	Close	418,000	Dec. 31	Close	48,000
			31	Close	370,000

Income Summary

Dec. 31	Close	622,100	Dec. 31	Close	699,500
31	Close	77,400			

These data precisely track the closing entries. It also would be possible to post each account balance to the Manufacturing Summary account.

SUMMARY OF STUDY OBJECTIVE FOR APPENDIX 1A

❽ *Prepare a work sheet and closing entries for a manufacturing company.* Two additional columns are needed in the work sheet for the cost of goods manufactured. In these columns, the beginning inventories of raw materials and work in process are entered as debits, and the ending inventories are entered as credits; all manufacturing costs are entered as debits. To close all of the accounts that appear in the cost of goods manufactured schedule, a Manufacturing Summary account is used.

GLOSSARY

Conversion costs Direct labor and manufacturing overhead costs incurred in converting raw materials into finished goods. (p. 10)

Cost of goods manufactured Total cost of work in process less the cost of the ending work in process inventory. (p. 12)

Direct labor The work of factory employees that can be physically and conveniently associated with converting raw materials into finished goods. (p. 8)

Direct materials Raw materials that can be physically and conveniently associated with manufacturing the finished product. (p. 8)

Indirect labor Work of factory employees that has no physical association with the finished product, or it is impractical to trace the costs to the goods produced. (p. 8)

Indirect materials Raw materials that do not physically become part of the finished product or cannot be traced because their physical association with the finished product is too small. (p. 8)

Managerial accounting A field of accounting that provides economic and financial information for managers and other internal users. (p. 4)

Manufacturing overhead Manufacturing costs that are indirectly associated with the manufacture of the finished product. (p. 9)

Period costs Costs that are identified with a specific time period and charged to expense as incurred. (p. 10)

Prime costs Direct materials and direct labor. (p. 10)

Product costs Costs that are a necessary and integral part of producing the finished product. (p. 10)

Total cost of work in process Cost of the beginning work in process plus total manufacturing costs for the current period. (p. 12)

Total manufacturing costs The sum of direct materials, direct labor, and manufacturing overhead incurred in the current period. (p. 12)

DEMONSTRATION PROBLEM

Superior Manufacturing Company has the following cost and expense data for the year ending December 31, 1999.

Raw materials, 1/1/99	$ 30,000	Insurance, factory	$ 14,000
Raw materials, 12/31/99	20,000	Property taxes, factory building	6,000
Raw materials purchased	205,000	Sales (net)	1,500,000
Indirect materials	15,000	Delivery expenses	100,000
Work in process, 1/1/99	80,000	Sales commissions	150,000
Work in process, 12/31/99	50,000	Indirect labor	90,000
Finished goods, 1/1/99	110,000	Factory machinery rent	40,000
Finished goods, 12/31/99	120,000	Factory utilities	65,000
Direct labor	350,000	Depreciation, factory building	24,000
Factory manager's salary	35,000	Administrative expenses	300,000

Instructions

(a) Prepare a cost of goods manufactured schedule for Superior Company for 1999.

(b) Prepare an income statement for Superior Company for 1999.

(c) Assume that Superior Company's ledgers show the balances of the following current asset accounts: Cash, $17,000, Accounts Receivable (net), $120,000, Prepaid Expenses, $13,000, and Short-term Investments, $26,000. Prepare the current assets section of the balance sheet for Superior Company as of December 31, 1999.

Problem-Solving Strategies

1. Beginning work in process is the first item in the cost of goods manufactured schedule.

2. Total manufacturing costs are the sum of direct materials used, direct labor, and total manufacturing overhead.

3. Total cost of work in process is the sum of beginning work in process and total manufacturing costs.

4. Cost of goods manufactured is the total cost of work in process less ending work in process.

5. The cost of goods sold section of the income statement shows beginning and ending finished goods inventory and cost of goods manufactured.

6. In the balance sheet, manufacturing inventories are listed in the order of their expected realization in cash, with finished goods first.

Solution to Demonstration Problem

(a)
SUPERIOR MANUFACTURING COMPANY
Cost of Goods Manufactured Schedule
For the Year Ended December 31, 1999

Work in process, 1/1			$ 80,000
Direct materials			
Raw materials inventory, 1/1	$ 30,000		
Raw materials purchased	205,000		
Total raw materials available for use	235,000		
Less: Raw materials inventory, 12/31	20,000		
Direct materials used		$215,000	
Direct labor		350,000	
Manufacturing overhead			
Indirect labor	90,000		
Factory utilities	65,000		
Factory machinery rent	40,000		
Factory manager's salary	35,000		
Depreciation on building	24,000		
Indirect materials	15,000		
Factory insurance	14,000		
Property taxes	6,000		
Total manufacturing overhead		289,000	
Total manufacturing costs			854,000
Total cost of work in process			934,000
Less: Work in process, 12/31			50,000
Cost of goods manufactured			$884,000

(b)

SUPERIOR MANUFACTURING COMPANY
Income Statement
For the Year Ended December 31, 1999

Sales (net)		$1,500,000
Cost of goods sold		
Finished goods inventory, January 1	$110,000	
Cost of goods manufactured	884,000	
Cost of goods available for sale	994,000	
Less: Finished goods inventory, December 31	120,000	
Cost of goods sold		874,000
Gross profit		626,000
Operating expenses		
Administrative expenses	300,000	
Sales commissions	150,000	
Delivery expenses	100,000	
Total operating expenses		550,000
Net income		$ 76,000

(c)

SUPERIOR MANUFACTURING COMPANY
Balance Sheet (partial)
December 31, 1999

Current assets		
Cash		$ 17,000
Short-term investments		26,000
Accounts receivable (net)		120,000
Inventories		
Finished goods	$120,000	
Work in process	50,000	
Raw materials	20,000	190,000
Prepaid expenses		13,000
Total current assets		$366,000

This would be a good time to return to the Student Owner's Manual at the beginning of the book (or look at it for the first time if you skipped it before) to read about the various types of homework materials that appear at the ends of chapters. Knowing the purpose of different assignments will help you appreciate what each contributes to your accounting skills and competencies.

SELF-STUDY QUESTIONS

Answers are at the end of the chapter.

(SO 1) 1. Managerial accounting:
   (a) is governed by generally accepted accounting principles.
   (b) places emphasis on special-purpose information.
   (c) pertains to the entity as a whole and is highly aggregated.
   (d) is limited to cost data.

(SO 1) 2. Which of the following is *not* one of the categories in *Standards of Ethical Conduct for Management Accountants*?
   (a) Confidentiality.
   (b) Competence.
   (c) Integrity.
   (d) Independence.

3. The management of an organization performs three broad functions. They are: (SO 2)
   (a) planning, directing and motivating, and selling.
   (b) planning, directing and motivating, and controlling.
   (c) planning, manufacturing, and controlling.
   (d) directing and motivating, manufacturing, and controlling.

4. Direct materials are a: (SO 3)

	Conversion Cost	Manufacturing Cost	Prime Cost
(a)	Yes	Yes	No
(b)	No	Yes	Yes
(c)	Yes	Yes	Yes
(d)	No	No	No

(SO 3)   5. Which of the following costs would be included in manufacturing overhead of a computer manufacturer?
   (a) The cost of the $3\frac{1}{2}$-inch disk drives.
   (b) The wages earned by computer assemblers.
   (c) The cost of the memory chips.
   (d) Depreciation on testing equipment.

(SO 3)   6. Which of the following is *not* an element of manufacturing overhead?
   (a) Sales manager's salary.
   (b) Plant manager's salary.
   (c) Factory repairman's wages.
   (d) Product inspector's salary.

(SO 4)   7. Indirect labor is a:
   (a) nonmanufacturing cost.
   (b) prime cost.
   (c) product cost.
   (d) period cost.

(SO 5)   8. For the year, Redder Company has cost of goods manufactured of $600,000, beginning finished goods inventory of $200,000, and end

ing finished goods inventory of $250,000. The cost of goods sold is:
   (a) $450,000
   (b) $500,000
   (c) $550,000
   (d) $600,000

9. A cost of goods manufactured schedule shows   (SO 6)
beginning and ending inventories for:
   (a) raw materials and work in process only.
   (b) work in process only.
   (c) raw materials only.
   (d) raw materials, work in process, and finished goods.

10. In a manufacturing company balance sheet,   (SO 7)
three inventories may be reported: (1) raw materials, (2) work in process, and (3) finished goods. Indicate in what sequence these inventories generally appear on a balance sheet.
   (a) (1), (2), (3)
   (b) (2), (3), (1)
   (c) (3), (1), (2)
   (d) (3), (2), (1)

THE NAVIGATOR

*****Note:** All asterisked Questions, Exercises, and Problems relate to material in the appendix to the chapter.

QUESTIONS

1. (a) "Managerial accounting is a field of accounting that provides economic information for all interested parties." Do you agree? Explain.
   (b) Pat Gonzalez believes that managerial accounting serves only manufacturing firms. Is Pat correct? Explain.

2. Distinguish between managerial and financial accounting as to (a) primary users of reports, (b) types and frequency of reports, and (c) purpose of reports.

3. How does the content of reports and the verification of reports differ between managerial and financial accounting?

4. (a) Identify the four categories of ethical standards for management accountants.
   (b) Is the responsibility of the management accountant limited to only his or her own acts? Explain.

5. Karen Pedigo is studying for the next accounting midterm examination. Summarize for Karen what she should know about management functions.

6. "Decision making is management's most important function." Do you agree? Why or why not?

7. Sue McCabe is studying for her next accounting examination. Explain to Sue what she should know about the differences between the income statements for a manufacturing company and a merchandising company.

8. Bob Segar is unclear as to the difference between the balance sheets of a merchandising company and a manufacturing company. Explain the difference to Bob.

9. How are manufacturing costs classified?

10. Gene Decker claims that the distinction between direct and indirect materials is based entirely on physical association with the product. Is Gene correct? Why?

11. Andrea Leite is confused about the differences between a product cost and a period cost. Explain the differences to Andrea.

12. Amy Haas asks your help with the terms (a) prime costs and (b) conversion costs. Distinguish between the terms.

13. In Modine Molding Company, direct materials are $12,000, direct labor is $15,000, and manufacturing overhead is $9,000. What is the amount of (a) prime costs and (b) conversion costs?

14. Identify the differences in the cost of goods sold section of an income statement between a merchandising company and a manufacturing company.

15. The determination of the cost of goods manufactured involves the following factors: (A) beginning work in process inventory, (B) total manufacturing costs, and (C) ending work in process inventory. Identify the meaning of x in the following formulas:
   (a) A + B = x
   (b) A + B − C = x

16. Sajjad Manufacturing has beginning raw materials inventory $24,000, ending raw materials inventory $18,000, and raw materials purchases $180,000. What is the cost of direct materials used?

17. Griggs Manufacturing Inc. has beginning work in process $27,200, direct materials used $240,000, di-

rect labor $200,000, total manufacturing overhead $120,000, and ending work in process $32,000. What are total manufacturing costs?

18. Using the data in Q17, what are (a) the total cost of work in process and (b) the cost of goods manufactured?

19. In what order should manufacturing inventories be listed in a balance sheet?

*20. How, if at all, does the accounting cycle differ between a manufacturing company and a merchandising company?

*21. What typical account balances are carried into the cost of goods manufactured columns of the manufacturing work sheet?

*22. Prepare the closing entries for (a) ending work in process and raw materials inventories and (b) manufacturing summary. Use XXXs for amounts.

BRIEF EXERCISES

BE1-1 Complete the following comparison table between managerial and financial accounting.

Distinguish between managerial and financial accounting.

(SO 1)

	Financial Accounting	**Managerial Accounting**
Primary users		
Type of reports		
Frequency of reports		
Purpose of reports		
Reporting standards		
Verification		

BE1-2 The Institute of Management Accountants has promulgated ethical standards for managerial accountants. Identify the four areas addressed by these standards.

Identify ethical standards.

(SO 1)

BE1-3 Listed below are three functions of the management of an organization:

(a) Planning (b) Directing and motivating (c) Controlling

Identify the three management functions.

(SO 2)

Identify each of the following statements that best describes each of the above functions.

1. ____ require(s) management to look ahead and to establish objectives. A key objective of management appears to be to add value to the business.

2. ____ involve(s) coordinating the diverse activities and human resources of a company to produce a smooth-running operation. This function relates to the implementation of planned objectives.

3. ____ is the process of keeping the activities on track. Management must determine whether goals are being met and what changes are necessary when there are deviations.

BE1-4 Determine whether each of the following costs should be classified as direct materials (DM), direct labor (DL), or manufacturing overhead (MO):

(a) ____ Frames and tires used in manufacturing bicycles.
(b) ____ Wages paid to production workers.
(c) ____ Insurance on factory equipment and machinery.
(d) ____ Depreciation on factory equipment.

Classify manufacturing costs.

(SO 3)

BE1-5 Indicate whether each of the following costs of an automobile manufacturer would be classified as direct materials, direct labor, or manufacturing overhead:

(a) ____ Windshield.
(b) ____ Engine.
(c) ____ Wages of assembly line worker.
(d) ____ Depreciation of factory machinery.
(e) ____ Factory machinery lubricants.
(f) ____ Tires.
(g) ____ Steering wheel.
(h) ____ Salary of painting supervisor.

Classify manufacturing costs.

(SO 3)

BE1-6 Identify whether each of the following costs should be classified as product costs or period costs:

(a) ____ Manufacturing overhead.
(b) ____ Selling expenses.
(c) ____ Administrative expenses.
(d) ____ Advertising expenses.
(e) ____ Direct labor.
(f) ____ Direct material.

Identify product and period costs.

(SO 4)

Classify manufacturing costs.
(SO 3, 4)

BE1-7   Presented below are Sabino Company's monthly manufacturing cost data related to its personal computer product:
(a) Utilities for manufacturing equipment $116,000
(b) Raw material (CPU, chips, etc.) $ 85,000
(c) Depreciation on manufacturing building $880,000
(d) Wages for production workers $191,000

Enter each cost item on the following table, placing an "X" under the appropriate headings.

| | **Product Costs** | | | | |
	Direct Material	Direct Labor	Factory Overhead	Prime Costs	Conversion Costs
(a)					
(b)					
(c)					
(d)					

Compute total manufacturing costs and total cost of work in process.
(SO 6)

BE1-8   Chinn Manufacturing Company has the following data: direct labor $250,000, direct materials used $180,000, total manufacturing overhead $208,000, and beginning work in process $25,000. Compute (a) total manufacturing costs and (b) total cost of work in process.

Prepare current assets section.
(SO 7)

BE1-9   In alphabetical order below are current asset items for Judd Company's balance sheet at December 31, 1999. Prepare the current asset section (including a complete heading).

Accounts receivable	$200,000
Cash	62,000
Finished goods	75,000
Prepaid expenses	38,000
Raw materials	68,000
Work in process	91,000

Determine missing amounts in computing total manufacturing costs.
(SO 6)

BE1-10   Presented below are incomplete 1999 manufacturing cost data for Kelser Corporation. Determine the missing amounts.

	Direct Material Used	Direct Labor Used	Factory Overhead	Total Manufacturing Costs
(a)	$49,000	$61,000	$ 50,000	?
(b)	?	$88,000	$120,000	$296,000
(c)	$55,000	?	$ 95,000	$300,000

Determine missing amounts in computing cost of goods manufactured.
(SO 6)

BE1-11   Use the same data from BE1-10 above. Compute the cost of goods manufactured for Kelser Corporation in 1999.

	Total Manufacturing Costs	Work in Process (1/1)	Work in Process (12/31)	Cost of Goods Manufactured
(a)	?	$120,000	$86,000	?
(b)	$296,000	?	$98,000	$318,000
(c)	$300,000	$470,000	?	$715,000

Identify work sheet columns for selected accounts.
(SO 8)

*BE1-12   A work sheet is used in preparing financial statements for Lawney Manufacturing Company. The following accounts are included in the adjusted trial balance: Finished Goods Inventory $28,000, Work in Process Inventory $21,600, Raw Materials Purchases $175,000, and Direct Labor $140,000. Indicate the work sheet column(s) to which each account should be extended.

EXERCISES

E1-1   Presented below is a list of costs and expenses usually incurred by Mauer Corporation, a manufacturer of furniture, in its factory:

Classify costs into three classes of manufacturing costs.

(SO 3)

1. Salaries for assembly line inspectors.
2. Insurance on factory machines.
3. Property taxes on the factory building.
4. Factory repairs.
5. Upholstery used in manufacturing furniture.
6. Wages paid to assembly line workers.
7. Factory machinery depreciation.
8. Glue, nails, paint, and other small parts used in production.
9. Factory supervisors' salaries.
10. Wood used in manufacturing furniture.

Instructions
Classify the above items into the following categories: (a) direct materials, (b) direct labor, and (c) manufacturing overhead.

E1-2   Nevitt Company reports the following costs and expenses in May:

Determine the total amount of various types of costs.

(SO 3, 4)

Factory utilities	$ 8,500	Direct labor	$69,100
Depreciation on factory		Sales salaries	49,400
equipment	12,650	Property taxes on factory	
Depreciation on delivery trucks	3,500	building	2,500
Indirect factory labor	48,900	Repairs to office equipment	1,300
Indirect materials	96,200	Factory repairs	2,000
Direct materials used	137,600	Advertising	18,000
Factory manager's salary	8,000	Office supplies used	3,000

Instructions
From the information, determine the total amount of:
(a) Prime costs.
(b) Manufacturing overhead.
(c) Conversion costs.
(d) Product costs.
(e) Period costs.

E1-3   Caudell Company is a manufacturer of personal computers. Various costs and expenses associated with its operations are as follows:

Classify various costs into different cost categories.

(SO 3, 4)

1. Property taxes on the factory building. (c)
2. Production superintendents' salaries. (c)
3. Memory boards and chips used in assembling computers. (a)
4. Depreciation on the factory equipment. (c)
5. Salaries for assembly line quality control inspectors. (b)
6. Sales commissions paid to sell personal computers. (d)
7. Electrical wiring in assembling computers. (a)
8. Wages of workers assembling personal computers. (b)
9. Soldering materials used on factory assembly lines. (c)
10. Salaries for the night security guards for the factory building. (c)

The company intends to classify these costs and expenses into the following categories:
(a) direct materials, (b) direct labor, (c) manufacturing overhead, and (d) period costs.

Instructions
List the items (1)–(10). For each item, indicate the cost category to which the item belongs.

Indicate in which schedule or financial statement(s) different cost items will appear.

(SO 5, 6, 7)

E1-4 Piazza Manufacturing Company produces blankets. From its accounting records it prepares the following schedule and financial statements on a yearly basis:
(a) Cost of goods manufactured schedule
(b) Income statement
(c) Balance sheet

The following items are found in its ledger and accompanying data:

1. Direct labor
2. Raw materials inventory, 1/1
3. Work in process inventory, 12/31
4. Finished goods inventory, 1/1
5. Indirect labor
6. Depreciation on factory machinery
7. Work in process, 1/1
8. Finished goods inventory, 12/31

9. Factory maintenance salaries
10. Cost of goods manufactured
11. Depreciation on delivery equipment
12. Cost of goods available for sale
13. Direct materials used
14. Heat and electricity for factory
15. Repairs to roof of factory building
16. Cost of raw materials purchases

Instructions
List the items (1)–(16). For each item, indicate by using the appropriate letter or letters, the schedule and/or financial statement(s) in which the item will appear.

Determine the missing amount of different cost items.

(SO 6)

E1-5 Manufacturing cost data for Rathke Company are presented below:

	Case A	Case B	Case C
Direct materials used	(a)	$70,000	$130,000
Direct labor	$ 60,000	86,000	(g)
Manufacturing overhead	42,500	81,600	102,000
Total manufacturing costs	180,650	(d)	260,000
Work in process 1/1/00	(b)	16,500	(h)
Total cost of work in process	221,500	(e)	327,000
Work in process 12/31/00	(c)	9,000	70,000
Cost of goods manufactured	185,275	(f)	(i)

Instructions
Indicate the missing amount for each letter.

Determine the missing amount of different cost items and prepare a condensed cost of goods manufactured schedule.

(SO 5, 6)

E1-6 Incomplete manufacturing cost data for Cepada Company for 2000 are presented as follows:

	Direct Materials Used	Direct Labor Used	Manufacturing Overhead	Total Manufacturing Costs	Work in Process 1/1	Work in Process 12/31	Cost of Goods Manufactured
(1)	$120,000	$140,000	$ 77,000	(a)	$30,000	(b)	$360,000
(2)	(c)	200,000	130,000	$440,000	(d)	$40,000	470,000
(3)	80,000	100,000	(e)	260,000	60,000	80,000	(f)
(4)	70,000	(g)	75,000	290,000	45,000	(h)	270,000

Instructions
(a) Indicate the missing amount for each letter.
(b) Prepare a condensed cost of goods manufactured schedule for situation (1) for the year ended December 31, 2000.

Prepare a cost of goods manufactured schedule and a partial income statement.

(SO 5, 6)

E1-7 Tressler Corporation has the following cost records for June 2000:

Indirect factory labor	$ 4,500	Factory utilities	$ 400
Direct materials used	20,000	Depreciation, factory equipment	1,700
Work in process, 6/1/00	3,000	Direct labor	25,000
Work in process, 6/30/00	3,500	Manufacture, factory equipment	1,300
Finished goods, 6/1/00	5,000	Indirect materials	2,200
Finished goods, 6/30/00	6,000	Factory manager's salary	3,000

Instructions
(a) Prepare a cost of goods manufactured schedule for June 2000.
(b) Prepare an income statement through gross profit for June 2000 assuming net sales are $98,100.

E1-8 An analysis of the accounts of Salazar Manufacturing reveals the following manufacturing cost data for the month ended June 30, 2000:

Prepare a cost of goods manufactured schedule and present the ending inventories of the balance sheet.

(SO 5, 6, 7)

Inventories:	Beginning	Ending
Raw materials	$9,000	$10,000
Work in process	5,000	8,000
Finished goods	8,000	6,000

Costs incurred:
  Raw material purchases $64,000, direct labor $50,000, manufacturing overhead $19,200. The specific overhead costs were: indirect labor $5,500, factory insurance $4,000, machinery depreciation $4,000, machinery repairs $1,800, factory utilities $2,400, miscellaneous factory costs $1,500.

Instructions
(a) Prepare the cost of goods manufactured schedule for the month ended June 30, 2000.
(b) Show the presentation of the ending inventories on the June 30, 2000, balance sheet.

E1-9 The cost of goods manufactured schedule shows each of the cost elements. Complete the following schedule for Lanier Manufacturing Company:

Determine missing amounts in cost of goods manufactured schedule.

(SO 5, 6)

LANIER MANUFACTURING COMPANY
Cost of Goods Manufactured Schedule
For the Year Ended December 31, 2000

Work in process (1/1)			$200,000
Direct materials			
Raw materials inventory (1/1)	$?		
Add: Raw material purchases	158,000		
Less: Raw material inventory (12/31)	6,500		
Direct materials used		$190,000	
Direct labor		?	
Manufacturing overhead			
Indirect labor	$ 18,000		
Factory depreciation	36,000		
Factory utilities	68,000		
Total overhead		122,000	
Total manufacturing costs			?
Total cost of work in process			$?
Less: Work in process (12/31)			87,000
Cost of goods manufactured			$560,000

E1-10 Fiero Motor Company manufactures automobiles. During September 2000 the company purchased 5,000 head lamps at a cost of $8 per lamp. Fiero withdrew 4,650 lamps from the warehouse during the month. Fifty of these lamps were used to replace the head lamps in autos used by traveling sales staff. The remaining 4,600 lamps were put in autos manufactured during the month.

Determine the amount of cost to appear in various accounts and indicate in which financial statements these accounts would appear.

(SO 5, 6, 7)

 Of the autos put into production during September 2000, 90% were completed and transferred to the company's storage lot. Eighty percent of the cars completed during the month were sold by September 30.

Instructions
(a) Determine the cost of head lamps that would appear in each of the following accounts at September 30, 2000: Raw Materials, Work in Process, Finished Goods, Cost of Goods Sold, and Selling Expenses.
(b) ▭▭▭▷ Write a short memorandum to the chief accountant, indicating whether and where each of the accounts in (a) would appear on the income statement or on the balance sheet at September 30, 2000.

Prepare a partial work sheet for a manufacturing firm.
(SO 8)

*E1-11 Data for Salazar Manufacturing are presented in Exercise 1-8.

Instructions
Prepare a partial work sheet for Salazar Manufacturing.

PROBLEMS: SET A

Classify manufacturing costs into different categories and compute the unit cost.
(SO 3, 4)

P1-1A Glazier Company specializes in manufacturing motorcycles. The model is well accepted by consumers, and the company has a large number of orders to keep the factory production at 1,000 motorcycles per month. Glazier's monthly manufacturing costs and other expense data are as follows:

Maintenance costs on factory building	$ 300
Factory manager's salary	5,000
Advertising for motorcycles	10,000
Sales commissions	5,000
Depreciation on factory building	700
Rent on factory equipment	5,000
Insurance on factory building	3,000
Raw materials (frames, tires, etc.)	20,000
Utility costs for factory	800
Supplies for general office	200
Wages for assembly line workers	35,000
Depreciation on office equipment	500
Miscellaneous materials (lubricants, solders, etc.)	700

Instructions
(a) Prepare an answer sheet with the following column headings:

	Product Costs					
Cost Item	Direct Materials	Direct Labor	Manufacturing Overhead	Period Costs	Prime Costs	Conversion Costs

Enter each cost item on your answer sheet, placing the dollar amount under the appropriate headings. Total the dollar amounts in each of the columns.
(b) Compute the cost to produce one motorcycle.

Classify manufacturing costs into different categories and compute the unit cost.
(SO 3, 4)

P1-2A Hewitt Company, a manufacturer of tennis rackets, started its production in November 1999. For the preceding 5 years Hewitt had been a retailer of sports equipment. After a thorough survey of tennis racket markets, Hewitt Company decided to turn its retail store into a tennis racket factory.

Raw materials cost for a tennis racket will total $20 per racket. Workers on the production lines are on average paid $12 per hour. A racket usually takes two hours to complete. In addition, the rent on the equipment used to produce rackets amounts to $1,000 per month. Indirect materials cost $3 per racket. A supervisor was hired to oversee production; her monthly salary will be $2,000.

Janitorial costs were $1,200 monthly. Advertising costs for the rackets will be $6,000 per month. The factory building depreciation expense is $8,400 per year. Property taxes on the factory building will be $3,600 per year.

Instructions
(a) Prepare an answer sheet with the following column headings:

	Product Costs					
Cost Item	Direct Materials	Direct Labor	Manufacturing Overhead	Period Costs	Prime Costs	Conversion Costs

Assuming that Hewitt manufactures, on average, 2,000 tennis rackets per month, enter each cost item on your answer sheet, placing the dollar amount per month under the appropriate headings. Total the dollar amounts in each of the columns.
(b) Compute the cost to produce one racket.

P1-3A Incomplete manufacturing costs, expenses, and selling data for two different cases are as follows:

Indicate the missing amount of different cost items; prepare a condensed cost of goods manufactured schedule, an income statement, and a partial balance sheet.

(SO 5, 6, 7)

	Case 1	Case 2
Direct Materials Used	$ 9,000	(g)
Direct Labor	3,000	4,000
Manufacturing Overhead	4,000	5,000
Total Manufacturing Costs	(a)	20,000
Beginning Work in Process Inventory	1,000	(h)
Ending Work in Process Inventory	(b)	2,000
Sales	21,500	(i)
Sales Discounts	1,500	1,200
Cost of Goods Manufactured	13,500	21,000
Beginning Finished Goods Inventory	(c)	3,500
Goods Available for Sale	18,000	(j)
Cost of Goods Sold	(d)	(k)
Ending Finished Goods Inventory	1,000	2,500
Gross Profit	(e)	6,000
Operating Expenses	2,700	(l)
Net Income	(f)	2,200

Instructions

(a) Indicate the missing amount for each letter.
(b) Prepare a condensed cost of goods manufactured schedule for Case 1.
(c) Prepare an income statement and the current assets section of the balance sheet for Case 1, assuming that in Case 1 the other items in the current assets section are as follows: Cash, $3,000, Receivables (net), $10,000, Raw Materials, $700, and Prepaid Expenses, $200.

P1-4A The following data were taken from the records of Buckley Manufacturing Company for the year ended December 31, 2000.

Prepare a cost of goods manufactured schedule, a partial income statement, and a partial balance sheet.

(SO 5, 6, 7)

Raw Materials		Factory Insurance	$ 5,400
Inventory 1/1/00	$ 43,500	Factory Machinery	
Raw Materials		Depreciation	7,700
Inventory 12/31/00	44,200	Freight-in on Raw Materials	
Finished Goods		Purchased	3,900
Inventory 1/1/00	85,000	Factory Utilities	15,900
Finished Goods		Office Utilities Expense	8,600
Inventory 12/31/00	77,800	Sales	475,000
Work in Process		Sales Discounts	3,200
Inventory 1/1/00	10,200	Plant Manager's Salary	30,000
Work in Process		Factory Property Taxes	6,100
Inventory 12/31/00	6,500	Factory Repairs	800
Direct Labor	145,100	Raw Materials Purchases	64,600
Indirect Labor	19,100	Cash	28,000
Accounts Receivable	27,000		

Instructions

(a) Prepare a cost of goods manufactured schedule.
(b) Prepare an income statement through gross profit.
(c) Prepare the current assets section of the balance sheet at December 31.

P1-5A Hawkinson Company is a manufacturer of toys. Its controller, Al Duryea, resigned in August 2000. An inexperienced assistant accountant has prepared the following income statement for the month of August 2000.

Prepare a cost of goods manufactured schedule and a correct income statement.

(SO 5, 6)

HAWKINSON COMPANY
Income Statement
For the Month Ended August 31, 2000

Sales (net)		$670,000
Less: Operating expenses		
Raw materials purchased	$200,000	
Direct labor cost	150,000	
Advertising expense	80,000	
Selling and administrative salaries	70,000	
Rent on factory facilities	60,000	
Depreciation on sales equipment	55,000	
Depreciation on factory equipment	40,000	
Indirect labor cost	20,000	
Factory utilities	10,000	
Factory insurance	5,000	690,000
Net loss		$ (20,000)

Prior to August 2000 the company had been profitable every month. The company's president is concerned about the accuracy of the income statement above. As a friend of the president, you have been asked to review the income statement and make necessary corrections. After examining other manufacturing cost data, you have acquired additional information as follows:

1. Inventory balances at the beginning and end of August were:

	August 1	**August 31**
Raw materials	$18,000	$33,000
Work in process	25,000	21,000
Finished goods	40,000	62,000

2. Only 70% of the utilities expense and 80% of the insurance expense apply to factory operations; the remaining amounts should be charged to selling and administrative activities.

Instructions
(a) Prepare a cost of goods manufactured schedule for August 2000.
(b) Prepare a correct income statement for August 2000.

Complete a work sheet; prepare a cost of goods manufactured schedule, an income statement, and a balance sheet; journalize and post the closing entries.

(SO 8)

*P1-6A Everheart Manufacturing Company uses a simple manufacturing accounting system. At the end of its fiscal year on August 31, 2000, the adjusted trial balance contains the following accounts.

Debits			**Credits**	
Cash	$ 16,700		Accumulated Depreciation	$353,000
Accounts Receivable (net)	62,900		Notes Payable	45,000
Finished Goods Inventory	56,000		Accounts Payable	38,200
Work in Process Inventory	27,800		Income Taxes Payable	9,000
Raw Materials Inventory	37,200		Common Stock	352,000
Plant Assets	890,000		Retained Earnings	205,300
Raw Materials Purchased	236,500		Sales	996,000
Direct Labor	280,900			
Indirect Labor	27,400			
Factory Repairs	17,200			
Factory Depreciation	19,000			
Factory Manager's Salary	40,000			
Factory Insurance	11,000			
Factory Property Taxes	12,900			
Factory Utilities	13,300			
Selling Expenses	98,500			
Administrative Expenses	115,200			
Income Tax Expense	36,000			
	$1,998,500			$1,998,500

Physical inventory accounts on August 31, 2000, show the following inventory amounts: Finished Goods $54,600, Work in Process $23,400, and Raw Material $46,500.

Instructions
(a) Enter the adjusted trial balance data on a work sheet in financial statement order and complete the work sheet.
(b) Prepare a cost of goods manufactured schedule for the year.
(c) Prepare an income statement for the year and a balance sheet at August 31, 2000.
(d) Journalize the closing entries.
(e) Post the closing entries to Manufacturing Summary and to Income Summary.

PROBLEMS: SET B

P1-1B Marek Company specializes in manufacturing a unique model of bicycle helmet. The model is well accepted by consumers, and the company has a large number of orders to keep the factory production at 10,000 helmets per month (80% of its full capacity). Marek's monthly manufacturing costs and other expense data are as follows.

Classify manufacturing costs into different categories and compute the unit cost.
(SO 3, 4)

Rent on factory equipment	$ 6,000
Insurance on factory building	1,500
Raw materials (plastics, polystyrene, etc.)	70,000
Utility costs for factory	900
Supplies for general office	300
Wages for assembly line workers	46,000
Depreciation on office equipment	800
Miscellaneous materials (lubricants, solders, etc.)	1,100
Factory manager's salary	5,700
Property taxes on factory building	400
Advertising for helmets	11,000
Sales commissions	7,000
Depreciation on factory building	1,500

Instructions
(a) Prepare an answer sheet with the following column headings:

	Product Costs					
Cost Item	Direct Materials	Direct Labor	Manufacturing Overhead	Period Costs	Prime Costs	Conversion Costs

Enter each cost item on your answer sheet, placing the dollar amount under the appropriate headings. Total the dollar amounts in each of the columns.
(b) Compute the cost to produce one helmet.

P1-2B Vargas Company, a manufacturer of stereo systems, started its production in October 1999. For the preceding 3 years Vargas had been a retailer of stereo systems. After a thorough survey of stereo system markets, Vargas Company decided to turn its retail store into a stereo equipment factory.

Classify manufacturing costs into different categories and compute the unit cost.
(SO 3, 4)

Raw materials cost for a stereo system will total $70 per unit. Workers on the production lines are on average paid $10 per hour. A stereo system usually takes five hours to complete. In addition, the rent on the equipment used to assemble stereo systems amounts to $1,200 per month. Indirect materials cost $5 per system. A supervisor was hired to oversee production; her monthly salary will be $2,400.

Janitorial costs were $1,300 monthly. Advertising costs for the stereo system will be $8,500 per month. The factory building depreciation expense is $7,200 per year. Property taxes on the factory building will be $6,000 per year.

Instructions
(a) Prepare an answer sheet with the following column headings:

	Product Costs					
Cost Item	Direct Materials	Direct Labor	Manufacturing Overhead	Period Costs	Prime Costs	Conversion Costs

Assuming that Vargas manufactures, on average, 1,200 stereo systems per month, enter each cost item on your answer sheet, placing the dollar amount per month under the appropriate headings. Total the dollar amounts in each of the columns.
(b) Compute the cost to produce one stereo system.

Indicate the missing amount of different cost items; prepare a condensed cost of goods manufactured schedule, an income statement, and a partial balance sheet.
(SO 5, 6, 7)

P1-3B Incomplete manufacturing costs, expenses, and selling data for two different cases are as follows.

	Case 1	Case 2
Direct Materials Used	$ 8,000	(g)
Direct Labor	6,000	8,000
Manufacturing Overhead	5,000	4,000
Total Manufacturing Costs	(a)	21,000
Beginning Work in Process Inventory	1,000	(h)
Ending Work in Process Inventory	(b)	3,000
Sales	24,500	(i)
Sales Discounts	2,500	1,400
Cost of Goods Manufactured	16,500	22,000
Beginning Finished Goods Inventory	(c)	3,500
Goods Available for Sale	18,000	(j)
Cost of Goods Sold	(d)	(k)
Ending Finished Goods Inventory	3,000	2,500
Gross Profit	(e)	7,000
Operating Expenses	2,500	(l)
Net Income	(f)	2,800

Instructions
(a) Indicate the missing amount for each letter.
(b) Prepare a condensed cost of goods manufactured schedule for Case 1.
(c) Prepare an income statement and the current assets section of the balance sheet for Case 1, assuming that in Case 1 the other items in the current assets section are as follows: Cash, $4,000, Receivables (net) $15,000, Raw Materials, $600, and Prepaid Expenses, $400.

Prepare a cost of goods manufactured schedule, a partial income statement, and a partial balance sheet.
(SO 5, 6, 7)

P1-4B The following data were taken from the records of Scheve Manufacturing Company for the fiscal year ended June 30, 2000.

Raw Materials Inventory 7/1/99	$ 46,500	Factory Insurance	$ 4,600
Raw Materials Inventory 6/30/00	39,600	Factory Machinery Depreciation	15,000
Finished Goods Inventory 7/1/99	96,000	Freight-in on Raw Materials Purchased	8,600
Finished Goods Inventory 6/30/00	95,900	Factory Utilities	24,600
Work in Process Inventory 7/1/99	21,000	Office Utilities Expense	8,650
Work in Process Inventory 6/30/00	18,700	Sales	547,000
Direct Labor	147,250	Sales Discounts	3,300
Indirect Labor	24,460	Plant Manager's Salary	29,000
Accounts Receivable	27,000	Factory Property Taxes	9,600
		Factory Repairs	1,400
		Raw Materials Purchases	89,800
		Cash	32,000

Instructions
(a) Prepare a cost of goods manufactured schedule.
(b) Prepare an income statement through gross profit.
(c) Prepare the current assets section of the balance sheet at June 30, 2000.

P1-5B Noonan Company is a manufacturer of computers. Its controller, Jason Petry, re-signed in October 2000. An inexperienced assistant accountant has prepared the follow-ing income statement for the month of October 2000.

Prepare a cost of goods man-ufactured schedule and a correct income statement.
(SO 5, 6)

NOONAN COMPANY
Income Statement
For the Month Ended October 31, 2000

Sales (net)		$780,000
Less: Operating expenses		
Raw materials purchased	$260,000	
Direct labor cost	190,000	
Advertising expense	90,000	
Selling and administrative salaries	75,000	
Rent on factory facilities	60,000	
Depreciation on sales equipment	45,000	
Depreciation on factory equipment	30,000	
Indirect labor cost	25,000	
Factory utilities	12,000	
Factory insurance	8,000	795,000
Net loss		$ (15,000)

Prior to October 2000 the company had been profitable every month. The company's president is concerned about the accuracy of the income statement above. As a friend of the president, you have been asked to review the income statement and make necessary corrections. After examining other manufacturing cost data, you have acquired additional information as follows:
1. Inventory balances at the beginning and end of October were:

	October 1	October 31
Raw materials	$15,000	$31,000
Work in process	16,000	14,000
Finished goods	30,000	48,000

2. Only 80% of the utilities expense and 70% of the insurance expense apply to factory operations; the remaining amounts should be charged to selling and administrative activities.

Instructions
(a) Prepare a schedule of cost of goods manufactured for October 2000.
(b) Prepare a correct income statement for October 2000.

BROADENING YOUR PERSPECTIVE

GROUP DECISION CASE

BYP1-1 Deskins Manufacturing Company specializes in producing fashion outfits. On July 31, 1999, a tornado touched down at its factory and general office. The inventories in the warehouse and the factory were totally damaged due to heavy rain and moisture. The general office nearby was completely destroyed. Next morning, through a careful search over the disaster site, however, Ed Loder, the company's controller, and Susan

Manning, the cost accountant, were able to recover a small part of manufacturing cost data for the current month.

"What a horrible experience," sighed Ed. "And the worst part is that we may not have enough records to use in filing an insurance claim."

"It was terrible," replied Susan. "However, I managed to recover some of the manufacturing cost data that I was working on yesterday afternoon. The data indicate that our direct labor cost in July totaled $250,000 and that we had purchased $345,000 of raw materials. In addition, I recall that the raw materials used for July was $350,000. But I'm not sure this information will help; the rest of our records are blown away."

"Well, not exactly," said Ed. "I was working on the year-to-date income statement when the tornado warning was announced. My recollection is that our sales in July were $1,250,000 and our gross profit ratio has been 40% of sales. Also, I can remember that our cost of goods available for sale was $790,000 for July."

"Maybe we can work something out from this information!" exclaimed Susan. "My experience tells me that our manufacturing overhead is usually 60% of direct labor."

"Hey, look what I just found," cried Susan. "It's a copy of this June's balance sheet, and it shows that our inventories as of June 30 are Finished goods, $36,000, Work in process, $22,000, and Raw materials, $19,000."

"Super," yelled Ed. "Let's go work something out."

In order to file an insurance claim Deskins Company must determine the amount of its inventories as of July 31, 1999, the date of the tornado touchdown.

Instructions

With the class divided into groups, determine the amount of cost in the Raw Materials, Work in Process, and Finished Goods inventory accounts as of the date of the tornado touchdown.

MANAGERIAL ANALYSIS

BYP1-2 Tennis, Anyone? is a fairly large manufacturing company located in the southern United States. The company manufactures tennis rackets, tennis balls, tennis clothing, and tennis shoes, all bearing the company's distinctive logo, a large green question mark on a white flocked tennis ball. The company's sales have been increasing over the past 10 years. The tennis racket division has recently implemented several advanced manufacturing techniques. Robot arms hold the tennis rackets in place while glue dries, machine vision systems check for defects, and the engineering and design team use computerized drafting and testing of new products. The following managers work in the tennis racket division:

Wayne Gryer, Sales Manager (supervises all sales representatives)
Tommye Stevens, technical specialist (supervises computer programmers)
Martie Lefever, cost accounting manager (supervises cost accountants)
Jack Marler, production supervisor (supervises all manufacturing employees)
Tina Roy, engineer (supervises all new product design teams)

Instructions

With the class divided into groups, answer the following questions:
(a) What are the primary information needs of each manager?
(b) Which, if any, financial accounting report(s) is each likely to use?
(c) Name one special-purpose management accounting report that could be designed for each manager. Include the name of the report, the information it contains, and how frequently it should be issued.

REAL-WORLD FOCUS

ANCHOR GLASS CONTAINER CORPORATION

BYP1-3 **Anchor Glass Container Corporation,** the third largest manufacturer of glass containers in the U.S., supplies beverage and food producers and consumer products manufacturers nationwide. Based in Tampa, Florida, Anchor employs 4,500 at ten U.S.

locations. Parent company Consumers Packaging, Inc. (*Toronto Stock Exchange:* CGC) is a leading international designer and manufacturer of glass containers.

The following management discussion appeared in a recent annual report of Anchor Glass:

ANCHOR GLASS CONTAINER CORPORATION
Management Discussion

Cost of Products Sold   Cost of products sold as a percentage of net sales was 89.3% in the current year compared to 87.6% in the prior year. The increase in cost of products sold as a percentage of net sales principally reflected the impact of operational problems during the second quarter of the current year at a major furnace at one of the Company's plants, higher downtime, and costs and expenses associated with an increased number of scheduled capital improvement projects, increases in labor, and certain other manufacturing costs (with no corresponding selling price increases in the current year). Reduced fixed costs from the closing of the Streator, Illinois, plant in June of the current year and productivity and efficiency gains partially offset these cost increases.

Financial statements of real companies, like this one, are accompanied by either a company logo or an associated photograph.

Instructions
What factors affect the costs of products sold at Anchor Glass Container Corporation?

COMMUNICATION ACTIVITY

BYP1-4   Refer to Problem 1-5A and add the following requirement:

Prepare a letter to the president of the company, Marie Klinger, describing the changes you made. Explain clearly why net income is different after the changes. Keep the following points in mind as you compose your letter:
1. This is a letter to the president of a company, who is your friend. The style should be generally formal, but you may relax some requirements; for example, you may call the president by her first name.
2. Executives are very busy. Your letter should tell the president your main results first (for example, the amount of net income).
3. You should include brief explanations so that the president can understand the changes you made in the calculations.

RESEARCH ASSIGNMENT

BYP1-5   The December 1995 issue of *Management Accounting* includes an article by William L. Ferrara entitled "Cost/Management Accounting: The 21st Century Paradigm." The article contains a historical perspective on management accounting as well as a prediction of the future.

Instructions
Read the article and answer the following questions:
(a) What are the four eras into which management accounting is divided? (Identify the dates of each era. These are labeled paradigm A, B, C, and D in the article.)
(b) What is the costing/pricing formula shown in Table 1 for paradigm (model) D, the fourth era?
(c) What are the three "provocative new issues" created by the future model of management accounting (paradigm D)?

ETHICS CASE

BYP1-6 Carlos Morales, controller for Tredway Industries, was reviewing production cost reports for the year. One amount in these reports continued to bother him—advertising. During the year, the company had instituted an expensive advertising campaign to sell some of its slower moving products. It was still too early to tell whether the advertising campaign was successful. There had been much internal debate as how to report advertising costs. The Vice President of Finance argued that advertising costs should be reported as a cost of production, just like direct materials and direct labor. He therefore recommended that this cost be identified as manufacturing overhead and reported as part of inventory costs until sold. Others disagreed. Morales believed that this cost should be reported as an expense of the current period based on the conservatism principle. Others argued that it should be reported as Prepaid Advertising and reported as a current asset.

The president finally had to decide the issue. He argued that these costs should be reported as inventory. His arguments were practical ones. He noted that the company was experiencing financial difficulty and expensing this amount in the current period might jeopardize a planned bond offering. Also by reporting the advertising costs as inventory rather than as prepaid advertising, less attention would be directed to it by the financial community.

Instructions
(a) Who are the stakeholders in this situation?
(b) What are the ethical issues involved in this situation?
(c) What would you do if you were Carlos Morales?

SURFING THE NET

BYP1-7 Dofasco Inc., located in Hamilton, Ontario, is one of Canada's largest integrated steelmakers. The home page of Dofasco Inc., includes information about the company, its markets, people, technology, and the environment, in addition to a wealth of financial information.

Address: https://www.dofasco.ca/

Instructions
At Dofasco's home page, choose the current **Annual Report** and locate the answers to the following questions:
(a) What does Dofasco produce? How much of this product did it produce in the current year?
(b) Explain the term "a shipped yield." What is Dofasco's current shipped yield? What are the factors influencing its increase or decrease?
(c) Did revenue per ton increase or decrease in the current year? Did cost per ton increase or decrease? What are the factors influencing these changes?
(d) How much was Dofasco's cost of sales in the current year? Its inventory? What inventory valuation method does Dofasco use?

Answers to Self-Study Questions
1. b   2. d   3. b   4. b   5. d   6. a   7. c   8. c   9. a   10. d

Remember to go back to the Navigator box on the chapter-opening page and check off your completed work.

CHAPTER 2

Job Order Cost Accounting

STUDY OBJECTIVES

After studying this chapter, you should be able to:

1. Explain the characteristics and purposes of cost accounting.

2. Describe the flow of costs in a job order cost accounting system.

3. Explain the nature and importance of a job cost sheet.

4. Indicate how the predetermined overhead rate is determined and used.

5. Prepare entries for jobs completed and sold.

6. Distinguish between under- and overapplied manufacturing overhead.

THE
NAVIGATOR

FEATURE STORY

"We'd Like It in Red"

Western States Fire Apparatus, Inc., of Cornelius, Oregon, is one of the few American companies that makes fire trucks. The company builds about 25 trucks per year. Founded in 1941, the company is run by the children and grandchildren of the original founder.

"We buy the chassis, which is the cab and the frame," says Susan Scott, the company's bookkeeper. "In our computer, we set up an account into which all of the direct material that is purchased for that particular job is charged." Other direct materi-

als include the water pump—which can cost $10,000—the lights, the siren, ladders, and hoses.

As for direct labor, the production workers fill out job sheets that tell what jobs they worked on. Usually, the company is building four trucks at any one time. On payday, the controller allocates the payroll to the appropriate job record.

Indirect materials, such as nuts and bolts, wiring, lubricants, and abrasives are allocated to each job in proportion to direct material dollars. Other costs, such as insurance and supervisors' salaries, are allocated based on direct labor hours. "We

need to allocate overhead in order to know what kind of price we have to charge when we submit our bids," she says.

Western gets orders through a "blind-bidding" process; that is, Western submits its bid without knowing the bid prices made by its competitors. "If we bid too low, we won't make a profit. If we bid too high, we don't get the job."

Regardless of the final price for the truck, the quality had better be first-rate. "The fire departments let you know if they don't like what you did, and you usually end up fixing it."

THE
NAVIGATOR

44

IX

THE NAVIGATOR ✔

- Scan *Study Objectives* ☐
- Read *Feature Story* ☐
- Read *Preview* ☐
- Read text and answer *Before You Go On*
  p. 48 ☐ p. 58 ☐ p. 64 ☐
- Work *Using the Decision Toolkit* ☐
- Review *Summary of Study Objectives* ☐
- Work *Demonstration Problem* ☐
- Answer *Self-Study Questions* ☐
- Complete assignments ☐

Having read the story about Western States Fire Apparatus, Inc., you should now be familiar with the manufacturing costs used in making a fire truck. This chapter illustrates how these manufacturing costs are assigned to specific jobs, such as the manufacture of individual fire trucks. We begin the discussion in this chapter with an overview of the flow of costs in a job order cost accounting system. We then use a case study to explain and illustrate the documents, entries, and accounts in this type of cost accounting system. The content and organization of this chapter are as follows:

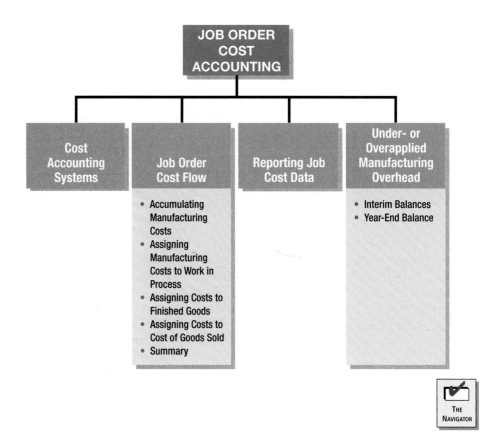

COST ACCOUNTING SYSTEMS

STUDY OBJECTIVE

❶

Explain the characteristics and purposes of cost accounting.

Cost accounting involves the measuring, recording, and reporting of product costs. From the data accumulated, both the total cost and the unit cost of each product is determined.

A cost accounting system consists of manufacturing cost accounts that are fully integrated into the general ledger of a company. **An important feature of a cost accounting system is the use of a perpetual inventory system that provides information immediately on the cost of a product.** There are two basic types of cost accounting systems: (1) a job order cost system and (2) a process cost system. Although cost accounting systems differ widely from company to company, most are based on one of these two traditional product costing systems.

#3

#4

Under a job order cost system, costs are assigned to each **job,** such as the manufacture of a high-speed drilling machine, or to each **batch** of goods, such as 500 wedding invitations. Jobs or batches may be completed to fill a specific customer order or to replenish inventory. An important feature of job order costing is that each job (or batch) has its own distinguishing characteristics. For example, each house is custom built, each motion picture is unique, and each printing job is different. **The objective is to compute the cost per job.** At each point in the manufacturing process, the job and its associated costs can be identified. A job order cost system measures costs for each completed job, rather than for set time periods. The recording of costs in a job order cost system is shown in Illustration 2-1.

Illustration 2-1   Job order cost system

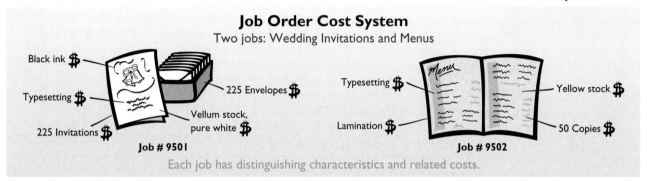

Job Order Cost System
Two jobs: Wedding Invitations and Menus

Black ink $ — Typesetting $ — 225 Invitations $ — 225 Envelopes $ — Vellum stock, pure white $ — **Job # 9501**

Typesetting $ — Lamination $ — Yellow stock $ — 50 Copies $ — **Job # 9502**

Each job has distinguishing characteristics and related costs.

#5

A process cost system is used when a series of connected manufacturing processes or departments produce a large volume of uniform or relatively homogeneous products. Production is continuous to ensure that adequate inventories of the finished product(s) are on hand. A process cost system is used in the manufacture of cereal, the refining of petroleum, and the production of automobiles. Process costing accounts for and accumulates product-related costs **for a period of time** (such as a week or a month) as opposed to assigning costs to specific products or job orders. In process costing, the costs are assigned to or accumulated by departments or processes for a set period of time. The recording of costs in a process cost system is shown in Illustration 2-2. The process cost system will be discussed further in Chapter 3.

Illustration 2-2   Process cost system

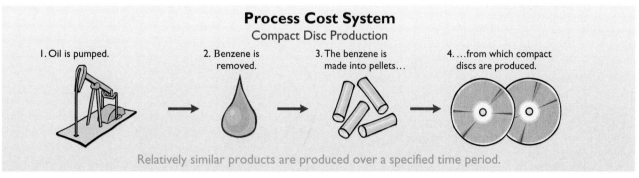

Process Cost System
Compact Disc Production

1. Oil is pumped.   2. Benzene is removed.   3. The benzene is made into pellets...   4. ...from which compact discs are produced.

Relatively similar products are produced over a specified time period.

#3

✳ A company may use both types of cost systems. For example, General Motors uses process cost accounting for its standard model cars, such as Saturns and Corvettes, and job order cost accounting for a custom-made limousine for the President of the United States. The objective of both systems is to provide product unit cost information for product pricing, cost control, inventory valuation, and financial statement presentation. End-of-period inventory values are computed by using product unit cost data.

BUSINESS INSIGHT
Management Perspective

Many companies suffer from poor cost accounting. As a result, companies sometimes make products they ought not to be selling at all and buy others, often from overseas suppliers, that they could more profitably make themselves. Moreover, inaccurate cost data lead companies to misallocate capital and frustrate efforts by plant managers to improve efficiency.

For example, consider a diversified company in the business of rebuilding diesel locomotives. The managers thought they were making money until a consulting firm determined that costs had been seriously underestimated. The company bailed out of the business, and not a moment too soon. Says the consultant who advised the company: "The more contracts it won, the more money it lost."

BEFORE YOU GO ON . . .

THE
NAVIGATOR

● **Review It**
   1. What is cost accounting?
   2. What is a cost accounting system?
   3. How does a job order cost system differ from a process cost system?

STUDY OBJECTIVE
②
Describe the flow of costs in a job order cost accounting system.

JOB ORDER COST FLOW

The flow of costs (direct materials, direct labor, and manufacturing overhead) in job order cost accounting parallels the physical flow of the materials as they are converted into finished goods. As shown in Illustration 2-3, manufacturing costs are assigned to the Work in Process Inventory account. When a job is completed, the cost of the job is transferred to Finished Goods Inventory. Later when the goods are sold, their cost is transferred to Cost of Goods Sold.

Illustration 2-3 Flow of costs in job order cost accounting

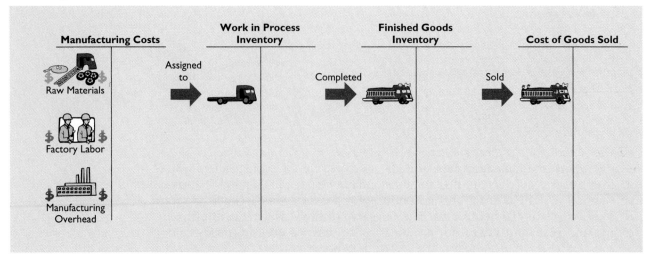

A more detailed presentation of the flow of costs is shown in Illustration 2-4. Illustration 2-4 indicates that there are two major steps in the flow of costs: (1) *accumulating* the manufacturing costs incurred and (2) *assigning* the accumulated costs to the work done. As shown, manufacturing costs incurred are accumulated in entries 1–3 by debits to Raw Materials Inventory, Factory Labor, and Manufacturing Overhead. No attempt is made when costs are incurred to associate the costs with specific jobs. The remaining entries (entries 4–8) pertain to the assignment of manufacturing costs incurred. We will use a case study to explain and illustrate how a job order system operates.

Illustration 2-4 Job order cost accounting system

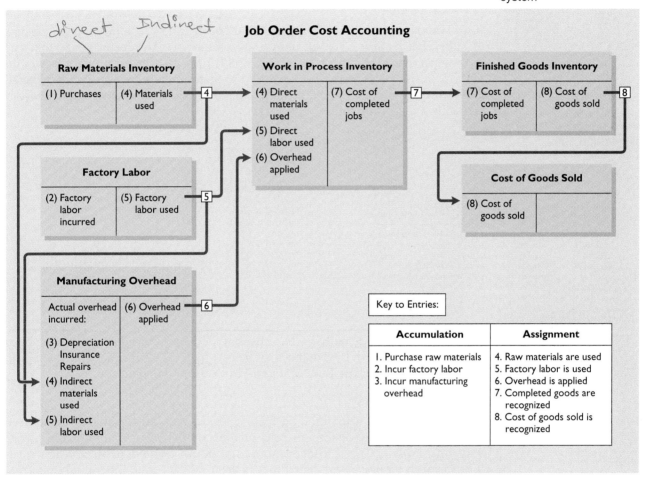

ACCUMULATING MANUFACTURING COSTS

In a job order cost system, manufacturing costs are recorded in the period in which they are incurred. To illustrate, we will use the January transactions of Wallace Manufacturing Company, which makes tools and dies.

Raw Materials Costs

The costs of raw materials purchased are debited to Raw Materials Inventory when materials are received. This account is debited for the invoice cost and freight costs chargeable to the purchaser. It is credited for purchase discounts taken and purchase returns and allowances. **No effort is made at this point to associate the cost of materials with specific jobs.** The procedures for ordering, receiving, recording, and paying for raw materials are similar to the purchasing procedures of a merchandising company.

To illustrate the purchase of raw materials, assume that Wallace Manufacturing Company purchases 2,000 handles (Stock No. AA2746) at $5 per unit ($10,000) and 800 modules (Stock No. AA2850) at $40 per unit ($32,000) for a total cost of $42,000 ($10,000 + $32,000). The entry to record this purchase on January 4 is:

#1

(1)
Jan. 4	Raw Materials Inventory	42,000	
	Accounts Payable		42,000
	(Purchase of raw materials on account)		

Raw Materials Inventory is a control account. The subsidiary ledger consists of individual records for each item of raw materials. The records may take the form of accounts (or cards) that are manually or mechanically prepared, or computer data files. The records are referred to as **materials inventory records** (or **stores ledger cards**). The card for Stock No. AA2746 following the purchase is shown in Illustration 2-5.

Illustration 2-5
Materials inventory card

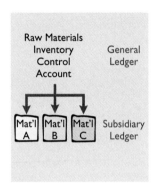

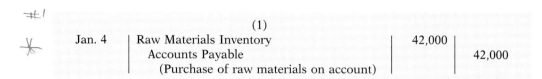

Item: Handles								Part No: AA2746	
	Receipts			Issues			Balance		
Date	Units	Cost	Total	Units	Cost	Total	Units	Cost	Total
1/4	2,000	$5	$10,000				2,000	$5	$10,000

Postings are made daily to the subsidiary ledger. After all postings have been completed, the sum of the balances in the raw materials subsidiary ledger should equal the balance in the Raw Materials Inventory control account.

Factory Labor Costs

The procedures for accumulating factory labor costs are similar to those used in computing the payroll for a merchandising company. For example, time clocks and time cards are used to determine total hours worked; gross and net earnings for each employee are listed in a payroll register; and individual employee earnings records are maintained. To help ensure the accuracy of payroll data, a company should follow basic principles of internal control.

In a manufacturing company, the cost of factory labor consists of (1) gross earnings of factory workers, (2) employer payroll taxes on such earnings, and (3) fringe benefits (such as sick pay, pensions, and vacation pay) incurred by the employer. **Labor costs are debited to Factory Labor when they are incurred.** To illustrate, assume that Wallace Manufacturing incurs $32,000 of factory labor costs, of which $27,000 relates to wages payable and $5,000 relates to payroll taxes payable in January. The entry is:

#2

(2)
Jan. 31	Factory Labor	32,000	
	Factory Wages Payable		27,000
	Employer Payroll Taxes Payable		5,000
	(To record factory labor costs)		

Factory labor is subsequently assigned to work in process and manufacturing overhead, as explained later in the chapter.

Manufacturing Overhead Costs

A company may have many types of overhead costs. The accumulation of these costs may be recognized **daily,** as in the case of machinery repairs and the use of indirect materials and indirect labor. Alternatively, overhead costs may be recorded **periodically** through adjusting entries, as in the case of property taxes, depreciation, and insurance. Using assumed data, a summary entry for manufacturing overhead in Wallace Manufacturing Company is:

		(3)	
Jan. 31	Manufacturing Overhead	13,800	
	Utilities Payable		4,800
	Prepaid Insurance		2,000
	Accounts Payable (for repairs)		2,600
	Accumulated Depreciation		3,000
	Property Taxes Payable		1,400
	(To record overhead costs)		

Manufacturing Overhead is a control account. The subsidiary ledger consists of individual accounts for each type of cost, such as Factory Utilities, Factory Insurance, and Factory Repairs.

ASSIGNING MANUFACTURING COSTS TO WORK IN PROCESS

Assigning manufacturing costs to work in process results in **debits** to Work in Process Inventory and **credits** to Raw Materials Inventory, Factory Labor, and Manufacturing Overhead. Journal entries for the assignment of costs to work in process are usually made and posted **monthly.** An indispensable accounting record in assigning costs to jobs is the job cost sheet, shown in Illustration 2-6.

STUDY OBJECTIVE

3

Explain the nature and importance of a job cost sheet.

Illustration 2-6 Job cost sheet

Job Cost Sheet

Job No. _____   Quantity _____
Item _____   Date Requested _____
For _____   Date Completed _____

Date	Direct Materials	Direct Labor	Manufacturing Overhead

Cost of completed job
   Direct materials $ _____
   Direct labor   _____
   Manufacturing overhead   _____
Total cost $ _____
Unit cost (total dollars ÷ quantity) $ _____

A job cost sheet is a form used to record the costs chargeable to a specific job and to determine the total and unit cost of the completed job. **Postings to job cost sheets are made daily,** directly from supporting documentation that shows the cost and job to be charged.

BUSINESS INSIGHT
Management Perspective

At Federal Express Corp., the job order is to deliver the shipper's package to the right customer on time. To make his deliveries, Santa may still rely on Rudolph, but more and more shippers are relying on FedEx. FedEx expects that its 608 planes and 40,500-vehicle fleet will have their busiest days each year in the week preceding Christmas. In a recent year, for instance, the company handled a record 3 million packages in a single day during that busy pre-holiday week.

A separate job cost sheet is kept for each job. Job cost sheets constitute the subsidiary ledger for the Work in Process Inventory account. **Each entry to Work in Process Inventory must be accompanied by a corresponding posting to one or more job cost sheets.**

Raw Materials Costs

Raw materials costs are assigned when the materials are issued by the storeroom. To achieve effective internal control over the issuance of materials, the storekeeper should obtain a written authorization each time materials are released to production. The authorization for issuing raw materials is made on a prenumbered materials requisition slip signed by an authorized employee such as a department supervisor. Materials may be used directly on a job, or they may be considered to be indirect materials. As shown in Illustration 2-7, the requisition should indicate the quantity and type of materials withdrawn and

Illustration 2-7
Materials requisition slip

Helpful Hint The internal control principle of documentation includes prenumbering to enhance subsequent accountability.

Wallace Manufacturing Company
Materials Requisition Slip

Deliver to: _____Assembly Department_____   Req. No. __R247__
Charge to: __Work in Process—Job No. 101__   Date: __1/6/99__

Quantity	Description	Stock No.	Cost per Unit	Total
200	Handles	AA2746	$5.00	$1,000

Requested by _Bruce Howart_   Received by _Herb Crowley_
Approved by _Kap Shin_   Costed by _Heather Remmers_

the account to be charged. The account is Work in Process Inventory for direct materials and Manufacturing Overhead for indirect materials.

Helpful Hint Approvals are an important part of a materials requisition slip because they help to establish individual accountability over inventory.

The requisition is prepared in duplicate. A copy is retained in the storeroom as evidence of the materials released; the original is sent to accounting, where the cost per unit and total cost of the materials used are determined. Any of the inventory costing methods (FIFO, LIFO, or average cost) may be used in costing the requisitions; the method selected by management should be followed consistently. After the requisition slips have been costed, they are posted daily to the materials inventory records. In addition, **requisitions for direct materials are posted daily to the individual job cost sheets.**

Periodically, the requisitions are sorted, totaled, and journalized. For example, if $24,000 of direct materials and $6,000 of indirect materials are used in Wallace Manufacturing in January, the entry is:

#4

	(4)		
Jan. 31	Work in Process Inventory	24,000	
	Manufacturing Overhead	6,000	
	Raw Materials Inventory		30,000
	(To assign materials to jobs and overhead)		

The requisition slips show total direct materials costs of $12,000 for Job No. 101, $7,000 for Job No. 102, and $5,000 for Job No. 103. The posting of requisition slip R247 and other assumed postings to the job cost sheets for materials are shown in Illustration 2-8. After all postings have been completed, the sum of the totals of the direct materials columns of the job cost sheets should equal the direct materials debited to Work in Process Inventory.

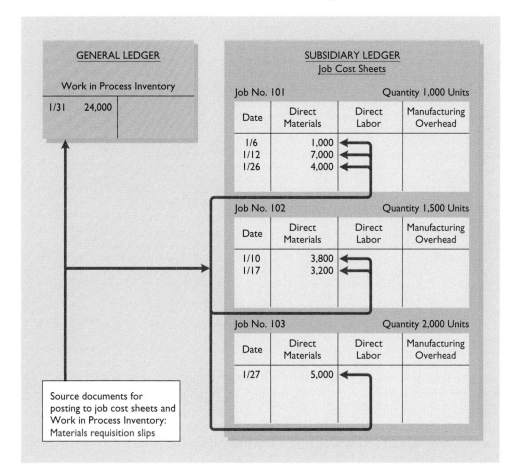

Illustration 2-8 Job cost sheets—direct materials

Helpful Hint Postings to control accounts are made monthly, and postings to job cost sheets are made daily.

The materials inventory record for Part No. AA2746, after posting requisition slip R247 and an assumed requisition slip for 760 handles costing $3,800 on January 10 for Job 102, is shown in Illustration 2-9.

Illustration 2-9
Materials inventory card
following issuances

Item: Handles									Part No: AA2746
	Receipts			Issues			Balance		
Date	Units	Cost	Total	Units	Cost	Total	Units	Cost	Total
1/4	2,000	$5	$10,000				2,000	$5	$10,000
1/6				200	$5	$1,000	1,800	$5	9,000
1/10				760	$5	3,800	1,040	$5	5,200

Factory Labor Costs

Factory labor costs are assigned to jobs on the basis of time tickets prepared when the work is performed. The time ticket should indicate the employee, the hours worked, the account and job to be charged, and the total labor cost. The account Work in Process Inventory is debited for direct labor, and Manufacturing Overhead is debited for indirect labor. When direct labor is involved, the job number must be indicated as shown in Illustration 2-10. In some companies, different colored time tickets are used for direct and indirect labor. All time tickets should be approved by the employee's supervisor.

Illustration 2-10 Time
ticket

Wallace Manufacturing Company
Time Ticket

Date: 1/6/99

Employee	John Nash	Employee No.	124
Charge to:	Work in Process	Job No.	101

Time			Hourly Rate	Total Cost
Start	Stop	Total Hours		
0800	1200	4	10.00	40.00

Approved by _Bob Kadler_   Costed by _M Cher_

The time tickets are later sent to the payroll department where the total time reported for an employee for a pay period is reconciled with total hours worked, shown on the employee's time card. Then the employee's hourly wage rate is applied and the total labor cost is computed. Subsequently, the time tickets are sorted, totaled, and journalized. For example, if the total factory labor cost incurred of $32,000 consists of $28,000 of direct labor and $4,000 of indirect labor, the entry is:

#5

	(5)		
Jan. 31	Work in Process Inventory	28,000	
	Manufacturing Overhead	4,000	
	Factory Labor		32,000
	(To assign labor to jobs and overhead)		

As a result of this entry, Factory Labor is left with a zero balance, and gross earnings are assigned to the appropriate manufacturing accounts.

We will assume that the labor costs chargeable to the three jobs are $15,000, $9,000, and $4,000. The Work in Process Inventory and job cost sheets after posting are shown in Illustration 2-11. As in the case of direct materials, the postings to the direct labor columns of the job cost sheets should equal the posting of direct labor to Work in Process Inventory.

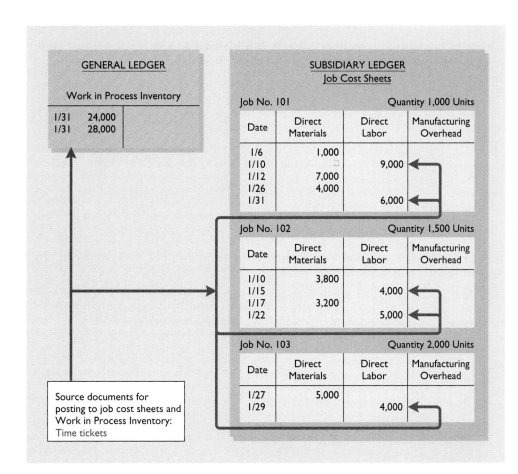

Illustration 2-11 Job cost sheets—direct labor

Helpful Hint Prove the $28,000 by totaling the charges by jobs:

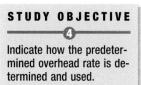

101	$15,000
102	9,000
103	4,000
	$28,000

Manufacturing Overhead Costs

Unlike direct materials and direct labor that apply to specific jobs, manufacturing overhead relates to production operations as a whole. Consequently, these costs cannot be assigned to specific jobs on the basis of actual costs incurred. Instead, **manufacturing overhead is assigned to work in process and to specific jobs on an estimated basis through the use of a predetermined overhead rate.**

STUDY OBJECTIVE

④

Indicate how the predetermined overhead rate is determined and used.

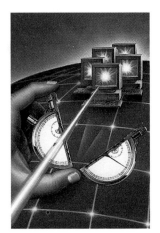

BUSINESS INSIGHT
Management Perspective

A job cost computer program provides summaries of material and labor expenses by job. The program enables the company to accumulate costs by jobs, provide data to accounts receivable for billings, assign overhead costs, and provide up-to-date management reports. The paperwork and reports generated by such systems are basically the same as shown for Wallace Manufacturing Company. The major difference between manual and computerized systems is the time involved in converting data into information and in getting feedback (reports) to management.

The predetermined overhead rate is based on the relationship between estimated annual overhead costs and expected annual operating activity, expressed in terms of a common **activity base.** The common activity base may be stated in terms of direct labor costs, direct labor hours, machine hours, or any other measure that will provide an equitable basis for applying overhead costs to jobs. **The predetermined overhead rate is established at (or prior to) the beginning of the year.** The formula for a predetermined overhead rate is shown in Illustration 2-12.

Illustration 2-12 Formula for predetermined overhead rate

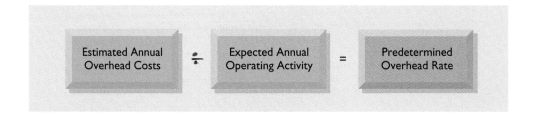

Helpful Hint In contrast to overhead, actual costs for direct materials and direct labor are used to assign costs to Work in Process because the time delay to get cost information is short.

A predetermined overhead rate is used to assign costs because overhead costs are not incurred uniformly each month, and not all actual overhead invoices are received at the end of each month. Therefore, using a predetermined overhead rate enables a cost to be determined for the job immediately. Illustration 2-13 indicates how manufacturing overhead is assigned to work in process.

Illustration 2-13 Using predetermined overhead rates

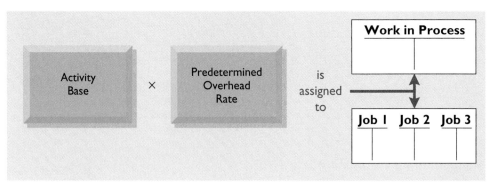

At Wallace Manufacturing, direct labor cost is the activity base. Assuming that annual overhead costs are expected to be $280,000 and that $350,000 of direct labor costs are anticipated, the overhead rate is 80%, computed as follows:

$$\$280,000 \div \$350,000 = 80\%$$

This means that for every dollar of direct labor, 80 cents of manufacturing overhead will be assigned to a job. The use of a predetermined overhead rate enables the company to determine the approximate total cost of each job **when the job is completed.**

Historically, direct labor costs or direct labor hours have often been used as the activity base because of the relatively high correlation between direct labor and manufacturing overhead. In recent years, however, **there has been a significant trend toward use of machine hours or a combination of other activity measures as the activity base because of increased reliance on automation in manufacturing operations.**

A company may use more than one activity base. For example, if a job order is manufactured in more than one factory department, each department may have its own overhead rate. In the opening story about fire trucks, two bases were used in assigning overhead to jobs: direct material dollars for indirect materials, and direct labor hours for such costs as insurance and supervisors' salaries.

For Wallace Manufacturing, manufacturing overhead is assigned to work in process and **charged to jobs when direct labor costs are assigned.** Overhead applied for January is $22,400 ($28,000 × 80%), and the application is recorded through the following entry.

#6

		(6)		
Jan. 31	Work in Process Inventory		22,400	
	Manufacturing Overhead			22,400
	(To assign overhead to jobs)			

After posting, the Work in Process Inventory account and the job cost sheets will appear as shown in Illustration 2-14.

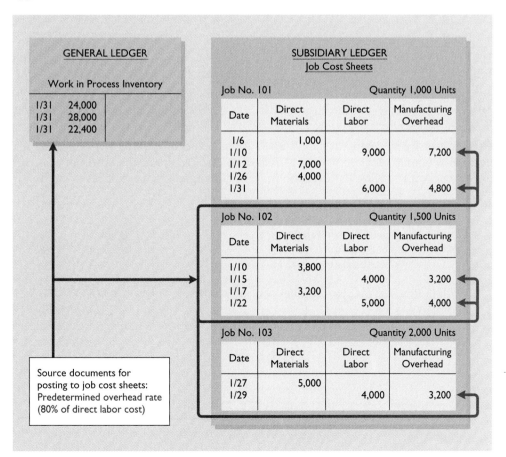

Illustration 2-14 Job cost sheets—manufacturing overhead applied

Note that the debit of $22,400 to Work in Process Inventory equals the sum of the overhead assigned to jobs: Job 101 $12,000 + Job 102 $7,200 + Job 103 $3,200.

At the end of each month, **the balance in Work in Process Inventory should equal the sum of the costs shown on the job cost sheets of unfinished jobs.** Assuming that all jobs are unfinished, proof of the agreement of the control and subsidiary accounts in Wallace Manufacturing is shown below.

Illustration 2-15 Proof of job cost sheets to work in process inventory

Work in Process Inventory		Job Cost Sheets	
Jan. 31	24,000	No. 101	$ 39,000
31	28,000	102	23,200
31	22,400	103	12,200
	74,400	←	$74,400

BEFORE YOU GO ON . . .

● **Review It**

1. What source documents are used in assigning manufacturing costs to Work in Process Inventory?
2. What is a job cost sheet, and what is its primary purpose?
3. What is the formula for computing a predetermined overhead rate?

● **Do It**

Danielle Company is working on two job orders. The job cost sheets show the following: direct materials—Job 120 $6,000, Job 121 $3,600; direct labor—Job 120 $4,000, Job 121 $2,000; and manufacturing overhead—Job 120 $5,000, Job 121 $2,500. Prepare the three summary entries to record the assignment of costs to Work in Process from the data on the job cost sheets.

Reasoning: Each cost charged to a job must be accompanied by a debit to the control account, Work in Process Inventory. The credits in the summary entries are the accounts debited when the manufacturing costs were accumulated.

Solution: The three summary entries are:

Work in Process Inventory ($6,000 + $3,600)	9,600	
Raw Materials Inventory		9,600
(To assign materials to jobs)		
Work in Process Inventory ($4,000 + $2,000)	6,000	
Factory Labor		6,000
(To assign labor to jobs)		
Work in Process Inventory ($5,000 + $2,500)	7,500	
Manufacturing Overhead		7,500
(To assign overhead to jobs)		

THE
NAVIGATOR

Related exercise material: BE2-3, BE2-4, BE2-7, E2-2, E2-3, E2-7, and E2-8.

DECISION TOOLKIT

Decision Checkpoints	Info Needed for Decision	Tool to Use for Decision	How to Evaluate Results
What is the cost of a job?	Cost of material, labor, and overhead assigned to a specific job	Job cost sheet	Compare costs to those of previous periods and to those of competitors to ensure that costs are in line. Compare costs to expected selling price to determine overall profitability.

ASSIGNING COSTS TO FINISHED GOODS

When a job is completed, the costs of direct materials, direct labor, and manufacturing overhead are summarized and the lower portion of the applicable job cost sheet is completed. For example, if we assume that Job No. 101 is completed on January 31, the completed job cost sheet will show the following:

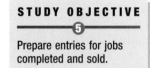

STUDY OBJECTIVE
5
Prepare entries for jobs completed and sold.

Illustration 2-16
Completed job cost sheet

Job Cost Sheet

Job No. _____ 101 _____   Quantity _____ 1,000 _____
Item _____ Magnetic Sensors _____   Date Requested _____ February 5 _____
For _____ Tanner Company _____   Date Completed _____ January 31 _____

Date	Direct Materials	Direct Labor	Manufacturing Overhead
1/6	$ 1,000		
1/10		$ 9,000	$ 7,200
1/12	7,000		
1/26	4,000		
1/31		6,000	4,800
	$12,000	$15,000	$12,000

Cost of completed job		
Direct materials	$	12,000
Direct labor		15,000
Manufacturing overhead		12,000
Total cost	$	39,000
Unit cost ($39,000 ÷ 1,000)	$	39.00

When a job is finished, an entry is made to transfer its total cost to finished goods inventory. The entry for Wallace Manufacturing is:

#7

		(7)		
Jan. 31	Finished Goods Inventory		39,000	
	Work in Process Inventory			39,000
	(To record completion of Job No. 101)			

Finished Goods Inventory is a control account that controls individual finished goods records in a finished goods subsidiary ledger. Postings to the receipts columns are made directly from completed job cost sheets. The finished goods inventory record for Job No. 101 is shown below in Illustration 2-17.

Illustration 2-17
Finished goods record

Item: Magnetic Sensors									Job No: 101	
	Receipts			Issues			Balance		
Date	Units	Cost	Total	Units	Cost	Total	Units	Cost	Total
1/31	1,000	$39	$39,000				1,000	$39	$39,000
2/2				1000	$39	$39,000			−0−

ASSIGNING COSTS TO COST OF GOODS SOLD

Recognition of the cost of goods sold is made when each sale occurs. To illustrate the entries when a completed job is sold, we will assume that on January 31 Wallace Manufacturing sells, on account, Job 101, costing $39,000, for $50,000. The entries are:

#8

		(8)		
Jan. 31	Accounts Receivable		50,000	
	Sales			50,000
	(To record sale of Job No. 101)			
31	Cost of Goods Sold		39,000	
	Finished Goods Inventory			39,000
	(To record cost of Job No. 101)			

The units sold, the cost per unit, and the total cost of goods sold for each job sold are recorded in the issues section of the finished goods record as shown in Illustration 2-17.

SUMMARY OF JOB ORDER COST FLOWS

A completed flow chart for a job order cost accounting system is shown in Illustration 2-18 on the next page. All postings are keyed to entries 1–8 in Wallace Manufacturing Company's accounts presented in the cost flow graphic in Illustration 2-4. The graphic also provides a summary of the inventory control accounts, subsidiary ledgers, and source documents for assigning costs to jobs.

Illustration 2-18   Job order cost system—flow of costs and documents

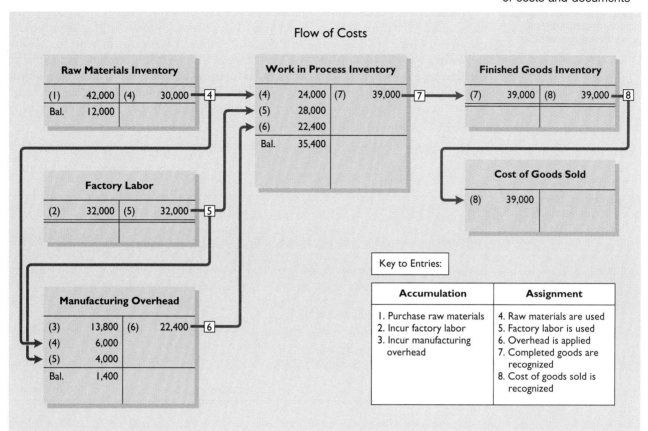

Flow of Costs

Raw Materials Inventory

(1)	42,000	(4)	30,000	▢4
Bal.	12,000			

Work in Process Inventory

(4)	24,000	(7)	39,000	▢7
(5)	28,000			
(6)	22,400			
Bal.	35,400			

Finished Goods Inventory

(7)	39,000	(8)	39,000	▢8

Factory Labor

(2)	32,000	(5)	32,000	▢5

Cost of Goods Sold

(8)	39,000

Manufacturing Overhead

(3)	13,800	(6)	22,400	▢6
(4)	6,000			
(5)	4,000			
Bal.	1,400			

Key to Entries:

Accumulation	Assignment
1. Purchase raw materials	4. Raw materials are used
2. Incur factory labor	5. Factory labor is used
3. Incur manufacturing overhead	6. Overhead is applied
	7. Completed goods are recognized
	8. Cost of goods sold is recognized

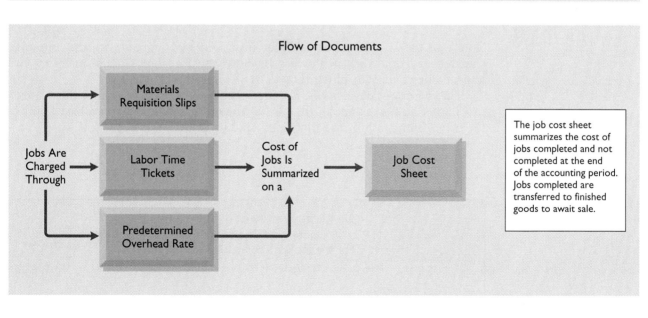

Flow of Documents

Jobs Are Charged Through → Materials Requisition Slips / Labor Time Tickets / Predetermined Overhead Rate → Cost of Jobs Is Summarized on a → Job Cost Sheet

The job cost sheet summarizes the cost of jobs completed and not completed at the end of the accounting period. Jobs completed are transferred to finished goods to await sale.

REPORTING JOB COST DATA

At the end of a period, financial statements are prepared that present aggregate data on all jobs manufactured and sold. The cost of goods manufactured schedule in job order costing is the same as in Chapter 1 with one exception: **Manufacturing overhead applied, rather than actual overhead costs, is added to direct materials and direct labor in determining total manufacturing costs.** The schedule is prepared directly from the Work in Process Inventory account. A condensed schedule for Wallace Manufacturing Company for January is as follows:

Illustration 2-19   Cost of goods manufactured schedule

WALLACE MANUFACTURING COMPANY Cost of Goods Manufactured Schedule For the Month Ended January 31, 1999		
Work in process, January 1		$ –0–
Direct materials used	$24,000	
Direct labor	28,000	
Manufacturing overhead applied	22,400	
Total manufacturing costs		74,400
Total cost of work in process		74,400
Less: Work in process, January 31		35,400
Cost of goods manufactured		$39,000

Note that the cost of goods manufactured ($39,000) agrees with the amount transferred from Work in Process Inventory to Finished Goods Inventory in journal entry No. 7 in Illustration 2-18.

The income statement and balance sheet are the same as those illustrated in Chapter 1. For example, the partial income statement for Wallace Manufacturing Company for the month of January is as follows:

Illustration 2-20   Partial income statement

WALLACE MANUFACTURING COMPANY Income Statement (partial) For the Month Ending January 31, 1999		
Sales		$50,000
Cost of goods sold		
Finished goods inventory, January 1	$ –0–	
Cost of goods manufactured (See Illustration 2-19)	39,000	
Cost of goods available for sale	39,000	
Finished goods inventory, January 31	–0–	
Cost of goods sold		39,000
Gross profit		$11,000

UNDER- OR OVERAPPLIED MANUFACTURING OVERHEAD

When Manufacturing Overhead has a **debit balance,** overhead is said to be underapplied. Underapplied overhead means that the overhead assigned to work in process is less than the overhead incurred. Conversely, when manufacturing overhead has a **credit balance,** overhead is overapplied. Overapplied overhead means that the overhead assigned to work in process is greater than the overhead incurred. These concepts are shown in Illustration 2-21:

Illustration 2-21   Under- and overapplied overhead

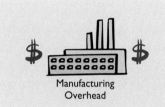

Manufacturing Overhead		If actual is *greater* than applied, manufacturing overhead is underapplied.
Actual (Costs incurred)	Applied (Costs assigned)	
Underapplied Debit Balance	overapplied credit balance	If actual is *less* than applied, manufacturing overhead is overapplied.

Manufacturing Overhead

INTERIM BALANCES

The existence of under- or overapplied overhead at the end of a month is expected and usually does not require corrective action by management. It is anticipated that monthly differences between actual and applied overhead will be offsetting over the course of the year.

When monthly financial statements are prepared, under- or overapplied overhead is reported on the balance sheet. **Underapplied overhead is shown as a prepaid expense in the current asset section. Overapplied overhead is reported as unearned revenue in the current liability section.**

YEAR-END BALANCE

At the end of the year, all manufacturing overhead transactions are complete; thus, there is no further opportunity for offsetting events to occur. Accordingly, any balance in Manufacturing Overhead is eliminated by an adjusting entry. Usually, under- or overapplied overhead is considered to be an **adjustment to cost of goods sold.** Thus, **underapplied overhead is debited to Cost of Goods Sold, and overapplied overhead is credited to Cost of Goods Sold.** To illustrate, assume that Wallace Manufacturing has a $2,500 credit balance in Manufacturing Overhead at December 31. The adjusting entry for the overapplied overhead is:

Dec. 31	Manufacturing Overhead	2,500	
	Cost of Goods Sold		2,500
	(To transfer overapplied overhead to cost of goods sold)		

After this entry is posted, Manufacturing Overhead will have a zero balance. In preparing an income statement for the year, the amount reported for cost of

BUSINESS INSIGHT
Management Perspective

Overhead also applies in nonmanufacturing companies. The State of Michigan found that auto dealers were charging documentary and service fees ranging from $18 to $445 per automobile and inspection fees from $88 to $360. These fees often were charged auto buyers after a base price had been negotiated. The Attorney General of the State of Michigan ruled that auto dealers cannot charge customers additional fees for routine overhead costs. The attorney general said: "Overhead is part of the sales price of a motor vehicle. Processing paper work, dealer incurred costs, and inspection fees to qualify cars for extended warranty plans are ordinary overhead expenses."

goods sold will be the account balance after the adjustment for either under- or overapplied overhead.

Conceptually, it can be argued that under- or overapplied overhead at the end of the year should be allocated among ending work in process, finished goods, and cost of goods sold. However, most management accountants do not believe allocation is worth the cost and effort. The bulk of the under- or overapplied amount will be allocated to cost of goods sold anyway, because most of the jobs will be sold during the year.

DECISION TOOLKIT

Decision Checkpoints	Info Needed for Decision	Tool to Use for Decision	How to Evaluate Results
Has the company over- or underapplied overhead for the period?	Actual overhead costs and overhead applied	Manufacturing overhead account	If the account balance is a credit, overhead applied exceeded actual overhead costs. If the account balance is a debit, overhead applied was less than actual overhead costs.

BEFORE YOU GO ON . . .

● **Review It**

1. When are entries made to record the completion and sale of a job?
2. What costs are included in total manufacturing costs in the cost of goods manufactured schedule?
3. How is under- or overapplied manufacturing overhead reported in monthly financial statements?

THE NAVIGATOR

USING THE DECISION TOOLKIT

Martinez Building Products Company is one of the largest manufacturers and marketers of unique, custom-made residential garage doors in the U.S. as well as a major supplier of industrial and commercial doors, grills, and counter shutters for the new construction, repair, and remodel markets. Martinez has developed plans for continued expansion of a network of service operations that sell, install, and service manufactured fireplaces, garage doors, and related products.

Martinez uses a job cost system and applies overhead to production on the basis of direct labor cost. In computing a predetermined overhead rate for the year 1999, the company estimated manufacturing overhead to be $24 million and direct labor costs to be $20 million. In addition the following information is provided:

Actual costs incurred during 1999:

Direct materials used	$30,000,000
Direct labor cost incurred	21,000,000

Manufacturing costs incurred during 1999:

Insurance, factory	$ 500,000
Indirect labor	7,500,000
Maintenance	1,000,000
Rent on building	11,000,000
Depreciation on equipment	2,000,000

Instructions

Answer each of the following:

(a) Why is Martinez Building Products Company using a job order costing system?

(b) On what basis does Martinez allocate its manufacturing overhead? Compute the predetermined overhead for the current year.

(c) Compute the amount of the under- or overapplied overhead for 1999.

(d) Martinez had balances in the beginning and ending work in process and finished goods accounts as follows:

	1/1/99	12/31/99
Work in process	$ 5,000,000	$ 4,000,000
Finished goods	13,000,000	11,000,000

Determine the (1) cost of goods manufactured and (2) cost of goods sold for Martinez during 1999. Assume that any under- or overapplied overhead should be included in the cost of goods sold.

(e) During 1999, Job G408 was started and completed. Its cost sheet showed a total cost of $100,000, and the company prices its product at 50% above its cost. What is the price to the customer if the company follows this pricing strategy?

Solution

(a) The company is using a job order system because each job (or batch) must have its own distinguishing characteristics. For example, each type of garage door would be different, and therefore a different cost per garage should be assigned.

(b) The company allocates its overhead on the basis of direct labor cost. The predetermined overhead rate is 120%, computed as follows:

$$\$24,000,000 \div \$20,000,000 = 120\%$$

(c)			
	Actual manufacturing overhead	$22,000,000	
	Applied overhead cost ($21,000,000 × 120%)	25,200,000	
	Overapplied overhead	$ 3,200,000	

(d) (1)	Work in process, 1/1/99		$ 5,000,000
	Direct materials used	$30,000,000	
	Direct labor	21,000,000	
	Manufacturing overhead applied	25,200,000	
	Total manufacturing costs		76,200,000
	Total cost of work in process		81,200,000
	Less: Work in process, 12/31/99		4,000,000
	Cost of goods manufactured		$77,200,000
(2)	Finished goods inventory, 1/1/99	$13,000,000	
	Cost of goods manufactured (see above)	77,200,000	
	Cost of goods available for sale	90,200,000	
	Finished goods inventory, 12/31/99	11,000,000	
	Cost of goods sold (unadjusted)	79,200,000	
	Less: Overapplied overhead	3,200,000	
	Cost of goods sold	$76,000,000	

(e)			
	G408 cost	$ 100,000	
	Markup percentage	× 50%	
	Profit	$ 50,000	

Price to customer: $150,000 ($100,000 + $50,000)

SUMMARY OF STUDY OBJECTIVES

❶ Explain the characteristics and purposes of cost accounting. Cost accounting involves the procedures for measuring, recording, and reporting product costs. From the data accumulated, the total cost and the unit cost of each product is determined.

❷ Describe the flow of costs in a job order cost accounting system. In job order cost accounting, manufacturing costs are first accumulated in three accounts: Raw Materials Inventory, Factory Labor, and Manufacturing Overhead. The accumulated costs are then assigned to Work in Process Inventory and eventually to Finished Goods Inventory and Cost of Goods Sold.

❸ Explain the nature and importance of a job cost sheet. A job cost sheet is a form used to record the costs chargeable to a specific job and to determine the total and unit cost of the completed job. Job cost sheets constitute the subsidiary ledger for the Work in Process Inventory control account.

❹ Indicate how the predetermined overhead rate is determined and used. The predetermined overhead rate is based on the relationship between estimated annual overhead costs and expected annual operating capacity expressed in terms of a common activity base, such as direct labor cost. The rate is used in assigning overhead costs to work in process and to specific jobs.

❺ Prepare entries for jobs completed and sold. When jobs are completed, the cost is debited to Finished Goods Inventory and credited to Work in Process Inventory. When a job is sold the entries are: (a) debit Cash or Accounts Receivable and credit Sales for the selling price and (b) debit Cost of Goods Sold and credit Finished Goods Inventory for the cost of the goods.

❻ Distinguish between under- and overapplied manufacturing overhead. Underapplied manufacturing overhead means that the overhead assigned to work in process is less than the overhead incurred. Conversely, overapplied overhead means that the overhead assigned to work in process is greater than the overhead incurred.

DECISION TOOLKIT—A SUMMARY

Decision Checkpoints	Info Needed for Decision	Tool to Use for Decision	How to Evaluate Results
What is the cost of a job?	Cost of material, labor, and overhead assigned to a specific job	Job cost sheet	Compare costs to those of previous periods and to those of competitors to ensure that costs are in line. Compare costs to expected selling price to determine overall profitability.
Has the company over- or underapplied overhead for the period?	Actual overhead costs and overhead applied	Manufacturing overhead account	If the account balance is a credit, overhead applied exceeded actual overhead costs. If the account balance is a debit, overhead applied was less than actual overhead costs.

GLOSSARY

Cost accounting An area of accounting that involves the measuring, recording, and reporting of product costs. (p. 46)

Cost accounting system Manufacturing cost accounts that are fully integrated into the general ledger of a company. (p. 46)

Job cost sheet A form used to record the costs chargeable to a job and to determine the total and unit cost of the completed job. (p. 52)

Job order cost system A cost accounting system in which costs are assigned to each job or batch. (p. 47)

Materials requisition slip A document authorizing the issuance of raw materials from the storeroom to production. (p. 52)

Overapplied overhead A situation in which overhead assigned to work in process is greater than the overhead incurred. (p. 63)

Predetermined overhead rate A rate based on the relationship between estimated annual overhead costs and expected annual operating activity, expressed in terms of a common activity base. (p. 56)

Process cost system A system of accounting used by companies that manufacture relatively homogeneous products through a series of continuous processes or operations. (p. 47)

Time ticket A document that indicates the employee, the hours worked, the account and job to be charged, and the total labor cost. (p. 54)

Underapplied overhead A situation in which overhead assigned to work in process is less than the overhead incurred. (p. 63)

DEMONSTRATION PROBLEM

During February, Cardella Manufacturing works on two jobs: Numbers A16 and B17. Summary data concerning these jobs are as follows:

Manufacturing Costs Incurred:

Purchased $54,000 of raw materials on account.
Factory labor $76,000 plus $4,000 employer payroll taxes.
Manufacturing overhead exclusive of indirect materials and indirect labor $59,800.

Assignment of Costs:

Direct materials:	Job A16 $27,000, Job B17 $21,000
Indirect materials:	$3,000
Direct labor:	Job A16 $52,000, Job B17 $26,000
Indirect labor:	$2,000

Manufacturing overhead rate 80% of direct labor costs.

Job A16 was completed and sold on account for $150,000. Job B17 was only partially completed.

Instructions

(a) Journalize the February transactions in the sequence followed in the chapter.

(b) What was the amount of under- or overapplied manufacturing overhead?

Solution to Demonstration Problem

Problem-Solving Strategies

1. In accumulating costs, three accounts are debited: Raw Materials Inventory, Factory Labor, and Manufacturing Overhead.

2. When Work in Process Inventory is debited, one of the three accounts in strategy (1), above, must be credited.

3. Finished Goods Inventory is debited for the cost of completed jobs, and Cost of Goods Sold is debited for the cost of jobs sold.

4. Overhead is underapplied when Manufacturing Overhead has a debit balance.

(a)

1.

Feb. 28	Raw Materials Inventory	54,000	
	Accounts Payable		54,000
	(Purchase of raw materials on account)		

2.

28	Factory Labor	80,000	
	Factory Wages Payable		76,000
	Employer Payroll Taxes Payable		4,000
	(To record factory labor costs)		

3.

28	Manufacturing Overhead	59,800	
	Accounts Payable, Accumulated		
	Depreciation, and Prepaid Insurance		59,800
	(To record overhead costs)		

4.

28	Work in Process Inventory	48,000	
	Manufacturing Overhead	3,000	
	Raw Materials Inventory		51,000
	(To assign raw materials to production)		

5.

28	Work in Process Inventory	78,000	
	Manufacturing Overhead	2,000	
	Factory Labor		80,000
	(To assign factory labor to production)		

6.

28	Work in Process Inventory	62,400	
	Manufacturing Overhead		62,400
	(To assign overhead to jobs—80% × $78,000)		

7.

28	Finished Goods Inventory	120,600	
	Work in Process Inventory		120,600
	(To record completion of Job A16: direct		
	materials $27,000, direct labor $52,000,		
	and manufacturing overhead $41,600)		

8.

28	Accounts Receivable	150,000	
	Cost of Goods Sold	120,600	
	Sales		150,000
	Finished Goods Inventory		120,600
	(To record sale of Job A16)		

(b) Manufacturing Overhead has a debit balance of $2,400 as shown below:

Manufacturing Overhead

(3)	59,800	(6)	62,400
(4)	3,000		
(5)	2,000		
Bal.	2,400		

Thus, manufacturing overhead is underapplied for the month.

SELF-STUDY QUESTIONS

Answers are at the end of the chapter.

(SO 1) 1. Cost accounting involves the measuring, recording, and reporting of:
(a) product costs.
(b) future costs.
(c) manufacturing processes.
(d) managerial accounting decisions.

(SO 2) 2. In accumulating raw materials costs, the cost of raw materials purchased in a perpetual system is debited to:
(a) Raw Material Purchases.
(b) Raw Materials Inventory.
(c) Purchases.
(d) Work in Process.

(SO 2) 3. When incurred, factory labor costs are debited to:
(a) Work in Process.
(b) Factory Wages Expense.
(c) Factory Labor.
(d) Factory Wages Payable.

(SO 3) 4. The source documents for assigning costs to job cost sheets are:
(a) invoices, time tickets, and the predetermined overhead rate.
(b) materials requisition slips, time tickets, and the actual overhead costs.
(c) materials requisition slips, payroll register, and the predetermined overhead rate.
(d) materials requisition slips, time tickets, and the predetermined overhead rate.

(SO 3) 5. In recording the issuance of raw materials in a job order cost system, it would be *incorrect* to:
(a) debit Work in Process Inventory.
(b) debit Finished Goods Inventory.
(c) debit Manufacturing Overhead.
(d) credit Raw Materials Inventory.

(SO 3) 6. The entry when direct factory labor is assigned to jobs is a debit to:
(a) Work in Process Inventory and a credit to Factory Labor.
(b) Manufacturing Overhead a credit to Factory Labor.

(c) Factory Labor and a credit to Manufacturing Overhead.
(d) Factory Labor and a credit to Work in Process Inventory.

(SO 4) 7. The formula for computing the predetermined manufacturing overhead rate is estimated annual overhead costs divided by an expected annual operating activity, expressed as:
(a) direct labor cost.
(b) direct labor hours.
(c) machine hours.
(d) any of the above.

(SO 4) 8. In the Cleo Company, the predetermined overhead rate is 80% of direct labor cost. During the month, $210,000 of factory labor costs are incurred, of which $180,000 is direct labor and $30,000 is indirect labor. Actual overhead incurred was $200,000. The amount of overhead debited to Work in Process Inventory should be:
(a) $120,000.
(b) $144,000.
(c) $168,000.
(d) $160,000.

(SO 5) 9. In BAC Company, Job No. 26 is completed at a cost of $4,500 and later sold for $7,000 cash. A correct entry is:
(a) Debit Finished Goods Inventory $7,000 and credit Work in Process Inventory $7,000.
(b) Debit Cost of Goods Sold $7,000 and credit Finished Goods Inventory $7,000.
(c) Debit Finished Goods Inventory $4,500 and credit Work in Process Inventory $4,500.
(d) Debit Accounts Receivable $7,000 and credit Sales $7,000.

(SO 6) 10. In preparing monthly financial statements, overapplied overhead is reported in the balance sheet as a(an):
(a) prepaid expense.
(b) unearned revenue.
(c) noncurrent asset.
(d) noncurrent liability.

QUESTIONS

1. Kenna Quayle is studying for an accounting midterm examination. What should Kenna know about how management may use job cost data?

2. (a) Nels Hoadley is not sure about the differences between cost accounting and a cost accounting system. Explain the difference to Nels. (b) What is an important feature of a cost accounting system?

3. (a) Distinguish between the two types of cost accounting systems. (b) May a company use both types of cost accounting systems? *yes*

4. What type of industry is likely to use a job order cost system? Give some examples.

5. What type of industry is likely to use a process cost system? Give some examples.

6. Your roommate asks your help in understanding the major steps in the flow of costs in a job order cost system. Identify the steps for your roommate.

7. There are three inventory control accounts in a job order system. Identify the control accounts and their subsidiary ledgers.

8. What source documents are used in accumulating direct labor costs?

9. Entries to manufacturing overhead normally are only made daily. Do you agree? Explain.

10. Elaine Gould is confused about the source documents used in assigning materials and labor costs. Identify the documents and give the entry for each document.

11. What is the purpose of a job cost sheet?

12. Indicate the source documents that are used in charging costs to specific jobs.

13. Differentiate between a "materials inventory record" and a "materials requisition slip" as used in a job order cost system.

14. Phil Agler believes actual manufacturing overhead should be charged to jobs. Do you agree? Why or why not?

15. What relationships are involved in computing a predetermined overhead rate?

16. How can the agreement of Work in Process Inventory and job cost sheets be verified?

17. Judy Jansen believes that the cost of goods manufactured schedule in job order cost accounting is the same as in manufacturing accounting. Is Judy correct? Explain. *Incorrect there's is a difference computing manuf. cost.*

18. Ron Patten is confused about under- and overapplied manufacturing overhead. Define the terms for Ron and indicate the balance in the manufacturing overhead account applicable to each term.

19. Under- or overapplied overhead is reported in the income statement when monthly financial statements are prepared. Do you agree? If not, indicate the proper presentation. *No!*

20. At the end of the year, under- or overapplied overhead is closed to Income Summary. Is this correct? If not, indicate the customary treatment of this account.

BRIEF EXERCISES

Prepare a flowchart of a job order cost accounting system, and identify transactions.
(SO 2)

BE2-1 Redeker Tool & Die begins operations on January 1. Because all work is done to customer specifications, the company decides to use a job cost accounting system. Prepare a flow chart of a typical job order system with arrows showing the flow of costs. Identify the eight transactions.

Prepare entries in accumulating manufacturing costs.
(SO 2)

BE2-2 During the first month of operations, Redeker Tool & Die accumulated the following manufacturing costs: raw materials $8,000 on account, factory labor $4,000 of which $3,600 relates to factory wages payable and $400 relates to payroll taxes payable, and utilities payable $2,000. Prepare separate journal entries for each type of manufacturing cost.

Prepare entry for the assignment of raw materials costs.
(SO 2)

BE2-3 In January, Redeker Tool & Die requisitions raw materials for production as follows: Job 1 $1,000, Job 2 $1,200, Job 3 $1,600, and general factory use $600. Prepare a summary journal entry to record raw materials used.

Prepare entry for the assignment of factory labor costs.
(SO 2)

BE2-4 Factory labor data for Redeker Tool & Die is given in BE2-2. During January, time tickets show that the factory labor of $4,000 was used as follows: Job 1 $1,200, Job 2 $1,300, Job 3 $1,000, and general factory use $500. Prepare a summary journal entry to record factory labor used.

Prepare job cost sheets.
(SO 3)

BE2-5 Data pertaining to job cost sheets for Redeker Tool & Die are given in BE2-3 and BE2-4. Prepare the job cost sheets for each of the three jobs. (Note: You may omit the column for Manufacturing Overhead.)

BE2-6 Oliva Company estimates that annual manufacturing overhead costs will be $300,000. Estimated annual operating activity bases are: direct labor cost $500,000, direct labor hours 50,000, and machine hours 100,000. Compute the predetermined overhead rate for each activity base.

Compute predetermined overhead rates.

(SO 4)

BE2-7 During the first quarter, Oliva Company incurs the following direct labor costs: January $40,000, February $30,000, and March $50,000. For each month, prepare the entry to assign overhead to production using a predetermined rate of 60% of direct labor cost.

Assign manufacturing overhead to production.

(SO 4)

BE2-8 In March, Glendo Company completes Jobs 10 and 11 costing $28,000 and $32,000, respectively. On March 31, Job 10 is sold to the customer for $35,000 in cash. Journalize the entries for the completion of the two jobs and the sale of Job 10.

Prepare entries for completion and sale of completed jobs.

(SO 5)

BE2-9 On September 30, balances in Manufacturing Overhead are: Oliva Company—Debit $1,500, Glendo Company—Credit $3,000. Indicate how each company should report its balance at September 30, assuming each company prepares annual financial statements on December 31.

Indicate statement classification of under- or overapplied overhead.

(SO 6)

BE2-10 At December 31, balances in Manufacturing Overhead are: Oliva Company—Debit $1,000, Glendo Company—Credit $1,200. Prepare the adjusting entry for each company at December 31, assuming the adjustment is made to cost of goods sold.

Prepare adjusting entries for under- and overapplied overhead.

(SO 6)

*E*XERCISES

E2-1 The gross earnings of the factory workers for Gaetti Company during the month of January are $90,000. The employer's payroll taxes for the factory payroll are $9,000 and the fringe benefits to be paid by the employer on this payroll are $4,000. Of the total accumulated cost of factory labor, 90% is related to direct labor and 10% is attributable to indirect labor.

Prepare entries for factory labor.

(SO 2)

Instructions
(a) Prepare the entry to record the factory labor costs for the month of January.
(b) Prepare the entry to assign factory labor to production.

E2-2 Lorenzo Manufacturing uses a job order cost accounting system. On May 1, the company has a balance in Work in Process Inventory of $3,200 and two jobs in process: Job No. 429 $2,000, and Job No. 430 $1,200. During May, a summary of source documents reveals the following:

Prepare journal entries for manufacturing costs.

(SO 2, 3, 4, 5)

Job Number	Materials Requisition Slips	Labor Time Tickets	manufacture overhead
429	$2,500	$ 2,400	1680
430	2,000	3,000	2100
431	4,400	7,600	5320
General use	800	1,200	840
	$9,700	$14,200	9100

Lorenzo Manufacturing applies manufacturing overhead to jobs at an overhead rate of 70% of direct labor cost. Job No. 429 is completed during the month.

Instructions
(a) Prepare summary journal entries to record the requisition slips, time tickets, the assignment of manufacturing overhead to jobs, and the completion of Job No. 429.
(b) Post the entries to Work in Process Inventory and prove the agreement of the control account with the job cost sheets.

Analyze a job cost sheet and prepare entries for manufacturing costs.

(SO 2, 3, 4, 5)

E2-3 A job order cost sheet for Free Company is shown below.

Job No. 92			For 2,000 Units
Date	Direct Materials	Direct Labor	Manufacturing Overhead
Beg. bal. Jan. 1	5,000	6,000	4,200
8	6,000		
12		8,000	6,000
25	2,000		
27		4,000	3,000
	13,000	18,000	13,200

Cost of completed job:	
Direct materials	$13,000
Direct labor	18,000
Manufacturing overhead	13,200
Total cost	$44,200
Unit cost ($44,200 ÷ 2,000)	$22.10

Instructions

(a) ▭▭▭▷ On the basis of the foregoing data answer the following questions:
  (1) What was the balance in Work in Process Inventory on January 1 if this was the only unfinished job?
  (2) If manufacturing overhead is applied on the basis of direct labor cost, what overhead rate was used in each year?
(b) Prepare summary entries at January 31 to record the current year's transactions pertaining to Job No. 92.

Analyze costs of manufacturing and determine missing amounts.

(SO 2, 5)

E2-4 Manufacturing cost data for Kosko Company, which uses a job order cost system, are presented below:

	Case A	Case B	Case C
Direct materials	(a)	$83,000	$ 65,000
Direct labor used	$ 50,000	90,000	(h)
Manufacturing overhead applied	42,500	(d)	(i)
Total manufacturing costs	190,650	(e)	287,000
Work in process 1/1/99	(b)	15,500	18,000
Total cost of work in process	201,500	(f)	(j)
Work in process 12/31/99	(c)	11,800	(k)
Cost of goods manufactured	192,300	(g)	262,000

Instructions

Indicate the missing amount for each letter. Assume that in all cases manufacturing overhead is applied on the basis of direct labor cost and the rate is the same.

Compute the manufacturing overhead rate and under- or overapplied overhead.

(SO 4, 6)

E2-5 Gomez Company applies manufacturing overhead to jobs on the basis of machine hours used. Overhead costs are expected to total $275,000 for the year, and machine usage is estimated at 125,000 hours.

In January, $26,000 of overhead costs are incurred and 10,000 machine hours are used. For the remainder of the year, $274,000 of overhead costs are incurred and 120,000 machine hours are worked.

Instructions

(a) Compute the manufacturing overhead rate for the year.
(b) What is the amount of under- or overapplied overhead at January 31? How should this amount be reported in the financial statements prepared on January 31?
(c) What is the amount of under- or overapplied overhead at December 31?
(d) Assuming the under- or overapplied overhead for the year is not allocated to inventory accounts, prepare the adjusting entry to assign the amount to cost of goods sold.

E2-6   A job cost sheet of Duc Mai Company is given below:

Job Cost Sheet

JOB NO.   469   Quantity   2,000

ITEM   White Lion Cages   Date Requested   7/2

FOR   Tesla Company   Date Completed   7/31

Date	Direct Materials	Direct Labor	Manufacturing Overhead
7/10	825		
12	900		
15		440	550
22		380	475
24	1,600		
27	1,500		
31		540	675

Cost of completed job:

   Direct materials   _____

   Direct labor   _____

   Manufacturing overhead _____

Total cost   _____

Instructions

(a)   ⬛▭▭▭▭▷ Answer the following questions:

   (1) What are the source documents for direct materials, direct labor, and manufacturing overhead costs assigned to this job?

   (2) What is the predetermined manufacturing overhead rate?

   (3) What is the total cost and unit cost of the completed job?

(b) Prepare the entry to record the completion of the job.

E2-7   Kiefer Corporation incurred the following transactions.

1. Purchased raw materials on account, $48,900.
2. Raw Materials of $36,000 were requisitioned to the factory. An analysis of the materials requisition slips indicated that $8,800 was classified as indirect materials.
3. Factory labor costs incurred were $64,900 of which $59,000 pertained to factory wages payable and $5,900 pertained to employer payroll taxes payable.
4. Time tickets indicated that $60,000 was direct labor and $4,900 was indirect labor.
5. Overhead costs incurred on account were $80,500.
6. Manufacturing overhead was applied at the rate of 150% of direct labor cost.
7. Goods costing $88,000 were completed and transferred to finished goods.
8. Finished goods costing $68,000 to manufacture were sold on account for $103,000.

Instructions

Journalize the transactions. (Omit explanations.)

E2-8   Ikerd Printing Corp. uses a job order cost system. The following data summarize the operations related to the first quarter's production:

1. Materials purchased on account $172,000 and factory wages incurred $87,300.
2. Materials requisitioned and factory labor used by job:

Job Number	Materials	Factory Labor
A20	$ 32,240	$18,000
A21	40,920	26,000
A22	36,100	15,000
A23	39,270	25,000
General factory use	4,470	3,300
	$153,000	$87,300

3. Manufacturing overhead costs incurred on account $39,500.
4. Depreciation on machinery and equipment $14,550.
5. Manufacturing overhead rate is 75% of direct labor cost.
6. Jobs completed during the quarter: A20, A21, and A23.

Instructions

Prepare entries to record the operations summarized above. (Prepare a schedule showing the individual cost elements and total cost for each job in item 6.)

Prepare a cost of goods manufactured schedule and partial financial statements.

(SO 2, 5)

E2-9 At May 31, the accounts of Ginavan Manufacturing Company show the following:
1. May 1 inventories—finished goods $12,600, work in process $14,700, and raw materials $8,200.
2. May 31 inventories—finished goods $10,500, work in process $16,900, and raw materials $7,100.
3. Debit postings to work in process were: direct materials $62,400, direct labor $32,000, and manufacturing overhead applied $64,000.
4. Sales totaled $200,000.

Instructions

(a) Prepare a condensed cost of goods manufactured schedule.
(b) Prepare an income statement for May through gross profit.
(c) Indicate the balance sheet presentation of the manufacturing inventories at May 31, 1999.

Compute work in process and finished goods from job cost sheets.

(SO 3, 5)

E2-10 Krumme Company begins operations on April 1. Information from job cost sheets shows the following:

| Job Number | **Manufacturing Costs Assigned** | | |
	April	May	June
10	$5,200	$4,400	
11	4,100	3,900	$3,000
12	1,200		
13		4,700	4,500
14		3,900	3,600

Job 12 was completed in April. Job 10 was completed in May, and Jobs 11 and 13 were completed in June. Each job was sold for 50% above its cost in the month following completion.

Instructions

Answer the following questions:
1. What is the balance in Work in Process Inventory at the end of each month?
2. What is the balance in Finished Goods Inventory at the end of each month?
3. What is the gross profit for May, June, and July?

PROBLEMS: SET A

Prepare entries in a job cost system and job costs sheets

(SO 2, 3, 4, 5, 6)

P2-1A Good Manufacturing uses a job order cost system and applies overhead to production on the basis of direct labor hours. On January 1, 1999, Job No. 25 was the only job in process. The costs incurred prior to January 1 on this job were as follows: direct materials, $10,000; direct labor, $6,000; and manufacturing overhead, $10,500. In addition, Job No. 23 had been completed at a cost of $45,000 and was part of finished goods inventory, and there was a $5,000 balance in the Raw Materials inventory account.

During the month of January, Good Manufacturing began production on Jobs 26 and 27, and completed Jobs 25 and 26. Jobs 23 and 25 were also sold on account during the month for $52,000 and $58,000 respectively. The following additional events occurred during the month:
1. Purchased additional raw materials of $45,000 on account.
2. Incurred factory labor costs of $31,500. Of this amount $6,500 related to employer payroll taxes.

3. Incurred manufacturing overhead costs as follows; indirect materials, $10,000; indirect labor, $7,500; depreciation expense, $10,000; and various other manufacturing overhead costs on account, $15,000.
4. Assigned direct materials and direct labor to jobs as follows:

(handwritten note:) est. manuf OHD Exp $500,000

Activities Base   20,000 hrs

= $25 per hours

Job No.	Direct Materials	Direct Labor
25	$ 5,000	$ 3,000
26	20,000	12,000
27	15,000	9,000

5. The company uses direct labor hours as the activity base to assign overhead. Direct labor hours incurred on each job were as follows: Job No. 25, 200; Job No. 26, 800; and Job No. 27, 600.

Instructions

(a) Calculate the predetermined overhead rate for the year 1999, assuming Good Manufacturing estimates total manufacturing overhead costs of $500,000, direct labor costs of $300,000, and direct labor hours of 20,000 for the year.
(b) Open job cost sheets for Jobs 25, 26, and 27. Enter the January 1 balances on the job cost sheet for Job No. 25.
(c) Prepare the journal entries to record the purchase of raw materials, the factory labor costs incurred, and the manufacturing overhead costs incurred during the month of January.
(d) Prepare the journal entries to record the assignment of direct materials, direct labor, and manufacturing overhead costs to production. In assigning manufacturing overhead costs, use the overhead rate calculated in (a). Post all costs to the job cost sheets as necessary.
(e) Total the job cost sheets for any job(s) completed during the month. Prepare the journal entry (or entries) to record the completion of any job(s) during the month.
(f) Prepare the journal entry (or entries) to record the sale of any job(s) during the month.
(g) What is the balance in the Work-In-Process Inventory account at the end of the month? What does this balance consist of?
(h) What is the amount of over- or underapplied overhead for the month? How would this be reported on the financial statements for the month of January?

P2-2A For the year ended December 31, 1999, the job cost sheets of Asticio Company contained the following data.

Prepare entries in a job cost system and partial income statement.

(SO 2, 3, 4, 5, 6)

Job Number	Explanation	Direct Materials	Direct Labor	Manufacturing Overhead	Total Costs
7650	Balance 1/1	$18,000	$20,000	$25,000	$ 63,000
	Current year's costs	22,000	30,000	37,500	89,500
7651	Balance 1/1	12,000	18,000	22,500	52,500
	Current year's costs	28,000	40,000	50,000	118,000
7652	Current year's costs	40,000	60,000	75,000	175,000

Other data:
1. Raw materials inventory totaled $20,000 on January 1. During the year, $100,000 of raw materials were purchased on account.
2. Finished goods on January 1 consisted of Job No. 7648 for $98,000 and Job No. 7649 for $62,000.
3. Job No. 7650 and Job No. 7651 were completed during the year.
4. Job Nos. 7648, 7649, and 7650 were sold on account for $390,000.
5. Manufacturing overhead incurred on account totaled $120,000.
6. Other manufacturing overhead consisted of indirect materials $12,000, indirect labor $18,000, and depreciation on factory machinery $6,000.

Instructions

(a) Prove the agreement of Work in Process Inventory with job cost sheets pertaining to unfinished work.

(b) Prepare the adjusting entry for manufacturing overhead, assuming the balance is allocated entirely to cost of goods sold.

(c) Determine the gross profit to be reported for 1999.

Prepare entries in a job cost system and cost of goods manufactured schedule.

(SO 2, 3, 4, 5)

P2-3A Joe Witten is a contractor specializing in custom-built jacuzzis. On May 1, 1999, his ledger contains the following data:

Raw Materials Inventory	$30,000
Work in Process Inventory	12,200
Manufacturing Overhead	2,500 (dr.)

The Manufacturing Overhead account has debit totals of $12,500 and credit totals of $10,000. Subsidiary data for Work in Process Inventory on May 1 include:

Job Cost Sheets

Job by Customer	Direct Materials	Manufacturing Direct Labor	Overhead
Jovi	$2,500	$2,000	$1,400
Roth	2,000	1,200	840
Nicks	900	800	560
	$5,400	$4,000	$2,800

A summary of materials requisition slips and time tickets for the month of May reveals the following:

Job by Customer	Materials Requisition Slips	Time Tickets
Jovi	$ 500	$ 400
Roth	600	1,000
Nicks	2,300	1,300
Jett	2,400	3,300
	5,800	6,000
General use	1,500	2,600
	$7,300	$8,600

During May, the following costs were incurred: (a) raw materials purchased on account, $5,000; (b) labor paid, $8,200; (c) manufacturing overhead paid, $1,400. Overhead was charged to jobs on the basis of direct labor cost at the same rate as in the previous month.

The jacuzzis for customers Jovi, Roth, and Nicks were completed during May. Each jacuzzi was sold for $12,500 cash.

Instructions

(a) Prepare journal entries for the May transactions.

(b) Post the entries to Work in Process Inventory.

(c) Reconcile the balance in Work in Process Inventory with the costs of unfinished jobs.

(d) Prepare a cost of goods manufactured schedule for May.

Compute predetermined overhead rates, apply overhead, and indicate statement presentation of under- or overapplied overhead.

(SO 4, 6)

P2-4A Navarro Manufacturing uses a job order cost system in each of its three manufacturing departments. Manufacturing overhead is applied to jobs on the basis of direct labor cost in Department A, direct labor hours in Department B, and machine hours in Department C.

In establishing the predetermined overhead rates for 1999 the following estimates were made for the year:

	Department		
	A	**B**	**C**
Manufacturing overhead	$900,000	$760,000	$780,000
Direct labor cost	$600,000	$100,000	$600,000
Direct labor hours	50,000	40,000	50,000
Machine hours	100,000	120,000	150,000

During January, the job cost sheets showed the following costs and production data:

	Department		
	A	**B**	**C**
Direct materials used	$92,000	$86,000	$64,000
Direct labor cost	$48,000	$35,000	$50,400
Manufacturing overhead incurred	$76,000	$67,000	$64,500
Direct labor hours	4,000	3,500	4,200
Machine hours	8,000	10,500	12,600

Instructions
(a) Compute the predetermined overhead rate for each department.
(b) Compute the total manufacturing cost assigned to jobs in January in each department.
(c) Compute the under- or overapplied overhead for each department at January 31.
(d) Indicate the statement presentation of the under- or overapplied overhead at January 31.
(e) If the amount in (d) was the same at December 31, how would it be reported in the year-end financial statements?

P2-5A Wagaman Company's fiscal year ends on June 30. The following accounts are found in its job order cost accounting system for the first month of the new fiscal year.

Analyze manufacturing cost accounts and determine missing amounts.
(SO 2, 3, 4, 5, 6)

Raw Materials Inventory

July 1	Beginning balance	19,000	July 31	Requisitions	(a) 83,900		
31	Purchases	88,400			(75,000 + 8,900)		
July 31	Ending balance	(b) 23,500					

Work in Process Inventory

July 1	Beginning balance 25,200	(c)	July 31	Jobs completed	(f) 255,750	
31	Direct materials	75,000			(91,000 manufacturing overhead applied)	
31	Direct labor 91,000 × 130%	(d) 70,000 (manufacturing ov			+130%	
31	Overhead	(e) 91,000 (manufacturing overhead applied)				
July 31	Ending balance 5,450	(g)	(2,000 + 1500 + 1950)			

7,000
8,200
5,200

Finished Goods Inventory

July 1	Beginning balance 135,000	(h)	July 31	Cost of goods sold	(j) 247,750	
31	Completed jobs (same as (f)) 255,750	(i)			(135,000 + 255,750 − 143,000)	
July 31	Ending balance 143,000	(k)				

Factory Labor

July 31	Factory wages 86,000	(l)	July 31	Wages assigned	(m) 86,000	
	(70,000 + 16,000) see (d)				(same as (l))	

Manufacturing Overhead

July 31	Indirect materials	8,900	July 31	Overhead applied	91,000
31	Indirect labor	16,000			
31	Other overhead	(n) 70,100	(91,000 + 4,200 − 8,900 − 16,000)		

Other data:
1. On July 1, two jobs were in process: Job No. 4085 and Job No. 4086 with costs of $17,000 and $8,200, respectively.
2. During July, Job Nos. 4087, 4088, and 4089 were started. On July 31, only Job No. 4089 was unfinished. This job had charges for direct materials $2,000, direct labor $1,500 plus manufacturing overhead.
3. On July 1, Job No. 4084, costing $135,000, was in the finished goods warehouse. On July 31, Job No. 4088, costing $143,000, was in finished goods.

4. Manufacturing overhead was applied at the rate of 130% of direct labor cost. Over-head was $4,000 underapplied in July.

Instructions
List the letters (a) through (n) and indicate the amount pertaining to each letter. Show computations.

PROBLEMS: SET B

Prepare entries in a job cost system and job cost sheets.

(SO 2, 3, 4, 5)

P2-1B   Great Manufacturing uses a job order cost system and applies overhead to pro-duction on the basis of direct labor costs. On January 1, 1999, Job No. 50 was the only job in process. The costs incurred prior to January 1 on this job were as follows: direct materials, $20,000; direct labor, $12,000; and manufacturing overhead, $21,000. In addi-tion as of January 1, Job No. 49 had been completed at a cost of $90,000 and was part of finished goods inventory, and there was a $15,000 balance in the Raw Materials In-ventory account.

During the month of January, Great Manufacturing began production on Jobs 51 and 52, and completed Jobs 50 and 51. Jobs 49 and 50 were also sold on account during the month for $89,000 and $115,000 respectively. The following additional events occurred during the month:
1. Purchased additional raw materials of $90,000 on account.
2. Incurred factory labor costs of $63,000. Of this amount $13,000 related to employer payroll taxes.
3. Incurred manufacturing overhead costs as follows: indirect materials, $14,000; indi-rect labor, $15,000; depreciation expense, $18,000; and various other manufacturing overhead costs on account, $23,000.
4. Assigned direct materials and direct labor to jobs as follows:

Job No.	Direct Materials	Direct Labor
50	$10,000	$ 6,000
51	39,000	24,000
52	30,000	18,000

5. The company uses direct labor hours as the activity base to assign overhead. Direct labor hours incurred on each job were as follows: Job No. 50, 400; Job No. 51, 1,600; and Job No. 52, 1,200.

Instructions
(a) Calculate the predetermined overhead rate for the year 1999, assuming Great Man-ufacturing estimates total manufacturing overhead costs of $1,050,000, direct labor costs of $700,000 and direct labor hours of 20,000 for the year.
(b) Open job cost sheets for Jobs 50, 51, and 52. Enter the January 1 balances on the job cost sheet for Job No. 50.
(c) Prepare the journal entries to record the purchase of raw materials, the factory la-bor costs incurred, and the manufacturing overhead costs incurred during the month of January.
(d) Prepare the journal entries to record the assignment of direct materials, direct labor, and manufacturing overhead costs to production. In assigning manufacturing over-head costs, use the overhead rate calculated in (a). Post all costs to the job cost sheets as necessary.
(e) Total the job cost sheets for any job(s) completed during the month. Prepare the jour-nal entry (or entries) to record the completion of any job(s) during the month.
(f) Prepare the journal entry (or entries) to record the sale of any job(s) during the month.
(g) What is the balance in the Finished Goods Inventory account at the end of the month? What does this balance consist of?
(h) What is the amount of over- or underapplied overhead for the month? How would this be reported on the financial statements for the month of January?

P2-2B For the year ended December 31, 1999, the job cost sheets of Brazil Company contained the following data.

Prepare entries in a job cost system and partial income statement.

(SO 2, 3, 4, 5, 6)

Job Number	Explanation	Direct Materials	Direct Labor	Manufacturing Overhead	Total Costs
7640	Balance 1/1	$25,000	$24,000	$28,800	$ 77,800
	Current year's costs	34,000	36,000	43,200	113,200
7641	Balance 1/1	11,000	18,000	21,600	50,600
	Current year's costs	40,000	48,000	57,600	145,600
7642	Current year's costs	48,000	55,000	66,000	169,000

Other data:
1. Raw materials inventory totaled $15,000 on January 1. During the year, $140,000 of raw materials were purchased on account.
2. Finished goods on January 1 consisted of Job No. 7638 for $87,000 and Job No. 7639 for $92,000.
3. Job No. 7640 and Job No. 7641 were completed during the year.
4. Job Nos. 7638, 7639, and 7641 were sold on account for $530,000.
5. Manufacturing overhead incurred on account totaled $135,000.
6. Other manufacturing overhead consisted of indirect materials $14,000, indirect labor $20,000, and depreciation on factory machinery $8,000.

Instructions
(a) Prove the agreement of Work in Process Inventory with job cost sheets pertaining to unfinished work.
(b) Prepare the adjusting entry for manufacturing overhead, assuming the balance is allocated entirely to Cost of Goods Sold.
(c) Determine the gross profit to be reported for 1999.

P2-3B Ehrlich Inc. is a construction company specializing in custom patios. The patios are constructed of concrete, brick, fiberglass, and lumber, depending upon customer preference. On June 1, 1999, the general ledger for Ehrlich Inc. contains the following data:

Prepare entries in a job cost system and cost of goods manufactured schedule.

(SO 2, 3, 4, 5)

Raw Material Inventory	$4,200	Manufacturing Overhead Applied	$27,200
Work in Process Inventory	$5,540	Manufacturing Overhead Incurred	$26,375

Subsidiary data for Work in Process Inventory on June 1 are as follows:

Job Cost Sheets

	Customer Job		
Cost Element	Dion	Cole	Kix
Direct materials	$ 600	$ 800	$ 900
Direct labor	320	540	580
Manufacturing overhead	400	675	725
	$1,320	$2,015	$2,205

A summary of materials requisition slips and time tickets for June shows the following:

Customer Job	Materials Requisition Slips	Time Tickets
Dion	$ 800	$ 450
Lock	2,000	800
Cole	500	360
Kix	1,300	800
Dion	300	250
	4,900	2,660
General use	1,500	1,200
	$6,400	$3,860

During June, raw materials purchased on account were $3,900 and all wages were paid. Additional overhead costs consisted of depreciation on equipment $700 and miscellaneous costs of $400 incurred on account. Overhead was charged to jobs at the same rate that was used in May. The patios for customers Dion, Cole, and Kix were completed during June and sold for a total of $18,900. Each customer paid in full.

Instructions
(a) Journalize the June transactions.
(b) Post the entries to Work in Process Inventory.
(c) Reconcile the balance in Work in Process Inventory with the costs of unfinished jobs.
(d) Prepare a cost of goods manufactured schedule for June.

Compute predetermined over-head rate, apply overhead, and indicate statement pre-sentation of under- or over-applied overhead.

(SO 4, 6)

P2-4B Salinas Manufacturing Company uses a job order cost system in each of its three manufacturing departments. Manufacturing overhead is applied to jobs on the basis of direct labor cost in Department X, direct labor hours in Department Y, and machine hours in Department Z.

In establishing the predetermined overhead rates for 2000 the following estimates were made for the year:

	Department		
	X	**Y**	**Z**
Manufacturing overhead	$1,170,000	$1,500,000	$960,000
Direct labor cost	$1,500,000	$1,250,000	$450,000
Direct labor hours	100,000	125,000	40,000
Machine hours	400,000	500,000	120,000

During January, the job cost sheets showed the following costs and production data:

	Department		
	X	**Y**	**Z**
Direct materials used	$140,000	$126,000	$78,000
Direct labor costs	$120,000	$110,000	$37,500
Manufacturing overhead incurred	$98,000	$129,000	$80,000
Direct labor hours	8,000	11,000	3,500
Machine hours	34,000	45,000	10,400

Instructions
(a) Compute the predetermined overhead rate for each department.
(b) Compute the total manufacturing costs assigned to jobs in January in each depart-ment.
(c) Compute the under- or overapplied overhead for each department at January 31.
(d) Indicate the statement presentation of the under- or overapplied overhead at Janu-ary 31.
(e) If the amount in (d) was the same at December 31, how would it be reported in the year-end financial statements?

Analyze manufacturing ac-counts and determine miss-ing amounts.

(SO 2, 3, 4, 5, 6)

P2-5B Laguna Corporation's fiscal year ends on November 30. The following accounts are found in its job order cost accounting system for the first month of the new fiscal year.

Raw Materials Inventory

Dec. 1	Beginning balance	(a)	Dec. 31	Requisitions	14,850
31	Purchases	17,225			
Dec. 31	Ending balance	7,975			

Work in Process Inventory

Dec. 1	Beginning balance	(b)	Dec. 31	Jobs completed	(f)
31	Direct materials	(c)			
31	Direct labor	8,100			
31	Overhead	(d)			
Dec. 31	Ending balance	(e)			

Finished Goods Inventory

Dec.	1	Beginning balance	(g)	Dec.	31	Cost of goods sold	(i)
	31	Completed jobs	(h)				
Dec.	31	Ending balance	(j)				

Factory Labor

Dec.	31	Factory wages	10,600	Dec.	31	Wages assigned	(k)

Manufacturing Overhead

Dec.	31	Indirect materials	1,900	Dec.	31	Overhead applied	(m)
	31	Indirect labor	(l)				
	31	Other overhead	1,445				

Other data:
1. On December 1, two jobs were in process: Job No. 154 and Job No. 155. These jobs had combined direct materials cost of $9,750 and direct labor costs of $12,000. Overhead was applied at a rate that was 75% of direct labor cost.
2. During December, Job Nos. 156, 157, and 158 were started. On December 31, Job No. 158 was unfinished. This job had charges for direct materials $3,800, direct labor $4,400 plus manufacturing overhead. All jobs, except for Job No. 158, were completed in December.
3. On December 1, Job No. 153 was in the finished goods warehouse. It had a total cost of $5,000. On December 31, Job No. 157 was the only job finished that was not sold. It had a cost of $4,000.
4. Manufacturing overhead was $230 overapplied in December.

Instructions
List the letters (a) through (m) and indicate the amount pertaining to each letter.

BROADENING YOUR PERSPECTIVE

GROUP DECISION CASE

BYP2-1 Costello Products Company uses a job order cost system. For a number of months there has been an ongoing rift between the sales department and the production department concerning a special-order product, TC-1. TC-1 is a seasonal product that is manufactured in batches of 1,000 units. TC-1 is sold at cost plus a markup of 40% of cost.

The sales department is unhappy because fluctuating unit production costs significantly affect selling prices. Sales personnel complain that this has caused excessive customer complaints and the loss of considerable orders for TC-1.

The production department maintains that each job order must be fully costed on the basis of the costs incurred during the period in which the goods are produced. Production personnel maintain that the only real solution to the problem is for the sales department to increase sales in the slack periods.

Linda Gurney, president of the company, asks you as the company accountant to collect quarterly data for the past year on TC-1. From the cost accounting system, you accumulate the following production quantity and cost data:

Costs	Quarter			
	1	**2**	**3**	**4**
Direct materials	$100,000	$220,000	$ 80,000	$200,000
Direct labor	60,000	132,000	48,000	120,000
Manufacturing overhead	105,000	123,000	97,000	125,000
Total	$265,000	$475,000	$225,000	$445,000
Production in batches	5	11	4	10
Unit cost (per batch)	$ 53,000	$ 43,182	$ 56,250	$ 44,500

Instructions

With the class divided into groups, answer the following questions:

(a) What manufacturing cost element is responsible for the fluctuating unit costs? Why?

(b) What is your recommended solution to the problem of fluctuating unit cost?

(c) Restate the quarterly data on the basis of your recommended solution.

MANAGERIAL ANALYSIS

BYP2–2 In the course of routine checking of all journal entries prior to preparing month-end reports, Li Chin discovered several strange entries. She recalled that the president's son Jeff had come in to "help out" during an especially busy time and that he had recorded some journal entries. She was relieved that there were only a few of his entries, and even more relieved that he had included rather lengthy explanations. The entries Jeff made were:

Work in Process	20,000	
Cash		20,000

(This is for materials put into process. I don't find the record that we paid for these, so I'm crediting Cash, because I know we'll have to pay for them sooner or later.)

Manufacturing Overhead	12,000	
Cash		12,000

(This is for bonuses paid to salespeople. I know they're part of overhead, and I can't find an account called "Non-factory Overhead" or "Other Overhead" so I'm putting it in Manufacturing Overhead. I have the check stubs, so I know we paid these.)

Wages Expense	120,000	
Cash		120,000

(This is for the factory workers' wages. I have a note that payroll taxes are $8,000. I still think that's part of wages expense, and that we'll have to pay it all in cash sooner or later, so I credited Cash for the wages and the taxes.)

Work in Process	3,000	
Raw Materials Inventory		3,000

(This is for the glue used in the factory. I know we used this to make the products, even though we didn't use very much on any one of the products. I got it out of inventory, so I credited an inventory account.)

Instructions

Using the information above, answer the following questions:

(a) How should Jeff have recorded each of the four events?

(b) If the entry was not corrected, which financial statements (income statement or balance sheet) would be affected? What balances would be overstated or understated?

REAL-WORLD FOCUS

PARLEX COMPANY

BYP2-3 Founded in 1970, **Parlex Corporation** is a world leader in the design and manufacture of flexible interconnect products. Parlex produces custom flexible circuits and laminated cables utilizing proprietary processes and patented technologies which are designed to satisfy the unique requirements of a wide range of customers. Its facilities are located in Methuen, Mass., Salem, N.H., Shanghai, China, and Empalmè, Mexico. Parlex provides its products and engineering services to a variety of markets including automotive, computer, telecommunications, industrial controls, medical, consumer, and military-aerospace. Parlex's common stock trades on the Nasdaq stock market under the symbol PRLX.

The following information was provided in the company's annual report:

PARLEX COMPANY
Notes to the Financial Statements

The Company's products are manufactured on a job order basis to customers' specifications. Customers submit requests for quotations on each job, and the Company prepares bids based on its own cost estimates. The Company attempts to reflect the impact of changing costs when establishing prices. However, during the past several years, the market conditions for flexible circuits and the resulting price sensitivity haven't always allowed this to transpire. Although still not satisfactory, the Company was able to reduce the cost of products sold as a percentage of sales to 85% this year versus 87% that was experienced in the two immediately preceding years. Management continues to focus on improving operational efficiency and further reducing costs.

Instructions
(a) Parlex management discusses the job order cost system employed by their company. What are several advantages of using the job order approach to costing?
(b) Contrast the products produced in a job order environment, like Parlex, to those produced when process cost systems are used.

COMMUNICATION ACTIVITY

BYP2-4 You are the management accountant for Modine Manufacturing. Your company does custom carpentry work and uses a job order cost accounting system. Modine sends detailed job cost sheets to its customers, along with an invoice. The job cost sheets show the date materials were used, the dollar cost of materials, and the hours and cost of labor. A predetermined overhead application rate is used, and the total overhead applied is also listed.

Cindy Ross is a customer who recently had custom cabinets installed. Along with her check in payment for the work done, she included a letter. She thanked the company for including the detailed cost information but questioned why overhead was estimated. She stated that she would be interested in knowing exactly what costs were included in overhead, and she thought that other customers would, too.

Instructions

Prepare a letter to Ms. Ross (address: 123 Cedar Lane, Altoona, Kansas 66651) and tell her why you did not send her information on exact costs of overhead included in her job. Respond to her suggestion that you provide this information.

RESEARCH ASSIGNMENT

BYP2-5 The February 1994 issue of *Ohio CPA Journal* includes an article by Eun-Sup Shim and Joseph M. Larkin entitled "A Survey of Current Managerial Accounting Practices: Where Do We Stand?"

Instructions

Read the article and answer the following questions:
(a) What percent of manufacturers surveyed used job order costing?
(b) What was the smallest cost component of the three factors of production? What portion of total manufacturing costs does it represent?
(c) What percent of manufacturers surveyed operate in a single product environment—that is, what percent produce only one product?
(d) What two managerial decisions were considered most affected by overhead allocation?

ETHICS CASE

BYP2-6 Roblez Printing provides printing services to many different corporate clients. Although Roblez bids most jobs, some jobs, particularly new ones, are often negotiated on a cost plus basis. Cost plus means that the buyer is willing to pay the actual cost plus a return (profit) on these costs to Roblez.

Kristi Peat, controller for Roblez, has recently returned from a meeting where Roblez's president stated that he wanted her to find a way to charge most costs to any project that was on a cost plus basis. The president noted that the company needed more profits to meet its stated goals this period. By charging more costs to the cost plus projects and therefore less costs to the jobs that were bid, the company should be able to increase its profits for the current year.

Kristi knew why the president wanted to take this action. Rumors were that he was looking for a new position and if the company reported strong profits the president's opportunities would be enhanced. Kristi also recognized that she could probably increase the cost of certain jobs by changing the basis used to allocate manufacturing overhead.

Instructions

(a) Who are the stakeholders in this situation?
(b) What are the ethical issues in this situation?
(c) What would you do if you were Kristi Peat?

SURFING THE NET

BYP2-7 The Institute of Management Accountants sponsors a certification for management accountants, allowing them to obtain the title of Certified Management Accountant.

Address: http://www.rutgers.edu/Accounting/raw/ima/certletter.htm

Steps:
1. Go to the site shown above.
2. Under the heading "About the Certification Programs," choose **Objectives.**

Instructions

Answer the following questions:

(a) What are the objectives of the certification program?

(b) What is the "experience requirement"?

(c) How many hours of continuing education are required, and what types of courses qualify?

Answers to Self-Study Questions

1. a   2. b   3. c   4. d   5. b   6. a   7. d   8. b   9. c   10. b

Remember to go back to the Navigator box on the chapter-opening page and check off your completed work.

CHAPTER 3

Process Cost Accounting

STUDY OBJECTIVES

After studying this chapter, you should be able to:

1. Understand who uses process cost systems.

2. Explain the similarities and differences between job order cost and process cost systems.

3. Explain the flow of costs in a process cost system.

4. Make the journal entries to assign manufacturing costs in a process cost system.

5. Compute equivalent units.

6. Explain the four steps necessary to prepare a production cost report.

7. Prepare a production cost report.

THE NAVIGATOR

FEATURE STORY

Ben & Jerry's Tracks Its Mix-Ups

At one time, one of the fastest growing companies in the nation was Ben & Jerry's Homemade, Inc., based in Waterbury, Vermont. The ice cream company that started out of a garage in 1978 is now a public company with sales exceeding $174 million.

Making ice cream is a process—a movement of product from a mixing department to a prepping department to a pint department. The mixing department is where the ice cream is created. The prep area is where extras such as cherries and walnuts are added to make plain ice cream into "Cherry Garcia." And

the pint department is where the ice cream is actually put into containers. As the product is processed from one department to the next, the appropriate materials, labor, and overhead are added to it.

"The incoming ingredients from the shipping and receiving departments are stored in certain locations, either in a freezer or dry warehouse," says Beecher Eurich, staff accountant. "As ingredients get added, so do the costs associated with them." How much ice cream is actually produced? Running the plant around the clock, 24,000 pints are produced per 8-hour shift, or 72,000 pints per day.

Using a process costing system, Eurich can tell you how

much a certain batch of ice cream costs to make — its materials, labor, and overhead in each of the production departments. She generates reports for the production department heads, but makes sure not to overdo it. "You can get bogged down in numbers," says Eurich. "If you're generating a report that no one can use, then that's a waste of time." More likely, though, Ben & Jerry's production people want to know how efficient they are. Why? Many own stock in the company.

THE NAVIGATOR

On the World Wide Web:
http://www.benjerry.com

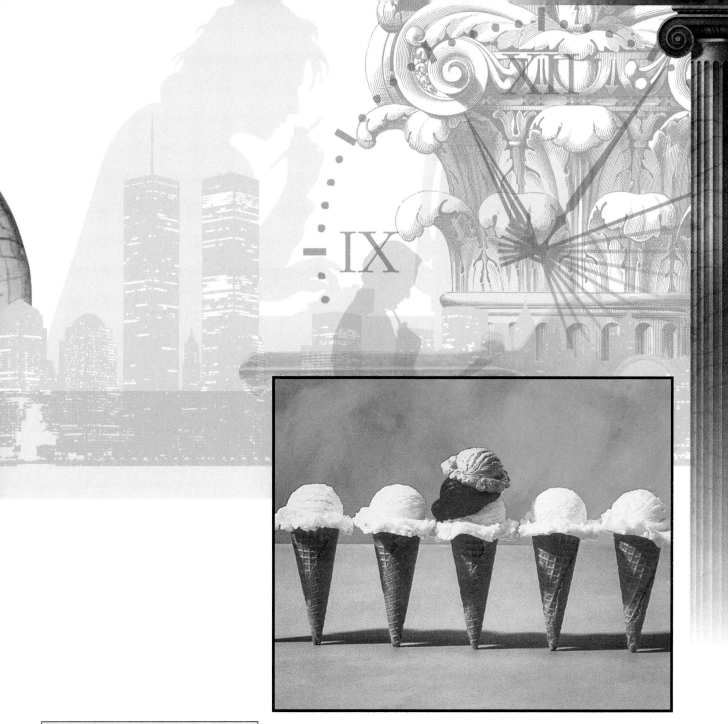

THE NAVIGATOR ✔

- Scan *Study Objectives* ☐
- Read *Feature Story* ☐
- Read *Preview* ☐
- Read text and answer *Before You Go On*
  p. 94 ☐   p. 103 ☐
- Work *Using the Decision Toolkit* ☐
- Review *Summary of Study Objectives* ☐
- Work *Demonstration Problem* ☐
- Answer *Self-Study Questions* ☐
- Complete assignments ☐

The cost accounting system used by companies such as Ben & Jerry's is called a **process cost accounting** system. In contrast to job order cost accounting, which focuses on the individual job, process cost accounting focuses on the processes involved in mass-producing products that are identical or very similar in nature. The primary objective of the chapter is to explain and illustrate process cost accounting. The content and organization of this chapter are as follows:

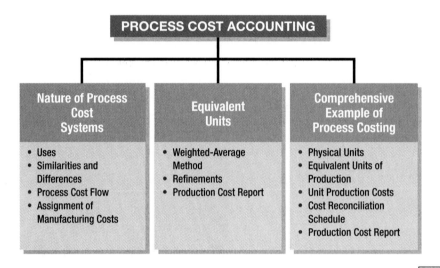

PROCESS COST ACCOUNTING

Nature of Process Cost Systems	Equivalent Units	Comprehensive Example of Process Costing
• Uses • Similarities and Differences • Process Cost Flow • Assignment of Manufacturing Costs	• Weighted-Average Method • Refinements • Production Cost Report	• Physical Units • Equivalent Units of Production • Unit Production Costs • Cost Reconciliation Schedule • Production Cost Report

THE NAVIGATOR

*T*HE NATURE OF PROCESS COST SYSTEMS

USES OF PROCESS COST SYSTEMS

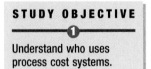

STUDY OBJECTIVE
❶
Understand who uses process cost systems.

Process cost systems are used to apply costs to similar products that are mass-produced in a continuous fashion. Ben & Jerry's uses a process cost system: production of the ice cream, once it begins, continues until the ice cream emerges, and the processing is the same for the entire run—with precisely the same amount of materials, labor, and overhead. Each finished pint of ice cream is indistinguishable from another.

A company such as USX uses process costing in the manufacturing of steel; Kellogg and General Mills use process costing for cereal production; Exxon uses process costing for its oil refining; and Sherwin Williams uses process costing for its paint products. At a bottling company like Coca-Cola, the manufacturing process begins with the blending of the beverages. Next the beverage is dispensed into bottles that are moved into position by automated machinery. The bottles are then capped, packaged, and forwarded to the finished goods warehouse. This process is shown in Illustration 3-1.

Illustration 3-1
Manufacturing processes

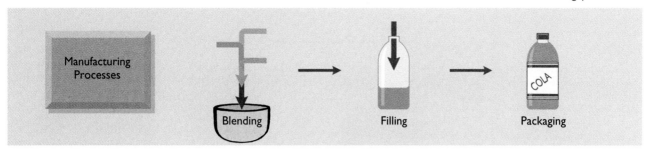

For Coca-Cola, as well as the other companies just mentioned, once the production begins, it continues until the finished product emerges, and each unit of finished product is like every other unit.

In comparison, costs in a job order cost system are assigned to a specific job, such as the construction of a customized home, the making of a motion picture, or the manufacturing of a specialized machine. Illustration 3-2 provides examples of companies that primarily use either a process cost system or a job order cost system.

Illustration 3-2   Process cost and job order cost companies and products

Process Cost System Company	Product		Job Order Cost System Company	Product	
Coca-Cola, PepsiCo	Soft drinks		Young & Rubicam, J. Walter Thompson	Advertising	
Exxon, Shell Oil	Oil		Walt Disney, Warner Brothers	Motion pictures	
Intel, Advanced Micro Devices	Computer chips		Center Ice Consultants, Ice Pro	Ice rinks	
Dow Chemical, DuPont	Chemicals		Kaiser, Mayo Clinic	Patient health care	

SIMILARITIES AND DIFFERENCES BETWEEN JOB ORDER COST AND PROCESS COST SYSTEMS

In a job order cost system, costs are assigned to each job. In a process cost system, costs are tracked through a series of connected manufacturing processes or departments, rather than by individual jobs. Thus, process cost systems are used when a large volume of uniform or relatively homogeneous products are produced. The basic flow of costs in these two systems is shown in Illustration 3-3.

STUDY OBJECTIVE
2
Explain the similarities and differences between job order cost and process cost systems.

Illustration 3-3 Job
order cost and process
cost flow

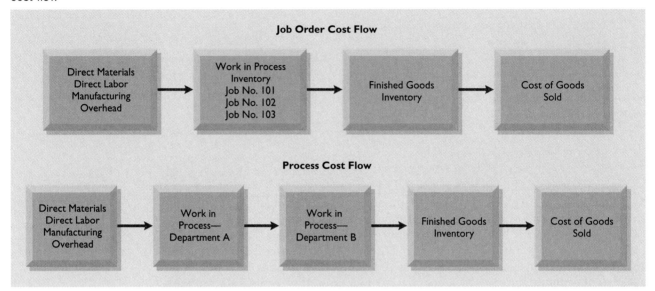

The basic similarities and differences between these two systems are highlighted in the following analysis.

Similarities

Job order cost and process cost systems are similar in three ways:

1. **The manufacturing cost elements.** Both a job order cost and a process cost system track the same three manufacturing cost elements—direct materials, direct labor, and manufacturing overhead.
2. **The accumulation of the costs of materials, labor, and overhead.** In both costing systems, all raw materials are debited to Raw Materials Inventory; all factory labor is debited to Factory Labor; and all manufacturing overhead costs are debited to Manufacturing Overhead.
3. **The flow of costs.** As noted above, all manufacturing costs are accumulated by debits to Raw Materials Inventory, Factory Labor, and Manufacturing Overhead. These costs are then assigned to the same accounts in both costing systems—Work in Process, Finished Goods Inventory, and Cost of Goods Sold. **The methods of assigning costs, however, differ significantly.** These differences are explained and illustrated later in the chapter.

Differences

The differences between a job order cost and a process cost system are as follows:

1. **The number of work in process accounts used.** In a job order cost system, only one work in process account is used. In a process cost system, multiple work in process accounts are used; separate accounts are maintained for each production department or manufacturing process.
2. **Documents used to track costs.** In a job order cost system, costs are charged to individual jobs and summarized in a job cost sheet. In a process cost system, costs are summarized in a production cost report for each department.

3. **The point at which costs are totaled.** In a job order cost system, total costs are determined when the job is completed. In a process cost system, total costs are determined at the end of a period of time, such as a month or year.

4. **Unit cost computations.** In a job order cost system, the unit cost is the total cost per job divided by the units produced. In a process cost system, the unit cost is total manufacturing costs for the period divided by the units produced during the period.

The major differences between a job order cost and a process cost system are summarized in Illustration 3-4.

Features	Job Order Cost System	Process Cost System
Work in process accounts	• One for multiple jobs	• One for each process
Documents used	• Job cost sheets	• Production cost reports
Determination of total manufacturing costs	• Each job	• Each period
Unit-cost computations	• Cost of each job ÷ Units produced for the job	• Total manufacturing costs ÷ Units produced during the period

Illustration 3-4   Job order versus process cost systems

PROCESS COST FLOW

Illustration 3-5 shows the flow of costs in the process cost system for Tyler Company. Tyler Company manufactures automatic can openers that are sold to retail outlets. Manufacturing consists of two processes: machining and assembly. In the Machining Department, the raw materials are shaped, honed, and drilled. In the Assembly Department, the parts are assembled and packaged.

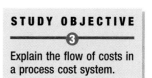

STUDY OBJECTIVE

3

Explain the flow of costs in a process cost system.

Illustration 3-5   Flow of costs in process cost system

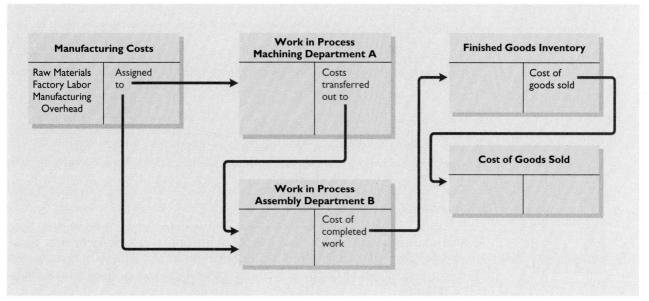

As the flow of costs indicates, materials, labor, and manufacturing overhead can be added in both the Machining and Assembly Departments. When the Machining Department finishes its work, the partially completed units are transferred to the Assembly Department. In the Assembly Department, the goods are finished and are then transferred to the finished goods inventory. Upon sale, the goods are removed from the finished goods inventory. Within each department, a similar set of activities is performed on each unit processed.

ASSIGNMENT OF MANUFACTURING COSTS— JOURNAL ENTRIES

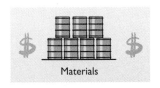

STUDY OBJECTIVE

④

Make the journal entries to assign manufacturing costs in a process cost system.

As indicated earlier, the accumulation of the costs of materials, labor, and manufacturing overhead is the same in a process cost system as in a job order cost system. All raw materials are debited to Raw Materials Inventory when the materials are purchased. All factory labor is debited to Factory Labor when the labor costs are incurred. And overhead costs are debited to Manufacturing Overhead as they are incurred. However, the assignment of the three manufacturing cost elements to Work in Process in a process cost system is different from a job order cost system. Here we'll look at how these manufacturing cost elements are assigned in a process cost system.

Materials Costs

All raw materials issued for production are a materials cost to the producing department. Materials requisition slips may be used in a process cost system, but **fewer requisitions are generally required than in a job order cost system, because the materials are used for processes rather than for specific jobs.** Requisitions are issued less frequently in a process cost system because the requisitions are for larger quantities.

Materials are usually added to production at the beginning of the first process. However, in subsequent processes, other materials may be added at various points. For example, in the manufacture of Hershey candy bars, the chocolate and other ingredients are added at the beginning of the first process, and the wrappers and cartons are added at the end of the packaging process. At Tyler Company, materials are entered at the beginning of each process. The entry to record the materials used is:

Work in Process—Machining	XXXX	
Work in Process—Assembly	XXXX	
Raw Materials Inventory		XXXX
(To record materials used)		

In our ice cream story at the beginning of the chapter, materials are added in three departments: milk and flavoring in the mixing department; extras such as cherries and walnuts in the prepping department; and cardboard containers in the pinting (packaging) department.

Factory Labor Costs

In a process cost system, as in a job order cost system, time tickets may be used in determining the cost of labor assignable to the production departments. Since labor costs are assigned to a process rather than a job, the labor cost chargeable to a process can be obtained from the payroll register or departmental payroll summaries.

All labor costs incurred within a producing department are a cost of processing the raw materials. Thus, labor costs for the Machining Department will include the wages of employees who shape, hone, and drill the raw materials. The entry to assign these costs for Tyler Company is:

Work in Process—Machining	XXXX	
Work in Process—Assembly	XXXX	
Factory Labor		XXXX
(To assign factory labor to production)		

Manufacturing Overhead Costs

The objective in assigning overhead in a process cost system is to allocate the overhead costs to the production departments on an objective and equitable basis. That basis is the activity that "drives" or causes the costs. A primary driver of overhead costs in continuous manufacturing operations is **machine time used,** not direct labor. Thus, **machine hours are widely used** in allocating manufacturing overhead costs. The entry to allocate overhead to the two processes is:

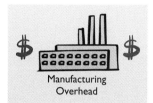
Manufacturing Overhead

Work in Process—Machining	XXXX	
Work in Process—Assembly	XXXX	
Manufacturing Overhead		XXXX
(To assign overhead to production)		

BUSINESS INSIGHT
Management Perspective

In one of Caterpillar's automated cost centers, work is fed into the cost center, processed by robotic machines, and transferred to the next cost center without human intervention. One person tends all of the machines and spends more time maintaining machines than operating them. In such cases, overhead rates based on direct labor hours may be misleading. Surprisingly, some companies continue to assign manufacturing overhead on the basis of direct labor despite the fact that there is no cause-and-effect relationship between labor and overhead.

Transfer to Next Department

At the end of the month, an entry is needed to record the cost of the goods transferred out of the department. In this case, the transfer is to the Assembly Department, and the following entry is made:

Work in Process—Assembly	XXXXX	
Work in Process—Machining		XXXXX
(To record transfer of units to the Assembly		
Department)		

Transfer to Finished Goods

The units completed in the Assembly Department are transferred to the finished goods warehouse. The entry for this transfer is as follows:

Finished Goods Inventory	XXXXX	
Work in Process—Assembly		XXXXX
(To record transfer of units to finished goods)		

Transfer to Cost of Goods Sold

When finished goods are sold, the entry to record the cost of goods sold is as follows:

Cost of Goods Sold	XXXXX	
Finished Goods Inventory		XXXXX
(To record cost of units sold)		

BEFORE YOU GO ON . . .

● **Review It**

1. What type of manufacturing companies might use a process cost accounting system?
2. What are the principal similarities and differences between a job order cost system and a process cost system?

● **Do It**

Ruth Company manufactures ZEBO through two processes: Blending and Bottling. In June, raw materials used were Blending $18,000 and Bottling $4,000; factory labor costs were Blending $12,000 and Bottling $5,000; manufacturing overhead costs were Blending $6,000 and Bottling $2,500. Units completed at a cost of $19,000 in the Blending Department are transferred to the Bottling Department. Units completed at a cost of $11,000 in the Bottling Department are transferred to Finished Goods. Journalize the assignment of these costs to the two processes and the transfer of units as appropriate.

Reasoning: In process cost accounting, separate work in process accounts are kept for each process. Raw materials are accumulated in the account titled Raw Materials Inventory. Factory labor is accumulated in the account titled Factory Labor. Overhead is accumulated in the account titled Manufacturing Overhead. These accounts are credited when the costs are assigned to production. When units are completed, they are transferred to the next process or to Finished Goods.

Solution: The entries are:

Work in Process—Blending	18,000	
Work in Process—Bottling	4,000	
Raw Materials Inventory		22,000
(To record materials used)		
Work in Process—Blending	12,000	
Work in Process—Bottling	5,000	
Factory Labor		17,000
(To assign factory labor to production)		

Work in Process—Blending	6,000	
Work in Process—Bottling	2,500	
Manufacturing Overhead		8,500
(To assign overhead to production)		
Work in Process—Bottling	19,000	
Work in Process—Blending		19,000
(To record transfer of units to the Bottling		
Department)		
Finished Goods Inventory	11,000	
Work in Process—Bottling		11,000
(To record transfer of units to finished goods)		

THE
NAVIGATOR

Related exercise material: BE3-1, BE3-2, BE3-3, E3-7, and E3-10.

EQUIVALENT UNITS

STUDY OBJECTIVE
5
Compute equivalent units.

Suppose you were asked to compute the cost of instruction at your college per full-time equivalent student. You are provided the following information:

Illustration 3-6
Information for full-time student example

Costs:	
Total cost of instruction	$900,000
Student population:	
Full-time students	900
Part-time students	1,000

Part-time students take 60% of the classes of a full-time student during the year. To compute the number of full-time equivalent students per year, you would make the following computation:

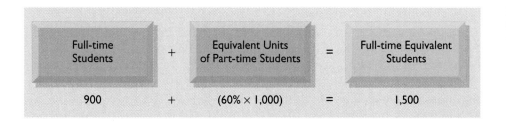

Illustration 3-7 Full-time equivalent unit computation

The cost of instruction per full-time equivalent student is therefore the total cost of instruction ($900,000) divided by the number of full-time equivalent students (1,500), which is $600 ($900,000 ÷ 1,500).

In a process cost system, the same idea, called equivalent units of production, is used. **Equivalent units of production** measure the work done during the period, expressed in fully completed units. This concept is used to determine the cost per unit of completed product.

WEIGHTED-AVERAGE METHOD

The formula to compute equivalent units of production is as follows:

Illustration 3-8
Equivalent units of
production formula

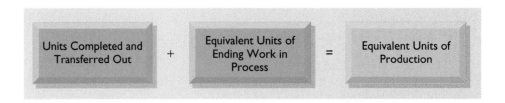

To better understand this concept of equivalent units, consider the following two examples:

Example 1: The Blending Department's entire output during the period consists of ending work in process of 4,000 units which are 60% complete as to materials, labor, and overhead. The equivalent units of production for the Blending Department are therefore 2,400 units (4,000 × 60%).

Example 2: The Packaging Department's output during the period consists of 10,000 units completed and transferred out, and 5,000 units in ending work in process which are 70% completed. The equivalent units of production are therefore 13,500 [10,000 + (5,000 × 70%)].

This method of computing equivalent units is referred to as the **weighted-average method.** It considers the degree of completion (weighting) of the units completed and transferred out and the ending work in process. It is the method most widely used in practice. A lesser used method, called the FIFO method, is discussed in advanced cost accounting courses.

REFINEMENTS ON THE WEIGHTED-AVERAGE METHOD

Kellogg Company has produced Eggo® Waffles since 1970. Three departments are used to produce these waffles: Mixing, Baking, and Freezing and Packaging. In the Mixing Department dry ingredients, including flour, salt, and baking powder, are mixed with liquid ingredients, including eggs and vegetable oil, to make waffle batter. Information related to the Mixing Department at the end of June is provided in Illustration 3-9.

Illustration 3-9
Information for Mixing
Department

	Mixing Department		
		Percentage Complete	
	Physical Units	**Materials**	**Conversion Costs**
Work in process, June 1	100,000	100%	70%
Started into production	800,000		
Total units	900,000		
Units transferred out	700,000		
Work in process, June 30	200,000	100%	60%
Total units	900,000		

Illustration 3-9 indicates that the beginning work in process is 100% complete as to materials cost and 70% complete as to conversion costs. In other words, both the dry and liquid ingredients (materials) are added at the beginning of the process to make Eggo® Waffles. The conversion costs (labor and overhead) related to the mixing of these ingredients were incurred uniformly and are 70% complete. The ending work in process is 100% complete as to materials cost and 60% complete as to conversion costs.

We then use the Mixing Department information to determine equivalent units. **In computing equivalent units, the beginning work in process is not**

part of the equivalent units of production formula. The units transferred out to the Baking Department are fully complete as to both materials and conversion costs. The ending work in process is fully complete as to materials, but only 60% complete as to conversion cost. **Two equivalent unit computations are therefore necessary:** one for materials and the other for conversion costs. Illustration 3-10 shows these computations.

	Equivalent Units	
	Materials	**Conversion Costs**
Units transferred out	700,000	700,000
Work in process, June 30		
200,000 × 100%	200,000	
200,000 × 60%		120,000
Total equivalent units	900,000	820,000

Illustration 3-10
Computation of equivalent units—Mixing Department

The earlier formula used to compute equivalent units of production can be refined to show the computations for materials and for conversion costs, as follows:

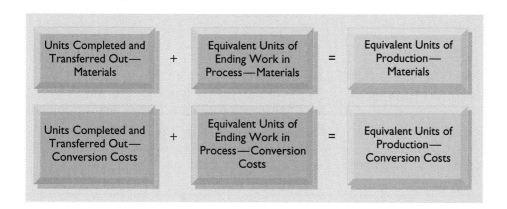

Illustration 3-11 Refined equivalent unit of production formula

PRODUCTION COST REPORT

As mentioned earlier, a production cost report is prepared for each department in a process cost system. A production cost report is the key document used by management to understand the activities in a department because it shows the production quantity and cost data related to that department. For example, in producing Eggo® Waffles, Kellogg Company would have three production cost reports: Mixing, Baking, and Freezing and Packaging. Illustration 3-12 shows the flow of costs to make an Eggo® Waffle and the related production cost reports for each department.

In order to be ready to complete a production cost report, the company must perform four steps:

1. Compute the physical unit flow.
2. Compute the equivalent units of production.
3. Compute unit production costs.
4. Prepare a cost reconciliation schedule.

As a whole, these four steps make up the process costing system. The next section explores these steps in an extended example.

STUDY OBJECTIVE
━━━━━━❻━━━━━━
Explain the four steps necessary to prepare a production cost report.

Illustration 3-12 Flow of costs in making Eggo® Waffles

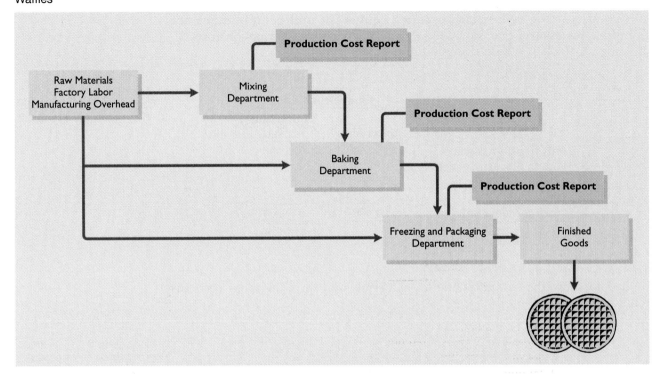

COMPREHENSIVE EXAMPLE OF PROCESS COSTING

Assumed data for the Mixing Department at Kellogg Company for the month of June are shown in Illustration 3-13. We will use this information to complete a production cost report for the Mixing Department.

Illustration 3-13 Unit and cost data—Mixing Department

Mixing Department	
Units:	
Work in process, June 1	100,000
Direct materials: 100% complete	
Conversion costs: 70% complete	
Units started into production during June	800,000
Units completed and transferred out to Baking Department	700,000
Work in process, June 30	200,000
Direct materials: 100% complete	
Conversion costs: 60% complete	
Costs:	
Work in process, June 1	
Direct materials: 100% complete	$50,000
Conversion costs: 70% complete	35,000
Cost of work in process, June 1	$85,000
Costs incurred during production in June	
Direct materials	$400,000
Conversion costs	170,000
Costs incurred in June	$570,000

COMPUTE THE PHYSICAL UNIT FLOW (STEP 1)

Physical units are the actual units to be accounted for during a period, irrespective of any work performed. To keep track of these units, it is necessary to add the units started (or transferred) into production during the period to the units in process at the beginning of the period. This amount is referred to as the total units to be accounted for.

These units then are accounted for by the output of the period, which consists of units transferred out during the period and any units in process at the end of the period. This amount is referred to as the total units accounted for. Illustration 3-14 shows the flow of physical units for Kellogg Company for the month of June for the Mixing Department.

Mixing Department	
	Physical Units
Units to be accounted for	
Work in process, June 1	100,000
Started (transferred) into production	800,000
Total units	900,000
Units accounted for	
Completed and transferred out	700,000
Work in process, June 30	200,000
Total units	900,000

Illustration 3-14
Physical unit flow—Mixing Department

The records indicate that 900,000 units must be accounted for in the Mixing Department. Of this sum, 700,000 units were transferred to the Baking Department and 200,000 units were still in process.

COMPUTE EQUIVALENT UNITS OF PRODUCTION (STEP 2)

Once the physical flow of the units is established, it is necessary to measure the Mixing Department's productivity in terms of equivalent units of production. In the Mixing Department, materials are added at the beginning of the process, and conversion costs are incurred uniformly during the process. Thus, two computations of equivalent units are required: one for materials and one for conversion costs. The equivalent unit computation is as follows:

Helpful Hint Materials are not always added at the beginning of the process. For example, materials are sometimes added uniformly during the process.

	Equivalent Units	
	Materials	**Conversion Costs**
Units transferred out	700,000	700,000
Work in process, June 30		
200,000 × 100%	200,000	
200,000 × 60%		120,000
Total equivalent units	900,000	820,000

Illustration 3-15
Computation of equivalent units—Mixing Department

Remember that the beginning work in process is ignored in this computation.

COMPUTE UNIT PRODUCTION COSTS (STEP 3)

Armed with the knowledge of the equivalent units of production, we can now compute the unit production costs. **Unit production costs** are costs expressed in terms of equivalent units of production. When equivalent units of production are different for materials and conversion costs, three unit costs are computed: (1) materials, (2) conversion, and (3) total manufacturing.

The computation of total materials cost related to Eggo® Waffles is as follows:

Illustration 3-16 Materials cost computation

Work in process, June 1	
Direct materials cost	$ 50,000
Costs added to production during June	
Direct materials cost	400,000
Total materials cost	**$450,000**

The computation of unit materials cost is as follows:

Illustration 3-17 Unit materials cost computation

Total Materials Cost	÷	Equivalent Units of Materials	=	Unit Materials Cost
$450,000	÷	900,000	=	$.50

The computation of total conversion costs is as follows:

Illustration 3-18 Conversion costs computation

Work in process, June 1	
Conversion costs	$ 35,000
Costs added to production during June	
Conversion costs	170,000
Total conversion costs	**$205,000**

The computation of unit conversion cost is as follows:

Illustration 3-19 Unit conversion cost computation

Total Conversion Costs	÷	Equivalent Units of Conversion Costs	=	Unit Conversion Cost
$205,000	÷	820,000	=	$.25

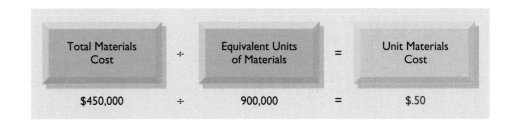

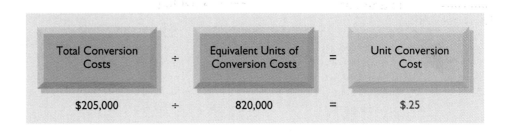

Total manufacturing cost per unit is therefore computed as follows:

Illustration 3-20 Total manufacturing cost per unit

PREPARE A COST RECONCILIATION SCHEDULE (STEP 4)

We are now ready to determine the cost of goods transferred out of the Mixing Department to the Baking Department and the costs in ending work in process. The total costs that were charged to the Mixing Department in June are as follows:

Costs to be accounted for	
Work in process, June 1	$ 85,000
Started into production	570,000
Total costs	$655,000

Illustration 3-21 Costs charged to Mixing Department

The total costs charged to the Mixing Department in June are therefore $655,000. A cost reconciliation schedule is then prepared to assign these costs to (1) units transferred out to the Baking Department and (2) ending work in process.

Mixing Department
Cost Reconciliation Schedule

Costs accounted for		
Transferred out (700,000 × $.75)		$ 525,000
Work in process, June 30		
Materials (200,000 × $.50)	$100,000	
Conversion costs (120,000 × $.25)	30,000	130,000
Total costs		$655,000

Illustration 3-22 Cost reconciliation schedule— Mixing Department

The total manufacturing cost per unit, $.75, is used in costing the units completed and transferred to the Baking Department. In contrast, the unit cost of materials and the unit cost of conversion are needed in costing units in process. The **cost reconciliation schedule** shows that the **total costs accounted for** (Illustration 3-22) equal the **total costs to be accounted for** (see Illustration 3-21).

PREPARING THE PRODUCTION COST REPORT

At this point, we are ready to prepare the production cost report for the Mixing Department. As indicated earlier, this report is an internal document for management that shows production quantity and cost data for a production department.

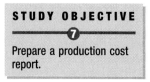

STUDY OBJECTIVE
7
Prepare a production cost report.

There are four steps in preparing a production cost report. They are: (1) preparing a physical unit schedule, (2) computing equivalent units, (3) computing unit costs, and (4) preparing a cost reconciliation schedule. The production cost report for the Mixing Department is shown in Illustration 3-23. The four steps are identified in the report.

Illustration 3-23
Production cost report

Mixing Department
Production Cost Report
For the Month Ended June 30, 1999

Equivalent Units

QUANTITIES	Physical Units (Step 1)	Materials	Conversion Costs (Step 2)
Units to be accounted for			
Work in process, June 1	100,000		
Started into production	800,000		
Total units	900,000		
Units accounted for			
Transferred out	700,000	700,000	700,000
Work in process, June 30	200,000	200,000	120,000 (200,000 × 60%)
Total units	900,000	900,000	820,000

COSTS		Materials	Conversion Costs	Total
Unit costs (Step 3)				
Costs in June	(a)	$450,000	$205,000	$655,000
Equivalent units	(b)	900,000	820,000	
Unit costs (a) ÷ (b)		$.50	$.25	$.75

Costs to be accounted for	
Work in process, June 1	$ 85,000
Started into production	570,000
Total costs	$655,000

Cost Reconciliation Schedule (Step 4)

Costs accounted for		
Transferred out (700,000 × $.75)		$525,000
Work in process, June 30		
Materials (200,000 × $.50)	$100,000	
Conversion costs (120,000 × $.25)	30,000	130,000
Total costs		$655,000

Production cost reports provide a basis for evaluating the productivity of a department. In addition, the cost data can be used to assess whether unit costs and total costs are reasonable. When the quantity and cost data are compared with predetermined goals, top management can also ascertain whether current performance is meeting planned objectives.

DECISION TOOLKIT

Decision Checkpoints	Info Needed for Decision	Tool to Use for Decision	How to Evaluate Results
What is the cost of a product?	Costs of materials, labor, and overhead assigned to processes used to make the product	Production cost report	Compare costs to previous periods and to competitors to ensure that costs are in line. Compare to expected selling price to determine overall profitability.

BEFORE YOU GO ON . . .

● **Review It**

1. How do physical units differ from equivalent units of production?
2. What are the formulas for computing unit costs of production?
3. How are costs assigned to units transferred out and in process?
4. What are the four sections of a production cost report?

● **Do It**

In March, Rodayo Manufacturing had the following unit production costs: materials $6 and conversion costs $9. On March 1, it had zero work in process. During March, 12,000 units were transferred out, and 800 units that were 25% completed as to conversion costs and 100% complete as to materials were in ending work in process at March 31. Assign the costs to the units transferred out and in process.

Reasoning: The 12,000 units transferred should be assigned the total manufacturing cost of $15 per unit. The assignment of costs to units in process consists of the materials cost and conversion cost based on equivalent units of production.

Solution: The assignment of costs is as follows:

Costs accounted for		
Transferred out (12,000 × $15)		$180,000
Work in process, March 31		
Materials (800 × $6)	$4,800	
Conversion costs (200ᵃ × $9)	1,800	6,600
Total costs		$186,600

ᵃ800 × 25%

Related exercise material: BE3-4, BE3-5, BE3-6, BE3-7, BE3-8, E3-1, E3-2, E3-4, E3-6, E3-8, E3-9, and E3-10.

THE
NAVIGATOR

*F*INAL COMMENTS

Companies often use a combination of a process cost and a job order cost system, called operations costing. Operations costing is similar to process costing in that standardized methods are used to manufacture the product. At the same time, the product may have some customized, individual features that require the use of a job order cost system. Consider, for example, the automobile manufacturer Ford Motor Company. Each automobile at a given plant goes through the same assembly line, but different materials (such as seat coverings, paint, and tinted glass) may be used for different automobiles. Similarly, Kellogg's

Pop-Tarts Toaster Pastries® go through numerous processes—mixing, filling, baking, frosting, and packaging. The pastry dough, however, comes in three flavors—plain, chocolate, and graham—and fillings include Smucker's® real fruit, chocolate fudge, vanilla creme, brown sugar cinnamon, and S'mores.

A cost–benefit tradeoff occurs as a company decides which costing system to use. A job order system, for example, provides detailed information related to the cost of the product. Because each job has its own distinguishing characteristics, an accurate cost per job can be provided. This information is useful in controlling costs and pricing products. However, the cost of implementing a job order cost system is often expensive because of the accounting costs involved.

Conversely, for a company like Intel, which makes computer chips, is there a benefit in knowing whether the cost of the one hundredth chip produced is different from the one thousandth chip produced? Probably not. An average cost of the product will suffice for control and pricing purposes. In summary, when deciding to use one of these systems, or a combination system, a company must weigh the cost of implementing the system against the benefits from the additional information provided.

DECISION TOOLKIT

Decision Checkpoints	Info Needed for Decision	Tool to Use for Decision	How to Evaluate Results
What costing method should be used?	Type of product produced	Cost of accounting system; benefits of additional information	The benefits of providing the additional information should exceed the costs of the accounting system needed to develop the information.

*U*SING THE DECISION TOOLKIT

Essence Company manufactures a high end after-shave lotion, called Eternity, in 10-ounce plastic bottles. Because the market for after-shave lotion is highly competitive, the company is very concerned about keeping its costs under control. Eternity is manufactured through three processes: mixing, filling, and corking. Materials are added at the beginning of the process, and labor and overhead are incurred uniformly throughout each process. The company uses a weighted-average method to cost its product. A partially completed production cost report for the month of May for the Mixing Department is shown below.

ESSENCE COMPANY
Mixing Department
Production Cost Report
For the Month Ended May 31, 1999

		Equivalent Units	
QUANTITIES	Physical Units	Materials	Conversion Costs
Units to be accounted for	Step 1		Step 2
Work in process, May 1	1,000		
Started into production	2,000		
Total units	3,000		

Units accounted for				
Transferred out	2,200	?	?	
Work in process, May 31	800	?	?	
Total units	3,000	?	?	

COSTS		Materials	Conversion Costs	Total
Unit costs Step 3				
Costs in May	(a)	?	?	?
Equivalent units	(b)	?	?	
Unit costs (a) ÷ (b)		?	?	?

Costs to be accounted for	
Work in process, May 1	$ 56,300
Started into production	119,320
Total costs	$175,620

Cost Reconciliation Schedule Step 4

Costs accounted for		
Transferred out		?
Work in process, May 31		
Materials	?	
Conversion costs	?	?
Total costs		?

Additional information:

Work in process, May 1, 1000 units

Materials cost, 1,000 units (100% complete)	$49,100	
Conversion costs, 1,000 units (70% complete)	7,200	$ 56,300
Materials cost for May, 2,000 units		$100,000

Work in process, May 31, 800 units, 100% complete as to materials and 50% complete as to conversion costs.

Instructions

(a) Prepare a production cost report for the Mixing Department for the month of May.

(b) Prepare the journal entry to record the transfer of goods from the Mixing Department to the Filling Department.

(c) Explain why Essence Company is using a process cost system to account for its costs.

Solution

(a) A completed production cost report for the Mixing Department is shown below. Computations to support the amounts reported follow the report.

ESSENCE COMPANY
Mixing Department
Production Cost Report
For the Month ended May 31, 1999

		Equivalent Units	
QUANTITIES	Physical Units	Materials	Conversion Costs
Units to be accounted for	Step 1	Step 2	
Work in process, May 1	1,000		
Started into production	2,000		
Total units	3,000		

Units accounted for

Transferred out	2,200	2,200	2,200
Work in process, May 31	800	800	400
Total units	3,000	3,000	2,600

COSTS			Conversion	
Unit costs Step 3		Materials	Costs	Total
Costs in May	(a)	$149,100	$26,520	$175,620
Equivalent units	(b)	3,000	2,600	
Unit costs (a) ÷ (b)		$49.70	$10.20	$59.90

Costs to be accounted for	
Work in process, May 1	$ 56,300
Started into production	119,320
Total costs	$175,620

Cost Reconciliation Schedule Step 4

Costs accounted for		
Transferred out (2,200 × $59.90)		$131,780
Work in process, May 31		
Materials (800 × $49.70)	$39,760	
Conversion costs (400 × $10.20)	4,080	43,840
Total costs		$175,620

Additional computations to support production cost report data:
Conversion cost equivalent units—2,200 + (50% × 800)
Materials cost—$49,100 + $100,000
Conversion costs—$7,200 + $19,320: ($119,320 − $100,000)

(b) Work in Process—Filling   131,780
          Work in Processing—Mixing   131,780

THE
NAVIGATOR

(c) Process cost systems are used to apply costs to similar products that are mass-produced in a continuous fashion. Essence Company uses a process cost system: production of the after-shave lotion, once it begins, continues until the after-shave lotion emerges, and the processing is the same for the entire run—with precisely the same amount of materials, labor, and overhead. Each bottle of Eternity after-shave lotion is indistinguishable from another.

SUMMARY OF STUDY OBJECTIVES

1 *Understand who uses process cost systems.* Process cost systems are used by companies that mass-produce similar products in a continuous fashion. Once production begins, it continues until the finished product emerges, and each unit of finished product is indistinguishable from every other unit.

2 *Explain the similarities and differences between job order cost and process cost systems.* Job order cost systems are similar to process cost systems in three ways: (1) Both systems track the same cost elements—direct materials, direct labor, and manufacturing overhead. (2) Costs are accumulated in the same accounts—Raw Materials Inventory, Factory Labor, and Manufacturing Overhead. (3) Accumulated costs are assigned to the same accounts—Work in Process, Finished Goods Inventory, and Cost of Goods Sold. However, the method of assigning costs differs significantly. There are four main differences between the two cost systems: (1) A process cost system uses separate accounts for each production process department or manufacturing process, rather than only one work in process account used in a job order cost system. (2) In a process cost system, costs are summarized in a production cost report for each department; in a job cost system, costs are charged to individual jobs and summarized in a job cost sheet. (3) Costs are totaled at the end of a time period in a process cost system and at the completion of a job in a job cost system. (4) In a process cost system, unit cost is calculated as total manufacturing costs for the period ÷ the units produced during the period. Unit cost in a job cost system is total cost per job ÷ units produced.

3 Explain the flow of costs in a process cost system. Manufacturing costs for raw materials, labor, and overhead are assigned to work in process accounts for various departments or manufacturing processes, and the costs of units completed in a department are transferred from one department to another as those units move through the manufacturing process. The costs of completed work are transferred to Finished Goods Inventory. When inventory is sold, costs are transferred to Cost of Goods Sold.

4 Make the journal entries to assign manufacturing costs in a process cost system. Entries to assign the costs of raw materials, labor, and overhead consist of a credit to Raw Materials Inventory, Factory Labor, and

Manufacturing Overhead, and a debit to Work in Process for each of the departments doing the processing. Entries to record the cost of goods transferred to another department are a credit to Work in Process for the department whose work is finished and a debit to the department to which the goods are transferred. The entry to record units completed and transferred to the warehouse is a credit for the department whose work is finished and a debit to Finished Goods Inventory. Finally, the entry to record the sale of goods is a credit to Finished Goods Inventory and a debit to Cost of Goods Sold.

5 Compute equivalent units. Equivalent units of production measure work done during a period, expressed in fully completed units. This concept is used to determine the cost per unit of completed product. Equivalent units are the sum of units completed and transferred out plus equivalent units of ending work in process.

6 Explain the four steps necessary to prepare a production cost report. The four steps to complete a production cost report are: (1) Compute the physical unit flow—that is, the total units to be accounted for. (2) Compute the equivalent units of production. (3) Compute the unit production costs, expressed in terms of equivalent units of production. (4) Prepare a cost reconciliation schedule, which shows that the total costs accounted for equal the total costs to be accounted for.

7 Prepare a production cost report. The production cost report contains both quantity and cost data for a production department. There are four sections in the report: (a) number of physical units, (b) equivalent units determination, (c) unit costs, and (d) cost reconciliation schedule.

DECISION TOOLKIT—A SUMMARY

Decision Checkpoints	Info Needed for Decision	Tool to Use for Decision	How to Evaluate Results
What is the cost of a product?	Costs of materials, labor, and overhead assigned to processes used to make the product	Production cost report	Compare costs to previous periods and to competitors to ensure that costs are in line. Compare to expected selling price to determine overall profitability.
Which costing method should be used?	Types of product produced	Cost of accounting system; benefits of additional information	The benefits of providing the additional information should exceed the costs of the accounting system needed to develop the information.

GLOSSARY

Cost reconciliation schedule A schedule that shows that the total costs accounted for equal the total costs to be accounted for. (p. 101)

Equivalent units of production A measure of the work done during the period, expressed in fully completed units. (p. 95)

Operations costing A combination of a process cost and a job order cost system, in which products are manufactured primarily by standardized methods, with some customization. (p. 103)

Physical units Actual units to be accounted for during a period, irrespective of any work performed. (p. 99)

Process cost systems An accounting system used to apply costs to similar products that are mass-produced in a continuous fashion. (p. 88)

Production cost report An internal report for management that shows both production quantity and cost data for a production department. (p. 97)

Total units (costs) accounted for The sum of the units (costs) transferred out during the period plus the units (costs) in process at the end of the period. (pp. 99, 101)

Total units (costs) to be accounted for The sum of the units (costs) started (or transferred) into production during the period plus the units (costs) in process at the beginning of the period. (pp. 99, 101)

Unit production costs Costs expressed in terms of equivalent units of production. (p. 100)

Weighted-average method Method used to compute equivalent units of production which consider the degree of completion (weighting) of the units completed and transferred out and the ending work in process. (p. 96)

DEMONSTRATION PROBLEM

Karlene Industries produces plastic ice cube trays in two processes: heating and stamping. All materials are added at the beginning of the Heating Department.

On November 1, 1,000 trays that were 70% complete were in process in the Heating Department. During November 12,000 trays were started into production. On November 30, 2,000 trays that were 60% complete were in process.

The following cost information for the Heating Department was also available:

Work in process, November 1		Costs incurred in November	
Materials	$640	Material	$3,000
Conversion costs	360	Labor	2,300
Cost of work in process, Nov. 1	$1,000	Overhead	4,050

Instructions

(a) Prepare a production cost report for the Heating Department for the month of November 1999.

(b) Journalize the transfer of costs to the Stamping Department.

Problem-Solving Strategies

1. Remember that total units accounted for must equal total units charged.
2. Similarly, total costs accounted for must equal total costs charged.
3. Equivalent units used for unit costs must equal equivalent units shown under total units accounted for.
4. The total costs charged must equal the debit total in work in process.

Solution to Demonstration Problem

(a)

KARLENE INDUSTRIES
Heating Department
Production Cost Report
For the Month Ended November 30, 1999

| | | | Equivalent Units | |
QUANTITIES	Physical Units	Materials	Conversion Costs
Units to be accounted for	Step 1	Step 2	
Work in process, November 1	1,000		
Started into production	12,000		
Total units	13,000		
Units accounted for			
Transferred out	11,000	11,000	11,000
Work in process, November 30	2,000	2,000	1,200
Total units	13,000	13,000	12,200

COSTS		Materials	Conversion Costs	Total
Unit costs Step 3				
Costs in November	(a)	$3,640	$6,710	$10,350
Equivalent units	(b)	13,000	12,200	
Unit costs (a) ÷ (b)		$.28	$.55	$.83

Costs to be accounted for
 Work in process, November 1 $ 1,000
 Started into production   9,350
Total costs $10,350

Cost Reconciliation Schedule Step 4

Costs accounted for
 Transferred out (11,000 × $.83) $ 9,130
 Work in process, November 30
  Materials (2,000 × $.28) $560
  Conversion costs (1,200 × $.55)   660   1,220
Total costs $10,350

THE
NAVIGATOR

SELF-STUDY QUESTIONS

Answers are at the end of the chapter.

(SO 1) 1. Which of the following items is *not* a characteristic of a process cost system?
 (a) Once production begins, it continues until the finished product emerges.
 (b) The products produced are heterogeneous in nature.
 (c) The focus is on continually producing homogeneous products.
 (d) When the finished product emerges, all units have precisely the same amount of materials, labor, and overhead.

(SO 2) 2. Indicate which of the following statements is *not* correct.
 (a) Both a job order and a process cost system track the same three manufacturing cost elements—direct materials, direct labor, and manufacturing overhead.
 (b) In a job order cost system, only one work in process account is used, whereas in a process cost system, multiple work in process accounts are used.
 (c) Manufacturing costs are accumulated the same way in a job order and in a process cost system.
 (d) Manufacturing costs are assigned the same way in a job order and in a process cost system.

(SO 3) 3. In a process cost system, costs are assigned only:
 (a) to one work in process account.
 (b) to work in process and finished goods inventory.
 (c) to work in process, finished goods, and cost of goods sold.

 (d) to work in process accounts.

(SO 4) 4. In making the journal entry to assign raw materials costs:
 (a) the debit is to Finished Goods Inventory.
 (b) the debit is often to two or more work in process accounts.
 (c) the credit is generally to two or more work in process accounts.
 (d) the credit is to Finished Goods Inventory.

(SO 5) 5. The Mixing Department's output during the period consists of 20,000 units completed and transferred out, and 5,000 units in ending work in process 60% complete as to materials and conversion costs. Beginning inventory is 1,000 units, 40% complete as to materials and conversion costs. The equivalent units of production are:
 (a) 22,600.
 (b) 23,000.
 (c) 24,000.
 (d) 25,000.

(SO 6) 6. In the RYZ Company, there are zero units in beginning work in process, 7,000 units started into production, and 500 units in ending work in process 20% completed. The physical units to be accounted for are:
 (a) 7,000.
 (b) 7,360.
 (c) 7,600.
 (d) 7,340.

(SO 6) 7. The Mora Company has 2,000 units in beginning work in process, 20% complete as to conversion costs, 23,000 units transferred out to finished goods, and 3,000 units in ending work in process $33\frac{1}{3}\%$ complete as to conversion costs.

The beginning and ending inventory is fully complete as to materials costs. Equivalent units for materials and conversion costs are, respectively:
(a) 22,000, 24,000.
(b) 24,000, 26,000.
(c) 26,000, 24,000.
(d) 26,000, 26,000.

(SO 6)   8. KLM Company has no beginning work in process; 9,000 units are transferred out and 3,000 units in ending work in process are one-third finished as to conversion costs and fully complete as to materials cost. If total materials cost is $60,000, the unit materials cost is:
(a) $5.00.
(b) $5.45 rounded.
(c) $6.00.
(d) No correct answer is given.

9. Toney Company has unit costs of $10 for materials and $30 for conversion costs. If there are 2,500 units in ending work in process, 40% complete as to conversion costs, and fully complete as to materials cost, the total cost assignable to the ending work in process inventory is: (SO 6)
(a) $45,000.
(b) $55,000.
(c) $75,000.
(d) $100,000.

10. A production cost report   (SO 7)
(a) is an external report.
(b) shows costs charged to department and costs accounted for.
(c) shows equivalent units of production but not physical units.
(d) contains six sections.

THE NAVIGATOR

QUESTIONS

1. Identify which costing system—job order or process cost—the following companies would use: (a) Quaker Oats, (b) Ford Motor Company, (c) Kinko's Print Shop, and (d) Warner Bros. Motion Pictures.

2. Contrast the primary focus of job order cost accounting and of process cost accounting.

3. What are the similarities between a job order and a process cost system?

4. Your roommate is confused about the features of process cost accounting. Identify and explain the distinctive features for your roommate.

5. Yang Woo believes there are no significant differences in the flow of costs between job order cost accounting and process cost accounting. Is Yang correct? Explain.

6. (a) What source documents are used in assigning (1) materials and (2) labor to production?
   (b) What criterion and basis are commonly used in allocating overhead to processes?

7. In Renfro Company, overhead is assigned to production departments at the rate of $15 per machining hour. In July, machine hours were 3,000 in the Machining Department and 2,400 in the Assembly Department. Prepare the entry to assign overhead to production.

8. Penny Griffen is uncertain about the steps used to prepare a production cost report. State the procedures that are required in the sequence in which they are performed.

9. Karl Lange is confused about computing physical units. Explain to Karl how physical units to be accounted for and physical units accounted for are determined.

10. What is meant by the term "equivalent units of production"?

11. How are equivalent units of production computed?

12. Irvine Company had zero units of beginning work in process. During the period, 8,000 units were completed, and there were 500 units of ending work in process. What were the units started into production?

13. Tabaras Co. has zero units of beginning work in process. During the period 10,000 units were completed, and there were 500 units of ending work in process one-fifth complete as to conversion cost and 100% complete as to materials cost. What were the equivalent units of production for (a) materials and (b) conversion costs?

14. Sielert Co. started 2,000 units for the period. Its beginning inventory is 600 units one-fourth complete as to conversion costs and 100% complete as to materials cost. Its ending inventory is 400 units one-fifth complete as to conversion cost and 100% complete as to materials costs. How many units were transferred out this period?

15. Osgood Company transfers out 12,000 units and has 2,000 units of ending work in process that are 25% complete. Materials are entered at the beginning of the process and there is no beginning work in process. Assuming unit materials costs of $3 and unit conversion costs of $9, what are the costs to be assigned to units (a) transferred out and (b) in ending work in process?

16. (a) Lori Lang believes the production cost report is an external report for stockholders. Is Lori correct? Explain.
    (b) Identify the sections in a production cost report.

17. What purposes are served by a production cost report?

18. In Mercer Company, there are 800 units of ending work in process that are 100% complete as to mate-

rials and 25% complete as to conversion costs. If the unit cost of materials is $4 and the costs assigned to the 800 units is $6,600, what is the per-unit conversion cost?

19. What is the difference between operations costing and a process costing system?

20. How does a company decide whether to use a job order or a process cost system?

BRIEF EXERCISES

BE3-1 Petty Manufacturing purchases $40,000 of raw materials on account, and it incurs $30,000 of factory labor costs. Journalize the two transactions on March 31 assuming the labor costs are not paid until April.

Journalize entries for accumulating costs.
(SO 4)

BE3-2 Data for Petty Manufacturing are given in BE3-1. Supporting records show that (a) the Assembly Department used $14,000 of raw materials and $18,000 of the factory labor, and (b) the Finishing Department used the remainder. Journalize the assignment of the costs to the processing departments on March 31.

Journalize the assignment of materials and labor costs.
(SO 4)

BE3-3 Factory labor data for Petty Manufacturing are given in BE3-2. Manufacturing overhead is assigned to departments on the basis of 200% of labor costs. Journalize the assignment of overhead to the Assembly and Finishing Departments.

Journalize the assignment of overhead costs.
(SO 4)

BE3-4 Sorvino Manufacturing Company has the following production data for selected months:

Compute physical units of production.
(SO 6)

| | | | Ending Work in Process | |
| | Beginning | Units | | % Complete as to |
Month	Work in Process	Transferred Out	Units	Conversion Cost
January	–0–	30,000	10,000	40%
March	–0–	50,000	4,000	75
July	–0–	40,000	6,000	25

Compute the physical units for each month.

BE3-5 Using the data in BE3-4, compute equivalent units of production for materials and conversion costs, assuming materials are entered at the beginning of the process.

Compute equivalent units of production.
(SO 5)

BE3-6 In Unger Company, total material costs are $48,000, and total conversion costs are $60,000. Equivalent units of production are materials 12,000 and conversion costs 10,000. Compute the unit costs for materials, conversion costs, and total manufacturing costs.

Compute unit costs of production.
(SO 6)

BE3-7 Motta Company has the following production data for April: units transferred out 40,000, and ending work in process 5,000 units that are 100% complete for materials and 40% complete for conversion costs. If unit materials cost is $8 and unit conversion cost is $12, determine the costs to be assigned to the units transferred out and the units in ending work in process.

Assign costs to units transferred out and in process.
(SO 6)

BE3-8 Production costs chargeable to the Finishing Department in June in Berger Company are materials $8,000, labor $20,000, overhead $18,000. Equivalent units of production are materials 20,000 and conversion costs 19,000. Compute the unit costs for materials and conversion costs.

Compute unit costs.
(SO 6)

BE3-9 Data for Berger Company are given in BE3-8. Production records indicate that 18,000 units were transferred out, and 2,000 units in ending work in process were 50% completed as to conversion cost and 100% complete as to materials. Prepare a cost reconciliation schedule.

Prepare cost reconciliation schedule.
(SO 6)

BE3-10 The Smelting Department of Agler Manufacturing Company has the following production and cost data for November:

Production: Beginning work in process 2,000 units that are 100% complete as to materials and 20% complete as to conversion costs; units transferred out 9,000 units; and ending work in process 1,000 units that are 100% complete as to materials and 40% com-

Compute equivalent units of production.
(SO 5)

plete as to conversion costs. Compute the equivalent units of production for (a) materials and (b) conversion costs for the month of November.

EXERCISES

Compute physical units and equivalent units of production.

(SO 5, 6)

E3-1   In Estes Company, materials are entered at the beginning of each process. Work in process inventories, with the percentage of work done on conversion costs, and production data for its Sterilizing Department in selected months during 1999 are as follows:

Month	Beginning Work in Process		Units Transferred Out	Ending Work in Process	
	Units	**Conversion Cost %**		**Units**	**Conversion Cost %**
January	–0–	—	7,000	1,000	60
March	–0–	—	10,000	3,000	30
May	–0–	—	16,000	2,500	80
July	–0–	—	9,000	1,500	40

Instructions
(a) Compute the physical units for January and May.
(b) Compute the equivalent units of production for (1) materials and (2) conversion costs for each month.

Determine equivalent units, unit costs, and assignment of costs.

(SO 5, 6)

E3-2   The Cutting Department of Cruz Manufacturing has the following production and cost data for July:

Production	Costs	
1. Transferred out 9,000 units.	Beginning work in process	$ –0–
2. Started 1,000 units that are 40%	Materials	45,000
completed as to conversion	Labor	14,000
costs and 100% completed as	Manufacturing overhead	18,900
to materials at July 31.		

Materials are entered at the beginning of the process. Conversion costs are incurred uniformly during the process.

Instructions
(a) Determine the equivalent units of production for (1) materials and (2) conversion costs.
(b) Compute unit costs and prepare a cost reconciliation schedule.

Prepare a production cost report.

(SO 5, 6, 7)

E3-3   The Sanding Department of Lore Furniture Company has the following production and manufacturing cost data for March 1999:

Production: 12,000 units finished and transferred out; 4,000 units started that are 100% completed as to materials and 25% completed as to conversion costs.
Manufacturing costs: Materials $32,000; labor $30,000; overhead $35,000.

Instructions
Prepare a production cost report.

Determine equivalent units, unit costs, and assignment of costs.

(SO 5, 6)

E3-4   The Blending Department of Dion Company has the following cost and production data for the month of April:

Costs:
  Work in process, April 1
    Direct materials: 100% complete $100,000
    Conversion costs: 20% complete   70,000
  Cost of work in process, April 1 $170,000

Costs incurred during production in April	
Direct materials	$ 800,000
Conversion costs	353,000
Costs incurred in April	$1,153,000

Units transferred out 9,000 units; and ending work in process 1,000 units that are 100% complete as to materials and 40% complete as to conversion costs.

Instructions
(a) Compute the equivalent units of production for (1) materials and (2) conversion costs for the month of April.
(b) Compute the unit costs for the month.
(c) Determine the costs to be assigned to the units transferred out and in ending work in process.

E3-5 Jerry Lundy has recently been promoted to production manager, and so he has just started to receive various managerial reports. One of the reports he has received is the production cost report that you prepared. It showed that his department had 1,000 equivalent units in ending inventory. His department has had a history of not keeping enough inventory on hand to meet demand. He has come to you, very angry, and wants to know why you credited him with only 1,000 units when he knows he had at least twice that many on hand.

Explain the production cost report.
(SO 7)

Instructions
⬛══▷ Explain to him why his production cost report showed only 1,000 equivalent units in ending inventory. Write an informal memo. Be kind and explain very clearly why he is mistaken.

E3-6 The ledger of Grogan Company has the following work in process account:

Answer questions on costs and production.
(SO 3, 5, 6)

Work in Process—Painting

5/1	Balance	3,680	5/31	Transferred out	?
5/31	Materials	6,030			
5/31	Labor	2,500			
5/31	Overhead	1,350			
5/31	Balance	?			

Production records show that there were 800 units in the beginning inventory, 30% complete, 1,100 units started, and 1,300 units transferred out. The beginning work in process had materials cost of $2,140 and conversion costs of $1,540. The units in ending inventory were 40% complete. Materials are entered at the beginning of the painting process.

Instructions
Answer the following questions:
(a) How many units are in process at May 31?
(b) What is the unit materials cost for May?
(c) What is the unit conversion cost for May?
(d) What is the total cost of units transferred out in May?
(e) What is the cost of the May 31 inventory?

E3-7 Hendrix Manufacturing Company has two production departments: Cutting and Assembly. July 1 inventories are Raw Materials $4,200, Work in Process—Cutting $2,900, Work in Process—Assembly $10,600, and Finished Goods $31,000. During July, the following transactions occurred:
1. Purchased $35,600 of raw materials on account.
2. Incurred $56,000 of factory labor. (Credit Wages Payable.)
3. Incurred $70,000 of manufacturing overhead; $42,000 was paid and the remainder is unpaid.
4. Requisitioned materials for Cutting $15,700 and Assembly $8,900.
5. Used factory labor for Cutting $29,000 and Assembly $27,000.
6. Applied overhead at the rate of $20 per machine hour. Machine hours were Cutting 1,740 and Assembly 1,620.
7. Transferred goods costing $67,700 from the Cutting Department to the Assembly Department.

Journalize transactions for two processes.
(SO 4)

8. Transferred goods costing $134,900 from Assembly to Finished Goods.
9. Sold goods costing $130,000 for $200,000 on account.

Instructions
Journalize the transactions. (Omit explanations.)

Compute equivalent units, unit costs, and costs assigned.

(SO 5, 6)

E3-8 The Polishing Department of Longbine Manufacturing Company has the following production and manufacturing cost data for September. Materials are entered at the beginning of the process.

Production: Beginning inventory 1,600 units that are 100% complete as to materials and 30% complete as to conversion costs; units started during the period are 12,000; ending inventory of 3,000 units 10% complete as to conversion costs.

Manufacturing costs: Beginning inventory costs, comprised of $20,000 of materials and $43,180 of conversion costs; materials costs added in Polishing during the month, $167,680; labor and overhead applied in Polishing during the month, $100,080 and $277,480 respectively.

Instructions
(a) Compute the equivalent units of production for materials and conversion costs for the month of September.
(b) Compute the unit costs for materials and conversion costs for the month.
(c) Determine the costs to be assigned to the units transferred out and in process.

Prepare a production cost report.

(SO 5, 6, 7)

E3-9 The Welding Department of Nagano Manufacturing Company has the following production and manufacturing cost data for February 1999. All materials are added at the beginning of the process.

Manufacturing Costs			Production Data	
Beginning work in process			Beginning work in process	15,000 units
Materials	$18,000			1/10 complete
Conversion costs	14,175	$32,175	Units transferred out	49,000
Materials		180,000	Units started	60,000
Labor		35,100	Ending work in process	26,000
Overhead		69,965		1/5 complete

Instructions
Prepare a production cost report for the Welding Department for the month of February.

Journalize transactions.

(SO 3, 4)

E3-10 Niemann Company manufactures pizza sauce through two production departments: Cooking and Canning. In each process, materials and conversion costs are incurred evenly throughout the process. For the month of April, the work in process accounts show the following debits:

	Cooking	Canning
Beginning work in process	$ –0–	$ 4,000
Materials	19,000	6,000
Labor	8,500	5,000
Overhead	29,500	21,800
Costs transferred in		50,000

Instructions
Journalize the April transactions.

PROBLEMS: SET A

Complete four steps necessary to prepare a production cost report.

(SO 5, 6, 7)

P3-1A Buehler Corporation manufactures water skis through two processes: Molding and Packaging. In the Molding Department fiber glass is heated and shaped into the form of a ski. In the Packaging Department, the skis are placed in cartons and sent to the finished goods warehouse. Materials are entered at the beginning of both processes. Labor and manufacturing overhead are incurred uniformly throughout each process. Production and cost data for the Molding Department for January 1999 are presented below.

Production Data	January
Beginning work in process units	–0–
Units started into production	42,500
Ending work in process units	2,500
Percent complete—ending inventory	40%

Cost Data	
Materials	$510,000
Labor	96,000
Overhead	150,000
Total	$756,000

Instructions
(a) Compute the physical units of production.
(b) Determine the equivalent units of production for materials and conversion costs.
(c) Compute the unit costs of production.
(d) Determine the costs to be assigned to the units transferred out and in process.
(e) Prepare a production cost report for the Molding Department for the month of January.

P3-2A Clemente Corporation manufactures in separate processes refrigerators and freezers for homes. In each process, materials are entered at the beginning and conversion costs are incurred uniformly. Production and cost data for the first process in making two products in two different manufacturing plants are as follows:

Complete four steps necessary to prepare a production cost report.
(SO 5, 6, 7)

	Stamping Department	
Production Data—June	Plant A R12 Refrigerators	Plant B F24 Freezers
Work in process units, June 1	–0–	–0–
Units started into production	21,000	20,000
Work in process units, June 30	4,000	2,500
Work in process percent complete	75	60

Cost Data—June		
Work in process, June 1	$ –0–	$ –0–
Materials	840,000	720,000
Labor	220,000	221,000
Overhead	420,000	292,000
Total	$1,480,000	$1,233,000

Instructions
(a) For each plant:
   (1) Compute the physical units of production.
   (2) Compute equivalent units of production for materials and for conversion costs.
   (3) Determine the unit costs of production.
   (4) Show the assignment of costs to units transferred out and in process.
(b) Prepare the production cost report for Plant A for June 1999.

P3-3A Pickard Company manufactures a nutrient, Everlife, through two manufacturing processes: Blending and Packaging. All materials are entered at the beginning of each process. On August 1, 1999, inventories consisted of Raw Materials $5,000, Work in Process—Blending $0, Work in Process—Packaging $3,945, and Finished Goods $7,500. The beginning inventory for Packaging consisted of 500 units, two-fifths complete as to conversion costs and fully complete as to materials. During August, 9,000 units were started into production in Blending and the following transactions were completed:
1. Purchased $25,000 of raw materials on account.
2. Issued raw materials for production: Blending $17,100 and Packaging $3,690.
3. Incurred labor costs of $17,880.
4. Used factory labor: Blending $13,320 and Packaging $4,560.

Journalize transactions.
(SO 3, 4)

5. Incurred $36,500 of manufacturing overhead on account.
6. Applied manufacturing overhead at the rate of $30 per machine hour. Machine hours were Blending 900 and Packaging 300.
7. Transferred 8,200 units from Blending to Packaging at a cost of $54,940.
8. Transferred 8,600 units from Packaging to Finished Goods at a cost of $74,490.
9. Sold goods costing $62,000 for $90,000 on account.

Instructions
Journalize the August transactions.

Assign costs and prepare production cost report.

(SO 5, 6, 7)

P3-4A   Cheng Company has several processing departments. Costs charged to the Assembly Department for October 1999 totaled $1,335,400 as follows:

Work in process, October 1		
Materials	$29,800	
Conversion costs	25,600	$ 55,400
Materials added		1,079,000
Labor		80,000
Overhead		121,000

Production records show that 25,000 units were in beginning work in process 40% complete as to conversion cost, 415,000 units were started into production, and 35,000 units were in ending work in process 20% complete as to conversion costs. Materials are entered at the beginning of each process.

Instructions
(a) Determine the equivalent units of production and the unit costs for the Assembly Department.
(b) Determine the assignment of costs to goods transferred out and in process.
(c) Prepare a production cost report for the Assembly Department.

Determine equivalent units and unit costs and assign costs.

(SO 5, 6, 7)

P3-5A   Jessica Company manufactures bicycles and tricycles. For both products, materials are added at the beginning of the production process, and conversion costs are incurred uniformly. Production and cost data for the month of May are as follows:

Production Data—Bicycles	**Units**	**Percent Complete**
Work in process units, May 1	200	80%
Units started in production	1,000	
Work in process units, May 31	300	30%

Cost Data—Bicycles		
Work in process, May 1		
Materials	$10,000	
Conversion costs	9,280	$19,280
Direct materials		50,000
Direct labor		18,140
Manufacturing overhead		30,000

add
for
conversion
cost

Instructions
(a) Calculate the following:
   (1) The equivalent units of production for materials and conversion.
   (2) The unit costs of production for materials and conversion costs.
   (3) The assignment of costs to units transferred out and in process at the end of the accounting period.
(b) Prepare a production cost report for the month of May for the bicycles.

Compute equivalent units and complete production cost report.

(SO 5, 7)

P3-6A   Fluid Cleaner Company uses a weighted-average process costing system and manufactures a single product—an all-purpose liquid cleaner. The manufacturing activity for the month of March has just been completed. A partially completed production cost report for the month of March for the mixing and blending department is shown below:

FLUID CLEANER COMPANY
Mixing and Blending Department
Production Cost Report
For the Month Ended March 31

		Equivalent Units	
QUANTITIES	Physical Units	Materials	Conversion Costs
Units to be accounted for			
Work in process, March 1 (40% materials, 20% conversion costs)	10,000		
Started into production	100,000		
Total units	110,000		
Units accounted for			
Transferred out	95,000	?	?
Work in process, March 31 (60% materials, 20% conversion costs)	15,000	?	?
Total units	110,000	?	?

COSTS			
Unit costs	Materials	Conversion Costs	Total
Costs in March	$156,000	$98,000	$254,000
Equivalent units	?	?	
Unit costs	$? +	$? =	$?

Costs to be accounted for	
Work in process, March 1	$ 8,700
Started into production	245,300
Total costs	$254,000

Cost Reconciliation Schedule

Costs accounted for		
Transferred out		$?
Work in process, March 31		
Materials	?	
Conversion costs	?	?
Total costs		?

Instructions
(a) Prepare a schedule that shows how the equivalent units were computed so that you can complete the "Quantities: Units accounted for" equivalent units section shown in the production cost report above, and compute March unit costs.
(b) Complete the "Cost Reconciliation Schedule" part of the production cost report above.

PROBLEMS: SET B

Complete four steps necessary to prepare a production cost report.
(SO 5, 6, 7)

P3-1B Fortner Company manufactures bowling balls through two processes: Molding and Packaging. In the Molding Department, the urethane, rubber, plastics, and other materials are molded into bowling balls. In the Packaging Department, the balls are placed in cartons and sent to the finished goods warehouse. All materials are entered at the beginning of each process. Labor and manufacturing overhead are incurred uniformly throughout each process. Production and cost data for the Molding Department during June 1999 are presented below.

Production Data	June
Beginning work in process units	–0–
Units started into production	22,000
Ending work in process units	2,000
Percent complete—ending inventory	45%

Cost Data	
Materials	$264,000
Labor	92,200
Overhead	116,800
Total	$473,000

Instructions
(a) Prepare a schedule showing physical units of production.
(b) Determine the equivalent units of production for materials and conversion costs.
(c) Compute the unit costs of production.
(d) Determine the costs to be assigned to the units transferred and in process for June.
(e) Prepare a production cost report for the Molding Department for the month of June only.

Complete four steps necessary to prepare a production cost report.
(SO 5, 6, 7)

P3-2B Enright Industries Inc. manufactures in separate processes furniture for homes. In each process, materials are entered at the beginning, and conversion costs are incurred uniformly. Production and cost data for the first process in making two products in two different manufacturing plants are as follows:

	Cutting Department	
	Plant 1	Plant 2
Production Data—July	T12-Tables	C10-Chairs
Work in process units, July 1	–0–	–0–
Units started into production	20,000	18,000
Work in process units, July 31	1,000	500
Work in process percent complete	60	80

Cost Data—July		
Work in process, July 1	$ –0–	$ –0–
Materials	360,000	270,000
Labor	180,000	110,200
Overhead	94,400	86,700
Total	$634,400	$466,900

Instructions
(a) For each plant:
   (1) Compute the physical units of production.
   (2) Compute equivalent units of production for materials and for conversion costs.
   (3) Determine the unit costs of production.
   (4) Show the assignment of costs to units transferred out and in process.
(b) Prepare the production cost report for Plant 1 for July 1999.

Journalize transactions.
(SO 3, 4)

P3-3B Vargas Company manufactures its product, Vitadrink, through two manufacturing processes: Mixing and Packaging. All materials are entered at the beginning of each process. On October 1, 2000, inventories consisted of Raw Materials $26,000, Work in

Process—Mixing $0, Work in Process—Packaging $250,000, and Finished Goods $89,000. The beginning inventory for Packaging consisted of 10,000 units that were 50% complete as to conversion costs and fully complete as to materials. During October, 50,000 units were started into production in the Mixing Department and the following transactions were completed:
1. Purchased $300,000 of raw materials on account.
2. Issued raw materials for production: Mixing $210,000 and Packaging $45,000.
3. Incurred labor costs of $238,900.
4. Used factory labor: Mixing $182,500 and Packaging $56,400.
5. Incurred $820,000 of manufacturing overhead on account.
6. Applied indirect manufacturing overhead on the basis of $25 per machine hour. Machine hours were 26,000 in Mixing and 6,600 in Packaging.
7. Transferred 45,000 units from Mixing to Packaging at a cost of $999,000.
8. Transferred 53,000 units from Packaging to Finished Goods at a cost of $1,455,000.
9. Sold goods costing $1,460,000 for $2,100,000 on account.

Instructions
Journalize the October transactions.

P3-4B Falcone Company has several processing departments. Costs charged to the Assembly Department for November 2000 totaled $2,097,750 as follows:

Assign costs and prepare production cost report.
(SO 5, 6, 7)

Work in process, November 1		
Materials	$69,000	
Conversion costs	39,950	$ 108,950
Materials added		1,472,000
Labor		185,920
Overhead		330,880

Production records show that 30,000 units were in beginning work in process 30% complete as to conversion costs, 640,000 units were started into production, and 25,000 units were in ending work in process 40% complete as to conversion costs. Materials are entered at the beginning of each process.

Instructions
(a) Determine the equivalent units of production and the unit costs for the Assembly Department.
(b) Determine the assignment of costs to goods transferred out and in process.
(c) Prepare a production cost report for the Assembly Department.

P3-5B Nicholas Company manufactures basketballs. Materials are added at the beginning of the production process and conversion costs are incurred uniformly. Production and cost data for the month of July are as follows:

Determine equivalent units and unit costs and assign costs.
(SO 5, 6, 7)

Production Data—Basketballs	Units	Percent Complete
Work in process units, July 1	500	60%
Units started into production	1,600	
Work in process units, July 31	600	40%

Cost Data—Basketballs		
Work in process, July 1		
Materials	$500	
Conversion costs	450	$950
Direct materials		1,600
Direct labor		1,160
Manufacturing overhead		1,000

Instructions
(a) Calculate the following:
   (1) The equivalent units of production for materials and conversion.
   (2) The unit costs of production for materials and conversion costs.

(3) The assignment of costs to units transferred out and in process at the end of the accounting period.

(b) Prepare a production cost report for the month of July for the basketballs.

Compute equivalent units and complete production cost report.

(SO 5, 7)

P3-6B   Bob and Ashley Thebeau Processing Company uses a weighted-average process costing system and manufactures a single product—a premium rug shampoo and cleaner. The manufacturing activity for the month of October has just been completed. A partially completed production cost report for the month of October for the mixing and cooking department is shown below:

BOB AND ASHLEY THEBEAU PROCESSING COMPANY
Mixing and Cooking Department
Production Cost Report
For the Month Ended October 31

| | | Equivalent Units | |
QUANTITIES	Physical Units	Materials	Conversion Costs
Units to be accounted for			
Work in process, October 1			
(all materials, 70%			
conversion costs)	20,000		
Started into production	200,000		
Total units	220,000		
Units accounted for			
Transferred out	180,000	?	?
Work in process, October 31			
(50% materials, 25%			
conversion costs)	40,000	?	?
Total units accounted for	220,000	?	?

| COSTS | | Conversion | |
Unit costs	Materials	Costs	Total
Costs in October	$240,000	$95,000	$335,000
Equivalent units	?	?	
Unit costs	$? +	$? =	$?

Costs to be accounted for		
Work in process, October 1		$ 30,000
Started into production		305,000
Total costs		$335,000

Cost Reconciliation Schedule

Costs accounted for		
Transferred out		$?
Work in process, October 31		
Materials	?	
Conversion costs	?	?
Total costs		?

Instructions

(a) Prepare a schedule that shows how the equivalent units were computed so that you can complete the "Quantities: Units accounted for" equivalent units section shown in the production cost report above, and compute October unit costs.

(b) Complete the "Cost Reconciliation Schedule" part of the production cost report above.

GROUP DECISION CASE

BYP3-1 Mendoza Company manufactures suntan lotion, called Surtan, in 11-ounce plastic bottles. Surtan is sold in a competitive market. As a result, management is very cost-conscious. Surtan is manufactured through two processes: mixing and filling. Materials are entered at the beginning of each process and labor and manufacturing overhead occur uniformly throughout each process. Unit costs are based on the cost per gallon of Surtan using the weighted average-costing approach.

On June 30, 1999, Sue Noller, the chief accountant for the past 20 years, opted to take early retirement. Her replacement, Jeff Mura, had extensive accounting experience with motels in the area but only limited contact with manufacturing accounting.

During July, Jeff correctly accumulated the following production quantity and cost data for the Mixing Department.

Production quantities: Work in process, July 1, 8,000 gallons 75% complete; started into production 100,000 gallons; work in process, July 31, 5,000 gallons 20% complete. Materials are added at the beginning of the process.

Production costs: Beginning work in process $88,000, comprised of $21,000 of materials costs and $67,000 of conversion costs; incurred in July: materials $600,000, conversion costs $785,800.

Jeff then prepared a production cost report on the basis of physical units started into production. His report showed a production cost of $14.738 per gallon of Surtan. The management of Mendoza was surprised at the high unit cost. The president comes to you, as Sue's top assistant, to review Jeff's report and prepare a correct report if necessary.

Instructions
With the class divided into groups, answer the following questions:
(a) Show how Jeff arrived at the unit cost of $14.738 per gallon of Surtan.
(b) What error(s) did Jeff make in preparing his production cost report?
(c) Prepare a correct production cost report for July.

MANAGERIAL ANALYSIS

BYP3-2 Dwyer Furniture Company manufactures living room furniture through two departments: Framing and Upholstering. Materials are entered at the beginning of each process. For May, the following cost data are obtained from the two work in process accounts.

	Framing	Upholstering
Work in process, May 1	$ –0–	$?
Materials	420,000	?
Conversion costs	210,000	330,000
Costs transferred in	–0–	550,000
Costs transferred out	550,000	?
Work in process, May 31	80,000	?

Instructions
Answer the following questions:
(a) If 3,000 sofas were started into production on May 1 and 2,500 sofas were transferred to Upholstering, what was the unit cost of materials for May in the Framing Department?
(b) Using the data in (a) above, what was the per unit conversion cost of the sofas transferred to Upholstering?
(c) Continuing the assumptions in (a) above, what is the percentage of completion of the units in process at May 31 in the Framing Department?

REAL-WORLD FOCUS

GENERAL MICROWAVE CORP.

BYP3-3   General Microwave Corp. is engaged primarily in the design, development, manufacture, and marketing of microwave, electronic, and fiber optic test equipment, components, and subsystems. A substantial portion of the company's microwave product is sold to manufacturers and users of microwave systems and equipment for applications in the defense electronics industry.

General Microwave Corp. reports the following information in one of the notes to its financial statements:

GENERAL MICROWAVE CORPORATION
5500 New Horizons Boulevard • Amityville, New York 11701

GENERAL MICROWAVE CORPORATION
Notes to the Financial Statement

Work in process inventory reflects all accumulated production costs, which are comprised of direct production costs and overhead, reduced by amounts attributable to units delivered. Work in process inventory is reduced to its estimated net realizable value by a charge to cost of sales in the period [in which] excess costs are identified. Raw materials and finished goods inventories are reflected at the lower of cost or market.

Instructions
(a) What types of manufacturing costs are accumulated in the work in process inventory account?
(b) What types of information must General Microwave have to be able to compute equivalent units of production?
(c) How does General Microwave assign costs to the units transferred out of work in process that are completed?

COMMUNICATION ACTIVITY

BYP3-4   Clara Pipken was a good friend of yours in high school and is from your home town. While you chose to major in accounting when you both went away to college, she majored in marketing and management. You have recently been promoted to accounting manager for the Snack Foods Division of Romero Enterprises, and your friend was promoted to regional sales manager for the same division of Romero. Clara recently telephoned you. She explained that she was familiar with job cost sheets, which had been used by the Special Projects division where she had formerly worked. She was, however, very uncomfortable with the production cost reports prepared by your division. She faxed you a list of her particular questions. These included the following:
1. Since Romero occasionally prepares snack foods for special orders in the Snack Foods Division, why don't we track costs of the orders separately?
2. What is an equivalent unit?
3. Why am I getting four production cost reports? Isn't there only one Work in Process account?

Instructions
Prepare a memorandum to Clara. Answer her questions, and include any additional information you think would be helpful. You may write informally, but be careful to use proper grammar and punctuation.

*E*THICS *C*ASE

BYP3-6 J. R. Snider Company manufactures a high-tech component that passes through two production processing departments, Molding and Assembly. Department managers are partially compensated on the basis of units of products completed and transferred out relative to units of product put into production. This was intended as encouragement to be efficient and to minimize waste.

Bill Fortuno is the department head in the Molding Department, and Steve Drummond is his quality control inspector. During the month of June, Bill had three new employees who were not yet technically skilled. As a result, many of the units produced in June had minor molding defects. In order to maintain the department's normal high rate of completion, Bill told Steve to pass through inspection and on to the Assembly Department all units that had defects nondetectable to the human eye. "Company and industry tolerances on this product are too high anyway," says Bill. "Less than 2% of the units we produce are subjected in the market to the stress tolerance we've designed into them. The odds of those 2% being any of this month's units are even less. Anyway, we're saving the company money."

Instructions
(a) Who are the potential stakeholders involved in this situation?
(b) What alternatives does Steve have in this situation? What might the company do to prevent this from occurring?

*S*URFING THE *N*ET

BYP3-7 Search the Internet and find the Web sites of two manufacturers that you think are likely to use process costing. Are there any specifics included in their Web sites that confirm the use of process costing for each of these companies?

Answers to Self-Study Questions
1. b   2. d   3. c   4. b   5. b   6. a   7. c   8. a   9. b   10. b

 Remember to go back to the Navigator box on the chapter-opening page and check off your completed work.

C H A P T E R 4
Activity-Based Costing

STUDY OBJECTIVES

After studying this chapter, you should be able to:

1. Recognize the difference between traditional costing and activity-based costing.

2. Identify the steps in the development of an activity-based costing system.

3. Identify the activity cost pools used in activity-based costing.

4. Identify and use the activity cost drivers in activity-based costing.

5. Understand the benefits and limitations of activity-based costing.

6. Differentiate between value-added and nonvalue-added activities.

7. Understand the value of a hierarchy of activity levels to activity-based costing.

8. Explain just-in-time (JIT) processing.

THE NAVIGATOR

FEATURE STORY

The ABCs of Donut Making—Virtual Reality Style

Super Bakery, Inc., created in 1990 by former Pittsburgh Steelers' running back Franco Harris, is a nationwide supplier of mineral-, vitamin-, and protein-enriched donuts and other baked goods to the institutional food market, primarily school systems. Super Bakery is a *virtual corporation,* in which only the core, strategic functions of the business are performed inside the company. The remaining activities—selling, manufacturing, warehousing, and shipping—are outsourced to a network of external companies. Super Bakery draws these cooperating companies together and organizes the work flow.

The goal is to add maximum value to the company while making the minimum investment in permanent staff, fixed assets, and working capital. The results are notable: Super Bakery's sales have grown at an average rate of 20% for the past eight years.

One of Super Bakery's challenges has been to control the cost of the outsourced activities. Management suspected a wide variation in the cost of serving customers in different parts of the country. Yet its traditional costing methods were spreading costs over the entire customer base. Each customer's order appeared to cost the same amount to complete—orders that provided high profit margins thus subsidized orders with low profit margins. Super Bakery desired a system that would more

accurately assign the costs of each order. With such a system, pricing could be improved.

The company looked at and eventually changed to a system that could isolate the costs associated with the *activities* performed in the business— manufacturing, sales, warehousing, and shipping. Activity-based costing has shown that the costs and profit margins on each sale vary significantly. Super Bakery is now able to track the profitability of each customer's account and the performance of outsourced activities. This donut maker, as a result, even knows the cost of the donut holes!

THE NAVIGATOR

Source: Tom R.V. Davis and Bruce L. Darling, "ABC in a Virtual Corporation," *Management Accounting,* Oct. 1996, pp. 18–26.

THE NAVIGATOR ✔

- Scan *Study Objectives* ☐
- Read *Feature Story* ☐
- Read *Preview* ☐
- Read text and answer *Before You Go On*
  p. 133 ☐   p. 140 ☐   p. 143 ☐
- Work *Using the Decision Toolkit* ☐
- Review *Summary of Study Objectives* ☐
- Work *Demonstration Problem* ☐
- Answer *Self-Study Questions* ☐
- Complete assignments ☐

As indicated in our feature story about Super Bakery, Inc., a traditional costing system, as described in earlier chapters, is not the answer for every company. Because Super Bakery suspected that the traditional system was masking significant differences in its real cost structure, it sought a new method of assigning costs. Similar searches by other companies for ways to improve their operations and gather more accurate data for decision-making purposes have resulted in the development of powerful new management tools, including **activity-based costing (ABC)** and **just-in-time (JIT) processing.** The primary objective of this chapter is to explain and illustrate activity-based costing. A brief overview of just-in-time processing is presented at the end of the chapter. The content and organization of this chapter are as follows:

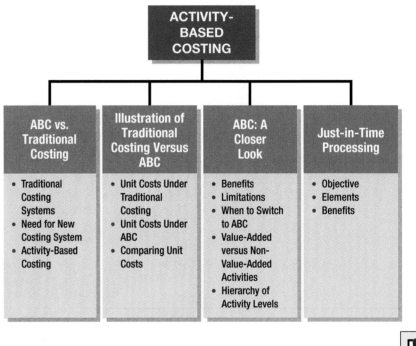

ACTIVITY-BASED COSTING VERSUS TRADITIONAL COSTING

TRADITIONAL COSTING SYSTEMS

STUDY OBJECTIVE

1

Recognize the difference between traditional costing and activity-based costing.

Although it may be impossible to determine the exact cost of a product or service, every effort to provide decision makers with the best possible cost estimates must be made. The best estimate of cost occurs when the costs are traceable directly to the product produced or the service rendered. Direct material and direct labor costs are the easiest to trace directly to the product through the use of material requisition forms and payroll time sheets. Overhead, however, is an indirect or common cost that generally cannot be directly traced to individual products or services.

Often the most difficult part of computing accurate unit costs is determining the proper amount of **overhead cost** to assign to each product, service, or job. In our coverage of job order costing and process costing in Chapters 2 and 3, respectively, a single overhead rate was used throughout the year for the entire factory operation. That rate was called the **predetermined overhead rate.** For job order costing we assumed that **direct labor cost** was the relevant activity base for the assignment of all overhead costs to jobs. For process costing, we assumed that **machine hours** was the relevant activity base for the assignment of all overhead.

When overhead cost allocation systems were first developed, direct labor made up a large part of total manufacturing cost. It was widely accepted that there was a high correlation between direct labor and the incurrence of overhead cost. As a result, direct labor became the most popular basis for overhead allocation. The results of one survey, shown in Illustration 4-1, indicate the overwhelming popularity of direct labor as the basis most used by U.S. companies to allocate overhead costs.

Allocation Basis	Companies Using Basis
Direct labor—hours	31%
Direct labor—dollars	31
Machine hours	12
Direct material dollars	4
Units of production	5
Other	17

Source: J. Cohen, and L. Paqueet, "Management Accounting Practices: Perception of Controllers," *Journal of Cost Management* (Fall 1991) © 1991 RIA Group. Used with permission..

Illustration 4-1 Bases used to allocate U.S. manufacturing overhead in 1990–91

Even in today's environment, direct labor is often the appropriate basis for assigning overhead cost to products. It is appropriate when (a) direct labor constitutes a significant part of total product cost, and (b) a high correlation exists between direct labor and changes in the amount of overhead costs. A simplified (one-stage) traditional costing system relying on direct labor to assign overhead is displayed in Illustration 4-2.

THE NEED FOR A NEW COSTING SYSTEM

Advances in computerized systems, technological innovation, international competition, and automation have changed the manufacturing environment drastically. The amount of direct labor used in many industries is now greatly reduced, and total overhead costs (for depreciation on expensive equipment and machinery, utilities, repairs, and maintenance) have significantly increased. Companies that continue to use plantwide predetermined overhead rates based on direct labor, where the correlation between direct labor and overhead no longer exists, experience significant product cost distortions.

Recognizing these distortions, many companies now use machine hours as the basis on which to allocate overhead in an automated manufacturing environment. But even machine hours may not suffice as the sole plantwide basis for allocating all overhead. If the manufacturing process is complex, then only multiple allocation bases can result in more accurate computations. In such situations, managers need a new overhead cost allocation method—*activity-based costing*.

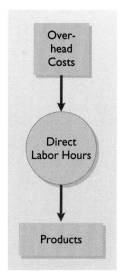

Illustration 4-2 Traditional one-stage costing system

ACTIVITY-BASED COSTING

Activities and Cost Drivers

Activity-based costing (ABC) allocates overhead to multiple activity cost pools and assigns the activity cost pools to products by means of cost drivers. In activity-based costing, an **activity** is any event, action, transaction, or work sequence that causes the incurrence of cost in the production of a product or the rendering of a service. A **cost driver** is any factor or activity that has a direct cause–effect relationship with the resources consumed.

ABC first allocates costs to activities, and then to the products based on each product's use of those activities. The reasoning behind ABC cost allocation is simple: **products consume activities; activities consume resources.**

ABC allocates overhead in a two-stage process: In the first stage, overhead is allocated to **activity cost pools,** each of which is a distinct type of activity (e.g., ordering materials, setting up machines, assembling, and inspecting), rather than to departments. In the second stage, the overhead allocated to the activity cost pools is assigned to products using **cost drivers** which represent and measure the number of individual activities undertaken or performed (e.g., number of purchase orders, number of setups, labor hours, or number of inspections) to produce products or render services. Examples of activities and the possible cost drivers that measure them are shown in Illustration 4-3.

Illustration 4-3 Activities and related cost drivers

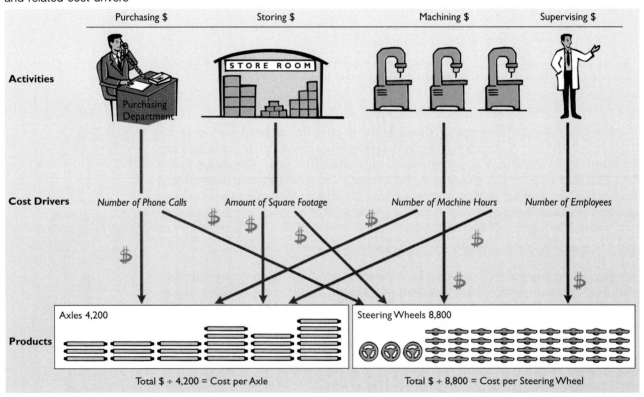

As you might imagine, not all products or services share equally in these activities. The more complex a product's manufacturing operation, the more activities and cost drivers it is likely to have. If there is little or no correlation between changes in the cost driver and consumption of the overhead cost, inaccurate product costs are inevitable.

The design of an activity-based costing system with seven activity cost pools is graphically shown in Illustration 4-4 for Lift Jack Company. Lift Jack Company manufactures two automotive jacks—an automobile scissors jack and a truck hydraulic jack.

Illustration 4-4
ABC system design—
Lift Jack Company

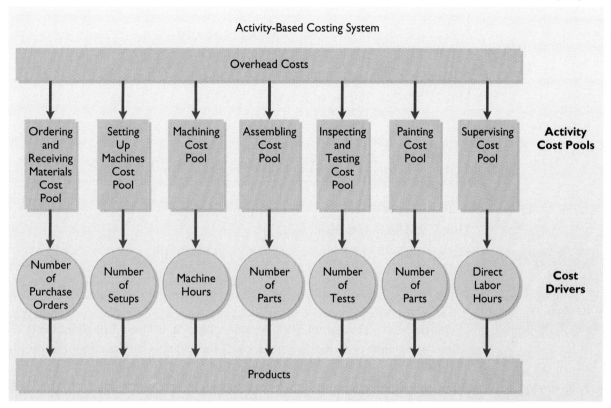

The Lift Jack Company illustration contains seven activity cost pools. In some companies the number of activities can be substantial. For example, at Clark-Hurth (a division of Clark Equipment Company), a manufacturer of axles and transmissions, over 170 activities were identified; at the Compumotor Division of Parker Hannifin over 80 activities were identified in just the procurement function of its Material Control Department.

Helpful Hint Computers alleviate the problems of huge numbers of activities and are delivering the potential of ABC to improve product costing.

ILLUSTRATION OF TRADITIONAL COSTING VERSUS ABC

In this section we present a simple case example that compares traditional costing and activity-based costing and illustrates the distortion that can occur in traditional overhead cost allocation.

UNIT COSTS UNDER TRADITIONAL COSTING

Atlas Company produces two automobile antitheft devices, The Boot and The Club. The Boot is a high-volume item totaling 25,000 units annually, and The Club is a low-volume item totaling only 5,000 units per year. Both products require one hour of direct labor for completion. Therefore, total annual direct labor hours are 30,000 (25,000 + 5,000). Expected annual manufacturing overhead costs are $900,000. Thus, the predetermined overhead rate is $30 ($900,000 ÷ 30,000) per direct labor hour.

The direct materials cost per unit is $40 for The Boot and $30 for The Club. The direct labor cost is $12 per unit for each product. The computation of the unit cost for The Boot and The Club under traditional costing is shown in Illustration 4-5.

Illustration 4-5
Computation of unit costs—traditional costing

ATLAS COMPANY		
	Products	
Manufacturing Costs	The Boot	The Club
Direct materials	$40	$30
Direct labor	12	12
Overhead	30*	30*
Total unit cost	$82	$72

*Predetermined overhead rate times direct labor hours ($30 × 1 hr. = $30).

UNIT COSTS UNDER ABC

Activity-based costing involves the following three steps:

1. Identify the major activities that pertain to the manufacture of specific products and allocate manufacturing overhead costs to activity cost pools.
2. Identify the cost drivers that accurately measure each activity's contribution to the finished product and compute the activity-based overhead rate.
3. Assign manufacturing overhead costs for each activity cost pool to products, using the activity-based overhead rates (cost per driver).

Identifying Activities and Allocating Overhead to Cost Pools

A well designed activity-based costing system starts with an analysis of the activities performed to manufacture a product or render a service. This analysis should identify all resource-consuming activities. It requires a detailed, step-by-step walk through of each operation, documenting every activity undertaken to accomplish a task. Anxious to compare activity-based costing with its traditional costing system, Atlas Company identified three activity-cost pools: setting up machines, machining, and inspecting.

After the activity cost pools are identified, overhead costs are assigned directly to activity cost pools. For example, all overhead costs directly associated with Atlas Company's machine setups (such as salaries, supplies, and depreciation) would be assigned to the machine setup cost pool as they are incurred. These activity cost pools, along with the estimated overhead allocated to each activity cost pool, are shown in Illustration 4-6.

Illustration 4-6 Activity cost pools and estimated overhead

ATLAS COMPANY	
Activity Cost Pools	Estimated Overhead
Setting up machines	$300,000
Machining	500,000
Inspecting	100,000
Total	$900,000

Identifying Cost Drivers and Computing Overhead Rates

After costs are allocated to the activity cost pools, the cost drivers for each activity cost pool must be identified. The cost driver must accurately measure the actual consumption of the activity by the various products. To achieve accurate costing, a high degree of correlation must exist between the activity cost driver and the actual consumption of the activity cost pool.

The cost drivers identified by Atlas and their total expected use per activity cost pool are shown in Illustration 4-7.

STUDY OBJECTIVE

4

Identify and use the activity cost drivers in activity-based costing.

ATLAS COMPANY

Activity Cost Pools	Cost Drivers	Expected Use of Cost Drivers per Activity
Setting up machine	Number of setups	1,500 setups
Machining	Machine hours	50,000 machine hours
Inspecting	Number of inspections	2,000 inspections

Illustration 4-7 Cost drivers and their expected use

Availability and ease of obtaining data relating to the activity cost driver is an important factor that must be considered in its selection. An activity-based overhead rate is then computed by dividing the estimated overhead per activity by the number of cost drivers expected to be used per activity. The formula for this computation is shown in Illustration 4-8.

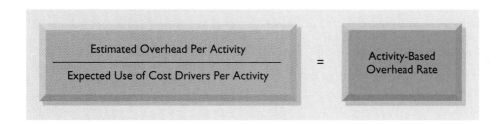

$$\frac{\text{Estimated Overhead Per Activity}}{\text{Expected Use of Cost Drivers Per Activity}} = \text{Activity-Based Overhead Rate}$$

Illustration 4-8 Formula for computing activity-based overhead rate

Atlas Company computes its activity-based overhead rates by using total estimated overhead per activity cost pool, shown in Illustration 4-6, and the total expected use of cost drivers per activity, shown in Illustration 4-7. The computations are presented in Illustration 4-9.

ATLAS COMPANY

Activity Cost Pools	Estimated ÷ Overhead	Expected Use of Cost Drivers per Activity	=	Activity-Based Overhead Rates
Setting up machines	$300,000	1,500 setups		$200 per setup
Machining	500,000	50,000 machine hours		$10 per machine hour
Inspecting	100,000	2,000 inspections		$50 per inspection
Total	$900,000			

Illustration 4-9 Computation of activity-based overhead rates

Assigning Overhead Costs to Products under ABC

In assigning overhead costs, it is necessary to know the expected use of cost drivers **for each product.** Because of its low volume, The Club requires more setups and inspections than The Boot. The expected use of cost drivers per product for each product is shown in Illustration 4-10.

Illustration 4-10
Expected use of cost drivers per product

ATLAS COMPANY

Activity Cost Pools	Cost Drivers	Expected Use of Cost Drivers for Activity	Expected Use of Cost Drivers per Product — The Boot	Expected Use of Cost Drivers per Product — The Club
Setting up machines	Number of setups	1,500 setups	500	1,000
Machining	Machine hours	50,000 machine hours	30,000	20,000
Inspection	Number of inspections	2,000 inspections	500	1,500

To assign overhead costs to each product, the activity-based overhead rates (Illustration 4-9) are multiplied by the number of cost drivers expected to be used per product (Illustration 4-10). The assignment of Atlas Company's estimated annual overhead cost to each product is then shown in Illustration 4-11.

Illustration 4-11
Assignment of activity cost pools to products

ATLAS COMPANY

Activity Cost Pools	The Boot — Expected Use of Cost Drivers per Product ×	The Boot — Activity-Based Overhead Rates =	The Boot — Cost Assigned	The Club — Expected Use of Cost Drivers per Product ×	The Club — Activity-Based Overhead Rates =	The Club — Cost Assigned
Setting up machines	500	$200	$100,000	1,000	$200	$200,000
Machining	30,000	$10	300,000	20,000	$10	200,000
Inspecting	500	$50	25,000	1,500	$50	75,000
Total assigned costs (a)			$425,000			$475,000
Units produced (b)			25,000			5,000
Overhead cost per unit (a) ÷ (b)			$17			$95

These data show that under ABC, overhead costs are shifted from the high-volume product (The Boot—25,000) to the low-volume product (The Club—5,000). This shift results in more accurate costing for two reasons:

1. Low-volume products often require more special handling, such as more machine setups and inspections, than high-volume products. This is true for Atlas Company, for example. Thus, the low-volume product frequently is responsible for more overhead costs per unit than a high-volume product.[1]

2. The overhead costs incurred by the low-volume product often are disproportionate to a traditional allocation base such as direct labor hours. There-

[1]Robin Cooper and Robert S. Kaplan, "How Cost Accounting Distorts Product Costs," *Management Accounting* 69, No. 10 (April 1988), pp. 20–27.

fore, direct labor hours is usually a poor cost driver for assigning overhead costs to low-volume products. When overhead is properly assigned in ABC, it will usually increase the unit cost of low-volume products.

COMPARING UNIT COSTS

A comparison of unit manufacturing costs under traditional costing and ABC shows the following significant differences:

Illustration 4-12
Comparison of unit product costs

	ATLAS COMPANY			
	The Boot		The Club	
Manufacturing Costs	Traditional Costing	ABC	Traditional Costing	ABC
Direct materials	$40	$40	$30	$30
Direct labor	12	12	12	12
Overhead	30	17	30	95
Total cost per unit	$82	$69	$72	$137

The comparison shows that unit costs under traditional costing are significantly distorted. The cost of producing The Boot is overstated $13 per unit ($82 − $69), and the cost of producing The Club is understated $65 per unit ($137 − $72). The differences are attributable entirely to how manufacturing overhead is assigned. A likely consequence of the differences is that Atlas Company has been overpricing The Boot and possibly losing market share to competitors. In addition, it has been sacrificing profitability by underpricing The Club.

BUSINESS INSIGHT
International Perspective

Activity-based costing was pioneered in the United States: John Deere Company coined the term less than 20 years ago. Although ABC has been adopted by numerous well-known U.S. companies including IBM, AT&T, Hewlett-Packard, Proctor and Gamble, Tektronix, John Deere, Hughes Aircraft, Caterpillar, American Express, and Compaq Computer, its use outside the U.S. is limited. The cost of implementation may discourage some foreign companies. In Japan, where activity-based costing is less used, companies prefer volume measures such as direct labor hours to assign overhead cost to products. Japanese managers are convinced that reducing direct labor is essential to continuous cost reduction. And, using direct labor as the basis for overhead allocation forces them to watch direct labor more closely. To the Japanese, labor cost reduction is apparently more of a priority than developing more accurate product costs.

BEFORE YOU GO ON . . .

● **Review It**

1. Why has direct labor been the most popular basis for allocating overhead to products?

2. What changes have occurred in the industrial environment to diminish the appeal of traditional volume-based overhead allocation systems?

3. What three steps are involved in developing an ABC system?

● **Do It**

Lift Jack Company, as shown in Illustration 4-4, page 129, has seven activity cost pools and two products (an automobile scissors jack, 200,000 units expected to be produced; and a truck hydraulic jack, 80,000 units expected to be produced). Having identified its activity cost pools and the cost drivers for each cost pool, Lift Jack Company accumulated the following data relative to those activity cost pools and cost drivers:

LIFT JACK COMPANY

	Annual Overhead Data			Expected Use of Cost Drivers per Product	
Activity Cost Pools	**Cost Drivers**	**Estimated Overhead**	**Expected Use of Cost Drivers per Activity**	**Scissors Jacks**	**Hydraulic Jacks**
Ordering and receiving	Purchase orders	$ 200,000	2,500 orders	1,000	1,500
Machine setup	Setups	600,000	1,200 setups	500	700
Machining	Machine hours	2,000,000	800,000 hours	300,000	500,000
Assembling	Parts	1,800,000	3,000,000 parts	1,800,000	1,200,000
Inspecting and testing	Inspections	700,000	35,000 inspections	20,000	15,000
Painting	Parts	300,000	3,000,000 parts	1,800,000	1,200,000
Supervising	Labor hours	1,200,000	200,000 hours	130,000	70,000
		$6,800,000			

Using the above data, (a) prepare a schedule showing the computations of the activity-based overhead rates, (b) prepare a schedule assigning each activity's overhead cost pool to each product, (c) compute the overhead cost per unit for each product, and (d) comment on the comparative overhead cost per unit.

Reasoning: Products consume activities; activities consume resources. All overhead costs related to the activity (1) must be consumed by the cost driver used to assign costs to products and (2) must respond proportionally to changes in the activity level of the cost driver.

Solution:

(a) Computations of activity-based overhead rates:

LIFT JACK COMPANY

Activity Cost Pools	**Estimated Overhead**	÷	**Expected Use of Cost Drivers per Activity**	=	**Activity-Based Overhead Rates**
Ordering and receiving	$ 200,000		2,500 purchase orders		$80 per order
Machine setup	600,000		1,200 setups		$500 per setup
Machining	2,000,000		800,000 machine hours		$2.50 per machine hour
Assembling	1,800,000		3,000,000 parts		$.60 per part
Inspecting and testing	700,000		35,000 inspections		$20 per inspection
Painting	300,000		3,000,000 parts		$.10 per part
Supervising	1,200,000		200,000 labor hours		$6 per labor hour
	$6,800,000				

(b) Assignment of activity cost pools to products:

LIFT JACK COMPANY

Activity Cost Pools	Scissors Jacks			Hydraulic Jacks		
	Expected Use of Cost Drivers per Product ×	Activity-Based Overhead Rates	= Cost Assigned	Expected Use of Cost Drivers per Product ×	Activity-Based Overhead Rates	= Cost Assigned
Ordering and receiving	1,000	$80	$ 80,000	1,500	$80	$ 120,000
Machine setup	500	$500	250,000	700	$500	350,000
Machining	300,000	$2.50	750,000	500,000	$2.50	1,250,000
Assembling	1,800,000	$.60	1,080,000	1,200,000	$.60	720,000
Inspecting and testing	20,000	$20	400,000	15,000	$20	300,000
Painting	1,800,000	$.10	180,000	1,200,000	$.10	120,000
Supervising	130,000	$6	780,000	70,000	$6	420,000
Total assigned costs			$3,520,000			$3,280,000

(c)

	Scissors Jack	Hydraulic Jack
Total costs assigned	$3,520,000	$3,280,000
Total units produced	200,000	80,000
Overhead cost per unit	$17.60	$41.00

(d) These data show that the total overhead assigned to 80,000 hydraulic jacks is nearly as great as the overhead assigned to 200,000 scissors jacks. But, the overhead cost per hydraulic jack is $41.00 and per scissors jack is only $17.60.

THE NAVIGATOR

ACTIVITY-BASED COSTING: A CLOSER LOOK

As the use of activity-based costing has grown, both its practical benefits and its limitations have now become apparent.

BENEFITS OF ABC

The primary benefit of ABC is **more accurate product costing** because:

1. **ABC leads to more cost pools** used to assign overhead costs to products. Instead of one plantwide pool (or even departmental pools) and a single cost driver, numerous activity cost pools with more relevant cost drivers are utilized. Costs are assigned more directly on a basis of the portion of multiple cost-driven activities that can be traced to each product.

2. **ABC leads to enhanced control over overhead costs.** Under ABC, many overhead costs can be traced directly to activities—some indirect costs become direct costs. Thus, managers become more aware of their responsibility to control the activities that generate those costs.

3. **ABC leads to better management decisions.** More accurate product costing should contribute to setting selling prices that will achieve desired product profitability levels. In addition, the more accurate cost data should be helpful in deciding whether to make or buy a product part or component.

Activity-based costing does not, in and of itself, change the amount of overhead costs, but it does in certain circumstances allocate those costs in a more accurate manner. And, if the score-keeping is more realistic, more accurate, and better understood, managers should be able to better understand cost behavior and overall profitability.

LIMITATIONS OF ABC

Although ABC systems often provide better product cost data than traditional volume-based systems, there are limitations:

1. **ABC can be expensive to use.** Many companies are discouraged from using ABC by the higher cost of identifying multiple activities and applying numerous cost drivers. Activity-based costing systems are more complex than traditional costing systems—sometimes significantly more complex. Is the cost of implementation greater than the benefits of greater accuracy? For some companies there may be no need to consider ABC at all because their existing system is sufficient, or because the costs of ABC outweigh the benefits.

2. **Some arbitrary allocations continue.** Even though more overhead costs can be assigned directly to products through multiple activity cost pools, certain overhead costs remain to be allocated by means of some arbitrary volume-based cost driver such as labor or machine hours.

BUSINESS INSIGHT
Management Perspective

Although most publicized ABC applications are in manufacturing companies or large service firms, ABC can be applied in a very small service business. Mahany Welding Supply, a small family-run welding service business in Rochester, NY, applied ABC to determine the cost of servicing customers and to identify feasible cost reduction opportunities.

Application of ABC to Mahany Welding provided information about the five employees who are involved in different activities of revenue generation—i.e., delivery of supplies (country versus city), welding services, repairs, telephone sales, field or door-to-door sales, repeat business sales, and cold call sales. Activity cost pools were assigned to the five revenue-producing employees using relevant cost drivers. ABC revealed annual net income by employee as follows: Employee #1, $65,431; Employee #2, $35,154; Employee #3, $13,731; Employee #4, ($10,957); Employee #5, ($46,180). This comparative information was an eye-opener to the owner of Mahany Welding—who was Employee #5!

Source: Michael Krupnicki and Thomas Tyson, "Using ABC to Determine the Cost of Servicing Customers," *Management Accounting,* December 31, 1997, pp. 40–46.

WHEN TO SWITCH TO ABC

Activity-based costing is a useful tool and under certain conditions is the appropriate costing system to use. The presence of one or more of the following factors indicates ABC as the superior costing system:

1. Product lines differ greatly in volume and manufacturing complexity.
2. Product lines are numerous, diverse, and require differing degrees of support services.
3. Overhead costs constitute a significant portion of total costs.

4. The manufacturing process or the number of products has changed significantly—for example, from labor-intensive to automated.

5. Production or marketing managers are ignoring data provided by the existing system and are instead using "bootleg" costing data or other alternative data when pricing or making other product decisions.

The redesign and installation of a new product-costing system is a significant decision that requires considerable cost and a major effort to accomplish. Therefore, financial managers need to be very cautious and deliberative when initiating changes in costing systems.

DECISION TOOLKIT

Decision Checkpoints	Info Needed for Decision	Tool to Use for Decision	How to Evaluate Results
When should we switch to ABC?	Knowledge of the products or product lines, the manufacturing process, overhead costs, and the needs of managers for accurate cost information	A detailed and accurate cost accounting system, cooperation between accountants and operating managers	Compare the results under both costing systems. If managers are better able to understand and control their operations using ABC, and the costs are not prohibitive, the switch would be beneficial.

VALUE-ADDED VERSUS NONVALUE-ADDED ACTIVITIES

Some companies that have experienced the benefits of activity-based costing have applied it to a broader range of management activities. **Activity-based management (ABM)** is an extension of ABC from a product costing system to a management function that focuses on reducing costs and improving processes and decision making. A refinement of activity-based costing used in ABM is the classification of activities as either value-added or nonvalue-added.

Value-added activities **increase the worth of a product or service** to customers; they involve resource usage and related costs that customers are willing to pay for. Value-added activities are the functions of actually manufacturing a product or performing a service—they increase the worth of the product or service. Examples of value-added activities in a manufacturing operation are engineering design, machining, assembly, painting, and packaging.

Nonvalue-added activities are production- or service-related activities that simply **add cost to, or increase the time spent on, a product or service without increasing its market value.** Examples typical of a manufacturing operation include the repair of machines; the storage of inventory; the moving of raw materials, assemblies, and finished product; building maintenance; inspections; and inventory control. Examples of nonvalue-added activities in service enterprises might include taking appointments, reception, bookkeeping, billing, traveling, ordering supplies, advertising, cleaning, and computer repair.

Identifying and labeling activities as value-added or nonvalue-added is part of the analysis of operations, the first step, in an ABC system. Illustration 4-13 is an activity flowchart. Activity flowcharts are often used to help identify the activities

STUDY OBJECTIVE
6
Differentiate between value-added and nonvalue-added activities.

that will be used in ABC costing. In the top part of this flowchart, activities are identified as value added or nonvalue added. The value added activities are highlighted in red, while the nonvalue added activities are highlighted in blue.

Note that in the lower part of the flowchart there are two rows showing the number of days spent on each activity. The first row shows the number of days spent on each activity under the current manufacturing process. The second row shows the number of days spent on each activity under management's proposed reengineered manufacturing process. The proposed changes would reduce time spent on nonvalue-added activities by 17 days. This 17-day improvement is entirely due to moving inventory more quickly through the processes—that is, by reducing inventory time in moving, storage, and waiting.

Illustration 4-13
Flowchart showing value-added and nonvalue-added activities

HEARTLAND MANUFACTURING COMPANY
Activity Flowchart

Activities

NVA	NVA	NVA	NVA	VA		NVA	NVA	VA	NVA	NVA	NVA	VA
Receive and Inspect Materials	Move and Store Materials	Move Materials to Production and Wait	Set up Machines	Machining: Drill	Machining: Lathe	Inspect	Move and Wait	Assembly	Inspect and Test	Move to Storage	Store Finished Goods	Package and Ship

Current Days 1 — 12 — 2.5 — 1.5 — 2 — 1 — .2 — 6 — 2 — .3 — .5 — 14 — 1

◄————————————— Total Current Average Time = 44 days —————————————►

Proposed Days 1 — 4 — 1.5 — 1.5 — 2 — 1 — .2 — 2 — 2 — .3 — .5 — 10 — 1

◄————————————— Total Proposed Average Time = 27 days —————————————►

Proposed reduction in nonvalue-added time = 17 days

VA = Value-added   NVA = Nonvalue-added

Not all activities labeled nonvalue-added are totally wasteful, nor can they be totally eliminated. For example, although inspection time is a nonvalue-added activity from a customer's perspective, few companies would eliminate their quality control functions. Similarly, moving and waiting time is nonvalue-added, but it would be impossible to completely eliminate. Nevertheless, because managers recognize the nonvalue-added characteristic of these activities, they are motivated to minimize them as much as possible. Attention to such matters is part of the growing practice of activity-based management which helps managers concentrate on **continuous improvement** of operations and activities.

HIERARCHY OF ACTIVITY LEVELS

STUDY OBJECTIVE
⑦
Understand the value of a hierarchy of activity levels to activity-based costing.

As previously mentioned, traditional costing systems are volume-driven—driven by units of output. Some activity costs are strictly variable and are caused by the production or acquisition of a single unit of product or the performance of a single unit of service. However, the recognition that other activity costs are not driven by output units has led to the development of a hierarchy of ABC activities, consisting of four levels. The four levels of activities are classified and defined as follows:

1. Unit-level activities. These are performed for each unit of production.
2. Batch-level activities. These are performed for each batch of products rather than each unit.

3. **Product-level activities.** These are performed in support of an entire product line, but are not always performed every time a new unit or batch of products is produced.

4. **Facility-level activities.** These are required to support or sustain an entire production process.

Greater accuracy in overhead cost allocation may be achieved by recognizing these four different levels of activities and, from them, developing specific activity cost pools and their related cost drivers. Illustration 4-14 graphically displays this four-level activity hierarchy, along with the types of activities and examples of costs traceable to those activities at each level.

Four Levels	Types of Activities	Examples of Costs
Unit-Level Activities		
	Machine-related: Drilling, cutting, milling, trimming, pressing	Direct material Depreciation of machines Power costs Machine maintenance
	Labor-related: Assembling, painting, sanding, sewing	Direct labor Fringe benefits Payroll taxes
Batch-Level Activities		
	Equipment setups Purchase ordering Inspection Material handling	Labor setup costs Purchasing clerical costs Material handling costs Quality control costs
Product-Level Activities		
	Product design Engineering changes Inventory management	Design costs Product engineering costs Inventory carrying costs
Facility-Level Activities		
	Plant management Personnel administration Training Security	Building depreciation Heating, air conditioning Property taxes Insurance

Illustration 4-14
Hierarchy of activity levels

This hierarchy provides managers and accountants a structured way of thinking about the relationships between activities and the resources they consume. In contrast, traditional volume-based costing recognizes only unit-level costs. **Failure to recognize this hierarchy of activities is one of the reasons that volume-based cost allocation causes distortions in product costing.**

As indicated earlier, allocating all overhead costs by bases that measure change in units produced can send false signals to managers: Dividing batch-, product-, or facility-level costs by the number of units produced gives the mistaken impression that these costs vary with the number of units. **The resources consumed by batch-, product-, and facility-level supporting ac-**

tivities do not vary at the unit level, nor can they be controlled at the unit level. The number of activities performed at the batch level goes up as the number of batches rises—not as the number of units within the batches changes. Similarly, what product-level activities are performed depends on the number of different products—not on how many units or batches are produced. And, facility-sustaining activity costs are not dependent upon the number of products, batches, or units produced. Batch-, product-, and facility-level costs can be controlled only by modifying batch-, product-, and facility-level activities.

B E F O R E   Y O U   G O   O N . . .

● Review It

1. What are the benefits of activity-based costing?
2. What are the limitations of activity-based costing?
3. What factors indicate the applicability of ABC as the superior costing system?
4. Of what benefit is classifying activities as value-added and nonvalue-added?
5. Of what importance to managers is the differentiation of activities into unit-level, batch-level, product-level, and facility-level?

● Do It

Morgan Toy Company manufactures six primary product lines in its Morganville plant. As a result of an activity analysis, the accounting department has identified eight activity cost pools. Each of the toy products is produced in large batches, with the whole plant devoted to one product at a time. Classify each of the following activities as either unit-level, batch-level, product-level, or facility-level: (a) engineering design, (b) machine setup, (c) inventory management, (d) plant cafeteria, (e) inspections after each setup, (f) polishing parts, (g) assembling parts, (h) health and safety.

Reasoning: Unit-, batch-, product- and facility-level costs can be controlled only by modifying unit-, batch-, product-, and facility-level activities. This hierarchy provides managers and accountants a structured way of thinking about the relationship between activities and the resources they consume.

THE
NAVIGATOR

Solution: (a) Product-level, (b) batch-level, (c) product-level, (d) facility-level, (e) batch-level, (f) unit-level, (g) unit-level, (h) facility-level.

DECISION TOOLKIT

Decision Checkpoints	Info Needed for Decision	Tool to Use for Decision	How to Evaluate Results
How can ABC help managers manage the business?	Activities classified as value-added and nonvalue-added; activities and costs classified by level of performance or incurrence	The activity analysis flowchart extended to identify each activity as value-added or non-value-added; activities and related costs classified as unit-level, batch-level, product-level, or facility-level	The flowchart should motivate managers to minimize nonvalue-added activities. Managers should better understand the relationship between activities and the resources they consume.

JUST-IN-TIME PROCESSING

The benefit of classifying activities as value-added and nonvalue-added is that managers know which activities to eliminate or minimize in order to reduce costs without affecting production efficiency or product quality. The activity analysis flowcharts shown in Illustration 4-13 revealed lots of inventory storage and waiting time—nonvalue-added activities—at several places in the operation. One way to minimize that inventory storage and waiting time is to implement **just-in-time processing.**

Traditionally, continuous process manufacturing has been based on a **just-in-case** philosophy: Inventories of raw materials are maintained **just in case** some items are of poor quality or a key supplier is shut down by a strike. Similarly, subassembly parts are manufactured and stored **just in case** they are needed later in the manufacturing process, and finished goods are completed and stored **just in case** unexpected and rush customer orders are received. This philosophy often results in a **push approach** in which raw materials and subassembly parts are pushed through each process. Traditional processing often results in the buildup of extensive manufacturing inventories.

Primarily in response to foreign competition, many U.S. firms have switched to **just-in-time (JIT) processing.** JIT manufacturing is dedicated to producing the right products (or parts) at the right time as they are needed. Under JIT processing, raw materials are received **just in time** for use in production, subassembly parts are completed **just in time** for use in finished goods, and finished goods are completed **just in time** to be sold. Illustration 4-15 shows the sequence of activities in just-in-time processing.

> **STUDY OBJECTIVE**
> ─────⑧─────
> Explain just-in-time (JIT) processing.

> **Helpful Hint** JIT is easier said than done. JIT requires a total commitment by management and employees, a complete change in philosophy, and significant changes in the way production is organized. JIT takes time to implement.

Illustration 4-15
Just-in-time processing

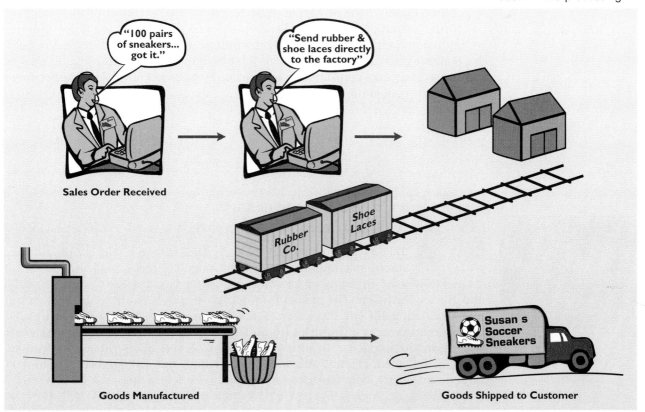

OBJECTIVE OF JIT PROCESSING

A primary objective of JIT is to eliminate all manufacturing inventories. Inventories are considered to have an adverse effect on net income because they tie up funds and storage space that could be made available for more productive purposes. JIT strives to eliminate inventories by using a **pull approach** in manufacturing. This approach begins at the final process (cell or work station) where a signal is sent via a computer to the next preceding work station indicating the exact materials (parts and subassemblies) needed for a time period, such as four hours or an eight-hour shift, to complete the production of a specified product. The preceding process, in turn, sends its signal to other processes so that there is a smooth continuous flow in the manufacturing process and no buildup of inventories at any point.

ELEMENTS OF JIT PROCESSING

There are three important elements in JIT processing:

Helpful Hint Buyer leverage is important in finding dependable suppliers. Companies like GM and GE have more success than smaller companies.

1. A company must have dependable suppliers who are willing to deliver on short notice exact quantities of raw materials according to precise quality specifications (even including multiple deliveries within the same day). Suppliers must also be willing to deliver the raw materials at specified work stations rather than at a central receiving department. This type of purchasing requires constant and direct communication with suppliers, which is facilitated by an on-line computer linkage between the company and its suppliers.

2. A multiskilled work force must be developed. Under JIT, machines are often strategically grouped around work cells or centers and much of the work is automated. As a result, one worker may have the responsibility to operate and maintain several different types of machines.

3. A total quality control system must be established throughout the manufacturing operations. Total quality control means **no defects.** Since only required quantities are signaled by the **pull approach,** any defects at any work station will shut down operations at subsequent work stations. Total quality control requires continuous monitoring by both employees and supervisors at each work station.

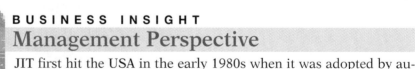

BUSINESS INSIGHT
Management Perspective

JIT first hit the USA in the early 1980s when it was adopted by automobile companies to meet foreign competition. It is now being successfully used in many companies, including General Electric, Caterpillar, and Harley-Davidson. The effects in most cases have been dramatic. For example, after using JIT for two years, a major division of Hewlett-Packard found that work in process inventories (in dollars) were down 82%, scrap/rework costs were down 30%, space utilization was down 40%, and labor efficiency improved 50%. As indicated, JIT not only reduces inventory but also enables a manufacturer to produce a better product faster and with less waste.

BENEFITS OF JIT PROCESSING

The major benefits of implementing JIT processing are:

1. Manufacturing inventories are significantly reduced or eliminated.
2. Product quality is enhanced.
3. Rework costs and inventory storage costs are reduced or eliminated.
4. Production cost savings are realized from the improved flow of goods through the processes.

> **Helpful Hint** Without its emphasis on quality control, JIT would be impractical or even impossible. In JIT, quality is engineered into the production process.

One of the major accounting benefits of JIT is the elimination of raw materials and work-in-process inventory accounts. In place of these accounts is one account, Raw and In-Process Inventory. All materials and conversion costs are charged to this account. Because of the reduction (or elimination) of in-process inventories, the computation of equivalent units of production is simplified.

DECISION TOOLKIT

Decision Checkpoints	Info Needed for Decision	Tool to Use for Decision	How to Evaluate Results
Can we benefit from installation and implementation of JIT processing?	Amounts of raw materials, work-in-process, and finished goods inventory; days that inventory is in storage or waiting to be processed or sold	Establish that we have dependable suppliers, a multi-skilled workforce, and a total quality control system	JIT should reduce or nearly eliminate inventories, storage, and waiting time and should minimize waste and defects. Inventory should be pulled rather than pushed through each production process.

BEFORE YOU GO ON . . .

● **Review It**
1. What is the difference between the push approach and the pull approach to handling inventories in a manufacturing operation?
2. What are the major benefits of implementing JIT?
3. What are the principal accounting effects of just-in-time processing?

THE NAVIGATOR

*U*SING THE DECISION TOOLKIT

Precor Company manufactures a line of high-end exercise equipment of commercial quality. The chief accountant has proposed changing from a traditional costing system to an activity-based costing system. The financial vice-president is not convinced of making the changes, so she requests that the next large order for equipment be costed under both systems for purposes of comparison and analysis. An order from Slim-Way Salons, Inc., for 150 low-impact treadmills is received and identified as the order to be subjected to dual costing. The following cost data relate to the Slim-Way order.

Data relevant to both costing systems

Direct materials	$55,500
Direct labor hours	820
Direct labor rate per hour	$18.00

Data relevant to the traditional costing system

Predetermined overhead rate is 300% of direct labor cost.

Data relevant to the activity-based costing system

Activity Cost Pools	Cost Drivers	Activity-Based Overhead Rate	Expected Use of Cost Drivers per Treadmill
Engineering design	Engineering hours	$30 per order	330
Machine setup	Setups	$200 per setup	22
Machining	Machine hours	$25 per hour	732
Assembly	Number of subassemblies	$8 per subassembly	1,450
Packaging and shipping	Packaging/shipping hours	$15 per hour	152
Building occupancy	Machine hours	$6 per hour	732

Instructions

Compute the total cost of the Slim-Way Salons, Inc., order under (a) the traditional costing system and (b) the activity-based costing system. As a result of this comparison, which costing system is Precor likely to adopt? Why?

Solution

(a) Traditional costing system:

Direct materials	$ 55,500
Direct labor (820 × $18)	14,760
Overhead assigned ($14,760 × 300%)	44,280
Total costs assigned to Slim-Way order	$114,540
Number of low-impact treadmills	150
Cost per unit	$763.60

(b) Activity-based costing system:

Direct materials		$ 55,500
Direct labor (820 × $18)		14,760
Overhead activities costs:		
Engineering design (330 hours @ $30)	9,900	
Machine setup (22 setups @ $200)	4,400	
Machining (732 machine hours @ $25)	18,300	
Assembly (1,450 subassemblies @ $8)	11,600	
Packaging and shipping (152 hours @ $15)	2,280	
Building occupancy (732 hours @ $6)	4,392	50,872
Total costs assigned to Slim-Way order		$121,132
Number of low-impact treadmills		150
Cost per unit		$807.55

(c) Precor Company will likely adopt ABC because of the differences in the cost per unit. More importantly, ABC provides greater insight into the sources and causes of the cost per unit. Managers are given greater insight into which activities to control in order to reduce costs.

THE NAVIGATOR

SUMMARY OF STUDY OBJECTIVES

1 **Recognize the difference between traditional costing and activity-based costing.** A traditional costing system allocates overhead to products on the basis of predetermined plantwide or department-wide volume of output rates such as direct labor or machine hours. An ABC system allocates overhead to identified activity cost pools which are then assigned to products using related cost drivers that measure the activities (resources) consumed.

2 **Identify the steps in the development of an activity-based costing system.** The development of an activity-based costing system involves (1) identifying the major activities that pertain to the manufacture of specific products or rendering of specific services and allocating overhead costs to activity cost pools, (2) identifying the cost drivers that accurately measure the activities consumed, and (3) assigning overhead costs for each activity cost pool to products or services using the cost drivers.

3 **Identify the activity cost pools used in activity-based costing.** To identify activity cost pools, a company must perform an analysis of each operation or process, documenting and timing every task, action, or transaction.

4 **Identify and use the activity cost drivers in activity-based costing.** Cost drivers identified for assigning activity cost pools must (a) accurately measure the actual consumption of the activity by the various products and (b) have related data easily available.

5 **Understand the benefits and limitations of activity-based costing.** What makes ABC a more accurate product costing system is (1) the increased number of cost pools used to assign overhead, (2) the enhanced control over overhead costs, and (3) the better management decisions. The limitations of ABC are (1) the higher analysis and measurement costs that accompany multiple activity centers and cost drivers and (2) the necessity still to allocate some costs arbitrarily.

6 **Differentiate between value-added and nonvalue-added activities.** Value-added activities increase the worth of a product or service, for which the customer is willing to pay. Nonvalue-added activities simply add cost to, or increase the time spent on, a product or service without increasing its market value. Awareness of these classifications encourages managers to reduce or eliminate the time spent on the nonvalue-added activities.

7 **Understand the value of a hierarchy of activity levels to activity-based costing.** Activities may be classified as unit-level, batch-level, product-level, and facility-level. Unit-, batch-, product-, and facility-level overhead costs are controlled by modifying unit-, batch-, product-, and facility-level activities, respectively. Nonrecognition of this hierarchy of levels can result in distorted product costing.

8 **Explain just-in-time (JIT) processing.** JIT is a manufacturing technique that is dedicated to producing the right products at the right time as needed, thereby reducing the amount of inventory and the time inventory is held. One of the principal accounting effects is that one account, Raw and In-Process Inventory, replaces both the raw materials and work-in-process inventory accounts.

THE NAVIGATOR

DECISION TOOLKIT—A SUMMARY

Decision Checkpoints	Info Needed for Decision	Tool to Use for Decision	How to Evaluate Results
When should we switch to ABC?	Knowledge of the products or product lines, the manufacturing process, overhead costs, and the needs of managers for accurate cost information	A detailed and accurate cost accounting system, cooperation between accountants and operating managers	Compare the results under both costing systems. If managers are better able to understand and control their operations using ABC, and the costs are not prohibitive, the switch would be beneficial.
How can ABC help managers manage the business?	Activities classified as value-added and nonvalue-added; activities and costs classified by level of performance or incurrence	The activity analysis flowchart extended to identify each activity as value-added or nonvalue-added; activities and related costs classified as unit-level, batch-level, product-level, or facility-level	The flowchart should motivate managers to minimize nonvalue-added activities. Managers should better understand the relationship between activities and the resources they consume.
Can we benefit from installation and implementation of JIT processing?	Amounts of raw materials, work-in-process, and finished goods inventory; days that inventory is in storage or waiting to be processed or sold	Establish that we have dependable suppliers, a multiskilled work force, and a total quality control system.	JIT should reduce or nearly eliminate inventories, storage, and waiting time and should minimize waste and defects. Inventory should be pulled rather than pushed through each production process.

APPENDIX 4A

ACTIVITY-BASED COSTING IN SERVICE INDUSTRIES

STUDY OBJECTIVE

9

Apply activity-based costing to service industries.

Although initially developed and implemented by manufacturing companies that produce products, activity-based costing has been widely adopted in service industries. ABC has been found to be a useful tool in such diverse industries as airlines, railroads, hotels, hospitals, banks, insurance companies, telephone companies, and financial services firms. The overall objective of installing ABC in service firms is no different than it is in a manufacturing company: to identify the key activities that generate costs and to keep track of how many of those activities are performed for each service that is rendered (by job, service, contract, or customer).

The general approach to identifying activities, activity cost pools, and cost drivers is used by a service company in the same manner as a manufacturing company. Also, the labeling of activities as value-added and nonvalue-added and the attempt to reduce or eliminate nonvalue-added activities as much as possible is just as valid in service industries as in manufacturing operations. And, the classification of activities into unit-level, batch-level, product-level, and facility-level activities also applies to service industries. What sometimes makes implementation of activity-based costing difficult in service industries is that **a larger proportion of overhead costs are facility-level costs** that cannot be directly traced to specific services rendered by the company.

To illustrate the application of activity-based costing to a service enterprise contrasted to traditional costing, we use a public accounting firm. This illustration is equally applicable to a law firm, consulting firm, architect, or any service firm that performs numerous services for a client as part of a job.

TRADITIONAL COSTING EXAMPLE

Assume that the public accounting firm of Check and Doublecheck prepares the following condensed annual budget (see Illustration 4A-1).

CHECK AND DOUBLECHECK, CPAs
Annual Budget

Revenue		$2,000,000
Direct labor	$ 600,000	
Overhead (expected)	1,200,000	
Total costs		1,800,000
Operating income		$ 200,000

$$\frac{\text{Estimated Overhead}}{\text{Direct labor cost}} = \text{Predetermined overhead rate}$$

$$\frac{\$1,200,000}{\$600,000} = 200\%$$

Illustration 4A-1
Condensed annual budget of a service firm under traditional costing

Under traditional costing the direct professional labor is the service performed and is the basis for overhead application to each audit job. To determine the operating income earned on any job, overhead is applied at the rate of 200% of actual direct professional labor cost incurred. For example, assume that the firm of Check and Doublecheck records $70,000 of actual direct professional labor cost during its audit of Plano Molding Company, which was billed an audit fee of $260,000. Under traditional costing, using 200% as the rate for applying overhead to the job, operating income related to the Plano Molding Company audit would be computed as shown in Illustration 4A-2:

CHECK AND DOUBLECHECK, CPAs
Plano Molding Company Audit

Revenue		$260,000
Less: Direct professional labor	$ 70,000	
Applied overhead (200% × $70,000)	140,000	210,000
Operating income		$ 50,000

Illustration 4A-2
Overhead applied under traditional costing system

In this simple service industry example, under traditional costing, only one direct cost item and only one overhead application rate is used.

ACTIVITY-BASED COSTING EXAMPLE

Illustration 4A-3
Condensed annual budget
of a service firm under
activity-based costing

Under activity-based costing, Check and Doublecheck's estimated annual overhead costs of $1,200,000 are recast and related to several activity cost pools and cost drivers that relate to the firm's audit activities. Illustration 4A-3 shows an annual overhead budget using an ABC system.

CHECK AND DOUBLECHECK, CPAs
Annual Overhead Budget

Activity Cost Pools	Cost Drivers	Estimated Overhead ÷	Expected Use of Cost Drivers per Activity =	Activity-Based Overhead Rates
Secretarial support	Direct professional hours	$ 210,000	30,000	$7 per hour
Direct labor fringe benefits	Direct labor cost	240,000	$600,000	$.40 per $1 labor cost
Printing and photocopying	Working paper pages	20,000	20,000	$1 per page
Computer support	CPU minutes	200,000	50,000	$4 per minute
Telephone and postage	None (Traced directly)	71,000	$71,000	Based on usage
Legal support	Hours used	129,000	860	$150 per hour
Insurance (professional liability, etc.)	Revenue billed	120,000	$2,000,000	$.06 per $1 revenue
Recruiting and training	Direct professional hours	210,000	30,000	$7 per hour
		$1,200,000		

Note that some of the overhead can be directly assigned (see Telephone and postage). The assignment of the individual overhead activity rates to the actual number of activities used in the performance of the Plano Molding audit results in total overhead assigned of $165,100 as shown in Illustration 4A-4.

Illustration 4A-4
Assignment of overhead
in a service company

CHECK AND DOUBLECHECK, CPAs
Plano Molding Company Audit

Activity Cost Pools	Cost Drivers	Actual Use of Drivers	Activity-Based Overhead Rates	Costs Assigned
Secretarial support	Direct professional hours	3,800	$7.00	$ 26,600
Direct labor fringe benefits	Direct labor cost	$70,000	$ .40	28,000
Printing and photocopying	Working paper pages	1,800	$1.00	1,800
Computer support	CPU minutes	8,600	$4.00	34,400
Telephone and postage	None (Traced directly)			8,700
Legal support	Hours used	156	$150.00	23,400
Insurance (professional liability, etc.)	Revenue billed	$260,000	$ .06	15,600
Recruiting and training	Direct professional hours	3,800	$7.00	26,600
				$165,100

Under activity-based costing, overhead of $165,100 is assigned to the Plano Molding Company audit, as compared to $140,000 under traditional costing. A comparison of total costs and operating margins is shown in Illustration 4A-5.

CHECK AND DOUBLECHECK, CPAs
Plano Molding Company Audit

	Traditional Costing		ABC	
Revenue		$260,000		$260,000
Expenses				
Direct professional labor	$ 70,000		$ 70,000	
Applied overhead	140,000		165,100	
Total expenses		210,000		235,100
Operating income		$ 50,000		$ 24,900
Profit margin		19.2%		9.6%

The comparison shows that the assignment of overhead costs under traditional costing is distorted. The total cost assigned to performing the audit of Plano Molding Company is greater under activity-based costing by $25,100, or 18% higher, and the profit margin is only half as great. Traditional costing gives the false impression of an operating profit of $50,000, more than double what it really is at $24,900.

SUMMARY OF STUDY OBJECTIVE FOR APPENDIX 4A

9 Apply activity-based costing to service industries. The overall objective of using ABC in service industries is no different than for manufacturing industries, that is, improved costing of services rendered (by job, service, contract, or customer). The general approach to costing is the same—analyze operations, identify activities, accumulate overhead costs by activity cost pools, and identify and use cost drivers to assign the cost pools to the services.

GLOSSARY

Activity Any event, action, transaction, or work sequence that causes incurrence of cost in producing a product or rendering a service. (p. 128)

Activity-based costing (ABC) An overhead cost allocation system that allocates overhead to multiple activity cost pools and assigns the activity cost pools to products or services by means of cost drivers that represent the activities used. (p. 128)

Activity-based management (ABM) An extension of ABC from a product costing system to a management function that focuses on reducing costs and improving processes and decision making. (p. 137)

Activity cost pool The overhead cost allocated to a distinct type of activity or related activities. (p. 128)

Batch-level activities Activities performed for each batch of products. (p. 138)

Cost driver Any factor or activity that has a direct cause–effect relationship with the resources consumed. In ABC cost drivers are used to assign activity cost pools to products or services. (p. 128)

Facility-level activities Activities required to support or sustain an entire production process and not dependent on number of products, batches, or units produced. (p. 139)

Just-in-time processing (JIT) A processing system dedicated to producing the right products (or parts) as they are needed, thereby reducing the amount of inventory. (p. 141)

Nonvalue-added activity An activity that adds cost to, or increases the time spent on, a product or service without increasing its market value. (p. 137)

Product-level activities Activities performed for and identifiable with an entire product line. (p. 139)

Unit-level activities Activities performed for each unit of production. (p. 138)

Value-added activity An activity that increases the worth of a product or service. (p. 137)

DEMONSTRATION PROBLEM

Spreadwell Paint Company manufactures two high-quality base paints: an **oil-based** paint and a **latex** paint. Both paints are manufactured in neutral white color only. The white base paints are sold to franchised retail paint and decorating stores where pigments are added to tint (color) the paint as desired by the customer. The oil-based paint is made from, thinned, and cleaned with organic solvents (petroleum products) such as mineral spirits or turpentine. The latex paint is made from, thinned, and cleaned with water; synthetic resin particles are suspended in the water and dry and harden when exposed to the air. Both paints are housepaints. Spreadwell uses the same processing equipment to produce both paints in differing production runs. Between batches, the vats and other processing equipment must be washed and cleaned.

Problem-Solving Strategies

Step 1. Identify the major activities that pertain to the manufacture of specific products and allocate manufacturing overhead costs to activity cost pools.

After analyzing the company's entire operations, Spreadwell's accountants and production managers have identified activity cost pools and accumulated annual budgeted overhead costs by pool as follows:

Activity Cost Pools	Estimated Overhead
Purchasing	$ 240,000
Processing (weighing and mixing, grinding, thinning and drying, straining)	1,400,000
Packaging (quarts, gallons, and 5-gallons)	580,000
Testing	240,000
Storage and inventory control	180,000
Washing and cleaning equipment	560,000
Total annual budgeted overhead	$3,200,000

Step 3. (a) Identify the cost drivers that accurately measure each activity's contribution to the finished product.

Following further analysis, activity cost drivers were identified and their expected use by product and activity were scheduled as follows:

Activity Cost Pool	Cost Drivers	Expected Cost Drivers per Activity	Expected Use of Drivers per Product Oil-based	Latex
Purchasing	Purchase orders	1,500 orders	800	700
Processing	Gallons processed	1,000,000 gals.	400,000	600,000
Packaging	Containers filled	400,000 containers	180,000	220,000
Testing	Number of tests	4,000 tests	2,100	1,900
Storing	Avg. gals. on hand	18,000 gals.	10,400	7,600
Washing	Number of batches	800 batches	350	450

Spreadwell has budgeted 400,000 gallons of oil-based paint and 600,000 gallons of latex paint for processing during the year.

Instructions

(a) Prepare a schedule showing the computations of the activity-based overhead rates.
(b) Prepare a schedule assigning each activity's overhead cost pool to each product.
(c) Compute the overhead cost per unit for each product.
(d) Classify each activity cost pool as value added or nonvalue added.

Solution to Demonstration Problem

Step 3. (b) Compute the activity based overhead rates.

(a) Computations of activity-based overhead rates:

SPREADWELL PAINT COMPANY

Activity Cost Pools	Estimated Overhead	÷	Expected Use of Cost Drivers	=	Activity-Based Overhead Rates
Purchasing	$ 240,000		1,500 orders		$160 per order
Processing	1,400,000		1,000,000 gallons		$1.40 per gallon
Packaging	580,000		400,000 containers		$1.45 per container
Testing	240,000		4,000 tests		$60 per test
Storing	180,000		18,000 gallons		$10 per gallon
Washing	560,000		800 batches		$700 per batch
	$3,200,000				

(b) Assignment of activity cost pools to products:

Step 4. Assign manufacturing overhead costs for each activity cost pool to products, using the activity-based overhead rates.

SPREADWELL PAINT COMPANY

	Oil-Based Paint			Latex Paint		
Activity Cost Pools	Expected Use of Drivers	Overhead Rates	Cost Assigned	Expected Use of Drivers	Overhead Rates	Cost Assigned
Purchasing	800	$160	$ 128,000	700	$160	$ 112,000
Processing	400,000	$1.40	560,000	600,000	$1.40	840,000
Packaging	180,000	$1.45	261,000	220,000	$1.45	319,000
Testing	2,100	$60	126,000	1,900	$60	114,000
Storing	10,400	$10	104,000	7,600	$10	76,000
Washing	350	$700	245,000	450	$700	315,000
Total overhead assigned			$1,424,000			$1,776,000

(c) Computation of overhead cost assigned per unit:

	Oil-Based Paint	Latex Paint
Total overhead cost assigned	$1,424,000	$1,776,000
Total gallons produced	400,000	600,000
Overhead cost per gallon	$3.56	$2.96

(d) Value-added activities: Processing and Packaging
Nonvalue-added activities: Purchasing, Testing, Storing, and Washing

Note: All asterisked Questions, Exercises, and Problems relate to material in the appendix to the chapter.

SELF-STUDY QUESTIONS

Answers are at the end of the chapter.

(SO 1) 1. Activity-based costing (ABC):
(a) can be used only in a process cost system.
(b) focuses on units of production.
(c) focuses on activities performed to produce a product.
(d) uses only a single basis of allocation.

(SO 1) 2. Activity-based costing:
(a) is the initial phase of converting to a just-in-time operating environment.
(b) can be used only in a job order costing system.

(c) is a two-phase overhead cost allocation system that identifies activity cost pools and cost drivers.
(d) uses direct labor as its primary cost driver.

3. Any activity that causes resources to be consumed is called a: (SO 3)
(a) just-in-time activity.
(b) facility-level activity.
(c) cost driver.
(d) nonvalue-added activity.

4. The overhead rate for Machine Setups is $100   (SO 4)
per setup. Products A and B have 80 and 60 set-

ups, respectively. The overhead assigned to each product is:
(a) Product A $8,000, Product B $8,000.
(b) Product A $8,000, Product B $6,000.
(c) Product A $6,000, Product B $6,000.
(d) Product A $6,000, Product B $8,000.

(SO 4)   5. A relevant facility-level cost driver for heating costs is:
(a) machine hours.
(b) direct material.
(c) floor space.
(d) direct labor cost.

(SO 6)   6. An activity that adds costs to the product but does not increase its market value is a:
(a) value-added activity.
(b) cost driver.
(c) cost–benefit activity.
(d) nonvalue-added activity.

(SO 6)   7. The following activity is value-added:
(a) Storage of raw materials.
(b) Moving parts from machine to machine.
(c) Turning a piece of metal on a lathe.
(d) All of the above.

(SO 4)   8. Donna Crawford Co. has identified an activity cost pool to which it has allocated estimated overhead of $1,920,000 and determined the expected use of cost drivers per that activity to be 160,000 inspections. Widgets require 40,000

inspections, Gadgets 30,000 inspections, and Targets, 90,000 inspections. The overhead assigned to each product is:
(a) Widgets $40,000, Gadgets $30,000, Targets $90,000.
(b) Widgets $480,000, Gadgets $360,000, Targets $108,000.
(c) Widgets $360,000, Gadgets $480,000, Targets $1,080,000.
(d) Widgets $480,000, Gadgets $360,000, Targets $1,080,000.

9. Under just-in-time processing: (SO 8)
(a) raw materials are received just in time for use in production.
(b) subassembly parts are completed just in time for use in assembling finished goods.
(c) finished goods are completed just in time to be sold.
(d) All of the above.

10. The primary objective of just-in-time processing is to: (SO 8)
(a) accumulate overhead in activity cost pools.
(b) eliminate or reduce all manufacturing inventories.
(c) identify relevant activity cost drivers.
(d) identify value-added activities.

THE NAVIGATOR

QUESTIONS

1. Under what conditions is direct labor a valid basis for allocating overhead?

2. What has happened in recent industrial history to invalidate direct labor as the primary basis for allocating overhead to products?

3. In an automated manufacturing environment, what basis of overhead allocation is frequently more relevant than direct labor hours? *machine hours*

4. Why is it generally true that high-volume products subsidize low-volume products under a traditional costing system? *Overhead is allocated in a direct-cost basis.*

5. (a) What are the principal differences between activity-based costing (ABC) and traditional product costing? *disadvantage = Too Expensive*
   (b) What assumptions must be met for ABC costing to be useful?

6. What is the formula for computing activity-based overhead rates?

7. What steps are involved in developing an activity-based costing system?

8. Explain the preparation and use of an activity flow-chart in an ABC system.

9. What is an activity cost pool?

10. What is a cost driver?

11. What makes a cost driver accurate and appropriate?

12. What is the formula for assigning activity cost pools to products?

13. What are the benefits of activity-based costing?

14. What are the limitations of activity-based costing?

15. Under what conditions is ABC generally the superior overhead costing system?

16. What two extensions or refinements have been made to enhance the efficiency and effectiveness of ABC for use in managing costs?

*17. Of what benefit is classifying activities as value-added and nonvalue-added?

18. What is the relevance of the hierarchy of levels of activity to ABC?

19. (a) Describe the philosophy and approach of just-in-time processing.
    (b) Identify the major elements of JIT processing.

20. In what ways is the application of ABC to service industries the same as its application to manufacturing companies?

BRIEF EXERCISES

BE4-1 Apex Co. identifies the following activities that pertain to manufacturing overhead: Materials Handling, Machine Setups, Factory Machine Maintenance, Factory Supervision, and Quality Control. For each activity, identify an appropriate cost driver.

Identify cost drivers.
(SO 4)

BE4-2 Safety Products Company manufactures four products in a single production facility. The company uses activity-based costing. The following activities have been identified through the company's activity analysis: (a) inventory maintenance, (b) machine setups, (c) employee training, (d) quality inspections, (e) material ordering, (f) drilling operations, and (g) building maintenance. For each activity, name a cost driver that might be used to assign overhead costs to products.

Identify cost drivers.
(SO 4)

BE4-3 Dooley Company identifies three activities in its manufacturing process: machine setups, machining, and inspections. Estimated annual overhead cost for each activity is $180,000, $300,000, and $70,000, respectively. The cost driver for each activity and the expected annual usage are: number of setups 1,000, machine hours 25,000, and number of inspections 1,400. Compute the overhead rate for each activity.

Compute activity-based overhead rates.
(SO 4)

BE4-4 Trimline Coat Company uses activity-based costing as the basis for information to set prices for its six lines of seasonal coats. Compute the activity-based overhead rates using the following budgeted data for each of the activity cost pools.

Compute activity-based overhead rates.
(SO 4)

Activity Cost Pool	Estimated Overhead	Expected Use of Cost Drivers per Activity
Designing	$ 480,000	12,000 Designer hours
Sizing and cutting	3,200,000	160,000 Machine hours
Stitching and trimming	1,400,000	70,000 Labor hours
Blocking and packing	320,000	32,000 Finished units

BE4-5 Platinum Technology, Inc., a manufacturer of woofers and chips for computers, employs activity-based costing. Compute activity-based overhead rates from the following budgeted data for each of the activity cost pools.

Compute activity-based overhead rates.
(SO 4)

Activity Cost Pool	Estimated Overhead	Expected Use of Cost Drivers per Activity
Ordering and receiving	$ 90,000	10,000 Orders
Annealing	102,400	32,000 Pounds
Etching	441,000	60,000 Machine hours
Soldering	1,298,000	441,000 Labor hours
Packing and shipping	439,600	28,000 Boxes

BE4-6 Dewey Yaeger Novelty Company identified the following activities in its production and support operations. Classify each of these activities as either value added or nonvalue added.

Classify activities as value or nonvalue added.
(SO 6)

1. Purchasing
2. Receiving
3. Design engineering
4. Storing inventory
5. Cost accounting
6. Moving work-in-process
7. Inspecting and testing
8. Painting and packing

BE4-7 Holiday Construction Company, a builder of pole barns on order for farm machinery storage, identifies the six activities: (1) receiving and handling materials, (2) setting up and moving scaffolding, (3) setting poles, (4) siding, (5) roofing, (6) inspecting. Classify each of their activities as value added or nonvalue added.

Classify activities as value or nonvalue added.
(SO 6)

BE4-8 Richard's Photo Center is a large film developing and processing center that serves 130 outlets in grocery stores, service stations, camera and photo shops, and drug stores in 16 nearby towns. The Center operates 24 hours a day, six days a week. Classify each of the following activity costs of the Center as either unit-level, batch-level, product-level, or facility-level.

Classify activities according to level.
(SO 7)

(a) Developing fluids
(b) Photocopy paper
(c) Depreciation of machinery
(d) Setups for enlargements
(e) Supervisor's salary

(f) Ordering materials
(g) Pickup and delivery
(h) Commission to dealers
(i) Insurance on building
(j) Loading developing machines

Classify activities according to level.

(SO 7)

BE4-9 Elburn Plastics Company operates 20 injection molding machines in the production of fishing tackle boxes of four different sizes: appropriately named, the minnow, the bass, the mackerel, and the shark. Classify each of the following costs as unit-level, batch-level, product-level, or facility-level.
(a) First shift supervisor's salary
(b) Powdered raw plastic
(c) Dyes for costing plastic components
(d) Depreciation on injection molding machines
(e) Changing dyes on machines
(f) Moving components to assembly department
(g) Engineering design
(h) Employee health and medical insurance coverage

Classify service company activities as value or nonvalue added.

(SO 6, 9)

*BE4-10 Moyer and Stevenson is an architectural firm that is contemplating the installation of activity-based costing. The following activities are performed daily by staff architects. Classify these activities as value added or nonvalue added: (1) designing and drafting, 3 hours; (2) staff meetings, 1 hour; (3) on-site supervision, 2 hours; (4) lunch, 1 hour; (5) consultation with client on specifications, 1.5 hours; (6) entertaining a prospective client for dinner, 2 hours.

*E*XERCISES

Assign overhead using traditional costing and ABC.

(SO 1, 4)

E4-1 Baseler Corporation manufactures safes, large mobile safes, and large walk-in stationary bank safes. As part of its annual budgeting process, Baseler is analyzing the profitability of its two products. Part of this analysis involves estimating the amount of overhead to be allocated to each product line. The following information relates to overhead:

	Mobile Safes	Walk-in Safes
Units planned for production	200	50
Material moves per product line	300	200
Purchase orders per product line	450	350
Direct labor hours per unit	600	1,800
Estimated material-handling costs	$120,000	
Estimated purchasing activity costs	$ 84,000	

Instructions
(a) Under traditional costing, which assigns overhead on the basis of direct-labor hours:
   (1) What material handling costs are assigned to:
      (a) One mobile safe?
      (b) One walk-in safe?
   (2) What purchasing activity costs are assigned to:
      (a) One mobile safe?
      (b) One walk-in safe?
(b) Under activity-based costing (ABC):
   (1) What material handling costs are assigned to:
      (a) One mobile safe?
      (b) One walk-in safe?
   (2) What purchasing activity costs are assigned to:
      (a) One mobile safe?
      (b) One walk-in safe?

E4-2 Waterman Clothing Company manufactures its own designed and labeled sports attire and sells its products through catalog sales and retail outlets. While Waterman has for years used activity-based costing in its manufacturing activities, it has always used traditional costing in assigning its selling costs to its product lines. Selling costs have traditionally been assigned to Waterman's product lines at a rate of 55% of direct material costs. Its direct material costs for the month of January for Waterman's "high intensity" line of attire are $395,000. The company has decided to extend activity-based costing to its selling costs. Data relating to the "high intensity" line of products for the month of January are as follows:

Assign overhead using traditional costing and ABC; classify activities as value or nonvalue added and by level.
(SO 1, 4, 6)

Activity Cost Pool	Cost Driver	Overhead Rates	Number of Cost Drivers Used per Activity
Sales commissions	Dollar sales	$.04 per dollar sales	$940,000
Advertising—TV/Radio	Minutes	$400 per minute	200
Advertising—Newspaper	Column inches	$10 per column inch	1,800
Catalogs	Catalogs mailed	$3 per catalog	50,000
Cost of catalog sales	Catalog orders	$1 per catalog order	8,400
Credit and collection	Dollar sales	$.03 per dollar sales	$940,000

Instructions
(a) Compute the selling costs to be assigned to the "high-intensity" line of attire for the month of January: (1) using the traditional product costing system (direct material cost is the cost driver), and (2) using activity-based costing.
(b) By what amount does the traditional product costing system undercost or overcost the "high-intensity" product line?
(c) Classify each of the activities as value added or nonvalue added.

E4-3 Dietary Products, Inc., uses a traditional product costing system to assign overhead costs uniformly to all products. To meet Food and Drug Administration requirements and to assure its customers of safe, sanitary, and nutritious food, Dietary engages in a high level of quality control. Dietary assigns its quality-control overhead costs to all products at a rate of 18% of direct-labor costs. Its direct-labor cost for the month of July for its low-calorie dessert line is $55,000. In response to repeated requests from its financial vice president, Dietary's management agrees to adopt activity-based costing. Data relating to the low-calorie dessert line for the month of July are as follows:

Assign overhead using traditional costing and ABC; classify activities as value or nonvalue added and by level.
(SO 1, 4, 6)

Activity Cost Pool	Cost Driver	Overhead Rate	Number of Cost Drivers Used per Activity
Material receiving inspections	Number of pounds	$.63 per pound	5,800 pounds
In-process inspections	Number of servings	$.32 per serving	10,000 servings
FDA certification	Customer orders	$11.80 per order	400 orders

Instructions
(a) Compute the quality-control overhead cost to be assigned to the low-calorie dessert product line for the month of July: (1) using the traditional product costing system (direct labor cost is the cost driver), and (2) using activity-based costing.
(b) By what amount does the traditional product costing system undercost or overcost the low-calorie dessert line?
(c) Classify each of the activities as value added or nonvalue added.

E4-4 Speedy Prints Company is a small printing and copying firm with three high-speed offset printing presses, five copiers, (two color and three black and white), one collator, one cutting and folding machine, and one FAX machine. Interested in improving its pricing practices, owner-manager Cole Sondgeroth is installing activity-based accounting. Additionally, Cole employs five employees—two printers/designers, one receptionist/bookkeeper, one sales and copy machine operator, and one janitor/delivery clerk. Cole can operate any of the machines and, in addition to managing the entire operation, he performs the training, designing, selling, and marketing functions.

Identify activity cost pools.
(SO 3)

Instructions

As Speedy Prints' independent accountant who prepares payroll tax forms, state and federal income and sales tax forms, and quarterly financial statements, you have been asked to identify the activities that would be used to accumulate overhead costs for assignment to jobs and customers. Using your knowledge (and imagination) of a small printing and copying firm, identify at least twelve activity cost pools as the start of an activity-based costing system for Speedy Prints Company.

Identify activity cost pools and cost drivers.

(SO 3, 4)

E4-5   Nofftz Corporation manufactures snowmobiles in its Rhinelander, Wisconsin plant. The following costs are budgeted for the first quarter's operations:

Direct factory labor-wages	$ 860,000
Raw material and purchased components	1,200,000
Engineering design	140,000
Engineering development	60,000
Depreciation, plant	210,000
Depreciation, machinery	520,000
Machine setup, wages	15,000
Machine setup, supplies	4,000
Inspections	16,000
Tests	4,000
Insurance, plant	110,000
Property taxes	29,000
Natural gas, heating	19,000
Electricity, plant lighting	21,000
Electricity, machinery	36,000
Custodial wages	17,000

Instructions

Classify the above costs of Nofftz Corporation into activity cost pools and identify a cost driver that may be used to assign each cost pool to each line of snowmobiles.

Identify activity cost drivers.

(SO 4)

E4-6   Henry Anderson's Valhalla Vineyards in Paso Robles, California, produces three varieties of wine: Merlot, Viognier, and Pinot Noir. His winemaster, Sue, has identified the following activities as cost pools for accumulating overhead and assigning it to products:

1. Culling and replanting—dead or overcrowded vines are culled and new vines are planted or relocated. (Separate vineyards by variety.)
2. Trimming—at the end of the harvest the vines are cut and trimmed back in preparation for the next season.
3. Tying—the posts and wires are reset and vines are tied to the wires for the dormant season.
4. Spraying—the vines are sprayed with chemicals for protection against insects and fungi.
5. Harvesting—the grapes are hand-picked, placed in carts, and transported to the crushers.
6. Stemming and crushing—cartfuls of bunches of grapes of each variety are separately loaded into machines which remove stems and gently crush the grapes.
7. Pressing and filtering—the crushed grapes are transferred to presses which mechanically remove the juices and filter out bulk and impurities.
8. Fermentation—the grape juice, by variety, is fermented in either stainless-steel tanks or oak barrels.
9. Aging—the wines are aged in either stainless-steel tanks or oak barrels for one to three years depending on variety.
10. Bottling and corking—bottles are machine-filled and corked.
11. Labeling and boxing—each bottle is labeled normally as is each nine-bottle case with the name of the vintner, vintage, and variety.
12. Storing—packaged and boxed bottles are stored awaiting shipment.
13. Shipping—the wine is shipped to distributors and private retailers.
14. Maintenance of buildings and equipment—printing, repairs, replacements, and general maintenance are performed in the off-season.
15. Heating and air-conditioning of plant and offices.

Instructions
For each of Valhalla's fifteen activity cost pools, identify a probable cost driver that might be used to assign overhead costs to its three wine varieties.

E4-7 In an effort to expand the usefulness of its activity-based costing system, Henry Anderson's Valhalla Vineyards employs activity-based management techniques. One of these ABM techniques is qualifying its activities as either value added or nonvalue added.

Classify activities as value added or nonvalue added.
(SO 6)

Instructions
Using Valhalla's list of fifteen activity cost pools in Exercise 4-6, classify each of the activities as either value added or nonvalue added.

E4-8 Amend Instrument, Inc., manufactures two products: missile range instruments and space pressure gauges. During January, 50 range instruments and 300 pressure gauges were produced, and overhead costs of $81,000 were incurred. An analysis of overhead costs reveals the following activities:

Compute overhead rates and assign overhead using ABC.
(SO 4, 5)

Activity	Cost Driver	Total Cost
1. Materials handling	Number of requisitions	$30,000
2. Machine setups	Number of setups	27,000
3. Quality inspections	Number of inspections	24,000

The cost driver volume for each product was as follows:

Cost Driver	Instruments	Gauges	Total
Number of requisitions	400	600	1,000
Number of setups	150	300	450
Number of inspections	200	400	600

Instructions
(a) Determine the overhead rate for each activity.
(b) Assign the manufacturing overhead costs for January to the two products using activity-based costing.
(c) ▭▭▭▷ Write a memorandum to the president of Amend Instrument explaining the benefits of activity-based costing.

E4-9 Malou Nelson, Inc., manufactures five models of kitchen appliances at its Peoria plant. The company is installing activity-based costing and has identified the following activities performed at its Peoria plant:

Classify activities by level.
(SO 7)

 1. Designing new models.
 2. Purchasing raw materials and parts.
 3. Receiving and inspecting raw materials and parts.
 4. Storing and managing inventory.
 5. Interviewing and hiring new personnel.
 6. Machine forming sheet steel into appliance parts.
 7. Manually assembling parts into appliances.
 8. Maintaining and repairing machinery and equipment.
 9. Insuring all tangible fixed assets.
10. Supervising production.
11. Training all employees of the company.
12. Painting and packaging finished appliances.

Instructions
Classify each activity as either unit-level, batch-level, product-level, or facility-level.

E4-10 Having analyzed its Peoria plant operations for purposes of installing activity-based costing, Malou Nelson, Inc., identified its activity cost centers. It now needs to identify relevant activity cost drivers in order to assign overhead costs to its products.

Identify activity cost drivers.
(SO 4)

Instructions
Using the activities listed in Exercise 4-9, identify for each activity one or more cost drivers that might be used to assign overhead to Malou Nelson's five products.

Classify activities as value added or nonvalue added.

(SO 6)

E4-11 Malou Nelson, Inc., is interested in using its activity-based costing system to improve its operating efficiency and its profit margins by applying activity-based management techniques. As part of this undertaking, you have been asked to classify its Peoria plant activities as value added or nonvalue added.

Instructions

Using the list of activities identified in Exercise 4-9, classify each activity as either value added or nonvalue added.

Classify activities by level.

(SO 7)

E4-12 Having itemized its costs for the first quarter of next year's budget, Nofftz Corporation desires to install an activity-based costing system. First it identified the activity cost pools in which to accumulate factory overhead; second, it identified the relevant cost drivers. (This was done in Exercise 4-5.)

Instructions

Using the activity cost pools identified in Exercise 4-5, classify each of those cost pools as either unit-level, batch-level, product-level, or facility-level.

Classify activities by level.

(SO 7)

E4-13 Tim Struthers & Sons, Inc., is a small manufacturing company in Naperville that uses activity-based costing. Struthers & Sons accumulates overhead in the following activity cost pools:

1. Managing parts inventory.
2. Hiring personnel.
3. Purchasing.
4. Designing products.
5. Testing prototypes.

6. Setting up equipment.
7. Inspecting machined parts.
8. Training employees.
9. Machining.
10. Assembling.

Instructions

For each activity cost pool, indicate whether the activity cost pool would be unit-level, batch-level, product-level, or facility-level.

Classify service company activities by level.

(SO 6, 9)

*E4-14 Groat and Groat is a law firm that is initiating an activity-based costing system. Jim Groat, the senior partner and strong supporter of ABC, has prepared the following list of activities performed by a typical attorney in a day at the firm.

Activity	Hours
Writing contracts and letters	1.0
Attending staff meetings	0.5
Taking depositions	2.0
Doing research	1.0
Traveling to/from court	1.0
Contemplating legal strategy	1.5
Eating lunch	0.5
Litigating a case in court	2.0
Entertaining a prospective client	1.5

Instructions

Classify each of the activities listed by Jim Groat as value added or nonvalue added; be able to defend your classification. How much was value-added time and how much was nonvalue-added?

Problems: Set A

Assign overhead using traditional costing and ABC; compute unit costs; classify activities as value or nonvalue added.

(SO 1, 4, 6)

P4-1A Spartan Safety Company manufactures steel cylinders and nozzles for two models of fire extinguishers: (1) a home fire extinguisher and (2) a commercial fire extinguisher. The **home model** is a high-volume (54,000 units) half-gallon cylinder that holds $2\frac{1}{2}$ pounds of multipurpose dry chemical at 480 PSI. The **commercial model** is a low-volume (10,000 units) two-gallon cylinder that holds 10 pounds of multi-purpose dry chemical at 390 PSI. Both products require 1.5 hours of direct labor for completion. Therefore, total annual direct labor hours are 96,000 [1.5 hrs. × (54,000 + 10,000)]. Expected annual manufacturing overhead is $1,478,320. Thus, the predetermined overhead rate is $15.40 ($1,478,320 ÷ 96,000) per direct labor hour. The direct materials cost per unit is $17.50 for the home model and $26.75 for the commercial model. The direct labor cost is $18 per unit for both the home and the commercial models.

Spartan's managers identified six activity cost pools and related cost drivers and accumulated overhead by cost pool as follows:

Activity Cost Pool	Cost Driver	Estimated Overhead	Expected Use of Cost Drivers	Expected Use of Drivers by Product	
				Home	Commercial
Receiving	Pounds	$ 73,920	336,000	216,000	120,000
Forming	Machine hours	147,000	35,000	27,000	8,000
Assembling	Number of parts	381,600	212,000	162,000	50,000
Testing	Number of tests	51,000	25,500	15,500	10,000
Painting	Gallons	52,080	6,510	4,510	2,000
Packing and shipping	Pounds	772,800	336,000	216,000	120,000
		$1,478,400			

Instructions

(a) Under traditional product costing, compute the total unit cost of both products using the information above. Prepare a simple comparative schedule of the individual costs by product (similar to Illustration 4-5).

(b) Under ABC, prepare a schedule showing the computations of the activity-based overhead rates (per cost driver), using the information above.

(c) Prepare a schedule assigning each activity's overhead cost pool to each product based on the use of cost drivers (include a computation of overhead cost per unit, rounding to the nearest cent).

(d) Compute the overhead cost per unit for each product under ABC.

(e) Classify each of the activities as a value-added activity or a nonvalue-added activity.

(f) Comment on (1) the comparative overhead cost per unit for the two products under ABC and (2) the comparative total costs per unit under traditional costing and ABC.

P4-2A Novacek Electronics manufactures two large-screen television models: the Royale which sells for $1,500, and a new model, the Majestic, which sells for $1,200. The production cost computed per unit under traditional costing for each model in 1999 was as follows:

Assign overhead to products using ABC and evaluate decision.

(SO 4)

Traditional Costing	Royale	Majestic
Direct materials	$ 700	$420
Direct labor ($20 per hour)	100	80
Manufacturing overhead ($40 per DLH)	200	160
Total per unit cost	$1,000	$660

In 1999, Novacek manufactured 30,000 units of the Royale and 10,000 units of the Majestic. The overhead rate of $40 per direct labor hour was determined by dividing total expected manufacturing overhead of $7,600,000 by the total direct labor hours (190,000) for the two models.

Under traditional costing, the gross profit on the models was: Royale $500 ($1,500 − $1,000) and Majestic $540 ($1,200 − $660). Because of this difference, management is considering phasing out the Royale model and increasing the production of the Majestic model.

Before finalizing its decision, management asks the controller of Novacek to prepare an analysis using activity-based costing (ABC). The controller accumulates the following information about overhead for the year ended December 31, 1999:

Activity	Cost Driver	Estimated Overhead	Expected Use of Cost Drivers	Activity-Based Overhead Rate
Purchasing	Number of orders	$1,200,000	30,000	$40
Machine setups	Number of setups	900,000	15,000	60
Machining	Machine hours	4,800,000	160,000	30
Quality control	Number of inspections	700,000	35,000	20

The cost drivers used for each product were:

Cost Driver	Royale	Majestic	Total
Purchase orders	10,000	20,000	30,000
Machine setups	5,000	10,000	15,000
Machine hours	100,000	60,000	160,000
Inspections	10,000	25,000	35,000

Instructions

(a) Assign the total 1999 manufacturing overhead costs to the two products using activity-based costing (ABC).

(b) What was the cost per unit and gross profit of each model using ABC costing?

(c) ▦▭▭▷ Are management's future plans for the two models sound? Explain.

Assign overhead costs using traditional costing and ABC; compare results.

(SO 1, 4)

P4-3A Designed Stairs Co. of Aurora designs and builds factory-made premium wooden stairs for homes. The manufactured stair components (spindles, risers, hangers, hand rails) permit installation of stairs of varying lengths and widths, but all are of white oak wood. Its budgeted manufacturing overhead costs for the year 2000 are as follows:

Overhead Cost Pools	Amount
Purchasing	$ 57,000
Handling materials	82,000
Production (cutting, milling, finishing)	200,000
Setting up machines	84,840
Inspecting	90,000
Inventory control (raw materials and finished goods)	126,000
Utilities	180,000
Total budget overhead costs	$819,840

For the last four years, Designed Stairs Co. has been charging overhead to products on the basis of machine hours. For the year 2000, 100,000 machine hours are budgeted.

Larry Rogers, owner-manager of Designed Stairs Co., recently directed his accountant, Denise Ramos, to implement the activity-based costing system that she has repeatedly proposed. At Larry Rogers' request, Denise and the production foreman identify the following cost drivers and their usage for the previously budgeted overhead cost pools:

Overhead Cost Pools	Activity Cost Drivers	Expected Use of Cost Drivers
Purchasing	Number of orders	600
Handling materials	Number of moves	8,000
Production (cutting, milling, finishing)	Direct labor hours	100,000
Setting up machines	Number of setups	1,200
Inspecting	Number of inspections	6,000
Inventory control (raw materials and finished goods)	Number of components	168,000
Utilities	Square feet occupied	90,000

Richard Way, sales manager, has received an order for 280 stairs from Mall Builders, Inc., a large housing development contractor. At Richard's request, Denise prepares cost estimates for producing components for 280 stairs so Richard can submit a contract price per stair to Mall Builders. She accumulates the following data for the production of 280 stairways:

Direct materials	$103,600
Direct labor	$112,000
Machine hours	14,500
Direct labor hours	5,000
Number of purchase orders	60
Number of material moves	800
Number of machine setups	100

Number of inspections	450
Number of components	16,000
Number of square feet occupied	8,000

Instructions
(a) Compute the predetermined overhead rate using traditional costing with machine hours as the basis.
(b) What is the manufacturing cost per stairway under traditional costing?
(c) What is the manufacturing cost per stairway under the proposed activity-based costing? (Prepare all of the necessary schedules.)
(d) ▭▭▭▭▷ Which of the two costing systems is preferable in pricing decisions and why?

P4-4A Wise and Otherwise is a public accounting firm that offers two primary services, auditing and tax return preparation. A controversy has developed between the partners of the two service lines as to who is contributing the greater amount to the bottom line. The contentious area is the assignment of overhead. The tax partners argue for assigning overhead on the basis of 37% of direct labor dollars while the audit partners argue for implementing activity-based costing. The partners agree to use next year's budgeted data for purposes of analysis and comparison. The following overhead data are collected to develop the comparison.

Assign overhead costs to services using traditional costing and ABC; compute overhead rates and unit costs; compare results.
(SO 1, 4, 6, 9)

			Expected Use of Cost	Expected Use of Cost Drivers per Service	
Activity Cost Pool	Cost Driver	Estimated Overhead	Drivers	Audit	Tax
Employee training	Direct labor dollars	$209,000	$1,900,000	$1,000,000	$900,000
Typing and secretarial	Number of reports/forms	73,200	2,400	550	1,850
Computing	Number of minutes	180,000	60,000	25,000	35,000
Facility rental	Number of employees	114,000	38	20	18
Travel	Per expense reports	126,800	Direct	86,800	40,000
		$703,000			

Instructions
(a) Using traditional product costing as proposed by the tax partners, compute the total cost of both services (audit and tax) of Wise and Otherwise.
(b) (1) Using activity-based costing, prepare a schedule showing the computations of the activity-based overhead rates (per cost driver).
  (2) Prepare a schedule assigning each activity's overhead cost pool to each service based on the use of the cost drivers.
  (3) Compute the overhead cost per unit for each product under ABC.
(c) Classify each of the activities as a value-added activity or a nonvalue-added activity.
(d) ▭▭▭▭▷ Comment on the comparative overhead cost per unit for the two products under both traditional costing and ABC.

PROBLEMS: SET B

P4-1B In-Hair-It, Inc., manufactures hair curlers and blow-dryers. The hand-held hair curler is In-Hair-Its' high volume product (80,000 units annually). It is a "large barrel," 20-watt, triple-heat appliance designed to appeal to the teenage market segment with its glow-in-the-dark handle. The handheld blow dryer is In-Hair-It's lower volume product (40,000 units annually). It is a three-speed, 2000 watt appliance with a "cool setting" a removable filter, and it also is designed for the teen market. Both products require one hour of direct labor for completion. Therefore, total annual direct labor hours are 120,000 (80,000 + 40,000). Expected annual manufacturing overhead is $468,000. Thus, the predetermined overhead rate is $3.90 per direct labor hour. The direct materials cost per unit is $5.15 for the hair curler and $9.50 for the blow-dryer. The direct labor cost is $7.50 per unit for the hair curler and the blow-dryer.

Assign overhead using traditional costing and ABC; compute unit costs; classify activities as value or nonvalue added.
(SO 1, 4, 6)

In-Hair-It purchases most of the parts from suppliers and assembles the finished product at its Cedar Rapids, Iowa plant. It recently adopted activity-based costing, which after this year-end will totally replace its traditional direct labor-based cost accounting system. In-Hair-It has identified the following six activity cost pools and related cost drivers and assembled the following information:

Activity Cost Pool	Cost Driver	Estimated Overhead	Expected Use of Cost Drivers	Expected Use of Cost Drivers per Product — Curlers	Expected Use of Cost Drivers per Product — Dryers
Purchasing	Orders	$ 57,000	500	170	330
Receiving	Pounds	36,960	168,000	70,000	98,000
Assembling	Parts	195,040	848,000	424,000	424,000
Testing	Tests	58,500	130,000	82,000	48,000
Finishing	Units	60,000	120,000	80,000	40,000
Packing and shipping	Cartons	60,500	12,100	8,040	4,060
		$468,000			

Instructions

(a) Under traditional product costing, compute the total unit cost of both products, using the information above. Prepare a simple comparative schedule of the individual costs by product (similar to Illustration 4-5).

(b) Under ABC, prepare a schedule showing the computations of the activity-based overhead rates (per cost driver), using the information above.

(c) Prepare a schedule assigning each activity's overhead cost pool to each product based on the use of cost drivers (include a computation of overhead cost per unit rounding to the nearest cent).

(d) Compute the overhead cost per unit for each product under ABC.

(e) Classify each of the activities as a value-added activity or a nonvalue-added activity.

(f) Comment on (1) the comparative overhead cost per unit for the two products under ABC and (2) the comparative total costs per unit under traditional costing and ABC.

Assign overhead to products using ABC and evaluate decision.

(SO 4)

P4-2B Leto Plastics, Inc., manufactures two plastic thermos containers at its plastic molding facility in Tilmock, Oregon. Its large container, called the Ice House, has a volume of five gallons, side carrying handles, a snap-down lid, and a side drain and plug. Its smaller container, called the Cool Chest, has a volume of two gallons, an over-the-top carrying handle which is part of a tilting lid, and a removable shelf. Both containers and their parts are made entirely of hard-molded plastic. The Ice House sells for $38.00 and the Cool Chest sells for $25.00. The production costs computed per unit under traditional costing for each model in 1999 were as follows:

Traditional Costing	Ice House	Cool Chest
Direct materials	$ 9.50	$ 4.00
Direct labor ($10 per hour)	7.50	5.00
Manufacturing overhead ($20 per DLH)	15.00	10.00
Total per unit cost	$32.00	$19.00

In 1999, Leto Plastics manufactured 60,000 units of the Ice House and 20,000 units of the Cool Chest. The overhead rate of $20 per direct labor hour was determined by dividing total expected manufacturing overhead of $1,100,000 by the total direct labor hours (55,000) for the two months.

Under traditional costing, the gross profit on the two containers was: Ice House $6 ($38 − $32) and Cool Chest $6 ($25 − $19). Although the gross profit amount is the same, the gross margins on cost are: Ice House 18.75% ($6 ÷ $32) and Cool Chest 31.58% ($6 ÷ $19). Because Leto can earn a gross margin nearly twice as great with less investment in inventory and labor costs, its management is urging its sales staff to put its efforts into selling the Cool Chest over the Ice House.

Before finalizing its decision, management asks the controller Janet Plote to prepare a product costing analysis using activity-based costing (ABC). Plote accumulates the following information about overhead for the year ended December 31, 1999:

Activity	Cost Driver	Estimated Total Overhead	Expected Cost Drivers	Activity-Based Overhead Rate
Purchasing	Number of orders	$200,000	5,000	$40 per order
Machine setups	Number of setups	300,000	1,200	$250 per setup
Extruding	Machine hours	400,000	100,000	$4 per machine hour
Quality control	Tests and inspections	200,000	10,000	$20 per test

The cost drivers used for each product were:

Cost Driver	Ice House	Cool Chest	Total
Purchase orders	2,800	2,200	5,000
Machine setups	700	500	1,200
Machine hours	70,000	30,000	100,000
Tests and inspections	6,000	4,000	10,000

Instructions
(a) Assign the total 1999 manufacturing overhead costs to the two products using activity-based costing (ABC).
(b) What was the cost per unit and gross profit of each model using ABC costing?
(c) ▭▭▭▷ Are management's future plans for the two models sound?

P4-3B Custom Cabinetry Company designs and builds upscale kitchen cabinets for luxury homes. Many of the kitchen cabinet and counter arrangements are custom made, but occasionally the company does mass production on order. Its budgeted manufacturing overhead costs for the year 2000 are as follows:

Assign overhead costs using traditional costing and ABC; compare results.
(SO 1, 4)

Overhead Cost Pools	Amount
Purchasing	$ 114,000
Handling materials	164,000
Production (cutting, milling, finishing)	400,000
Setting up machines	169,680
Inspecting	180,000
Inventory control (raw materials and finished goods)	252,000
Utilities	360,000
Total budget overhead costs	$1,639,680

For the last three years, Custom Cabinetry Company has been charging overhead to products on the basis of machine hours. For the year 2000, 100,000 machine hours are budgeted.

John Lewis, owner-manager of Custom Cabinetry, recently directed his accountant, Candy Mowinski, to implement the activity-based costing system she has repeatedly proposed. At John's request, Candy and the production foreman identify the following cost drivers and their usage for the previously budgeted overhead cost pools.

Overhead Cost Pools	Activity Cost Drivers	Total Drivers
Purchasing	Number of orders	600
Handling materials	Numbers of moves	8,000
Production (cutting, milling, finishing)	Direct labor hours	100,000
Setting up machines	Number of setups	1,200
Inspecting	Number of inspections	6,000
Inventory control (raw materials and finished goods)	Number of components	36,000
Utilities	Square feet occupied	90,000

Terry Duffy, sales manager, has received an order for 60 kitchen cabinet arrangements from Spoor Builders, a housing development contractor. At Terry's request, Candy prepares cost estimates for producing components for 60 cabinet arrangements so Terry can submit a contract price per kitchen arrangement to Spoor Builders. She accumulates the following data for the production of 60 kitchen cabinet arrangements:

Direct materials	$180,000
Direct labor	$200,000
Machine hours	15,000
Direct labor hours	12,000
Number of purchase orders	60
Number of material moves	800
Number of machine setups	100
Number of inspections	450
Number of components (cabinets and accessories)	3,000
Number of square feet occupied	8,000

Instructions

(a) Compute the predetermined overhead rate using traditional costing with machine hours as the basis (round to the nearest cent).

(b) What is the manufacturing cost per complete kitchen arrangement under traditional costing?

(c) What is the manufacturing cost per kitchen arrangement under the proposed activity-based costing? (Prepare all of the necessary schedules.)

(d) ▭▭▭▷ Which of the two costing systems is preferable in pricing decisions and why?

(SO 1, 4, 6)

4-4B   Cows and Cats Veterinary Clinic is a small-town partnership that offers two primary services, farm animal services and pet care services. Rendering veterinary care to farm animals requires travel to the farm animal (house calls), while veterinary care to pets generally requires that the pet be brought into the clinic. As part of an investigation to determine the contribution that each of these two types of services makes to overall profit, one partner argues for allocating overhead using activity-based costing while the other partner argues for a more simple overhead cost allocation on the basis of direct labor hours. The partners agree to use next year's budgeted data, as prepared by their public accountant for analysis and comparison purposes. The following overhead data are collected to develop the comparison.

Activity Cost Pool	Cost Driver	Estimated Overhead	Total Expected Cost Drivers	Expected Use of Drivers by Service Farm Animals	Pets
Drug treatment	Treatments	$ 60,000	4,000	1,800	2,200
Surgery	Operations	64,000	800	150	650
Travel	Mileage	28,000	28,000	26,000	2,000
Consultation	Appointment/Calls	30,000	3,000	600	2,400
Accounting/office	Direct labor hours	25,000	5,000	2,0000	3,000
Boarding and grooming	100% pets	40,000			
		$247,000			

Instructions

(a) Using traditional product costing as proposed by the one partner, compute the total cost of both services of Cows and Cats Veterinary Clinic.

(b) (1) Using activity-based costing, prepare a schedule showing the computations of the activity-based overhead rates (per cost driver).

(2) Prepare a schedule assigning each activity's overhead cost pool to each service based on the use of the cost drivers.

(3) Compute the overhead cost per unit for each product under ABC.

(c) Classify each of the activities as a value-added activity or a nonvalue-added activity.

(d) ▭▭▭▷ Comment on the comparative overhead cost assigned to the two services under both traditional costing and ABC.

BROADENING YOUR PERSPECTIVE

GROUP DECISION CASE

BYP4-1 Valley West Hospital is a primary medical health care facility, as well as trauma center, that serves eleven small rural Midwestern communities within a forty-mile radius. The hospital offers all the medical/surgical services of a typical small hospital. It has a staff of 18 full-time doctors and 20 part-time visiting specialists. Valley West has a payroll of 150 employees consisting of technicians, nurses, therapists, managers, directors, administrators, dieticians, secretaries, data processors, and janitors.

Instructions
With the class divided into groups, discuss and answer the following:
(a) Using your limited, moderate, or in-depth knowledge of a hospital's operations, identify as many **activities** as you can that would serve as the basis for implementing an activity-based costing system.
(b) For each of the activities listed in (a), identify a **cost driver** that would serve as a valid measure of the resources consumed by the activity.

MANAGERIAL ANALYSIS

BYP4-2 Ideal Manufacturing Company of Sycamore, Illinois, has supported a research and development (R & D) department that has for many years been the sole contributor to the company's new farm machinery products. The research and development activity is an overhead cost center that provides services only to in-house manufacturing departments (4 different product lines), all of which produce agricultural/farm/ranch related machinery products. The department has never sold its services outside, but because of its long history of success, larger manufacturers of agricultural products have approached Ideal to hire its R & D department for special projects. Because the costs of operating the R & D department have been spiraling uncontrollably, Ideal's management is considering entertaining these outside approaches to absorb the increasing costs. But, (1) management doesn't have any cost basis for charging R & D services to outsiders, and (2) it needs to gain control of its R & D costs. Management decides to implement an activity-based costing system in order to determine the charges for both outsiders and the in-house users of the department's services.

R & D activities fall into four pools with the following annual costs:

Market analysis	$1,050,000
Product design	2,280,000
Product development	3,600,000
Prototype testing	1,400,000

Activity analysis determines that the appropriate cost drivers and their usage for the four activities are:

Activity	Cost Drivers	Total Estimated Drivers
Market analysis	Hours of analysis	14,000 hours
Product design	Number of designs	2,400 designs
Product development	Number of products	80 products
Prototype testing	Number of redesigns	800 redesigns

Instructions
(a) Compute the activity-based overhead rate for each activity cost pool.
(b) How much cost would be charged to an in-house manufacturing department that consumed 1,800 hours of market analysis time, was provided 280 designs relating to 10 products, and requested 92 engineering redesigns?

(c) How much cost would serve as the basis for pricing an R & D bid with an outside company on a contract that would consume 800 hours of analysis time, require 178 designs relating to 3 products, and result in 70 engineering redesigns?

(d) What is the benefit to Ideal Manufacturing of applying activity-based costing to its R & D activity for both in-house and outside charging purposes?

REAL-WORLD FOCUS

HEWLETT-PACKARD

BYP4-3   Hewlett-Packard is considered one of the best managed and most innovative companies in the world. It continually has shown an ability to adapt to global competitive challenges through technical innovation and continual reassessment of its management and control mechanisms. Most applications of activity-based costing by Hewlett-Packard have been successful.

But, over the period August 1988 to August 1989, the Colorado Springs Division of Hewlett-Packard designed an activity-based costing system with the goal of providing for better product costing and inventory valuation. It began implementation in November 1989 but halted the process in the summer of 1992. Since then, the Colorado Springs Division has made no further attempts to re-implement a more expansive ABC approach.

Instructions
The March 1997 issue of Management Accounting contains an article by Steven P. Landry, Larry M. Wood, and Tim M. Linquist about the Colorado Springs Division entitled "Can ABC Bring Mixed Results?" Read the article and answer the following questions:

(a) What went wrong at HP's Colorado Springs Division in the design, development, and implementation of its activity-based costing system?

(b) What conclusions were drawn from HP's Colorado Springs Division experience? What does successful ABC implementation require?

COMMUNICATION ACTIVITY

BYP4-4   In our chapter opening feature story about Super Bakery, Inc., a virtual corporation was described as one which consists of a core unit that is supported by a network of outsourced activities. A virtual corporation minimizes investment in human resources, fixed assets, and working capital. The application of ABC to Super Bakery, Inc., is described in an article entitled "ABC in a Virtual Corporation" by Tom Davis and Bruce Darling, in *Management Accounting*, October 1996.

Instructions
Assume you are the controller of a virtual corporation. Using the article as a basis for your communication, write a summary that answers the following questions:

(a) What unique strategies and tactics did Super Bakery's management implement that caused sales to take off and continue to grow for eight years at an average rate of 20%?

(b) Why did Super Bakery's management feel that it was necessary to install an ABC system?

(c) What is the main difference between Super Bakery's ABC system and other manufacturers' ABC systems?

RESEARCH ASSIGNMENT

BYP4-5 The April 1998 issue of *Management Accounting* includes an article by Kip R. Krumwiede entitled "ABC: Why It's Tried and How It Succeeds."

Instructions
Read the article and answer the following questions:
(a) What is the adoption and implementation status of ABC according to the survey conducted in 1996 by the Cost Management Group of the Institute of Management Accountants?
(b) What did Krumwiede's survey attempt to determine?
(c) In Krumwiede's survey, what factors appeared to separate those companies that adopted ABC from those that did not adopt ABC?
(d) Identify at least five "Basic ABC Implementation Tips" recommended in the article.

ETHICS CASE

BYP4-6 Ernie Lobb, the cost accountant for Superior Mower Company, recently installed activity-based costing at its St. Louis lawn tractor (riding mower) plant where three models—the 8-horsepower Bladerunner, the 12-horsepower Quickcut, and the 18-horsepower Supercut—are manufactured. Ernie's new product costs for these three models show that the company's traditional costing system had been significantly undercosting the 18-horsepower Supercut. This was due primarily to the lower volume of the Supercut compared to the Bladerunner and the Quickcut. Before completing his analysis and reporting these results to management, Ernie is approached by his friend Eddie Polyester, who is the production manager for the 18-horsepower Supercut model. Eddie has heard from one of Ernie's staff about the new product costs and is upset and worried for his job because the new costs show the Supercut to be losing, rather than making, money.

At first Eddie condemns the new cost system, whereupon Ernie explains the practice of activity-based costing and why it is more accurate than the company's present system. Even more worried now, Eddie begs Ernie, "Massage the figures just enough to save the line from being discontinued. You don't want me to lose my job do you? Anyway, nobody will know."

Ernie holds firm but agrees to recompute all his calculations for accuracy before submitting his costs to management.

Instructions
(a) Who are the stakeholders in this situation?
(b) What, if any, are the ethical considerations in this situation?
(c) What are Ernie's ethical obligations to the company? To his friend?

SURFING THE NET

BYP4-7 Cost Technology describes itself as a "global consulting company specializing in profit management." They help manufacturing, service, and government organizations implement methods, such as activity-based costing and activity-based management, that will improve corporate profitability. The home page of Cost Technology includes infor-

mation about the company, its markets, and products. The following exercise investigates the company's training programs.

Address: http://costtechnology.com/training.htm

Instructions

This page refers to other pages that describe three different training courses. Read the descriptions of these courses to answer the following questions:

(a) List four types of employees that the company says would benefit from the course "Introduction of Activity-Based Management Solutions."
(b) What is target costing?
(c) What is the major cause of failure of many ABC implementations? Describe "Workforce Activity-Based Management."

Answers to Self-Study Questions
1. c   2. c   3. c   4. b   5. c   6. d   7. c   8. d   9. d   10. b

Remember to go back to the Navigator box on the chapter-opening page and check off your completed work.

CHAPTER 5

Cost-Volume-Profit Relationships

THE NAVIGATOR

STUDY OBJECTIVES

After studying this chapter, you should be able to:

1. Distinguish between variable and fixed costs.

2. Explain the meaning and importance of the relevant range.

3. Explain the concept of mixed costs.

4. State the five components of cost-volume-profit analysis.

5. Indicate the meaning of contribution margin and the ways it may be expressed.

6. Identify the three ways that the break-even point may be determined.

7. Define margin of safety and give the formulas for computing it.

8. Give the formulas for determining sales required to earn target net income.

9. Describe the essential features of a cost-volume-profit income statement.

THE NAVIGATOR

FEATURE STORY

Growing by Leaps and Leotards

When the last of her children went off to school, Amy began looking for a job. At this same time, her daughter asked to take dance classes. The nearest dance studio was 20 miles away, and Amy didn't know how she would balance a new job and driving to dance classes. Suddenly it hit her—why not start her own dance studio?

Amy sketched out a business plan: A local church would rent its basement for $6 per hour. The size of the basement limited the number of students she could teach, but the rent was low. Insurance was $50 per month. Initially she would teach classes only for young kids. She thought she could charge $2.50 for a one-hour class. There was room for 8 students per class. She wouldn't get rich—but she didn't have much at risk.

Amy soon realized that demand far exceeded her capacity. She began to consider renting a bigger space in which she could serve as many as 15 students per class. Rather than paying rent by the hour, she would have to pay $600 per month, even during summer months when demand for dance classes was low. She also would have to pay utilities—roughly $70 per month.

However, with a bigger space Amy could offer classes for teens and adults, at $5 per hour, though she could take only 8 such students per class. She would hire a part-time instructor, at about $18 per hour, to teach advanced classes. Insurance costs would increase to $100 per month, and she would need a part-time administrator at $100 per month to keep records. Amy also realized she could increase her income by selling dance shoes and leotards.

Amy laid out a new business plan based on these estimates and felt convinced she could make a go of it.

Within 10 years of starting business in a church basement Amy had 800 students, 7 instructors, two administrators, and three studios.

THE NAVIGATOR

THE NAVIGATOR ✔

- Scan *Study Objectives* ☐
- Read *Feature Story* ☐
- Read *Preview* ☐
- Read text and answer *Before You Go On*
  p. 178 ☐ p. 185 ☐ p. 191 ☐
- Work *Using the Decision Toolkit* ☐
- Review *Summary of Study Objectives* ☐
- Work *Demonstration Problem* ☐
- Answer *Self-Study Questions* ☐
- Complete assignments ☐

As the opening story indicates, to manage any size business you must understand how costs respond to changes in sales volume and the effect of the interaction of costs and revenues on profits. A prerequisite to understanding cost-volume-profit (CVP) relationships is knowledge of the behavior of costs. In this chapter, we first explain the considerations involved in cost behavior analysis. Then we discuss and illustrate CVP analysis and variable costing. The content and organization of the chapter are as follows:

THE NAVIGATOR

COST BEHAVIOR ANALYSIS

Cost behavior analysis is the study of how specific costs respond to changes in the level of activity within a company. As you might expect, some costs change and others remain the same. A knowledge of cost behavior helps management plan business operations and decide between alternative courses of action. Cost behavior analysis applies to all types of entities as the story about Amy's Dance Studio indicates.

The starting point in cost behavior analysis is measuring the key activities in the company's business. Activity levels may be expressed in terms of sales dollars (in a retail company), miles driven (in a trucking company), room occupancy (in a hotel), or dance classes taught (by a dance studio). Many companies use more than one measurement base. A manufacturing company, for example, may use direct labor hours or units of output for manufacturing costs and sales revenue or units sold for selling expenses.

For an activity level to be useful in cost behavior analysis, there should be correlation between changes in the level or volume of activity and changes in costs. The activity level selected is referred to as the activity (or volume) index. The activity index identifies the activity that causes changes in the behavior of costs. Once an appropriate activity index is selected, it is possible to classify the behavior of costs in response to changes in activity levels into three categories: variable, fixed, or mixed.

VARIABLE COSTS

Variable costs are costs that vary **in total** directly and proportionately with changes in the activity level. If the level increases 10%, total variable costs will increase 10%. If the level of activity decreases by 25%, variable costs will be reduced 25%. Examples of variable costs include direct materials and direct labor in a manufacturing company; cost of goods sold, sales commissions, and freight-out in a merchandising company; and gasoline in airline and trucking companies. A variable cost may also be defined as a cost that **remains the same *per unit* at every level of activity.**

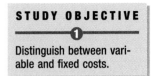

STUDY OBJECTIVE

❶

Distinguish between variable and fixed costs.

To illustrate the behavior of a variable cost, assume that Damon Company manufactures radios that contain a $10 digital clock. The activity index is the number of radios produced. As each radio is manufactured, the total cost of the clocks increases by $10. As shown in part (a) of Illustration 5-1, total cost of the clocks will be $20,000 if 2,000 radios are produced, and $100,000 when 10,000 radios are produced. The digital clocks can also be used to show that a variable cost remains the same per unit as the level of activity changes. As shown in part (b) of Illustration 5-1, the unit cost of $10 for the clocks is the same whether 2,000 or 10,000 radios are produced.

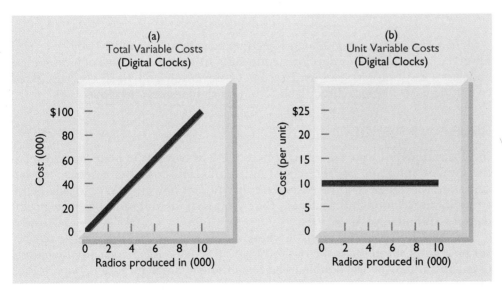

Illustration 5-1 Behavior of total and unit variable costs

Helpful Hint True or false: Variable cost per unit changes directly and proportionately with changes in activity. Answer: False; per unit cost remains constant at all levels of activity.

Companies that rely heavily on labor to manufacture a product or to render a service are likely to have many variable costs. In contrast, companies that use a high proportion of machinery and equipment in producing revenue, such as public utilities, may have few variable costs.

FIXED COSTS

Fixed costs are costs that **remain the same in total** regardless of changes in the activity level. Examples include property taxes, insurance, rent, supervisory salaries, and depreciation on buildings and equipment. Because fixed costs remain constant in total as activity changes, it follows that **fixed costs per unit vary inversely with activity. As volume increases, unit cost declines and vice versa.**

To illustrate the behavior of fixed costs, assume that Damon Company leases all of its productive facilities at a cost of $10,000 per month. Total fixed costs of the facilities will remain constant at every level of activity, as shown in part (a) of Illustration 5-2. However, on a per unit basis, the cost of rent will decline as activity increases, as shown in part (b) of Illustration 5-2. At 2,000 units, the unit cost is $5 ($10,000 ÷ 2,000); when 10,000 radios are produced, the unit cost is only $1 ($10,000 ÷ 10,000).

Illustration 5-2 Behavior of total and unit fixed costs

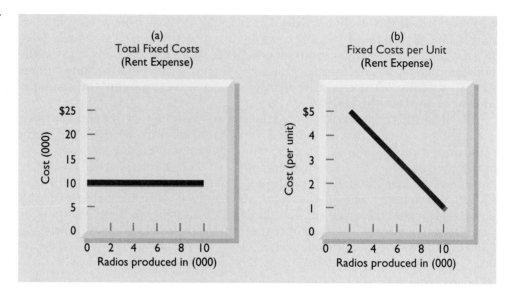

The trend in many manufacturing companies is to have more fixed costs and fewer variable costs. This development results from increased use of automation and less use of employees. As a result, depreciation and lease charges (fixed costs) increase whereas direct labor costs (variable costs) decrease.

RELEVANT RANGE

In Illustrations 5-1 and 5-2, straight lines were drawn throughout the entire activity index for total variable costs and total fixed costs. In essence, the assumption was made that the costs were **linear.** It is now necessary to ask: Is the straight-line relationship realistic? Can the linear assumption produce useful data for CVP analysis?

In most business situations, a straight-line relationship **does not exist** for variable costs throughout the entire range of activity. At abnormally low levels of activity, it may be impossible to be cost efficient, since the scale of operations may not allow the company to obtain quantity discounts in the purchase of raw materials or use specialization of labor. In contrast, at abnormally high levels of activity, labor costs may increase sharply because of overtime pay, and materials costs may jump significantly because of excess spoilage caused by worker fatigue. Consequently, in the real world, the relationship between the behavior of a variable cost and changes in the activity level is often **curvilinear,** as shown in part (a) of Illustration 5-3.

Total fixed costs also do not have a straight-line relationship over the entire range of activity. While some fixed costs will not change, it is possible for management to change other fixed costs. For example, in the feature story the dance studio's rent was originally variable, then became fixed at a certain level, then increased to a new fixed amount when the size of the studio increased beyond

Helpful Hint Fixed costs that may be changeable include research, such as new product development, and management training programs.

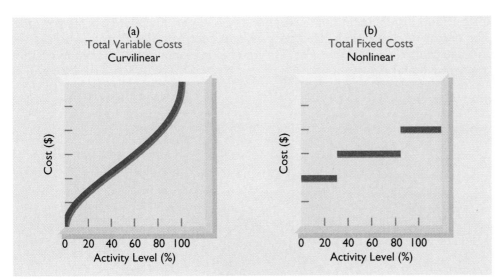

Illustration 5-3
Nonlinear behavior of
variable and fixed costs

a certain point. The behavior of total fixed costs through all levels of activity is
shown in part (b) of Illustration 5-3.

For most companies, operating at almost zero or at 100% capacity is the exception rather than the rule. Instead, companies often operate over a somewhat
narrower range, such as 40–80% of capacity. The range over which a company
expects to operate during a year is called the **relevant range** of the activity index. Within this range, as shown in both diagrams in Illustration 5-4, a straight-
line relationship generally exists for both variable and fixed costs.

Alternative Terminology The
relevant range is also called
the *normal* or *practical range.*

Illustration 5-4   Linear
behavior within relevant
range

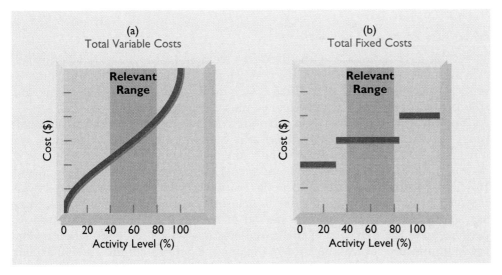

As you can see, although the straight-line relationship may not be completely
realistic, the linear assumption produces useful data for CVP analysis as long as
the level of activity remains within the relevant range.

MIXED COSTS

Mixed costs contain both a variable cost element and a fixed cost element. Sometimes called **semivariable costs, mixed costs change in total but not proportionately with changes in the activity level.** The rental of a U-Haul truck
is a good example of a mixed cost. To illustrate, assume that local rental terms

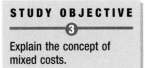

STUDY OBJECTIVE
3
Explain the concept of
mixed costs.

for a 17-foot truck, including insurance, are $50 per day plus 50 cents per mile. The per diem charge is a fixed cost with respect to miles driven, whereas the mileage charge is a variable cost. The graphic presentation of the rental cost for a one-day rental is as follows:

Illustration 5-5 Behavior of a mixed cost

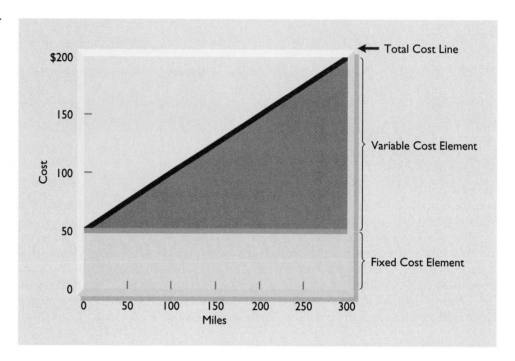

In this case, as in others, the fixed cost element is the cost of having the service available, whereas the variable cost element is the cost of actually using the service. Another example of a mixed cost is utility costs (electric, telephone, and so on), where there is a flat service fee plus a usage charge.

For purposes of CVP analysis, an underlying assumption is that **mixed costs must be classified into their fixed and variable elements.** Accordingly, we must ask: How does management make the classification? One possibility is to determine the variable and fixed components each time a mixed cost is incurred. However, because of time and cost constraints, this approach is rarely followed. Instead, the customary approach is to determine variable and fixed costs on an **aggregate basis at the end of a period of time,** using the company's past experience with the behavior of the mixed cost at various levels of activity. Management may use several methods in making the determination. We will explain the **high-low method** here; other methods are more appropriately explained in cost accounting courses.[1]

High-Low Method

The high-low method is a mathematical method that uses the total costs incurred at the high and low levels of activity. The difference in costs between the high and low levels represents variable costs, since only the variable cost element can change as activity levels change. The steps in computing fixed and variable costs under this method are as follows:

_____

[1]Other methods include the scatter diagram method and least squares regression analysis.

1. **Determine variable cost per unit from the following formula:**

Illustration 5-6   Formula for variable cost per unit using high-low method

To illustrate, assume that Metro Transit Company has the following maintenance costs and mileage data for its fleet of buses over a 4-month period:

Month	Miles Driven	Total Cost	Month	Miles Driven	Total Cost
January	20,000	$30,000	March	35,000	$49,000
February	40,000	48,000	April	50,000	63,000

Illustration 5-7   Assumed maintenance costs and mileage data

The high and low levels of activity are 50,000 miles in April and 20,000 miles in January. The maintenance costs at these two levels are $63,000 and $30,000, respectively. The difference in maintenance costs is $33,000 ($63,000 − $30,000) and the difference in miles is 30,000 (50,000 − 20,000). Therefore, for Metro Transit, variable cost per unit is $1.10, computed as follows:

$$\$33,000 \div 30,000 = \$1.10$$

2. **Determine the fixed cost by subtracting the total variable cost at either the high or the low activity level from the total cost at that activity level.**

For Metro Transit, the computations are shown in Illustration 5-8:

	Activity Level	
	High	Low
Total cost	$63,000	$30,000
Less: Variable costs		
50,000 × $1.10	55,000	
20,000 × $1.10		22,000
Total fixed costs	$ 8,000	$ 8,000

Illustration 5-8   High-low method computation of fixed costs

Maintenance costs are therefore $8,000 per month plus $1.10 per mile. For example, at 45,000 miles, estimated maintenance costs would be $49,500 variable (45,000 × $1.10) and $8,000 fixed. The high-low method generally produces a reasonable estimate for analysis. However, it does not produce a precise measurement of the fixed and variable elements in a mixed cost because other activity levels are ignored in the computation.

IMPORTANCE OF IDENTIFYING VARIABLE AND FIXED COSTS

Why is it important to segregate costs into variable and fixed elements? The answer may become apparent if we look at the following five business decisions:

1. If American Airlines is to make a profit when it reduces all domestic fares by 50%, what reduction in costs or increase in passengers will be required? **Answer:** To make a profit when it cuts domestic fares by 50%, American Airlines will have to increase the number of passengers or cut its variable costs for those flights. Its fixed costs will not change.

2. What increase in sales revenue will be needed to maintain current profit levels if Ford Motor Company meets the United Auto Workers' demands for higher wages? **Answer:** Higher wages to UAW members at Ford Motor Company will increase the variable costs of manufacturing automobiles. To maintain present profit levels, Ford will have to cut other variable costs or increase the price of its automobiles.

3. What level of sales will General Motors need to cover its costs exactly for the Saturn automobile in the next model year? **Answer:** To cover its costs exactly on the Saturn automobile for the next model year, General Motors must determine the sales volume at which sales revenue will equal total costs, both fixed and variable.

4. What will be the effect on the cost of producing one ton of steel at USX Corp. if its program to modernize plant facilities reduces the work force by 50%? **Answer:** The modernizing of plant facilities at USX Corp. changes the proportion of fixed and variable costs of producing one ton of steel. Fixed costs increase because of higher depreciation charges whereas variable costs decrease due to the reduction in the number of steelworkers.

5. What happens if Kellogg Company increases its advertising expenses? **Answer:** Sales volume must be increased to cover three items: (1) the increase in advertising, (2) the variable cost of the increased sales volume, and (3) the desired additional net income.

BEFORE YOU GO ON . . .

● **Review It**

1. What are the effects on (a) a variable cost and (b) a fixed cost due to a change in activity?
2. What is the relevant range and the behavior of costs within this range?
3. What are the steps in applying the high-low method to mixed costs?

● **Do It**

Helena Company reports the following total costs at two levels of production:

	10,000 units	**20,000 units**
Direct materials	$20,000	$40,000
Maintenance	8,000	10,000
Depreciation	4,000	4,000

Classify each cost as either variable, fixed, or mixed.

Reasoning: A variable cost varies in total directly and proportionately with each change. A fixed cost remains the same in total with each change. A mixed cost changes in total but not proportionately with each change.

Solution: Direct materials is a variable cost. Maintenance is a mixed cost. Depreciation is a fixed cost.

THE
NAVIGATOR

Related exercise material: BE5-1, E5-1, and E5-2.

COST-VOLUME-PROFIT ANALYSIS

Cost-volume-profit (CVP) analysis is the study of the effects of changes in costs and volume on a company's profits. CVP analysis is important in profit planning. It also is a critical factor in such management decisions as setting selling prices, determining the best product mix, and making maximum use of production facilities.

STUDY OBJECTIVE

4

State the five components of cost-volume-profit analysis.

BASIC COMPONENTS

CVP analysis involves a consideration of the interrelationships among the components shown in Illustration 5-9.

Illustration 5-9
Components of CVP analysis

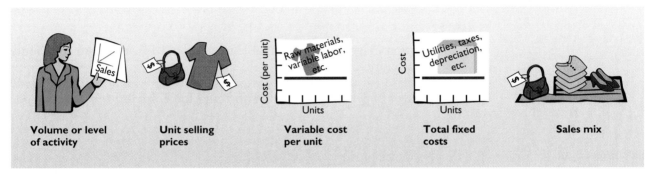

| Volume or level of activity | Unit selling prices | Variable cost per unit | Total fixed costs | Sales mix |

The following assumptions underlie each CVP application:

1. The behavior of both costs and revenues is linear throughout the relevant range of the activity index.
2. All costs can be classified as either variable or fixed with reasonable accuracy.
3. Changes in activity are the only factors that affect costs.
4. All units produced are sold.
5. When more than one type of product is sold, total sales will be in a constant sales mix. Sales mix complicates CVP analysis because different products will have different cost relationships. In this chapter we assume a single product. In Chapter 9 we address sales mix problems or issues created by multiple products.

When these five assumptions are not valid, the results of CVP analysis may be inaccurate.

In the applications of CVP analysis that follow, we will assume that the term "cost" includes **all** costs and expenses pertaining to production and sale of the product. That is, **cost includes manufacturing costs plus selling and administrative expenses.** We will use Vargo Video Company as an example. Relevant data for the videocassette recorders (VCRs) made by this company are as follows:

Unit selling price	$500
Unit variable costs	$300
Total monthly fixed costs	$200,000

Illustration 5-10
Assumed selling price and cost data for Vargo Video

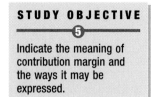
CONTRIBUTION MARGIN

One of the key relationships in CVP analysis is contribution margin (CM). **Contribution margin is the amount of revenue remaining after deducting variable costs.** For example, if we assume that Vargo Video sells 1,000 VCRs in one month, sales are $500,000 (1,000 × $500) and variable costs are $300,000 (1,000 × $300). Thus, contribution margin is $200,000 computed as follows:

Illustration 5-11
Formula for and computation of contribution margin

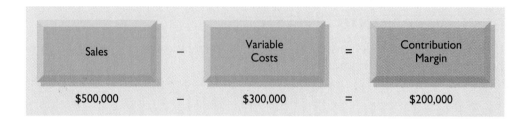

This contribution margin is then available to cover fixed costs and to contribute income for the company.

Views differ as to the best way to express contribution margin (CM). Some individuals favor a per unit basis. The formula for **contribution margin per unit** is:

Illustration 5-12
Formula for contribution margin per unit

At Vargo Video, the contribution margin per unit is $200, computed as follows:

$$\$500 - \$300 = \$200$$

Contribution margin per unit indicates that for every VCR sold, Vargo will have $200 to cover fixed costs and contribute to income. Since fixed costs are $200,000, Vargo Video must sell 1,000 VCRs ($200,000 ÷ $200) before there is any income. Above that sales volume, every sale will contribute $200 to income. Thus, if 1,500 units are sold, income will be $100,000 (500 × $200).

Others prefer to use a **contribution margin ratio.** The formula for this ratio is:

Illustration 5-13
Formula for contribution margin ratio

Helpful Hint The same ratio results from dividing total CM by total sales; i.e., $200,000 ÷ $500,000 = 40%.

At Vargo Video, the ratio is 40%, as shown below.

$$\$200 \div \$500 = 40\%$$

The CM ratio of 40% means that 40 cents of each sales dollar ($1 × 40%) is available to apply to fixed costs and to contribute to income. This expression of contribution margin is very helpful in determining the effect of changes in sales on income. To illustrate, if the management of Vargo Video wants to know the effect of a $50,000 increase in sales, they simply multiply $50,000 by the CM ratio (40%) to determine that income will increase $20,000.

DECISION TOOLKIT

Decision Checkpoints	Info Needed for Decision	Tool to Use for Decision	How to Evaluate Results
What was the contribution toward fixed costs and income from each unit sold?	Selling price per unit and variable cost per unit	$\text{Contribution margin per unit} = \text{Unit selling price} - \text{Unit variable cost}$	Every unit sold will increase income by the contribution margin.

BREAK-EVEN ANALYSIS

A second key relationship in CVP analysis is the level of activity at which total revenues equal total costs, both fixed and variable. This level of activity is called the **break-even point.** At this volume of sales, the company will realize no income and suffer no loss. Since no income is involved when the break-even point is the objective, the analysis is often referred to simply as **break-even analysis.** Knowledge of the break-even point is useful to management in deciding whether to introduce new product lines, change sales prices on established products, or enter new market areas.

STUDY OBJECTIVE

6

Identify the three ways that the break-even point may be determined.

The break-even point can be:

1. Computed from a mathematical equation.
2. Computed by using contribution margin.
3. Derived from a cost-volume-profit (CVP) graph.

The break-even point can be expressed **either in sales dollars or sales units.**

BUSINESS INSIGHT
Management Perspective

It pays to know how break-even is defined. For example, *Forrest Gump*, a highly successful film, provided little return to the movie producers initially because of the definitions used for profits. As one producer noted, "The studios do not cheat and they do not lie—they just have very creative accounting methods. A studio, for example, has at least four ways to define 'break-even' and 24 different types of 'gross,' and they're all legitimate." Perhaps the Hollywood bookkeeper is right when he observed, "Most of the creative work in this business is done in the accounting department."

Mathematical Equation

In its simplest form, the equation for break-even sales is:

Illustration 5-14
Break-even equation

The break-even point **in dollars** is found by expressing **variable costs as a percentage of unit selling price.** For Vargo Video, the percentage is 60% ($300 ÷ $500). The computation to determine sales dollars at the break-even point is:

Illustration 5-15
Computation of break-even point in dollars

$$X = .60X + \$200,000$$
$$.40X = \$200,000$$
$$X = \mathbf{\$500,000}$$

where:

X = sales dollars at the break-even point
.60 = variable costs as a percentage of unit selling price
$200,000 = total fixed costs

Sales, therefore, must be $500,000 for Vargo Video to break even.

BUSINESS INSIGHT
Investor Perspective

As the accompanying chart shows, the level of break-even sales of the Big Three automakers moved lower in recent years. This meant increased profits for Detroit.

Source: Fortune, December 12, 1994, p. 32.

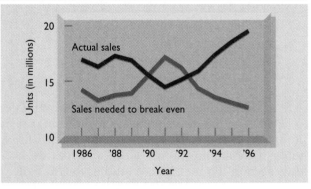

The break-even point **in units** can be computed directly from the mathematical equation by **using unit selling prices** and **unit variable costs.** The computation is:

Illustration 5-16
Computation of break-even point in units

$$\$500X = \$300X + \$200,000$$
$$\$200X = \$200,000$$
$$X = \textbf{1,000 units}$$

where:

$$X = \text{sales volume}$$
$$\$500 = \text{unit selling price}$$
$$\$300 = \text{variable cost per unit}$$
$$\$200,000 = \text{total fixed costs}$$

Thus, Vargo Video must sell 1,000 units to break even. The accuracy of the computations can be proved as follows:

Illustration 5-17
Break-even proof

Sales (1,000 × $500)		$500,000
Total costs:		
Variable (1,000 × $300)	$300,000	
Fixed	200,000	500,000
Net income		**$ –0–**

Contribution Margin Technique

Because we know that contribution margin equals total revenues less variable costs, it follows that at the break-even point, **contribution margin must equal total fixed costs.** On the basis of this relationship, the break-even point can be computed by using either the contribution margin per unit or the contribution margin ratio.

When the contribution margin per unit is used, the formula to compute break-even point in units is as follows:

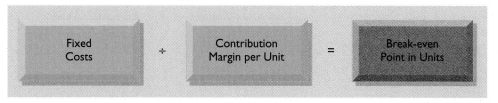

For Vargo Video, the contribution margin per unit is $200, as explained above. Thus, the computation is:

$$\$200,000 \div \$200 = 1,000 \text{ units}$$

When the contribution margin ratio is used, the formula to compute break-even point in dollars is:

We know that the contribution margin ratio for Vargo Video is 40%. Thus, the computation is:

$$\$200,000 \div 40\% = \$500,000$$

Graphic Presentation

An effective way to derive the break-even point is to prepare a break-even graph. Because this graph also shows costs, volume, and profits, it is referred to as the **cost-volume-profit (CVP) graph.**

In the graph in Illustration 5-20, sales volume is recorded along the horizontal axis. This axis should extend to the maximum level of expected sales. Both total revenues (sales) and total costs (fixed plus variable) are recorded on the vertical axis.

Illustration 5-20 CVP graph

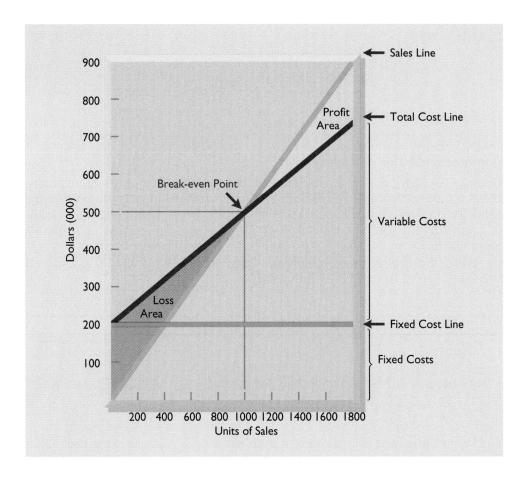

The construction of the graph, using the data for Vargo Video, is as follows:

1. Plot the total revenue line starting at the zero activity level. For every VCR sold, total revenue increases by $500. For example, at 200 units, sales are $100,000, and at the upper level of activity (1,800 units), sales are $900,000. Note that the revenue line is assumed to be linear throughout the full range of activity.

2. Plot the total fixed cost by a horizontal line. For the VCRs, this line is plotted at $200,000, and it is the same at every level of activity.

3. Plot the total cost line starting at the fixed cost line at zero activity and increasing the amount by the variable cost at each level of activity. For each VCR, variable costs are $300. Thus, at 200 units, total variable cost is $60,000 and the total cost is $260,000; at 1,800 units total variable cost is $540,000,

and total cost is $740,000. On the graph, the amount of the variable cost can be derived from the difference between the total cost and fixed cost lines at each level of activity.

4. Determine the break-even point from the intersection of the total cost line and the total revenue line. The break-even point in dollars is found by drawing a horizontal line from the break-even point to the vertical axis. The break-even point in units is obtained by drawing a vertical line from the break-even point to the horizontal axis. For the VCRs, the break-even point is $500,000 of sales, or 1,000 units. At this sales level, Vargo Video will cover costs but make no profit.

In addition to identifying the break-even point, the CVP graph shows both the net income and net loss areas. Thus, the amount of income or loss at each level of sales can be derived from the total sales and total cost lines.

A CVP graph is especially useful in management meetings because the effects of a change in any element in the CVP analysis can be promptly portrayed. For example, a 10% increase in selling price will change the location of the total revenue line. Likewise, the effects on total costs of wage increases to both office employees and factory workers can be quickly observed.

DECISION TOOLKIT

Decision Checkpoints	Info Needed for Decision	Tool to Use for Decision	How to Evaluate Results
How far can sales drop before the company becomes unprofitable?	Unit selling price, unit variable cost, and total fixed costs	Break-even point analysis *In units:* $$\text{Break-even point} = \frac{\text{Fixed costs}}{\text{Unit contribution margin}}$$ *In dollars:* $$\text{Break-even point} = \frac{\text{Fixed costs}}{\text{Contribution margin ratio}}$$	Below the break-even point— the point at which total sales equal total costs— the company is unprofitable.

BEFORE YOU GO ON . . .

● **Review It**

1. What are the assumptions that underlie each CVP application?
2. What is contribution margin and how may it be expressed?
3. How can the break-even point be determined?

● **Do It**

Lombardi Company has a unit selling price of $400, variable costs per unit of $240, and fixed costs of $160,000. Compute the break-even point in units using (a) a mathematical equation and (b) contribution margin per unit.

Reasoning: The mathematical equation is Break-even Sales = Variable Costs + Fixed Costs. Using contribution margin per unit, the formula is Fixed Costs ÷ Contribution Margin per Unit = Break-even Point in Units.

Solution: (a) The equation is $400X = $240X + $160,000. Thus, the break-even point in units is 1,000 ($160,000 ÷ $160). (b) Contribution margin per unit is $160 ($400 − $240). The formula is $160,000 ÷ $160, and the break-even point in units is 1,000.

Related exercise material: BE5-5, BE5-6, E5-3, E5-4, E5-5, E5-6, and E5-7.

THE
NAVIGATOR

MARGIN OF SAFETY

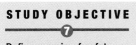

The margin of safety is another relationship that may be calculated in CVP analysis. Margin of safety is the difference between actual or expected sales and sales at the break-even point. This relationship measures the "breathing room" or "cushion" that management has in order to break even if actual or expected sales fail to materialize. The margin of safety may be expressed in dollars or as a ratio.

The formula for stating the **margin of safety in dollars** is:

Illustration 5-21
Formula for margin of safety in dollars

Assuming that actual (expected) sales for Vargo Video are $750,000, the computation is:

$$\$750,000 - \$500,000 = \$250,000$$

In contrast, the formula and computation for determining the **margin of safety ratio** are:

Illustration 5-22
Formula for margin of safety ratio

BUSINESS INSIGHT
Management Perspective

Computation of break-even and margin of safety is important for various types of business. Consider how the promoter for the Rolling Stones' tour used the break-even point and margin of safety. For example, one outdoor show should bring 70,000 individuals for a gross of $2.45 million. The promoter guarantees $1.2 million to the Rolling Stones. In addition, 20% of gross or approximately $500,000 goes to the stadium in which the performance is staged. Add another $400,000 for other expenses such as ticket takers, parking attendants, advertising, and so on. This leaves $350,000 per show to the promoter, if it sells out. At 75%, the promoter breaks about even, and at 50%, the promoter loses hundreds of thousands of dollars. However, the promoter also shares in sales of T-shirts and memorabilia for which the promoter will net over $7 million during the tour. From a successful tour, the promoter could make $35 million!

The higher the dollars or the percentage, the greater the margin of safety. The adequacy of the margin of safety should be evaluated by management in terms of such factors as the vulnerability of the product to competitive pressures and to downturns in the economy.

TARGET NET INCOME

Management usually sets an income objective for individual product lines. This objective called target net income is extremely useful to management because it indicates the sales necessary to achieve a specified level of income. The amount of sales necessary to achieve target net income can be determined from each of the approaches used in determining break-even sales.

> **STUDY OBJECTIVE**
> ——— 8 ———
> Give the formulas for determining sales required to earn target net income.

Mathematical Equation

We know that at the break-even point no profit or loss results for the company. By adding a factor for target net income to the break-even equation, we obtain the following formula for determining required sales:

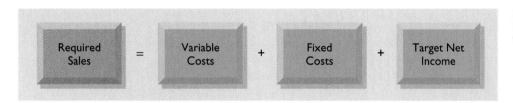

Illustration 5-23
Formula for required sales to meet target net income

Required sales may be expressed in **either sales dollars or sales units.** Assuming that target net income is $120,000 for Vargo Video, the computation of required sales in dollars is as follows:

$$X = .60X + \$200,000 + \$120,000$$
$$.40X = \$320,000$$
$$X = \mathbf{\$800,000}$$

where:

X = required sales
.60 = variable costs as a percentage of unit selling price
$200,000 = total fixed costs
$120,000 = target net income

Illustration 5-24
Computation of required sales

Helpful Hint Alternatively, the required sales units can be computed directly by using unit prices in the equation: 500X$ = 300X$ + $200,000 + $120,000; 200X$ = $320,000 or 1,600 units.

The sales volume in units at the targeted income level is found by dividing the sales dollars by the unit selling price ($800,000 ÷ $500) = 1,600 units.

Contribution Margin Technique

As in the case of break-even sales, the sales required to meet a target net income can be computed in either dollars or units. The formula using the contribution margin ratio is as follows:

Illustration 5-25
Formula for required sales in dollars using contribution margin ratio

The computation for Vargo Video is as follows:

$$\$320{,}000 \div 40\% = \$800{,}000$$

Graphic Presentation

The CVP graph presented in Illustration 5-20 can also be used to derive the sales required to meet target net income. In the profit area of the graph, the distance between the sales line and the total cost line at any point equals net income. Required sales are found by analyzing the differences between the two lines until the desired net income is found.

CVP AND CHANGES IN THE BUSINESS ENVIRONMENT

When the IBM personal computer (PC) was introduced, it sold for $2,500; today the same type of computer sells for much less. When high oil prices fell, the break-even point for airline and trucking companies dropped dramatically. Because of lower prices for imported steel, the demand for domestic steel dropped significantly. The point should be clear: Business conditions change rapidly, and management must respond intelligently to these changes. CVP analysis can help.

To illustrate how CVP analysis can be used in responding to change, we will use the following independent situations that might occur at Vargo Video. Each case is based on the original VCR sales and cost data, which were:

Illustration 5-26   Original VCR sales and cost data

Unit selling price	$500
Unit variable cost	$300
Total fixed costs	$200,000
Break-even sales	$500,000 or 1,000 units

Case I. A competitor is offering a 10% discount on the selling price of its VCRs. Management must decide whether to offer a similar discount. **Question:** What effect will a 10% discount on selling price have on the break-even point for VCRs? **Answer:** A 10% discount on selling price reduces the selling price per unit to $450 [$500 − ($500 × 10%)]. Variable costs per unit remain unchanged at $300. Thus, the contribution margin per unit is $150. Assuming no change in fixed costs, break-even sales are 1,333 units, computed as follows:

Illustration 5-27 Computation of break-even sales in units

Fixed Costs	÷	**Contribution Margin per Unit**	=	**Break-even Sales**
$200,000	÷	$150	=	1,333 units (rounded)

For Vargo Video, this change would require monthly sales to increase by 333 units or $33\frac{1}{3}\%$ in order to break even. In reaching a conclusion about offering a 10% discount to customers, management must determine the likelihood of achieving the increased sales. Also, management should estimate the possible loss of sales if the competitor's discount price is not matched.

Case II. To meet the continuing threat of foreign competition, management invests in new robotic equipment that will significantly lower the amount of direct labor required to make the VCRs. It is estimated that total fixed costs will increase 30% and that variable cost per unit will decrease 30%. **Question:** What effect will the new equipment have on the sales volume required to break even? **Answer:** Total fixed costs become $260,000 [$200,000 + (30% × $200,000)], and variable cost per unit is now $210 [$300 − (30% × $300)]. The new break-even point is approximately 900 units, computed as follows:

Fixed Costs	÷	**Contribution Margin per Unit**	=	**Break-even Sales**
$260,000	÷	($500 − $210)	=	900 units (rounded)

Illustration 5-28
Computation of break-even sales in units

These changes appear to be advantageous for Vargo Video because the break-even point is reduced by 10%, or 100 units.

Case III. The principal supplier of raw materials has just announced a price increase. It is estimated that the higher cost will increase the variable cost of VCRs by $25 per unit. Management would like to hold the line on the selling price of VCRs. It plans a cost-cutting program that will save $17,500 in fixed costs per month. Vargo is currently realizing monthly net income of $80,000 on sales of 1,400 VCRs. **Question:** What increase in sales will be needed to maintain the same level of net income? **Answer:** The variable cost per unit increases to $325 ($300 + $25), and fixed costs are reduced to $182,500 ($200,000 − $17,500). Because of the change in variable cost, the variable cost becomes 65% of sales ($325 ÷ $500). Using the equation for target net income, we find that required sales are $750,000, computed as follows:

$$\text{Required Sales} = \text{Variable Costs} + \text{Fixed Costs} + \text{Target Net Income}$$
$$X = .65X + \$182,500 + \$80,000$$
$$.35X = \$262,500$$
$$X = \$750,000$$

Illustration 5-29 Computation of required sales

To achieve the required sales, 1,500 VCRs will have to be sold ($750,000 ÷ $500), an increase of 100 units. If this does not seem to be a reasonable expectation, management will either have to effect further reductions in costs or accept less net income if the selling price remains unchanged.

DECISION TOOLKIT

Decision Checkpoints	**Info Needed for Decision**	**Tool to Use for Decision**	**How to Evaluate Results**
How can a company increase its total contribution margin to improve profitability?	Data on what effect a price decrease, a fixed-cost increase, or a trade-off between fixed and variable costs, would have on volume	Measurement of contribution margin at new volume levels	If contribution margin increases under proposed change, adopt change.

CVP INCOME STATEMENT

STUDY OBJECTIVE
——9——
Describe the essential features of a cost-volume-profit income statement.

As you have learned, cost behavior and contribution margin are key factors in CVP analysis. Because management makes its decisions on these factors, it often wants the results of these decisions reported in a similar format. This has led to the development for **internal use only** of a **CVP** or **contribution margin format** for the income statement. The CVP income statement classifies costs and expenses as variable or fixed and specifically reports contribution margin in the body of the statement. This is in contrast to the income statement traditionally prepared for external use, in which no disclosure is made of the behavior of costs and expenses. In the traditional statement, costs and expenses are classified only by function, such as cost of goods sold, selling expenses, and administrative expenses.

To illustrate the CVP income statement, we will assume that Vargo Video reaches its target net income of $120,000 (see page 187). From an analysis of the transactions, the following information is obtained on the $680,000 of costs that were incurred in June:

Illustration 5-30
Assumed cost and expense data

	Variable	Fixed	Total
Cost of goods sold	$400,000	$120,000	$520,000
Selling expenses	60,000	40,000	100,000
Administrative expenses	20,000	40,000	60,000
	$480,000	$200,000	$680,000

Illustration 5-31
Traditional versus CVP income statement

The CVP income statement and the conventional income statement based on these data are shown side-by-side for comparative purposes in Illustration 5-31.

VARGO VIDEO COMPANY
Income Statements
For the Month Ended June 30, 1999

Traditional Format			CVP Format		
Sales		$ 800,000	Sales		$ 800,000
Cost of goods sold		520,000	Variable expenses		
Gross profit		280,000	Cost of goods sold	$400,000	
Operating expenses			Selling expenses	60,000	
Selling expenses	$100,000		Administrative expenses	20,000	
Administrative expenses	60,000		Total variable expenses		480,000
Total operating expenses		160,000	**CONTRIBUTION MARGIN**		320,000
Net income		$120,000	Fixed expenses		
			Cost of goods sold	120,000	
			Selling expenses	40,000	
			Administrative expenses	40,000	
			Total fixed expenses		200,000
			Net income		$120,000

Note that net income is the same ($120,000) in both of the statements. The major difference is the format for the expenses. As illustrated, the CVP statement classifies costs and expenses as either variable or fixed. Another difference is that the traditional statement shows gross profit, whereas the CVP statement shows contribution margin. Study the CVP format carefully. It will be used in remaining chapters, and it is often used in business in internal reporting to management.

BEFORE YOU GO ON . . .

● **Review It**

1. What is the formula for computing the margin of safety (a) in dollars and (b) as a ratio?
2. How does a CVP income statement differ from a traditional income statement?

THE
NAVIGATOR

---

*U*SING THE DECISION TOOLKIT

B.T. Hernandez Company, maker of high-quality pipes, has experienced steady growth over the last six years. However, increased competition has led Mr. Hernandez, the president, to believe that an aggressive campaign is needed next year to maintain the company's present growth. The company's accountant has presented Mr. Hernandez with the following data for the current year, 1999, for use in preparing next year's advertising campaign:

Cost Schedules

Variable costs	
Direct labor per pipe	$ 8.00
Direct materials	4.00
Variable overhead	3.00
Variable cost per pipe	$15.00
Fixed costs	
Manufacturing	$ 25,000
Selling	40,000
Administrative	70,000
Total fixed costs	$135,000
Selling price per pipe	$25.00
Expected sales, 1999 (20,000 pipes)	$500,000

Mr. Hernandez has set the sales target for the year 2000 at a level of $550,000 (22,000 pipes).

Instructions

(Ignore any income tax considerations.)

(a) What is the projected operating income for 1999?

(b) What is the contribution margin per unit for 1999?

(c) What is the break-even point in units for 1999?

(d) Mr. Hernandez believes that to attain the sales target in the year 2000 requires an additional selling expense of $10,000 for advertising in 2000, with all other costs remaining constant. What will be the break-even point in dollar sales for 2000 if the company spends the additional $10,000?

(e) If the company spends the additional $10,000 for advertising in 2000, what is the sales level in dollars required to equal 1999 operating income?

Solution

(a)

Expected sales	$500,000
Less:	
Variable cost (20,000 pipes × $15)	300,000
Fixed costs	135,000
Projected operating income	$ 65,000

(b) $500,000 ÷ 20,000 = $25 selling price per pipe

Selling price per pipe	$25
Variable cost per pipe	15
Contribution margin per unit	$10

(c) Fixed costs ÷ Contribution margin per unit = Break-even point in units
$135,000 ÷ $10 = 13,500 units

(d) Fixed costs ÷ Contribution margin ratio = Break-even point in dollars
$145,000 ÷ 40% = $362,500

Fixed costs (from 1999)	$135,000
Additional advertising expense	10,000
Fixed costs (2000)	$145,000

Contribution margin = Sales − Variable costs

Expected sales	$550,000
Variable costs (22,000 × $15)	330,000
Contribution margin	$220,000

Contribution margin ratio = Contribution margin ÷ Sales
40% = $220,000 ÷ $550,000

(e) Required sales = Variable costs + Fixed costs + Target net income
$$X = .6X + \$145,000 + \$65,000$$
$$.40X = \$210,000$$
$$X = \$525,000$$

THE
NAVIGATOR

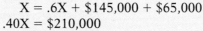

SUMMARY OF STUDY OBJECTIVES

❶ Distinguish between variable and fixed costs. Variable costs are costs that vary in total directly and proportionately with changes in the activity index. Fixed costs are costs that remain the same in total regardless of changes in the activity index.

❷ Explain the meaning and importance of the relevant range. The relevant range is the range of activity in which a company expects to operate during a year. It is important in CVP analysis because the behavior of costs is linear throughout the relevant range.

❸ Explain the concept of mixed costs. Mixed costs increase in total but not proportionately with changes in the activity level. For purposes of CVP analysis, mixed costs must be classified into their fixed and variable elements. One method that management may use is the high-low method.

❹ State the five components of cost-volume-profit analysis. The five components of CVP analysis are (a) volume or level of activity, (b) unit selling prices, (c) variable cost per unit, (d) total fixed costs, and (e) sales mix.

⑤ *Indicate the meaning of contribution margin and the ways it may be expressed.* Contribution margin is the amount of revenue remaining after deducting variable costs. It can be expressed as a per unit amount or as a ratio.

⑥ *Identify the three ways that the break-even point may be determined.* The break-even point can be (a) computed from a mathematical equation, (b) computed by using a contribution margin technique, and (c) derived from a CVP graph.

⑦ *Define margin of safety and give the formulas for computing it.* Margin of safety is the difference between actual or expected sales and sales at the break-even point. The formulas for margin of safety are Actual (Expected) Sales − Break-even Sales = Margin of Safety

in Dollars; Margin of Safety in Dollars ÷ Actual (Expected) Sales = Margin of Safety Ratio.

⑧ *Give the formulas for determining sales required to earn target net income.* One formula is: Required Sales = Variable Costs + Fixed Costs + Target Net Income. Another formula is: Fixed Costs + Target Net Income ÷ Contribution Margin Ratio = Required Sales.

⑨ *Describe the essential features of a cost-volume-profit income statement.* The CVP income statement classifies costs and expenses as variable or fixed and reports contribution margin in the body of the statement.

DECISION TOOLKIT — A SUMMARY

Decision Checkpoints	Info Needed for Decision	Tool to Use for Decision	How to Evaluate Results
What was the contribution toward fixed costs and income from each unit sold?	Selling price per unit and variable cost per unit	$\text{Contribution margin} = \text{Unit selling price} - \text{Unit variable cost}$	Every unit sold will increase income by the contribution margin.
How far can sales drop before the company becomes unprofitable?	Unit selling price, unit variable cost, and total fixed costs	Break-even point analysis *In units:* $\text{Break-even point} = \dfrac{\text{Fixed costs}}{\text{Unit contribution margin}}$ *In dollars:* $\text{Break-even point} = \dfrac{\text{Fixed costs}}{\text{Unit contribution ratio}}$	Below the break-even point—the point at which total sales equal total costs—the company is unprofitable.
How can a company increase its total contribution margin to improve profitability?	Data on what effect a price decrease, a fixed-cost increase, or a trade-off between fixed and variable costs would have on volume	Measurement of contribution margin at new volume levels	If contribution margin increases under proposed change, adopt change.

APPENDIX 5A

VARIABLE COSTING

In earlier chapters, both variable and fixed manufacturing costs have been classified as product costs. In job order costing, for example, a job is assigned the costs of direct materials, direct labor, and both variable and fixed manufacturing overhead. This costing approach is referred to as full or **absorption costing,** because all manufacturing costs are charged to, or absorbed by, the product. An alternative approach is to use variable costing. Under **variable costing** only direct materials, direct labor, and variable manufacturing overhead costs are considered product costs; fixed manufacturing overhead costs are recognized as period costs (expenses) when incurred. The difference between absorption costing and variable costing is graphically shown as follows:

Illustration 5A-1
Difference between absorption costing and variable costing

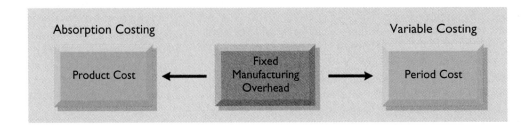

Selling and administrative expenses are period costs under both absorption and variable costing.

To illustrate the computation of unit production cost under absorption and variable costing, assume that Premium Products Corporation manufactures a polyurethane sealant, called Fix-it, for car windshields. Relevant data for Fix-it in January 1999, the first month of production, are as follows:

Selling price: $20 per unit.

Units: Produced 30,000; sold 20,000; beginning inventory zero.

Variable unit costs: Manufacturing $9 (direct materials $5, direct labor $3, and variable overhead $1), and selling and administrative expenses $2.

Fixed costs: Manufacturing overhead $120,000 and selling and administrative expenses $15,000.

The per unit production cost under each costing approach is:

Illustration 5A-2
Computation of per unit production cost

Type of Cost	Absorption Costing	Variable Costing
Direct materials	$ 5	$ 5
Direct labor	3	3
Variable manufacturing overhead	1	1
Fixed manufacturing overhead ($120,000 ÷ 30,000 units produced)	4	0
Total unit cost	**$13**	**$9**

The difference in total unit cost of $4 ($13 − $9) occurs because fixed manufacturing costs are a product cost under absorption costing and a period cost under variable costing. Based on these data, each unit sold and each unit remaining in inventory is costed at $13 under absorption costing and at $9 under variable costing.

EFFECTS ON INCOME

The income statements under the two costing approaches are shown in Illustrations 5A-3 and 5A-4. The conventional income statement format is used with absorption costing, and the cost-volume-profit format is used with variable costing. Computations are inserted parenthetically in the statements to facilitate your understanding of the amounts.

Illustration 5A-3
Absorption costing income statement

PREMIUM PRODUCTS COMPANY
Income Statement
For the Month Ended January 31, 1999
(Absorption Costing)

Sales (20,000 units × $20)		$400,000
Cost of goods sold		
Inventory, January 1	$ –0–	
Cost of goods manufactured (30,000 units × $13)	390,000	
Cost of goods available for sale	390,000	
Inventory, January 31 (10,000 units × $13)	**130,000**	
Cost of goods sold (20,000 units × $13)		260,000
Gross profit		140,000
Selling and administrative expenses		
[(Variable 20,000 units × $2) + (fixed $15,000)]		55,000
Income from operations		**$ 85,000**

Illustration 5A-3
Absorption costing income statement

Helpful Hint This is the conventional statement that would result from job order and processing costing explained in Chapters 2 and 3.

Income from operations under absorption costing, shown in Illustration 5A-3, is $40,000 higher than under variable costing ($85,000 − $45,000), shown in Illustration 5A-4.

As highlighted in the two income statements, there is a $40,000 difference in the ending inventories ($130,000 under absorption costing and $90,000 under variable costing). Under absorption costing, $40,000 of the fixed overhead costs (10,000 units × $4) have been deferred to a future period as a product cost. In contrast, under variable costing the entire fixed manufacturing costs are expensed when incurred.

Illustration 5A-4
Variable costing income statement

PREMIUM PRODUCTS COMPANY
Income Statement
For the Month Ended January 31, 1999
(Variable Costing)

Sales (20,000 units × $20)		$ 400,000
Variable expenses		
Variable cost of goods sold		
Inventory, January 1	$ –0–	
Variable manufacturing costs (30,000 units × $9)	270,000	
Cost of goods available for sale	270,000	
Inventory, January 31 (10,000 units × $9)	**90,000**	
Variable cost of goods sold	180,000	
Variable selling and administrative expenses		
(20,000 units × $2)	40,000	
Total variable expenses		220,000
Contribution margin		180,000
Fixed expenses		
Manufacturing overhead	120,000	
Selling and administrative expenses	15,000	
Total fixed expenses		135,000
Income from operations		**$ 45,000**

Helpful Hint Note the difference in the computation of the ending inventory: $9 per unit here, $13 per unit above.

As shown, when units produced exceed units sold, income under absorption costing is higher than under variable costing. Conversely, when units produced are less than units sold, income under absorption costing is lower than under variable costing. The reason is that the cost of the **beginning inventory will be higher under absorption costing** than under variable costing. For example, if 30,000 units of Fix-it are sold in February and only 20,000 units are produced, income from operations will be $40,000 less under absorption costing than under variable costing because of the $40,000 difference ($130,000 vs. $90,000) in the beginning inventories.

When units produced and sold are the same, income from operations will be equal under the two costing approaches. Since there is no increase in ending inventory, fixed overhead costs of the current period are not deferred to future periods through the ending inventory. The foregoing effects of the two costing approaches on income from operations may be summarized as follows:

Illustration 5A-5
Summary of income effects

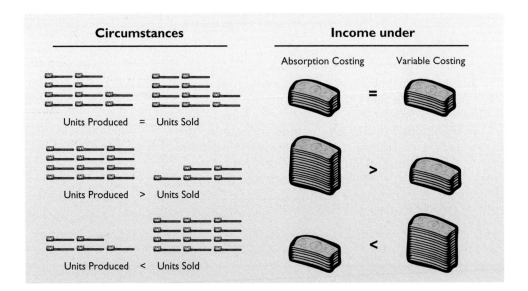

RATIONALE FOR VARIABLE COSTING

The rationale for variable costing centers on the purpose of fixed manufacturing costs, which is **to have productive facilities available for use.** Conceptually, these costs are incurred whether a company operates at zero or at 100% of capacity. Thus, proponents of variable costing argue that these costs should be expensed in the period in which they are incurred.

Supporters of absorption costing defend the assignment of fixed manufacturing overhead costs to inventory on the basis that these costs are as much a cost of getting a product (such as Fix-it) ready for sale as direct materials or direct labor. Accordingly, these costs should not be matched with revenues until the product is sold.

The use of variable costing in product costing is acceptable **only for internal use by management.** It cannot be used in determining product costs in financial statements prepared in accordance with generally accepted accounting principles because it understates inventory costs. To comply with the matching principle, a company must use absorption costing for its work in process and finished goods inventories. Similarly, absorption costing must be used for income tax purposes.

SUMMARY OF STUDY OBJECTIVE FOR APPENDIX 5A

⑩ *Explain the difference between absorption costing and variable costing.* Under absorption costing, fixed manufacturing costs are product costs; under variable costing, fixed manufacturing costs are period costs.

GLOSSARY

Absorption costing A costing approach in which all manufacturing costs are charged to the product. (p. 193)

Activity index The activity that causes changes in the behavior of costs. (p. 173)

Break-even point The level of activity at which total revenues equal total costs. (p. 181)

Contribution margin (CM) The amount of revenue remaining after deducting variable costs. (p. 180)

Cost behavior analysis The study of how specific costs respond to changes in the level of activity within a company. (p. 172)

Cost-volume-profit (CVP) analysis The study of the effects of changes in costs and volume on a company's profits. (p. 179)

Cost-volume-profit (CVP) graph A graph showing the relationship between costs, volume, and profits. (p. 184)

Cost-volume-profit (CVP) income statement A statement for internal use that classifies costs and expenses as fixed or variable and reports contribution margin in the body of the statement. (p. 190)

Fixed costs Costs that remain the same in total regardless of changes in the activity level. (p. 173)

High-low method A mathematical method that uses the total costs incurred at the high and low levels of activity. (p. 176)

Margin of safety The difference between actual or expected sales and sales at the break-even point. (p. 186)

Mixed costs Costs that contain both a variable and a fixed cost element and change in total but not proportionately with changes in the activity level. (p. 175)

Relevant range The range of the activity index over which the company expects to operate during the year. (p. 175)

Target net income The income objective for individual product lines. (p. 187)

Variable costing A costing approach in which only variable manufacturing costs are product costs and fixed manufacturing costs are period costs (expenses). (p. 193)

Variable costs Costs that vary in total directly and proportionately with changes in the activity level. (p. 173)

DEMONSTRATION PROBLEM

Mabo Company makes calculators that sell for $20 each. For the coming year, management expects fixed costs to total $220,000 and variable costs to be $9.00 per unit.

Instructions

(a) Compute break-even sales in dollars using the mathematical equation.
(b) Compute break-even sales using the contribution margin (CM) ratio.
(c) Compute the margin of safety percentage assuming actual sales are $500,000.
(d) Compute the sales required to earn net income of $165,000.

Problem-Solving Strategies

1. Know the formulas.
2. Recognize that variable costs change with sales volume; fixed costs do not.
3. Avoid computational errors.
4. Prove your answers.

Solution to Demonstration Problem

(a) Break-even sales = Variable costs + Fixed costs

$$X = .45X + \$220,000$$
$$.55X = \$220,000$$
$$X = \$400,000$$

(b) Contribution margin per unit = Unit selling price − Unit variable costs

$$\$11 = \$20 - \$9$$

Contribution margin ratio = Contribution margin per unit ÷ Unit selling price

$$55\% = \$11 \div \$20$$

Break-even sales = Fixed cost ÷ Contribution margin ratio
$$X = \$220,000 \div 55\%$$
$$X = \$400,000$$

(c) Margin of safety =

=

= 20%

(d) Required sales = Variable costs + Fixed costs + Net income
$$X = .45X + \$220,000 + \$165,000$$
$$.55X = \$385,000$$
$$X = \$700,000$$

THE
NAVIGATOR

Note: All asterisked Questions, Exercises, and Problems relate to material contained in the appendix to the chapter.

SELF-STUDY QUESTIONS

Answers are at the end of the chapter.

(SO 1) **1.** Variable costs are costs that:
  (a) vary in total directly and proportionately with changes in the activity level.
  (b) remain the same per unit at every activity level.
  (c) None of the above.
  (d) Both (a) and (b) above.

(SO 2) **2.** The relevant range is:
  (a) the range of activity in which variable costs will be curvilinear.
  (b) the range of activity in which fixed costs will be curvilinear.
  (c) the range over which the company expects to operate during a year.
  (d) usually from zero to 100% of operating capacity.

(SO 3) **3.** Mixed costs consist of a:
  (a) variable cost element and a fixed cost element.
  (b) fixed cost element and a controllable cost element.
  (c) relevant cost element and a controllable cost element.
  (d) variable cost element and a relevant cost element.

(SO 4) **4.** One of the following is *not* involved in CVP analysis. That factor is:
  (a) sales mix.
  (b) unit selling prices.
  (c) fixed costs per unit.
  (d) volume or level of activity.

(SO 5) **5.** Contribution margin:
  (a) is revenue remaining after deducting variable costs.
  (b) may be expressed as contribution margin per unit.
  (c) is selling price less cost of goods sold.
  (d) Both (a) and (b) above.

(SO 6) **6.** Gossen Company is planning to sell 200,000 pliers for $4.00 per unit. The contribution margin ratio is 25%. If Gossen will break even at this level of sales, what are the fixed costs?
  (a) $100,000.
  (b) $160,000.
  (c) $200,000.
  (d) $300,000.

(SO 7) **7.** Marshall Company had actual sales of $600,000 when break-even sales were $420,000. What is the margin of safety ratio?
  (a) 25%.
  (b) 30%.
  (c) $33\frac{1}{3}\%$.
  (d) 45%.

(SO 8) **8.** The mathematical equation for computing required sales to obtain target net income is: Required sales =
  (a) Variable costs + Target net income.
  (b) Variable costs + Fixed costs + Target net income.
  (c) Fixed costs + Target net income.
  (d) No correct answer is given.

(SO 9) **9.** Cournot Company sells 100,000 wrenches for $12.00 a unit. Fixed costs are $300,000 and net income is $200,000. What should be reported as variable expenses in the CVP income statement?
  (a) $700,000.
  (b) $900,000.
  (c) $500,000.
  (d) $1,000,000.

(SO 10) *10. Under variable costing, fixed manufacturing costs are classified as:
  (a) period costs.
  (b) product costs.
  (c) both (a) and (b).
  (d) neither (a) nor (b).

THE
NAVIGATOR

QUESTIONS

1. (a) What is cost behavior analysis?
   (b) Why is cost behavior analysis important to management?

2. (a) Jenny Beason asks your help in understanding the term "activity index." Explain the meaning and importance of this term for Jenny.
   (b) State the two ways that variable costs may be defined.

3. Contrast the effects of changes in the activity level on total and on unit fixed costs.

4. R.E. Chang claims that the relevant range concept is important only for variable costs.
   (a) Explain the relevant range concept.
   (b) Do you agree with R.E.'s claim? Explain.

5. "The relevant range is indispensable in cost behavior analysis." Is this true? Why?

6. Bart Detar is confused. He does not understand why rent on his apartment is a fixed cost and rent on a Hertz rental truck is a mixed cost. Explain the difference to Bart.

7. How should mixed costs be classified in CVP analysis? What approach is used to effect the appropriate classification?

8. At the high and low levels of activity during the month, direct labor hours are 90,000 and 40,000, respectively, and the related costs are $150,000 and $100,000. What are the fixed and variable costs at any level of activity?

9. "Cost-volume-profit (CVP) analysis is based entirely on unit costs." Do you agree? Explain.

10. Patty Dye defines contribution margin as the amount of profit available to cover operating expenses. Is there any truth in this definition? Discuss.

11. In Eusey Company, the Speedo pocket calculator sells for $40, and variable costs per unit are estimated to be $22. What is the contribution margin per unit and the contribution margin ratio?

12. "Break-even analysis is of limited use to management because a company cannot survive by just breaking even." Do you agree? Explain.

13. Total fixed costs are $18,000 for Froelich Inc.; it has a contribution margin per unit of $15, and a contribution margin ratio of 20%. Compute the break-even sales in dollars.

14. Linda Gibbons asks your help in constructing a CVP graph. Explain to Linda how (a) the break-even point is plotted and (b) the level of activity and dollar sales at the break-even point are determined.

15. Define the term "margin of safety." If Hancock Company expects to sell 1,250 units of its product at $12 per unit, and break-even sales for the product are $12,000, what is the margin of safety ratio?

16. Inwood Company's break-even sales are $600,000. Assuming fixed costs are $210,000, what sales dollars are needed to achieve a target net income of $56,000?

17. What are the similarities and differences between a CVP income statement and a traditional income statement?

18. The traditional income statement for Reeves Company shows sales $900,000, cost of goods sold $500,000, and operating expenses $200,000. Assuming all costs and expenses are 70% variable and 30% fixed, prepare a CVP income statement through contribution margin.

*19. Distinguish between absorption costing and variable costing.

*20. (a) What is the major rationale for the use of variable costing? (b) Discuss why variable costing may not be used for financial reporting purposes.

BRIEF EXERCISES

BE5-1 Monthly production costs in Kasnic Company for two levels of production are as follows:

Classify costs as variable, fixed, or mixed.
(SO 1, 3)

Cost	2,000 units	4,000 units
Indirect labor	$10,000	$20,000
Supervisory salaries	5,000	5,000
Maintenance	3,000	3,600

Indicate which costs are variable, fixed, and mixed, and give the reason for each answer.

BE5-2 In Manhart Company, the relevant range of production is 40–80% of capacity. At 40% of capacity, a variable cost is $2,000 and a fixed cost is $4,000. Diagram the behavior of each cost within the relevant range assuming the behavior is linear.

Diagram the behavior of costs within the relevant range.
(SO 2)

Diagram the behavior of a mixed cost.
(SO 3)

BE5-3 In Leyva Company, a mixed cost is $40,000 plus $8 per direct labor hour. Diagram the behavior of the cost using increments of 1,000 hours up to 5,000 hours on the horizontal axis and increments of $20,000 up to $80,000 on the vertical axis.

Determine variable and fixed cost elements using the high-low method.
(SO 3)

BE5-4 Neufeld Company accumulates the following data concerning a mixed cost, using miles as the activity level.

	Miles Driven	Total Cost		Miles Driven	Total Cost
January	8,000	$14,100	March	8,500	$14,800
February	7,500	13,400	April	8,200	14,400

Compute the variable and fixed cost elements using the high-low method.

Determine missing amounts for contribution margin.
(SO 5)

BE5-5 Determine the missing amounts.

	Unit Selling Price	Unit Variable Costs	Contribution Margin per Unit	Contribution Margin Ratio
1.	$250	$180	(a)	(b)
2.	$500	(c)	$140	(d)
3.	(e)	(f)	$360	40%

Compute the break-even point.
(SO 6)

BE5-6 Cajun Company has a unit selling price of $400, variable costs per unit of $280, and fixed costs of $120,000. Compute the break-even point using (a) a mathematical equation and (b) contribution margin per unit.

Compute the margin of safety and the margin of safety ratio.
(SO 7)

BE5-7 In Petry Company actual sales are $1,200,000 and break-even sales are $840,000. Compute (a) the margin of safety in dollars and (b) the margin of safety ratio.

Compute sales for target net income.
(SO 8)

BE5-8 In Riddell Company, variable costs are 75% of sales, fixed costs are $160,000, and management's net income goal is $60,000. Compute the required sales needed to achieve management's target net income of $60,000. (Use the mathematical equation approach.)

Prepare CVP income statement.
(SO 9)

BE5-9 Zimmerman Manufacturing Inc. has sales of $1,900,000 for the first quarter of 1999. In making the sales, the company incurred the following costs and expenses:

	Variable	Fixed
Cost of goods sold	$760,000	$540,000
Selling expenses	95,000	60,000
Administrative expenses	79,000	66,000

Prepare a CVP income statement for the quarter ended March 31, 1999.

Compute net income under absorption and variable costing.
(SO 10)

*BE5-10 Sayler Company's fixed overhead costs are $5 per unit, and its variable overhead costs are $8 per unit. In the first month of operations, 50,000 units are produced, and 45,000 units are sold. Write a short memorandum to the chief financial officer of Sayler Company explaining which costing approach will produce the higher income and what the difference will be.

EXERCISES

Define and classify variable, fixed, and mixed costs.
(SO 1, 3)

E5-1 Massey Company manufactures a single product. Annual production costs incurred in the manufacturing process are shown below for two levels of production:

	Costs Incurred				
Production in Units	5,000			10,000	
Production Costs	Total Cost	Cost/ Unit		Total Cost	Cost/ Unit
Direct materials	$8,250	$1.65		$16,500	$1.65
Direct labor	9,500	1.90		19,000	1.90

Utilities	1,400	.28	2,300	.23
Rent	4,000	.80	4,000	.40
Maintenance	800	.16	1,100	.11
Supervisory salaries	1,000	.20	1,000	.10

Instructions
(a) Define the terms variable costs, fixed costs, and mixed costs.
(b) Classify each cost above as either variable, fixed, or mixed.

E5-2 The controller of Jimenez Industries has collected the following monthly expense data for use in analyzing the cost behavior of maintenance costs:

Determine fixed and variable costs using the high-low method and prepare graph.
(SO 1, 3)

Month	Total Maintenance Costs	Total Machine Hours
January	$2,900	3,000
February	3,000	4,000
March	3,600	6,000
April	4,500	7,900
May	3,200	5,000
June	4,650	8,000

Instructions
(a) Determine the fixed and variable cost components using the high-low method.
(b) Prepare a graph showing the behavior of maintenance costs and identify the fixed and variable cost elements. Use 2,000 unit increments and $1,000 cost increments.

E5-3 In the month of June, Jan's Beauty Salon gave 2,400 haircuts, shampoos, and permanents at an average price of $30. During the month, fixed costs were $18,000 and variable costs were 60% of sales.

Compute contribution margin, break-even point, and margin of safety.
(SO 5, 6, 7)

Instructions
(a) Determine the contribution margin in dollars, per unit, and as a ratio.
(b) Using the contribution margin technique, compute the break-even point in dollars and in units.
(c) Compute the margin of safety in dollars and as a ratio.

E5-4 Unruh Company estimates that variable costs will be 50% of sales and fixed costs will total $700,000. The selling price of the product is $4.

Prepare a CVP graph and compute break-even point and margin of safety.
(SO 6, 7)

Instructions
(a) Prepare a CVP graph, assuming maximum sales of $3,200,000. (Note: Use $400,000 increments for sales and costs and 100,000 increments for units.)
(b) Compute the break-even point in (1) units and (2) dollars.
(c) Compute the margin of safety in (1) dollars and (2) as a ratio, assuming actual sales are $2 million.

E5-5 In 1999, Wiggins Company had a break-even point of $350,000 based on a selling price of $7 per unit and fixed costs of $105,000. In 2000, the selling price and the variable cost per unit did not change, but the break-even point increased to $455,000.

Compute variable cost per unit, contribution margin ratio, and increase in fixed costs.
(SO 5)

Instructions
(a) Compute the variable cost per unit and the contribution margin ratio for 1999.
(b) Compute the increase in fixed costs for 2000.

E5-6 Vowell Company had $90,000 of net income in 1999 when the selling price per unit was $150, the variable costs per unit were $90, and the fixed costs were $630,000. Management expects per unit data and total fixed costs to remain the same in 2000. The president of Vowell Company is under pressure from stockholders to increase net income by $60,000 in 2000.

Compute various components to derive target net income under different assumptions.
(SO 6, 8)

Instructions
(a) Compute the number of units sold in 1999.
(b) Compute the number of units that would have to be sold in 2000 to reach the stockholders' desired profit level.
(c) Assume that Vowell Company sells the same number of units in 2000 as it did in 1999. What would the selling price have to be in order to reach the stockholders' desired profit level?

Compute net income under different alternatives.

(SO 8)

E5-7 Angell Company reports the following operating results for the month of August: Sales $300,000 (units 5,000); variable costs $210,000; and fixed costs $80,000. Management is considering the following independent courses of action to increase net income.
1. Increase selling price by 15% with no change in total variable costs.
2. Reduce variable costs to 60% of sales.
3. Reduce fixed costs by $20,000.

Instructions
Compute the net income to be earned under each alternative. Which course of action will produce the highest net income?

Prepare a CVP income statement before and after changes in business environment.

(SO 9)

E5-8 Healy Company had sales in 1999 of $1,500,000 on 60,000 units. Variable costs totaled $720,000, and fixed costs totaled $500,000.

A new raw material is available that will decrease the variable costs per unit by 20% (or $2.40). However, to process the new raw material, fixed operating costs will increase by $50,000. Management feels that one-half of the decline in the variable costs per unit should be passed on to the company's customers in the form of a sales price reduction. The marketing department expects that this sales price reduction will result in a 10% increase in the number of units sold.

Instructions
Prepare a CVP income statement for 1999, assuming the changes are made as described.

Compute total product cost and prepare an income statement using variable costing.

(SO 10)

*E5-9 DeLong Equipment Company manufactures and distributes industrial air compressors. The following costs are available for the year ended December 31, 1999. The company has no beginning inventory. In 1999, 1,500 units were produced, but only 1,200 units were sold. The unit selling price was $4,500. Costs and expenses were:

Variable costs per unit	
Direct materials	$ 600
Direct labor	1,500
Variable manufacturing overhead	300
Variable selling and administrative expenses	70
Annual fixed costs and expenses	
Manufacturing overhead	$1,200,000
Selling and administrative expenses	100,000

Instructions
(a) Compute the manufacturing cost of one unit of product using variable costing.
(b) Prepare a 1999 income statement for DeLong Company using variable costing.

PROBLEMS: SET A

Determine variable and fixed costs, compute break-even point, prepare a CVP graph, and determine net income.

(SO 1, 3, 5, 6)

P5-1A The College Barber Shop employs four barbers. One barber, who also serves as the manager, is paid a salary of $1,600 per month. The other barbers are paid $1,200 per month. In addition, each barber is paid a commission of $4 per haircut. Other monthly costs are: store rent $800 plus 60 cents per haircut, depreciation on equipment $500, barber supplies 40 cents per haircut, utilities $300, and advertising $200. The price of a haircut is $10.

Instructions
(a) Determine the variable cost per haircut and the total monthly fixed costs.
(b) Compute the break-even point in units and dollars.
(c) Prepare a CVP graph, assuming a maximum of 1,800 haircuts in a month. Use increments of 300 haircuts on the horizontal axis and $3,000 increments on the vertical axis.
(d) Determine the net income, assuming 1,600 haircuts are given in a month.

P5-2A Corbin Company bottles and distributes LOKAL, a fruit drink. The beverage is sold for 50 cents per 16-oz. bottle to retailers, who charge customers 70 cents per bottle. At full (100%) plant capacity, management estimates the following revenues and costs.

Prepare a CVP income statement, compute break-even point, contribution margin ratio, margin of safety ratio, and sales for target net income.

(SO 5, 6, 7, 8, 9)

Net sales	$2,000,000	Selling expenses—variable	$ 90,000
Direct materials	360,000	Selling expenses—fixed	150,000
Direct labor	450,000	Administrative expenses—	
Manufacturing overhead—		variable	30,000
variable	270,000	Administrative expenses—	
Manufacturing overhead—		fixed	70,000
fixed	380,000		

Instructions
(a) Prepare a CVP income statement for the year 1999 based on management's estimates.
(b) Compute the break-even point in (1) units and (2) dollars.
(c) Compute the contribution margin ratio and the margin of safety ratio.
(d) Determine the sales required to earn net income of $220,000.

P5-3A Griffey Manufacturing had a bad year in 1999. For the first time in its history it operated at a loss. The company's income statement showed the following results from selling 60,000 units of product: Net sales $1,500,000; total costs and expenses $1,890,000; and net loss $390,000. Costs and expenses consisted of the following:

Compute break-even point under alternative courses of action.

(SO 5, 6)

	Total	Variable	Fixed
Cost of goods sold	$1,350,000	$ 930,000	$420,000
Selling expenses	420,000	75,000	345,000
Administrative expenses	120,000	45,000	75,000
	$1,890,000	$1,050,000	$840,000

Management is considering the following independent alternatives for 2000:
1. Increase unit selling price 40% with no change in costs, expenses, and sales volume.
2. Change the compensation of salespersons from fixed annual salaries totaling $200,000 to total salaries of $50,000 plus a 6% commission on net sales.
3. Purchase new high-tech factory machinery that will change the proportion between variable and fixed cost of goods sold to 50:50.

Instructions
(a) Compute the break-even point in dollars for the year 1999.
(b) Compute the break-even point in dollars under each of the alternative courses of action. Which course of action do you recommend?

P5-4A Cindy Henning is the advertising manager for Thrifty Shoe Store. She is currently working on a major promotional campaign. Her ideas include the installation of a new lighting system and increased display space that will add $37,000 in fixed costs to the $210,000 currently spent. In addition, Cindy is proposing that a $6\frac{2}{3}\%$ price decrease (from $30.00 to $28.00) will produce an increase in sales volume from 16,000 to 21,000 units. Variable costs will remain at $15.00 per pair of shoes. Management is impressed with Cindy's ideas but concerned about the effects that these changes will have on the break-even point and the margin of safety.

Compute break-even point and margin of safety ratio and prepare a CVP income statement before and after changes in business environment.

(SO 6, 7, 9)

Instructions
(a) Compute the current break-even point in units, and compare it to the break-even point in units if Cindy's ideas are used.
(b) Compute the margin of safety ratio for current operations and after Cindy's changes are introduced. (Round to nearest full percent.)
(c) Prepare a CVP income statement for current operations and after Cindy's changes are introduced. Would you make the changes suggested?

*****P5-5A** Karmik Metal Company produces the steel wire that goes into the production of paper clips. In 1999, the first year of operations, Karmik produced 40,000 miles of wire and sold 30,000 miles. In 2000, the production and sales results were exactly reversed. In each year, selling price per mile was $80, variable manufacturing costs were 20% of the sales price, variable selling expenses were $8.00 per mile sold, fixed manufacturing costs were $1,200,000, and fixed administrative expenses were $200,000.

Prepare income statements under absorption and variable costing.

(SO 10)

Instructions
(a) Prepare comparative income statements for each year using variable costing.
(b) Prepare comparative income statements for each year using absorption costing.
(c) Reconcile the differences each year in income from operations under the two costing approaches.
(d) Comment on the effects of production and sales on net income under the two costing approaches.

PROBLEMS: SET B

Determine variable and fixed costs, compute break-even point, prepare a CVP graph, and determine net income.

(SO 1, 3, 5, 6)

P5-1B Joe Wong owns the Peace Barber Shop. He employs five barbers and pays each a base rate of $1,000 per month. One of the barbers serves as the manager and receives an extra $400 per month. In addition to the base rate, each barber also receives a commission of $3.50 per haircut.

Other costs are as follows:

Advertising	$200 per month
Rent	$800 per month
Barber supplies	$.30 per haircut
Utilities	$175 per month plus $.20 per haircut
Magazines	$25 per month

Joe currently charges $10 per haircut.

Instructions
(a) Determine the variable cost per haircut and the total monthly fixed costs.
(b) Compute the break-even point in units and dollars.
(c) Prepare a CVP graph, assuming a maximum of 1,800 haircuts in a month. Use increments of 300 haircuts on the horizontal axis and $3,000 on the vertical axis.
(d) Determine net income, assuming 1,500 haircuts are given in a month.

Prepare a CVP income statement, compute break-even point, contribution margin ratio, margin of safety ratio, and sales for target net income.

(SO 5, 6, 7, 8, 9)

P5-2B Newsom Company bottles and distributes NOKAL, a diet soft drink. The beverage is sold for 40 cents per 16-oz. bottle to retailers, who charge customers 60 cents per bottle. At full (100%) plant capacity, management estimates the following revenues and costs.

Net sales	$1,800,000	Selling expenses—variable	$80,000
—Direct materials	400,000	Selling expenses—fixed	65,000
–Direct labor	460,000	Administrative expenses—	
— Manufacturing overhead—		variable	20,000
variable	300,000	Administrative expenses—	
Manufacturing overhead—		fixed	52,000
fixed	243,000		

Instructions
(a) Prepare a CVP income statement for the year 1999 based on management's estimates.
(b) Compute the break-even point in (1) units and (2) dollars.
(c) Compute the contribution margin ratio and the margin of safety ratio. (Round to full percents.)
(d) Determine the sales required to earn net income of $150,000.

Compute break-even point under alternative courses of action.

(SO 5, 6)

P5-3B Masoni Manufacturing's sales slumped badly in 1999. For the first time in its history, it operated at a loss. The company's income statement showed the following results from selling 600,000 units of product: Net sales $2,400,000; total costs and expenses $2,490,000; and net loss $90,000. Costs and expenses consisted of the following:

	Total	Variable	Fixed
Cost of goods sold	$1,980,000	$1,320,000	$660,000
Selling expenses	310,000	72,000	238,000
Administrative expenses	200,000	48,000	152,000
	$2,490,000	$1,440,000	$1,050,000

Management is considering the following independent alternatives for 2000:
1. Increase unit selling price 20% with no change in costs, expenses, and sales volume.
2. Change the compensation of salespersons from fixed annual salaries totaling $210,000 to total salaries of $70,000 plus a 5% commission on net sales.
3. Purchase new automated equipment that will change the proportion between variable and fixed cost of goods sold to 60% variable and 40% fixed.

Instructions
(a) Compute the break-even point in dollars for the year 1999.
(b) Compute the break-even point in dollars under each of the alternative courses of action. (Round to full percents.) Which course of action do you recommend?

P5-4B Kathy Short is the advertising manager for Value Shoe Store. She is currently working on a major promotional campaign. Her ideas include the installation of a new lighting system and increased display space that will add $48,000 in fixed costs to the $240,000 currently spent. In addition, Kathy is proposing that a 5% price decrease ($40.00 to $38.00) will produce a 20% increase in sales volume (20,000 to 24,000). Variable costs will remain at $20.00 per pair of shoes. Management is impressed with Kathy's ideas but concerned about the effects that these changes will have on the break-even point and the margin of safety.

Compute break-even point and margin of safety ratio and prepare a CVP income statement before and after changes in business environment.
(SO 6, 7, 9)

Instructions
(a) Compute the current break-even point in units, and compare it to the break-even point in units if Kathy's ideas are used.
(b) Compute the margin of safety ratio for current operations and after Kathy's changes are introduced. (Round to nearest full percent.)
(c) Prepare a CVP income statement for current operations and after Kathy's changes are introduced. Would you make the changes suggested?

*P5-5B ADC produces plastic that is used for injection molding applications such as gears for small motors. In 1999, the first year of operations, ADC produced 4,000 tons of plastic and sold 3,000 tons. In 2000, the production and sales results were exactly reversed. In each year, selling price per ton was $2,500, variable manufacturing costs were 15% of the sales price of units produced, variable selling expenses were 10% of the selling price of units sold, fixed manufacturing costs were $3,000,000, and fixed administrative expenses were $600,000.

Prepare income statements under absorption and variable costing.
(SO 10)

Instructions
(a) Prepare comparative income statements for each year using variable costing.
(b) Prepare comparative income statements for each year using absorption costing.
(c) Reconcile the differences each year in income from operations under the two costing approaches.
(d) Comment on the effects of production and sales on net income under the two costing approaches.

BROADENING YOUR PERSPECTIVE

GROUP DECISION CASE

BYP5-1 Cedeno Company has decided to introduce a new product. The new product can be manufactured by either a capital-intensive method or a labor-intensive method.

The manufacturing method will not affect the quality of the product. The estimated manufacturing costs by the two methods are as follows:

	Capital-Intensive	Labor-Intensive
Raw materials	$5 per unit	$5.50 per unit
Direct labor	$6 per unit	$7.20 per unit
Variable overhead	$3 per unit	$4.80 per unit
Fixed manufacturing costs	$2,300,000	$1,285,000

Cedeno's market research department has recommended an introductory unit sales price of $30. The incremental selling expenses are estimated to be $500,000 annually plus $2 for each unit sold, regardless of manufacturing method.

Instructions
With the class divided into groups, answer the following:
(a) Calculate the estimated break-even point in annual unit sales of the new product if Cedeno Company uses the:
   (1) capital-intensive manufacturing method.
   (2) labor-intensive manufacturing method.
(b) Determine the annual unit sales volume at which Cedeno Company would be indifferent between the two manufacturing methods.
(c) Explain the circumstances under which Cedeno should employ each of the two manufacturing methods.

(CMA adapted)

*M*ANAGERIAL ANALYSIS

BYP5-2 The condensed income statement for the Rivera and Santos partnership for 1999 is as follows:

RIVERA AND SANTOS COMPANY
Income Statement
For the Year Ended December 31, 1999

Sales (200,000 units)		$1,200,000
Cost of goods sold		800,000
Gross profit		400,000
Operating expenses		
Selling	320,000	
Administrative	160,000	480,000
Net loss		($80,000)

A cost behavior analysis indicates that 75% of the cost of goods sold are variable; 50% of the selling expenses are variable; and 25% of the administrative expenses are variable.

Instructions
(Round to nearest unit, dollar, and percentage, where necessary. Use the CVP income statement format in computing profits.)
(a) Compute the break-even point in total sales dollars and in units for 1999.
(b) Rivera has proposed a plan to get the partnership "out of the red" and improve its profitability. She feels that the quality of the product could be substantially improved by spending $0.55 more per unit on better raw materials. The selling price per unit could be increased to only $6.50 because of competitive pressures. Rivera estimates that sales volume will increase by 30%. What effect will Rivera's plan have on the profits and the break-even point in dollars of the partnership?
(c) Santos was a marketing major in college. He believes that sales volume can be increased only by intensive advertising and promotional campaigns. He therefore proposed the following plan as an alternative to Rivera's: (1) increase variable selling expenses to $0.85 per unit, (2) lower the selling price per unit by $0.20, and (3) increase

fixed selling expenses by $20,000. Santos quoted an old marketing research report that said that sales volume would increase by 50% if these changes were made. What effect will Santos's plan have on the profits and the break-even point in dollars of the partnership?

(d) Which plan should be accepted? Explain your answer.

REAL-WORLD FOCUS

THE COCA-COLA COMPANY

BYP5-3   The **Coca-Cola Company** hardly needs an introduction. A line taken from the cover of its 1996 annual report says it all: If you measured time in servings of Coca-Cola, "a billion Coca-Cola's ago was yesterday morning." On average, every U.S. citizen drinks 363 eight-ounce servings of Coca-Cola products each year. Coca-Cola's primary line of business is the making and selling of syrup to bottlers. These bottlers then sell the finished bottles and cans of Coca-Cola to the consumer.

In the 1996 annual report of Coca-Cola, the following information was provided:

THE COCA-COLA COMPANY
Management Discussion

Our gross margin declined to 61 percent in 1995 from 62 percent in 1994, primarily due to costs for materials such as sweeteners and packaging.

The increases (in selling expenses) in 1996 and 1995 were primarily due to higher marketing expenditures in support of our Company's volume growth.

We measure our sales volume in two ways: (1) gallon shipments of concentrates and syrups and (2) unit cases of finished product (bottles and cans of Coke sold by bottlers).

Instructions

Answer the following questions:

(a) Are sweeteners and packaging a variable cost or a fixed cost? What is the impact on the contribution margin of an increase in the per unit cost of sweeteners or packaging? What are the implications for profitability?

(b) In your opinion, are marketing expenditures a fixed cost, variable cost, or mixed cost to The Coca-Cola Company? Give justification for your answer.

(c) Which of the two measures cited for measuring volume represents the activity index as defined in this chapter? Why might Coca-Cola use two different measures?

COMMUNICATION ACTIVITY

BYP5-4   In CVP analysis there are many formulas. Your roommate asks your help on the following questions:

(a) How can the mathematical equation for break-even sales show both sales dollars and sales units?

(b) How do the formulas differ, if at all, for contribution margin per unit and contribution margin ratio?

(c) How can contribution margin be used to determine break-even sales in dollars and in units?

Instructions

Write a memorandum to your roommate stating the relevant formulas and the answers to each of the foregoing questions.

RESEARCH ASSIGNMENT

BYP5-5 The February 1998 issue of *Management Accounting* includes an article by Bonnie Stivers, Teresa Covin, Nancy Green Hall, and Steven Smalt entitled "How Nonfinancial Performance Measures Are Used."

Instructions
Read the article and answer the following questions:

(a) The article is based on a study and survey. What is the objective of this study? Describe the specific nature of the survey that was conducted.

(b) What were the five categories of nonfinancial performance measures identified and surveyed in this study?

(c) What factors were identified, as a result of the survey, to be the most important nonfinancial measures?

(d) What are the "three red flags" (conclusions) that the study results highlight?

ETHICS CASE

BYP5-6 Donny Blake is an accountant for Swenson Company. Early this year Donny made a highly favorable projection of sales and profits over the next 3 years for its hot-selling computer PLEX. As a result of the projections Donny presented to senior management, they decided to expand production in this area. This decision led to dislocations of some plant personnel who were reassigned to one of the company's newer plants in another state. However, no one was fired, and in fact the company expanded its work force slightly.

Unfortunately Donny rechecked his computations on the projections a few months later and found that he had made an error that, if corrected, would have reduced his projections substantially. Luckily, sales of PLEX have exceeded projections so far, and management is satisfied with its decision. Donny, however, is not sure what to do. Should he confess his honest mistake and jeopardize his possible promotion? He suspects that no one will catch the error because sales of PLEX have exceeded his projections, and it appears that profits will materialize close to his projections.

Instructions

(a) Who are the stakeholders in this situation?

(b) Identify the ethical issues involved in this situation.

(c) What are the possible alternative actions for Donny? What would you do in Donny's position?

SURFING THE NET

BYP5-7 Ganong Bros. Ltd., located in St. Stephen, New Brunswick, is Canada's oldest independent candy company. Its products are distributed worldwide. In 1885, Ganong invented the popular "chicken bone," a cinnamon flavored, pink, hard candy jacket over a chocolate center. The home page of Ganong, listed below, includes information about the company and its products.

Address: http://www.gulliver.nb.ca/pcsolve/ganong/index.htm

Instructions
Choose the **Ganong Times,** and answer the following:
(a) Describe the steps in making "chicken bones."
(b) Identify at least two variable and two fixed costs that are likely to affect the production of "chicken bones."

Answers to Self-Study Questions
1. d   2. c   3. a   4. c   5. d   6. c   7. b   8. b   9. a   10. a

 Remember to go back to the Navigator box on the chapter-opening page and check off your completed work.

CHAPTER 6
Budgetary Planning

STUDY OBJECTIVES

After studying this chapter, you should be able to:

1. Indicate the benefits of budgeting.
2. State the essentials of effective budgeting.
3. Identify the budgets that comprise the master budget.
4. Describe the sources for preparing the budgeted income statement.
5. Explain the principal sections of a cash budget.
6. Indicate the applicability of budgeting in nonmanufacturing companies.

THE
NAVIGATOR

FEATURE STORY

Big Red's Biennial Budget

Every university has a budget. Usually, there's a capital budget for big projects such as new buildings, and there's an operating budget for the day-to-day expenditures.

At the University of Nebraska, the operating budget request takes up four volumes totaling nearly 900 pages. Because the university is funded by the state of Nebraska, the budget must be submitted to the state legislature for approval. That means the university has to pay lobbyists to plead its case with legislators. The budget is due September 15th of every other year. The lawmakers consider it during their sessions, which begin in January.

As you might expect, increases in expenses are resisted because money is tight. "Roughly 70% of our budget goes toward salaries," says Paula Boroff, budget officer at the Omaha campus. "A university is a very labor-intensive institution," she observes. The total budget for a recent fiscal year is about $95 million, reflecting a 1% cut in state funds from the prior year.

One budget item of interest to students is the "remission" category. That's where scholarships are funded. "This year, the budget for honor students and needy students is nearly $2 million—$1,994,488 to be exact," says Boroff, who recently received her MBA from the University of Nebraska graduate school. "Of our 16,000 students, we had 8,274 on some kind of aid," she says.

THE
NAVIGATOR

210

THE NAVIGATOR ✔

- Scan *Study Objectives* ☐
- Read *Feature Story* ☐
- Read *Preview* ☐
- Read text and answer *Before You Go On*
  p. 217 ☐   *p. 228* ☐   *p. 231* ☐
- Work *Using the Decision Toolkit* ☐
- Review *Summary of Study Objectives* ☐
- Work *Demonstration Problem* ☐
- Answer *Self-Study Questions* ☐
- Complete assignments ☐

As the story about the University of Nebraska indicates, budgeting is an integral part of our society. As students, you budget your study time and your money. Families budget income and expenses, and governmental agencies budget revenues and expenditures. Business enterprises use budgets in planning and controlling their operations.

Our primary focus in this chapter is budgeting—specifically, how budgeting is used as a *planning tool* by management. Through budgeting, it should be possible for management to maintain enough cash to pay creditors, to have sufficient raw materials to meet production requirements, and to have adequate finished goods to meet expected sales. The content and organization of this chapter are as follows:

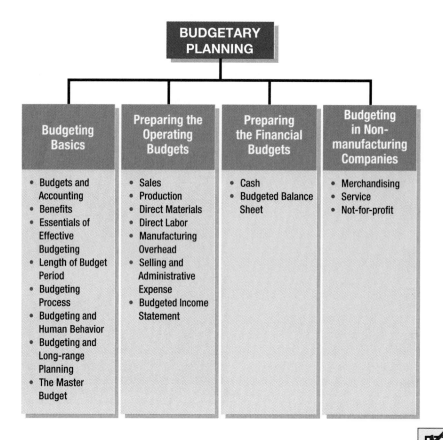

THE NAVIGATOR

*B*UDGETING BASICS

One of management's major responsibilities is planning. As explained in Chapter 1, **planning** is the process of establishing enterprise objectives. A successful organization establishes both long-term and short-term plans that set forth the objectives of the company and the proposed means of accomplishing them.

A **budget** is a formal written summary (or statement) of management's plans for a specified future time period, expressed in financial terms. It normally represents the primary means of communicating agreed-upon objectives throughout the business organization. Once adopted, a budget becomes an important basis for evaluating performance. Thus, it promotes efficiency and serves as a deterrent to waste and inefficiency. We consider the role of budgeting as a **control device** in Chapter 7.

BUDGETING AND ACCOUNTING

Accounting information makes major contributions to the budgeting process. From the accounting records, historical data on revenues, costs, and expenses can be obtained. These data may be helpful in formulating future budget goals.

Normally, accounting has the responsibility for expressing management's budgeting goals in financial terms. In this role, it becomes the translator of management's plans, and it provides the means of communicating the budget to all areas of responsibility. Accounting also prepares periodic budget reports that provide the basis for measuring performance and comparing actual results with planned objectives. The budget itself, and the administration of the budget, however, are entirely management responsibilities.

BUSINESS INSIGHT
Management Perspective

In large firms, the computer is an essential tool in the budgeting process. Entire computer programs are designed to aid in budget preparation. These systems can also be integrated into the general ledger and provide a complete reporting package for monitoring budgeted vs. actual results. Packages with similar features are available for microcomputers so even small companies can adopt the budgeting practices found in major companies.

A powerful feature of many spreadsheet packages is the ability to merge and consolidate budget data as they flow up the organizational chain of command.

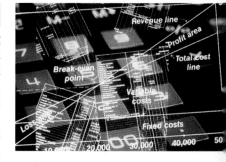

THE BENEFITS OF BUDGETING

The primary benefits of budgeting are:

1. It requires all levels of management to **plan ahead** and to formalize their future goals on a recurring basis.

2. It provides **definite objectives** for evaluating performance at each level of responsibility.

3. It creates an **early warning system** for potential problems. With early warning, management has time to solve the problem before things get out of hand. For example, the cash budget may reveal the need for outside financing several months before an actual cash shortage occurs.

4. It facilitates the **coordination of activities** within the business by correlating the goals of each segment with overall company objectives. Thus, production and sales promotion can be integrated with expected sales.

5. It results in greater **management awareness** of the entity's overall operations and the impact of external factors, such as economic trends, on the company's operations.

6. It contributes to **positive behavior patterns** throughout the organization by motivating personnel to meet planned objectives.

STUDY OBJECTIVE
①
Indicate the benefits of budgeting.

A budget is an aid to management; it is not a substitute for management. A budget cannot operate or enforce itself. The benefits of budgeting will be realized only when budgets are carefully prepared and properly administered by management.

ESSENTIALS OF EFFECTIVE BUDGETING

STUDY OBJECTIVE

②

State the essentials of effective budgeting.

Effective budgeting depends on a **sound organizational structure** in which authority and responsibility over all phases of operations are clearly defined. Budgets based on **research and analysis** should result in realistic goals that will contribute to the growth and profitability of a company. And, the effectiveness of a budget program is directly related to its **acceptance by all levels of management.**

Once the budget has been adopted, it should be an important basis for evaluating performance. Variations between actual and expected results should be systematically and periodically reviewed to determine their cause(s). However, care should be exercised to see that individuals are not held responsible for variations that are beyond their control.

LENGTH OF THE BUDGET PERIOD

As indicated in the opening story about the University of Nebraska budget, the budget period is not necessarily one year in length. **A budget may be prepared for any period of time.** Such factors as the type of budget, the nature of the organization, the need for periodic appraisal, and prevailing business conditions will influence the length of the budget period. For example, cash may be budgeted monthly, whereas a plant expansion program budget may cover a 10-year period.

The budget period should be long enough to provide an attainable goal under normal business conditions. Ideally, the time period should minimize the impact of seasonal and cyclical business fluctuations. On the other hand, the budget period should not be so long that reliable estimates are impossible.

The **most common budget period is one year.** The annual budget, in turn, is often supplemented by monthly and quarterly budgets. Many companies today use **continuous 12-month budgets** by dropping the month just ended and adding a future month. One advantage of continuous budgeting is that it keeps management planning a full year ahead.

THE BUDGETING PROCESS

The development of the budget for the coming year generally starts several months before the end of the current year. The budgeting process usually begins with the collection of data from each of the organizational units of the company. Past performance is often the starting point in budgeting, from which future budget goals are formulated.

The budget is developed within the framework of a sales forecast that shows potential sales for the industry and the company's expected share of such sales. Sales forecasting involves a consideration of such factors as (1) general economic conditions, (2) industry trends, (3) market research studies, (4) anticipated advertising and promotion, (5) previous market share, (6) changes in prices, and (7) technological developments. The input of sales personnel and top management are essential in preparing the sales forecast.

In many companies, responsibility for coordinating the preparation of the budget is assigned to a budget committee. The committee, often headed by a budget director, ordinarily includes the president, treasurer, chief accountant (controller), and management personnel from each of the major areas of the company, such as sales, production, and research. The budget committee serves as a review board where managers and supervisors can defend their budget goals and requests. After differences are reviewed, modified if necessary, and reconciled, the budget is prepared by the budget committee, put in its final form, approved, and distributed.

BUDGETING AND HUMAN BEHAVIOR

A budget can have a significant effect on human behavior. On the one hand, a budget may have a strong positive influence that inspires a manager to higher levels of performance. On the other hand, a budget may discourage additional effort and have a negative impact on the morale of a manager. Why do these diverse effects occur? The answer is found in the manner in which the budget is developed and administered.

In **developing the budget,** each level of management should be invited and encouraged to participate. The overall objective is to reach agreement on a budget that the manager considers to be fair and achievable. When this objective is met, the budget will have a positive effect on the manager. In contrast, if the manager views the budget as being unfair and unrealistic, he or she may become discouraged and uncommitted to the budget goals. The risk of having unrealistic budgets is generally greater when the budget is developed from top management down to lower management than vice versa. Illustration 6-1 graphically displays the flow of budget data from bottom to top in an organization.

Illustration 6-1 Flow of budget data from lower levels of management to top

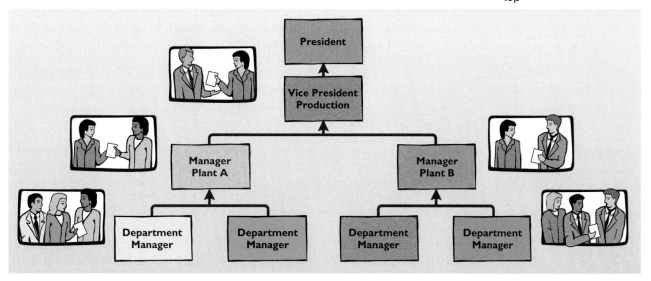

Administering the budget relates to the manner in which the budget is used by top management. As explained earlier, the budget should have the complete support of top management. In addition, the budget should be an important basis for evaluating performance. The effect of an evaluation on a manager will be positive when top management tempers criticism with advice and assistance. In contrast, the response of a manager is likely to be negative when the budget is used exclusively to assess blame. Top management should also be sensitive to the behavioral implications of its actions. An understanding and flexible attitude

Helpful Hint Unrealistic budgets can lead to unethical employee behavior such as cutting corners on the job or distorting internal financial reports.

has a positive influence on human behavior. Conversely, a rigid and inflexible attitude has a negative effect on the manager who is being evaluated.

A budget may be used improperly as a pressure device to force improved performance. Alternatively, it can be used as a positive aid in achieving projected goals. In sum, a budget can become a friend or a foe to the manager.

BUDGETING AND LONG-RANGE PLANNING

In business, you may hear management talk about the need for long-range planning. Budgeting and long-range planning are not the same. One important difference is the **time period involved.** The maximum length of a budget is usually one year, and budgets are often prepared for shorter periods of time, such as a month or a quarter. In contrast, long-range planning usually encompasses a period of at least five years.

A second significant difference is **in emphasis.** Budgeting is concerned with the achievement of specific short-term goals, such as meeting annual profit objectives. **Long-range planning,** on the other hand, is a formalized process of selecting strategies to achieve long-term goals and developing policies and plans to implement the strategies. In long-range planning, management also considers anticipated trends in the economic and political environment and policies the company should follow to cope with them.

The final difference between budgeting and long-range planning pertains to the **amount of detail presented.** Budgets, as you will see later in this chapter, can be very detailed. The detail is needed to provide a basis for control. Long-range plans contain considerably less detail, because the data are intended more for a review of progress toward long-term goals than for an evaluation of specific results to be achieved. The primary objective of long-range planning is to develop the best strategy to maximize the company's performance over an extended future period.

Helpful Hint In comparing a budget with a long-range plan: (1) Which has more detail? (2) Which is done for a longer period of time? (3) Which is more concerned with short-term goals? Answer: (1) Budget. (2) Long-range plan. (3) Budget.

THE MASTER BUDGET

STUDY OBJECTIVE

3

Identify the budgets that comprise the master budget.

When we discuss a "budget," we actually are using a shorthand term to describe a variety of budget documents, all of which are combined into a master budget. The **master budget** is a set of interrelated budgets that constitutes a plan of action for a specified time period. The individual budgets included in a master budget for Hayes Company, which sells a single product, Kitchen-mate, are shown in Illustration 6-2.

As shown in the illustration, there are two classes of budgets in the master budget. **Operating budgets** include the individual budgets that culminate in the preparation of the budgeted income statement. The primary objective of these budgets is to establish goals for the company's sales and production personnel. In contrast, **financial budgets** include the cash budget and the budgeted balance sheet. These budgets focus primarily on the cash resources needed to fund expected operations and planned capital expenditures.

The master budget is prepared in the sequence shown in Illustration 6-2. The operating budgets are developed first, beginning with the sales budget. After these budgets have been determined, the financial budgets are prepared. We will explain and illustrate each budget shown in Illustration 6-2 except the capital expenditure budget. This budget is discussed under the topic Capital Budgeting in Chapter 10.

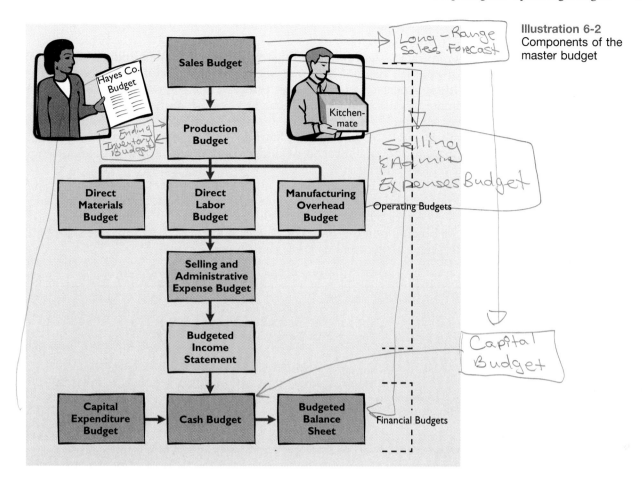

Illustration 6-2
Components of the master budget

BEFORE YOU GO ON . . .

● **Review It**

1. What are the benefits of budgeting?
2. What are the factors essential to effective budgeting?
3. How does the budget process work?
4. How does budgeting differ from long-range planning?
5. What is a master budget?

THE
NAVIGATOR

PREPARING THE OPERATING BUDGETS

A case study of Hayes Company will be used in preparing the operating budgets. Hayes Company manufactures and sells a single product, Kitchen-mate. The budgets will be prepared by quarters for the year ending December 31, 1999. Hayes Company begins its annual budgeting process on September 1, 1998, and it completes the budget for 1999 by December 1, 1998.

SALES BUDGET

As shown in the master budget in Illustration 6-2, **the sales budget is the first budget prepared.** Each of the other budgets depends on the sales budget. The sales budget is derived from the sales forecast, and it represents management's best estimate of sales revenue for the budget period. An inaccurate sales budget may adversely affect net income. For example, an overly optimistic sales budget may result in excessive inventories that may have to be sold at reduced prices. In contrast, an unduly conservative budget may result in loss of sales revenue due to inventory shortages.

The sales budget is prepared by multiplying the expected unit sales volume for each product by its anticipated unit selling price. For Hayes Company, sales volume is expected to be 3,000 units in the first quarter with 500-unit increments in each succeeding quarter. Based on a sales price of $60 per unit, the sales budget for the year, by quarters, is shown in Illustration 6-3.

Illustration 6-3 Sales budget

HAYES COMPANY
Sales Budget
For the Year Ending December 31, 1999

| | \multicolumn{5}{c}{Quarter} |
	1	2	3	4	Year
Expected unit sales	3,000	3,500	4,000	4,500	15,000
Unit selling price	× $60	× $60	× $60	× $60	× $60
Total sales	$180,000	$210,000	$240,000	$270,000	$900,000

The anticipated sales revenue may be classified as cash or credit sales and by geographical regions, territories, or salespersons.

PRODUCTION BUDGET

The production budget shows the units that must be produced to meet anticipated sales. Production requirements are determined from the following formula:[1]

Illustration 6-4 Production requirements formula

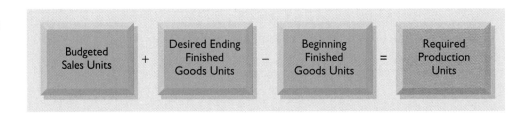

A realistic estimate of ending inventory is essential in scheduling production requirements. Excessive inventories in one quarter may lead to cutbacks in production and layoffs of employees in a subsequent quarter. Conversely, inadequate inventories may result either in added costs for overtime work or in lost sales in a later period. On the basis of past experience, Hayes Company believes

---

[1]This formula ignores any work in process inventories, which are assumed to be nonexistent in Hayes Company.

it can meet future sales requirements by maintaining an ending inventory equal to 20% of the next quarter's budgeted sales volume. For example, the ending finished goods inventory for the first quarter is 700 units (20% × anticipated second-quarter sales of 3,500 units). The production budget is shown in Illustration 6-5.

Illustration 6-5
Production budget

HAYES COMPANY
Production Budget
For the Year Ending December 31, 1999

	Quarter				
	1	2	3	4	Year
Expected unit sales (Illustration 6-3)	3,000	3,500	4,000	4,500	
Add: Desired ending finished goods units[a]	700	800	900	1,000[b]	
Total required units	3,700	4,300	4,900	5,500	
Less: Beginning finished goods units	600[c]	700	800	900	
Required production units	**3,100**	**3,600**	**4,100**	**4,600**	15,400

[a]20% of next quarter's sales
[b]Expected 2000 first-quarter sales, 5,000 units × 20%
[c]20% of estimated first-quarter 1999 sales units

The production budget, in turn, provides the basis for determining the budgeted costs for each manufacturing cost element, as explained in the following pages.

BUSINESS INSIGHT
Management Perspective

Wrong move, wrong time, poor planning. Recently, Fruit of the Loom Inc. saw underwear and apparel sales slowing. It cut back production sharply. Too sharply, in fact: almost overnight, demand soared. Caught with its shorts down, the company hired back thousands of workers and frantically increased production. The mistimed production cuts contributed to a 43% fall in first-quarter profits. For the year, Fruit stood to lose $200 million in sales, and analysts expected an 11% drop in profits for the year.

Source: Business Week, June 6, 1994, p. 38.

DIRECT MATERIALS BUDGET

The **direct materials budget** contains both the quantity and cost of direct materials to be purchased. The quantities of direct materials are derived from the following formula:

Illustration 6-6 Formula for direct materials quantities

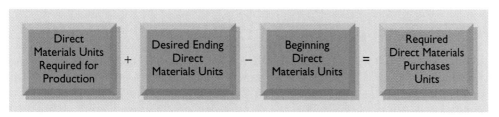

| Direct Materials Units Required for Production | + | Desired Ending Direct Materials Units | − | Beginning Direct Materials Units | = | Required Direct Materials Purchases Units |

The budgeted cost of direct materials to be purchased is then computed by multiplying the required units of direct materials by the anticipated cost per unit.

The desired ending inventory is again a critical component in the budgeting process. For example, inadequate inventories could result in temporary shutdowns of production. Because of its close proximity to suppliers, Hayes Company has found that an ending inventory of raw materials equal to 10% of the next quarter's production is sufficient. The manufacture of each Kitchen-mate requires 2 pounds of raw materials and the expected cost per pound is $4. The direct materials budget is shown in Illustration 6-7.

Illustration 6-7 Direct materials budget

HAYES COMPANY					
Direct Materials Budget					
For the Year Ending December 31, 1999					

	Quarter				
	1	2	3	4	Year
Units to be produced (Illustration 6-5)	3,100	3,600	4,100	4,600	
Direct materials per unit	× 2	× 2	× 2	× 2	
Total pounds needed for production	6,200	7,200	8,200	9,200	
Add: Desired ending direct materials (pounds)^a	720	820	920	1,020^b	
Total materials required	6,920	8,020	9,120	10,220	
Less: Beginning direct materials (pounds)	620^c	720	820	920	
Direct materials purchases	6,300	7,300	8,300	9,300	
Cost per pound	× $4	× $4	× $4	× $4	
Total cost of direct materials purchases	**$25,200**	**$29,200**	**$33,200**	**$37,200**	**$124,800**

^{a}10% of next quarter's production
^{b}Estimated 2000 first-quarter pounds needed for production, 10,200 × 10%
^{c}10% of estimated first-quarter pounds needed for production

BUSINESS INSIGHT
Management Perspective

The successful manufacturers of the twenty-first century will be fully computerized. A crucial step on the way is material requirements planning (MRP) systems. Early MRP systems accepted a sales forecast and computed quantities of materials, inventory, people, and machinery needed to manufacture the product. Current MRP systems link the company's manufacturing resource planning with its financial management, creating a powerful system of control over the entire business planning and operating process. With MRP, management can make decisions on facts rather than on "hunches" and "instinct."

DIRECT LABOR BUDGET

Like the direct materials budget, the direct labor budget contains the quantity (hours) and cost of direct labor necessary to meet production requirements. Direct labor hours are determined from the production budget. At Hayes Company, two hours of direct labor are required to produce each unit of finished goods, and the anticipated hourly wage rate is $10. These data are shown in

Illustration 6-8. The direct labor budget is critical in maintaining a labor force that can meet the expected levels of production.

Illustration 6-8 Direct labor budget

HAYES COMPANY
Direct Labor Budget
For the Year Ending December 31, 1999

	Quarter				
	1	2	3	4	Year
Units to be produced (Illustration 6-5)	3,100	3,600	4,100	4,600	
Direct labor time (hours) per unit	× 2	× 2	× 2	× 2	
Total required direct labor hours	6,200	7,200	8,200	9,200	
Direct labor cost per hour	× $10	× $10	× $10	× $10	
Total direct labor cost	**$62,000**	**$72,000**	**$82,000**	**$92,000**	**$308,000**

Helpful Hint An important assumption here is that the company can add and subtract from its work force as needed so that the $10 per hour labor cost applies to a wide range of possible production activity.

MANUFACTURING OVERHEAD BUDGET

The manufacturing overhead budget shows the expected manufacturing overhead costs for the budget period. As shown in Illustration 6-9, **this budget distinguishes between variable and fixed overhead costs.** From previous experience, Hayes Company expects variable costs to fluctuate with production volume on the basis of the following rates per direct labor hour: indirect materials $1.00, indirect labor $1.40, utilities $0.40, and maintenance $0.20. Thus, for 6,200 direct labor hours, budgeted indirect materials are $6,200 (6,200 × $1), and budgeted indirect labor is $8,680 (6,200 × $1.40). Hayes Company also recognizes that some maintenance is fixed. The amounts reported for fixed costs are assumed. At Hayes, overhead is applied to production on the basis of direct labor hours. Thus, as shown in Illustration 6-9, the annual rate is $8 per hour ($246,400 ÷ 30,800).

Illustration 6-9 Manufacturing overhead budget

HAYES COMPANY
Manufacturing Overhead Budget
For the Year Ending December 31, 1999

	Quarter				
	1	2	3	4	Year
Variable costs					
Indirect materials	$ 6,200	$ 7,200	$ 8,200	$ 9,200	$ 30,800
Indirect labor	8,680	10,080	11,480	12,880	43,120
Utilities	2,480	2,880	3,280	3,680	12,320
Maintenance	1,240	1,440	1,640	1,840	6,160
Total variable	18,600	21,600	24,600	27,600	92,400
Fixed costs					
Supervisory salaries	20,000	20,000	20,000	20,000	80,000
Depreciation	3,800	3,800	3,800	3,800	15,200
Property taxes and insurance	9,000	9,000	9,000	9,000	36,000
Maintenance	5,700	5,700	5,700	5,700	22,800
Total fixed	38,500	38,500	38,500	38,500	154,000
Total manufacturing overhead	**$57,100**	**$60,100**	**$63,100**	**$66,100**	**$246,400**
Direct labor hours	**6,200**	**7,200**	**8,200**	**9,200**	**30,800**
Manufacturing overhead rate per direct labor hour ($246,400 ÷ 30,800)					**$8.00**

SELLING AND ADMINISTRATIVE EXPENSE BUDGET

Hayes Company combines its operating expenses into one budget, the **selling and administrative expense budget.** This budget is a projection of anticipated selling and administrative expenses for the budget period. In this budget, as in the preceding budget, expenses are classified as either variable or fixed. In this case, the variable expense rates per unit of sales are sales commissions $3.00, and freight-out $1.00. Variable expenses per quarter are based on the unit sales projected in the sales budget (Illustration 6-3). For example, sales in the first quarter are expected to be 3,000 units. Thus, Sales Commissions Expense is $9,000 (3,000 × $3), and Freight-out is $3,000 (3,000 × $1). Fixed expenses are based on assumed data. The selling and administrative expense budget is shown in Illustration 6-10.

Illustration 6-10 Selling and administrative expense budget

HAYES COMPANY					
Selling and Administrative Expense Budget					
For the Year Ending December 31, 1999					
	Quarter				
	1	2	3	4	Year
Variable expenses					
Sales commissions	$ 9,000	$ 10,500	$ 12,000	$ 13,500	$ 45,000
Freight-out	3,000	3,500	4,000	4,500	15,000
Total variable	12,000	14,000	16,000	18,000	60,000
Fixed expenses					
Advertising	5,000	5,000	5,000	5,000	20,000
Sales salaries	15,000	15,000	15,000	15,000	60,000
Office salaries	7,500	7,500	7,500	7,500	30,000
Depreciation	1,000	1,000	1,000	1,000	4,000
Property taxes and insurance	1,500	1,500	1,500	1,500	6,000
Total fixed	30,000	30,000	30,000	30,000	120,000
Total selling and administrative expenses	$42,000	$44,000	$46,000	$48,000	$180,000

BUDGETED INCOME STATEMENT

STUDY OBJECTIVE
4
Describe the sources for preparing the budgeted income statement.

The **budgeted income statement** is the important end-product in preparing operating budgets. This budget indicates the expected profitability of operations for the budget period. Once established, the budgeted income statement provides the basis for evaluating company performance. As you would expect, this budget is prepared from the previous budgets. For example, to find the cost of goods sold, it is first necessary to determine the total unit cost of producing one Kitchen-mate as follows:

Illustration 6-11 Computation of total unit cost

	Cost of One Kitchen-mate			
Cost Element	**Illustration**	**Quantity**	**Unit Cost**	**Total**
Direct materials	6-7	2 pounds	$ 4.00	$ 8.00
Direct labor	6-8	2 hours	$10.00	20.00
Manufacturing overhead	6-9	2 hours	$ 8.00	16.00
Total unit cost				**$44.00**

Cost of goods sold can then be determined by multiplying the units sold by the unit cost. For Hayes Company, budgeted cost of goods sold is $660,000 (15,000 × $44). All data for the statement are obtained from the individual operating budgets except the following: (1) interest expense is expected to be $100 and (2) income taxes are estimated to be $12,000. The budgeted income statement is shown in Illustration 6-12.

HAYES COMPANY Budgeted Income Statement For the Year Ending December 31, 1999	
Sales (Illustration 6-3)	$900,000
Cost of goods sold (15,000 × $44)	660,000
Gross profit	240,000
Selling and administrative expenses (Illustration 6-10)	180,000
Income from operations	60,000
Interest expense	100
Income before income taxes	59,900
Income tax expense	12,000
Net income	$ 47,900

Illustration 6-12
Budgeted income statement

DECISION TOOLKIT

Decision Checkpoints	Info Needed for Decision	Tool to Use for Decision	How to Evaluate Results
Has the company met its targets for sales, production expenses, selling and administrative expenses, and net income?	Sales forecasts, inventory levels, projected materials, labor, overhead, and selling and administrative requirements	Master budget—a set of interrelated budgets including sales, production, materials, labor, overhead, and selling and administrative budgets	Results are favorable if revenues exceed budgeted amounts, or if expenses are less than budgeted amounts.

PREPARING THE FINANCIAL BUDGETS

As shown in Illustration 6-2, the financial budgets consist of the capital expenditure budget, the cash budget, and the budgeted balance sheet. The capital expenditure budget is discussed in Chapter 10; the other budgets are explained in the following sections.

CASH BUDGET

The **cash budget** shows anticipated cash flows. Because cash is so vital in a company, this budget is considered to be the most important output in preparing financial budgets. The cash budget contains three sections (cash receipts,

STUDY OBJECTIVE

5

Explain the principal sections of a cash budget.

cash disbursements, and financing) and the beginning and ending cash balances as shown in Illustration 6-13.

Illustration 6-13 Basic form of a cash budget

ANY COMPANY Cash Budget	
Beginning cash balance	$X,XXX
Add: Cash receipts (Itemized)	X,XXX
Total available cash	X,XXX
Less: Cash disbursements (Itemized)	X,XXX
Excess (deficiency) of available cash over cash disbursements	X,XXX
Financing	X,XXX
Ending cash balance	$X,XXX

The **cash receipts section** includes expected receipts from the company's principal source(s) of revenue such as cash sales and collections from customers on credit sales. This section also shows anticipated receipts of interest and dividends, and proceeds from planned sales of investments, plant assets, and the company's capital stock.

The **cash disbursements section** shows expected payments for direct materials, direct labor, manufacturing overhead, and selling and administrative expenses. This section also includes projected payments for income taxes, dividends, investments, and plant assets.

The **financing section** shows expected borrowings and the repayment of the borrowed funds plus interest. This section is needed when there is a cash deficiency or when the cash balance is below management's minimum required balance.

Helpful Hint Why is the cash budget prepared after the other budgets are prepared? Answer: Because the information generated by the other budgets dictates the need for and the inflows and outflows of cash.

Data in the cash budget must be prepared in sequence because the ending cash balance of one period becomes the beginning cash balance for the next period. Data for preparing the cash budget are obtained from other budgets and from information provided by management. In practice, cash budgets are often prepared for the year on a monthly basis.

BUSINESS INSIGHT
Management Perspective

Douglas Roberson, president of Atlantic Network, woke up one morning to find that his company was out of cash. At that point, Roberson realized that managing cash flow is different from simply accumulating sales. He says: "If you don't do serious projections about how much cash you will need to handle sales—and how long it will take to collect on invoices—you can end up out of business no matter how fast you are growing." In fact, Roberson says, fast growth exacerbates cash flow problems because the company can be spending cash on supplies and payroll at an accelerated pace while waiting 45 days or longer to collect receivables.

To minimize detail, we will assume that Hayes Company prepares an annual cash budget by quarters. The cash budget for Hayes Company is based on the following assumptions:

1. The January 1, 1999, cash balance is expected to be $38,000.

2. Sales (Illustration 6-3)—60% are collected in the quarter sold and 40% are collected in the following quarter. Accounts receivable of $60,000 at December 31, 1998, are expected to be collected in full in the first quarter of 1999.

3. Marketable securities are expected to be sold for $2,000 cash in the first quarter.

4. Direct materials (Illustration 6-7)—50% are paid in the quarter purchased and 50% are paid in the following quarter. Accounts payable of $10,600 at December 31, 1998, are expected to be paid in full in the first quarter of 1999.

5. Direct labor (Illustration 6-8)—100% is paid in the quarter incurred.

6. Manufacturing overhead (Illustration 6-9) and selling and administrative expenses (Illustration 6-10). All items except depreciation are paid in the quarter incurred.

7. Management plans to purchase a new truck in the second quarter for $10,000 cash.

8. The company makes equal quarterly payments of its estimated annual income taxes.

9. Loans are repaid in the first subsequent quarter in which there is sufficient cash.

Preparing schedules for collections from customers (assumption No. 2, above) and cash payments for direct materials (assumption No. 4, above) is useful in preparing the cash budget. The schedules are shown in Illustrations 6-14 and 6-15.

Illustration 6-14
Collections from customers

Schedule of Expected Collections from Customers			
	Quarter		
	1	2	3	4
Accounts receivable, 12/31/98	$ 60,000			
First quarter ($180,000)	108,000	$ 72,000		
Second quarter ($210,000)		126,000	$ 84,000	
Third quarter ($240,000)			144,000	$ 96,000
Fourth quarter ($270,000)				162,000
Total collections	$168,000	$198,000	$228,000	$258,000

Illustration 6-15
Payments for direct
materials

Schedule of Expected Payments for Direct Materials				
	Quarter			
	1	2	3	4
Accounts payable, 12/31/98	$10,600			
First quarter ($25,200)	12,600	$12,600		
Second quarter ($29,200)		14,600	$14,600	
Third quarter ($33,200)			16,600	$16,600
Fourth quarter ($37,200)				18,600
Total payments	$23,200	$27,200	$31,200	$35,200

The cash budget for the Hayes Company is shown in Illustration 6-16. The budget indicates that $3,000 of financing will be needed in the second quarter to maintain a minimum cash balance of $15,000. Since there is an excess of available cash over disbursements of $22,500 at the end of the third quarter, the borrowing is repaid in this quarter plus $100 interest.

Illustration 6-16 Cash budget

HAYES COMPANY Cash Budget For the Year Ending December 31, 1999					
		Quarter			
	Assumption	1	2	3	4
Beginning cash balance	1	$ 38,000	$ 25,500	$ 15,000	$ 19,400
Add: Receipts					
Collections from customers	2	168,000	198,000	228,000	258,000
Sale of securities	3	2,000	0	0	0
Total receipts		170,000	198,000	228,000	258,000
Total available cash		208,000	223,500	243,000	277,400
Less: Disbursements					
Direct materials	4	23,200	27,200	31,200	35,200
Direct labor	5	62,000	72,000	82,000	92,000
Manufacturing overhead	6	53,300[1]	56,300	59,300	62,300
Selling and administrative expenses	6	41,000[2]	43,000	45,000	47,000
Purchase of truck	7	0	10,000	0	0
Income tax expense	8	3,000	3,000	3,000	3,000
Total disbursements		182,500	211,500	220,500	239,500
Excess (deficiency) of available cash over disbursements		25,500	12,000	22,500	37,900
Financing					
Borrowings		0	3,000	0	0
Repayments—plus $100 interest	9	0	0	3,100	0
Ending cash balance		$ 25,500	$ 15,000	$ 19,400	$ 37,900

[1]$57,100 − $3,800 depreciation
[2]$42,000 − $1,000 depreciation

A cash budget contributes to more effective cash management. For example, it can show when additional financing will be necessary well before the actual need arises. Conversely, it can indicate when excess cash will be available for investments or other purposes.

DECISION TOOLKIT

Decision Checkpoints	Info Needed for Decision	Tool to Use for Decision	How to Evaluate Results
Is the company going to need to borrow funds in the coming quarter?	Beginning cash balance, cash receipts, cash disbursements, and desired cash balance	Cash budget	The company will need to borrow money if the cash budget indicates a projected cash deficiency of available cash over cash disbursements for the quarter.

BUDGETED BALANCE SHEET

The **budgeted balance sheet** is a projection of financial position at the end of the budget period. This budget is developed from the budgeted balance sheet for the preceding year and the budgets for the current year. Pertinent data from the budgeted balance sheet at December 31, 1998, are as follows:

Building and equipment	$182,000	Common stock	$225,000
Accumulated depreciation	$ 28,800	Retained earnings	$ 46,480

The budgeted balance sheet at December 31, 1999, is shown below.

HAYES COMPANY
Budgeted Balance Sheet
December 31, 1999

Assets

Cash		$ 37,900
Accounts receivable		108,000
Finished goods inventory		44,000
Raw materials inventory		4,080
Buildings and equipment	$192,000	
Less: Accumulated depreciation	48,000	144,000
Total assets		$337,980

Liabilities and Stockholders' Equity

Accounts payable		$ 18,600
Common stock		225,000
Retained earnings		94,380
Total liabilities and stockholders' equity		$337,980

Illustration 6-17
Budgeted balance sheet

The computations and sources of the amounts are explained below.

Cash—Ending cash balance $37,900, shown in the cash budget (Illustration 6-16).

Accounts receivable—40% of fourth-quarter sales $270,000, shown in the schedule of expected collections from customers (Illustration 6-14).

Finished goods inventory—Desired ending inventory 1,000 units, shown in production budget (Illustration 6-5) times the total unit cost $44 (shown in Illustration 6-11).

Raw materials inventory—Desired ending inventory 1,020 pounds, times the cost per pound $4, shown in the direct materials budget (Illustration 6-7).

Buildings and equipment—December 31, 1998, balance $182,000, plus purchase of truck for $10,000.

Accumulated depreciation—December 31, 1998, balance $28,800, plus $15,200 depreciation shown in manufacturing overhead budget (Illustration 6-9) and $4,000 depreciation shown in selling and administrative expense budget (Illustration 6-10).

Accounts payable—50% of fourth-quarter purchases $37,200, shown in schedule of expected payments for direct materials (Illustration 6-15).

Common stock—Unchanged from the beginning of the year.

Retained earnings—December 31, 1998, balance $46,480, plus net income $47,900, shown in budgeted income statement (Illustration 6-12).

BUSINESS INSIGHT
Management Perspective

After the budgeting data are entered into the computer, the various budgets (sales, cash, etc.) can be prepared, as well as the budgeted financial statements. Management can also manipulate the budgets in "what if" (sensitivity) analyses based on different hypothetical assumptions. For example, suppose that sales were budgeted to be 10 percent higher in the coming quarter. What impact would the change have on the rest of the budgeting process and the financing needs of the business? The computer can quickly "play out" the impact of the various assumptions on the budgets. Armed with these analyses, management can make more informed decisions about the impact of various projects and anticipate future problems and business opportunities. Budgeting is one of the top uses of electronic spreadsheets. Template versions of every one of the Hayes Company budgets shown in this chapter could easily be prepared.

BEFORE YOU GO ON . . .

● **Review It**

1. How may the individual budgets in the master budget be classified?
2. What is the sequence for preparing the budgets that comprise the operating budgets?
3. What are the three principal sections of the cash budget?

● **Do It**

In Martian Company, management wants to maintain a minimum monthly cash balance of $15,000. At the beginning of March, the cash balance is $16,500, expected cash receipts for March are $210,000, and cash disbursements are expected to be $220,000. How much cash, if any, must be borrowed to maintain the desired minimum monthly balance?

Reasoning: The best way to answer this question is to insert the dollar data into the basic form of the cash budget.

Solution:

MARTIAN COMPANY
Cash Budget
For the Month Ending March 31, 1999

Beginning cash balance	$ 16,500
Add: Cash receipts for March	210,000
Total available cash	226,500
Less: Cash disbursements for March	220,000
Excess of available cash over cash disbursements	6,500
Financing	8,500
Ending cash balance	$ 15,000

To maintain the desired minimum cash balance of $15,000, $8,500 of cash must be borrowed.

THE
NAVIGATOR

Related exercise material: BE6-9 and E6-9.

BUDGETING IN NONMANUFACTURING COMPANIES

Budgeting is not limited to manufacturing companies. Budgets may also be used in profit planning by merchandising companies, service enterprises, and not-for-profit organizations.

MERCHANDISING COMPANIES

As in manufacturing operations, the sales budget is both the starting point and the key factor in the development of the master budget for a merchandising company. The major differences between the master budgets of a merchandising company and a manufacturing company are that a merchandiser **(1) uses a merchandise purchases budget instead of a production budget and (2) does not use the manufacturing budgets (direct materials, direct labor, and manufacturing overhead).** The merchandise purchases budget shows the estimated cost of goods to be purchased to meet expected sales. The formula for determining budgeted merchandise purchases is:

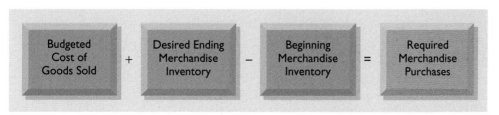

Illustration 6-18
Merchandise purchases formula

To illustrate, assume that the budget committee of Lima Company is preparing the merchandise purchases budget for July. It estimates that budgeted sales will be $300,000 in July and $320,000 in August. Cost of goods sold is expected to be 70% of sales, and the company's desired ending inventory is 30% of the following month's cost of goods sold. Required merchandise purchases for July are $214,200, computed as follows:

Illustration 6-19
Computation of required merchandise purchases

Budgeted cost of goods sold (budgeted sales for July, $300,000 \times 70\%$)	$ 210,000
Desired ending merchandise inventory (budgeted cost of goods sold for August, $320,000 \times 70\% \times 30\%$)	67,200
Total	277,200
Less: Beginning merchandise inventory (budgeted sales for July, $300,000 \times 70\% \times 30\%$)	63,000
Required merchandise purchases for July	**$214,200**

Departmentalized budgets

When the merchandising company is departmentalized, separate budgets are prepared for each department. For example, a grocery store may start by preparing sales budgets and purchases budgets for each of its major departments, such as meats, dairy, and produce. These budgets are then combined into a master budget for the store. When a retailer has branch stores, separate master budgets are prepared for each store. Then these budgets are incorporated into master budgets for the company as a whole.

SERVICE ENTERPRISES

In service enterprises, such as a public accounting firm, a law office, or a medical practice, the critical factor in budgeting is **coordinating professional staff needs with anticipated services.** If a firm is overstaffed, (1) labor costs will be disproportionately high, (2) profits will be lower because of the additional salaries, and (3) staff turnover may increase because of lack of challenging work. In contrast, if an enterprise is understaffed, revenue may be lost because existing and prospective client needs for service cannot be met, and professional staff may seek other positions because of excessive work loads.

Budget data for service revenue may be obtained from expected output or expected input. When output is used, it is necessary to determine the expected billings of clients for services rendered. In a public accounting firm, for example, output would be the sum of its billings in auditing, tax, and consulting services. When service revenue is derived from input data, each professional staff member is required to project his or her billable time. Billing rates are then applied to billable time to produce expected service revenue.

BUSINESS INSIGHT
Management Perspective

Lucy Carter, managing partner of a small CPA firm in Nashville, uses formal budgets as the principal tool for keeping cash flow on an even keel throughout the year. The firm budgets annually for both revenues and expenses on a month-by-month basis. For example, the revenue budget is derived from chargeable-hour goals set by the staff, with a threshold of 1,800 hours for each staff member and 1,700 hours for each manager. Each month the budget is compared with the financial statements, and adjustments are made if necessary.

NOT-FOR-PROFIT ORGANIZATIONS

Budgeting is just as important for not-for-profit organizations as for profit-oriented enterprises. The budget process, however, is significantly different. In most cases not-for-profit entities budget **on the basis of cash flows (expenditures and receipts), rather than on a revenue and expense basis.** Further, the starting point in the process is usually expenditures, not receipts. For the not-for-profit entity, management's task generally is to find the receipts needed to support the planned expenditures. This was the case for the University of Nebraska in the Feature Story. The activity index is also likely to be significantly different. For example, in a not-for-profit entity, such as a university, budgeted faculty positions may be based on full-time equivalent students or credit hours expected to be taught in a department.

For some governmental units, the budget must be approved by voters. In other cases, such as state governments and the federal government, legislative approval is required. After the budget is adopted, it must be strictly followed, and overspending is often illegal. In governmental budgets, authorizations tend to be on a line-by-line basis. That is, the budget for a municipality may have a specified authorization for police and fire protection, garbage collection, street paving, and so on. The line item authorization of governmental budgets significantly limits the amount of discretion management can exercise. The city manager often cannot use savings in one line item, such as street paving, to cover increased spending in another line item, such as snow removal.

BEFORE YOU GO ON . . .

● **Review It**

1. What is the formula for computing required merchandise purchases?
2. How does budgeting in service and not-for-profit organizations differ from budgeting in manufacturing and merchandising companies?

THE
NAVIGATOR

*U*SING THE DECISION TOOLKIT

Like the University of Nebraska in the Feature Story, the University of Wisconsin and its subunits must prepare budgets. One unique subunit of the University of Wisconsin is Babcock Ice Cream, a functioning producer of dairy products (and famous, at least on campus, for its delicious ice cream).

Assume that Babcock Ice Cream prepares monthly cash budgets. Relevant data from assumed operating budgets for 2000 are:

	January	February
Sales	$460,000	$412,000
Direct materials purchases	185,000	210,000
Direct labor	70,000	85,000
Manufacturing overhead	50,000	65,000
Selling and administrative expenses	85,000	95,000

Babcock sells 50% of its ice cream in its shops on campus, as well as selling to local stores. Collections from local stores are expected to be 50% in the month of sale, and 50% in the month following sale. Sixty percent (60%) of direct materials purchases are paid in cash in the month of purchase, and the balance due is paid in the month following the purchase. All other items above are paid in the month incurred. (Depreciation has been excluded from manufacturing overhead and selling and administrative expenses.)

Other data:

(1) Sales: November 1999, $370,000; December 1999, $320,000

(2) Purchases of direct materials: December 1999, $175,000

(3) Other receipts: January—Donation received, $2,000

                 February—Sale of used equipment, $4,000

(4) Other disbursements: February—Purchased equipment, $10,000

(5) Repaid debt: January, $30,000

The company's cash balance on January 1, 2000, is expected to be $50,000. The company wants to maintain a minimum cash balance of $45,000.

Instructions

(a) Prepare schedules for (1) expected collections from customers and (2) expected payments for direct materials purchases.

(b) Prepare a cash budget for January and February in columnar form.

Solution

(a) (1)

Expected Collections from Customers

	January	February
December ($320,000)	$ 80,000	$ 0
January ($460,000)	345,000	115,000
February ($412,000)	0	309,000
Totals	$425,000	$424,000

(2)

Expected Payments for Direct Materials

	January	February
December ($175,000)	$ 70,000	$ 0
January ($185,000)	111,000	74,000
February ($210,000)	0	126,000
Totals	$181,000	$200,000

(b)

BABCOCK ICE CREAM
Cash Budget
For the Two Months Ending February 28, 2000

	January	February
Beginning cash balance	$ 50,000	$ 61,000
Add: Receipts		
Collections from customers	425,000	424,000
Donations received	2,000	0
Sale of used equipment	0	4,000
Total receipts	427,000	428,000
Total available cash	477,000	489,000
Less: Disbursements		
Direct materials	181,000	200,000
Direct labor	70,000	85,000
Manufacturing overhead	50,000	65,000
Selling and administrative expenses	85,000	95,000
Purchase of equipment	0	10,000
Total disbursements	386,000	455,000
Excess (deficiency) of available cash over disbursements	91,000	34,000
Financing		
Borrowings	0	11,000
Repayments	30,000	0
Ending cash balance	$ 61,000	$ 45,000

THE
NAVIGATOR

SUMMARY OF STUDY OBJECTIVES

❶ Indicate the benefits of budgeting. The primary advantages of budgeting are that it (a) requires management to plan ahead, (b) provides definite objectives for evaluating performance, (c) creates an early warning system for potential problems, (d) facilitates coordination of activities, (e) results in greater management awareness, and (f) contributes to positive behavior patterns.

❷ State the essentials of effective budgeting. The essentials of effective budgeting are (a) sound organizational structure, (b) research and analysis, and (c) acceptance by all levels of management.

❸ Identify the budgets that comprise the master budget. The master budget consists of the following budgets: (a) sales, (b) production, (c) direct materials, (d) direct labor, (e) manufacturing overhead, (f) selling and administrative expense, (g) budgeted income statement, (h) capital expenditure budget, (i) cash budget, and (j) budgeted balance sheet.

❹ Describe the sources for preparing the budgeted income statement. The budgeted income statement is prepared from (a) the sales budget, (b) the budgets for direct materials, direct labor, and manufacturing overhead, and (c) the selling and administrative expense budget.

❺ Explain the principal sections of a cash budget. The cash budget has three sections (receipts, disbursements, and financing) and the beginning and ending cash balances.

❻ Indicate the applicability of budgeting in non-manufacturing companies. Budgeting may be used in merchandising companies for development of a master budget. In service enterprises budgeting is a critical factor in coordinating staff needs with anticipated services. In not-for-profit organizations, the starting point in budgeting is usually expenditures, not receipts.

DECISION TOOLKIT—A SUMMARY

Decision Checkpoints	Info Needed for Decision	Tool to Use for Decision	How to Evaluate Results
Has the company met its targets for sales, production expenses, selling and administrative expenses, and net income?	Sales forecasts, inventory levels, projected materials, labor, overhead, and selling and administrative requirements	Master budget—a set of interrelated budgets including sales, production, materials, labor, overhead, and selling and administrative budgets	Results are favorable if revenues exceed budgeted amounts, or if expenses are less than budgeted amounts.
Is the company going to need to borrow funds in the coming quarter?	Beginning cash balance, cash receipts, cash disbursements, and desired cash balance	Cash budget	The company will need to borrow money if the cash budget indicates a projected cash deficiency of available cash over cash disbursements for the quarter.

GLOSSARY

Budget A formal written summary of management's plans for a specified future time period, expressed in financial terms. (p. 212)

Budget committee A group responsible for coordinating the preparation of the budget. (p. 214)

Budgeted balance sheet A projection of financial position at the end of the budget period. (p. 227)

Budgeted income statement An estimate of the expected profitability of operations for the budget period. (p. 222)

Cash budget A projection of anticipated cash flows. (p. 223)

Direct labor budget A projection of the quantity and cost of direct labor to be incurred to meet production requirements. (p. 220)

Direct materials budget An estimate of the quantity and cost of direct materials to be purchased. (p. 219)

Financial budgets Individual budgets that indicate the cash resources needed for expected operations and planned capital expenditures. (p. 216)

Long-range planning A formalized process of selecting strategies to achieve long-term goals and developing policies and plans to implement the strategies. (p. 216)

Manufacturing overhead budget An estimate of expected manufacturing overhead costs for the budget period. (p. 221)

Master budget A set of interrelated budgets that constitutes a plan of action for a specific time period. (p. 216)

Merchandise purchases budget The estimated cost of goods to be purchased in a merchandising company to meet expected sales. (p. 229)

Operating budgets Individual budgets that culminate in a budgeted income statement. (p. 216)

Production budget A projection of the units that must be produced to meet anticipated sales. (p. 218)

Sales budget An estimate of expected sales for the budget period. (p. 218)

Sales forecast The projection of potential sales for the industry and the company's expected share of such sales. (p. 214)

Selling and administrative expense budget A projection of anticipated selling and administrative expenses for the budget period. (p. 222)

DEMONSTRATION PROBLEM

The Soroco Company is preparing its master budgets for 1999. Relevant data pertaining to its sales and production budgets are as follows:

Sales: Sales for the year are expected to total 1,200,000 units. Quarterly sales are 20%, 25%, 30%, and 25%, respectively. The sales price is expected to be $50 per unit for the first three quarters and $55 per unit beginning in the fourth quarter. Sales in the first quarter of 2000 are expected to be 10% higher than the budgeted sales volume for the first quarter of 1999.

Production: Management desires to maintain ending finished goods inventories at 25% of the next quarter's budgeted sales volume.

Instructions

Prepare the sales budget and production budget by quarters for 1999.

Problem-Solving Strategies

1. For the sales budget, know the form and content.

2. The sales budget is the first budget prepared.

3. Each of the other budgets is dependent on the sales budget.

4. The production budget shows the units that must be produced to meet anticipated sales.

5. The production budget provides the bases for determining the budgeted cost for each manufacturing cost element.

6. Know how to compute the beginning and ending finished goods units.

Solution to Demonstration Problem

SOROCO COMPANY
Sales Budget
For the Year Ending December 31, 1999

	Quarter				
	1	2	3	4	Year
Expected unit sales	240,000	300,000	360,000	300,000	1,200,000
Unit selling price	× $50	× $50	× $50	× $55	—
	$12,000,000	$15,000,000	$18,000,000	$16,500,000	$61,500,000

SOROCO COMPANY
Production Budget
For the Year Ending December 31, 1999

	Quarter				
	1	2	3	4	Year
Expected unit sales	240,000	300,000	360,000	300,000	
Add: Desired ending finished goods units	75,000	90,000	75,000	66,000[1]	
Total required units	315,000	390,000	435,000	366,000	
Less: Beginning finished goods units	60,000[2]	75,000	90,000	75,000	
Units to be produced	255,000	315,000	345,000	291,000	1,206,000

THE
NAVIGATOR

[1]Estimated first-quarter 2000 sales volume 240,000 + (240,000 × 10%) = 264,000; 264,000 × 25%.
[2]25% of estimated first-quarter 1999 sales units.

SELF-STUDY QUESTIONS

Answers are at the end of the chapter.

(SO 1) 1. The benefits of budgeting include *all but one* of the following:
(a) Management can plan ahead.
(b) An early warning system is provided for potential problems.
(c) It enables disciplinary action to be taken at every level of responsibility.
(d) The coordination of activities is facilitated.

(SO 2) 2. The essentials of effective budgeting do *not* include:
(a) top down budgeting.
(b) management acceptance.
(c) research and analysis.
(d) sound organizational structure.

(SO 2) 3. Compared to budgeting, long-range planning generally has the:
(a) same amount of detail.
(b) longer time period.
(c) same emphasis.
(d) same time period.

(SO 3) 4. A sales budget is:
(a) derived from the production budget.
(b) management's best estimate of sales revenue for the year.
(c) not the starting point for the master budget.
(d) prepared only for credit sales.

(SO 3) 5. The formula for the production budget is budgeted sales in units plus:
(a) desired ending merchandise inventory less beginning merchandise inventory.
(b) beginning finished goods units less desired ending finished goods units.
(c) desired ending direct materials units less beginning direct materials units.

(d) desired ending finished goods units less beginning finished goods units.

(SO 3) 6. Direct materials inventories are kept in pounds in Byrd Company, and the total pounds of direct materials needed for production is 9,500. If the beginning inventory is 1,000 pounds and the desired ending inventory is 2,200 pounds, the total pounds to be purchased is:
(a) 9,400.
(b) 9,500.
(c) 9,700.
(d) 10,700.

(SO 3) 7. The formula for computing the direct labor cost budget is to multiply the direct labor cost per hour by the:
(a) total required direct labor hours.
(b) physical units to be produced.
(c) equivalent units to be produced.
(d) no correct answer is given.

(SO 4) 8. Each of the following budgets is used in preparing the budgeted income statement *except* the:
(a) sales budget.
(b) selling and administrative budget.
(c) capital expenditure budget.
(d) direct labor budget.

(SO 5) 9. Expected direct materials purchases in Read Company are $70,000 in the first quarter and $90,000 in the second quarter. Forty percent of the purchases are paid in cash as incurred, and the balance is paid in the following quarter. The budgeted cash payments for purchases in the second quarter are:
(a) $96,000.
(b) $90,000.
(c) $78,000.
(d) $72,000.

(SO 6) 10. The budget for a merchandising company differs from a budget for a manufacturing company because:
(a) a merchandise purchases budget replaces the production budget.

(b) the manufacturing budgets are not applicable.
(c) None of the above.
(d) Both (a) and (b) above.

QUESTIONS

1. (a) What is a budget?
   (b) How does a budget contribute to good management?

2. Alemeda and Delino are discussing the benefits of budgeting. They ask you to identify the primary advantages of budgeting. Comply with their request.

3. Ramon Martinez asks your help in understanding the essentials of effective budgeting. Identify the essentials for Ramon.

4. (a) "Accounting plays a relatively unimportant role in budgeting." Do you agree? Explain.
   (b) What responsibilities does management have in budgeting?

5. What criteria are helpful in determining the length of the budget period? What is the most common budget period?

6. Kathy Fernetti maintains that the only difference between budgeting and long-range planning is time. Do you agree? Why or why not?

7. Distinguish between a master budget and a sales forecast.

8. What budget is the starting point in preparing the master budget? What may result if this budget is inaccurate?

9. "The production budget shows both unit production data and unit cost data." Is this true? Explain.

10. Klaus Company has 6,000 beginning finished goods units. Budgeted sales units are 150,000. If management desires 10,000 ending finished goods units, what are the required units of production?

11. In preparing the direct materials budget for Matsakis Company, management concludes that required purchases are 48,000 units. If 46,000 direct materials units are required in production and there are 4,000 units of beginning direct materials, what is the desired units of ending direct materials?

12. The production budget of Piper Company calls for 80,000 units to be produced. If it takes 30 minutes to make one unit and the direct labor rate is $14 per hour, what is the total budgeted direct labor cost?

13. Schultz Company's manufacturing overhead budget shows total variable costs of $186,000 and total fixed costs of $174,000. Total production in units is expected to be 160,000. It takes 15 minutes to make one unit, and the direct labor rate is $15 per hour. Express the manufacturing overhead rate as (a) a percentage of direct labor cost and (b) an amount per direct labor hour.

14. Tabor Company's variable selling and administrative expenses are 10% of net sales and fixed expenses are $60,000 per quarter. The sales budget shows expected sales of $200,000 and $250,000 in the first and second quarters, respectively. What are the total budgeted selling and administrative expenses for each quarter?

15. For Franco Company, the budgeted cost for one unit of product is direct materials $10, direct labor $20, and manufacturing overhead 75% of direct labor cost. If 25,000 units are expected to be sold at $77 each, what is the budgeted gross profit?

16. Indicate the supporting schedules used in preparing a budgeted income statement through gross profit for a manufacturing company.

17. Identify the three sections of a cash budget. What balances are also shown in this budget?

18. Garcia Company has credit sales of $400,000 in January. Past experience suggests that 40% is collected in the month of sale, 50% in the month following the sale, and 4% in the second month following the sale. Compute the cash collections from January sales in January, February, and March.

19. What is the formula for determining required merchandise purchases in a merchandising company?

20. How may expected revenues in a service enterprise be computed?

BRIEF EXERCISES

Prepare a diagram of a master budget.

(SO 3)

BE6-1 O'Connor Manufacturing Company uses the following budgets: Balance Sheet, Capital Expenditure, Cash, Direct Labor, Direct Materials, Income Statement, Manufacturing Overhead, Production, Sales, and Selling and Administrative. Prepare a diagram of the interrelationships of the budgets in the master budget. Indicate whether each budget is an operating or a financial budget.

BE6-2   Delgado Company estimates that unit sales will be 10,000 in quarter 1; 12,000 in quarter 2; 14,000 in quarter 3; and 15,000 in quarter 4. Using a sales price of $60 per unit, prepare the sales budget, by quarters, for the year ending December 31, 1999.

Prepare a sales budget.
(SO 3)

BE6-3   Sales budget data for Delgado Company are given in BE6-2. Management desires to have an ending finished goods inventory equal to 25% of the next quarter's expected unit sales. Prepare a production budget, by quarters, for the first 6 months of 1999.

Prepare a production budget for 2 quarters.
(SO 3)

BE6-4   Fosdick Company has 1,200 pounds of raw materials in its December 31, 1999, ending inventory. Required production for January and February are 4,000 and 5,000 units, respectively. Three pounds of raw materials are needed for each unit, and the estimated cost per pound is $6. Management desires an ending inventory equal to 10% of next month's materials requirements. Prepare the direct materials budget for January.

Prepare a direct materials budget for one month.
(SO 3)

BE6-5   For Haught Company, units to be produced are 5,000 in quarter 1 and 6,000 in quarter 2. It takes 1.5 hours to make a finished unit, and the expected hourly wage rate is $12 per hour. Prepare a direct labor budget, by quarters, for the 6 months ending June 30, 1999.

Prepare a direct labor budget for 2 quarters.
(SO 3)

BE6-6   For McNulty, Inc., variable manufacturing overhead costs are expected to be $30,000 in the first quarter of 1999 with $4,000 increments in each of the remaining three quarters. Fixed overhead costs are estimated to be $35,000 in each quarter. Prepare the manufacturing overhead budget, by quarters, for the year.

Prepare a manufacturing overhead budget.
(SO 3)

BE6-7   Newlin Company classifies its selling and administrative expense budget into variable and fixed components. Variable expenses are expected to be $21,000 in the first quarter, and $3,000 increments are expected in the remaining quarters of 1999. Fixed expenses are expected to be $40,000 in each quarter. Prepare the selling and administrative expense budget, by quarters, for 1999.

Prepare a selling and administrative expense budget.
(SO 3)

BE6-8   Markowitz Company has completed all of its operating budgets. The sales budget for the year shows 50,000 units and total sales of $2,000,000. The total unit cost of making one unit of sales is $30. Selling and administrative expenses are expected to be $300,000, and income taxes are estimated to be $50,000. Prepare a budgeted income statement for the year ending December 31, 1999.

Prepare a budgeted income statement for the year.
(SO 4)

BE6-9   Liang Industries expects credit sales for January, February, and March to be $200,000, $275,000, and $310,000, respectively. It is expected that 60% of the sales will be collected in the month of sale, and 40% will be collected in the following month. Compute cash collections from customers for each month.

Prepare data for a cash budget.
(SO 5)

BE6-10   GRS Wholesalers is preparing its merchandise purchases budget. Budgeted sales are $400,000 for April and $450,000 for May. Cost of goods sold is expected to be 70% of sales, and the company's desired ending inventory is 20% of the following month's cost of goods sold. Compute the required purchases for April.

Determine required merchandise purchases for one month.
(SO 6)

EXERCISES

E6-1   Kohler Electronics Inc. produces and sells two models of pocket calculators, XQ-103 and XQ-104. The calculators sell for $10 and $15, respectively. Because of the intense competition Kohler faces, management budgets sales semiannually. Its projections for the first 2 quarters of 1999 are as follows:

Prepare a sales budget for 2 quarters.
(SO 3)

	Unit Sales	
Product	**Quarter 1**	**Quarter 2**
XQ-103	30,000	27,000
XQ-104	12,000	13,000

No changes in selling prices are anticipated.

Instructions
Prepare a sales budget for the two quarters ending June 30, 1999. List the products and show for each quarter and for the 6 months, units, selling price, and total sales by product and in total.

Prepare quarterly production budgets.

(SO 3)

E6-2   Ghosh Company produces and sells two types of automobile batteries, the heavy-duty HD-240 and the long-life LL-250. The 1999 sales budget for the two products is as follows:

Quarter	HD-240	LL-250
1	5,000	10,000
2	7,000	18,000
3	8,000	20,000
4	10,000	35,000

The January 1, 1999, inventory of HD-240 and LL-250 units is 4,000 and 8,000, respectively. Management desires an ending inventory each quarter equal to 70% of the next quarter's sales. Sales in the first quarter of 2000 are expected to be 40% higher than sales in the same quarter in 1999.

Instructions
Prepare separate quarterly production budgets for each product by quarters for 1999.

Prepare a direct materials purchases budget.

(SO 3)

E6-3   Herrara Industries has adopted the following production budget for the first 4 months of 2000.

Month	Units	Month	Units
January	10,000	March	6,000
February	8,000	April	4,000

Each unit requires 6 pounds of raw materials costing $1.50 per pound. On December 31, 1999, the ending raw materials inventory was 36,000 pounds. Management wants to have a raw materials inventory at the end of the month equal to 60% of next month's production requirements.

Instructions
Prepare a direct materials purchases budget by months for the first quarter.

Prepare production and direct materials budgets by quarters for 6 months.

(SO 3)

E6-4   The Kasper Company budget committee has reached agreement on the following data for the 6 months ending June 30, 2000:

Sales units (by quarters):   (1) 5,000, (2) 8,000
Ending raw materials inventory: 50% of the next quarter's production requirements
Ending finished goods inventory: 25% of the next quarter's expected sales units

The ending raw materials and finished goods inventories at December 31, 1999, follow the same percentage relationships to production and sales that occur in 2000. Three pounds of raw materials are required to make each unit of finished goods. Raw materials purchased are expected to cost $4 per pound. Sales of 7,000 units and required production of 7,250 units are expected in the third quarter of 2000.

Instructions
(a) Prepare a production budget by quarters for the 6 months.
(b) Prepare a direct materials budget by quarters for the 6 months.

Prepare a direct labor budget.

(SO 3)

E6-5   Manies, Inc., is preparing its direct labor budget for 1999 from the following production budget based on a calendar year:

Quarter	Units	Quarter	Units
1	20,000	3	35,000
2	25,000	4	30,000

Each unit requires 1.6 hours of direct labor.

Instructions
Prepare a direct labor cost budget for 1999. Wage rates are expected to be $14 for the first 2 quarters and $15 for quarters 3 and 4.

E6-6   Napier Company is preparing its manufacturing overhead budget for 1999. Relevant data consist of the following:

Prepare a manufacturing overhead budget for the year.
(SO 3)

Units to be produced (by quarters):   10,000; 12,000; 14,000; 16,000.

Direct labor: Time is 1.5 hours per unit.

Variable overhead costs per direct labor hour: Indirect materials $0.70; indirect labor $1.20; and maintenance $0.30.

Fixed overhead costs per quarter: Supervisory salaries $30,000; depreciation $8,000; and maintenance $6,000.

Instructions
Prepare the manufacturing overhead budget for the year, showing quarterly data.

E6-7   Ortega Company combines its operating expenses for budget purposes in a selling and administrative expense budget. For the first 6 months of 1999, the following data are developed:
1. Sales: 12,000 units quarter 1; 15,000 units quarter 2.
2. Variable costs per dollar of sales: Sales commissions 5%; delivery expense 2%; and advertising 3%.
3. Fixed costs per quarter: Sales salaries $10,000; office salaries $6,000; depreciation $4,200; insurance $1,500; utilities $800; and repairs expense $600.
4. Unit selling price: $20.

Prepare a selling and administrative expense budget for 2 quarters.
(SO 3)

Instructions
Prepare a selling and administrative expense budget by quarters for the first 6 months of 1999.

E6-8   Renfro Company has accumulated the following budget data for the year 1999:
1. Sales: 25,000 units; unit selling price $80.
2. Cost of one unit of finished goods: Direct materials 2 pounds at $5 per pound; direct labor 3 hours at $12 per hour; and manufacturing overhead $6 per direct labor hour.
3. Inventories (raw materials only):   Beginning, 10,000 pounds; ending, 15,000 pounds.
4. Raw materials cost: $5 per pound.
5. Selling and administrative expenses: $150,000.
6. Income taxes: 30% of income before income taxes.

Prepare a budgeted income statement for the year.
(SO 3, 4)

Instructions
Prepare a budgeted income statement for 1999. Show the computation of cost of goods sold.

E6-9   Peres Company expects to have a cash balance of $46,000 on January 1, 1999. Relevant monthly budget data for the first 2 months of 1999 are as follows:

Prepare a cash budget for 2 months.
(SO 5)

Collections from customers: January $70,000; February $150,000.

Payments to suppliers: January $40,000; February $75,000.

Direct labor: January $30,000; February $40,000. Wages are paid in the month they are incurred.

Manufacturing overhead: January $21,000; February $30,000. These costs include depreciation of $1,000 per month. All other overhead costs are paid as incurred.

Selling and administrative expenses: January $15,000; February $20,000. These costs are exclusive of depreciation. They are paid as incurred.

Sales of marketable securities in January are expected to realize $10,000 in cash. Peres Company has a line of credit at a local bank that enables it to borrow up to $25,000. The company wants to maintain a minimum monthly cash balance of $20,000.

Instructions
Prepare a cash budget for January and February.

Prepare a purchases budget and budgeted income statement for a merchandising company.

(SO 6)

E6-10   In May 1999, the budget committee of Union Street Stores assembles the following data in preparation of budgeted merchandise purchases for the month of June.
1. Expected sales: June $500,000, July $600,000.
2. Cost of goods sold is expected to be 60% of sales.
3. Desired ending merchandise inventory is 30% of the following (next) month's cost of goods sold.
4. The beginning inventory at June 1 will be the desired amount.

Instructions
(a) Compute the budgeted merchandise purchases for June.
(b) Prepare the budgeted income statement for June through gross profit on sales.

PROBLEMS: SET A

Prepare a budgeted income statement and supporting budgets.

(SO 3, 4)

P6-1A   Bluestem Farm Supply Company manufactures and sells a fertilizer called Basic II. The following data are developed for preparing budgets for Basic II for the first 2 quarters of 1999:
1. Sales: Quarter 1, 40,000 bags; quarter 2, 60,000 bags. Selling price is $60 per bag.
2. Direct materials: Each bag of Basic II requires 6 pounds of Crup at a cost of $3 per pound and 10 pounds of Dert at $1.50 per pound.
3. Desired inventory levels:

Type of Inventory	January 1	April 1	July 1
Basic II (bags)	10,000	15,000	20,000
Crup (pounds)	9,000	12,000	15,000
Dert (pounds)	15,000	20,000	25,000

4. Direct labor: Direct labor time is 15 minutes per bag at an hourly rate of $10 per hour.
5. Selling and administrative expenses are expected to be 10% of sales plus $150,000 per quarter.
6. Income taxes are expected to be 30% of income from operations.

   Your assistant has prepared two budgets: the manufacturing overhead budget that shows expected costs to be 100% of direct labor cost, and the direct materials budget for Dert which shows the cost of Dert to be $682,500 in quarter 1 and $982,500 in quarter 2.

Instructions
Prepare the budgeted income statement for the first 6 months of 1999 and all required supporting budgets by quarters. (*Note:* Use variable and fixed in the selling and administrative expense budget.)

Prepare sales, production, direct materials, direct labor, and income statement budgets.

(SO 3, 4)

P6-2A   Reneau Inc. is preparing its annual budgets for the year ending December 31, 1999. Accounting assistants furnish the following data:

	Product LN 35	Product LN 40
Sales budget:		
Anticipated volume in units	400,000	180,000
Unit selling price	$20.00	$30.00
Production budget:		
Desired ending finished goods units	30,000	25,000
Beginning finished goods units	20,000	15,000

	Product LN 35	Product LN 40
Direct materials budget:		
Direct materials per unit (pounds)	2	3
Desired ending direct materials pounds	50,000	20,000
Beginning direct materials pounds	40,000	10,000
Cost per pound	$2.00	$3.00

Direct labor budget:

Direct labor time per unit	.5	.75
Direct labor rate per hour	$8.00	$8.00

Budgeted income statement:

Total unit cost	$10.00	$20.00

An accounting assistant has prepared the detailed manufacturing overhead budget and the selling and administrative expense budget. The latter shows selling expenses of $460,000 for product LN 35 and $440,000 for product LN 40, and administrative expenses of $420,000 for product LN 35 and $380,000 for product LN 40. Income taxes are expected to be 30%.

Instructions
Prepare the following budgets for the year. Show data for each product. Quarterly budgets should not be prepared.
(a) Sales   (d) Direct labor
(b) Production   (e) Income statement (*Note:* Income taxes are not allocated to
(c) Direct materials   the products.)

P6-3A Prothe Industries had sales in 1999 of $5,250,000 (875,000 units) and gross profit of $1,587,500. Management is considering two alternative budget plans to increase its gross profit in 2000.

Prepare sales and production budgets and compute cost per unit under two plans.
(SO 3, 4)

Plan A would increase the selling price per unit from $6.00 to $6.60. Sales volume would decrease by 10% from its 1999 level. Plan B would decrease the selling price per unit by 5%. The marketing department expects that the sales volume would increase by 100,000 units.

At the end of 1999, Prothe has 75,000 units on hand. If Plan A is accepted, the 2000 ending inventory should be equal to 87,500 units. If Plan B is accepted, the ending inventory should be equal to 100,000 units. Each unit produced will cost $2.00 in direct materials, $1.00 in direct labor, and $.50 in variable overhead. The fixed overhead for 2000 should be $1,000,000.

Instructions
(a) Prepare a sales budget for 2000 under (1) Plan A and (2) Plan B.
(b) Prepare a production budget for 2000 under (1) Plan A and (2) Plan B.
(c) Compute the cost per unit under (1) Plan A and (2) Plan B. Explain why the cost per unit is different for each of the two plans. (Round to two decimals.)
(d) Which plan should be accepted? (*Hint:* Compute the gross profit under each plan.)

P6-4A Sielert Company prepares monthly cash budgets. Relevant data from operating budgets for 2000 are:

Prepare cash budget for 2 months.
(SO 5)

	January	February
Sales	$350,000	$400,000
Direct materials purchases	95,000	110,000
Direct labor	80,000	95,000
Manufacturing overhead	60,000	75,000
Selling and administrative expenses	75,000	85,000

All sales are on account. Collections are expected to be 50% in the month of sale, 30% in the first month following the sale, and 20% in the second month following the sale. Forty percent (40%) of direct material purchases are paid in cash in the month of purchase, and the balance due is paid in the month following the purchase. All other items above are paid in the month incurred. Depreciation has been excluded from manufacturing overhead and selling and administrative expenses.

Other data:
(1) Credit sales: November 1999, $200,000; December 1999, $280,000.
(2) Purchases of direct materials: December 1999, $90,000.
(3) Other receipts: January—Collection of December 31, 1999, interest receivable $3,000;
                      February—Proceeds from sale of securities $5,000.
(4) Other disbursements: February—payment of $20,000 for land.
   The company's cash balance on January 1, 2000, is expected to be $60,000. The company wants to maintain a minimum cash balance of $50,000.

Instructions
(a) Prepare schedules for (1) expected collections from customers and (2) expected payments for direct materials purchases.
(b) Prepare a cash budget for January and February in columnar form.

Prepare purchases and income statement budgets for a merchandising company.

(SO 6)

P6-5A The budget committee of Taberes Company collects the following data for its Westwood Store in preparing budgeted income statements for July and August 1999.
1. Expected sales: July $400,000, August $450,000, September $500,000.
2. Cost of goods sold is expected to be 70% of sales.
3. Company policy is to maintain ending merchandise inventory at 25% of the following month's cost of goods sold.
4. Operating expenses are estimated to be:

Sales salaries	$20,000 per month
Advertising	4% of monthly sales
Delivery expense	2% of monthly sales
Sales commissions	3% of monthly sales
Rent expense	$3,000 per month
Depreciation	$700 per month
Utilities	$500 per month
Insurance	$300 per month

5. Income taxes are estimated to be 30% of income from operations.

Instructions
(a) Prepare the merchandise purchases budget for each month in columnar form.
(b) Prepare budgeted income statements for each month in columnar form. Show the details of cost of goods sold in the statements.

Prepare budgeted income statement and balance sheet.

(SO 3, 4)

P6-6A Viola Industries' balance sheet at December 31, 1999, is presented below.

VIOLA INDUSTRIES
Balance Sheet
December 31, 1999

Assets

Current assets		
Cash		$ 7,500
Accounts receivable		82,500
Finished goods inventory (2,000 units)		30,000
Total current assets		120,000
Property, plant, and equipment		
Equipment	$40,000	
Less: Accumulated depreciation	10,000	30,000
Total assets		$150,000

Liabilities and Stockholders' Equity

Liabilities		
Notes payable		$ 25,000
Accounts payable		45,000
Total liabilities		70,000
Stockholders' equity		
Common stock	$50,000	
Retained earnings	30,000	
Total stockholders' equity		80,000
Total liabilities and stockholders' equity		$150,000

Additional information accumulated for the budgeting process:
Budgeted data for the year 2000 include the following:

	4th Qtr. of 2000	Year 2000 Total
Sales budget (8,000 units at $35)	$80,000	$280,000
Direct materials used	17,000	67,200
Direct labor	8,500	33,600
Manufacturing overhead applied	10,000	42,000
Selling and administrative expenses	18,000	76,000

To meet sales requirements and to have 2,400 units of finished goods on hand at December 31, 2000, the production budget shows 8,400 required units of output. The total unit cost of production is expected to be $17. Viola Industries uses the first-in, first-out (FIFO) inventory costing method. Selling and administrative expenses include $4,000 for depreciation on equipment. Interest expense is expected to be $3,500 for the year. Income taxes are expected to be 30% of income before income taxes.

All sales and purchases are on account. It is expected that 60% of quarterly sales are collected in cash within the quarter and the remainder is collected in the following quarter. Direct materials purchased from suppliers are paid 50% in the quarter incurred and the remainder in the following quarter. Purchases in the fourth quarter were the same as the materials used. In 2000, the company expects to purchase additional equipment costing $24,000. It expects to pay $8,000 on notes payable plus all interest due and payable to December 31 (included in interest expense $3,500 above). Accounts payable at December 31, 2000, includes amounts due suppliers (see above) plus other accounts payable of $7,500. In 2000, the company expects to declare and pay a $2,000 cash dividend. Unpaid income taxes at December 31 will be $5,000. The company's cash budget shows an expected cash balance of $41,150 at December 31, 2000.

Instructions
Prepare a budgeted income statement for 2000 and a budgeted balance sheet at December 31, 2000. In preparing the income statement, you will need to compute cost of goods manufactured (materials + labor + overhead) and finished goods inventory (December 31, 2000).

PROBLEMS: SET B

P6-1B Hindi Farm Supply Company manufactures and sells a pesticide called Snare. The following data are developed for preparing budgets for Snare for the first 2 quarters of 2000.

Prepare budgeted income statement and supporting budgets.

(SO 3, 4)

1. Sales: Quarter 1, 32,000 bags: quarter 2, 48,000 bags. Selling price is $60 per bag.
2. Direct materials: Each bag of Snare requires 6 pounds of Gumm at a cost of $3 per pound and 8 pounds of Tarr at $1.50 per pound.
3. Desired inventory levels:

Type of Inventory	January 1	April 1	July 1
Snare (bags)	8,000	12,000	18,000
Gumm (pounds)	9,000	10,000	13,000
Tarr (pounds)	14,000	20,000	25,000

4. Direct labor: Direct labor time is 20 minutes per bag at an hourly rate of $12 per hour.
5. Selling and administrative expenses are expected to be 8% of sales plus $175,000 per quarter.
6. Income taxes are expected to be 30% of income from operations.

Your assistant has prepared two budgets: the manufacturing overhead budget that shows expected costs to be 150% of direct labor cost, and the direct materials budget for Tarr which shows the cost of Tarr to be $441,000 in quarter 1 and $655,500 in quarter 2.

Instructions

Prepare the budgeted income statement for the first 6 months and all required supporting budgets by quarters. (*Note:* Use variable and fixed in the selling and administrative expense budget.)

P6-2B   Kaminski Inc. is preparing its annual budgets for the year ending December 31, 2000. Accounting assistants furnish the following data:

	Product JB 50	Product JB 60
Sales budget:		
Anticipated volume in units	450,000	160,000
Unit selling price	$20.00	$25.00
Production budget:		
Desired ending finished goods units	25,000	15,000
Beginning finished goods units	30,000	10,000
Direct materials budget:		
Direct materials per unit (pounds)	2	3
Desired ending direct materials pounds	30,000	15,000
Beginning direct materials pounds	40,000	10,000
Cost per pound	$3.00	$4.00
Direct labor budget		
Direct labor time per unit	.4	.6
Direct labor rate per hour	$10.00	$10.00
Budgeted income statement:		
Total unit cost	$12.00	$20.00

An accounting assistant has prepared the detailed manufacturing overhead budget and the selling and administrative expense budget. The latter shows selling expenses of $660,000 for product JB 50 and $360,000 for product JB 60 and administrative expenses of $420,000 for product JB 50 and $340,000 for product JB 60. Income taxes are expected to be 30%.

Instructions

Prepare the following budgets for the year. Show data for each product. Quarterly budgets should not be prepared.
(a) Sales   (d) Direct labor
(b) Production   (e) Income statement (*Note:* Income taxes are not allocated to
(c) Direct materials   the products.)

P6-3B   Latham Industries had sales in 1999 of $6,000,000, and gross profit of $1,500,000. Management is considering two alternative budget plans to increase its gross profit in 2000.
   Plan A would increase the selling price per unit from $8.00 to $8.40. Sales volume would decrease by 5% from its 1999 level. Plan B would decrease the selling price per unit by $0.50. The marketing department expects that the sales volume would increase by 150,000 units.
   At the end of 1999, Latham has 30,000 units of inventory on hand. If Plan A is accepted, the 2000 ending inventory should be equal to 4% of the 2000 sales. If Plan B is accepted, the ending inventory should be equal to 40,000 units. Each unit produced will cost $1.50 in direct labor, $2.00 in direct materials, and $.90 in variable overhead. The fixed overhead for 2000 should be $1,800,000.

Instructions

(a) Prepare a sales budget for 2000 under each plan.
(b) Prepare a production budget for 2000 under each plan.
(c) Compute the production cost per unit under each plan. Why is the cost per unit different for each of the two plans? (Round to two decimals.)
(d) Which plan should be accepted? (*Hint:* Compute the gross profit under each plan.)

P6-4B Gagney Company prepares monthly cash budgets. Relevant data from operating budgets for 2000 are:

Prepare cash budget for 2 months.

(SO 5)

	January	February
Sales	$360,000	$400,000
Direct materials purchases	125,000	130,000
Direct labor	80,000	95,000
Manufacturing overhead	70,000	75,000
Selling and administrative expenses	79,000	86,000

All sales are on account. Collections are expected to be 50% in the month of sale, 40% in the first month following the sale, and 10% in the second month following the sale. Fifty percent (50%) of direct material purchases are paid in cash in the month of purchase, and the balance due is paid in the month following the purchase. All other items above are paid in the month incurred except for selling and administrative expenses that include $1,000 of depreciation per month.

    Other data: 26,000

(1) Credit sales: November 1999, $260,000; December 1999, $300,000.
(2) Purchases of direct materials: December 1999, $100,000.
(3) Other receipts: January—Collection of December 31, 1999, notes receivable $15,000;
                     February—Proceeds from sale of securities $6,000.
(4) Other disbursements: February—Withdrawal of $5,000 cash for personal use of owner, T. Kempen.

    The company's cash balance on January 1, 2000, is expected to be $55,000. The company wants to maintain a minimum cash balance of $50,000.

Instructions
(a) Prepare schedules for (1) expected collections from customers and (2) expected payments for direct materials purchases.
(b) Prepare a cash budget for January and February in columnar form.

P6-5B The budget committee of Hernandez Company collects the following data for its San Miguel Store in preparing budgeted income statements for May and June 2000.

Prepare purchases and income statement budgets for a merchandising company.

(SO 6)

1. Sales for May are expected to be $600,000. Sales in June and July are expected to be 10% higher than the preceding month.
2. Cost of goods sold is expected to be 75% of sales.
3. Company policy is to maintain ending merchandise inventory at 30% of the following month's cost of goods sold.
4. Operating expenses are estimated to be:

Sales salaries	$25,000 per month
Advertising	5% of monthly sales
Delivery expense	3% of monthly sales
Sales commissions	4% of monthly sales
Rent expense	$5,000 per month
Depreciation	$800 per month
Utilities	$600 per month
Insurance	$500 per month

5. Income taxes are estimated to be 30% of income from operations.

Instructions
(a) Prepare the merchandise purchases budget for each month in columnar form.
(b) Prepare budgeted income statements for each month in columnar form. Show the details of cost of goods sold in the statements.

BROADENING YOUR PERSPECTIVE

GROUP DECISION CASE

BYP6-1 Henigen Corporation operates on a calendar-year basis. It begins the annual budgeting process in late August when the president establishes targets for the total dollar sales and net income before taxes for the next year.

The sales target is given to the marketing department where the marketing manager formulates a sales budget by product line in both units and dollars. From this budget, sales quotas by product line in units and dollars are established for each of the corporation's sales districts. The marketing manager also estimates the cost of the marketing activities required to support the target sales volume and prepares a tentative marketing expense budget.

The executive vice president uses the sales and profit targets, the sales budget by product line, and the tentative marketing expense budget to determine the dollar amounts that can be devoted to manufacturing and corporate office expense. The executive vice president prepares the budget for corporate expenses, and then forwards to the production department the product-line sales budget in units and the total dollar amount that can be devoted to manufacturing.

The production manager meets with the factory managers to develop a manufacturing plan that will produce the required units when needed within the cost constraints set by the executive vice president. The budgeting process usually comes to a halt at this point because the production department does not consider the financial resources allocated to be adequate.

When this standstill occurs, the vice president of finance, the executive vice president, the marketing manager, and the production manager meet together to determine the final budgets for each of the areas. This normally results in a modest increase in the total amount available for manufacturing costs while the marketing expense and corporate office expense budgets are cut. The total sales and net income figures proposed by the president are seldom changed. Although the participants are seldom pleased with the compromise, these budgets are final. Each executive then develops a new detailed budget for the operations in his or her area.

None of the areas has achieved its budget in recent years. Sales often run below the target. When budgeted sales are not achieved, each area is expected to cut costs so that the president's profit target can still be met. However, the profit target is seldom met because costs are not cut enough. In fact, costs often run above the original budget in all functional areas (marketing, production, and corporate office). The president is disturbed that Henigen has not been able to meet the sales and profit targets. He hired a consultant with considerable experience with companies in Henigen's industry. The consultant reviewed the budgets for the past four years. He concluded that the product-line sales budgets were reasonable and that the cost and expense budgets were adequate for the budgeted sales and production levels.

Instructions

With the class divided into groups, answer the following:
(a) Discuss how the budgeting process employed by Henigen Corporation contributes to the failure to achieve the president's sales and profit targets.
(b) Suggest how Henigen Corporation's budgeting process could be revised to correct the problems.
(c) Should the functional areas be expected to cut their costs when sales volume falls below budget? Explain your answer. (CMA adapted.)

MANAGERIAL ANALYSIS

BYP6-2 Thebeau & Carlson Inc. manufactures ergonomic devices for computer users. Some of their more popular products include glare screens (for computer monitors), keyboard stands with wrist rests, and carousels that allow easy access to floppy disks. Over the past 5 years, they experienced rapid growth, with sales of all products increasing 20% to 50% each year.

Last year, some of the primary manufacturers of computers began introducing new products with some of the ergonomic designs, such as glare screens and wrist rests, already built in. As a result, sales of Thebeau & Carlson's accessory devices have declined somewhat. The company believes that the disk carousels will probably continue to show growth, but that the other products will probably continue to decline. When the next year's budget was prepared, increases were built in to research and development so that replacement products could be developed or the company could expand into some other product line. Some product lines being considered are general-purpose ergonomic devices including back supports, foot rests, and sloped writing pads.

The most recent results have shown that sales decreased more than was expected for the glare screens. As a result, the company may have a shortage of funds. Top management has therefore asked that all expenses be reduced 10% to compensate for these reduced sales. Summary budget information is as follows:

Raw materials	$240,000
Direct labor	110,000
Insurance	50,000
Depreciation	90,000
Machine repairs	30,000
Sales salaries	50,000
Office salaries	80,000
Factory salaries (indirect labor)	50,000
Total	$700,000

Instructions
Using the information above, answer the following questions:
(a) What are the implications of reducing each of the costs? For example, if the company reduces raw materials costs, it may have to do so by purchasing lower quality materials. This may affect sales in the long term.
(b) Based on your analysis in (a), what do you think is the best way to obtain the $70,000 in cost savings requested? Be specific. Are there any costs that cannot or should not be reduced? Why?

REAL-WORLD FOCUS

NETWORK COMPUTING DEVICES INC.

BYP6-3 Network Computing Devices Inc. was founded in 1988 in Mountain View, Calif. The company, which has 375 employees, develops software products such as X-terminals, Z-mail, PC X-ware, and related hardware products. Presented below is a discussion by management in its annual report.

NETWORK COMPUTING DEVICES, INC.
Management Discussion

NCD

The Company's operating results have varied significantly, particularly on a quarterly basis, as a result of a number of factors, including general economic conditions affecting industry demand for computer products, the timing and market acceptance of new product introductions by the Company and its competitors, the timing of significant orders from large customers, periodic changes in product pricing and discounting due to competitive factors, and the availability of key components, such as video monitors and electronic subassemblies, some of which require substantial order lead times. The Company's operating results may fluctuate in the future as a result of these and other factors, including the Company's success in developing and introducing new products, its product and customer mix, and the level of competition which it experiences. The Company operates with a small backlog. Sales and operating results, therefore, generally depend on the volume and timing of orders received, which are difficult to forecast. The Company has experienced slowness in orders from some customers during the first quarter of each calendar year due to budgeting cycles common in the computer industry. In addition, sales in Europe typically are adversely affected in the third calendar quarter as many European customers reduce their business activities during the month of August.

Due to the Company's rapid growth rate and the effect of new product introductions on quarterly revenues, these seasonal trends have not materially impacted the Company's results of operations to date. However, as the Company's product lines mature and its rate of revenue growth declines, these seasonal factors may become more evident. Additionally, the Company's international sales are denominated in U.S. dollars, and an increase or decrease in the value of the U.S. dollar relative to foreign currencies could make the Company's products less or more competitive in those markets.

Instructions
(a) Identify the factors that affect the budgeting process at Network Computing Devices, Inc.
(b) Explain the additional budgeting concerns created by the international operations of the Company.

Communication Activity

BYP6-4 In order to better serve their rural patients, Drs. Jim and Jeff Howell (brothers) began giving safety seminars. Especially popular were their "emergency-preparedness" talks given to farmers. Many people asked whether the "kit" of materials the doctors recommended for common farm emergencies was commercially available.

After checking with several suppliers, the doctors realized that no other company offered the supplies they recommended in their seminars, packaged in the way they described. Their wives, Marie and Pam, agreed to make a test package by ordering supplies from various medical supply companies and assembling them into a "kit" that could be sold at the seminars. When these kits proved a runaway success, the sisters-in-law decided to market them. At the advice of their accountant, they organized this venture as a separate company, called Life Protection Products (LPP), with Marie Howell as CEO and Pam Howell as Secretary-Treasurer.

LPP soon started receiving requests for the kits from all over the country, as word spread about their availability. Even without advertising, LPP was able to sell its full inventory every month. However, the company was becoming financially strained. Marie and Pam had about $100,000 in savings, and invested about half that amount initially. They believed that this venture would allow them to make money. However, at the present time, only about $30,000 of the cash remains, and the company is constantly short of cash.

Marie Howell has come to you for advice. She does not understand why the company is having cash flow problems. She and Pam have not even been withdrawing salaries. However, they have rented a local building and have hired two more full-time workers to help them cope with the increasing demand. They do not think they could handle the demand without this additional help.

Marie is also worried that the cash problems mean that the company may not be able to support itself. She has prepared the cash budget shown below. All seminar customers pay for their products in full at the time of purchase. In addition, several large companies have ordered the kits for use by employees who work in remote sites. They have requested credit terms and have been allowed to pay in the month following the sale. These large purchasers amount to about 25% of the sales at the present time. LPP purchases the materials for the kits about 2 months ahead of time. Marie and Pam are considering slowing the growth of the company by simply purchasing less materials, which will mean selling fewer kits.

The workers are paid in cash weekly. Marie and Pam need about $15,000 cash on hand at the beginning of the month to pay for purchases of raw materials. Right now they have been using cash from their savings, but as noted, only $30,000 is left.

The cash budget that Marie Howell has given you is as follows:

LIFE PROTECTION PRODUCTS
Cash Budget
For the Quarter Ending June 30, 2000

	April	May	June
Cash balance, beginning	$15,000	$15,000	$15,000
Cash received			
From prior month sales	5,000	7,500	12,500
From current sales	15,000	22,500	37,500
Total cash on hand	35,000	45,000	65,000
Cash payments			
To employees	3,000	3,000	3,000
For products	25,000	35,000	45,000
Miscellaneous expenses	5,000	6,000	7,000
Postage	1,000	1,000	1,000
Total cash payments	34,000	45,000	56,000
Cash balance	$ 1,000	$ 0	$ 9,000
Borrow from savings	$14,000	$15,000	$ 1,000
Borrow from bank?	$ 0	$ 0	$ 7,000

Instructions
Write a response to Marie Howell. Explain why LPP is short of cash. Will this company be able to support itself? Explain your answer. Make any recommendations you deem appropriate.

RESEARCH ASSIGNMENT

BYP6-5 The January 1997 issue of *Management Accounting* contains an article by Robert West and Amy Snyder entitled "How to Set Up a Budgeting and Planning System." The article is a description of Penn Fuel Gas, Inc.'s experience of initiating its first annual and long-range operating budget process.

Instructions
Read the article and answer the following questions:
(a) What were the "three primary tasks" first faced by the new budget director in developing the new budget process?
(b) After solving the initial challenges of developing and installing a new budget process, what were four ongoing challenges faced by the new budget director?
(c) What benefits has Penn Fuel Gas, Inc., derived from its budgeting process?

ETHICS CASE

BYP6-6 You are an accountant in the budgetary, projections, and special projects department of Vek-Tek Corp., a large manufacturing company. The president, Warren Bleeker, asks you on very short notice to prepare some sales and income projections covering the next 2 years of the company's much heralded new product lines. He wants these projections for a series of speeches he is making while on a 2-week trip to eight East Coast brokerage firms. The president hopes to bolster Vek-Tek's stock sales and price.

You work 23 hours in 2 days to compile the projections, hand deliver them to the president, and are swiftly but graciously thanked as he departs. A week later you find time to go over some of your computations and discover a miscalculation that makes the projections grossly overstated. You quickly inquire about the president's itinerary and learn that he has made half of his speeches and has half yet to make. You are in a quandary as to what to do.

Instructions
(a) What are the consequences of telling the president of your gross miscalculations?
(b) What are the consequences of *not* telling the president of your gross miscalculations?
(c) What are the ethical considerations to you and the president in this situation?

SURFING THE NET

BYP6-7 In its annual report Mark's Work Wearhouse Ltd. publishes a forecast for the upcoming year and a "post-mortem" on how well it met the prior year's forecast. The company also publishes senior management performance targets and corporate goals. Because of this, and other extensive disclosures, Mark's Work Wearhouse Ltd. received the gold prize in the merchandising category of the Canadian Institute of Chartered Accountants/Financial Post Annual Report Awards program.

Address: http://www.cica.ca/new/index.htm.

Steps:
1. Go to the Canadian Institute of Chartered Accountants web site, at the above address.
2. Choose the **Annual Report Awards** button. Explore each of the 1996 and 1997 Annual Report Awards. Choose **Merchandising** in each category. Highlight **Mark's Work Wearhouse Ltd.**

Instructions
(a) Explain, with particular emphasis on budgetary disclosures, what Mark's Work Wearhouse includes in its annual report that persuades the judges that it repeatedly deserves the gold prize.
(b) Relate Mark's Work Wearhouse's budget disclosures to the budget process outlined in Chapter 6. What has Mark's done right, in terms of the ideal budget process?

Answers to Self-Study Questions
1. c   2. a   3. b   4. b   5. d   6. d   7. a   8. c   9. c   10. d

Remember to go back to the Navigator box on the chapter-opening page and check off your completed work.

CHAPTER 7

Budgetary Control and Responsibility Accounting

STUDY OBJECTIVES

After studying this chapter, you should be able to:

1. Describe the concept of budgetary control.
2. Evaluate the usefulness of static budget reports.
3. Explain the development of flexible budgets and the usefulness of flexible budget reports.
4. Describe the concept of responsibility accounting.
5. Indicate the features of responsibility reports for cost centers.
6. Identify the content of responsibility reports for profit centers.
7. Explain the basis and formula used in evaluating performance in investment centers.

THE NAVIGATOR

FEATURE STORY

"If Money Is Low, We'll Take the Bus"

Virtually every department on a college campus develops a budget and then compares that budget to the amount actually spent. As the school term progresses, the person in charge of the budget can see how well the department is doing compared to expectations.

One of the most expensive departments on campus is the athletic department. That fact usually rankles the academic department heads. They argue that a university exists first and fore-most to educate. But the money for sports is often justified because the sports teams—particularly at big schools—generate large incomes from television contracts that can then be used for a variety of educational purposes.

At the University of Nevada, Las Vegas, each athletic team has its own budget and its own financial statements. This financial information "shows what the teams have spent for the month and for the year to date, and how the actual expenditures compare to the budget," says Merv Gupton, athletic account-ing manager. The biggest budget items: scholarships for student athletes, payroll, and travel costs.

UNLV sports teams include football, basketball, tennis, baseball, softball, soccer, track, cross country, golf, and swimming. Travel costs are usually the most uncontrollable item in the budget. What if you get two-thirds through the season and run out of money? "One sports team might be able to help out another," says Gupton. Or more likely, "if a coach is running low on money, the team won't fly—it'll take the bus."

THE NAVIGATOR

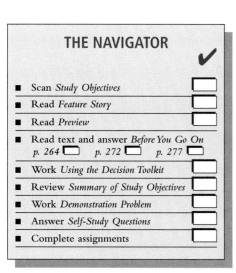

The opening story indicates not only that budgets are necessary for an athletic department, but also that they can be used to control the department's activities. For example, if you were the athletic director at UNLV, you might require periodic updates from each coach, showing actual and budgeted expenses.

In contrast to Chapter 6, we now consider how budgets are used by management to control operations. This chapter focuses on two aspects of management control: (1) budgetary control and (2) responsibility accounting. The content and organization of this chapter are as follows:

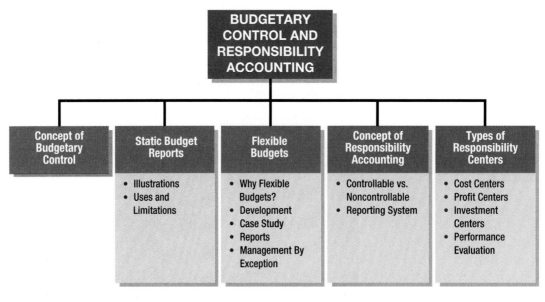

THE
NAVIGATOR

CONCEPT OF BUDGETARY CONTROL

As stated in Chapter One, one of management's major functions is controlling the operations of the company. Control was defined as the steps taken by management to see that planned objectives are met. We now ask: How do budgets assist management in controlling operations?

The use of budgets in controlling operations is known as **budgetary control.** The centerpiece of budgetary control is the use of **budget reports** that compare actual results with planned objectives. The preparation and use of budget reports is based on the belief that planned objectives lose much of their potential value without some monitoring of progress along the way. Just as your professors give midterm examinations to evaluate your progress, so top management requires periodic reports on the progress that department managers are making toward planned annual objectives.

Budget reports provide the feedback needed by management to see whether actual operations are on course. The feedback for a crucial objective, such as having enough cash on hand to pay bills, may be made daily. For other objectives, such as meeting budgeted annual sales and operating expenses, monthly budget reports may suffice. Because of the flexibility of managerial accounting, budget reports can be prepared as frequently as needed. On the basis of the budget reports, management first analyzes any differences between actual and planned results to determine their causes. From this analysis, management may take corrective action, or it may decide to modify future plans.

Budgetary control involves the following:

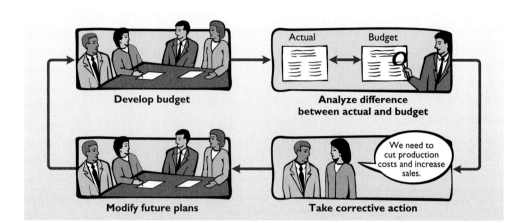

Illustration 7-1
Budgetary control

Budgetary control works best when a company has a formalized reporting system. The system should (1) identify the name of the budget report, such as the sales budget or the manufacturing overhead budget; (2) state the frequency of the report, such as weekly or monthly; (3) specify the purpose of the report; and (4) indicate the primary recipient(s) of the report. The following schedule illustrates a partial budgetary control system for a manufacturing company. Note the emphasis on control in the reports and the frequency of the reports. For example, there is a daily report on scrap and a weekly report on labor.

Illustration 7-2
Budgetary control reporting system

Name of Report	Frequency	Purpose	Primary Recipient(s)
Sales	Weekly	Determine whether sales goals are being met	Top management and sales manager
Labor	Weekly	Control direct and indirect labor costs	Vice president of production and production department managers
Scrap	Daily	Determine efficient use of materials	Production manager
Departmental overhead costs	Monthly	Control overhead costs	Department manager
Selling expenses	Monthly	Control selling expenses	Sales manager
Income statement	Monthly and quarterly	Determine whether income objectives are being met	Top management

Static Budget Reports

You learned in Chapter 6 that the master budget formalizes management's planned objectives for the coming year. When used in budgetary control, each budget included in the master budget is considered to be a static budget. A static budget is a projection of budget data at one level of activity. In such a budget, data for different levels of activity are ignored. As a result, actual results are always compared with budget data at the activity level used in developing the master budget.

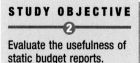

STUDY OBJECTIVE
②
Evaluate the usefulness of static budget reports.

ILLUSTRATIONS

To illustrate the role of a static budget in budgetary control, we will use selected budget data prepared for Hayes Company in Chapter 6. Budget and actual sales data for the Kitchen-mate product in the first and second quarters of 1999 are as follows:

Illustration 7-3 Budget and actual sales data

Sales	First Quarter	Second Quarter	Total
Budgeted	$180,000	$210,000	$390,000
Actual	179,000	199,500	378,500
Difference	$ 1,000	$ 10,500	$ 11,500

The sales budget report for Hayes Company's first quarter is shown below.

Illustration 7-4 Sales budget report—first quarter

HAYES COMPANY
Sales Budget Report
For the Quarter Ended March 31, 1999

Product Line	Budget	Actual	Difference Favorable F Unfavorable U
Kitchen-mate[a]	$180,000	$179,000	$1,000 U

[a]In practice, each product line would be included in the report.

The report shows that sales are $1,000 under budget—an unfavorable result. This difference is less than 1% of budgeted sales ($1,000 ÷ $180,000 = .0056). Top management's analysis of unfavorable differences is often influenced by the materiality (significance) of the difference. Since the difference of $1,000 is immaterial in this case, we will assume that the management of Hayes Company does not investigate the difference and takes no specific action.

The budget report for the second quarter presented in Illustration 7-5 contains one new feature: cumulative year-to-date information. This report indicates that sales for the second quarter were $10,500 below budget, which is 5% of budgeted sales ($10,500 ÷ $210,000). Top management may conclude that the difference between budgeted and actual sales in the second quarter merits investigation.

Illustration 7-5 Sales budget report—second quarter

HAYES COMPANY
Sales Budget Report
For the Quarter Ended June 30, 1999

	Second Quarter			Year-to-Date		
Product Line	Budget	Actual	Difference Favorable F Unfavorable U	Budget	Actual	Difference Favorable F Unfavorable U
Kitchen-mate	$210,000	$199,500	$10,500 U	$390,000	$378,500	$11,500 U

Management's analysis should start by asking the sales manager the cause(s) of the shortfall. The need for corrective action should be considered. For example, management may decide to spur sales by offering sales incentives to customers or by increasing the advertising of Kitchen-mates. On the other hand, if management concludes that a downturn in the economy is responsible for the lower sales, it may decide to modify planned sales and profit goals for the remainder of the year.

USES AND LIMITATIONS

From the examples just discussed, you can see that a master sales budget is useful in evaluating the performance of a sales manager. It is now necessary to ask: How appropriate is the master budget for evaluating a manager's performance in controlling costs? Recall that in a static budget, budget data are not modified or adjusted, regardless of changes in activity during the year. It follows, then, that a static budget is appropriate in evaluating a manager's effectiveness in controlling costs when:

1. The actual level of activity closely approximates the master budget activity level, and/or
2. The behavior of the costs in response to changes in activity is fixed.

A static budget report is, therefore, appropriate for fixed manufacturing costs and fixed selling and administrative expenses. However, static budget reports may not be a proper basis for evaluating a manager's performance in controlling variable costs.

Static budgets are best for fixed costs and expenses

FLEXIBLE BUDGETS

In contrast to a static budget, which is based on one level of activity, a flexible budget projects budget data for various levels of activity. In essence, **the flexible budget is a series of static budgets at different levels of activity.** The flexible budget recognizes that the budgetary process has greater usefulness if it is adaptable to changed operating conditions.

Flexible budgets can be prepared for each of the types of budgets included in the master budget. For example, Marriott Hotels can budget revenues and net income on the basis of 60%, 80%, and 100% of room occupancy. Similarly, American Van Lines can budget its operating expenses on the basis of various levels of truck miles driven. Likewise, the bottling department of Coca-Cola can budget manufacturing costs on the basis of 70%, 80%, and 100% of direct labor costs or machine hours. In the following pages, we will illustrate a flexible budget for manufacturing overhead.

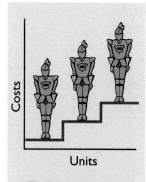

Flexible budgets are static budgets at different activity levels

WHY FLEXIBLE BUDGETS?

Assume that you are the manager in charge of manufacturing overhead in the Forging Department of Barton Steel. In preparing the manufacturing overhead budget for 1999, you prepare the following static budget based on a production volume of 10,000 units of steel ingots:

Illustration 7-6 Static
overhead budget

> **BARTON STEEL**
> **Manufacturing Overhead Budget (Static)**
> **Forging Department**
> **For the Year Ended December 31, 1999**
>
> | | |
> |---|---:|
> | Budgeted production in units (steel ingots) | 10,000 |
> | | |
> | Budgeted costs | |
> | Indirect materials | $ 250,000 |
> | Indirect labor | 260,000 |
> | Utilities | 190,000 |
> | Depreciation | 280,000 |
> | Property taxes | 70,000 |
> | Supervision | 50,000 |
> | | $1,100,000 |

Helpful Hint Which of the following is likely to be of little use when costs are variable— the static budget or the flexible budget? Answer: The static budget.

Fortunately for the company, the demand for steel ingots has increased, and 12,000 units are produced during the year, rather than 10,000. You are elated because increased sales means increased profitability, which should mean a large raise for you and the employees in your department. Unfortunately, a comparison of the actual costs incurred with the budgeted costs for the year in the Forging Department has put you on the spot. The budget report is shown below.

Illustration 7-7 Static
overhead budget report

> **BARTON STEEL**
> **Manufacturing Overhead Budget Report (Static)**
> **Forging Department**
> **For the Year Ended December 31, 1999**
>
> | | Budget | Actual | Difference
Favorable F
Unfavorable U |
> |---|---:|---:|---:|
> | Production in units | 10,000 | 12,000 | |
> | | | | |
> | Costs | | | |
> | Indirect materials | $ 250,000 | $ 295,000 | $ 45,000 U |
> | Indirect labor | 260,000 | 312,000 | 52,000 U |
> | Utilities | 190,000 | 225,000 | 35,000 U |
> | Depreciation | 280,000 | 280,000 | –0– |
> | Property taxes | 70,000 | 70,000 | –0– |
> | Supervision | 50,000 | 50,000 | –0– |
> | | $1,100,000 | $1,232,000 | $132,000 U |

Helpful Hint A static budget will not work if a company has substantial variable costs.

Note that this comparison is based on budget data based on the original activity level (10,000 steel ingots). The comparison indicates that the Forging Department is significantly **over budget** for three of the six overhead costs. Moreover, there is a total unfavorable difference of $132,000, which is 12% over budget ($132,000 ÷ $1,100,000). Your supervisor is very unhappy! Instead of sharing in the company's success, you may find yourself looking for another job. What would you do in this situation?

When you calm down and carefully examine the manufacturing overhead budget, you identify the problem: The budget data are not relevant! At the time the budget was developed, the company anticipated that only 10,000 units of steel ingots would be produced, **not** 12,000 ingots. As a result, the comparison of actual variable costs with budgeted costs is meaningless. The reason is that as production increases, the budget allowances for variable costs should increase both directly and proportionately. The variable costs in this example are indirect materials, indirect labor, and utilities.

An analysis of the budget data for these costs at 10,000 units produces the following per unit results:

Item	Total Cost	Per Unit
Indirect materials	$250,000	$25
Indirect labor	260,000	26
Utilities	190,000	19
	$700,000	$70

Illustration 7-8 Variable costs per unit

The budgeted variable costs at 12,000 units, therefore, are as follows:

Item	Computation	Total
Indirect materials	$25 × 12,000	$300,000
Indirect labor	26 × 12,000	312,000
Utilities	19 × 12,000	228,000
		$840,000

Illustration 7-9
Budgeted variable costs
(12,000 units)

Because fixed costs do not change in total as activity changes, the budgeted amounts for these costs remain the same. The budget report based on the flexible budget for 12,000 units of production is shown in Illustration 7-10. (Compare this to Illustration 7-7.)

Illustration 7-10 Flexible overhead budget report

BARTON STEEL
Manufacturing Overhead Budget Report (Flexible)
Forging Department
For the Year Ended December 31, 1999

	Budget	Actual	Difference Favorable F Unfavorable U
Production in units	12,000	12,000	
Variable costs			
Indirect materials	$ 300,000	$ 295,000	$5,000 F
Indirect labor	312,000	312,000	–0–
Utilities	228,000	225,000	3,000 F
Total variable	840,000	832,000	8,000 F
Fixed costs			
Depreciation	280,000	280,000	–0–
Property taxes	70,000	70,000	–0–
Supervision	50,000	50,000	–0–
Total fixed	400,000	400,000	–0–
Total costs	$1,240,000	$1,232,000	$8,000 F

This report indicates that the Forging Department is below budget—a favorable difference. Instead of worrying about being fired, you may be in line for a raise or a promotion after all! As indicated from the foregoing analysis, the only appropriate comparison is between actual costs at 12,000 units of production and budgeted costs at 12,000 units of production. Flexible budget reports provide this comparison.

DEVELOPING THE FLEXIBLE BUDGET

The flexible budget uses the master budget as its basis. To develop the flexible budget, management should take the following steps:

1. Identify the activity index and the relevant range of activity.
2. Identify the variable costs and determine the budgeted variable cost per unit of activity for each cost.
3. Identify the fixed costs and determine the budgeted amount for each cost.
4. Prepare the budget for selected increments of activity within the relevant range.

The activity index chosen should be one that significantly influences the costs that are being budgeted. For manufacturing overhead costs, for example, the activity index is usually the same as the index used in developing the predetermined overhead rate—that is, direct labor hours or machine hours. For selling and administrative expenses, the activity index usually is sales or net sales.

The choice of selected increments of activity is largely a matter of judgment. For example, if the relevant range is 8,000 to 12,000 direct labor hours, increments of 1,000 hours may be selected. The flexible budget is then prepared in columnar form for each increment within the relevant range.

DECISION TOOLKIT

Decision Checkpoints	Info Needed for Decision	Tool to Use for Decision	How to Evaluate Results
Are the increased costs resulting from increased production reasonable?	Variable costs projected at different levels of production	Flexible budget	After taking into account different production levels, results are favorable if expenses are less than budgeted amounts.

FLEXIBLE BUDGET—A CASE STUDY

To illustrate the preparation of the flexible budget, we will use Fox Manufacturing Company. The management of Fox Manufacturing wants to use the **flexible budget for monthly comparisons** of actual and budgeted manufacturing overhead costs of the Finishing Department. The master budget for the year ending December 31, 1999, shows expected annual operating capacity of 120,000 direct labor hours and the following overhead costs:

Illustration 7-11 Master budget data

Variable Costs		**Fixed Costs**	
Indirect materials	$180,000	Depreciation	$180,000
Indirect labor	240,000	Supervision	120,000
Utilities	60,000	Property taxes	60,000
Total	$480,000	Total	$360,000

The application of the four steps is as follows:

Step 1. Identify the activity index and the relevant range of activity. The activity index is direct labor hours. Management concludes that the relevant range is 8,000–12,000 direct labor hours per month.

Step 2. Identify the variable costs and determine the budgeted variable cost per unit of activity for each cost. There are three variable costs. The variable cost per unit is found by dividing each total budgeted cost by the direct labor hours used in preparing the master budget (120,000 hours). For Fox Manufacturing, the computations are:

Variable Cost	Computation	Variable Cost per Direct Labor Hour
Indirect materials	$180,000 ÷ 120,000	$1.50
Indirect labor	240,000 ÷ 120,000	2.00
Utilities	60,000 ÷ 120,000	.50
Total		$4.00

Illustration 7-12
Computation of variable costs per direct labor hour

Step 3. Identify the fixed costs and determine the budgeted amount for each cost. There are three fixed costs. Since Fox Manufacturing desires **monthly budget data**, the budgeted amount is found by dividing each annual budgeted cost by 12. For Fox Manufacturing, the monthly budgeted fixed costs are: Depreciation $15,000, Supervision $10,000, and Property taxes $5,000.

Step 4. Prepare the budget for selected increments of activity within the relevant range. Management decides that the budget be prepared in increments of 1,000 direct labor hours.

The flexible budget for the month of January, 1999 is shown in Illustration 7-13.

Illustration 7-13 Flexible monthly overhead budget

FOX MANUFACTURING COMPANY
Flexible Monthly Manufacturing Overhead Budget
Finishing Department
For the Month Ended January 31, 1999

Activity level					
Direct labor hours	8,000	9,000	10,000	11,000	12,000
Variable costs					
Indirect materials	$12,000	$13,500	$15,000	$16,500	$18,000
Indirect labor	16,000	18,000	20,000	22,000	24,000
Utilities	4,000	4,500	5,000	5,500	6,000
Total variable	32,000	36,000	40,000	44,000	48,000
Fixed costs					
Depreciation	15,000	15,000	15,000	15,000	15,000
Supervision	10,000	10,000	10,000	10,000	10,000
Property taxes	5,000	5,000	5,000	5,000	5,000
Total fixed	30,000	30,000	30,000	30,000	30,000
Total costs	$62,000	$66,000	$70,000	$74,000	$78,000

From the budget, the following formula may be used to determine total budgeted costs at any level of activity:

Illustration 7-14
Formula for total budgeted costs

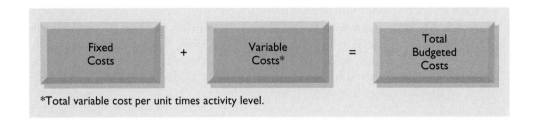

*Total variable cost per unit times activity level.

For Fox Manufacturing, fixed costs are $30,000, and total variable cost per unit is $4.00. Thus, at 9,000 direct labor hours, total budgeted costs are $66,000 [$30,000 + ($4.00 × 9,000)]. Similarly, at 8,622 direct labor hours, total budgeted costs are $64,488 [$30,000 + ($4.00 × 8,622)].

Total budgeted costs can also be shown graphically, as in Illustration 7-15. In the graph, the activity index is shown on the horizontal axis and costs are indicated on the vertical axis. The graph highlights two of the 1,000 increments (10,000 and 12,000). As shown in Illustration 7-15, total budgeted costs are $70,000 [$30,000 + ($4.00 × 10,000)] and $78,000 [$30,000 + ($4.00 × 12,000)], respectively.

Illustration 7-15
Graphic flexible budget data highlighting 10,000 and 12,000 activity levels

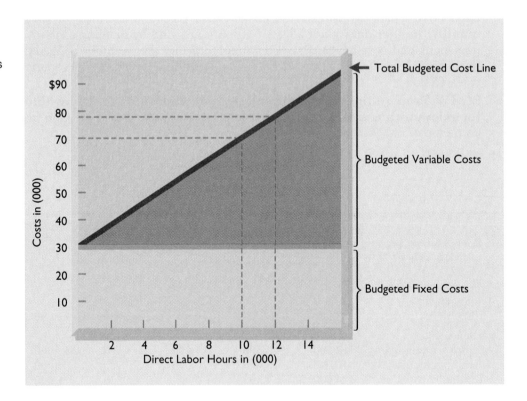

FLEXIBLE BUDGET REPORTS

Flexible budget reports represent another type of internal report produced by managerial accounting. The flexible budget report consists of two sections: (1) production data such as direct labor hours and (2) cost data for variable and fixed costs. Consequently, the report provides a basis for evaluating a manager's performance in two areas: production control and cost control. Flexible budgets are widely used in production and service departments.

A flexible overhead budget report for the Finishing Department of Fox Company for the month of January is shown in Illustration 7-16. In this month, 8,800 direct labor hours were expected but 9,000 hours were worked. The budget data are based on the flexible budget for 9,000 hours in Illustration 7-13. The actual cost data are assumed.

Helpful Hint An assembly department is a production department, and a maintenance department is a service department, as explained on page 269.

Illustration 7-16 Flexible overhead budget report

FOX MANUFACTURING COMPANY
Manufacturing Overhead Budget Report (Flexible)
Finishing Department
For the Month Ended January 31, 1999

Direct labor hours (DLH)				Difference
Expected	8,800	**Budget at**	Actual Costs	Favorable F
Actual	9,000	**9,000 DLH**	9,000 DLH	Unfavorable U
Variable costs				
Indirect materials		$13,500	$14,000	$ 500 U
Indirect labor		18,000	17,000	1,000 F
Utilities		4,500	4,600	100 U
Total variable		36,000	35,600	400 F
Fixed costs				
Depreciation		15,000	15,000	–0–
Supervision		10,000	10,000	–0–
Property taxes		5,000	5,000	–0–
Total fixed		30,000	30,000	–0–
Total costs		$66,000	$65,600	$ 400 F

How appropriate is this report in evaluating the Finishing Department manager's performance in controlling costs? The report clearly provides a reliable basis for this purpose. Both actual and budget costs are based on the activity level worked during January. Since variable costs generally are incurred directly by the department, the difference between the budget allowance for those hours and the actual costs are the responsibility of the department manager.

From the standpoint of production control, the report shows a 200-hour difference between actual direct labor hours and expected hours. This difference is favorable if actual production orders required 9,000 direct labor hours. The difference is unfavorable if actual production orders required only 8,800 direct labor hours. In either case, the budget for purposes of cost control is based on 9,000 direct labor hours.

In subsequent months, other flexible budget reports will be prepared. For each month, the budget data are based on the actual activity level attained. In February that level may be 11,000 direct labor hours, in July, 10,000, and so on.

MANAGEMENT BY EXCEPTION

Management by exception means that top management's review of a budget report is directed either entirely or primarily to differences between actual results and planned objectives. This approach enables top management to focus on problem areas that need attention. Management by exception does not mean that top management will investigate every difference. For this approach to be effective, there must be some guidelines for identifying an exception. The usual criteria are materiality and controllability of the item.

Materiality

Without quantitative guidelines, management would have to investigate every budget difference regardless of the amount. Materiality is usually expressed as a percentage difference from budget. For example, management may set the percentage difference at 5% for important items and 10% for other items. This means that all differences either over or under budget by the specified percentage will be investigated. Costs over budget warrant investigation to determine why they were not controlled. In contrast, costs under budget merit investigation to determine whether costs critical to the profitability of the division are being curtailed. For example, if maintenance costs are budgeted at $80,000 and only $40,000 is spent, major unexpected breakdowns in productive facilities may occur in the future.

Alternatively, a company may specify a single percentage difference from budget for all items and supplement this guideline with a minimum dollar limit. For example, the exception criteria may be stated at 5% of budget or more than $10,000.

Controllability of the Item

Exception guidelines are more restrictive for controllable items than for items that are not controllable by the manager being evaluated. In fact, there may be no guidelines for noncontrollable items. For example, a large unfavorable difference between actual and budgeted property tax expense may not be flagged by management for investigation because the only possible causes are an unexpected increase in the tax rate or in the assessed value of the property. An investigation into the difference will be useless because the manager cannot control either cause.

BEFORE YOU GO ON . . .

● Review It

1. What is the meaning of budgetary control?
2. When is a static budget appropriate for evaluating a manager's effectiveness in controlling costs?
3. What is a flexible budget?
4. How is a flexible budget developed?
5. What are the criteria used in management by exception?

● Do It

Your roommate asks your help in understanding how total budgeted costs are computed at any level of activity. Compute total budgeted costs at 30,000 direct labor hours, assuming that in the flexible budget graph, the fixed cost line and the total budgeted cost line intersect the vertical axis at $36,000 and that the total budget cost line is $186,000 at an activity level of 50,000 direct labor hours.

Reasoning: The formula for the computation is: Fixed Costs + Variable Costs (Total Variable Costs per Unit × Activity Level) = Total Budgeted Costs.

Solution: Using the graph, fixed costs are $36,000 and variable costs are $3 per direct labor hour [($186,000 − $36,000) ÷ 50,000]. Thus, at 30,000 direct labor hours total budgeted costs are $126,000 [$36,000 + ($3 × 30,000)].

THE NAVIGATOR

Related exercise material: BE7-3, BE7-4, BE7-5, E7-1, E7-2, E7-3, E7-4, E7-5, E7-6, and E7-7.

THE CONCEPT OF RESPONSIBILITY ACCOUNTING

Like budgeting, responsibility accounting is an important part of management accounting. **Responsibility accounting** involves accumulating and reporting costs (and revenues, where relevant) on the basis of the individual manager who has the authority to make the day-to-day decisions about the items. Under responsibility accounting, the evaluation of a manager's performance is based on matters directly under that manager's control. Responsibility accounting can be used at every level of management in which the following conditions exist:

1. Costs and revenues can be directly associated with the specific level of management responsibility.
2. The costs and revenues are controllable at the level of responsibility with which they are associated.
3. Budget data can be developed for evaluating the manager's effectiveness in controlling the costs and revenues.

The levels of responsibility for controlling costs are depicted in Illustration 7-17.

Illustration 7-17
Responsibility for controllable costs at varying levels of management

Responsibility accounting personalizes the managerial accounting system. Under responsibility accounting, any individual who has control and is accountable for a specified set of activities can be recognized as a responsibility center. Thus, responsibility accounting may extend from the lowest level of control to the top strata of management. Once responsibility has been established, the effectiveness of the individual's performance is first measured and reported for the specified activity, and it is then reported upward throughout the organization.

Responsibility accounting is especially valuable in a decentralized company. **Decentralization** means that the control of operations is delegated by top management to many individuals (managers) throughout the organization. The term **segment** is sometimes used to identify an area of responsibility in decentralized operations. Under responsibility accounting, reports are prepared periodically

Helpful Hint All companies use responsibility accounting. Without some form of responsibility accounting, there would be chaos in discharging management's control function.

such as monthly, quarterly, and annually, to provide a basis for evaluating the performance of each manager.

Responsibility accounting is an essential part of any effective system of budgetary control. The reporting of costs and revenues under responsibility accounting differs from budgeting in two respects:

1. A distinction is made between controllable and noncontrollable items.
2. Performance reports either emphasize or include only items controllable by the individual manager.

Responsibility accounting applies to both profit and not-for-profit entities. The former seek to maximize net income, whereas the latter wish to minimize the cost of providing the service.

BUSINESS INSIGHT

Management Perspective

Since developing its budgeting system, JKL, Inc., a large New York advertising agency, has become aware of which specific customer accounts are unprofitable and the reasons why. Since the budgeting and control system has been instituted, the agency has dropped several unprofitable accounts that otherwise would have gone unnoticed. Account managers and supervisors now feel responsible for the profitability of their accounts. They carefully monitor actual hours spent on each account to make sure the account is being managed and run as efficiently as possible. For example, an account manager noticed a large amount of supervisory creative time was being spent on an account. Further investigation showed that the supervisors, rather than the creative department, were doing the actual creative work. The account manager pointed this out, and a junior creative team was appointed to the account, saving a great deal of money.

CONTROLLABLE VERSUS NONCONTROLLABLE REVENUES AND COSTS

All costs and revenues are controllable at some level of responsibility within a company. This truth underscores the adage by the chief executive officer of any organization that "the buck stops here." Under responsibility accounting, the critical issue is **whether the cost or revenue is controllable at the level of responsibility with which it is associated.**

Helpful Hint Are there more or fewer controllable costs as you move to higher levels of management? Answer: More.

A cost is considered to be controllable at a given level of managerial responsibility if that manager has the power to incur it within a given period of time. From this criterion, it follows that

1. All costs are controllable by top management because of the broad range of its authority.
2. Fewer costs are controllable as one moves down to each lower level of managerial responsibility because of the manager's decreasing authority.

Helpful Hint The longer the time span, the more likely that the cost becomes controllable.

In general, **costs incurred directly by a level of responsibility are controllable at that level.** In contrast, costs incurred indirectly and allocated to a responsibility level are considered to be noncontrollable at that level.

RESPONSIBILITY REPORTING SYSTEM

A responsibility reporting system involves the preparation of a report for each level of responsibility shown in the company's organization chart. To illustrate a responsibility reporting system, we will use the partial organization chart and production departments of the Francis Chair Company in Illustration 7-18.

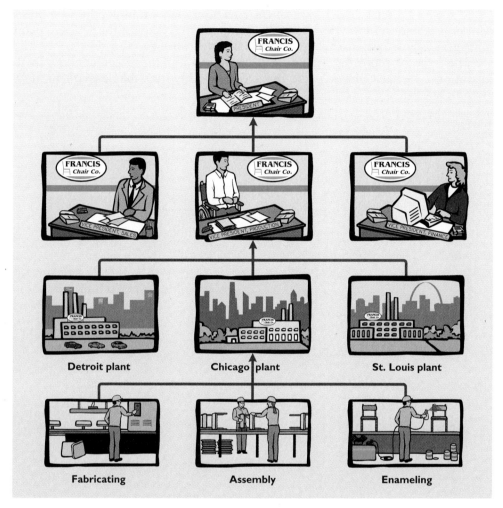

Illustration 7-18 Partial organization chart

Report A
President sees summary data of vice presidents.

Report B
Vice president sees summary of controllable costs in his/her functional area.

Report C
Plant manager sees summary of controllable costs for each department in plant.

Report D
Department manager sees controllable costs of his/her department.

The responsibility reporting system begins with the lowest level of responsibility for controlling costs and moves upward to each higher level, as detailed in Illustration 7-19. A brief description of the four reports follows.

1. **Report D** is typical of reports that go to managers at the lowest level of responsibility shown in the organization chart—department managers. In this report, additional detail may be presented for manufacturing overhead. Similar reports are prepared for the managers of the Enameling and Assembly Departments.

2. **Report C** is an example of reports that are sent to plant managers. This report shows the costs of the Chicago plant that are controllable at the second level of responsibility. In addition, Report C shows summary data for each department that is controlled by the plant manager. Similar reports are prepared for the Detroit and St. Louis plant managers.

3. **Report B** illustrates the reports at the third level of responsibility. It shows the controllable costs of the vice president of production and summary data on the three assembly plants for which this officer is responsible.

4. **Report A** is typical of the reports that go to the top level of responsibility—the president. This report shows the controllable costs and expenses of this office and summary data on the vice presidents that are accountable to the president.

A responsibility reporting system permits management by exception at each level of responsibility within the organization. In addition to the information shown in Illustration 7-19, each higher level of responsibility can obtain the detailed report for each lower level of responsibility. For example, the vice president of production in the Francis Chair Company may request the Chicago plant manager's report because this plant is $5,300 over budget.

This type of reporting system also permits comparative evaluations. In Illustration 7-19, the Chicago plant manager can easily rank the department man-

Illustration 7-19
Responsibility reporting system

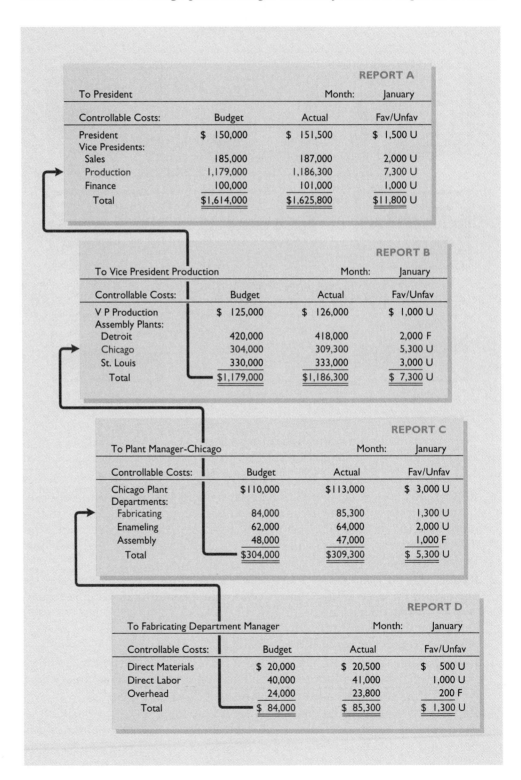

REPORT A

To President   Month: January

Controllable Costs:	Budget	Actual	Fav/Unfav
President	$ 150,000	$ 151,500	$ 1,500 U
Vice Presidents:			
Sales	185,000	187,000	2,000 U
Production	1,179,000	1,186,300	7,300 U
Finance	100,000	101,000	1,000 U
Total	$1,614,000	$1,625,800	$11,800 U

REPORT B

To Vice President Production   Month: January

Controllable Costs:	Budget	Actual	Fav/Unfav
V P Production	$ 125,000	$ 126,000	$ 1,000 U
Assembly Plants:			
Detroit	420,000	418,000	2,000 F
Chicago	304,000	309,300	5,300 U
St. Louis	330,000	333,000	3,000 U
Total	$1,179,000	$1,186,300	$ 7,300 U

REPORT C

To Plant Manager-Chicago   Month: January

Controllable Costs:	Budget	Actual	Fav/Unfav
Chicago Plant	$110,000	$113,000	$ 3,000 U
Departments:			
Fabricating	84,000	85,300	1,300 U
Enameling	62,000	64,000	2,000 U
Assembly	48,000	47,000	1,000 F
Total	$304,000	$309,300	$ 5,300 U

REPORT D

To Fabricating Department Manager   Month: January

Controllable Costs:	Budget	Actual	Fav/Unfav
Direct Materials	$ 20,000	$ 20,500	$ 500 U
Direct Labor	40,000	41,000	1,000 U
Overhead	24,000	23,800	200 F
Total	$ 84,000	$ 85,300	$ 1,300 U

agers' effectiveness in controlling manufacturing costs. Comparative rankings provide further incentive for a manager to control costs. For example, the Detroit plant manager will want to continue to be No. 1 in the report to the vice president of production, and the Chicago plant manager will not want to remain No. 3 in future reporting periods.

TYPES OF RESPONSIBILITY CENTERS

There are three basic types of responsibility centers: cost centers, profit centers, and investment centers. These centers indicate the degree of responsibility the manager has for the performance of the center.

A cost center incurs costs (and expenses) but does not directly generate revenues. Managers of cost centers have the authority to incur costs. They are evaluated on their ability to control costs. **Cost centers are usually either production departments or service departments.** The former participate directly in making the product whereas the latter provide only support services. In a Ford Motor Company automobile plant, the welding, painting, and assembling departments are production departments, and the maintenance, cafeteria, and personnel departments are service departments. All of these departments are cost centers.

A profit center incurs costs (and expenses) but also generates revenues. Managers of profit centers are judged on the profitability of their centers. Examples of profit centers include the individual departments of a retail store, such as clothing, furniture, and automotive products, and branch offices of banks.

Like a profit center, an investment center incurs costs (and expenses) and generates revenues. In addition, an investment center has control over the investment funds available for use. Managers of investment centers are evaluated on the profitability of the center and on the rate of return earned on the funds invested. Investment centers are often associated with subsidiary companies. For example, Kellogg produces several product lines including ready-to-eat cereals, toaster pastries, frozen waffles, cereal bars, and bagels; General Mills's product lines include cereals, helper dinner mixes, fruit snacks, popcorn, and yogurt. In each of these instances, the manager of the investment center (product line or segment) is able to control or significantly influence investment decisions pertaining to such matters as plant expansion and entry into new market areas. These three types of responsibility centers are depicted in Illustration 7-20.

Helpful Hint (1) Is the jewelry department of Marshall Field's department store a profit center or a cost center? (2) Is the props department of a movie studio a profit center or a cost center? Answers: (1) Profit center. (2) Cost center.

Illustration 7-20   Types of responsibility centers

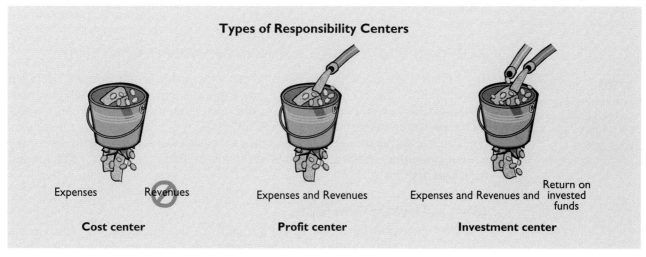

Types of Responsibility Centers

Expenses   ~~Revenues~~

Cost center

Expenses and Revenues

Profit center

Expenses and Revenues and   Return on invested funds

Investment center

The evaluation of a manager's performance in each type of responsibility center is explained in the remainder of this chapter.

RESPONSIBILITY ACCOUNTING FOR COST CENTERS

The evaluation of a manager's performance for cost centers is based on the manager's ability to meet budgeted goals for controllable costs. **Responsibility reports for cost centers compare actual controllable costs with flexible budget data.**

A manufacturing overhead responsibility report is illustrated in Illustration 7-21. The report is adapted from the budget report for Fox Manufacturing Company in Illustration 7-16 on page 263. It assumes that the Finishing Department manager is able to control all manufacturing overhead costs except depreciation, property taxes, and his own monthly supervisory salary of $6,000. The remaining $4,000 of supervision costs are assumed to apply to other supervisory personnel within the Finishing Department, whose salaries are controllable by the manager.

Illustration 7-21
Responsibility report for a cost center

FOX MANUFACTURING COMPANY
Finishing Department
Manufacturing Overhead Responsibility Report
For the Month Ended January 31, 1999

Controllable Cost	Budget	Actual	Difference Favorable F Unfavorable U
Indirect materials	$13,500	$14,000	$ 500 U
Indirect labor	18,000	17,000	1,000 F
Utilities	4,500	4,600	100 U
Supervision	4,000	4,000	–0–
	$40,000	$39,600	$ 400 F

Only controllable costs are included in the report, and no distinction is made between variable and fixed costs. As in budget reports, the responsibility report continues the concept of management by exception. In this case, top management may request an explanation of the $1,000 favorable difference in indirect labor and/or the $500 unfavorable difference in indirect materials.

RESPONSIBILITY ACCOUNTING FOR PROFIT CENTERS

To evaluate the performance of a manager of a profit center properly, detailed information is needed about both controllable revenues and controllable costs. The operating revenues earned by a profit center, such as sales, are controllable by the manager. All variable costs (and expenses) incurred by the center are also controllable by the manager because they vary with sales. However, to determine the controllability of fixed costs, it is necessary to distinguish between direct and indirect fixed costs.

Direct and Indirect Fixed Costs

A profit center may have both direct and indirect fixed costs. Direct fixed costs are costs that relate specifically to one center and are incurred for the sole benefit of that center. Examples of such costs include the salaries established by the profit center manager for supervisory personnel and the cost of maintaining a timekeeping department for the center's employees. Since these fixed costs can be traced directly to a center, they are also called **traceable costs. Most direct fixed costs are controllable by the profit center manager.**

In contrast, indirect fixed costs pertain to a company's overall operating activities and they are incurred for the benefit of more than one profit center. Indirect fixed costs are allocated to profit centers on some type of equitable basis. For example, property taxes on a building occupied by more than one center may be allocated on the basis of square feet of floor space used by each center. Alternatively, the costs of a company's personnel department may be allocated to profit centers on the basis of the number of employees in each center. Because these fixed costs apply to more than one center, they are also called **common costs. Most indirect fixed costs are not controllable by the profit center manager.**

Responsibility Report

The responsibility report for a profit center shows budgeted and actual **controllable revenues and costs.** The report is prepared using the cost-volume-profit income statement explained in Chapter 5. In the report:

1. Controllable fixed costs are deducted from contribution margin.
2. The excess of contribution margin over controllable fixed costs is identified as controllable margin.
3. Noncontrollable fixed costs are not reported.

The responsibility report for the manager of the Marine Division, a profit center of Mantle Manufacturing Company, is shown in Illustration 7-22. For the year, the Marine Division also had $60,000 of indirect fixed costs that were not controllable by the profit center manager.

Illustration 7-22
Responsibility report for profit center

MANTLE MANUFACTURING COMPANY
Marine Division
Responsibility Report
For the Year Ended December 31, 1999

	Budget	Actual	Difference Favorable F Unfavorable U
Sales	$1,200,000	$1,150,000	$50,000 U
Variable costs			
Cost of goods sold	500,000	490,000	10,000 F
Selling and administrative	160,000	156,000	4,000 F
Total	660,000	646,000	14,000 F
Contribution margin	540,000	504,000	36,000 U
Controllable fixed costs			
Cost of goods sold	100,000	100,000	–0–
Selling and administrative	80,000	80,000	–0–
Total	180,000	180,000	–0–
Controllable margin	$ 360,000	$ 324,000	$36,000 U

Helpful Hint Recognize that we are emphasizing financial measures of performance. More effort is now being made to stress nonfinancial performance measures such as product quality, labor productivity, market growth, material's yield, manufacturing flexibility, and technological capability.

Controllable margin is considered to be the best measure of the manager's performance **in controlling revenues and costs.** This report shows that the manager's performance was below budgeted expectations by approximately 10%

($36,000 ÷ $360,000). Top management would likely investigate the causes of this unfavorable result. Note that the report does not show the Marine Division's noncontrollable fixed costs of $60,000. These costs would be included in a report on the profitability of the profit center.

Responsibility reports for profit centers may also be prepared monthly. In addition, they may include cumulative year-to-date results.

DECISION TOOLKIT

Decision Checkpoints	Info Needed for Decision	Tool to Use for Decision	How to Evaluate Results
Have the individual managers been held accountable for the costs and revenues under their control?	Relevant costs and revenues, where the individual manager has authority to make day-to-day decisions about the items	Responsibility reports focused on cost centers, profit centers, and investment centers as appropriate	Compare budget to actual costs for controllable items.

BEFORE YOU GO ON . . .

● **Review It**

1. What conditions are essential for responsibility accounting?

2. What is involved in a responsibility reporting system?

3. What is the primary objective of a responsibility report for a cost center?

4. What is the difference between direct fixed costs and indirect fixed costs relative to a responsibility report for a profit center? Which of these costs are called traceable costs and which are called common costs?

5. How does contribution margin differ from controllable margin in a responsibility report for a profit center?

● **Do It**

Midwest Division, which operates as a profit center, reports the following actual results for the year: Sales $1,700,000, variable costs $800,000, controllable fixed costs $400,000, noncontrollable fixed costs $200,000. Annual budgeted amounts were $1,500,000, $700,000, $400,000, and $200,000, respectively. Prepare a responsibility report for the Midwest Division for December 31, 1999.

Reasoning: In the responsibility report, variable costs are deducted from sales to show contribution margin. Controllable fixed costs are then deducted to show controllable margin. Noncontrollable fixed costs are not reported; they would, however, be included in a report on the profitability of the profit center.

Solution:

MIDWEST DIVISION
Responsibility Report
For the Year Ended December 31, 1999

	Budget	Actual	Difference Favorable F Unfavorable U
Sales	$1,500,000	$1,700,000	$200,000 F
Variable costs	700,000	800,000	100,000 U
Contribution margin	800,000	900,000	100,000 F
Controllable fixed costs	400,000	400,000	–0–
Controllable margin	$ 400,000	$ 500,000	$100,000 F

Related exercise material: BE7-7 and E7-9.

THE
NAVIGATOR

RESPONSIBILITY ACCOUNTING FOR INVESTMENT CENTERS

As explained earlier, an important characteristic of an investment center is that the manager can control or significantly influence the investment funds available for use. Thus, the primary basis for evaluating the performance of a manager of an investment center is **return on investment (ROI).** The return on investment is considered to be superior to any other performance measurement because it shows the **effectiveness of the manager in utilizing the assets at the manager's disposal.**

STUDY OBJECTIVE
7
Explain the basis and formula used in evaluating performance in investment centers.

Return on Investment (ROI)

The formula for computing ROI for an investment center, together with assumed illustrative data, is shown in Illustration 7-23. Both factors in the formula are controllable by the investment center manager. Operating assets consist of current assets and plant assets used in operations by the center and controlled by the manager. Nonoperating assets such as idle plant assets and land held for future use are excluded. Average operating assets are usually based on the cost or book value of the assets at the beginning and end of the year.

Illustration 7-23
ROI formula

Responsibility Report

The scope of the investment center manager's responsibility significantly affects the content of the performance report. Since an investment center is an independent entity for operating purposes, **all fixed costs are controllable by the investment center manager.** For example, the manager is responsible for depreciation on investment center assets. Accordingly, more fixed costs are identified as controllable in the performance report for an investment center manager than in a performance report for a profit center manager. In addition, the report shows budgeted and actual ROI below controllable margin.

To illustrate the responsibility report, we will now assume that the Marine Division of Mantle Manufacturing Company is an investment center with budgeted and actual average operating assets of $2,000,000. In addition, we will assume that the manager can control the $60,000 of fixed costs that were not controllable when the division was a profit center. The responsibility report is shown in Illustration 7-24.

Illustration 7-24
Responsibility report for investment center

MANTLE MANUFACTURING COMPANY
Marine Division
Responsibility Report
For the Year Ended December 31, 1999

	Budget	Actual	Difference Favorable F Unfavorable U
Sales	$1,200,000	$1,150,000	$50,000 U
Variable costs			
Cost of goods sold	500,000	490,000	10,000 F
Selling and administrative	160,000	156,000	4,000 F
Total	660,000	646,000	14,000 F
Contribution margin	540,000	504,000	36,000 U
Controllable fixed costs			
Cost of goods sold	100,000	100,000	–0–
Selling and administrative	80,000	80,000	–0–
Other fixed costs	**60,000**	**60,000**	**–0–**
Total	240,000	240,000	–0–
Controllable margin	**$ 300,000**	**$ 264,000**	**$36,000 U**
Return on investment	15%	13.2%	1.8% U
	(a)	(b)	(c)

$$(a)\ \frac{\$300,000}{\$2,000,000} \qquad (b)\frac{\$264,000}{\$2,000,000} \qquad (c)\frac{\$36,000}{\$2,000,000}$$

The report shows that the manager's performance based on ROI was 12% below budget expectations (1.8% ÷ 15%). Top management would likely want an explanation of the reasons for this unfavorable result.

Improving ROI

The manager of an investment center can improve ROI in two ways: (1) increase controllable margin and/or (2) reduce average operating assets. To illustrate, we will use the following assumed data for the Marine Division of Mantle Manufacturing:

Illustration 7-25
Assumed data for Marine Division

Sales	$2,000,000
Variable cost	1,100,000
Contribution margin (45%)	900,000
Controllable fixed costs	300,000
Controllable margin (a)	$ 600,000
Average operating assets (b)	$5,000,000
Return on investment (a) ÷ (b)	12%

Increasing Controllable Margin. Controllable margin can be increased by increasing sales or by reducing variable and controllable fixed costs as follows:

1. **Increase sales 10%.** Sales will increase $200,000 ($2,000,000 × .10). Assuming no change in the contribution margin percentage of 45%, contribution margin will increase $90,000 ($200,000 × .45). Controllable margin will increase by the same amount because controllable fixed costs will not change. Thus, controllable margin becomes $690,000 ($600,000 + $90,000), and the new ROI is 13.8%, computed as follows:

$$\text{ROI} = \frac{\text{Controllable margin}}{\text{Average operating assets}} = \frac{\$690,000}{\$5,000,000} = 13.8\%$$

Illustration 7-26 ROI computation—increase in sales

An increase in sales benefits both the investment center and the company if it results in new business. It would not benefit the company if the increase was achieved at the expense of other investment centers.

2. **Decrease variable and fixed costs 10%.** Total costs will decrease $140,000 [($1,100,000 + $300,000) × .10]. This reduction will result in a corresponding increase in controllable margin. Thus, this margin becomes $740,000 ($600,000 + $140,000), and the new ROI is 14.8%, computed as follows:

$$\text{ROI} = \frac{\text{Controllable margin}}{\text{Average operating assets}} = \frac{\$740,000}{\$5,000,000} = 14.8\%$$

Illustration 7-27 ROI computation—decrease in costs

This course of action is clearly beneficial when waste and inefficiencies are eliminated. However, a reduction in vital costs such as required maintenance and inspections is not likely to be acceptable to top management.

Reducing Average Operating Assets. Assume that average operating assets are reduced 10% or $500,000 ($5,000,000 × .10). Average operating assets become $4,500,000 ($5,000,000 − $500,000). Since controllable margin remains unchanged at $600,000, the new ROI is 13.3%, computed as follows:

$$\text{ROI} = \frac{\text{Controllable margin}}{\text{Average operating assets}} = \frac{\$600,000}{\$4,500,000} = 13.3\%$$

Illustration 7-28 ROI computation—decrease in operating assets

Reductions in operating assets may or may not be prudent. It is beneficial to eliminate overinvestment in inventories and to dispose of excessive plant assets. However, it is unwise to reduce inventories below expected needs or to dispose of essential plant assets.

Judgmental Factors in ROI

The return on investment approach includes two judgmental factors:

1. **Valuation of operating assets.** Operating assets may be valued at acquisition cost, book value, appraised value, or market value. The first two bases are readily available from the accounting records.
2. **Margin (income) measure.** This measure may be controllable margin, income from operations, or net income.

Each of the alternative values for operating assets can provide a reliable basis for evaluating a manager's performance as long as it is consistently applied between reporting periods. However, the use of income measures other than controllable margin will not result in a valid basis for evaluating the performance of an investment center manager because they will include some noncontrollable revenues and costs.

DECISION TOOLKIT

Decision Checkpoints	Info Needed for Decision	Tool to Use for Decision	How to Evaluate Results
Has the investment center performed up to expectations?	Controllable margin (contribution margin minus controllable fixed costs), and average investment center operating assets		Compare actual ROI to expected ROI.

PRINCIPLES OF PERFORMANCE EVALUATION

Performance evaluation is at the center of responsibility accounting. **Performance evaluation** is a management function that compares actual results with budget goals. It is based on internal reports prepared by the managerial accountant. Performance evaluation involves both behavioral and reporting principles.

Behavioral Principles

The human factor is critical in evaluating performance. Behavioral principles include the following:

1. **Managers of responsibility centers should have direct input into the process of establishing budget goals of their area of responsibility.** Without such input, managers may view the goals as unrealistic or arbitrarily set by top management. Such views adversely affect the managers' motivation to meet the targeted objectives.

2. **The evaluation of performance should be based entirely on matters that are controllable by the manager being evaluated.** Criticism of a manager on matters outside his or her control reduces the effectiveness of the evaluation process. Moreover, it leads to negative reactions by a manager and to doubts about the fairness of the company's evaluation policies.

3. **Top management should support the evaluation process.** As explained earlier, the evaluation process begins at the lowest level of responsibility and extends upward to the highest level of management. Managers quickly lose faith in the process when top management ignores, overrules, or bypasses established procedures for evaluating a manager's performance.

4. **The evaluation process must allow managers to respond to their evaluations.** Evaluation is not a one-way street. Managers should have the op-

portunity to defend their performance. Evaluation without feedback is both impersonal and ineffective.

5. **The evaluation should identify both good and poor performance.** Praise for good performance is a powerful motivating factor for a manager. This is especially true when a manager's compensation includes rewards for meeting budget goals.

Reporting Principles

Performance evaluation under responsibility accounting also involves reporting principles. These principles pertain primarily to the internal reports that provide the basis for evaluating performance. Performance reports should:

1. Contain only data that are controllable by the manager of the responsibility center.
2. Provide accurate and reliable budget data to measure performance.
3. Highlight significant differences between actual results and budget goals.
4. Be tailor-made for the intended evaluation.
5. Be prepared at reasonable intervals.

B E F O R E   Y O U   G O   O N . . .

● **Review It**

1. What is the formula for computing return on investment (ROI)?
2. Identify three actions a manager may take to improve ROI.

THE
NAVIGATOR

*U*SING THE DECISION TOOLKIT

The manufacturing overhead budget for Reebles Company contains the following items:

Variable expenses	
Indirect materials	$25,000
Indirect labor	12,000
Maintenance expenses	10,000
Manufacturing supplies	6,000
Total variable	$53,000
Fixed expenses	
Supervision	$17,000
Inspection costs	1,000
Insurance expenses	2,000
Depreciation	15,000
Total fixed	$35,000

The budget was based on an estimated 2,000 units being produced. During the past month, 1,500 units were produced, and the following costs incurred:

Variable expenses	
Indirect materials	$25,200
Indirect labor	13,500
Maintenance expenses	8,200
Manufacturing supplies	5,100
Total variable	$52,000

	Fixed expenses	
	Supervision	$19,300
	Inspection costs	1,200
	Insurance expenses	2,200
	Depreciation	14,700
	Total fixed	$37,400

Instructions

(a) Determine which items would be controllable by Ed Lopat, the production manager (assume "supervision" excludes Lopat's own salary).

(b) How much should have been spent during the month for the manufacture of the 1,500 units?

(c) Prepare a flexible manufacturing overhead budget report for Mr. Lopat.

(d) Prepare a responsibility report. Include only the costs that would have been controllable by Mr. Lopat. In an attached memo, describe clearly for Mr. Lopat the areas in which his performance needs to be improved.

Solution

(a) Ed Lopat should be able to control all the variable expenses and the fixed expenses of supervision and inspection. Insurance and depreciation ordinarily are not the responsibility of the department manager.

(b) The total variable cost per unit is $26.50 ($53,000 ÷ 2,000). The total budgeted cost during the month to manufacture 1,500 units is variable costs $39,750 (1,500 × $26.50) plus fixed costs ($35,000), for a total of $74,750 ($39,750 + $35,000).

(c)

REEBLES COMPANY
Production Department
Manufacturing Overhead Budget Report (Flexible)
For the Month Ended _____

Units		Budget at	Actual at	Difference
Expected 2,000		Budget at	Actual at	Favorable F
Actual 1,500		1,500 units	1,500 units	Unfavorable U
Variable costs				
Indirect materials		$18,750	$25,200	$ 6,450 U
Indirect labor		9,000	13,500	4,500 U
Maintenance		7,500	8,200	700 U
Manufacturing supplies		4,500	5,100	600 U
Total variable		39,750	52,000	12,250 U
Fixed costs				
Supervision		17,000	19,300	2,300 U
Inspection		1,000	1,200	200 U
Insurance		2,000	2,200	200 U
Depreciation		15,000	14,700	300 F
Total fixed		35,000	37,400	2,400 U
Total costs		$74,750	$89,400	$14,650 U

(d) Because a production department is a cost center, the responsibility report should include only the costs that are controllable by the production manager. In this type of report, no distinction is made between variable and fixed costs. Budget data in the report should be based on the units actually produced.

REEBLES COMPANY
Production Department
Manufacturing Overhead Responsibility Report
For the Month Ended _____

Controllable Cost	Budget	Actual	Difference Favorable F Unfavorable U
Indirect materials	$18,750	$25,200	$ 6,450 U
Indirect labor	9,000	13,500	4,500 U
Maintenance	7,500	8,200	700 U
Manufacturing supplies	4,500	5,100	600 U
Supervision	17,000	19,300	2,300 U
Inspection	1,000	1,200	200 U
Total	$57,750	$72,500	$14,750 U

To: Mr. Ed Lopat, Production Manager

From: _____, Vice-President of Production

Subject: Performance Evaluation for the Month of XXXXX

Your performance in controlling costs that are your responsibility was very disappointing in the month of XXXXX. As indicated in the accompanying responsibility report, total costs were $14,750 over budget. On a percentage basis, costs were 26% over budget. As you can see, actual costs were over budget for every cost item. In three instances, costs were significantly over budget (indirect materials 34%, indirect labor 50%, and supervision 14%).

Ed, it is imperative that you get costs under control in your department as soon as possible.

I think we need to talk about ways to implement more effective cost control measures. I would like to meet with you in my office at 9 a.m. on Wednesday to discuss possible alternatives.

SUMMARY OF STUDY OBJECTIVES

❶ Describe the concept of budgetary control. Budgetary control consists of (a) preparing periodic budget reports that compare actual results with planned objectives, (b) analyzing the differences to determine their causes, (c) taking appropriate corrective action, and (d) modifying future plans, if necessary.

❷ Evaluate the usefulness of static budget reports. Static budget reports are useful in evaluating the progress toward meeting planned sales and profit goals. They are also appropriate in assessing a manager's effectiveness in controlling fixed costs and expenses when (a) actual activity closely approximates the master budget activity level and/or (b) the behavior of the costs in response to changes in activity is fixed.

❸ Explain the development of flexible budgets and the usefulness of flexible budget reports. To develop the flexible budget it is necessary to:
(a) Identify the activity index and the relevant range of activity.
(b) Identify the variable costs and determine the budgeted variable cost per unit of activity for each cost.
(c) Identify the fixed costs and determine the budgeted amount for each cost.
(d) Prepare the budget for selected increments of activity within the relevant range.

Flexible budget reports permit an evaluation of a manager's performance in controlling production and costs.

4 *Describe the concept of responsibility accounting.* Responsibility accounting involves the accumulation and reporting of revenues and costs on the basis of the individual manager who has the authority to make the day-to-day decisions about the items. Under responsibility accounting, the evaluation of a manager's performance is based on the matters directly under the manager's control. In responsibility accounting, it is necessary to distinguish between controllable and noncontrollable fixed costs and to identify three types of responsibility centers: cost, profit, and investment.

5 *Indicate the features of responsibility reports for cost centers.* Responsibility reports for cost centers compare actual costs with flexible budget data. The reports show only controllable costs and no distinction is made between variable and fixed costs.

6 *Identify the content of responsibility reports for profit centers.* Responsibility reports show contribution margin, controllable fixed costs, and controllable margin for each profit center.

7 *Explain the basis and formula used in evaluating performance in investment centers.* The primary basis for evaluating performance in investment centers is return on investment (ROI). The formula for computing ROI for investment centers is: Controllable Margin (in dollars) ÷ Average Operating Assets.

THE NAVIGATOR

DECISION TOOLKIT—A SUMMARY

Decision Checkpoints	Info Needed for Decision	Tool to Use for Decision	How to Evaluate Results
Are the increased costs resulting from increased production reasonable?	Variable costs projected at different levels of production	Flexible budget	After taking into account different production levels, results are favorable if expenses are less than budgeted amounts.
Have the individual managers been held accountable for the costs and revenues under their control?	Relevant costs and revenues, where the individual manager has authority to make day-to-day decisions about the items	Responsibility reports focused on cost centers, profit centers, and investment centers as appropriate	Compare budget to actual costs for controllable items.
Has the investment center performed up to expectations?	Controllable margin (contribution margin minus controllable fixed costs), and average investment center operating assets	Return on investment	Compare actual ROI to expected ROI.

GLOSSARY

Budgetary control The use of budgets to control operations. (p. 254)

Controllable costs Costs that a manager has the authority to incur within a given period of time. (p. 266)

Controllable margin Contribution margin less controllable fixed costs. (p. 271)

Cost center A responsibility center that incurs costs but does not directly generate revenues. (p. 269)

Decentralization Control of operations is delegated by top management to many managers throughout the organization. (p. 265)

Direct fixed costs Costs that relate specifically to a responsibility center and are incurred for the sole benefit of the center. (p. 270)

Flexible budget A projection of budget data for various levels of activity. (p. 257)

Indirect fixed costs   Costs that are incurred for the benefit of more than one profit center. (p. 271)

Investment center   A responsibility center that incurs costs, generates revenues, and has control over the investment funds available for use. (p. 269)

Management by exception   The review of budget reports by top management directed entirely or primarily to differences between actual results and planned objectives. (p. 263)

Noncontrollable costs   Costs incurred indirectly and allocated to a responsibility center that are not controllable at that level. (p. 266)

Profit center   A responsibility center that incurs costs and also generates revenues. (p. 269)

Responsibility accounting   A part of management accounting that involves accumulating and reporting revenues and costs on the basis of the individual manager who has the authority to make the day-to-day decisions about the items. (p. 265)

Responsibility reporting system   The preparation of reports for each level of responsibility shown in the company's organization chart. (p. 266)

Return on investment (ROI)   A measure of management's effectiveness in utilizing assets at its disposal in an investment center. (p. 273)

Segment   An area of responsibility in decentralized operations. (p. 265)

Static budget   A projection of budget data at one level of activity. (p. 255)

DEMONSTRATION PROBLEM

Glenda Company uses a flexible budget for manufacturing overhead based on direct labor hours. For 1999 the master overhead budget for the Packaging Department at normal capacity of 300,000 direct labor hours was as follows:

Variable Costs		Fixed Costs	
Indirect labor	$360,000	Supervision	$ 60,000
Supplies and lubricants	150,000	Depreciation	24,000
Maintenance	210,000	Property taxes	18,000
Utilities	120,000	Insurance	12,000
	$840,000		$114,000

During July, 24,000 direct labor hours were worked when 25,000 hours were expected to be worked. The company incurred the following variable costs in July: Indirect labor $30,200, supplies and lubricants $11,600, maintenance $17,500, and utilities $9,200. Actual fixed overhead costs were the same as monthly budgeted fixed costs.

Instructions

Prepare a flexible budget report for the Packaging Department for July.

Solution to Demonstration Problem

GLENDA COMPANY
Manufacturing Overhead Budget Report (Flexible)
Packaging Department
For the Month Ended July 31, 1999

Direct labor hours (DLH)			Difference
Expected 25,000	Budget	Actual Costs	Favorable F
Actual 24,000	24,000 DLH	24,000 DLH	Unfavorable U
Variable costs			
Indirect labor	$28,800	$30,200	$1,400 U
Supplies and lubricants	12,000	11,600	400 F
Maintenance	16,800	17,500	700 U
Utilities	9,600	9,200	400 F
Total variable	67,200	68,500	1,300 U

Problem-Solving Strategies

1. Use budget data for actual direct labor hours worked.
2. Classify each cost as variable or fixed.
3. Determine the difference between budgeted and actual costs.
4. Identify the difference as favorable or unfavorable.
5. Determine the difference in total variable costs, total fixed costs, and total costs.

Fixed costs			
Supervision	5,000	5,000	–0–
Depreciation	2,000	2,000	–0–
Property taxes	1,500	1,500	–0–
Insurance	1,000	1,000	–0–
Total fixed	9,500	9,500	–0–
Total costs	$76,700	$78,000	$1,300 U

SELF-STUDY QUESTIONS

Answers are at the end of the chapter.

(SO 1) 1. Budgetary control involves all but one of the following:
   (a) modifying future plans.
   (b) analyzing differences.
   (c) using static budgets.
   (d) determining differences between actual and planned results.

(SO 2) 2. A static budget is useful in controlling costs when cost behavior is:
   (a) mixed.
   (b) fixed.
   (c) variable.
   (d) linear.

(SO 3) 3. At zero direct labor hours in a flexible budget graph, the total budgeted cost line intersects the vertical axis at $30,000. At 10,000 direct labor hours, the line drawn from the total budgeted cost line intersects the vertical axis at $90,000. Fixed and variable costs may be expressed as:
   (a) $30,000 fixed plus $6 per direct labor hour variable.
   (b) $30,000 fixed plus $9 per direct labor hour variable.
   (c) $60,000 fixed plus $3 per direct labor hour variable.
   (d) $60,000 fixed plus $6 per direct labor hour variable.

(SO 3) 4. At 9,000 direct labor hours, the flexible budget for indirect materials is $27,000. If $28,000 of indirect materials costs are incurred at 9,200 direct labor hours, the flexible budget report should show the following difference for indirect materials:
   (a) $1,000 unfavorable.
   (b) $1,000 favorable.
   (c) $400 favorable.
   (d) $400 unfavorable.

(SO 4) 5. Under responsibility accounting, the evaluation of a manager's performance is based on matters that the manager:
   (a) directly controls.
   (b) directly and indirectly controls.
   (c) indirectly controls.
   (d) has shared responsibility with another manager.

(SO 4) 6. Responsibility centers include:
   (a) cost centers.
   (b) profit centers.
   (c) investment centers.
   (d) all of the above.

(SO 5) 7. Responsibility reports for cost centers:
   (a) distinguish between fixed and variable costs.
   (b) use static budget data.
   (c) include both controllable and noncontrollable costs.
   (d) include only controllable costs.

(SO 6) 8. In a responsibility report for a profit center, controllable fixed costs are deducted from contribution margin to show:
   (a) profit center margin.
   (b) controllable margin.
   (c) net income.
   (d) income from operations.

(SO 7) 9. In the formula for return on investment (ROI), the factors for controllable margin and operating assets are, respectively:
   (a) controllable margin percentage and total operating assets.
   (b) controllable margin dollars and average operating assets.
   (c) controllable margin dollars and total assets.
   (d) controllable margin percentage and average operating assets.

(SO 7) 10. A manager of an investment center can improve ROI by:
   (a) increasing average operating assets.
   (b) reducing sales.
   (c) increasing variable costs.
   (d) reducing variable and/or controllable fixed costs.

QUESTIONS

1. (a) What is budgetary control?
   (b) Tony Crespino is describing budgetary control. What steps should be included in Tony's description?

2. The following purposes are part of a budgetary reporting system: (a) determine efficient use of materials, (b) control overhead costs, and (c) determine whether income objectives are being met. For each purpose, indicate the name of the report, the frequency of the report, and the primary recipient(s) of the report.

3. How may a budget report for the second quarter differ from a budget report for the first quarter?

4. Don Cox questions the usefulness of a master sales budget in evaluating sales performance. Is there justification for Don's concern? Explain. *No, Budget is for a reason*

5. Under what circumstances may a static budget be an appropriate basis for evaluating a manager's effectiveness in controlling costs?

6. "A flexible budget is really a series of static budgets." Is this true? Why? *≠ False*

7. The static manufacturing overhead budget based on 40,000 direct labor hours shows budgeted indirect labor costs of $56,000. During March, the department incurs $66,000 of indirect labor while working 45,000 direct labor hours. Is this a favorable or unfavorable performance? Why?

8. A static overhead budget based on 40,000 direct labor hours shows Factory Insurance $6,500 as a fixed cost. At the 50,000 direct labor hours worked in March, factory insurance costs were $6,200. Is this a favorable or unfavorable performance? Why? *Sales budget*

9. Kate Coulter is confused about how a flexible budget is prepared. Identify the steps for Kate.

10. Alou Company has prepared a graph of flexible budget data. At zero direct labor hours, the total budgeted cost line intersects the vertical axis at $25,000. At 10,000 direct labor hours, the line drawn from the total budgeted cost line intersects the vertical axis at

$85,000. How may the fixed and variable costs be expressed?

11. The flexible budget formula is fixed costs $40,000 plus variable costs of $2 per direct labor hour. What is the total budgeted cost at (a) 9,000 hours and (b) 12,345 hours?

12. What is management by exception? What criteria may be used in identifying exceptions?

13. What is responsibility accounting? Explain the purpose of responsibility accounting.

14. Ann Wilkins is studying for an accounting examination. Describe for Ann what conditions are necessary for responsibility accounting to be used effectively.

15. Distinguish between controllable and noncontrollable costs.

16. How do responsibility reports differ from budget reports?

17. What is the relationship, if any, between a responsibility reporting system and a company's organization chart?

18. Distinguish among the three types of responsibility centers.

19. (a) What costs are included in a performance report for a cost center? (b) In the report, are variable and fixed costs identified?

20. How do direct fixed costs differ from indirect fixed costs? Are both types of fixed costs controllable?

21. Lori Quan is confused about controllable margin reported in an income statement for a profit center. How is this margin computed, and what is its primary purpose?

22. What is the primary basis for evaluating the performance of the manager of an investment center? Indicate the formula for this basis.

23. Explain the ways that ROI can be improved.

24. Indicate two behavioral principles that pertain to (a) the manager being evaluated and (b) top management.

BRIEF EXERCISES

BE7-1 For the quarter ended March 31, 1999, Elsie Company accumulates the following sales data for its product, Garden-Tools: $315,000 budget; $300,000 actual. Prepare a static budget report for the quarter.

Prepare static budget report.
(SO 2)

BE7-2 Data for Elsie Company are given in BE7-1. In the second quarter, budgeted sales were $380,000, and actual sales were $390,000. Prepare a static budget report for the second quarter and for the year to date.

Prepare static budget report for two quarters.
(SO 2)

BE7-3 In Finney Company, direct labor is $20 per hour, and the company expects to operate at 10,000 direct labor hours each month. In January 1999, direct labor totaling $207,000 is incurred in working 10,800 hours. Prepare a static budget report and a flexible budget report. Evaluate the usefulness of each report.

Show usefulness of flexible budgets in evaluating performance.
(SO 3)

Prepare a flexible budget for variable costs.
(SO 3)

BE7-4 Kandt Company expects to produce 1,200,000 units of Product XX in 1999. Monthly production is expected to range from 80,000 to 120,000 units. Budgeted variable manufacturing costs per unit are: direct materials $5, direct labor $6, and overhead $3. Prepare a flexible manufacturing budget for the relevant range value using 20,000 unit increments.

Prepare flexible budget report.
(SO 3)

BE7-5 Data for Kandt Company are given in BE7-4. In March 1999, the company incurs the following costs in producing 100,000 units: direct materials $520,000, direct labor $590,000, and variable overhead $305,000. Prepare a flexible budget report for March. Were costs controlled?

Prepare a responsibility report for a cost center.
(SO 5)

BE7-6 In the Assembly Department of Jurgens Company, budgeted and actual manufacturing overhead costs for the month of April 1999 were as follows:

	Budget	**Actual**
Indirect materials	$150,00	$14,500
Indirect labor	20,000	20,800
Utilities	10,000	10,600
Supervision	5,000	5,000

All costs are controllable by the department manager. Prepare a responsibility report for April for the cost center.

Prepare a responsibility report for a profit center.
(SO 6)

BE7-7 Lehman Manufacturing Company accumulates the following summary data for the year ending December 31, 1999, for its Aqua Division which it operates as a profit center: Sales—$2,000,000 budget, $2,080,000 actual; variable costs—$1,000,000 budget, $1,050,000 actual; and controllable fixed costs—$300,000 budget, $310,000 actual. Prepare a responsibility report for the Aqua Division.

Prepare a responsibility report for an investment center.
(SO 7)

BE7-8 For the year ending December 31, 1999, Ming Chow Company accumulates the following data for the Plastics Division which it operates as an investment center: contribution margin—$700,000 budget, $715,000 actual; controllable fixed costs—$300,000 budget, $295,000 actual. Average operating assets for the year were $2,000,000. Prepare a responsibility report for the Plastics Division beginning with contribution margin.

Compute return on investment using the ROI formula.
(SO 7)

BE7-9 For its three investment centers, Huskey Company accumulates the following data:

	I	**II**	**III**
Sales	$2,000,000	$3,000,000	$ 4,000,000
Controllable margin	1,500,000	2,400,000	3,200,000
Average operating assets	6,000,000	8,000,000	10,000,000

Compute the return on investment (ROI) for each center.

Compute return on investment under changed conditions.
(SO 7)

BE7-10 Data for the investment centers for Huskey Company are given in BE7-9. The centers expect the following changes in the next year: (I) increase sales 10%; (II) decrease costs $200,000; (III) decrease average operating assets $400,000. Compute the expected return on investment (ROI) for each center. Assume center I has a contribution margin percentage of 80%.

EXERCISES

Prepare flexible manufacturing overhead budget.
(SO 3)

E7-1 Paola Company uses a flexible budget for manufacturing overhead based on direct labor hours. Variable manufacturing overhead costs per direct labor hour are as follows:

Indirect labor	$1.00
Indirect materials	.50
Utilities	.30

Fixed overhead costs per month are: Supervision $3,000, Depreciation $1,500, and Property Taxes $800. The company believes it will normally operate in a range of 7,000–10,000 direct labor hours per month.

Instructions
Prepare a monthly flexible manufacturing overhead budget for 1999 for the expected range of activity, using increments of 1,000 direct labor hours.

E7-2 Using the information in E7-1, assume that in July 1999, Paola Company incurs the following manufacturing overhead costs:

Prepare flexible budget reports for manufacturing overhead costs and comment on findings.
(SO 3)

Actual

Variable Costs		Fixed Costs	
Indirect labor	$8,700	Supervision	$3,000
Indirect materials	4,300	Depreciation	1,500
Utilities	2,500	Property taxes	800

Instructions
(a) Prepare a flexible budget performance report, assuming that the company worked 9,000 direct labor hours during the month. The company expected to work 9,000 direct labor hours.
(b) Prepare a flexible budget performance report, assuming that the company worked 8,500 direct labor hours during the month. The company expected to work 8,500 direct labor hours.
(c) ▭▭▭▭▷ Comment on your findings.

E7-3 Mallory Company uses flexible budgets to control its selling expenses. Monthly sales are expected to range from $170,000 to $200,000. Variable costs and their percentage relationship to sales are: Sales Commissions (5%), Advertising (4%), Traveling (3%), and Delivery (2%). Fixed selling expenses will consist of Sales Salaries $30,000, Depreciation on Delivery Equipment $5,000, and Insurance on Delivery Equipment $1,000.

Prepare flexible selling expense budget.
(SO 3)

Instructions
Prepare a monthly flexible budget for each $10,000 increment of sales within the relevant range for the year ending December 31, 1999.

E7-4 The actual selling expenses incurred in March 1999 by Mallory Company are as follows:

Prepare flexible budget reports for selling expenses.
(SO 3)

Variable Expenses		Fixed Expenses	
Sales commissions	$9,200	Sales salaries	$30,000
Advertising	7,000	Depreciation	5,000
Travel	5,100	Insurance	1,000
Delivery	3,500		

Instructions
(a) Prepare a flexible budget performance report for March using the budget data in E7-3, assuming that March sales were $170,000. Expected and actual sales are the same.
(b) Prepare a flexible budget performance report, assuming that March sales were $180,000. Expected sales and actual sales are the same.
(c) Comment on the importance of using flexible budgets in evaluating the performance of the sales manager.

E7-5 Jabarra Company's manufacturing overhead budget for the first quarter of 1999 contained the following data: *Budget*

Prepare flexible budget and responsibility report for manufacturing overhead.
(SO 3, 5)

Variable Costs		Fixed Costs	
Indirect materials	$12,000	Supervisory salaries	$30,000
Indirect labor	10,000	Depreciation	7,000
Utilities	8,000	Property taxes and insurance	8,000
Maintenance	5,000	Maintenance	5,000

Actual variable costs were: indirect materials $14,200, indirect labor $9,600, utilities $8,700, and maintenance $4,200. Actual fixed costs equaled budgeted costs except for property taxes and insurance, which were $8,100.

All costs are considered controllable by the production department manager except for depreciation, property taxes, and insurance.

Instructions
(a) Prepare a flexible overhead budget report for the first quarter.
(b) Prepare a responsibility report for the first quarter.

Prepare flexible budget report and answer question.

(SO 2, 3)

E7-6 As sales manager, Todd Keyser was given the following static budget report for selling expenses in the Clothing Department of O'Keefe Company for the month of October.

O'KEEFE COMPANY
Clothing Department
Budget Report
For the Month Ended October 31, 1999

	Budget	Actual	Difference Favorable F Unfavorable U
Sales in units	8,000	10,000	2,000 F
Variable costs			
Sales commissions	$ 2,000	$ 2,200	$ 200 U
Advertising expense	800	850	50 U
Travel expense	4,400	4,900	500 U
Free samples given out	1,000	1,300	300 U
Total variable	8,200	9,250	1,050 U
Fixed costs			
Rent	1,500	1,500	–0–
Sales salaries	1,200	1,200	–0–
Office salaries	800	800	–0–
Depreciation—autos (sales staff)	500	500	–0–
Total fixed	4,000	4,000	–0–
Total costs	$11,800	$13,250	$1,050 U

As a result of this budget report, Todd was called into the president's office and congratulated on his fine sales performance. He was reprimanded, however, for allowing his costs to get out of control. Todd knew something was wrong with the performance report that he had been given. However, he was not sure what to do, and comes to you for advice.

Instructions
(a) Prepare a budget report based on flexible budget data to help Todd.
(b) Should Todd have been reprimanded? Explain.

State total budgeted cost formulas and prepare flexible budget graph.

(SO 3)

E7-7 Gonzalez Company has two production departments, Fabricating and Assembling. At a department managers' meeting, the controller uses flexible budget graphs to explain total budgeted costs. Separate graphs based on direct labor hours are used for each department. The graphs show the following:
1. At zero direct labor hours, the total budgeted cost line and the fixed cost line intersect the vertical axis at $50,000 in the Fabricating Department and $48,000 in the Assembling Department.
2. At normal capacity of 50,000 direct labor hours, the line drawn from the total budgeted cost line intersects the vertical axis at $160,000 in the Fabricating Department, and $108,000 in the Assembling Department.

Instructions
(a) State the total budgeted cost formula for each department.
(b) Compute the total budgeted cost for each department, assuming actual direct labor hours worked were 53,000 and 47,000, in the Fabricating and Assembling Departments, respectively.

(c) Prepare the flexible budget graph for the Fabricating Department, assuming the maximum direct labor hours in the relevant range is 100,000. Use increments of 10,000 direct labor hours on the horizontal axis and increments of $50,000 on the vertical axis.

E7-8   Abotteen Company's organization chart includes the president; the vice president of production; three assembly plants—Dallas, Atlanta, and Tucson; and two departments within each plant—Machining and Finishing. Budget and actual manufacturing cost data for July 1999 are as follows: *Prepare reports in a responsibility reporting system.* *(SO 4)*

Finishing Department—Dallas: Direct materials $42,000 actual, $46,000 budget; direct labor $83,000 actual, $82,000 budget; manufacturing overhead $51,000 actual, $49,200 budget.

Machining Department—Dallas: Total manufacturing costs $218,000 actual, $214,000 budget.

Atlanta Plant: Total manufacturing costs $426,000 actual, $421,000 budget.

Tucson Plant: Total manufacturing costs $494,000 actual, $499,000 budget.

The Dallas plant manager's office costs were $95,000 actual and $92,000 budget. The vice president of production's office costs were $132,000 actual and $130,000 budget. Office costs are not allocated to departments and plants.

Instructions
Prepare the reports in a responsibility system for (a) the Finishing Department—Dallas, (b) the plant manager—Dallas, and (c) the vice president of production. Use the format on page 268.

E7-9   Pavlik Manufacturing Inc. has three divisions which are operated as profit centers. Operating data for the divisions listed alphabetically are as follows: *Compute missing amounts in responsibility reports for three profit centers and prepare a report.* *(SO 6)*

Operating Data	Women's Shoes	Men's Shoes	Children's Shoes
Contribution margin	$250,000	(3)	$160,000
Controllable fixed costs	100,000	(4)	(5)
Controllable margin	(1)	$ 90,000	96,000
Sales	600,000	450,000	(6)
Variable costs	(2)	310,000	250,000

Instructions
(a) Compute the missing amounts. Show computations.
(b) Prepare a responsibility report for the Women's Shoe Division assuming (1) the data are for the month ended June 30, 1999, and (2) all data equal budget except variable costs which are $10,000 over budget.

E7-10   The Mastercraft Division of Nunez Company reported the following data for the current year: *Compute ROI for current year and for possible future changes.* *(SO 7)*

Sales	$3,000,000
Variable costs	1,800,000
Controllable fixed costs	600,000
Average operating assets	5,000,000

Top management is unhappy with the investment center's return on investment (ROI). It asks the manager of the Mastercraft Division to submit plans to improve ROI in the next year. The manager believes it is feasible to consider the following independent courses of action.
1. Increase sales by $320,000 with no change in the contribution margin percentage.
2. Reduce variable costs by $100,000.
3. Reduce average operating assets by 5%.

Instructions
(a) Compute the return on investment (ROI) for the current year.
(b) Using the ROI formula, compute the ROI under each of the proposed courses of action. (Round to one decimal.)

Problems: Set A

Prepare flexible budget and budget report for manufacturing overhead.

(SO 3)

P7-1A   Rossi Company estimates that 240,000 direct labor hours will be worked during 1999 in the Assembly Department. On this basis, the following budgeted manufacturing overhead data are computed:

Variable Overhead Costs		Fixed Overhead Costs	
Indirect labor	$ 72,000	Supervision	$ 72,000
Indirect materials	48,000	Depreciation	30,000
Repairs	24,000	Insurance	9,600
Utilities	14,400	Rent	7,200
Lubricants	9,600	Property taxes	6,000
	$168,000		$124,800

It is estimated that direct labor hours worked each month will range from 18,000 to 24,000 hours.

During January, 20,000 direct labor hours were worked and the following overhead costs were incurred.

Variable Overhead Costs		Fixed Overhead Costs	
Indirect labor	$ 6,200	Supervision	$ 6,000
Indirect materials	3,600	Depreciation	2,500
Repairs	1,600	Insurance	800
Utilities	900	Rent	700
Lubricants	830	Property taxes	500
	$13,130		$10,500

Instructions

(a) Prepare a monthly flexible manufacturing overhead budget for each increment of 2,000 direct labor hours over the relevant range for the year ending December 31, 1999.

(b) Prepare a manufacturing overhead budget report for January, assuming 20,500 direct labor hours were expected.

(c) Comment on management's efficiency in controlling manufacturing overhead costs in January.

Prepare flexible budget, budget report, and graph for manufacturing overhead.

(SO 3)

P7-2A   Tariq Manufacturing Company produces one product, Kebo. Because of wide fluctuations in demand for Kebo, the Assembly Department experiences significant variations in monthly production levels.

The master manufacturing overhead budget **for the year,** based on 300,000 direct labor hours, and the actual overhead costs incurred in July in which 27,500 labor hours were worked, and 27,500 hours were expected to be worked, are as follows:

Overhead Costs	Master Budget (annual)	Actual in July
Variable		
Indirect labor	$ 360,000	$32,000
Indirect materials	210,000	17,000
Utilities	90,000	8,100
Maintenance	60,000	5,400
Fixed		
Supervision	180,000	15,000
Depreciation	120,000	10,000
Insurance and taxes	60,000	5,000
Total	$1,080,000	$92,500

Instructions

(a) Prepare a monthly flexible overhead budget for the year ending December 31, 1999, assuming monthly production levels range from 22,500 to 30,000 direct labor hours. Use increments of 2,500 direct labor hours.

(b) Prepare a budget performance report for the month of July 1999 comparing actual results with budget data based on the flexible budget.

(c) ◼◼◼▶ Were costs effectively controlled? Explain.

(d) State the formula for computing the total monthly budgeted costs in Tariq Company.

(e) Prepare the flexible budget graph showing total budgeted costs at 25,000 and 27,500 direct labor hours. Use increments of 5,000 on the horizontal axis and increments of $10,000 on the vertical axis.

P7-3A Uphoff Company uses budgets in controlling costs. The May 1999 budget report for the company's Packaging Department is as follows:

State total budgeted cost formula and prepare flexible budget reports for two time periods.

(SO 2, 3)

UPHOFF COMPANY
Budget Report
Packaging Department
For the Month Ended May 31, 1999

Manufacturing Costs	Budget	Actual	Difference Favorable F Unfavorable U
Variable costs			
Direct materials	$ 30,000	$ 32,000	$2,000 U
Direct labor	40,000	43,000	3,000 U
Indirect materials	15,000	15,200	200 U
Indirect labor	12,500	13,000	500 U
Utilities	7,500	7,100	400 F
Maintenance	5,000	5,200	200 U
Total variable	110,000	115,500	5,500 U
Fixed costs			
Rent	9,000	9,000	–0–
Supervision	8,000	8,000	–0–
Depreciation	5,000	5,000	–0–
Total fixed	22,000	22,000	–0–
Total costs	$132,000	$137,500	$5,500 U

TMU =

The budget amounts in the report were on the master budget for the year, which assumed that 600,000 units would be produced. (*Hint:* The budget amounts above are one-twelfth of the master budget for the year.)

The company president was displeased with the department manager's performance. The department manager, who thought he had done a good job, could not understand the unfavorable results. In May, 55,000 units were produced.

Instructions

(a) State the total budgeted cost formula.

(b) Prepare a budget report for May using flexible budget data. Why does this report provide a better basis for evaluating performance than the report based on static budget data? Assume 57,000 units were expected to be produced in the Packaging Department.

(c) In June, 40,000 units were produced when 39,000 were expected. Prepare the budget report using flexible budget data, assuming (1) each variable cost was 20% less in June than its actual cost in May, and (2) fixed costs were the same in the month of June as in May.

P7-4A McCluskey Manufacturing Inc. operates the Home Appliance Division as a profit center. Operating data for this division for the year ended December 31, 1999, are as follows:

Prepare responsibility report for a profit center.

(SO 6)

	Budget	Difference from Budget
Sales	$2,400,000	$100,000 U
Costs of goods sold		
Variable	1,200,000	60,000 U
Controllable fixed	200,000	10,000 F

	Budget	Difference from Budget
Selling and administrative		
Variable	240,000	10,000 F
Controllable fixed	60,000	6,000 U
Noncontrollable fixed costs	50,000	2,000 U

In addition, McCluskey Manufacturing incurs $150,000 of indirect fixed costs that were budgeted at $155,000. Twenty percent (20%) of these costs are allocated to the Home Appliance Division. None of these costs are controllable by the division manager.

Instructions
(a) Prepare a responsibility report for the Home Appliance Division (a profit center) for the year.
(b) ▭▭▭▭▷Comment on the manager's performance in controlling revenues and costs.
(c) Identify any costs excluded from the responsibility report and explain why they were excluded.

Prepare responsibility report for an investment center and compute ROI.
(SO 7)

P7-5A Ninemire Manufacturing Company manufactures a variety of garden and lawn equipment. The company operates through three divisions. Each division is an investment center. Operating data for the Lawnmower Division for the year ended December 31, 1999, and relevant budget data are as follows:

	Actual	Comparison with Budget
Sales	$2,800,000	$200,000 unfavorable
Variable cost of goods sold	1,400,000	150,000 unfavorable
Variable selling and administrative expenses	300,000	50,000 favorable
Controllable fixed cost of goods sold	270,000	On target
Controllable fixed selling and administrative expenses	130,000	On target

Average operating assets for the year for the Lawnmower Division were $5,000,000 which was also the budgeted amount.

Instructions
(a) Prepare a responsibility report (in thousands of dollars) for the Lawnmower Division.
(b) Evaluate the manager's performance. Which items will likely be investigated by top management?
(c) Compute the expected ROI in 2000 for the Lawnmower Division, assuming the following changes:
  (1) Variable cost of goods sold is decreased by 15%.
  (2) Average operating assets are decreased by 20%.
  (3) Sales are increased by $500,000 and this increase is expected to increase contribution margin by $200,000.

Prepare reports for cost centers under responsibility accounting and comment on performance of managers.
(SO 4)

P7-6A Ohse Company uses a responsibility reporting system. It has divisions in Denver, Seattle, and San Diego. Each division has three production departments: Cutting, Shaping, and Finishing. The responsibility for each department rests with a manager who reports to the division production manager. Each division manager reports to the vice president of production. There are also vice presidents for marketing and finance. All vice presidents report to the president.

In January 1999, controllable actual and budget manufacturing overhead cost data for the departments and divisions were as follows:

Manufacturing Overhead	Actual	Budget
Individual costs—Cutting Department—Seattle		
Indirect labor	$ 73,000	$ 70,000
Indirect materials	46,700	46,000
Maintenance	20,500	18,000
Utilities	20,100	17,000
Supervision	20,000	20,000
	$ 180,300	$ 171,000

Manufacturing Overhead	Actual	Budget
Total costs		
Shaping Department—Seattle	$ 158,000	$ 148,000
Finishing Department—Seattle	210,000	208,000
Denver division	676,000	673,000
San Diego division	722,000	715,000
	$1,766,000	$1,744,000

Additional overhead costs were incurred as follows: Seattle division production manager—actual costs $52,500, budget $51,000; vice president of production—actual costs $65,000, budget $64,000; president—actual costs $76,400, budget $74,200. These expenses are not allocated.

The vice presidents who report to the president, other than the vice president of production, had the following expenses:

Vice President	Actual	Budget
Marketing	$133,600	$130,000
Finance	107,000	105,000

Instructions
(a) Prepare the following responsibility reports:
    (1) Manufacturing overhead—Cutting Department manager—Seattle division.
    (2) Manufacturing overhead—Seattle division manager.
    (3) Manufacturing overhead—vice president of production.
    (4) Manufacturing overhead and expenses—president. Use the format on page 268.
(b) Comment on the comparative performances of
    (1) Department managers in the Seattle division.
    (2) Division managers.
    (3) Vice presidents.

PROBLEMS: SET B

P7-1B Petrova Company estimates that 360,000 direct labor hours will be worked during the coming year, 1999, in the Packaging Department. On this basis, the following budgeted manufacturing overhead cost data are computed for the year:

Prepare flexible budget and budget report for manufacturing overhead.
(SO 3)

Fixed Overhead Costs		Variable Overhead Costs	
Supervision	$ 90,000	Indirect labor	$144,000
Depreciation	54,000	Indirect materials	90,000
Insurance	27,000	Repairs	54,000
Rent	36,000	Utilities	72,000
Property taxes	18,000	Lubricants	18,000
	$225,000		$378,000

It is estimated that direct labor hours worked each month will range from 27,000 to 36,000 hours.

During October, 27,000 direct labor hours were worked and the following overhead costs were incurred:

Fixed overhead costs: Supervision $7,500, Depreciation $4,500, Insurance $2,225, Rent $3,000, and Property taxes $1,500.

Variable overhead costs: Indirect labor $11,760, Indirect materials, $6,400, Repairs $4,000, Utilities $5,900, and Lubricants $1,640.

Instructions
(a) Prepare a monthly flexible manufacturing overhead budget for each increment of 3,000 direct labor hours over the relevant range for the year ending December 31, 1999.

(b) Prepare a flexible budget report for October, when 27,500 direct labor hours were expected.

(c) Comment on management's efficiency in controlling manufacturing overhead costs in October.

Prepare flexible budget, budget report, and graph for manufacturing overhead.
(SO 3)

P7-2B Matheny Company manufactures tablecloths. Sales have grown rapidly over the past 2 years. As a result, the president has installed a budgetary control system for 1999. The following data were used in developing the master manufacturing overhead budget for the Ironing Department, which is based on an activity index of direct labor hours.

Variable Costs	Rate per Direct Labor Hour	Annual Fixed Costs	
Indirect labor	$.40	Supervision	$30,000
Indirect materials	.50	Depreciation	18,000
Factory utilities	.30	Insurance	12,000
Factory repairs	.20	Rent	24,000

The master overhead budget was prepared on the expectation that 480,000 direct labor hours will be worked during the year. In June, 42,000 direct labor hours were worked and 42,000 were expected. At that level of activity, actual costs were as follows:

Variable—per direct labor hour: Indirect labor $.42, Indirect materials $.50, Factory utilities $.32, and Factory repairs $.21.

Fixed: same as budgeted.

Instructions

(a) Prepare a monthly flexible manufacturing overhead budget for the year ending December 31, 1999, assuming production levels range from 35,000 to 50,000 direct labor hours. Use increments of 5,000 direct labor hours.

(b) Prepare a budget performance report for June comparing actual results with budget data based on the flexible budget.

(c) Were costs effectively controlled? Explain.

(d) State the formula for computing the total budgeted costs for Matheny Company.

(e) Prepare the flexible budget graph, showing total budgeted costs at 35,000 and 45,000 direct labor hours. Use increments of 5,000 direct labor hours on the horizontal axis and increments of $10,000 on the vertical axis.

State total budgeted cost formula and prepare flexible budget reports for two time periods.
(SO 2, 3)

P7-3B Fernandez Company uses budgets in controlling costs. The August 1999 budget report for the company's Assembling Department is as follows:

FERNANDEZ COMPANY
Budget Report
Assembling Department
For the Month Ended August 31, 1999

Manufacturing Costs	Budget	Actual	Difference Favorable F Unfavorable U
Variable costs			
Direct materials	$ 48,000	$ 47,000	$1,000 F
Direct labor	72,000	68,000	4,000 F
Indirect materials	24,000	24,200	200 U
Indirect labor	18,000	17,500	500 F
Utilities	15,000	14,900	100 F
Maintenance	9,000	9,200	200 U
Total variable	186,000	180,800	5,200 F
Fixed costs			
Rent	10,000	10,000	–0–
Supervision	15,000	15,000	–0–
Depreciation	7,000	7,000	–0–
Total fixed	32,000	32,000	–0–
Total costs	$218,000	$212,800	$5,200 F

The budget data in the report are based on the master budget for the year, which assumed that 720,000 units would be produced. The Assembling Department manager is pleased with the report and expects a raise, or at least praise for a job well done. The company president, however, is unhappy with the results for August, because only 58,000 units were produced. (*Hint:* The budget amounts above are one-twelfth of the master budget.)

Instructions
(a) State the total budgeted cost formula.
(b) Prepare a budget report for August using flexible budget data. Why does this report provide a better basis for evaluating performance than the report based on static budget data? Assume 62,000 units were expected to be produced.
(c) In September, 64,000 units were produced when 65,000 were expected. Prepare the budget report using flexible budget data, assuming (1) each variable cost was 10% higher than its actual cost in August, and (2) fixed costs were the same in September as in August.

P7-4B Kohler Manufacturing Inc. operates the Patio Furniture Division as a profit center. Operating data for this division for the year ended December 31, 1999, are as follows:

Prepare responsibility report for a profit center.
(SO 6)

	Budget	Difference from Budget
Sales	$2,500,000	$50,000 F
Cost of goods sold		
Variable	1,300,000	40,000 F
Controllable fixed	200,000	5,000 U
Selling and administrative		
Variable	220,000	5,000 U
Controllable fixed	50,000	2,000 U
Noncontrollable fixed costs	70,000	4,000 U

In addition, Kohler Manufacturing incurs $180,000 of indirect fixed costs that were budgeted at $175,000. Twenty percent (20%) of these costs are allocated to the Patio Furniture Division.

Instructions
(a) Prepare a responsibility report for the Patio Furniture Division for the year.
(b) Comment on the manager's performance in controlling revenues and costs.
(c) Identify any costs excluded from the responsibility report and explain why they were excluded.

P7-5B Ingalls Manufacturing Company manufactures a variety of tools and industrial equipment. The company operates through three divisions. Each division is an investment center. Operating data for the Home Division for the year ended December 31, 1999, and relevant budget data are as follows:

Prepare responsibility report for an investment center and compute ROI.
(SO 7)

	Actual	Comparison with Budget
Sales	$1,500,000	$100,000 favorable
Variable cost of goods sold	700,000	100,000 unfavorable
Variable selling and administrative expenses	125,000	25,000 unfavorable
Controllable fixed cost of goods sold	170,000	On target
Controllable fixed selling and administrative expenses	100,000	On target

Average operating assets for the year for the Home Division were $2,500,000 which was also the budgeted amount.

Instructions
(a) Prepare a responsibility report (in thousands of dollars) for the Home Division.
(b) Evaluate the manager's performance. Which items will likely be investigated by top management?
(c) Compute the expected ROI in 2000 for the Home Division, assuming the following changes:
   (1) Variable cost of goods sold is decreased by 6%.
   (2) Average operating assets are decreased by 10%.
   (3) Sales are increased by $200,000, and this increase is expected to increase contribution margin by $90,000.

BROADENING YOUR PERSPECTIVE

GROUP DECISION CASE

BYP7-1 Green Pastures is a 400-acre farm on the outskirts of the Kentucky Bluegrass, specializing in the boarding of broodmares and their foals. A recent economic downturn in the thoroughbred industry has led to a decline in breeding activities, and it has made the boarding business extremely competitive. To meet the competition, Green Pastures planned in 1999 to entertain clients, advertise more extensively, and absorb expenses formerly paid by clients such as veterinary and blacksmith fees.

The budget report for 1999 is presented below. As shown, the static income statement budget for the year is based on an expected 21,900 boarding days at $25 per mare. The variable expenses per mare per day were budgeted: Feed $5, Veterinary fees $3, Blacksmith fees $0.30, and Supplies $0.40. All other budgeted expenses were either semifixed or fixed.

During the year, management decided not to replace a worker who quit in March, but it did issue a new advertising brochure and did more entertaining of clients.[1]

GREEN PASTURES
Static Budget Income Statement
Year Ended December 31, 1999

	Actual	Master Budget	Difference
Number of mares	52	60	8*
Number of boarding days	18,980	21,900	2,920*
Sales	$379,600	$547,500	$167,900*
Less variable expenses:			
Feed	104,390	109,500	5,110
Veterinary fees	58,838	65,700	6,862
Blacksmith fees	6,074	6,570	496
Supplies	7,402	8,760	1,358
Total variable expenses	176,704	190,530	13,826
Contribution margin	202,896	356,970	154,074*
Less fixed expenses:			
Depreciation	40,000	40,000	-0-
Insurance	11,000	11,000	-0-
Utilities	12,000	14,000	2,000
Repairs and maintenance	10,000	11,000	1,000
Labor	88,000	96,000	8,000
Advertisement	12,000	8,000	4,000*
Entertainment	7,000	5,000	2,000*
Total fixed expense	180,000	185,000	5,000
Net income	$ 22,896	$171,970	$149,074*

*Unfavorable.

Instructions
With the class divided into groups, answer the following:
(a) Based on the static budget report,
    (1) What was the primary cause(s) of the loss in net income?
    (2) Did management do a good, average, or poor job of controlling expenses?
    (3) Were management's decisions to stay competitive sound?

---

[1]Data for this case are based on Hans Sprohge and John Talbott, "New Applications for Variance Analysis," *Journal of Accountancy* (AICPA, New York), April 1989, pp. 137–41.

(b) Prepare a flexible budget report for the year.
(c) Based on the flexible budget report, answer the three questions in part (a) above.
(d) What course of action do you recommend for the management of Green Pastures?

Managerial Analysis

BYP7-2 Lakenvelder Dutch manufactures expensive watch cases sold as souvenirs. Three of its sales departments are: Retail Sales, Wholesale Sales, and Outlet Sales. The Retail Sales Department is a profit center. The Wholesale Sales Department, however, is a cost center, because its managers merely take orders from customers who purchase through the company's wholesale catalog. The Outlet Sales Department is an investment center, because each manager is given full responsibility for an outlet store location. The manager can hire and discharge employees, purchase, maintain, and sell equipment, and in general is fairly independent of company control.

Rena Worthington is a manager in the Retail Sales Department; Winston Hillhouse manages the Wholesale Sales Department; Oscar Hadley manages the Golden Gate Club outlet store in San Francisco. The following are the budget responsibility reports for each of the three departments:

Budget			
	Retail Sales	Wholesale Sales	Outlet Sales
Sales	$ 750,000	$ 400,000	$200,000
Variable costs			
Cost of goods sold	150,000	100,000	25,000
Advertising	100,000	30,000	5,000
Sales salaries	75,000	15,000	3,000
Printing	10,000	20,000	5,000
Travel	20,000	30,000	2,000
Fixed costs			
Rent	50,000	30,000	10,000
Insurance	5,000	2,000	1,000
Depreciation	75,000	100,000	40,000
Investment in assets	$1,000,000	$1,200,000	$800,000

Actual Results			
	Retail Sales	Wholesale Sales	Outlet Sales
Sales	$ 750,000	$ 400,000	$200,000
Variable costs			
Cost of goods sold	195,000	120,000	26,250
Advertising	100,000	30,000	5,000
Sales salaries	75,000	15,000	3,000
Printing	10,000	20,000	5,000
Travel	15,000	20,000	1,500
Fixed costs			
Rent	40,000	50,000	12,000
Insurance	5,000	2,000	1,000
Depreciation	80,000	90,000	60,000
Investment in assets	$1,000,000	$1,200,000	$800,000

Instructions
(a) Determine which of the items should be included in the responsibility report for each of the three managers.
(b) Compare the budgeted measures with the actual results. Decide which results should be called to the attention of each manager.

REAL-WORLD FOCUS

COMPUTER ASSOCIATES INTERNATIONAL, INC.

BYP7-3 Computer Associates International was incorporated in 1974. Today it designs, develops, markets, and supports standardized computer software products for use with mainframe, midrange, and desktop computers. The company has 6,900 employees who work in its 55 offices in the U.S. or its 62 offices throughout the world including Europe, Asia, Russia, Israel, South America, and New Zealand.

Presented below is information from the company's annual report:

COMPUTER ASSOCIATES INTERNATIONAL
Management Discussion

The Company has experienced a pattern of business whereby revenue for its third and fourth fiscal quarters reflects an increase over first- and second-quarter revenue. The Company attributes this increase to clients' increased spending at the end of their calendar year budgetary periods and the culmination of its annual sales plan. Since the Company's costs do not increase proportionately with the third- and fourth-quarters' increase in revenue, the higher revenue in these quarters results in greater profit margins and income. Fourth-quarter profitability is traditionally affected by significant new hirings, training, and education expenditures for the succeeding year.

Instructions
(a) Why don't the company's costs increase proportionately as the revenues increase in the third and fourth quarters?
(b) What type of budgeting seems appropriate for Computer Associates' situation?

COMMUNICATION ACTIVITY

BYP7-4 Refer to the opening story about the athletic department of UNLV, and answer the following questions.
1. Would you expect a static or a flexible budget to be used in comparing actual and budgeted expenditures for each team?
2. Which of the biggest budget items are variable and which are fixed?
3. What is the relationship, if any, of the budgets used at UNLV and the allocation of cash to each team?

RESEARCH ASSIGNMENT

BYP7-5 The January 1998 issue of *Management Accounting* contains an article by Guy Haddleton entitled "10 Rules for Selecting Budget Management Software."

Instructions
Read the article and answer the following questions:
(a) In December 1996, International Data Corp. identified a new category of business management software—budget management. What is the meaning of budget management? Why is budget management complicated for any mid- to large-scale organization?
(b) As the foundation for the budget management system, why is the spreadsheet solution failing?
(c) The author of the article classifies his 10 rules into four categories that identify the demands of a budget management system, the demands that the spreadsheet solution fails to satisfy. What are these four categories of demands?
(d) What are the 10 requirements for a budget management system?

ETHICS CASE

BYP7-6   National Products Corporation participates in a highly competitive industry. In order to meet this competition and achieve profit goals, the company has chosen the decentralized form of organization. Each manager of a decentralized investment center is measured on the basis of profit contribution, market penetration, and return on investment. Failure to meet the objectives established by corporate management for these measures has not been acceptable and usually has resulted in demotion or dismissal of an investment center manager.

An anonymous survey of managers in the company revealed that the managers feel the pressure to compromise their personal ethical standards to achieve the corporate objectives. For example, at certain plant locations there was pressure to reduce quality control to a level which could not assure that all unsafe products would be rejected. Also, sales personnel were encouraged to use questionable sales tactics to obtain orders, including gifts and other incentives to purchasing agents.

The chief executive officer is disturbed by the survey findings. In his opinion such behavior cannot be condoned by the company. He concludes that the company should do something about this problem.

Instructions
(a) Who are the stakeholders (the affected parties) in this situation?
(b) Identify the ethical implications, conflicts, or dilemmas in the above described situation.
(c) What might the company do to reduce the pressures on managers and decrease the ethical conflicts?

(CMA adapted)

SURFING THE NET

BYP7-7   Genelle and Doug have recorded the story of their wedding planning. They are on a strict budget and need help in preparing what they call "a somewhat flexible budget."

Address: http://www.wednet.com/inspire/wedstory/story1.htm

Steps:
1. Go to Genelle and Doug's Web site and read about their trials and tribulations in planning a wedding.
2. Review the **Planning and Budgeting** section in "Part 1" of their story. They mention that this is a "somewhat flexible budget" for 250 guests, totalling $7,150. They would like to reduce their total costs to $7,000, if at all possible.

Instructions
Recast Genelle and Doug's budget into a truly flexible budget so that they can see the effects on their total costs of reducing the number of invited guests to 225 or 200.

Answers to Self-Study Questions
1. c   2. b   3. a   4. d   5. a   6. d   7. d   8. b   9. b   10. d

 Remember to go back to the Navigator box on the chapter-opening page and check off your completed work.

CHAPTER 8

Performance Evaluation through Standard Costs

THE NAVIGATOR

FEATURE STORY

Highlighting Performance Efficiency

There's a very good chance that the highlighter you're holding in your hand was made by Sanford, a maker of markers and other writing instruments. Sanford, headquartered in Illinois, annually sells hundreds of millions of dollars' worth of ACCENT highlighters, fine-point pens, Sharpie markers for overhead projectors, and other writing instruments.

Since Sanford makes literally billions of writing utensils per year, the company must keep tight control over manufacturing costs. As a result, a very important part of Sanford's manufacturing process is the de-termination of how much direct materials, labor, and overhead should cost. These costs are then compared to actual costs to assess performance efficiency. Raw materials for Sanford's markers include a barrel, plug, cap, ink reservoir, and a nib (tip). These parts are assembled by machine to produce thousands of units per hour. A major component of manufacturing overhead, then, includes machine maintenance—some fixed, some variable.

There's still a labor component, though: the machine operator, who makes or breaks productivity. "We try to control labor efficiency the best we can," says Tom Beyer, Sanford's vice president–controller. "But excessive labor time is often due to malfunctioning equipment—which is difficult to control."

In contrast, labor rates are more predictable because the hourly workers are covered by a union contract. The story is the same with the fringe benefits and some supervisory salaries. Even volume levels are fairly predictable—demand for the product is high—so that fixed overhead is efficiently absorbed. Raw material standard costs are based on the previous year's actual prices plus any anticipated inflation. Lately, though, inflation has been so low that the company is considering any price increase in raw material to be unfavorable.

THE NAVIGATOR

On the World Wide Web
http://www.sanfordcorp.com

298

n this chapter we continue the study of controlling costs by considering additional measures that permit the evaluation of performance. The content and organization of this chapter are as follows:

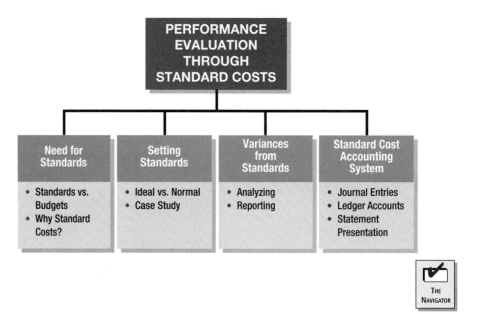

THE NEED FOR STANDANDS

Standards are a fact of life. You met the admission standards for the college or university you are attending. The automobile that you drive had to meet certain governmental emissions standards. The hamburgers and salads you eat in a restaurant have to meet certain health and nutritional standards before they can be sold. The reason for standards in these cases is very simple: They help to ensure that the overall quality of the product produced is high. Without standards, quality control is lost.

Standards are also common in business. Those imposed by government agencies are often called **regulations.** They include the Fair Labor Standards Act, the Equal Employment Opportunity Act, and a multitude of environmental standards. Standards established internally by a company may extend to personnel matters, such as employee absenteeism and ethical codes of conduct, quality control standards for products, and standard costs for goods and services. In managerial accounting, standard costs are predetermined unit costs, which are used as measures of performance.

Although we will focus on manufacturing operations in the remainder of this chapter, you should also recognize that standard costs are also applicable to many other types of businesses. For example, a fast-food restaurant such as McDonald's knows not only the price it should pay for pickles, beef, buns, and other ingredients, but also how much time it should take an employee to flip hamburgers. If too much is paid for pickles or too much time is taken to prepare Big Macs, the deviations are noticed and corrective action is taken. Moreover, standard costs may be used in not-for-profit enterprises such as universities, charitable organizations, and governmental agencies.

DISTINGUISHING BETWEEN STANDARDS AND BUDGETS

In concept, **standards** and **budgets** are essentially the same. Both are predetermined costs and both contribute significantly to management planning and control. There is a difference, however, in the way the terms are expressed. A standard is a **unit** amount, whereas a budget is a **total** amount. Thus, it is customary to state that the standard cost of direct labor for a unit of product is $10. However, if 5,000 units of the product are produced, the $50,000 of direct labor is the budgeted labor cost. In this context, a standard is the budgeted cost per unit of product. A standard is, therefore, concerned with each individual cost component that makes up the entire budget.

There are important accounting differences between budgets and standards. Except in the application of manufacturing overhead to jobs and processes, budget data are not journalized in cost accounting systems. In contrast, as will be illustrated later in the chapter, standard costs may be incorporated into cost accounting systems. It is also possible for a company to report its inventories at standard cost in its financial statements, but it is not possible to report inventories at budgeted costs.

WHY STANDARD COSTS?

Standard costs offer a number of advantages to an organization, as shown in Illustration 8-1. These advantages will be realized only when standard costs are carefully established and prudently used. Using standards solely as a means of

Illustration 8-1
Advantages of standard costs

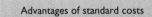
Advantages of standard costs

Facilitate management planning

Promote greater economy by making employees more "cost-conscious"

Useful in setting selling prices

Contribute to management control by providing basis for evaluation of cost control

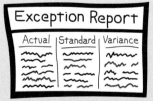
Useful in highlighting variances in management by exception

Simplify costing of inventories and reduce clerical costs

finding fault or placing blame can have a negative effect on managers and employees. In an effort to minimize this effect, many companies offer wage incentives to those who meet their standards.

SETTING STANDARD COSTS— A DIFFICULT TASK

STUDY OBJECTIVE

③

Describe how standards are set.

The setting of standard costs to produce a unit of product is a difficult task. It requires input from all persons who have responsibility for costs and quantities. To determine the standard cost of direct materials, management may have to consult the purchasing agents, product managers, quality control engineers, and production supervisors. In setting the cost standard for direct labor, pay rate data are obtained from the payroll department, and the labor time requirements may be determined by industrial engineers. The managerial accountant provides input into the standards-setting process by accumulating historical cost data and by knowing how costs respond to changes in activity levels. The decision as to what the standard cost should be is, of course, a management responsibility.

To be effective in controlling costs, standard costs need to be current at all times. Thus, standards should be under continuous review and should be changed whenever it is determined that the existing standard is not a good measure of performance. Circumstances that may warrant revision of a standard include changed wage rates resulting from a new union contract, a change in product specifications, or the implementation of a new manufacturing method.

BUSINESS INSIGHT

Management Perspective

Computerized standard cost systems represent one of the most complex accounting systems to develop and maintain. The standard cost system must be fully integrated into the general ledger, allow for the creation and timely maintenance of the data base of standard usage and costs for every product, and perform various variance computations. Such systems must also produce variance reports by product, department, or employee. With the increased use of automation and robotics, the computerized standard cost system may even be tied directly into these systems to gather variance information.

IDEAL VERSUS NORMAL STANDARDS

Standards may be set at one of two levels: ideal or normal. **Ideal standards** represent optimum levels of performance under perfect operating conditions. In contrast, **normal standards** represent efficient levels of performance that are attainable under expected operating conditions.

Some managers believe ideal standards will stimulate the conscientious worker to ever-increasing improvement. However, most managers believe that because these standards are so difficult, if not impossible, to meet, they discourage self-improvement and lower the morale of the entire workforce. Very few companies use ideal standards.

Helpful Hint When standards are set too high, employees sometimes feel pressure to consider unethical practices to meet these standards.

Most companies that use standards set them at a normal level. Properly set, normal standards should be **rigorous but attainable.** Normal standards allow for rest periods, machine breakdowns, and other "normal" contingencies in the production process. It will be assumed in the remainder of this chapter that standard costs are set at a normal level.

A CASE STUDY

To establish the standard cost of producing a product, it is necessary to establish standards for each manufacturing cost element—direct materials, direct labor, and manufacturing overhead. The standard for each element is derived from a consideration of the standard price to be paid and the standard quantity to be used. To illustrate, in the remainder of this section we will look at a case study of how standard costs are set. In this extended example, we will assume that Xonic, Inc., wishes to use standard costs to measure performance in filling an order for 1,000 gallons of Weed-O, a liquid weed killer.

Direct Materials

The direct materials price standard is the cost per unit of direct materials that should be incurred. This standard should be based on the purchasing department's best estimate of the **cost of raw materials.** This is frequently based on an analysis of current purchase prices. The price standard should also include an amount for related costs such as receiving, storing, and handling. The materials price standard per pound of material for Xonic's weed killer is:

Item	Price
Purchase price, net of discounts	$2.70
Freight	.20
Receiving and handling	.10
Standard direct materials price per pound	**$3.00**

Illustration 8-2 Setting direct materials price standard

The direct materials quantity standard is the quantity of direct materials that should be used per unit of finished goods. This standard is expressed as a physical measure, such as pounds, barrels, or board feet. In setting the standard, management should consider both the quality and quantity of materials required to manufacture the product. The standard should include allowances for unavoidable waste and normal spoilage. To illustrate, the standard quantity per unit for Xonic, Inc., is as follows:

Item	Quantity (Pounds)
Required materials	3.5
Allowance for waste	.4
Allowance for spoilage	.1
Standard direct materials quantity per unit	**4.0**

Illustration 8-3 Setting direct materials quantity standard

The standard direct materials cost per unit is the standard direct materials price times the standard direct materials quantity. For Xonic, Inc., the standard direct materials cost per gallon of Weed-O is $12.00 ($3.00 × 4.0 pounds).

Direct Labor

The direct labor price standard is the rate per hour that should be incurred for direct labor. This standard is based on current wage rates adjusted for anticipated changes, such as cost of living adjustments (COLAs) included in many union contracts. In addition, the price standard generally includes employer pay-

Alternative Terminology The direct labor price standard is also called the *direct labor rate standard.*

roll taxes and fringe benefits, such as paid holidays and vacations. For Xonic, Inc., the direct labor price standard is as follows:

Illustration 8-4 Setting direct labor price standard

Item	Price
Hourly wage rate	$ 7.50
COLA	.25
Payroll taxes	.75
Fringe benefits	1.50
Standard direct labor rate per hour	**$10.00**

Alternative Terminology The direct labor quantity standard is also called the *direct labor efficiency standard.*

The **direct labor quantity standard** is the time that should be required to make one unit of the product. This standard is especially critical in labor-intensive (as opposed to capital-intensive) companies. Allowances should be made in this standard for rest periods, cleanup, machine setup, and machine downtime. For Xonic, Inc., the direct labor quantity standard is as follows:

Illustration 8-5 Setting direct labor quantity standard

Item	Quantity (Hours)
Actual production time	1.5
Rest periods and cleanup	.2
Setup and downtime	.3
Standard direct labor hours per unit	**2.0**

The standard direct labor cost per unit is the standard direct labor rate times the standard direct labor hours. For Xonic, Inc., the standard direct labor cost per gallon of Weed-O is $20 ($10.00 × 2.0 hours).

Manufacturing Overhead

For manufacturing overhead, a **standard predetermined overhead rate** is used in setting the standard. This overhead rate is determined by dividing budgeted overhead costs by an expected standard activity index. For example, the index may be standard direct labor hours or standard machine hours or some other index or combination of indexes. Xonic, Inc., uses standard direct labor hours as the activity index. The company expects to produce 13,200 gallons of Weed-O during the year at normal capacity. Since it takes two direct labor hours for each gallon, total standard direct labor hours are 26,400 (13,200 × 2). At this level of activity, overhead costs are expected to be $132,000, of which $79,200 are variable and $52,800 are fixed. The standard predetermined overhead rates, therefore, are computed as shown in Illustration 8-6:

Calculating the overhead rate

Overhead ÷ Labor hours

Illustration 8-6 Computing predetermined overhead rates

Budgeted Overhead Costs	Amount	÷	Standard Direct Labor Hours	=	Overhead Rate per Direct Labor Hour
Variable	$ 79,200		26,400		$3.00
Fixed	52,800		26,400		2.00
Total	$132,000		26,400		$5.00

The standard manufacturing overhead rate per unit is the predetermined overhead rate times the activity index quantity standard. For Xonic, Inc., which uses direct labor hours as its activity index, the standard manufacturing overhead rate per gallon of Weed-O is $10 ($5 × 2 hours).

Total Standard Cost per Unit

Now that the standard quantity and price have been established per unit of product, the total standard cost can be determined. The total standard cost per unit is the sum of the standard costs of direct materials, direct labor, and manufacturing overhead. For Xonic, Inc., the total standard cost per gallon of Weed-O is $42, as shown on the following standard cost card:

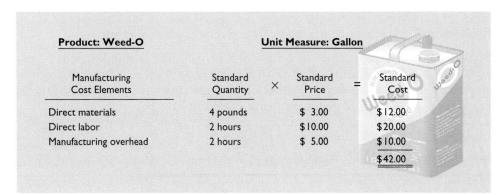

Illustration 8-7
Standard cost per gallon of Weed-O

Product: Weed-O			Unit Measure: Gallon
Manufacturing Cost Elements	Standard Quantity	× Standard Price	= Standard Cost
Direct materials	4 pounds	$ 3.00	$12.00
Direct labor	2 hours	$10.00	$20.00
Manufacturing overhead	2 hours	$ 5.00	$10.00
			$42.00

A standard cost card is prepared for each product. This card provides the basis for determining variances from standards.

BUSINESS INSIGHT
Management Perspective

Setting standards can be difficult. Consider Susan's Chili Factory, which manufactures and sells chili. The cost of manufacturing Susan's chili consists of the costs of raw materials, labor to convert the basic ingredients to chili, and overhead. We will use material cost as an example. Three standards need to be developed: (1) What should be the formula (mix) of ingredients for one gallon of chili? (2) What should be the normal amount of waste (or shrinkage) for the individual ingredients? (3) What should be the standard cost for the individual ingredients that go into the chili?

Susan's Chili Factory also illustrates how standard costs can be used by management in controlling costs. Suppose that summer droughts have reduced crop yields and, as a result, prices have doubled for beans, onions, and peppers. In such a case, actual costs will be significantly higher than standard costs, which will cause management to evaluate the situation. Such an evaluation might lead to an increase in the price charged for a gallon of chili, reexamination of the product mix to see if other types of ingredients can be used, or curtailment of production until ingredients can be purchased at or near standard costs. Similarly, assume that poor maintenance procedures caused the onion-dicing blades to become dull. As a result, usage of onions to make a gallon of chili tripled. Because this deviation is quickly highlighted through standard costs, corrective action can be promptly taken.

Source: Adapted from David R. Beran, "Cost Reduction Through Control Reporting," *Management Accounting*, April 1982, pp. 29–33.

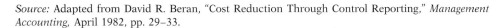

Before You Go On . . .

● Review It

1. How do standards differ from budgets?
2. What are the advantages of standard costs to an organization?
3. Distinguish between normal standards and ideal standards. Which standard is more widely used? Why?

● Do It

The management of Arapahoe Company has decided to use standard costs. Management asks you to explain the components used in setting the standard cost per unit for direct materials, direct labor, and manufacturing overhead.

Reasoning: Each standard has two components: price and quantity.

Solution: The standard direct materials cost per unit is the standard direct materials price times the standard direct materials quantity. The standard direct labor cost per unit is the standard direct labor rate times the standard direct labor hours. The standard manufacturing overhead rate per unit is the standard predetermined overhead rate times the activity index quantity standard.

Related exercise material: BE8-2, BE8-3, and E8-1.

VARIANCES FROM STANDARDS

Alternative Terminology In business, the term *variance* is also used to indicate differences between total budgeted and total actual costs.

One of the major management uses of standard costs is to identify variances from standards. Variances are the differences between total actual costs and total standard costs. To illustrate, we will assume that in producing 1,000 gallons of Weed-O in the month of June, Xonic, Inc., incurred the following costs:

Illustration 8-8 Actual production costs

Direct materials	$13,020
Direct labor	20,580
Variable overhead	6,500
Fixed overhead	4,400
Total actual costs	$44,500

Total standard costs are determined by multiplying the units produced by the standard cost per unit. The total standard cost of Weed-O is $42,000 (1,000 gallons × $42). Thus, the total variance is $2,500, as shown below:

Illustration 8-9 Computation of total variance

Actual costs	$44,500
Standard costs	42,000
Total variance	**$ 2,500**

Note that the variance is expressed in total dollars and not on a per unit basis.

When actual costs exceed standard costs, the variance is **unfavorable.** Thus, the $2,500 variance is unfavorable. An unfavorable variance has a negative connotation. It suggests that too much was paid for one or more of the manufacturing cost elements or that the elements were used inefficiently.

If actual costs are less than standard costs, the variance is **favorable.** A favorable variance has a positive inference. It suggests efficiencies in incurring manufacturing costs and in using direct materials, direct labor, and manufacturing overhead. However, be careful: A favorable variance could be obtained by using inferior materials. In printing wedding invitations, for example, a favorable variance could result from using an inferior grade of paper. Similarly, a favorable variance might be achieved in installing tires on an automobile assembly line by tightening only half of the lug nuts. The point should be obvious: **A variance is not favorable if quality control standards have been sacrificed.**

ANALYZING VARIANCES

To interpret properly the significance of a variance, you must analyze it to determine the underlying factors. Analyzing variances begins with a determination of the cost elements that comprise the variance. **For each manufacturing cost element, a total dollar variance is computed. Then this variance is analyzed into a price variance and a quantity variance.** The relationships are shown graphically as follows:

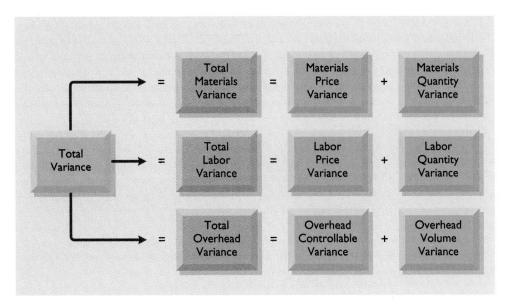

Illustration 8-10
Relationships of
variances

Each of the variances is explained below.

STUDY OBJECTIVE

4

Indicate the formulas for determining direct materials and direct labor variances.

Direct Materials Variances

In completing the order for 1,000 gallons of Weed-O, Xonic used 4,200 pounds of direct materials purchased at a cost of $3.10 per unit. The total materials variance is computed from the following formula:

Illustration 8-11 Formula for total materials variance

For Xonic, Inc., the total materials variance is $1,020 ($13,020 − $12,000) unfavorable as shown below:

$$(4{,}200 \times \$3.10) - (4{,}000 \times \$3.00) = \$1{,}020 \text{ U}$$

Next, the total variance is analyzed to determine the amount attributable to costs and to quantity (use). The materials price variance is computed from the formula shown in Illustration 8-12.[1]

Illustration 8-12
Formula for materials price variance

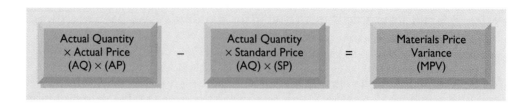

For Xonic, Inc., the materials price variance is $420 ($13,020 − $12,600) unfavorable as shown below:

$$(4{,}200 \times \$3.10) - (4{,}200 \times \$3.00) = \$420 \text{ U}$$

Helpful Hint The alternative formula is:

$$\boxed{AQ} \times \boxed{AP - SP} = \boxed{MPV}$$

The price variance can also be computed by multiplying the actual quantity purchased by the difference between the actual and standard price per unit. The computation in this case is 4,200 × ($3.10 − $3.00) = $420 U.

The materials quantity variance is determined from the following formula:

Illustration 8-13
Formula for materials quantity variance

For Xonic, Inc., the materials quantity variance is $600 ($12,600 − $12,000) unfavorable, as shown below:

$$(4{,}200 \times \$3.00) - (4{,}000 \times \$3.00) = \$600 \text{ U}$$

Helpful Hint The alternative formula is:

$$\boxed{SP} \times \boxed{AQ - SQ} = \boxed{MQV}$$

This variance can also be computed by applying the standard price to the difference between actual and standard quantities used. The computation in this example is $3.00 × (4,200 − 4,000) = $600 U.

The total materials variance of $1,020(U), therefore, consists of the following:

Illustration 8-14 Summary of materials variance

Materials price variance	$ 420 U
Materials quantity variance	600 U
Total materials variance	**$1,020 U**

---

[1]We will assume that all materials purchased during the period are used in production and that no units remain in inventory at the end of the period.

A matrix is sometimes used to determine and analyze a variance. **When the matrix is used, the formulas for each cost element are computed first and then the variances.** The completed matrix for the direct materials variance for Xonic, Inc., is shown in Illustration 8-15. The matrix provides a convenient structure for determining each variance.

Illustration 8-15 Matrix for direct materials variance

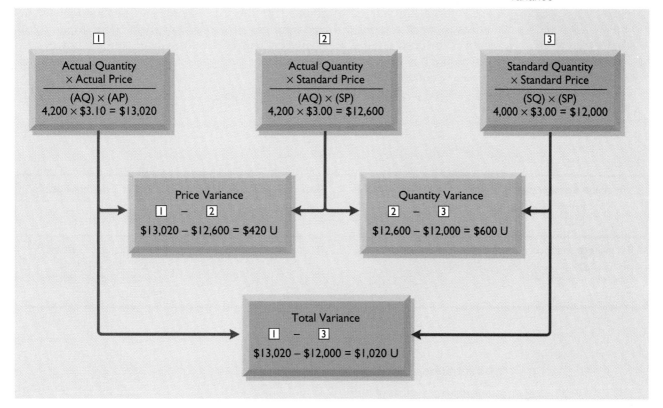

Causes of Materials Variances.   What are the causes of a variance? The causes may relate to both internal and external factors. **The investigation of a materials price variance usually begins in the purchasing department.** Many factors affect the price paid for raw materials. These include the delivery method used, availability of quantity and cash discounts, and the quality of the materials requested. To the extent that these factors have been considered in setting the price standard, the purchasing department should be responsible for any variances. However, a variance may be beyond the control of the purchasing department. In a period of inflation, prices may rise faster than expected. Moreover, actions over which the company has no control, such as governmental legislation and subsidies, may cause an unfavorable variance. There are also times when a production department may be responsible for the price variance. This may occur when a rush order forces the company to pay a higher price for the materials.

The starting point for determining the cause(s) of an unfavorable **materials quantity variance** is in the **production department.** If the variances are due to inexperienced workers, faulty machinery, or carelessness, the production department would be responsible. However, if the materials obtained by the purchasing department were of inferior quality, then the purchasing department should be responsible.

"What caused materials price variances?"

Purchasing Dept.

"What caused materials quantity variances?"

Production Dept.

DECISION TOOLKIT

Decision Checkpoints	Info Needed for Decision	Tool to Use for Decision	How to Evaluate Results
Has management accomplished its price and quantity objectives regarding materials?	Actual cost and standard cost of materials	Materials price and materials quantity variances	Positive (favorable) variances suggest that price and quantity objectives have been met.

Direct Labor Variances

The process of determining direct labor variances is the same as for determining the direct materials variances. In completing the Weed-O order, Xonic, Inc., incurred 2,100 direct labor hours at an average hourly rate of $9.80. The standard hours allowed for the units produced were 2,000 hours (1,000 units × 2 hours) and the standard rate was $10 per hour. The total labor variance is obtained from the following formula:

Illustration 8-16
Formula for total labor variance

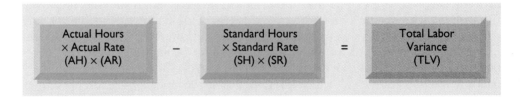

The total labor variance is $580 ($20,580 − $20,000) unfavorable, as shown below:

$$(2,100 \times \$9.80) - (2,000 \times \$10.00) = \$580 \text{ U}$$

The formula for the labor price variance is:

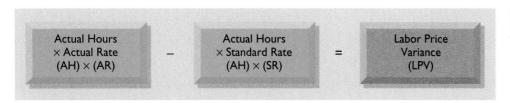

Illustration 8-17
Formula for labor price
variance

For Xonic, Inc., the labor price variance is $420 ($20,580 − $21,000) favorable as shown below.

$$(2,100 \times \$9.80) - (2,100 \times \$10.00) = \$420 \text{ F}$$

This variance can also be computed by multiplying actual hours worked by the difference between the actual pay rate and the standard pay rate. The computation in this example is $2,100 \times (\$10.00 - \$9.80) = \$420$ F.

The labor quantity variance is derived from the following formula:

Helpful Hint The alternative formula is:

$$AH \times \boxed{AR - SR} = \boxed{LPV}$$

Illustration 8-18
Formula for labor quantity
variance

For Xonic, Inc., the labor quantity variance is $1,000 ($21,000 − $20,000) unfavorable:

$$(2,100 \times \$10.00) - (2,000 \times \$10.00) = \$1,000 \text{ U}$$

The same result can be obtained by multiplying the standard rate by the difference between actual hours worked and standard hours allowed. In this case the computation is $\$10.00 \times (2,100 - 2,000) = \$1,000$ U.

The total direct labor variance of $580 U, therefore, consists of:

Helpful Hint The alternative formula is:

$$SR \times \boxed{AH - SH} = \boxed{LQV}$$

Labor price variance	$ 420 F
Labor quantity variance	$1,000 U
Total direct labor variance	**$ 580 U**

Illustration 8-19
Summary of labor
variances

These results can also be obtained from the matrix in Illustration 8-20.

Illustration 8-20 Matrix
for direct labor variances

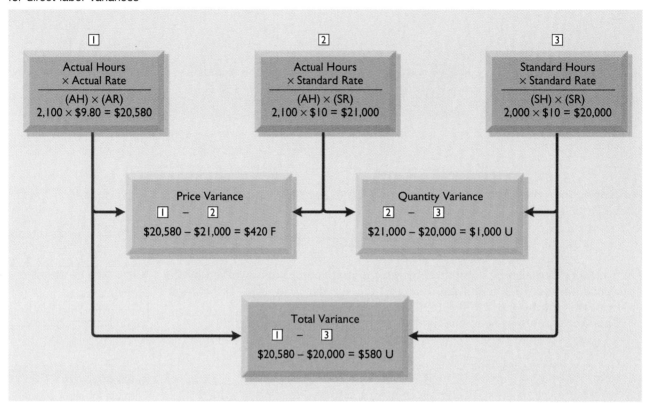

Causes of Labor Variances. **Labor price variances** usually result from two factors: (1) paying workers **higher wages than expected,** and (2) **misallocation of workers.** In companies where pay rates are determined by union contracts, labor price variances should be infrequent. When workers are not unionized, there is a much higher likelihood of such variances. The responsibility for these variances rests with the manager who authorized the wage increase. Misallocation of the workforce refers to using skilled workers in place of unskilled workers and vice versa. The use of an inexperienced worker instead of an experienced one will result in a favorable price variance because of the lower pay rate of the unskilled worker. An unfavorable price variance would result if the skilled worker were substituted for the inexperienced employee. The production department generally is responsible for labor price variances resulting from misallocation of the workforce.

Labor quantity variances relate to the **efficiency of workers.** An investigation of the causes of a quantity variance generally focuses on the production department. The causes of an unfavorable variance may be poor training, worker fatigue, faulty machinery, or carelessness. These causes are the responsibility of the **production department.** However, if the excess time is due to inferior materials, the responsibility falls outside the production department.

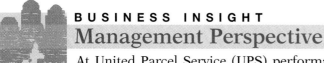

BUSINESS INSIGHT
Management Perspective

At United Parcel Service (UPS) performance standards are set by industrial engineers for many tasks performed by UPS employees. For example, a UPS driver is expected to walk at a pace of three feet per second when going to a customer's door and knock rather than take the time to look for a doorbell. UPS executives attribute the company's success to its ability to manage and hold labor accountable.

DECISION TOOLKIT

Decision Checkpoints	Info Needed for Decision	Tool to Use for Decision	How to Evaluate Results
Has management accomplished its price and quantity objectives regarding labor?	Actual cost and standard cost of labor	Labor price and labor quantity variances	Positive (favorable) variances suggest that price and quantity objectives have been met.

Manufacturing Overhead Variances

The computation of the manufacturing overhead variances is conceptually the same as the computation of the materials and labor variances. However, the task is more challenging for manufacturing overhead because both variable and fixed overhead costs must be considered.

STUDY OBJECTIVE
⑤
State the formulas for determining manufacturing overhead variances.

Total Overhead Variance. The total overhead variance is the difference between actual overhead costs and overhead costs applied to work done. As indicated earlier, manufacturing overhead costs incurred were $10,900, as follows:

Variable overhead	$ 6,500
Fixed overhead	4,400
Total actual overhead	$10,900

Illustration 8-21 Actual overhead costs

With standard costs, manufacturing overhead costs are applied to work in process on the basis of the **standard hours allowed** for the work done. **Standard hours allowed** are the hours that should have been worked for the units produced. For the Weed-O order, the standard hours allowed are 2,000 and the predetermined overhead rate is $5 per direct labor hour. Thus, overhead applied is $10,000 (2,000 × $5). **Note that actual hours of direct labor (2,100) are not used in applying manufacturing overhead.**

The formula for the total overhead variance is:

Illustration 8-22
Formula for total
overhead variance

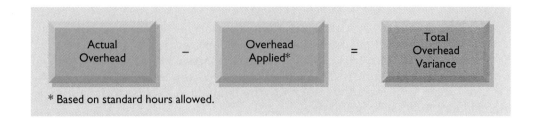

* Based on standard hours allowed.

Thus, for Xonic, Inc., the total overhead variance is $900 unfavorable as shown below:

$$\$10,900 - \$10,000 = \$900 \text{ U}$$

The overhead variance is generally analyzed through a price variance and a quantity variance. The name usually given to the price variance is the **overhead controllable variance,** whereas the quantity variance is referred to as the **overhead volume variance.**

Alternative Terminology The overhead controllable variance is also called the *budget* or *spending variance.*

Overhead Controllable Variance. The overhead controllable variance shows whether overhead costs were effectively controlled. To compute this variance, actual overhead costs incurred are compared with budgeted costs for the **standard hours allowed.** The budgeted costs are determined from the flexible manufacturing overhead budget. The budget for Xonic, Inc., is as follows:

Illustration 8-23 Flexible budget using standard direct labor hours

XONIC, INC.				
Flexible Manufacturing Overhead Budget				
Activity Index				
Standard direct labor hours	1,800	**2,000**	2,200	2,400
Costs				
Variable costs				
Indirect materials	$1,800	$ **2,000**	$ 2,200	$ 2,400
Indirect labor	2,700	**3,000**	3,300	3,600
Utilities	900	**1,000**	1,100	1,200
Total variable	5,400	**6,000**	6,600	7,200
Fixed costs				
Supervision	3,000	**3,000**	3,000	3,000
Depreciation	1,400	**1,400**	1,400	1,400
Total fixed	4,400	**4,400**	4,400	4,400
Total costs	$9,800	**$10,400**	$11,000	$11,600

As shown, the budgeted costs for 2,000 standard hours are $10,400 ($6,000 variable and $4,400 fixed).[2]

---

[2]The flexible budget formula is: fixed costs $4,400 plus variable costs $3 per hour. Thus, total budgeted costs are $4,400 + ($3 × 2,000), or $10,400.

The formula for the overhead controllable variance is:

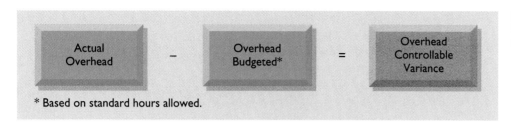

Illustration 8-24
Formula for overhead
controllable variance

The overhead controllable variance for Xonic, Inc., is $500 unfavorable as shown below:

$$\$10,900 - \$10,400 = \$500 \text{ U}$$

Most controllable variances are associated with variable costs which are controllable costs. Fixed costs are usually known at the time the budget is prepared. In Xonic, Inc., the variance is accounted for by comparing the actual variable overhead costs ($6,500) with the budgeted variable costs ($6,000).

   If management desires, actual and budgeted overhead for each manufacturing overhead cost that contributes to the controllable variance can be compared. In addition, cost and quantity variances can be developed for each overhead cost, such as indirect materials and indirect labor.

Overhead Volume Variance.   The **overhead volume variance** indicates whether plant facilities were efficiently used during the period. The formula for computing the volume variance is as follows:

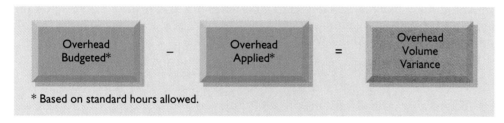

Illustration 8-25
Formula for overhead
volume variance

Both the factors in this formula have been explained above. The overhead budgeted is the same as the amount used in computing the controllable variance or $10,400 in our example. Overhead applied of $10,000 is the amount used in determining the total overhead variance. For Xonic, Inc., the overhead volume variance is $400 unfavorable as shown below:

$$\$10,400 - \$10,000 = \$400 \text{ U}$$

   Further insight into the volume variance can be obtained from a detailed analysis of the two factors. As shown in the flexible manufacturing overhead budget, the budgeted overhead of $10,400 consists of $6,000 variable and $4,400 fixed. As indicated in determining the predetermined overhead rate in Illustration 8-6 (p. 304), the rate of $5 consists of $3 variable and $2 fixed. The detailed analysis, therefore, is:

Illustration 8-26
Detailed analysis of
overhead volume
variance

Overhead budgeted		
Variable costs	$6,000	
Fixed costs	**4,400**	$10,400
Overhead applied		
Variable costs (2,000 × $3)	6,000	
Fixed costs (2,000 × $2)	**4,000**	10,000
Overhead volume variance—unfavorable		$ 400

A careful examination of this analysis indicates that **the overhead volume variance relates solely to fixed costs** (fixed costs budgeted $4,400 − fixed costs applied $4,000). Thus, **the volume variance measures the amount that fixed overhead costs are under- or overapplied.**

We have already established that total fixed costs remain the same at every level of activity within the relevant range. Since a predetermined overhead rate based on normal capacity is used in applying overhead, **it follows that if the standard hours allowed are less than the standard hours at normal capacity, fixed overhead costs will be underapplied.** In contrast, **if production exceeds normal capacity, fixed overhead costs will be overapplied.**

An alternative formula for computing the overhead volume variance is shown in Illustration 8-27.

Illustration 8-27
Alternative formula for
overhead volume
variance

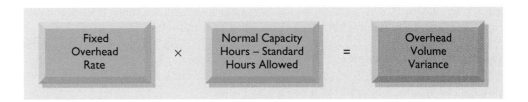

In Xonic, Inc., normal capacity is 26,400 hours for the year or 2,200 hours for a month (26,400 ÷ 12), and the fixed overhead rate is $2 per hour. Thus, the volume variance is $400 unfavorable as shown below:

$$\$2 \times (2,200 - 2,000) = \$400 \text{ U}$$

The total overhead variance of $900 unfavorable for Xonic, Inc., therefore, consists of the following:

Illustration 8-28
Summary of overhead
variance

Overhead controllable variance	$500 U
Overhead volume variance	400 U
Total overhead variance	**$900 U**

The results can also be obtained from the matrix in Illustration 8-29. In computing the overhead variances, it is important to remember the following:

1. Standard hours allowed are used in each of the variances.
2. Budgeted costs for the controllable variance are derived from the flexible budget.
3. The controllable variance generally pertains to variable costs.
4. The volume variance pertains solely to fixed costs.

Illustration 8-29 Matrix for manufacturing overhead variance

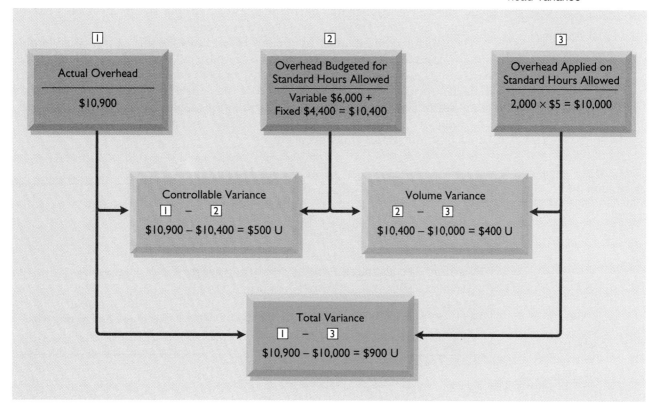

Causes of Manufacturing Overhead Variances.   Since the **controllable variance** relates to variable manufacturing costs, the responsibility for the variance rests with the **production department.** The cause of an unfavorable variance may be (1) **higher than expected use** of indirect materials, indirect labor, and factory supplies or (2) **increases in indirect manufacturing costs,** such as fuel and maintenance costs.

The **overhead volume variance** is the responsibility of the **production department** if the cause is inefficient use of direct labor or machine breakdowns. However, when the cause is a **lack of sales orders,** the responsibility rests **outside** the production department.

DECISION TOOLKIT

Decision Checkpoints	Info Needed for Decision	Tool to Use for Decision	How to Evaluate Results
Has management accomplished its price and quantity objectives regarding overhead?	Actual cost and standard cost of overhead	Overhead controllable variance and overhead volume variance	Positive (favorable) variances suggest that price and quantity objectives have been met.

REPORTING VARIANCES

STUDY OBJECTIVE
—————⑥—————
Discuss the reporting of variances.

All variances should be reported to appropriate levels of management as soon as possible. The sooner management is informed, the sooner problems can be evaluated and corrective actions taken if necessary.

The form, content, and frequency of variance reports vary considerably among companies. One approach is to prepare a weekly report for each department that has primary responsibility for cost control. Under this approach, materials price variances are reported to the purchasing department, and all other variances are reported to the production department that did the work. The following report for Xonic, Inc., with the materials for the Weed-O order listed first, illustrates this approach:

Illustration 8-30
Materials price variance report

					XONIC, INC.
					Variance Report—Purchasing Department
					For Week Ended June 8, 1999

Type of Materials	Quantity Purchased	Actual Price	Standard Price	Price Variance	Explanation
RM 100	4,200 lbs.	$3.10	$3.00	$420 U	Rush order
BW 142	1,200 units	2.75	2.80	60 F	Quantity discount
AZ 85	600 doz.	5.20	5.10	60 U	Regular supplier on strike
Total price variance				$420 U	

The explanation column is completed after consultation with the purchasing department manager.

Variance reports facilitate the principle of "management by exception" explained in Chapter 7. For example, the vice president of purchasing can use the report illustrated above to evaluate the effectiveness of the purchasing department manager. Similarly, the vice president of production can use production department variance reports to determine how well each production manager is controlling costs. In using variance reports, top management normally looks for **significant variances.** The significance of a variance may be judged on the basis of some quantitative measure, such as more than 10% of the standard or more than $1,000.

BEFORE YOU GO ON . . .

● **Review It**

1. What are the formulas for computing the total, price, and quantity variances for direct materials?
2. What are the formulas for computing the total, price, and quantity variances for direct labor?
3. What are the formulas for computing the total, controllable, and volume variances for manufacturing overhead?

● **Do It**

The standard cost of Product WD-80 includes two units of direct materials at $8.00 per unit. During July, 22,000 units of direct materials are purchased at $7.50 and used to produce 10,000 units. Compute the total, price, and quantity variances for materials.

Reasoning: It is necessary to know the formulas for computing each of the materials variances. The formulas are:

Total materials variance
= (actual quantity × actual price) − (standard quantity × standard price)
Materials price variance
= (actual quantity × actual price) − (actual quantity × standard price)
Materials quantity variance
= (actual quantity × standard price) − (standard quantity × standard price)

Solution: Substituting amounts into the formulas, the variances are:

Total materials variance
= (22,000 × $7.50) − (20,000 × $8.00) = $5,000 unfavorable.
Materials price variance
= (22,000 × $7.50) − (22,000 × $8.00) = $11,000 favorable.
Materials quantity variance
= (22,000 × $8.00) − (20,000 × $8.00) = $16,000 unfavorable.

Related exercise material: BE8-4, BE8-5, BE8-6, BE8-7, BE8-8, E8-2, E8-3, E8-4, E8-6, E8-7, E8-8, E8-9, and E8-12.

THE
NAVIGATOR

STANDARD COST ACCOUNTING SYSTEM

A **standard cost accounting system** is a double-entry system of accounting in which standard costs are used in making entries and variances are formally recognized in the accounts. A standard cost system may be used with either job order or process costing. At this point, we will explain and illustrate a **standard cost, job order cost accounting system.** The system includes two important assumptions: (1) variances from standards are recognized at the earliest opportunity, and (2) the Work in Process account is maintained exclusively on the basis of standard costs. In practice, there are many variations among standard cost systems. However, the system described here should facilitate your transition to a specific company's system.

STUDY OBJECTIVE

7

Identify the features of a standard cost accounting system.

JOURNAL ENTRIES

The transactions of Xonic, Inc., will be used to illustrate the journal entries. Note as you study the entries that the major difference between the entries here and those for the job order cost accounting system in Chapter 2 is the **variance accounts.**

1. Purchase raw materials on account for $13,020 when the standard cost is $12,600.

Raw Materials Inventory	12,600	
Materials Price Variance	420	
Accounts Payable		13,020
(To record purchase of materials)		

The inventory account is debited for actual quantities at standard cost. This enables the perpetual materials records to show actual quantities. The price variance, which is unfavorable, is debited to Materials Price Variance.

2. Incur direct labor costs of $20,580 when the standard labor cost is $21,000.

Factory Labor	21,000	
Labor Price Variance		420
Wages Payable		20,580
(To record direct labor costs)		

Like the raw materials inventory account, Factory Labor is debited for actual hours worked at the standard hourly rate of pay. In this case, the labor variance is favorable. Thus, Labor Price Variance is credited.

3. Incur actual manufacturing overhead costs of $10,900.

Manufacturing Overhead	10,900	
Accounts Payable/Cash/Acc. Depreciation		10,900
(To record overhead incurred)		

The controllable overhead variance is not recorded at this time. It depends on standard hours applied to work in process, which is not known at the time overhead is incurred.

4. Issue raw materials for production at a cost of $12,600 when the standard cost is $12,000.

Work in Process Inventory	12,000	
Materials Quantity Variance	600	
Raw Materials Inventory		12,600
(To record issuance of raw materials)		

Work in Process Inventory is debited for standard materials quantities used at standard prices. The variance account is debited because the variance is unfavorable. Raw Materials Inventory is credited for actual quantities at standard prices.

5. Assign factory labor to production at a cost of $21,000 when standard cost is $20,000.

Work in Process Inventory	20,000	
Labor Quantity Variance	1,000	
Factory Labor		21,000
(To assign factory labor to jobs)		

Work in Process Inventory is debited for standard labor hours at standard rates, and the unfavorable variance is debited to Labor Quantity Variance. The credit to Factory Labor produces a zero balance in this account.

6. Applying manufacturing overhead to production, $10,000.

Work in Process Inventory	10,000	
Manufacturing Overhead		10,000
(To assign overhead to jobs)		

Work in Process Inventory is debited for standard hours allowed multiplied by the standard overhead rate.

7. Transfer completed work to finished goods, $42,000.

Finished Goods Inventory	42,000	
Work in Process Inventory		42,000
(To record transfer of completed work to finished goods)		

In this example, both inventory accounts are at standard cost.

8. The 1,000 gallons of Weed-O are sold for $60,000.

Accounts Receivable	60,000	
Cost of Goods Sold	42,000	
Sales		60,000
Finished Goods Inventory		42,000
(To record sale of finished goods and the cost of goods sold)		

Cost of Goods Sold is debited at standard cost. Gross profit, in turn, is the difference between sales and the standard cost of goods sold.

9. Recognize unfavorable overhead variances: controllable, $500; volume, $400.

Overhead Controllable Variance	500	
Overhead Volume Variance	400	
Manufacturing Overhead		900
(To recognize overhead variances)		

Prior to this entry, a debit balance of $900 existed in Manufacturing Overhead. The above entry therefore produces a zero balance in the Manufacturing Overhead account. The information needed for this entry is often not available until the end of the accounting period.

LEDGER ACCOUNTS

The cost accounts for Xonic, Inc., after posting the entries, are shown in Illustration 8-31 on the next page. Note that six variance accounts are included in the ledger. The remaining accounts are the same as those illustrated for a job order cost system in Chapter 2 in which only actual costs were used.

Illustration 8-31 Cost accounts with variances

Helpful Hint All debit balances in variance accounts indicate unfavorable variances; all credit balances indicate favorable variances.

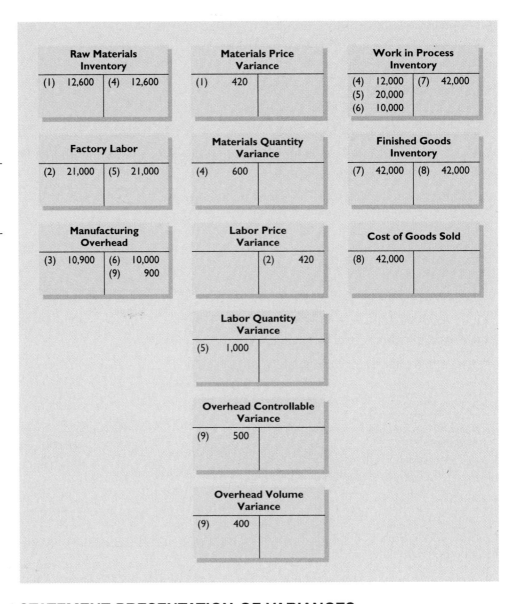

STATEMENT PRESENTATION OF VARIANCES

In income statements **prepared for management** under a standard cost accounting system, **cost of goods sold is stated at standard cost and the variances are separately disclosed,** as shown in Illustration 8-32 on page 323. The statement shown is based entirely on the production and sale of Weed-O and assumes selling and administrative costs of $3,000. Observe that each variance is shown, as well as the total net variance. In this example, variations from standard costs reduced net income by $2,500.

In financial statements prepared for stockholders and other external users, standard costs may be used. The costing of inventories at standard costs is in accordance with generally accepted accounting principles when there are no significant differences between actual costs and standard costs. However, if there are significant differences between actual and standard costs, inventories and cost of goods sold must be reported at actual costs.

It is also possible to show the variances in an income statement prepared in the contribution margin format. To do so, it is necessary to analyze the overhead variances into variable and fixed components. This type of analysis is explained in cost accounting textbooks.

Illustration 8-32
Variances in income
statement for
management

XONIC, INC.		
Income Statement (for Management)		
For the Month Ended June 30, 1999		
Sales		$60,000
Cost of goods sold (at standard)		42,000
Gross profit (at standard)		18,000
Variances		
Materials price	$ 420	
Materials quantity	600	
Labor price	(420)	
Labor quantity	1,000	
Overhead controllable	500	
Overhead volume	400	
Total variance unfavorable		2,500
Gross profit (actual)		15,500
Selling and administrative expenses		3,000
Net income		$12,500

BEFORE YOU GO ON . . .

- ● **Review It**

1. Does a debit balance in a variance account indicate favorable or unfavorable performance?
2. What entry is made to recognize overhead variances in the accounts?
3. How are standard costs and variances reported in income statements prepared for management?

THE
NAVIGATOR

*U*SING THE DECISION TOOLKIT

Assume that during the past month Sanford produced 10,000 cartons of Liquid ACCENT® highlighters. Liquid ACCENT® offers a translucent barrel and cap with a visible ink supply for see-through color. The special fluorescent ink is fade- and water-resistant. Each carton contains 100 boxes of markers, and each box contains five markers. The markers come in boxes of one of five fluorescent colors—orange, blue, yellow, green, and pink—and in a five-color set.

Assume the following additional facts: The standard cost for one carton of 500 markers is as follows:

Manufacturing Cost Elements	Standard			
	Quantity	× Price	=	Cost
Direct materials				
Tips (boxes of 500)	500	× $ .03	=	$ 15.00
Translucent barrels and caps (boxes of 500)	500	× $ .09	=	45.00
Fluorescent ink (100 oz. containers)	100 oz.	× $ .32	=	32.00
Total direct materials				92.00
Direct labor	0.25 hours	× $ 9.00	=	2.25
Overhead	0.25 hours	× $48.00	=	12.00
				$106.25

During the month, the following transactions occurred in manufacturing the 10,000 cartons of highlighters:

1. Purchased 10,000 boxes of tips for $148,000 ($14.80 per 500 tips); purchased 10,200 boxes of translucent barrels and caps for $453,900 ($44.50 per 500 barrels and caps); and purchased 9,900 containers of fluorescent ink for $328,185 ($33.15 per 100 ounces).
2. All materials purchased during the period were used to make markers during the period.
3. 2,300 direct labor hours were worked at a total labor cost of $20,240 (an average hourly rate of $8.80).
4. Variable manufacturing overhead incurred was $34,600, and fixed overhead incurred was $84,000.

The manufacturing overhead rate of $48.00 is based on a normal capacity of 2,600 direct labor hours. The total budget at this capacity is $83,980 fixed and $40,820 variable.

Instructions

Determine whether Sanford met its price and quantity objectives relative to materials, labor, and overhead.

Solution

To determine whether Sanford met its price and quantity objectives, compute the total variance and the variances for each of the manufacturing cost elements.

Total Variance

Actual cost incurred:
Direct materials
Tips $148,000
Translucent barrels and caps 453,900
Fluorescent ink 328,185

Total direct materials $ 930,085
Direct labor 20,240
Overhead 118,600

Total actual costs 1,068,925
Standard cost (10,000 × $106.25) 1,062,500
Total variance $ 6,425 U

Direct Materials Variances

Total	=	$930,085	−	$920,000 (10,000 × $92)	= $10,085 U
Price (Tips)	=	$148,000 (10,000 × $14.80)	−	$150,000 (10,000 × $15.00)	= $ 2,000 F
Price (Barrels and caps)	=	$453,900 (10,200 × $44.50)	−	$459,000 (10,200 × $45.00)	= $ 5,100 F
Price (Ink)	=	$328,185 (9,900 × $33.15)	−	$316,800 (9,900 × $32.00)	= $11,385 U
Quantity (Tips)	=	$150,000 (10,000 × $15.00)	−	$150,000 (10,000 × $15.00)	= $ 0
Quantity (Barrels and caps)	=	$459,000 (10,200 × $45.00)	−	$450,000 (10,000 × $45.00)	= $ 9,000 U
Quantity (Ink)	=	$316,800 (9,900 × $32.00)	−	$320,000 (10,000 × $32.00)	= $ 3,200 F

Direct Labor Variances

Total	=	$20,240	–	$22,500	= $ 2,260 F
		(2,300 × $8.80)		(2,500 × $9.00)	
Price	=	$20,240	–	$20,700	= $ 460 F
		(2,300 × $8.80)		(2,300 × $9.00)	
Quantity	=	$20,700	–	$22,500	= $ 1,800 F
		(2,300 × $9.00)		(2,500 × $9.00)	

Overhead Variances

Total	=	$118,600	–	$120,000	= $ 1,400 F
		($84,000 + $34,600)		(2,500 × $48)	
Controllable	=	$118,600	–	$123,230	= $ 4,630 F
		($84,000 + $34,600)		[(2,500 × $15.70) + $83,980]	
Volume	=	$123,230	–	$120,000	= $ 3,230 U
		[(2,500 × $15.70) + $83,980] – (2,500 × $48)			

Sanford's total variance was an unfavorable $6,425. The unfavorable materials variance outweighed the favorable labor and overhead variances. The primary determinants were an unfavorable price variance for ink and an unfavorable quantity variance for barrels and caps.

THE
NAVIGATOR

SUMMARY OF STUDY OBJECTIVES

❶ Distinguish between a standard and a budget. Both standards and budgets are predetermined costs. The primary difference is that a standard is a unit amount, whereas a budget is a total amount. A standard may be regarded as the budgeted cost per unit of product.

❷ Identify the advantages of standard costs. Standard costs offer a number of advantages to an organization. They (a) facilitate management planning, (b) promote greater economy and efficiency, (c) are useful in setting selling prices, (d) contribute to management control, (e) permit "management by exception," and (f) simplify the costing of inventories and reduce clerical costs.

❸ Describe how standards are set. The direct materials price standard should be based on the delivered cost of raw materials plus an allowance for receiving and handling. The direct materials quantity standard should establish the required quantity plus an allowance for waste and spoilage.

The direct labor price standard should be based on current wage rates and anticipated adjustments such as COLAs. In addition, it generally includes payroll taxes and fringe benefits. Direct labor quantity standards should be based on required production time plus an allowance for rest periods, cleanup, machine setup, and machine downtime.

For manufacturing overhead, a standard predetermined overhead rate is used based on an expected standard activity index such as standard direct labor hours or standard direct labor cost.

❹ Indicate the formulas for determining direct materials and direct labor variances. The formulas for the direct materials variances are:

$$\left(\begin{array}{c}\text{Actual quantity}\\ \times \text{ Actual price}\end{array}\right) - \left(\begin{array}{c}\text{Standard quantity}\\ \times \text{ Standard price}\end{array}\right) = \begin{array}{c}\text{Total}\\ \text{materials}\\ \text{variance}\end{array}$$

$$\left(\begin{array}{c}\text{Actual quantity}\\ \times \text{ Actual price}\end{array}\right) - \left(\begin{array}{c}\text{Actual quantity}\\ \times \text{ Standard price}\end{array}\right) = \begin{array}{c}\text{Materials}\\ \text{price}\\ \text{variance}\end{array}$$

$$\left(\begin{array}{c}\text{Actual quantity}\\ \times \text{ Standard price}\end{array}\right) - \left(\begin{array}{c}\text{Standard quantity}\\ \times \text{ Standard price}\end{array}\right) = \begin{array}{c}\text{Materials}\\ \text{quantity}\\ \text{variance}\end{array}$$

The formulas for the direct labor variances are:

$$\left(\begin{array}{c}\text{Actual hours}\\ \times \text{ Actual rate}\end{array}\right) - \left(\begin{array}{c}\text{Standard hours}\\ \times \text{ Standard rate}\end{array}\right) = \begin{array}{c}\text{Total}\\ \text{labor}\\ \text{variance}\end{array}$$

$$\left(\begin{array}{c}\text{Actual hours}\\ \times \text{ Actual rate}\end{array}\right) - \left(\begin{array}{c}\text{Actual hours}\\ \times \text{ Standard rate}\end{array}\right) = \begin{array}{c}\text{Labor}\\ \text{price}\\ \text{variance}\end{array}$$

$$\left(\begin{array}{c}\text{Actual hours}\\ \times \text{ Standard rate}\end{array}\right) - \left(\begin{array}{c}\text{Standard hours}\\ \times \text{ Standard rate}\end{array}\right) = \begin{array}{c}\text{Labor}\\ \text{quantity}\\ \text{variance}\end{array}$$

⑤ *State the formulas for determining manufacturing overhead variances.* The formulas for the manufacturing overhead variances are:

$$\begin{array}{l}
\text{Actual} \\
\text{overhead}
\end{array} - \begin{array}{l}
\text{Overhead} \\
\text{applied}
\end{array} = \begin{array}{l}
\text{Total overhead} \\
\text{variance}
\end{array}$$

$$\begin{array}{l}
\text{Actual} \\
\text{overhead}
\end{array} - \begin{array}{l}
\text{Overhead} \\
\text{budgeted}
\end{array} = \begin{array}{l}
\text{Overhead control-} \\
\text{lable variance}
\end{array}$$

$$\begin{array}{l}
\text{Overhead} \\
\text{budgeted}
\end{array} - \begin{array}{l}
\text{Overhead} \\
\text{applied}
\end{array} = \begin{array}{l}
\text{Overhead volume} \\
\text{variance}
\end{array}$$

⑥ *Discuss the reporting of variances.* Variances are reported to management in variance reports. The reports facilitate management by exception because significant differences can be highlighted.

⑦ *Identify the features of a standard cost accounting system.* In a standard cost accounting system, standard costs are journalized and posted and separate variance accounts are maintained in the ledger. When differences between actual costs and standard costs do not differ significantly, inventories may be reported at standard costs.

THE
NAVIGATOR

DECISION TOOLKIT—A SUMMARY

Decision Checkpoints	Info Needed for Decision	Tool to Use for Decision	How to Evaluate Results
Has management accomplished its price and quantity objectives regarding materials?	Actual cost and standard cost of materials	Materials price and materials quantity variances	Positive (favorable) variances suggest that price and quantity objectives have been met.
Has management accomplished its price and quantity objectives regarding labor?	Actual cost and standard cost of labor	Labor price and labor quantity variances	Positive (favorable) variances suggest that price and quantity objectives have been met.
Has management accomplished its price and quantity objectives regarding overhead?	Actual cost and standard cost of overhead	Overhead controllable variance and overhead volume variance	Positive (favorable) variances suggest that price and quantity objectives have been met.

GLOSSARY

Direct labor price standard The rate per hour that should be incurred for direct labor. (p. 303)

Direct labor quantity standard The time that should be required to make one unit of product. (p. 304)

Direct materials price standard The cost per unit of direct materials that should be incurred. (p. 303)

Direct materials quantity standard The quantity of direct materials that should be used per unit of finished goods. (p. 303)

Ideal standards Standards based on the optimum level of performance under perfect operating conditions. (p. 302)

Labor price variance The difference between the actual hours times the actual rate and the actual hours times the standard rate. (p. 311)

Labor quantity variance The difference between actual hours times the standard rate and standard hours times the standard rate. (p. 311)

Materials price variance The difference between the actual quantity times the actual price and the actual quantity times the standard price. (p. 308)

Materials quantity variance The difference between the actual quantity times the standard price and the standard quantity times the standard price. (p. 308)

Normal standards Standards based on an efficient level of performance that are attainable under expected operating conditions. (p. 302)

Overhead controllable variance The difference between actual overhead incurred and overhead budgeted for the standard hours allowed. (p. 314)

Overhead volume variance The difference between overhead budgeted for the standard hours allowed and the overhead applied. (p. 315)

Standard cost accounting system A double-entry system of accounting in which standard costs are used in making entries and variances are recognized in the accounts. (p. 319)

Standard costs Predetermined unit costs which are used as measures of performance. (p. 300)

Standard hours allowed The hours that should have been worked for the units produced. (p. 313)

Standard predetermined overhead rate An overhead rate determined by dividing budgeted overhead costs by an expected standard activity index. (p. 304)

Total labor variance The difference between actual hours times the actual rate and standard hours times the standard rate for labor. (p. 310)

Total materials variance The difference between the actual quantity times the actual price and the standard quantity times the standard price of materials. (p. 307)

Total overhead variance The difference between actual overhead costs and overhead costs applied to work done. (p. 313)

Variances The difference between total actual costs and total standard costs. (p. 306)

DEMONSTRATION PROBLEM

Manlow Company makes a cologne called Allure. The standard cost for one bottle of Allure is as follows:

	Standard				
Manufacturing Cost Elements	**Quantity**	×	**Price**	=	**Cost**
Direct materials	6 oz.	×	$ .90	=	$ 5.40
Direct labor	0.5 hrs.	×	$12.00	=	6.00
Manufacturing overhead	0.5 hrs.	×	$ 4.80	=	2.40
					$13.80

During the month, the following transactions occurred in manufacturing 10,000 bottles of Allure.

1. 58,000 ounces of materials were purchased at $1.00 per ounce.
2. All the materials purchased were used to produce the 10,000 bottles of Allure.
3. 4,900 direct labor hours were worked at a total labor cost of $56,350.
4. Variable manufacturing overhead incurred was $15,000 and fixed overhead incurred was $10,400.

The manufacturing overhead rate of $4.80 is based on a normal capacity of 5,200 direct labor hours. The total budget at this capacity is $10,400 fixed and $14,560 variable ($2.80 per labor hour).

Instructions

Compute the total variance and the variances for each of the manufacturing cost elements.

Solution to Demonstration Problem

Total Variance

Actual costs incurred:	
Direct materials	$ 58,000
Direct labor	56,350
Manufacturing overhead	25,400
	139,750
Standard cost (10,000 × $13.80)	138,000
Total variance	$ 1,750 (U)

Problem-Solving Strategies

1. Check to make sure the total variance and the sum of the individual variances are equal.
2. Find the price variance first, then the quantity variance.
3. Budgeted overhead costs are based on flexible budget data.
4. Overhead applied is based on standard hours allowed.
5. Actual hours worked is not relevant in computing overhead variances.
6. The overhead volume variance relates solely to fixed costs.

Direct Materials Variances

Total	=	$58,000	−	$54,000	= $4,000 U
		(58,000 × $1.00)		(60,000 × $.90)	
Price	=	$58,000	−	$52,200	= $5,800 U
		(58,000 × $1.00)		(58,000 × $.90)	
Quantity	=	$52,200	−	$54,000	= $1,800 F
		(58,000 × $.90)		(60,000 × $.90)	

Direct Labor Variances

Total	=	$56,350	−	$60,000	= $3,650 F
		(4,900 × $11.50)		(5,000 × $12.00)	
Price	=	$56,350	−	$58,800	= $2,450 F
		(4,900 × $11.50)		(4,900 × $12.00)	
Quantity	=	$58,800	−	$60,000	= $1,200 F
		(4,900 × $12.00)		(5,000 × $12.00)	

Overhead Variances

Total	= $25,400	−	$24,000	= $1,400 U
	($15,000 + $10,400)		(5,000 × $4.80)	
Controllable	= $25,400	−	$24,400	= $1,000 U
	($15,000 + $10,400)		[(5,000 × $2.80) + $10,400]	
Volume	= $24,400	−	$24,000	= $ 400 U
	[(5,000 × $2.80) + $10,400]		(5,000 × $4.80)	

THE NAVIGATOR

SELF-STUDY QUESTIONS

Answers are at the end of the chapter.

(SO 1) 1. Standards differ from budgets in that:
  (a) budgets may be used in valuing inventories but not standards.
  (b) budgets may be journalized and posted but not standards.
  (c) budgets are a total amount and standards are a unit amount.
  (d) only budgets contribute to management planning and control.

(SO 2) 2. The advantages of standard costs include all of the following *except:*
  (a) management by exception may be used.
  (b) management planning is facilitated.
  (c) they may simplify the costing of inventories.
  (d) management must use a static budget.

(SO 3) 3. The setting of standards is:
  (a) a managerial accountant decision.
  (b) a management decision.
  (c) a worker decision.
  (d) preferably set at the ideal level of performance.

(SO 4) 4. Each of the following formulas is correct except:
  (a) Labor price variance = (actual hours × actual rate) − (actual hours × standard rate).
  (b) Overhead controllable variance = actual overhead − overhead budgeted.
  (c) Materials price variance = (actual quantity × actual cost) − (standard quantity × standard cost).

  (d) Overhead volume variance = overhead budgeted − overhead applied.

(SO 4) 5. In producing product AA, 6,300 pounds of direct materials were used at a cost of $1.10 per pound when the standard was 6,000 pounds at $1 per pound. The direct materials quantity variance is:
  (a) $330 unfavorable.
  (b) $300 unfavorable.
  (c) $600 unfavorable.
  (d) $630 unfavorable.

(SO 4) 6. In producing product ZZ, 14,800 direct labor hours were used at a rate of $8.20 per hour when the standard was 15,000 hours at $8.00 per hour. Based on these data, the direct labor:
  (a) quantity variance is $1,600 favorable.
  (b) quantity variance is $1,600 unfavorable.
  (c) price variance is $2,960 favorable.
  (d) price variance is $3,000 unfavorable.

(SO 5) 7. Which of the following is *correct* about overhead variances?
  (a) The controllable variance generally pertains to fixed overhead costs.
  (b) The volume variance pertains solely to variable overhead costs.
  (c) Standard hours actually worked are used in each variance.
  (d) Budgeted overhead costs are based on the flexible overhead budget.

8. The formula for computing the total overhead variance is: _(SO 5)_
   (a) actual overhead less overhead applied.
   (b) overhead budgeted less overhead applied.
   (c) actual overhead less overhead budgeted.
   (d) no correct answer given.

9. Which of the following is *incorrect* about variance reports? _(SO 6)_
   (a) They facilitate "management by exception."
   (b) They should only be sent to the top level of management.
   (c) They should be prepared as soon as possible.
   (d) They may vary in form, content, and frequency among companies.

10. Which of the following is *incorrect* about a standard cost accounting system? _(SO 7)_
    (a) It is applicable to job order costing.
    (b) It is applicable to process costing.
    (c) It is a single-entry system.
    (d) It keeps separate accounts for each variance.

QUESTIONS

1. (a) "Standard costs are the expected total cost of completing a job." Is this correct? Explain.
   (b) "A standard imposed by a governmental agency is known as a regulation." Do you agree? Explain.

2. (a) Explain the similarities and differences between standards and budgets.
   (b) Contrast the accounting for standards and budgets.

3. Standard costs facilitate management planning. What are the other advantages of standard costs?

4. Contrast the roles of the management accountant and management in setting standard costs.

5. Distinguish between an ideal standard and a normal standard.

6. What factors should be considered in setting (a) the materials price standard and (b) the materials quantity standard?

7. "The objective in setting the direct labor quantity standard is to determine the aggregate time required to make one unit of product." Do you agree? What allowances should be made in setting this standard? *Yes, should include allowances*

8. How is the predetermined overhead rate determined when standard costs are used?

9. What is the difference between a favorable cost variance and an unfavorable cost variance?

10. In each of the following formulas, supply the words that should be inserted for each number in parentheses.
    (a) (Actual quantity × (1)) − (standard quantity × (2)) = Total materials variance
    (b) ((3) × actual price) − (actual quantity × (4)) = Materials price variance
    (c) (Actual quantity × (5)) − ((6) × standard price) = Materials quantity variance

11. In the direct labor variance matrix, there are three factors: (1) actual hours × actual rate, (2) actual hours × standard rate, and (3) standard hours × standard rate. Using the numbers, indicate the formulas for each of the direct labor variances.

12. Keene Company's standard predetermined overhead rate is $6.00 per direct labor hour. For the month of June, 26,000 actual hours were worked and 27,500 standard hours were allowed. Normal capacity hours were 28,000. How much overhead was applied?

13. If the $6.00 per hour overhead rate in question 12 consists of $4.00 variable, and actual overhead costs were $163,000, what is the overhead controllable variance for June? Is the variance favorable or unfavorable?

14. Using the data in questions 12 and 13, what is the overhead volume variance for June? Is the variance favorable or unfavorable?

15. What is the purpose of computing the overhead volume variance? What is the basic formula for this variance?

16. Ellen Landis does not understand why the overhead volume variance indicates that fixed overhead costs are under- or overapplied. Clarify this matter for Ellen.

17. Stan LaRue is attempting to outline the important points about overhead variances on a class examination. List four points that Stan should include in his outline.

18. How often should variances be reported to management? What principle may be used with variance reports?

19. What circumstances may cause the purchasing department to be responsible for both an unfavorable materials price variance and an unfavorable materials quantity variance? *Pay too much/or didn't meet standards*

20. (a) Explain the basic features of a standard cost accounting system. (b) What type of balance will exist in the variance account when (1) the materials price variance is unfavorable and (2) the labor quantity variance is favorable?

21. (a) How are variances reported in income statements prepared for management? (b) May standard costs be used in preparing financial statements for stockholders? Explain.

BRIEF EXERCISES

Distinguish between a standard and a budget.
(SO 1)

BE8-1   Valdez Company uses both standards and budgets. For the year, estimated production of Product X is 400,000 units. Total estimated cost for materials and labor are $1,200,000 and $1,600,000. Compute the estimates for (a) a standard cost and (b) a budgeted cost.

Set direct materials standard.
(SO 3)

BE8-2   Hideo Company accumulates the following data concerning raw materials in making one gallon of finished product: (1) Price—net purchase price $3.40, freight-in $0.20, and receiving and handling $0.10; (2) quantity—required materials 2.6 pounds, allowance for waste and spoilage 0.4 pounds. Compute the (a) standard direct materials price per gallon, (b) standard direct materials quantity per gallon, and (c) total standard material cost per gallon.

Set direct labor standard.
(SO 3)

BE8-3   Labor data for making one gallon of finished product in Hideo Company are as follows: (1) Price—hourly wage rate $10.00, payroll taxes $0.80, and fringe benefits $1.20; (2) Quantity—actual production time 1.4 hours, rest periods and clean up 0.25 hours, and setup and downtime 0.15 hours. Compute the (a) standard direct labor rate per hour, (b) standard direct labor hours per gallon, and (c) the standard labor cost per gallon.

Compute direct materials variances.
(SO 4)

BE8-4   Sprague Company's standard materials cost per unit of output is $10 (2 pounds × $5.00). During July, the company purchases and uses 3,300 pounds of materials costing $16,830 in making 1,500 units of finished product. Compute the total, price, and quantity materials variances.

Compute direct labor variances.
(SO 4)

BE8-5   Talbot Company's standard labor cost per unit of output is $20 (2 hours × $10.00 per hour). During August, the company incurs 1,850 hours of direct labor at an hourly cost of $9.60 per hour in making 1,000 units of finished product. Compute the total, price, and quantity labor variances.

Compute total manufacturing overhead variance.
(SO 5)

BE8-6   In October, Russo Company reports 21,000 actual direct labor hours and it incurs $101,000 of manufacturing overhead costs. Standard hours allowed for the work done is 20,000 hours and the predetermined overhead rate is $5.00 per direct labor hour. Compute the total manufacturing overhead variance.

Compute the manufacturing overhead controllable variance.
(SO 5)

BE8-7   Some overhead data for Russo Company are given in BE8-6. In addition, the flexible manufacturing overhead budget shows that budgeted costs are $4.00 variable per direct labor hour and $24,000 fixed. Compute the manufacturing overhead controllable variance.

Compute overhead volume variance.
(SO 5)

BE8-8   Using the data in BE8-6 and BE8-7, compute the manufacturing overhead volume variance.

Journalize materials variances.
(SO 7)

BE8-9   Journalize the following transactions for McBee Manufacturing:
1. Purchased 6,000 units of raw materials on account for $12,300 when the standard cost was $12,000.
2. Issued 6,000 units of raw materials for production when the standard units were 5,800.

Journalize labor variances.
(SO 7)

BE8-10   Journalize the following transactions for Worrel Manufacturing:
1. Incurred direct labor costs of $24,300 for 3,000 hours when the standard labor cost was $24,000.
2. Assigned 3,000 direct labor hours costing $24,300 to production when standard hours were 3,100.

EXERCISES

Compute standard materials costs.
(SO 3)

E8-1   Raul Montanez manufactures and sells homemade wine, and he wants to develop a standard cost per gallon. The following are required for production of a 50-gallon batch:

3,000 ounces of grape concentrate at $0.04 per ounce

55 pounds of granulated sugar at $0.30 per pound

60 lemons at $0.65 each

50 yeast tablets at $0.25 each

50 nutrient tablets at $0.20 each

2,500 ounces of water at $0.004 per ounce

Raul estimates that 4% of the grape concentrate is wasted, 12% of the sugar is lost, and 20% of the lemons cannot be used.

Instructions
Compute the standard cost of the ingredients for one gallon of wine. (Carry computations to three decimal places.)

E8-2   The standard cost of Product B manufactured by Nang Company includes three units of direct materials at $5.00 per unit. During June, 30,000 units of direct materials are purchased at a cost of $4.70 per unit, and 27,600 units of direct materials are used to produce 9,000 units of Product B.   *Compute materials price and quantity variances.*   (SO 4)

Instructions
(a) Compute the materials price and quantity variances.
(b) Repeat (a), assuming the purchase price is $5.20 and the quantity used is 26,600 units.

E8-3   Pagnozzi Company's standard labor cost of producing one unit of Product DD is 4 hours at the rate of $12.00 per hour. During August, 40,800 hours of labor are incurred at a cost of $12.20 per hour to produce 10,000 units of Product DD.   *Compute labor price and quantity variances.*   (SO 4)

Instructions
(a) Compute the labor price and quantity variances.
(b) Repeat (a), assuming the standard is 4.2 hours of direct labor at $12.40 per hour.

E8-4   Kopecky Inc., which produces a single product, has prepared the following standard cost sheet for one unit of the product.   *Compute materials and labor variances.*   (SO 4)

Direct materials (8 pounds at $2.50 per pound)	$20.00
Direct labor (3 hours at $12.00 per hour)	$36.00

During the month of April, the company manufactures 245 units and incurs the following actual costs:

Direct materials (1,900 pounds)	$4,940
Direct labor (700 hours)	$8,120

Instructions
Compute the total, price, and quantity variances for materials and labor.

E8-5   Data for Kopecky Inc. are given in E8-4.   *Journalize entries for materials and labor variances.*   (SO 7)

Instructions
Journalize the entries to record the materials and labor variances.

E8-6   The following direct materials and direct labor data pertain to the operations of Batista Manufacturing Company for the month of August.   *Compute the materials and labor variances and list reasons for unfavorable variances.*   (SO 4, 6)

Costs		Quantities	
Actual labor rate	$13.00 per hour	Actual hours incurred and used	4,250 hours
Actual materials price	$128.00 per ton	Actual quantity of materials purchased and used	1,225 tons
Standard labor rate	$12.00 per hour	Standard hours used	4,300 hours
Standard materials price	$130.00 per ton	Standard quantity of materials used	1,200 tons

Instructions
(a) Compute the total, price, and quantity variances for materials and labor.
(b) ▭▭▭▷ Provide two possible explanations for each of the unfavorable variances calculated above and suggest where responsibility for the unfavorable result might be placed.

Compute manufacturing overhead variances and interpret findings.

(SO 5)

E8-7   The following information was taken from the annual manufacturing overhead cost budget of Guardino Company:

Variable manufacturing overhead costs	$33,000
Fixed manufacturing overhead costs	$20,625
Normal production level in hours	16,500
Normal production level in units	4,125

During the year, 4,000 units were produced, 16,100 hours were worked, and the actual manufacturing overhead was $55,000. Actual fixed manufacturing overhead costs equaled budgeted fixed manufacturing overhead costs. Overhead is applied on the basis of direct labor hours.

Instructions
(a) Compute the total, fixed, and variable predetermined manufacturing overhead rates.
(b) Compute the total, controllable, and volume overhead variances.
(c) ▰▰▰▰▶ Briefly interpret the overhead controllable and volume variances computed in (b).

Compute overhead variances and journalize transactions and adjusting entry.

(SO 5, 7)

E8-8   Manufacturing overhead data for the production of Product H by DeDonder Company are as follows:

Overhead incurred for 51,000 actual direct labor hours worked	$213,000
Overhead rate (variable $3.00; fixed $1.00) at normal capacity of 54,000 direct labor hours	$ 4.00
Standard hours allowed for work done	52,000

Instructions
(a) Compute the total, controllable, and volume overhead variances.
(b) Journalize the incurrence of the overhead costs and the application of overhead to the job, assuming a standard cost accounting system is used.
(c) Prepare the adjusting entry for the overhead variances.

Prepare a variance report for direct labor.

(SO 4, 6)

E8-9   During March 1999, Tovar Tool & Die Company worked on four jobs. A review of direct labor costs reveals the following summary data:

Job Number	Actual Hours	Actual Costs	Standard Hours	Standard Costs	Total Variance
A257	220	$ 4,400	225	$4,500	$ 100 F
A258	450	10,350	420	8,400	1,950 U
A259	300	6,150	300	6,000	150 U
A260	115	2,070	110	2,200	130 F
Total variance					$1,870 U

Analysis reveals that Job A257 was a repeat job. Job A258 was a rush order that required overtime work at premium rates of pay. Job A259 required a more experienced replacement worker on one shift. Work on Job A260 was done for one day by a new trainee when a regular worker was absent.

Instructions
Prepare a report for the plant supervisor on direct labor cost variances for March. The report should have columns for (1) Job No., (2) Actual Hours, (3) Standard Hours, (4) Labor Quantity Variance, (5) Actual Rate, (6) Standard Rate, (7) Labor Price Variance, and (8) Explanations.

Prepare income statement for management.

(SO 7)

E8-10   Aladen Company uses a standard cost accounting system. During January, the company reported the following manufacturing variances:

Material price variance	$2,250 debit	Labor quantity variance	$ 725 debit
Material quantity variance	700 credit	Overhead controllable	200 credit
Labor price variance	525 debit	Overhead volume	1,000 debit

In addition, 6,000 units of product were sold at $8.00 per unit. Each unit sold had a standard cost of $6.00. Selling and administrative expenses were $7,000 for the month.

Instructions

Prepare an income statement for management for the month ending January 31, 1999.

E8-11 Frizell Company installed a standard cost system on January 1. Selected transactions for the month of January are as follows:

1. Purchased 18,000 units of raw materials on account at a cost of $4.30 per unit. Stan-
   dard cost was $4.00 per unit.
2. Issued 18,000 units of raw materials for jobs that required 17,500 standard units of
   raw materials.
3. Incurred 15,200 actual hours of direct labor at an actual rate of $4.90 per hour. The
   standard rate is $5.00 per hour. (Credit Wages Payable.)
4. Performed 15,200 hours of direct labor on jobs when standard hours were 15,300.
5. Applied overhead to jobs at the rate of 100% of direct labor cost for standard hours
   allowed.

*Journalize entries in a stan-
dard cost accounting system.*
(SO 7)

Instructions

Journalize the January transactions.

E8-12 Lacruz Company uses a standard cost accounting system. Some of the ledger accounts have been destroyed in a fire. The controller asks your help in reconstructing some
missing entries and balances.

*Answer questions concerning
missing entries and balances.*
(SO 4, 5, 7)

Instructions

Answer the following questions:

Credit

(a) Materials Price Variance shows a $2,000 favorable balance, and Accounts Payable
    shows $126,000 of raw materials purchases. What was the amount debited to Raw
    Materials Inventory for raw materials purchased?
(b) Materials Quantity Variance shows a $3,000 unfavorable balance, and Raw Materi-
    als Inventory shows a zero balance. What was the amount debited to Work in Process
    Inventory for direct materials used?
(c) Labor Price Variance shows a $1,500 unfavorable balance, and Factory Labor shows
    a debit of $153,000 for wages incurred. What was the amount credited to Wages
    Payable?
(d) Factory Labor shows a credit of $153,000 for direct labor used, and Labor Quantity
    Variance shows a $900 unfavorable balance. What was the amount debited to Work
    in Process for direct labor used?
(e) Overhead applied to Work in Process totaled $165,000. If the total overhead variance
    was $1,200 unfavorable, what was the amount of overhead costs debited to Manu-
    facturing Overhead?
(f) Overhead Controllable Variance shows a debit balance of $1,500. What was the
    amount and type of balance (debit or credit) in Overhead Volume Variance?

PROBLEMS: SET A

P8-1A Roniger Manufacturing Company uses a standard cost accounting system. In July
1999, it accumulates the following data relative to jobs started and finished:

*Compute variances, and pre-
pare income statement.*
(SO 4, 5, 7)

Cost and Production Data	Actual	Standard
Raw materials		
Units purchased	17,700	
Units used	17,700	18,000
Unit cost	$3.40	$3.00
Direct labor		
Hours worked	2,950	3,000
Hourly rate	$11.80	$12.00
Manufacturing overhead		
Incurred	$87,500	
Applied		$90,000

Manufacturing overhead was applied on the basis of direct labor hours. Normal capacity for the month was 2,800 direct labor hours. At normal capacity, budgeted overhead costs were: variable $56,000 and fixed $28,000.

Jobs finished during the month were sold for $240,000; selling and administrative expenses were $25,000.

Instructions

(a) Compute all of the variances for direct materials, direct labor, and manufacturing overhead.

(b) Prepare an income statement for management. Ignore income taxes.

Compute variances.
(SO 4, 5, 7)

P8-2A Moreno Corporation manufactures a single product. The standard cost per unit of product is as follows:

Direct materials—2 pounds of plastic at $5.00 per pound	$10.00
Direct labor—2 hours at $12.00 per hour	24.00
Variable manufacturing overhead	12.00
Fixed manufacturing overhead	6.00
Total standard cost per unit	$52.00

The master manufacturing overhead budget for the year based on normal productive capacity of 180,000 direct labor hours (90,000 units) shows total variable costs of $1,080,000 and total fixed costs of $540,000. Overhead is applied on the basis of direct labor hours. Actual costs for November in producing 7,600 units were as follows:

Direct materials (15,000 pounds)	$ 73,500
Direct labor (14,900 hours)	181,780
Variable overhead	88,990
Fixed overhead	44,000
Total manufacturing costs	$388,270

The purchasing department normally buys the quantities of raw materials that are expected to be used in production each month. Raw materials inventories, therefore, can be ignored.

Instructions
Compute all of the materials, labor, and overhead variances.

Compute variances, journalize entries, and identify significant variances.
(SO 4, 5, 6, 7)

P8-3A Harbaugh Clothiers manufactures women's business suits. The company uses a standard cost accounting system. In March 1999, 12,000 suits were made. The following standard and actual cost data applied to the month of March when normal capacity was 15,000 direct labor hours.

Cost Element	Standard (per unit)	Actual
Direct materials	5 yards at $7.00 per yard	$423,400 for 58,000 yards ($7.30 per yard)
Direct labor	1.0 hours at $12.00 per hour	$128,800 for 11,500 hours ($11.20 per hour)
Overhead	1.0 hours at $9.00 per hour (fixed $6.00; variable $3.00)	$90,000 fixed overhead $42,000 variable overhead

Overhead is applied on the basis of direct labor hours. At normal capacity, budgeted fixed overhead costs were $90,000 and budgeted variable overhead costs were $45,000.

Instructions

(a) Compute the total, price, and quantity variances for (1) materials and (2) labor, and compute the total, controllable, and volume variances for manufacturing overhead.

(b) Journalize the entries to record the variances assuming (1) all purchases of materials were on account and (2) Wages Payable was credited for factory labor incurred.

(c) ▭▭▭▶ Which of the materials and labor variances should be investigated if management considers a variance of more than 6% from standard to be significant?

P8-4A Soriano Manufacturing Company uses standard costs with its job order cost accounting system. In January, an order (Job 84) was received for 4,000 units of Product D. The standard cost of 1 unit of Product D is as follows:

Journalize and post standard cost entries and prepare income statement.
(SO 4, 5, 7)

Direct materials—1.5 pounds at $4.00 per pound	$ 6.00
Direct labor—1 hour at $9.00 per hour	9.00
Overhead—1 hour (variable $6.00; fixed $10.00)	16.00
Standard cost per unit	$31.00

Overhead is applied on the basis of direct labor hours. Normal capacity for the month of January was 4,500 direct labor hours. During January, the following transactions applicable to Job No. 84 occurred.
1. Purchased 6,200 pounds of raw materials on account at $3.60 per pound.
2. Requisitioned 6,200 pounds of raw materials for production.
3. Incurred 3,800 hours of direct labor at $9.20 per hour.
4. Worked 3,800 hours of direct labor on Job No. 84.
5. Incurred $67,650 of manufacturing overhead on account.
6. Applied overhead to Job No. 84 on the basis of direct labor hours.
7. Transferred Job No. 84 to finished goods.
8. Billed customer for Job No. 84 at a selling price of $250,000.
9. Incurred selling and administrative expenses on account $61,000.

Instructions
(a) Journalize the transactions.
(b) Post to the job order cost accounts.
(c) Prepare the entry to recognize the overhead variances.
(d) Prepare the income statement for management for January 1999.

P8-5A Inwood Manufacturing Company uses a standard cost accounting system. In 1999, 36,000 units were produced. Each unit took several pounds of direct materials and $1\frac{1}{3}$ standard hours of direct labor at a standard hourly rate of $12.00. Normal capacity was 42,000 direct labor hours. During the year, 140,000 pounds of raw materials were purchased at $0.94 per pound. All pounds purchased were used during the year.

Answer questions about variances.
(SO 4, 5, 7)

Instructions
Answer the following questions:
(a) If the materials price variance was $5,600 unfavorable, what was the standard materials price per pound?
(b) If the materials quantity variance was $3,600 favorable, what was the standard materials quantity per unit?
(c) What were the standard hours allowed for the units produced?
(d) If the labor quantity variance was $9,600 unfavorable, what were the actual direct labor hours worked?
(e) If the labor price variance was $7,320 favorable, what was the actual rate per hour?
(f) If total budgeted manufacturing overhead was $315,000 at normal capacity, what was the predetermined overhead rate?
(g) What was the standard cost per unit of product?
(h) How much overhead was applied to production during the year?
(i) If the fixed overhead rate was $2.50, what was the overhead volume variance?
(j) If the overhead controllable variance was $3,000 favorable, what were the total variable overhead costs incurred?
(k) Using selected answers above, what were the total costs assigned to work in process?

PROBLEMS: SET B

*Compute variances and pre-
pare income statement.*
(SO 4, 5, 7)

P8-1B Mattivi Manufacturing Corporation accumulates the following data relative to jobs started and finished during the month of June 1999:

Costs and Production Data	Actual	Standard
Raw materials purchases, 10,300 units	$22,660	$20,000
Raw materials units used	10,300	10,000
Direct labor payroll	$120,450	$120,000
Direct labor hours worked	14,600	15,000
Manufacturing overhead incurred	$178,500	
Manufacturing overhead applied		$180,000
Machine hours expected to be used at normal capacity		42,500
Budgeted fixed overhead for June		$42,500
Variable overhead rate per hour		$3.00

Overhead is applied on the basis of standard machine hours. Three hours of machine time are required for each direct labor hour. The jobs were sold for $400,000; selling and administrative expenses were $40,000.

Instructions
(a) Compute all of the variances for direct materials, direct labor, and manufacturing overhead.
(b) Prepare an income statement for management. Ignore income taxes.

Compute variances.
(SO 4, 5, 7)

P8-2B Fuqua Corporation manufactures a single product. The standard cost per unit of product is shown below:

Direct materials—1 pound plastic at $7.00 per pound	$ 7.00
Direct labor—1.5 hours at $12.00 per hour	18.00
Variable manufacturing overhead	11.25
Fixed manufacturing overhead	3.75
Total standard cost per unit	$40.00

The predetermined manufacturing overhead rate is $10 per direct labor hour ($15.00 ÷ 1.5). This rate was computed from a master manufacturing overhead budget based on normal production of 90,000 direct labor hours (60,000 units) for the year. The master budget showed total variable costs of $675,000 and total fixed costs of $225,000. Actual costs for October in producing 4,900 units were as follows:

Direct materials (5,100 pounds)	$ 37,230
Direct labor (7,000 hours)	87,500
Variable overhead	56,170
Fixed overhead	18,750
Total manufacturing costs	$199,650

The purchasing department normally buys the quantities of raw materials that are expected to be used in production each month. Raw materials inventories, therefore, can be ignored.

Instructions
Compute all of the materials, labor, and overhead variances.

*Compute variances, journal-
ize entries, and identify significant variances.*
(SO 4, 5, 6, 7)

P8-3B Drago Clothiers is a small company that manufactures tall men's suits. The company has used a standard cost accounting system. In May 2000, 11,250 suits were produced.
    The following standard and actual cost data applied to the month of May when normal capacity was 14,000 direct labor hours.

Cost Element	Standard (per unit)	Actual
Direct materials	8 yards at $4.50 per yard	$366,000 for 91,500 yards ($4.00 per yard)
Direct labor	1.2 hours at $13.00 per hour	$203,000 for 14,500 hours ($14.00 per hour)
Overhead	1.2 hours at $6.00 per hour (fixed $3.50; variable $2.50)	$49,000 fixed overhead $36,000 variable overhead

Overhead is applied on the basis of direct labor hours. At normal capacity, budgeted fixed overhead costs were $49,000 and budgeted variable overhead was $35,000.

Instructions
(a) Compute the total, price, and quantity variances for (1) materials and (2) labor, and the total, controllable, and volume variances for manufacturing overhead.
(b) Journalize the entries to record the variances assuming (1) all purchases of materials were on account and (2) Wages Payable was credited for factory labor incurred.
(c) ▦▦▦▶ Which of the materials and labor variances should be investigated if management considers a variance of more than 7% from standard to be significant?

P8-4B Grassie Corporation uses standard costs with its job order cost accounting system. In January, an order (Job No. 12) for 2,000 units of Product B was received. The standard cost of 1 unit of Product B is as follows:

Journalize and post standard cost entries and prepare income statement.
(SO 4, 5, 7)

Direct materials	3 pounds at $1.00 per pound	$ 3.00
Direct labor	1 hour at $8.00 per hour	8.00
Overhead	2 hours (variable $4.00 per machine hour; fixed $2.00 per machine hour)	12.00
Standard cost per unit		$23.00

Normal capacity for the month was 4,200 machine hours. During January, the following transactions applicable to Job No. 12 occurred:
1. Purchased 6,150 pounds of raw materials on account at $1.10 per pound.
2. Requisitioned 6,150 pounds of raw materials for Job No. 12.
3. Incurred 2,100 hours of direct labor at a rate of $7.80 per hour.
4. Worked 2,100 hours of direct labor on Job No. 12.
5. Incurred manufacturing overhead on account $24,200.
6. Applied overhead to Job No. 12 on basis of standard machine hours used.
7. Completed Job No. 12.
8. Billed customer for Job No. 12 at a selling price of $70,000.
9. Incurred selling and administrative expenses on account $2,000.

Instructions
(a) Journalize the transactions.
(b) Post to the job order cost accounts.
(c) Prepare the entry to recognize the overhead variances.
(d) Prepare the January 2000 income statement for management.

P8-5B Diego Manufacturing Company uses a standard cost accounting system. In 1999, 32,000 units were produced. Each unit took several pounds of direct materials and $1\frac{1}{2}$ standard hours of direct labor at a standard hourly rate of $12.00. Normal capacity was 50,000 direct labor hours. During the year, 133,000 pounds of raw materials were purchased at $0.96 per pound. All pounds purchased were used during the year.

Answer questions about variances.
(SO 4, 5, 7)

Instructions
Answer the following questions:
(a) If the materials price variance was $2,660 favorable, what was the standard materials price per pound?
(b) If the materials quantity variance was $4,900 unfavorable, what was the standard materials quantity per unit?
(c) What were the standard hours allowed for the units produced?
(d) If the labor quantity variance was $7,200 unfavorable, what were the actual direct labor hours worked?

(e) If the labor price variance was $9,720 favorable, what was the actual rate per hour?

(f) If total budgeted manufacturing overhead was $350,000 at normal capacity, what was the predetermined overhead rate?

(g) What was the standard cost per unit of product?

(h) How much overhead was applied to production during the year?

(i) If the fixed overhead rate was $2.00, what was the overhead volume variance?

(j) If the overhead controllable variance is $3,000 unfavorable, what were the total variable overhead costs incurred?

(k) Using one or more answers above, what were the total costs assigned to work in process?

BROADENING YOUR PERSPECTIVE

GROUP DECISION CASE

BYP8-1 Admar Professionals, a management consulting firm, specializes in strategic planning for financial institutions. Tim Adler and Joan Marley, partners in the firm, are assembling a new strategic planning model for use by clients. The model is designed for use on most microcomputers and replaces a rather lengthy manual model currently marketed by the firm. To market the new model Tim and Joan will need to provide clients with an estimate of the number of labor hours and computer time needed to operate the model. The model is currently being test marketed at five small financial institutions. These financial institutions are listed below, along with the number of combined computer/labor hours used by each institution to run the model one time.

Financial Institutions	Computer/Labor Hours Required
Midland National	25
First State	45
Financial Federal	40
Pacific America	30
Lakeview National	30
Total	170
Average	34

Any company that purchases the new model will need to purchase user manuals to access and operate the system. Also required are specialized computer forms that are sold only by Admar Professionals. User manuals will be sold to clients in cases of 20, at a cost of $400 per case. One manual must be used each time the model is run because each manual includes a nonreusable computer accessed password for operating the system. The specialized computer forms are sold in packages of 250, at a cost of $75 per package. One application of the model requires the use of 50 forms. This sum includes two forms that are generally wasted in each application due to printer alignment errors. The overall cost of the strategic planning model to user clients is $12,000. Most clients will use the model four times annually.

Admar Professionals must provide its clients with estimates of ongoing costs incurred in operating the new strategic planning model. They would like to provide this information in the form of standard costs.

Instructions

With the class divided into groups, answer the following:

(a) What factors should be considered in setting a standard for computer/labor hours?

(b) What alternatives for setting a standard for computer/labor hours might be used?

(c) What standard for computer/labor hours would you select? Justify your answer.

(d) Determine the standard material cost associated with the user manuals and computer forms for each application of the strategic planning model.

MANAGERIAL ANALYSIS

BYP8-2 Jake Ryan and Associates is a medium-sized company located near a large metropolitan area in the Midwest. The company manufactures cabinets of mahogany, oak, and other fine woods for use in expensive homes, restaurants, and hotels. Although some of the work is custom, many of the cabinets are a standard size. One such model is called Luxury Base Frame. Standard production is 1,000 units. Each unit has a direct labor hour standard of 5 hours. Overhead is applied to production based on standard direct labor hours. During the most recent month, only 900 units were produced; 4,500 direct labor hours were allowed for standard production, but only 4,000 hours were used. Standard and actual overhead costs were as follows:

	Standard (1,000 units)	Actual (900 units)
Indirect materials	$ 12,000	$ 12,300
Indirect labor	43,000	51,000
(Fixed) Manufacturing supervisors salaries	22,000	22,000
(Fixed) Manufacturing office employees salaries	13,000	11,500
(Fixed) Engineering costs	27,000	25,000
Computer costs	10,000	10,000
Electricity	2,500	2,500
(Fixed) Manufacturing building depreciation	8,000	8,000
(Fixed) Machinery depreciation	3,000	3,000
(Fixed) Trucks and forklift depreciation	1,500	1,500
Small tools	700	1,400
(Fixed) Insurance	500	500
(Fixed) Property taxes	300	300
Total	$143,500	$149,000

Instructions
(a) Determine the overhead application rate.
(b) Determine how much overhead was applied to production.
(c) Calculate the controllable overhead variance and the overhead volume variance.
(d) Decide which overhead variances should be investigated.
(e) Discuss causes of the overhead variances. What can management do to improve its performance next month?

REAL-WORLD FOCUS

GLASSMASTER COMPANY

BYP8-3 Glassmaster Co. was incorporated in 1946 as Koolvent Metal Awning Company. Its current name was adopted in 1982 to reflect the more general nature of its products. The company is organized as two divisions and one subsidiary. One division focuses on the manufacture of filaments such as fishing line and sewing thread; the other division manufactures antennas and specialty fiberglass products. Its subsidiary manufactures flexible steel wire controls and molded control panels.

The annual report of Glassmaster provides the following information:

GLASSMASTER COMPANY
Management Discussion

Gross profit margins for the year improved to 20.9% of sales compared to last year's 18.5%. All operations reported improved margins due in large part to improved operating efficiencies as a result of cost reduction measures implemented during the second and third quarters of the fiscal year and increased manufacturing throughout due to higher unit volume sales. Contributing to the improved margins was a favorable materials price variance due to competitive pricing by suppliers as a result of soft demand for petrochemical-based products. This favorable variance is temporary and will begin to reverse itself as stronger worldwide demand for commodity products improves in tandem with the economy. Partially offsetting these positive effects on profit margins were competitive pressures on sales prices of certain product lines. The company responded with pricing strategies designed to maintain and/or increase market share.

Instructions
(a) Is it apparent from the information whether Glassmaster utilizes standard costs?
(b) Do you think the price variance experienced should lead to changes in standard costs for the next fiscal year?

COMMUNICATION ACTIVITY

BYP8-4 The setting of standards is critical to the effective use of standards in evaluating performance.

Instructions
Explain in a memorandum to your instructor (a) the comparative advantages and disadvantages of ideal versus normal standards, and (b) the factors that should be included in setting the price and quantity standards for direct materials, direct labor, and manufacturing overhead.

RESEARCH ASSIGNMENT

BYP8-5 The December 1996 issue of *Accounting Horizons* contains an article by Carol B. Cheatham and Leo R. Cheatham entitled "Redesigning Cost Systems: Is Standard Costing Obsolete?"

Instructions
Read the article and answer the following questions:
(a) For what percent of U.S. manufacturing firms are standard cost systems still the cost system of choice?
(b) What are the major criticisms of standard cost systems?
(c) How does a standard cost system relate to activity-based costing (ABC)? And, how might activity-based costing (ABC) be used to enhance a company's costing system when standard costing is the primary system?
(d) What do the authors conclude from their study of standard cost systems?

ETHICS CASE

BYP8-6 In Corolla Manufacturing Company production workers in the Painting Department are paid on the basis of productivity. The labor time standard for a unit of production is established through periodic time studies conducted by the Manpower Management Department. In a time study, the actual time required to complete a specific task by a worker is observed. Allowances are then made for preparation time, rest periods, and clean up time. Jeff Jorden is one of several veterans in the Painting Department.

Jeff is informed by Manpower Management that he will be used in the time study for the painting of a new product. The findings will be the basis for establishing the labor time standard for the next 6 months. During the test, Jeff deliberately slows his normal work pace in an effort to obtain a labor time standard that will be easy to meet. Because it is a new product, the Manpower Management representative who conducted the test is unaware that Jeff did not give the test his best effort.

Instructions

(a) Who was benefited and who was harmed by Jeff's actions?

(b) Was Jeff ethical in the way he performed the time study test?

(c) What measure(s) might the company take to obtain valid data for setting the labor time standard?

SURFING THE NET

BYP8-7 Computer manufacturer Hewlett-Packard's Web site provides information about Hewlett-Packard's 25,000 electronic products and services, its worldwide operations, and its financial picture.

Address: http://www.hp.com/

Steps:

1. Choose **HP Financials.**
2. Choose the current **Annual Report.**
3. Review the Summary of Significant Accounting Policies in the Notes to the Financial Statements.

Instructions

(a) At what cost does Hewlett-Packard report its inventories?

(b) What inventory costing method does standard cost approximate for Hewlett-Packard?

(c) Has the lower-of-cost-or-market rule been applied to the Hewlett-Packard inventories?

(d) Why do you suppose that Hewlett-Packard accounts for and reports its inventories at standard cost?

Answers to Self-Study Questions

1. c   2. d   3. b   4. c   5. b   6. a   7. d   8. a   9. b   10. c

 Remember to go back to the Navigator box on the chapter-opening page and check off your completed work.

CHAPTER 9
Incremental Analysis

CLASS A
COMMON STOC

PAR VALUE
$1 PER SHARE

NUMBER
A

CUSIP 96822?

STUDY OBJECTIVES

After studying this chapter, you should be able to:

1. Identify the steps in management's decision-making process.
2. Describe the concept of incremental analysis.
3. Identify the relevant costs in accepting an order at a special price.
4. Indicate the relevant costs in a make-or-buy decision.
5. Give the decision rule in deciding whether to sell or process materials further.
6. Identify the factors to be considered in retaining or replacing equipment.
7. Explain the factors that are relevant in deciding whether to eliminate an unprofitable segment.
8. Explain the term "sales mix" and its effects in determining break-even sales.
9. Determine sales mix when a company has limited resources.

THE NAVIGATOR

FEATURE STORY

To Make It or To Buy It?

When is a manufacturer not a manufacturer? When it outsources. An extension of the classic "make or buy" decision, outsourcing involves hiring other companies to make all or part of a product or to perform services. Who is outsourcing? Nike, General Motors, Sara Lee, and Hewlett-Packard, to name a few. Even a recent trade journal article for small cabinet makers outlined the pros and cons of building cabinet doors and drawers internally, or outsourcing them to other shops.

Gibson Greetings, Inc., one of the country's largest sellers of greeting cards, has experienced both the pros and cons of outsourcing. In April one year it announced it would outsource the manufacturing of all of its cards and gift wrap. Gibson's stock price shot up quickly because investors believed the strategy could save the company $10 million a year, primarily by reducing manufacturing costs. But later in the same year Gibson Greetings also got a taste of the negative side of outsourcing: When one of its suppliers was unable to meet its production schedule, about $20 million of Christmas cards went to stores a month later than scheduled.

Outsourcing is often a point of dispute in labor negotiations. While many of the jobs lost to outsourcing go overseas, that is not always the case. In fact, a recent trend is to hire out work to vendors located close to the corporation. This reduces shipping costs and can improve coordination of efforts. One company that has benefited from outsourcing is Solectron Corporation in Silicon Valley. It makes things like cell phones, printers, and computers for high-tech companies in the region. To the surprise of many, it has kept 5,600 people employed in California, rather than watching those jobs go overseas. What is its secret? It produces high-quality products efficiently. Solectron has to be efficient because it operates on a very thin profit margin—that is, it makes a tiny amount of money on each part—but it makes millions and millions of parts. It has proved

342

the logic of outsourcing as a management decision, both for the companies for whom it makes parts and for its owners and employees.

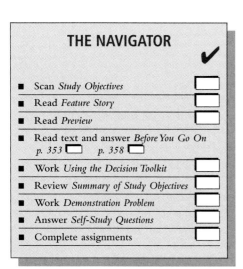

THE NAVIGATOR ✔

- Scan *Study Objectives* ☐
- Read *Feature Story* ☐
- Read *Preview* ☐
- Read text and answer *Before You Go On*
  p. 353 ☐   p. 358 ☐
- Work *Using the Decision Toolkit* ☐
- Review *Summary of Study Objectives* ☐
- Work *Demonstration Problem* ☐
- Answer *Self-Study Questions* ☐
- Complete assignments ☐

An important purpose of management accounting is to provide managers with relevant information for decision making. Companies of all sorts must make product decisions. Philip Morris decided to cut prices to raise market share. Oral-B Laboratories opted to produce a new, higher priced ($5) toothbrush. General Motors discontinued making the Buick Riviera and Oldsmobile 88. Quaker Oats decided to sell its Snapple line of beverages, at a price more than one billion dollars less than it paid for Snapple only a few years before. Ski manufacturers like Dynastar had to decide whether to use their limited resources to make snowboards instead of downhill skis.

This chapter explains management's decision-making process and a decision-making approach called incremental analysis. The use of incremental analysis is demonstrated in a variety of situations. The content and organization of this chapter are as follows:

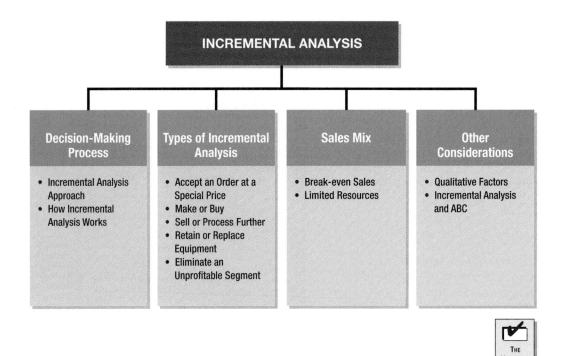

*T*HE DECISION-MAKING PROCESS

STUDY OBJECTIVE

1

Identify the steps in management's decision-making process.

Making decisions is an important part of management. Management's decision-making process does not always follow a set pattern, because decisions vary significantly in their scope, urgency, and importance. It is possible, however, to identify some steps that are frequently involved in the process. These steps are graphically shown in Illustration 9-1.

Accounting's contribution to the decision-making process occurs primarily in Steps 2 and 4. In Step 2, for each possible course of action, relevant revenue and cost data are provided to show the expected overall effect on net income. In Step 4, internal reports are prepared that review the actual impact of the decision.

Illustration 9-1
Management's decision-
making process

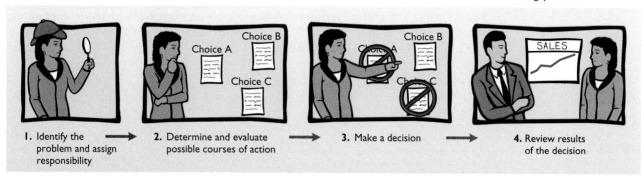

In making business decisions, management ordinarily considers both financial and nonfinancial information. **Financial** information is related to revenues and costs and their effect on the company's overall profitability. **Nonfinancial** information relates to such factors as the effect of the decision on employee turnover, the environment, or the overall image of the company in the community. Although nonfinancial information can be as important as, and in some cases more important than, financial information, we will limit our discussion primarily to financial information that is relevant to the decision.

INCREMENTAL ANALYSIS APPROACH

Decisions involve a choice among alternative courses of action. Suppose that you were deciding whether to purchase or lease a computer. The financial data relate to the cost of leasing versus the cost of purchasing. For example, leasing would involve periodic lease payments; purchasing would require payment of the purchase price. In other words, the financial data relevant to the decision are the data that would vary in the future among the possible alternatives. The process used to identify the financial data that change under alternative courses of action is called incremental analysis. In some cases, you will find that when you use incremental analysis, both costs **and** revenues will change. In other cases, only costs **or** revenues will vary.

Incremental analysis involves not only identifying relevant revenues and costs, but also determining the probable effects of decisions on future earnings. Such data inevitably involve estimates and uncertainty. Gathering data for incremental analyses may involve market analysts, engineers, and accountants. In quantifying the data, the accountant is expected to exercise professional judgment to produce the most reliable information available at the time the decision must be made.

> **STUDY OBJECTIVE**
> **2**
> Describe the concept of incremental analysis.

> **Alternative Terminology**
> Incremental analysis is also called *differential analysis* because the analysis focuses on differences.

HOW INCREMENTAL ANALYSIS WORKS

The basic approach in incremental analysis is illustrated in the following example:

	Alternative A	Alternative B	Net Income Increase (Decrease)
Revenues	$125,000	$110,000	$(15,000)
Costs	100,000	80,000	20,000
Net income	$ 25,000	$ 30,000	$ 5,000

Illustration 9-2 Basic approach in incremental analysis

In this example, alternative B is being compared with alternative A. The net income column shows the differences between the alternatives. In this case, incremental revenue will be $15,000 less under alternative B than under alternative A, but a $20,000 incremental cost saving will be realized.[1] Thus, alternative B will produce $5,000 more net income than alternative A.

In the following pages you will encounter three important cost concepts used in incremental analysis:

Illustration 9-3 Key cost concepts in incremental analysis

- **Relevant cost** In incremental analysis, the only factors to be considered are those costs and revenues that differ across alternatives. Those factors are called relevant costs. Costs and revenues that do not differ across alternatives can be ignored when trying to choose between alternatives.

- **Opportunity cost** Often in choosing one course of action, the company must give up the opportunity to benefit from some other course of action. For example, if a machine is used to make one type of product, the benefit of making another type of product with that machine is lost. This lost benefit is referred to as opportunity cost.

- **Sunk cost** Costs that have already been incurred and will not be changed or avoided by any future decision are referred to as sunk costs. For example, if you have already purchased a machine, and now a new, more efficient machine is available, the book value of the original machine is a sunk cost. It should have no bearing on your decision whether to buy the new machine. **Sunk costs are not relevant costs.**

In incremental analysis, it is also important to recognize that (1) variable costs may not change under the alternative courses of action, and (2) fixed costs may change. For example, direct labor, normally a variable cost, is not an incremental cost in deciding between two new factory machines if each asset requires the same amount of direct labor. In contrast, rent expense, normally a fixed cost, is an incremental cost in a decision to continue occupancy of a building or to purchase or lease a new building.

---

[1]Although income taxes are sometimes important in incremental analysis, they are ignored in the chapter for simplicity's sake.

TYPES OF INCREMENTAL ANALYSIS

A number of different types of decisions involve incremental analysis. The more common types of decisions are whether to:

1. Accept an order at a special price.
2. Make or buy component parts or finished products.
3. Sell products or process them further.
4. Retain or replace equipment.
5. Eliminate an unprofitable business segment.

We will consider each of these types of incremental analysis in the following pages.

ACCEPT AN ORDER AT A SPECIAL PRICE

Sometimes, a company may have an opportunity to obtain additional business if it is willing to make a major price concession to a specific customer. To illustrate, assume that Sunbelt Company produces 100,000 automatic blenders per month, which is 80% of plant capacity. Variable manufacturing costs are $8 per unit, and fixed manufacturing costs are $400,000, or $4 per unit. The blenders are normally sold directly to retailers at $20 each. Sunbelt has an offer from Mexico Co. (a foreign wholesaler) to purchase an additional 2,000 blenders at $11 per unit. Acceptance of the offer would not affect normal sales of the product, and the additional units can be manufactured without increasing plant capacity. What should management do?

> **STUDY OBJECTIVE**
> **3**
> Identify the relevant costs in accepting an order at a special price.

If management makes its decision on the basis of the total cost per unit of $12 ($8 + $4), the order would be rejected, because costs ($12) would exceed revenues ($11) by $1 per unit. However, since the units can be produced within existing plant capacity, the special order **will not increase fixed costs.** The relevant data for the decision, therefore, are the variable manufacturing costs per unit of $8 and the expected revenue of $11 per unit. Thus, as shown in Illustration 9-4, Sunbelt will increase its net income by $6,000 by accepting this special order.

> **Helpful Hint** This is a good example of different costs for different purposes. In the long-run all costs are relevant, but for this decision only costs that change are relevant.

	Reject Order	Accept Order	Net Income Increase (Decrease)
Revenues	$-0-	$22,000	$22,000
Costs	-0-	16,000	(16,000)
Net income	$-0-	$ 6,000	$ 6,000

Illustration 9-4
Incremental analysis—accepting an order at a special price

Two points should be emphasized: First, it is assumed that sales of the product in other markets would not be affected by this special order. If other sales were affected, then Sunbelt would have to consider the lost sales in making the decision. Second, if Sunbelt is operating at full capacity, it is likely that the special order would be rejected. Under such circumstances, the company would have to expand plant capacity, and the special order would have to absorb these additional fixed manufacturing costs, as well as the variable manufacturing costs.

MAKE OR BUY

When a manufacturer assembles component parts in producing a finished product, management must decide whether to make or buy the components. The decision to buy parts or services is often referred to as outsourcing. For example, as discussed in the *Feature Story*, a company such as General Motors Corporation may either make or buy the batteries, tires, and radios used in its cars. Similarly, Hewlett-Packard Corporation may make or buy the electronic circuitry, cases, and printer heads for its printers. The decision to make or buy components should be made on the basis of incremental analysis.

To illustrate the analysis, assume that Baron Company incurs the following annual costs in producing 25,000 ignition switches for motor scooters:

Illustration 9-5   Annual product cost data

Direct materials	$ 50,000
Direct labor	75,000
Variable manufacturing overhead	40,000
Fixed manufacturing overhead	60,000
Total manufacturing costs	$225,000
Total cost per unit ($225,000 ÷ 25,000)	**$9.00**

Alternatively, Baron Company may purchase the ignition switches from Ignition, Inc., at a price of $8 per unit. The question again is, "What should management do?"

On the one hand, it appears that management should purchase the ignition switches for $8, rather than make them at a cost of $9. However, a review of operations indicates that if the ignition switches are purchased from Ignition, Inc., all of Baron's variable costs but only $10,000 of its fixed manufacturing costs will be eliminated. Thus, $50,000 of the fixed manufacturing costs will remain if the ignition switches are purchased. The relevant costs for incremental analysis, therefore, are as follows:

Illustration 9-6 Incremental analysis— make or buy

	Make	Buy	Net Income Increase (Decrease)
Direct materials	$ 50,000	$ –0–	$ 50,000
Direct labor	75,000	–0–	75,000
Variable manufacturing costs	40,000	–0–	40,000
Fixed manufacturing costs	60,000	50,000	10,000
Purchase price (25,000 × $8)	–0–	200,000	(200,000)
Total annual cost	$225,000	$250,000	$ (25,000)

This analysis indicates that Baron Company will incur $25,000 of additional cost by buying the ignition switches. Therefore, Baron should continue to make the ignition switches, even though the total manufacturing cost is $1 higher than the purchase price. The reason is that if the company purchases the ignition switches, it will still have fixed costs of $50,000 to absorb.

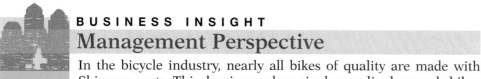

BUSINESS INSIGHT
Management Perspective

In the bicycle industry, nearly all bikes of quality are made with Shimano parts. This dominance by a single supplier has made bikes a sort of commodity. That is, if all bikes are made from the same parts, then what does it matter what brand of bike you buy? As a consequence, the majority of profits go to Shimano, with bike manufacturers that use Shimano parts having to accept an increasingly small profit margin. To break this trend, and increase its profit margins, Cannondale Corporation has decided to take "the approach that we manufacture the whole bicycle, not just taking a frame and putting somebody's parts on it." Similar steps are being taken by Trek Bicycle Corporation and Specialized Bicycle Components Inc. These companies recognize that they are taking a risk. In order to compete with Shimano, they will have to dramatically step up their research and development efforts and significantly increase their efficiency in the manufacture of parts. This will be difficult given Shimano's huge volume advantage.

Source: Ross Kerber, "Bike Maker Faces a Tactical Shift," *The Wall Street Journal,* October 12, 1998, p. B1.

Opportunity Cost

The foregoing make-or-buy analysis is complete only if it is assumed that the productive capacity used to make the ignition switches cannot be converted to another purpose. If there is an opportunity to use this productive capacity in some other manner, then this opportunity cost must be considered. **Opportunity cost** is the potential benefit that may be obtained by following an alternative course of action. To illustrate, assume that through buying the switches, Baron Company can use the released productive capacity to generate additional income of $28,000 producing a different product. This lost income is an additional cost of continuing to make the switches in the make-or-buy decision. This opportunity cost therefore is added to the "Make" column, for comparison. As shown, it is now advantageous to buy the ignition switches.

	Make	Buy	Net Income Increase (Decrease)
Total annual cost	$225,000*	$250,000*	$(25,000)
Opportunity cost	**28,000**	–0–	**28,000**
Total cost	$253,000	$250,000	$ 3,000

*From Illustration 9-6.

Illustration 9-7
Incremental analysis—make or buy, with opportunity cost

The qualitative factors in this decision include the possible loss of jobs for employees who produce the ignition switches. In addition, management must assess how long the supplier will be able to satisfy the company's quality control standards at the quoted price per unit.

SELL OR PROCESS FURTHER

STUDY OBJECTIVE

5

Give the decision rule in deciding whether to sell or process materials further.

Many manufacturers have the option of selling products at a given point in the production cycle or continuing to process with the expectation of selling them at a higher price. For example, a bicycle manufacturer such as Schwinn could sell its 10-speed bicycles to retailers either unassembled or assembled, and a furniture manufacturer such as Ethan Allen could sell its dining room sets to furniture stores either unfinished or finished. The sell-or-process further decision should be made on the basis of incremental analysis. The basic decision rule is: **Process further as long as the incremental revenue from such processing exceeds the incremental processing costs.**

Assume, for example, that Woodmasters Inc. makes tables. The cost to manufacture an unfinished table is $35, computed as follows:

Illustration 9-8 Per unit cost of unfinished table

Direct material	$15
Direct labor	10
Variable manufacturing overhead	6
Fixed manufacturing overhead	4
Manufacturing cost per unit	**$35**

The selling price per unfinished unit is $50. Woodmasters currently has unused productive capacity that is expected to continue indefinitely. Management concludes that some of this capacity may be used to finish the tables and sell them at $60 per unit. For a finished table, it is anticipated that direct materials and direct labor costs will increase $2 and $4, respectively. In addition, variable manufacturing overhead costs will increase by $2.40 (60% of direct labor). No increase is anticipated in fixed manufacturing overhead. The incremental analysis on a per unit basis is as follows:

Illustration 9-9 Incremental analysis—sell or process further

	Sell	Process Further	Net Income Increase (Decrease)
Sales per unit	$50.00	$60.00	$10.00
Cost per unit			
Direct materials	15.00	17.00	(2.00)
Direct labor	10.00	14.00	(4.00)
Variable manufacturing overhead	6.00	8.40	(2.40)
Fixed manufacturing overhead	4.00	4.00	–0–
Total	$35.00	$43.40	$ (8.40)
Net income per unit	$15.00	$16.60	$ 1.60

Helpful Hint Current net income is known. Net income from processing further is an estimate. In making its decision, management could add a "risk" factor for the estimate.

As indicated from the analysis, it would be advantageous for Woodmaster to process the tables further. In this case, the incremental revenue of $10.00 from the additional processing is $1.60 higher than the incremental processing costs of $8.40.

RETAIN OR REPLACE EQUIPMENT

STUDY OBJECTIVE

6

Identify the factors to be considered in retaining or replacing equipment.

Management often has to decide whether to continue using an asset or replace it. To illustrate, assume that Jeffcoat Company has a factory machine with a book value of $40,000 and a remaining useful life of four years. A new machine is available that costs $120,000 and is expected to have zero salvage value at the end of its 4-year useful life. If the new machine is acquired, variable manufacturing costs are expected to decrease from $160,000 to $125,000 annually and the old unit will be scrapped. The incremental analysis for the **4-year period** is as follows:

Illustration 9-10
Incremental analysis—
retain or replace
equipment

	Retain Equipment	Replace Equipment	Net Income Increase (Decrease)
Variable manufacturing costs	$640,000^a	$500,000^b	**$140,000**
New machine cost		120,000	**(120,000)**
Total	$640,000	$620,000	**$ 20,000**

^a(4 years × $160,000)
^b(4 years × $125,000)

In this case, it would be to the company's advantage to replace the equipment. The lower variable manufacturing costs due to replacement more than offset the cost of the new equipment.

One other point should be mentioned regarding Jeffcoat's decision: **The book value of the old machine does not affect the decision.** Book value is a sunk cost, which is a cost that cannot be changed by any present or future decision. Sunk costs, therefore, **are not relevant in incremental analysis.** In this example, if the asset is retained, book value will be depreciated over its remaining useful life. On the other hand, if the new unit is acquired, book value will be recognized as a loss of the current period. Thus, the effect of book value on current and future earnings is the same regardless of the replacement decision. **Any trade-in allowance or cash disposal value of the existing asset, however, is relevant** to the decision, because this value will not be realized if the asset is continued in use.

ELIMINATE AN UNPROFITABLE SEGMENT

Management sometimes needs to decide whether to eliminate an unprofitable business segment. Again, the key is to **focus on the data that change under the alternative courses of action.** To illustrate, assume that Martina Company manufactures tennis racquets in three models: Pro, Master, and Champ. Pro and Master are profitable lines, whereas Champ (highlighted in color in the table below) operates at a loss. Condensed income statement data are:

STUDY OBJECTIVE 7
Explain the factors that are relevant in deciding whether to eliminate an unprofitable segment.

Illustration 9-11
Segment income data

	Pro	Master	Champ	Total
Sales	$800,000	$300,000	$100,000	$1,200,000
Variable expenses	520,000	210,000	90,000	820,000
Contribution margin	280,000	90,000	10,000	380,000
Fixed expenses	80,000	50,000	30,000	160,000
Net income	$200,000	$ 40,000	$ (20,000)	$ 220,000

Helpful Hint A decision to discontinue a segment based solely on the bottom line—net loss—is inappropriate.

It might be expected that total net income will increase by $20,000 to $240,000 if the unprofitable line of racquets is eliminated. However, **it is possible for net income to decrease if the Champ line is discontinued.** The reason is that the fixed expenses allocated to the Champ racquets will have to be absorbed by the other products. To illustrate, assume that the $30,000 of fixed costs applicable to the unprofitable segment are allocated ⅔ and ⅓ to the Pro and Master product lines, respectively. Fixed expenses will increase to $100,000 ($80,000 + $20,000) in the Pro line and to $60,000 ($50,000 + $10,000) in the Master line. The revised income statement is:

Illustration 9-12 Income data after eliminating unprofitable product line

	Pro	Master	Total
Sales	$800,000	$300,000	$1,100,000
Variable expenses	520,000	210,000	730,000
Contribution margin	280,000	90,000	370,000
Fixed expenses	100,000	60,000	160,000
Net income	$180,000	$ 30,000	$ 210,000

Total net income has decreased $10,000 ($220,000 − $210,000). This result is also obtained in the following incremental analysis of the Champ racquets:

Illustration 9-13 Incremental analysis—eliminating an unprofitable segment

	Continue	Eliminate	Net Income Increase (Decrease)
Sales	$100,000	$ –0–	$(100,000)
Variable expenses	90,000	–0–	90,000
Contribution margin	10,000	–0–	(10,000)
Fixed expenses	30,000	30,000	–0–
Net income	$ (20,000)	$(30,000)	$ (10,000)

The loss in net income is attributable to the contribution margin ($10,000) that will not be realized if the segment is discontinued.

In deciding on the future status of an unprofitable segment, management should consider the effect of elimination on related product lines. It may be possible for continuing product lines to obtain some or all of the sales lost by the discontinued product line. In some businesses, services or products may be linked—for example, free checking accounts at a bank, or coffee at a donut shop. In addition, management should consider the effect of eliminating the product line on employees who may have to be discharged or retrained.

BUSINESS INSIGHT
Management Perspective

In 1994 Quaker Oats paid $1.7 billion for America's hottest new beverage company—Snapple. While some observers thought that Quaker Oats had overpaid, Quaker's management believed it was an exciting purchase because it would make a great strategic partner for Quaker Oats' famous sport drink—Gatorade. But Quaker Oats' timing couldn't have been worse. First, rather than buying Snapple when fruit drink consumption was on the rise, Quaker purchased Snapple when the trend had hit its peak. Second, at about the same time, Coke and Pepsi decided to begin producing and selling competing fruit and tea drinks. Worse yet, the processing methods used by Coke and Pepsi allowed them to produce their drinks much more inexpensively, undercutting Snapple's profit margin. In the end, Quaker Oats management decided to sell Snapple and take a $1.4 billion loss. Management stated that by ridding itself of Snapple, the company could reduce its debt burden and focus its remaining assets on its cereal brands and Gatorade.

DECISION TOOLKIT

Decision Checkpoints	Info Needed for Decision	Tool to Use for Decision	How to Evaluate Results
Which alternative should the company choose?	All relevant costs, opportunity costs, and sunk costs	Compare relevant cost of each alternative.	Choose the alternative that maximizes net income.

BEFORE YOU GO ON . . .

● **Review It**

1. Give three examples of how incremental analysis might be used.
2. What is the decision rule in deciding to sell or process products further?
3. How may the elimination of an unprofitable segment decrease the overall net income of a company?

● **Do It**

Cobb Company incurs a cost of $28 per unit, of which $18 is variable, to make a product that normally sells for $42. A foreign wholesaler offers to buy 5,000 units at $25 each. Cobb will incur shipping costs of $1 per unit. Compute the net income (loss) Cobb will realize by accepting the special order, assuming Cobb has excess operating capacity.

Reasoning: The decision in this case involves incremental analysis. Thus, Cobb must identify the revenues and costs that change by accepting the special order.

Solution:

	Reject	Accept	Net Income Increase (Decrease)
Revenues	$–0–	$125,000	$125,000
Costs	–0–	95,000*	(95,000)
Net income	$–0–	$ 30,000	$ 30,000

*(5,000 × $18) + (5,000 × $1)

Related exercise material: BE9-2, BE9-3, and E9-1.

SALES MIX

In our Chapter 5 discussion of cost-volume-profit analysis (CVP) we assumed that the company sold only a single product. One of the assumptions of CVP analysis is that if more than one product is involved, the sales mix of the products remains constant. **Sales mix** is the relative combination in which a company's products are sold. For example, if 2 units of Product A are sold for every 1 unit of Product B, the sales mix of the two products is 2:1.

STUDY OBJECTIVE

8

Explain the term "sales mix" and its effects in determining break-even sales.

BREAK-EVEN SALES

Break-even sales can be computed for a mix of two or more products by determining the **weighted average unit contribution margin of all the products.** To illustrate, we will assume that Vargo Video sells both VCRs and television sets (TVs) at the following per unit data:

Illustration 9-14 Per unit data—sales mix

Unit Data	VCRs	TVs
Selling price	$500	$800
Variable costs	300	400
Contribution margin	$200	$400
Sales mix	3	1

The total contribution margin for the sales mix of 3 VCRs to 1 TV is $1,000, which is computed as follows:

$$[(\$200 \times 3) + (\$400 \times 1)] = \$1,000$$

The weighted average unit contribution margin, which is total contribution margin divided by the number of units in the sales mix is $250, which is computed as follows:

$$\$1,000/4 \text{ units} = \$250$$

We then use the weighted average unit contribution margin to compute break-even sales as follows:

Illustration 9-15 Break-even formula—sales mix

Helpful Hint What are break-even sales in units if the sales mix is reversed? Answer: Total contribution margin = $1,400 ($200 + $1,200) Weighted average unit contrib. margin = $350 ($1,400 ÷ 4) Break-even units = 571 (rounded)

The computation of break-even sales in units for Vargo Video, assuming $200,000 of fixed costs, is as follows:

$$\$200,000 \div \$250 = 800 \text{ units}$$

Note that with our sales mix of 3 to 1, $\frac{3}{4}$ of the units sold will be VCRs and $\frac{1}{4}$ will be TVs. Therefore, in order to break even, Vargo Video must sell 600 VCRs ($\frac{3}{4} \times 800$) and 200 TVs ($\frac{1}{4} \times 800$). This can be verified by the following:

Illustration 9-16 Break-even proof—sales mix

Product	Unit Sales	×	Unit CM	=	Total CM
VCRs	600	×	$200	=	$120,000
TVs	200	×	400	=	80,000
	800				$200,000

Management should continually review the company's sales mix. At any level of units sold, **net income will be greater if more high contribution margin**

units are sold than low contribution margin units. For Vargo Video, the television sets produce the higher contribution margin. Consequently, if 300 TVs and 500 VCRs are sold, net income would be higher than in the current sales mix even though total units sold has not changed. An analysis of these relationships shows that a shift from low-margin sales to high-margin sales may increase net income, even though there is a decline in total units sold. Likewise, a shift from high- to low-margin sales may result in a decrease in net income, even though there is an increase in total units sold.

Helpful Hint Continue the preceding Helpful Hint: How many VCRs and TVs must be sold? Answer:
VCRs 143 (571 × $\frac{1}{4}$)
TVs 428 (571 × $\frac{3}{4}$)

DECISION TOOLKIT

Decision Checkpoints	Info Needed for Decision	Tool to Use for Decision	How to Evaluate Results
✔			👍
How many units of product A and product B do we need to sell to break even?	Fixed costs, weighted average contribution margin, sales mix	$\text{Break-even point in units} = \dfrac{\text{Fixed costs}}{\text{Weighted average contribution margin}}$	To determine number of units of Product A and B, allocate total units based on sales mix.

LIMITED RESOURCES

Everyone's resources are limited. The limited resource may be floor space in a retail store, or raw materials, direct labor hours, or machine capacity in a manufacturing company. When a company has limited resources, management must decide which products to make and sell in order to maximize net income.

To illustrate, assume that Collins Company manufactures deluxe and standard pen and pencil sets. The limiting resource is machine capacity, which is 3,600 hours per month. Relevant data consist of the following:

STUDY OBJECTIVE
9
Determine sales mix when a company has limited resources.

	Deluxe Sets	**Standard Sets**
Contribution margin per unit	$8	$6
Machine hours required per unit	.4	.2

Illustration 9-17
Contribution margin and machine hours

The deluxe sets may appear to be more profitable since they have a higher contribution margin ($8) than the standard sets ($6). However, note that the standard sets take fewer machine hours to produce than the deluxe sets. Therefore, it is necessary to find the **contribution margin per unit of limited resource,** in this case, contribution margin per machine hour. This is obtained by dividing the contribution margin per unit of each product by the number of units of the limited resource required for each product as shown in Illustration 9-18.

Helpful Hint CM alone is not enough to make this decision. The key factor is CM per limited resource.

	Deluxe Sets	**Standard Sets**
Contribution margin per unit (a)	$8	$6
Machine hours required (b)	.4	.2
Contribution margin per unit of limited resource (a) ÷ (b)	**$20**	**$30**

Illustration 9-18
Contribution margin per unit of limited resource

The computation shows that the standard sets have a higher contribution margin per unit of limited resource. This would suggest that, given sufficient demand for standard sets, the company should shift the sales mix to standard sets or increase machine capacity.

If Collins Company is able to increase machine capacity from 3,600 hours to 4,200 hours, the additional 600 hours could be used to produce either the standard or deluxe pen and pencil sets. The total contribution margin under each alternative is found by multiplying the machine hours by the contribution margin per unit of limited resource as shown below.

Illustration 9-19
Incremental analysis—
computation of total
contribution margin

	Produce Deluxe Sets	Produce Standard Sets
Machine hours (a)	600	600
Contribution margin per unit of limited resource (b)	$20	$30
Contribution margin (a) × (b)	$12,000	$18,000

From this analysis, we can see that to maximize net income, all of the increased capacity should be used to make and sell the standard sets.

BUSINESS INSIGHT
Management Perspective

When fragrance sales recently went flat, retailers turned up the heat on fragrance manufacturers. The amount of floor space devoted to fragrances was reduced, leaving fragrance manufacturers fighting each other for a smaller space. The retailer doesn't just choose the fragrance with the highest contribution margin, but instead, the fragrance with the highest contribution margin per square foot. In this game, a product with a lower contribution margin, but a higher turnover, could well be the winner.

DECISION TOOLKIT

Decision Checkpoints	Info Needed for Decision	Tool to Use for Decision	How to Evaluate Results
How many units of product A and B should we produce in light of a limited resource?	Contribution margin per unit, limited resource required per unit	$$\text{Contribution margin per unit of limited resource} = \frac{\text{Contribution margin per unit}}{\text{Limited resource per unit}}$$	Any additional capacity of limited resource should be applied toward the product with higher contribution margin per unit of limited resource.

OTHER CONSIDERATIONS IN DECISION MAKING

QUALITATIVE FACTORS

In this chapter we have focused primarily on the quantitative factors that affect a decision—those attributes that can be easily expressed in terms of numbers or dollars. However, many of the decisions involving incremental analysis have important qualitative features that, while not easily measured, should not be ignored. Consider, for example, the potential effects of the make-or-buy decision *or* of the decision to eliminate a line of business on existing employees and the community in which the plant is located. The cost savings that may be obtained from outsourcing or from eliminating a plant should be weighed against these qualitative attributes. Consider the cost of lost morale that might result. Al "Chainsaw" Dunlap was a so-called "turnaround" artist who went into many companies, identified inefficiencies (using incremental analysis techniques), and tried to correct these problems to improve corporate profitability. Along the way he laid off thousands of employees at numerous companies. At his most recent position as head of Sunbeam, it was Al Dunlap who eventually lost his job because his Draconian approach failed to improve Sunbeam's profitability. It was widely reported that Sunbeam's employees openly rejoiced for days after his departure. Clearly, qualitative factors can matter.

RELATIONSHIP OF INCREMENTAL ANALYSIS AND ACTIVITY-BASED COSTING

In Chapter 4 we noted that many companies have shifted to activity-based costing to allocate overhead costs to products. The primary reason for using activity-based costing is that it results in a more accurate allocation of overhead. That is, activity-based costing better associates the actual increase in overhead costs that results from the manufacture of each product. The concepts presented in this chapter are completely consistent with the use of activity-based costing. In fact, activity-based costing will result in better identification of relevant costs and, therefore, better incremental analysis.

BUSINESS INSIGHT
Management Perspective

The existence of excess plant capacity is frequently the incentive for management to add new products. Adding one new product may not add much incremental cost, but continuing to add products will at some point create new constraints, perhaps requiring additional investments in people, equipment, and facilities. The effects of product and product line proliferation are generally understood, but the effect on incremental overhead costs of *changes in servicing customers* is less understood. For example, if a company newly offers its customers the option of product delivery by case or by pallet, the new service may appear to be simple and low in cost. But, if the manufacturing process must be realigned to package in two different forms; if two sets of inventory records must be maintained; and if warehousing, handling, and shipping require two different arrangements or sets of equipment, the additional costs of this new option could be as high as a whole new product. If the customer service option were adopted for all products, the product line could effectively be doubled—but so might many overhead costs.

Source: Elizabeth Haas Edersheim and Joan Wilson, "Complexity at Consumer Goods Companies: Naming and Taming the Beast," *Journal of Cost Management*, Fall 1992, p. 27.

BEFORE YOU GO ON . . .

● **Review It**

1. State the formula for computing break-even sales in units when a company sells more than one product.
2. Explain how a company that shifts its sales mix might actually increase its net income even though the total number of units it sells declines.
3. What is the critical factor in allocating limited resources to various product lines?

*U*SING THE DECISION TOOLKIT

Suppose Hewlett-Packard Company must decide whether to make or buy some of its components from Solectron Corp. The cost of producing 50,000 electrical connectors for its printers is $110,000, broken down as follows:

| Direct materials | $60,000 | Variable overhead | $12,000 |
| Direct labor | 30,000 | Fixed overhead | 8,000 |

Instead of making the electrical connectors at an average cost per unit of $2.20 ($110,000 ÷ 50,000), the company has an opportunity to buy the connectors at $2.30 per unit. If the connectors are purchased, all variable costs and one-half of the fixed costs will be eliminated.

Instructions

(a) Prepare an incremental analysis showing whether the company should make or buy the electrical connectors.

(b) Will your answer be different if the released productive capacity will generate additional income of $25,000?

Solution

(a)	Make	Buy	Net Income Increase (Decrease)
Direct materials	$ 60,000	$ –0–	$ 60,000
Direct labor	30,000	–0–	30,000
Variable manufacturing costs	12,000	–0–	12,000
Fixed manufacturing costs	8,000	4,000	4,000
Purchase price	–0–	115,000	(115,000)
Total cost	$110,000	$119,000	$ (9,000)

This analysis indicates that Hewlett-Packard Company will incur $9,000 of additional costs if it buys the electrical connectors.

(b)	Make	Buy	Net Income Increase (Decrease)
Total cost	$110,000	$119,000	$(9,000)
Opportunity cost	25,000		25,000
Total cost	$135,000	$119,000	$16,000

Yes, the answer is different because the analysis shows that net income will be increased by $16,000 if the electrical connectors are purchased.

SUMMARY OF STUDY OBJECTIVES

1 *Identify the steps in management's decision-making process.* Management's decision-making process consists of (a) identifying the problem or opportunity, (b) assigning responsibility for the decision, (c) determining possible courses of action, (d) developing data relevant to each course of action, (e) making the decision, and (f) reviewing the results of the decision.

2 *Describe the concept of incremental analysis.* Incremental analysis is the process that is used to identify financial data that change under alternative courses of action. These data are relevant to the decision because they will vary in the future among the possible alternatives.

3 *Identify the relevant costs in accepting an order at a special price.* The relevant information in accepting an order at a special price is the difference between the variable manufacturing costs to produce the special order and expected revenues.

4 *Indicate the relevant costs in a make-or-buy decision.* In a make-or-buy decision, the relevant costs are (a) the variable manufacturing costs that will be saved, (b) the purchase price, and (c) opportunity costs.

5 *Give the decision rule in deciding whether to sell or process materials further.* The decision rule in deciding whether to sell or process materials further is:

process further as long as the incremental revenue from processing exceeds the incremental processing costs.

6 *Identify the factors to be considered in retaining or replacing equipment.* The factors to be considered in determining whether equipment should be retained or replaced are the effects on variable costs and the cost of the new equipment. In addition, any disposal value of the existing asset must be considered.

7 *Explain the factors that are relevant in deciding whether to eliminate an unprofitable segment.* In deciding whether to eliminate an unprofitable segment, it is necessary to determine the contribution margin, if any, produced by the segment and the disposition of the segment's fixed expenses.

8 *Explain the term "sales mix" and its effects in determining break-even sales.* Sales mix is the relative combination in which a company's products are sold. Break-even sales are determined by using the weighted average unit contribution margin of all the products.

9 *Determine sales mix when a company has limited resources.* When a company has limited resources, it is necessary to find the contribution margin per unit of limited resource. This amount is then multiplied by the units of limited resource to determine which product maximizes net income.

THE NAVIGATOR

DECISION TOOLKIT—A SUMMARY

Decision Checkpoints	Info Needed for Decision	Tool to Use for Decision	How to Evaluate Results
Which alternative should the company choose?	All relevant costs, opportunity costs, and sunk costs	Compare relevant cost of each alternative.	Choose the alternative that maximizes net income.
How many units of product A and product B do we need to sell to break even?	Fixed costs, weighted average contribution margin, sales mix	$$\text{Break-even point in units} = \frac{\text{Fixed costs}}{\text{Weighted average contribution margin}}$$	To determine number of units of Product A and B, allocate total units based on sales mix.
How many units of product A and B should we produce in light of a limited resource?	Contribution margin per unit, limited resource required per unit	$$\text{Contribution margin per unit of limited resource} = \frac{\text{Contribution margin per unit}}{\text{Limited resource per unit}}$$	Any additional capacity of limited resource should be applied toward the product with higher contribution margin per unit of limited resource.

GLOSSARY

Incremental analysis The process of identifying the financial data that change under alternative courses of action. (p. 345)

Opportunity cost The potential benefit that may be obtained from following an alternative course of action. (p. 346)

Relevant cost Those costs and revenues that differ across alternatives. (p. 346)

Sales mix The relative combination in which a company's products are sold. (p. 353)

Sunk cost A cost that cannot be changed by any present or future decision. (p. 346)

DEMONSTRATION PROBLEM

Carolina Corporation manufactures and sells three different types of high-quality sealed ball bearings. The bearings vary in terms of their quality specifications—primarily in terms of their smoothness and roundness. They are referred to as Fine, Extra-Fine, and Super-Fine bearings. Machine time is limited, and more machine time is required to manufacture the Extra-Fine and Super-Fine bearings. Additional information is provided below:

	Product		
	Fine	**Extra-Fine**	**Super-Fine**
Selling price	$6.00	$10.00	$16.00
Variable costs and expenses	4.00	6.50	11.00
Contribution margin	$2.00	$ 3.50	$ 5.00
Machine hours required	.02	.04	.08
Units sold	100,000	40,000	10,000
Sales mix	10	4	1

Total fixed costs: $234,000

Instructions

Answer each of the following questions:
1. What is the weighted-average unit contribution margin?
2. What is the break-even point using the current sales mix?
3. Ignoring the machine time constraint, what strategy would appear optimal?
4. What is the contribution margin per unit of limited resource for each type of bearing?
5. If additional machine time could be obtained, how should the additional capacity be used?

Problem-Solving Strategies

1. To compute the break-even point for a given sales mix, divide total fixed costs by the weighted-average unit contribution margin.

2. To determine how best to use a limited resource, calculate the contribution margin per unit of limited resource for each product type.

Solution to Demonstration Problem

1. The weighted-average unit contribution margin is determined by dividing the total contribution margin for this sales mix by the number of units:

Total contribution margin = $(10 \times \$2) + (4 \times \$3.50) + (1 \times \$5) = \$39$

Weighted-average unit contribution margin is computed as:

$$\frac{\text{Total contribution margin}}{\text{Number of units}} = \frac{\$39}{10 + 4 + 1} = \$2.60 \text{ per unit}$$

2. The break-even point given this sales mix is computed as:

$$\frac{\text{Fixed costs}}{\begin{array}{c}\text{Weighted-average unit}\\\text{contribution margin}\end{array}} = \frac{\$234,000}{\$2.60} = 90,000 \text{ units}$$

3. The Super-Fine bearings have the highest contribution margin per set. Thus, ignoring any manufacturing constraints, it would appear that the company should shift toward production of more Super-Fine units.

4. The contribution margin per unit of limited resource is calculated as:

	Fine	Extra-Fine	Super-Fine
$\dfrac{\text{Contribution margin per unit}}{\text{Limited resource consumed per unit}}$	$\dfrac{\$2}{.02} = \$100$	$\dfrac{\$3.5}{.04} = \$87.50$	$\dfrac{\$5}{.08} = \$62.50$

5. The Fine bearings have the highest contribution margin per limited resource, even though they have the lowest contribution margin per unit. Given the resource constraint, any additional capacity should be used to make Fine bearings.

THE
NAVIGATOR

SELF-STUDY QUESTIONS

Answers are at the end of the chapter.

(SO 1) 1. Three of the steps in management's decision process are (1) review results of decision, (2) determine and evaluate possible courses of action, and (3) make the decision. The steps are prepared in the following order:
(a) (1), (2), (3).
(b) (3), (2), (1).
(c) (2), (1), (3).
(d) (2), (3), (1).

(SO 2) 2. Incremental analysis is the process of identifying the financial data that:
(a) do not change under alternative courses of action.
(b) change under alternative courses of action.
(c) are mixed under alternative courses of action.
(d) No correct answer is given.

(SO 3) 3. It costs a company $14 of variable costs and $6 of fixed costs to produce product A that sells for $30. A foreign buyer offers to purchase 3,000 units at $18 each. If the special offer is accepted and produced with unused capacity, net income will:
(a) decrease $6,000.
(b) increase $6,000.
(c) increase $12,000.
(d) increase $9,000.

(SO 4) 4. In a make-or-buy decision, relevant costs are:
(a) manufacturing costs that will be saved.
(b) the purchase price of the units.
(c) opportunity costs.
(d) all of the above.

5. The decision rule in a sell-or-process-further (SO 5) decision is: process further as long as the incremental revenue from processing exceeds:
(a) incremental processing costs.
(b) variable processing costs.
(c) fixed processing costs.
(d) No correct answer is given.

6. In a decision to retain or replace equipment, (SO 6) the book value of the old equipment is a (an):
(a) opportunity cost.
(b) sunk cost.
(c) incremental cost.
(d) marginal cost.

7. If an unprofitable segment is eliminated: (SO 7)
(a) net income will always increase.
(b) variable expenses of the eliminated segment will have to be absorbed by other segments.
(c) fixed expenses allocated to the eliminated segment will have to be absorbed by other segments.
(d) net income will always decrease.

8. Keynes Company sells both radios and cassette (SO 8) players at the following per unit data:

Unit Data	Radios	Cassette Players
Selling price	$40	$70
Variable costs	35	50
Contribution margin	$ 5	$20
Sales mix	2	1

What is the number of radios and cassette players that Keynes must sell in order to break even if fixed costs are $45,000?

	Radios	Cassette Players
(a)	1,000	500
(b)	1,500	750
(c)	2,000	1,000
(d)	3,000	1,500

9. If the contribution margin per unit is $15 and (SO 9) it takes 3.0 machine hours to produce the unit, the contribution margin per unit of limited resource is:
(a) $25.
(b) $5.
(c) $4.
(d) No correct answer is given.

QUESTIONS

1. What steps are frequently involved in management's decision-making process?

2. Your roommate, John Ross, contends that accounting contributes to most of the steps in management's decision-making process. Is your roommate correct? Explain.

3. "Incremental analysis involves the accumulation of information concerning a single course of action." Do you agree? Why?

4. Ron Schoffer asks your help concerning the relevance of variable and fixed costs in incremental analysis. Help Ron with his problem.

5. What data are relevant in deciding whether to accept an order at a special price?

6. Roland Carlson Company has an opportunity to buy parts at $7 each that currently cost $10 to make. What manufacturing costs are relevant to this make-or-buy decision?

7. Define the term "opportunity cost." How may this cost be relevant in a make-or-buy decision?

8. What is the decision rule in deciding whether to sell a product or process it further?

9. Your roommate, John Lewis, is confused about sunk costs. Explain to your roommate the meaning of sunk costs and their relevance to a decision to retain or replace equipment.

10. Anita Ferraro Inc. has one product line that is unprofitable. What circumstances may cause overall company net income to be lower if the unprofitable product line is eliminated?

11. The sales mix of Oxford Company's two products is 5:2. What does 5:2 mean? What effect, if any, does a company's sales mix have on CVP analysis?

12. Zurhoff Company sells two products, X and Y. Their unit contribution margins are $52 and $70, respectively, and their sales mix is 2:1. What is the weighted average unit contribution margin?

13. How is the contribution margin per unit of limited resources computed?

BRIEF EXERCISES

Identify the steps in management's decision-making process.
(SO 1)

BE9-1 The steps in management's decision-making process are listed in random order below. Indicate the order in which the steps should be executed.

_____ Make decision
_____ Identify the opportunity or problem
_____ Assign responsibility for decision

_____ Review results of decision
_____ Determine possible courses of action
_____ Develop data relevant to each course of action

Determine incremental changes.
(SO 2)

BE9-2 Jeong Company is considering two alternatives. Alternative A will have sales of $150,000 and costs of $100,000. Alternative B will have sales of $180,000 and costs of $125,000. Compare Alternative A to Alternative B showing incremental revenues, costs, and net income.

Determine whether to accept a special order.
(SO 3)

BE9-3 In Essex Company it costs $30 per unit ($20 variable and $10 fixed) to make a product that normally sells for $45. A foreign wholesaler offers to buy 4,000 units at $25 each. Essex will incur special shipping costs of $1 per unit. Assuming that Essex has excess operating capacity, indicate the net income (loss) Essex would realize by accepting the special order.

BE9-4 Wirtz Manufacturing incurs unit costs of $8 ($5 variable and $3 fixed) in making a sub-assembly part for its finished product. A supplier offers to make 10,000 of the assembly part at $5.50 per unit. If the offer is accepted, Wirtz will save all variable costs but no fixed costs. Prepare an analysis showing the total cost saving, if any, Wirtz will realize by buying the part.

Determine whether to make or buy a part.
(SO 4)

BE9-5 Trujillo Inc. makes unfinished bookcases that it sells for $60. Production costs are $30 variable and $10 fixed. Because it has unused capacity, Trujillo is considering finishing the bookcases and selling them for $70. Variable finishing costs are expected to be $8 per unit with no increase in fixed costs. Prepare an analysis on a per unit basis showing whether Trujillo should sell unfinished or finished bookcases.

Determine whether to sell or process further.
(SO 5)

BE9-6 Roark Company has a factory machine with a book value of $90,000 and a remaining useful life of 4 years. A new machine is available at a cost of $200,000. This machine will have a 4-year useful life with no salvage value. The new machine will lower annual variable manufacturing costs from $600,000 to $420,000. Prepare an analysis showing whether the old machine should be retained or replaced.

Determine whether to retain or replace equipment.
(SO 6)

BE9-7 Parmely, Inc., manufactures golf clubs in three models. For the year, the Eagle line has a net loss of $20,000 from sales $200,000, variable expenses $180,000, and fixed expenses $40,000. If the Eagle line is eliminated, $28,000 of fixed costs will remain. Prepare an analysis showing whether the Eagle line should be eliminated.

Determine whether to eliminate an unprofitable segment.
(SO 7)

BE9-8 Loos Company sells three units of AA to one unit of BB; the two products have contribution margins of $100 and $200, respectively. Fixed costs are $300,000. Compute the unit sales at the break-even point. How many units of each product must be sold?

Compute break-even sales units for two products.
(SO 8)

BE9-9 In Cruz Company, data concerning two products are: Contribution margin per unit—Product A $10, Product B $12; machine hours required for one unit—Product A 2, Product B 3. Compute the contribution margin per unit of limited resource for each product.

Show allocation of limited resources.
(SO 9)

EXERCISES

E9-1 Giraldi Company manufactures toasters. For the first 8 months of 2000, the company reported the following operating results while operating at 75% of plant capacity:

Make incremental analysis for special order.
(SO 3)

Sales (400,000 units)	$4,000,000
Cost of goods sold	2,400,000
Gross profit	1,600,000
Operating expenses	900,000
Net income	$ 700,000

Cost of goods sold was 70% variable and 30% fixed; operating expenses were 60% variable and 40% fixed.

In September, Giraldi Company receives a special order for 15,000 toasters at $6.00 each from Alazar Company of Mexico City. Acceptance of the order would result in $3,000 of shipping costs but no increase in fixed operating expenses.

Instructions
(a) Prepare an incremental analysis for the special order.
(b) Should Giraldi Company accept the special order? Why or why not?

E9-2 Cinelli Inc. has been manufacturing its own shades for its table lamps. The company is currently operating at 100% of capacity, and variable manufacturing overhead is charged to production at the rate of 50% of direct labor cost. The direct materials and direct labor cost per unit to make the lamp shades are $4.00 and $6.00, respectively. Normal production is 30,000 table lamps per year.

A supplier offers to make the lamp shades at a price of $13.50 per unit. If Cinelli Inc. accepts the supplier's offer, all variable manufacturing costs will be eliminated, but the $40,000 of fixed manufacturing overhead currently being charged to the lamp shades will have to be absorbed by other products.

Make incremental analysis for make-or-buy decision.
(SO 4)

Instructions
(a) Prepare the incremental analysis for the decision to make or buy the lamp shades.
(b) ▭▭▭▷ Should Cinelli Inc. buy the lamp shades? *No*
(c) ▭▭▭▷ Would your answer be different in (b) if the productive capacity released by
not making the lamp shades could be used to produce income of $35,000?
yes — saving $20,000

Make incremental analysis for further processing of materials.
(SO 5)

E9-3   Debbie Sondgeroth recently opened her own basketweaving studio. She sells finished baskets in addition to the raw materials needed by customers to weave baskets of
their own. Debbie has put together a variety of raw material kits, each including materials at various stages of completion. Unfortunately, owing to space limitations, Debbie
is unable to carry all varieties of kits originally assembled and must choose between two
basic packages.

The basic introductory kit includes undyed, uncut reeds (with dye included) for weav-
ing one basket. This basic package costs Debbie $12 and sells for $27. The second kit,
called Stage 2, includes cut reeds that have already been dyed. With this kit the customer
need only soak the reeds and weave the basket. Debbie is able to produce the second kit
by using the basic materials included in the first kit and adding one hour of her own
time, which she values at $16 per hour. Because she is more efficient at cutting and dy-
ing reeds than her average customer, Debbie is able to make two kits of the dyed reeds,
in one hour, from one kit of undyed reeds. The kit of dyed and cut reeds sells for $32.

Instructions
Determine whether Debbie's basketweaving shop should carry the basic introductory kit
with undyed and uncut reeds or the Stage 2 kit with reeds already dyed and cut. Prepare
an incremental analysis to support your answer.

Make incremental analysis for retaining or replacing equipment.
(SO 6)

E9-4   Yan Enterprises uses a word processing computer to handle its sales invoices.
Lately, business has been so good that it takes an extra 3 hours per night, plus every third
Saturday, to keep up with the volume of sales invoices. Management is considering
updating its computer with a faster model that would eliminate all of the overtime
processing.

	Current Machine	**New Machine**
Original purchase cost	$15,000	$24,000
Accumulated depreciation	$ 6,000	—
Estimated operating costs	$21,000	$16,000
Useful life	5 years	5 years

If sold now, the current machine would have a salvage value of $3,000. If operated for
the remainder of its useful life, the current machine would have zero salvage value. The
new machine is expected to have zero salvage value after five years.

Instructions
Should the current machine be replaced? (Ignore the time value of money.)

Make incremental analysis concerning elimination of division.
(SO 7)

E9-5   Lisa Hollern, a recent graduate of Rolling's accounting program, evaluated the operating performance of Winser Company's six divisions. Lisa made the following presentation to Winser's Board of Directors and suggested the Hudson Division be eliminated.
"If the Hudson Division is eliminated," she said, "our total profits would increase by
$16,870."

	The Other Five Divisions	**Hudson Division**	**Total**
Sales	$1,664,200	$ 98,200	$1,762,400
Cost of goods sold	978,520	76,470	1,054,990
Gross profit	685,680	21,730	707,410
Operating expenses	527,940	38,600	566,540
Net income	$ 157,740	$(16,870)	$ 140,870

In the Hudson Division, cost of goods sold is $60,000 variable and $16,470 fixed, and operating expenses are $12,000 variable and $24,600 fixed. None of the Hudson Division's
fixed costs will be eliminated if the division is discontinued.

Instructions

◧▦▦▷ Is Lisa right about eliminating the Hudson Division? Prepare a schedule to support your answer.

E9-6   The following information is selected from the records of Oneida Company, which produces and sells two products:

Compute sales mix, weighted average unit contribution margin, and break-even point.

(SO 8)

	Product A	Product B
Selling price per unit	$ 9.00	$ 17.00
Units sold	100,000	50,000
Variable manufacturing cost per unit	$ 4.00	$ 9.00

Fixed manufacturing overhead costs are $248,000, and fixed selling and administrative expenses are $94,000.

Instructions

(a) Compute the sales mix for Oneida Company.
(b) Calculate the weighted average unit contribution margin.
(c) Compute the break-even point in units, assuming the sales mix computed in part (a).

E9-7   The Home Appliance Center sells three models of Super Clean dishwashers. Selling price and variable cost data for the models are as follows:

Compute and prove the break-even point in units with sales mix.

(SO 8)

	Economy	Standard	Deluxe
Unit selling price	$600	$750	$1,000
Unit variable costs	$400	$500	$ 600
Expected sales volume (units)	500	300	200

Instructions

(a) Compute the break-even point in units, assuming total fixed costs are $229,500.
(b) Prove the correctness of your answer.

E9-8   Lazarus Company manufactures and sells three products. Relevant per unit data concerning each product are given below:

Compute contribution margin and determine the product to be manufactured.

(SO 9)

	Product		
	A	B	C
Selling price	$8	$12	$14
Variable costs and expenses	$4	$ 9	$12
Machine hours to produce	2	1	2

Instructions

(a) Compute the contribution margin per unit of the limited resource (machine hour) for each product.
(b) Assuming 1,500 additional machine hours are available, which product should be manufactured?
(c) Prepare an analysis showing the total contribution margin if the additional hours are (1) divided equally among the products, and (2) allocated entirely to the product identified in (b) above.

PROBLEMS: SET A

P9-1A   All Sports Inc. manufactures basketballs for the National Basketball Association (NBA). For the first 6 months of 2000, the company reported the following operating results while operating at 90% of plant capacity.

Make incremental analysis for special order and identify nonfinancial factors in decision.

(SO 3)

	Amount	Per Unit
Sales	$4,500,000	$50.00
Cost of goods sold	3,600,000	40.00
Selling and administrative expenses	360,000	4.00
Net income	$ 540,000	$ 6.00

Fixed costs for the period were: cost of goods sold $900,000, and selling and administrative expenses $180,000.

In July, normally a slack manufacturing month, All Sports receives a special order for 10,000 basketballs at $34 each from the Italian Basketball Association (IBA). Acceptance of the order would increase variable selling and administrative expenses $.35 per unit because of shipping costs but would not increase fixed costs and expenses.

Instructions
(a) Prepare an incremental analysis for the special order.
(b) Should All Sports Inc. accept the special order?
(c) What is the minimum selling price on the special order to produce net income of $2.50 per ball?
(d) ▭▭▭▷ What nonfinancial factors should management consider in making its decision?

Make incremental analysis related to make or buy; consider opportunity cost and identify nonfinancial factors.
(SO 4)

P9-2A The management of Francona Manufacturing Company is trying to decide whether to continue manufacturing a part or to buy it from an outside supplier. The part, called WISCO, is a component of the company's finished product.

The following information was collected from the accounting records and production data for the year ending December 31, 2000:
1. 7,000 units of WISCO were produced in the Machining Department.
2. Variable manufacturing costs applicable to the production of each WISCO unit were: direct materials $4.75, direct labor $4.60, indirect labor $0.45, utilities $0.35.
3. Fixed manufacturing costs applicable to the production of WISCO were:

Cost Item	Direct	Allocated
Depreciation	$1,600	$ 900
Property taxes	400	200
Insurance	900	600
	$2,900	$1,700

All variable manufacturing and direct fixed costs will be eliminated if WISCO is purchased. Allocated costs will have to be absorbed by other production departments.
4. The lowest quotation for 7,000 WISCO units from a supplier is $75,000.
5. If WISCO units are purchased, freight and inspection costs would be $0.30 per unit, and receiving costs totaling $750 per year would be incurred by the Machining Department.

Instructions
(a) Prepare an incremental analysis for WISCO. Your analysis should have columns for (1) Make WISCO, (2) Buy WISCO, and (3) Net Income Increase/Decrease.
(b) Based on your analysis, what decision should management make?
(c) Would the decision be different if Francona Company has the opportunity to produce $4,000 of net income with the facilities currently being used to manufacture WISCO? Show computations.
(d) ▭▭▭▷ What nonfinancial factors should management consider in making its decision?

Compute contribution margin and prepare incremental analysis concerning elimination of divisions.
(SO 7)

P9-3A Bailor Manufacturing Company has four operating divisions. During the first quarter of 2000, the company reported aggregate income from operations of $145,000 and the following divisional results:

	Division			
	I	**II**	**III**	**IV**
Sales	$490,000	$410,000	$300,000	$190,000
Cost of goods sold	300,000	250,000	280,000	180,000
Selling and administrative expenses	60,000	80,000	35,000	60,000
Income (loss) from operations	$130,000	$ 80,000	$ (15,000)	$ (50,000)

Analysis reveals the following percentages of variable costs in each division.

	I	II	III	IV
Cost of goods sold	70%	80%	75%	90%
Selling and administrative expenses	40	50	60	70

Discontinuance of any division would save 50% of the fixed costs and expenses for that division.

Top management is very concerned about the unprofitable divisions (III and IV). Consensus is that one or both of the divisions should be discontinued.

Instructions
(a) Compute the contribution margin for Divisions III and IV.
(b) Prepare an incremental analysis concerning the possible discontinuance of (1) Division III and (2) Division IV. What course of action do you recommend for each division?
(c) Prepare a columnar condensed income statement for Bailor Manufacturing, assuming Division IV is eliminated. Use the CVP format. Division IV's unavoidable fixed costs are allocated equally to the continuing divisions.
(d) Reconcile the total income from operations ($145,000) with the total income from operations without Division IV.

P9-4A Bret Shumway Company manufactures two models of televisions, Superclear and Ultraclear. Unit data for each model are as follows:

Compute contribution margin ratio, break-even point, and sales to meet target net income.

(SO 8)

	Superclear	**Ultraclear**
Selling price	$360	$480
Variable costs and expenses:		
Direct materials	90	95
Direct labor	50	60
Manufacturing overhead	60	68
Selling	32	36
Administrative	20	29
Total variable	$252	$288

Monthly fixed costs are: manufacturing overhead $72,000; selling expenses $46,000; and administrative expenses $26,000.

Instructions
(a) Compute the contribution margin ratio for each model.
(b) Compute the break-even point in dollars for each model using the contribution margin ratio, assuming fixed costs are divided equally between the products.
(c) Compute the sales necessary to make net income of $36,000 on Superclear and $48,000 on Ultraclear. Each model incurs 50% of all fixed costs.

PROBLEMS: SET B

P9-1B Escobar Company is currently producing 15,000 units per month, which is 75% of its production capacity. Variable manufacturing costs are currently $11.00 per unit, and fixed manufacturing costs are $48,000 per month. Escobar pays a 9% sales commission to its sales people, has $30,000 in fixed administrative expenses per month, and is averaging $300,000 in sales per month.

Make incremental analysis for special order and identify nonfinancial factors in decisions.

(SO 3)

A special order received from a foreign company would enable Escobar Company to operate at 100% capacity. The foreign company offered to pay 75% of Escobar's current selling price per unit. If the order is accepted, Escobar will have to spend an extra $2.00 per unit to package the product for overseas shipping. Also, Escobar Company would need to lease a new stamping machine to imprint the foreign company's logo on the product, at a monthly cost of $2,500. The special order would require a sales commission of $3,000.

Instructions

(a) Compute the number of units involved in the special order and the foreign company's offered price per unit.

(b) What is the manufacturing cost of producing one unit of Escobar's product for regular customers?

(c) Prepare an incremental analysis of the special order. Should management accept the order?

(d) What is the lowest price that Escobar could accept for the special order to earn net income of $1.20 per unit?

(e) ▭▭▭▭▶ What nonfinancial factors should management consider in making its decision?

Make incremental analysis related to make or buy, consider opportunity cost, and identify nonfinancial factors.

(SO 4)

P9-2B   The management of Mareno Manufacturing Company has asked for your assistance in deciding whether to continue manufacturing a part or to buy it from an outside supplier. The part, called Tropica, is a component of Mareno's finished product.

An analysis of the accounting records and the production data revealed the following information for the year ending December 31, 1999:

1. The Machinery Department produced 36,000 units of Tropica.

2. Each Tropica unit requires 10 minutes to produce. Three people in the Machinery Department work full time (2,000 hours per year) producing Tropica. Each person is paid $10.00 per hour.

3. The cost of materials per Tropica unit is $2.00.

4. Manufacturing costs directly applicable to the production of Tropica are: indirect labor, $5,500; utilities, $1,300; depreciation, $1,600; property taxes and insurance, $1,000. All of the costs will be eliminated if Tropica is purchased.

5. The lowest price for a Tropica from an outside supplier is $3.50 per unit. Freight charges will be $0.30 per unit, and a part-time receiving clerk at $8,500 per year will be required.

6. If Tropica is purchased, the excess space will be used to store Mareno's finished product. Currently, Mareno rents storage space at approximately $0.60 per unit stored per year. Approximately 4,500 units per year are stored in the rented space.

Instructions

(a) Prepare an incremental analysis for the make or buy decision. Should Mareno make or buy the part? Why?

(b) Prepare an incremental analysis, assuming the released facilities can be used to produce $10,000 of net income in addition to the savings on the rental of storage space. What decision should now be made?

(c) ▭▭▭▭▶ What nonfinancial factors should be considered in the decision?

Compute contribution margin and prepare incremental analysis concerning elimination of divisions.

(SO 7)

P9-3B   Modine Manufacturing Company has four operating divisions. During the first quarter of 1999, the company reported total income from operations of $61,000 and the following results for the divisions:

	Division			
	Denver	**Helena**	**Portland**	**Seattle**
Sales	$440,000	$730,000	$920,000	$520,000
Cost of goods sold	380,000	480,000	576,000	420,000
Selling and administrative expenses	120,000	207,000	246,000	120,000
Income (loss) from operations	$ (60,000)	$ 43,000	$ 98,000	$ (20,000)

Analysis reveals the following percentages of variable costs in each division.

	Denver	**Helena**	**Portland**	**Seattle**
Cost of goods sold	95%	80%	90%	90%
Selling and administrative expenses	80	60	70	60

Discontinuance of any division would save 60% of the fixed costs and expenses for that division.

Top management is deeply concerned about the unprofitable divisions (Denver and Seattle). The consensus is that one or both of the divisions should be eliminated.

Instructions

(a) Compute the contribution margin for the two unprofitable divisions.

(b) Prepare an incremental analysis concerning the possible elimination of (1) the Denver Division and (2) the Seattle Division. What course of action do you recommend for each division?

(c) Prepare a columnar condensed income statement using the CVP format for Modine Manufacturing Company, assuming (1) the Denver Division is eliminated, and (2) the unavoidable fixed costs and expenses of the Denver Division are allocated 30% to Helena, 50% to Portland, and 20% to Seattle.

(d) Compare the total income from operations with the Denver Division ($61,000) to total income from operations without this division.

P9-4B Precision Electronics manufactures two models of cameras, Superfast and Ultrafast. Unit data for each model are as follows:

Compute contribution margin ratio, break-even point, and sales to meet target net income.

(SO 8)

	Superfast	Ultrafast
Selling price	$240	$330
Variable costs and expenses:		
Direct materials	60	60
Direct labor	40	70
Manufacturing overhead	34	36
Selling	20	25
Administrative	26	29
Total variable	$180	$220

Monthly fixed costs are: manufacturing overhead $45,000; selling expenses $35,000; and administrative expenses $20,000.

Instructions

(a) Compute the contribution margin ratio for each model.

(b) Compute the break-even point in dollars for each model using the contribution margin ratio, assuming fixed costs are divided equally between the products.

(c) Compute the sales necessary to make net income of $25,000 on Superfast and $40,000 on Ultrafast. Each model incurs 50% of the fixed costs.

BROADENING YOUR PERSPECTIVE

GROUP DECISION CASE

BYP9-1 Sanchez Company is considering the purchase of a new machine. The invoice price of the machine is $115,000, freight charges are estimated to be $4,000, and installation costs are expected to be $6,000. Salvage value of the new equipment is expected to be zero after a useful life of 4 years. Existing equipment could be retained and used for an additional 4 years if the new machine is not purchased. At that time, the salvage value of the equipment would be zero. If the new machine is purchased now, the existing machine would have to be scrapped. Sanchez's accountant, Diane Gallup, has accumulated the following data regarding annual sales and expenses with and without the new machine:

1. Without the new machine, Sanchez can sell 11,000 units of product annually at a per unit selling price of $100. If the new unit is purchased, the number of units produced and sold would increase by 20%, and the selling price would remain the same.

2. The new machine is faster than the old machine, and it is more efficient in its usage of materials. With the old machine the gross profit rate will be 27.5% of sales, whereas the rate will be 29% of sales with the new machine.

3. Annual selling expenses are $180,000 with the current equipment. Because the new equipment would produce a greater number of units to be sold, annual selling expenses are expected to increase by 10% if it is purchased.

4. Annual administrative expenses are expected to be $100,000 with the old machine, and $113,000 with the new machine.

5. The current book value of the existing machine is $36,000. Sanchez uses straight-line depreciation.

Instructions

With the class divided into groups, prepare an incremental analysis for the 4 years showing whether Sanchez should keep the existing machine or buy the new machine. (Ignore income tax effects.)

MANAGERIAL ANALYSIS

BYP9-2 Electro-More manufactures private-label small electronic products, such as alarm clocks, calculators, kitchen timers, stopwatches, and automatic pencil sharpeners. Some of the products are sold as sets, and others are sold individually. Products are studied as to their sales potential, and then cost estimates are made. The Engineering Department develops production plans, and then production begins. The company has generally had very successful product introduction. Only two products introduced by the company have been discontinued.

One of the products currently sold is a multi-alarm alarm clock. The clock has four alarms that can be programmed to sound at various times and for varying lengths of time. The company has experienced a great deal of difficulty in making the circuit boards for the clocks. The production process has never operated smoothly. The product is unprofitable at the present time, primarily because of warranty repairs and product recalls. Two models of the clocks were recalled, for example, because they sometimes caused an electric shock when the alarms were being shut off. The Engineering Department is attempting to revise the manufacturing process, but the revision will take another 6 months at least.

The clocks were very popular when they were introduced, and since they are private-label, the company has not suffered much from the recalls. Presently, the company has a very large order for several items from Kmart Stores. The order includes 5,000 of the multi-alarm clocks. When the company suggested that Kmart purchase the clocks from another manufacturer, Kmart threatened to rescind the entire order unless the clocks were included.

The company has therefore investigated the possibility of having another company make the clocks for them. The clocks were bid for the Kmart order based on an estimated $5 cost to manufacture:

Circuit board, 1 each @ $1.50	$1.50
Plastic case, 1 each @ $0.50	0.50
Alarms, 4 @ $0.10 each	0.10
Labor, 15 minutes @ $10/hour	2.50
Overhead, $1.60 per labor hour	0.40

Electro-More could purchase clocks to fill the Kmart order for $10 from Silver Star, a Korean manufacturer with a very good quality record. Silver Star has offered to reduce the price to $7.50 after Electro-More has been a customer for 6 months, placing an order of at least 1,000 units per month. If Electro-More becomes a "preferred customer" by purchasing 15,000 units per year, the price would be reduced still further to $4.50.

Alpha Products, a local manufacturer, has also offered to make clocks for Electro-More. They have offered to sell 5,000 clocks for $3 each. However, Alpha Products has been in business for only 6 months. They have experienced significant turnover in their labor force, and the local press has reported that the owners may face tax evasion charges soon. The owner of Alpha Products is an electronic engineer, however, and the quality of the clocks is likely to be good.

If Electro-More decides to purchase the clocks from either Silver Star or Alpha, all the costs to manufacture could be avoided, except a total of $5,000 in overhead costs for machine depreciation. The machinery is fairly new, and has no alternate use.

Instructions
(a) What is the difference in profit under each of the alternatives if the clocks are to be sold for $12.50 each to Kmart?
(b) What are the most important nonfinancial factors that Electro-More should consider when making this decision?
(c) What do you think Electro-More should do in regard to the Kmart order? What should it do in regard to continuing to manufacture the multi-alarm alarm clocks? Be prepared to defend your answer.

REAL-WORLD FOCUS

BEVERLY HILLS FAN COMPANY

BYP9-3 Founded in 1983, the **Beverly Hills Fan Company** is located in Woodland Hills, California. With 23 employees and sales of less than $10 million, the company is relatively small. Management feels that there is potential for growth in the upscale market for ceiling fans and lighting. They are particularly optimistic about growth in Mexican and Canadian markets.

Presented below is information from the president's letter in the company's annual report:

BEVERLY HILLS FAN COMPANY
President's Letter

An aggressive product development program was initiated during the past year resulting in new ceiling fan models planned for introduction in 1993. Award winning industrial designer Ron Rezek created several new fan models for the Beverly Hills Fan and L.A. Fan lines, including a new Showroom Collection, designed specifically for the architectural and designer markets. Each of these models has received critical acclaim, and order commitments for 1993 have been outstanding. Additionally, our Custom Color and special order fans continued to enjoy increasing popularity and sales gains as more and more customers desire fans that match their specific interior decors. Currently, Beverly Hills Fan Company offers a product line of over 100 models of contemporary, traditional, and transitional ceiling fans.

Instructions
(a) What points did the company management need to consider before deciding to offer the special-order fans to customers?
(b) How would incremental analysis be employed to assist in this decision?

COMMUNICATION ACTIVITY

BYP9-4 Harvey Mudd is a production manager at a metal fabricating plant. Last night he read an article about a new piece of equipment that would dramatically reduce his divisions costs. Harvey was very excited about the prospect, and the first thing he did this morning was to bring the article to his supervisor, Nathan Peas, the plant manager. The following conversation occurred:

Harvey: Nathan, I thought you would like to see this article on the new PDD1130; they've made some fantastic changes that could save us millions of dollars.

Nathan: I appreciate your interest Harvey, but I actually have been aware of the new machine for two months. The problem is that we just bought a new machine last year. We spent $2 million on that machine, and it was supposed to last us 12 years. If we replace it now we would have to write its book value off of the books for a huge loss. If I go to top management now and say that I want a new machine, they will fire me. I think we should use our existing machine for a couple of years, and then when it becomes obvious that we have to have a new machine, I will make the proposal.

Instructions
Harvey just completed a course in managerial accounting, and he believes that Nathan is making a big mistake. Write a memo from Harvey to Nathan explaining Nathan's decision making error.

RESEARCH ASSIGNMENT

BYP9-5 The April 1998 issue of *Management Accounting* includes an article by Julie Hertenstein and Marjorie Platt entitled "Why Product Development Teams Need Management Accountants."

Instructions
Read the article and answer the following questions:
(a) What percentage of a product's cost are determined at the design stage?
(b) Why do the authors say that management accountants can provide a broader perspective on costs than purchasing managers?
(c) What are some of the roles and responsibilities that management accountants can have on a design team?
(d) What are some nonfinancial measures used to evaluate industrial design performance?

ETHICS CASE

BYP9-6 Harold Dean became Chief Executive Officer of Wriston Manufacturing two years ago. At the time, the company was reporting lagging profits, and Harold was brought in to "stir things up." The company has three divisions, electronics, fiber optics, and plumbing supplies. Harold has no interest in plumbing supplies, and one of the first things he did was to put pressure on his accountants to reallocate some of the company's fixed costs away from the other two divisions to the plumbing division. This had the effect of causing the plumbing division to report losses during the last two years; in the past it had always reported low, but acceptable, net income. Harold felt that this reallocation would shine a favorable light on him in front of the board of directors because it meant that the electronics and fiber optics divisions would look like they were improving. Given that these are "businesses of the future," he believed that the stock market would react favorably to these increases, while not penalizing the poor results of the plumbing division. Without this shift in the allocation of fixed costs, the profits of the electronics and fiber optics divisions would not have improved. But now the board of directors has suggested that the plumbing division be closed because it is reporting losses. This would mean that nearly 500 employees, many of whom have worked for Wriston their whole lives, would lose their jobs.

Instructions
(a) If a division is reporting losses, does that necessarily mean that it should be closed?
(b) Was the reallocation of fixed costs across divisions unethical?
(c) What should Harold do?

SURFING THE NET

BYP9-7 Productivity Enhancement Products (PEP), Inc., specializes in providing rapid, made-to-order product outsourcing from start to finish for hand-held devices and single-board computers. PEP also offers a variety of specialized products and services, including fast data encryption devices and "smart card" systems. PEP's products have applications in the security, factory data collection, and telecommunications industries.

Address: http://www.pepinc.com

Steps:
Go to the web page of PEP, Inc., at the address shown above.

Instructions
Answer the following questions:
1. What are four types of problems that PEP says it can solve for its clients?
2. Name five clients that PEP has served.
3. Where is PEP's headquarters located? In order for PEP to provide design and manufacturing assistance, must the client be in close proximity?

Answers to Self-Study Questions
1. d   2. b   3. c   4. d   5. a   6. b   7. c   8. d   9. b

Remember to go back to the Navigator box on the chapter-opening page and check off your completed work.

CHAPTER 10

Capital Budgeting

STUDY OBJECTIVES

After studying this chapter, you should be able to:

1. Discuss the capital budgeting evaluation process and explain what inputs are used in capital budgeting.

2. Describe the cash payback technique.

3. Explain the net present value method.

4. Identify the challenges presented by intangible benefits in capital budgeting.

5. Describe the profitability index.

6. Indicate the benefits of performing a post-audit.

7. Explain the internal rate of return method.

8. Describe the annual rate of return method.

THE NAVIGATOR

FEATURE STORY

Soup Is Good Food

When you hear the word *Campbell's,* what is the first thing that comes to mind? Soup. Campbell's *is* soup. It sells 38 percent of all the soup—including homemade—consumed in the United States. But can a company survive on soup alone? In an effort to expand its operations and to lessen its reliance on soup, Campbell Soup Company began searching for an additional line of business in 1990. Campbell's management believed it saw an opportunity in convenient meals that were low in fat, nutritionally rich, and had therapeutic value for heart patients and diabetics. This venture would require a huge investment—but the rewards were potentially tremendous.

The initial investment required building food labs, hiring nutritional scientists, researching prototype products, constructing new production facilities, and marketing the new products. Management predicted that with an initial investment of roughly $55 million, the company might generate sales of $200 million per year.

By 1994 the company had created 24 meals, and an extensive field-study revealed considerable health benefits from the products. Unfortunately, initial sales of the new product line, called Intelligent Quisine, were less than stellar. In 1997 a consulting firm was hired to evaluate whether the project should be continued. Product development of the new line was costing $20 million per year—a sum that

some managers felt could be better spent developing new products in other divisions, or expanding overseas operations. In 1998 the project was discontinued.

Campbell's is not giving up on growth, but simply has decided to refocus its efforts on soup. The company's annual report stated management's philosophy: "Soup will be our growth engine." Campbell's will sell many of its non-soup businesses and in a recent year introduced 20 new soup products.

THE NAVIGATOR

Source: Vanessa O'Connell, "Food for Thought: How Campbell Saw a Breakthrough Menu Turn into Leftovers," *The Wall Street Journal,* October 6, 1998.

On the World Wide Web
http://www.campbellsoup.com

374

THE NAVIGATOR ✔

- Scan *Study Objectives* ☐
- Read *Feature Story* ☐
- Read *Preview* ☐
- Read text and answer *Before You Go On*
  p. 383 ☐   p. 393 ☐
- Work *Using the Decision Toolkit* ☐
- Review *Summary of Study Objectives* ☐
- Work *Demonstration Problem* ☐
- Answer *Self-Study Questions* ☐
- Complete assignments ☐

Companies like Campbell Soup must constantly determine how to invest their resources. Other examples: Hollywood studios recently built 25 new sound stage projects to allow for additional filming in future years. Starwood Hotels and Resorts Worldwide, Inc., committed a total of $1 billion in 1998 and 1999 to renovate its existing hotel properties, while, at roughly the same time, the hotel industry canceled about $2 billion worth of *new* construction scheduled through the year 2000. And Union Pacific Resources Group Inc. announced that it would cut its 1998 capital budget by 19 percent in order to use the funds to reduce its outstanding debt.

The process of making such capital expenditure decisions is referred to as **capital budgeting.** Capital budgeting involves choosing among various capital projects to find the one(s) that will maximize a company's return on its financial investment. The purpose of this chapter is to discuss the various techniques used to make effective capital budgeting decisions. The content and organization of this chapter are as follows:

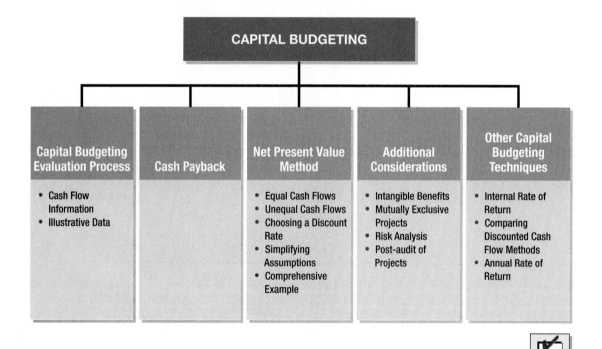

THE NAVIGATOR

THE CAPITAL BUDGETING EVALUATION PROCESS

STUDY OBJECTIVE
1

Discuss the capital budgeting evaluation process, and explain what inputs are used in capital budgeting.

Many companies follow a carefully prescribed process in capital budgeting. At least once a year, proposals for projects are requested from each department and plant and from authorized personnel. The proposals are screened by a capital budgeting committee, which submits its findings to the officers of the company. The officers, in turn, select the projects they believe to be most worthy of funding and submit them to the board of directors. Ultimately, the directors approve the capital expenditure budget for the year. This process is shown in Illustration 10-1.

Illustration 10-1
Corporate capital budget
authorization process

1. Project proposals are requested from departments, plants, and authorized personnel.

2. Proposals are screened by a capital budget committee.

3. Officers determine which projects are worthy of funding.

4. Board of directors approves capital budget.

The involvement of top management and the board of directors in the process demonstrates the importance of capital budgeting decisions. These decisions often have a significant impact on a company's future profitability. Indeed, poor capital budgeting decisions can cost a lot of money, as the Campbell Soup story demonstrated, and have even led to the bankruptcy of some companies.

BUSINESS INSIGHT
Investor Perspective

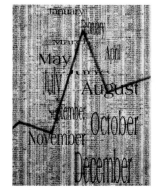

Monitoring capital expenditure amounts is one way to learn about a company's growth potential. Few companies can grow if they don't make significant capital investments. Here is a list of well-known companies and their amounts and types of capital expenditures in recent years.

Company Name	Amount	Type of Expenditure
Dell Computer Corporation	$180 million	Construct and equip manufacturing and office facilities
Sears Roebuck and Co.	$1,400 million	Opening 30 new full-line stores and 100 speciality stores
NIKE, Inc.	$466 million	Warehouse locations, management information systems, and world headquarters expansion
Campbell Soup Company	$375 million	Acquisitions and plant expansions
Barrick Gold Corporation	$510 million	Land acquisition and mine expansion

CASH FLOW INFORMATION

In this chapter we will look at several methods that help companies make effective capital budgeting decisions. Most of these methods employ **cash flow numbers** rather than accrual accounting revenues and expenses. Remember from your financial accounting course that accrual accounting records *revenues* and *expenses,* rather than cash inflows and cash outflows. In fact, revenues and expenses measured during a period often differ significantly from their cash flow counterparts. While accrual accounting has advantages over cash accounting in many contexts, **for purposes of capital budgeting, estimated cash inflows and outflows are preferred** for inputs into the capital budgeting decision tools. Ultimately, the value of all financial investments is determined by the value of cash flows received and paid. Some typical cash outflows and inflows related to equipment purchase and replacement are listed in Illustration 10-2.

Illustration 10-2   Typical cash flows relating to capital budgeting decisions

Cash Outflows

Initial investment
Repairs and maintenance
Increased operating costs
Overhaul of equipment

Cash Inflows

Sale of old equipment
Increased cash received from customers
Reduced cash outflows related to operating costs
Salvage value of equipment when project is complete

These cash flows are the inputs that are considered relevant in capital budgeting decisions.

The capital budgeting decision, under any technique, depends in part on a variety of considerations:

- *The availability of funds:* Does the company have unlimited funds or will it have to ration capital investments?
- *Relationships among proposed projects:* Are proposed projects independent of each other, or does the acceptance/rejection of one depend on the acceptance/rejection of another?
- *The company's basic decision-making approach:* Does the company want to produce an accept-reject decision, or a ranking of desirability among possible projects?
- *The risk associated with a particular project:* How certain are the projected returns? The certainty of estimates varies with such issues as market considerations or the length of time before returns are expected.

ILLUSTRATIVE DATA

For our initial discussion of quantitative techniques, we will use a continuing example so that we can easily compare the results of the various techniques. Assume that Stewart Soup Company is considering an investment of $130,000 in new equipment. The new equipment is expected to last 10 years and have a zero salvage value at the end of its useful life. The annual cash inflows are $200,000 and the annual net cash outflows are $176,000. These data are summarized in Illustration 10-3.

Illustration 10-3
Investment information for Stewart Soup example

Initial investment	$130,000
Estimated useful life	10 years
Estimated salvage value	–0–
Estimated annual cash flows:	
Cash inflows from customers	$200,000
Cash outflows for operating costs	176,000
Net annual cash inflow	$ 24,000

In the following two sections we will examine two popular techniques: cash payback and the net present value method.

CASH PAYBACK

The **cash payback technique** identifies the time period required to recover the cost of the capital investment from the annual cash inflow produced by the investment. The formula for computing the cash payback period is:

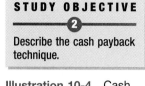

Illustration 10-4   Cash payback formula

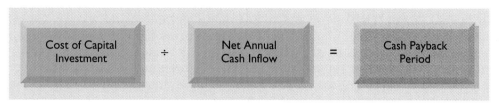

The cash payback period in the Stewart Soup example is therefore 5.42 years, computed as follows:

$$\$130{,}000 \div \$24{,}000 = 5.42 \text{ years}$$

The evaluation of the payback period is often related to the expected useful life of the asset. For example, assume that at Stewart Soup a project is unacceptable if the payback period is longer than 60% of the asset's expected useful life. The 5.42-year payback period in this case is a bit over 50% of the project's expected useful life. Thus, the project is acceptable. It follows that when the payback technique is used to decide among acceptable alternative projects, **the shorter the payback period, the more attractive the investment.** The reason is that: (1) the earlier the investment is recovered, the sooner the cash funds can be used for other purposes, and (2) the risk of loss from obsolescence and changed economic conditions is less in a shorter payback period.

The cash payback technique may be useful as an initial screening tool. It also may be the most critical factor in the capital budgeting decision for a company that desires a fast turnaround of its investment because of a weak cash position. It also is relatively easy to compute and understand. However, cash payback should not ordinarily be the only basis for the capital budgeting decision because it ignores the expected profitability of the project. To illustrate, assume that Projects A and B have the same payback period, but Project A's useful life is double the useful life of Project B. Project A's earning power, therefore, is twice as long as Project B's. A further disadvantage of this technique is that it ignores the time value of money.

NET PRESENT VALUE METHOD

Recognition of the time value of money can make a significant difference in the long-term impact of the capital budgeting decision. For example, cash flows that occur early in the life of an investment will be worth more than those that occur later—because of the time value of money. Therefore it is useful to recognize the timing of cash flows when evaluating projects. Capital budgeting techniques that take into account both the time value of money and the estimated total cash flows from an investment are called **discounted cash flow techniques.** They are gen-

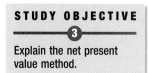

erally recognized as the most informative and best conceptual approaches to making capital budgeting decisions. The expected total cash inflow calculated in discounted cash flow techniques consists of the sum of the annual cash inflows plus the estimated liquidation proceeds—**salvage value**—when the asset is sold for salvage at the end of its useful life. The primary capital budgeting method that uses discounted cash flow techniques is called **net present value.** A second method, discussed later in the chapter, is the **internal rate of return.** At this point, before you read on, **we recommend that you examine Appendix C** to review time value of money concepts, upon which these methods are based.

Under the net present value (NPV) method, cash inflows are discounted to their present value and then compared with the capital outlay required by the investment. The difference between these two amounts is referred to as **net present value (NPV).** The interest rate to be used in discounting the future cash inflows is the required minimum rate of return. **A proposal is acceptable when net present value is zero or positive.** At either of those values, the rate of return on the investment equals or exceeds the required rate of return. When net present value is negative, the project is unacceptable. Illustration 10-5 shows the net present value decision criteria.

Illustration 10-5 Net present value decision criteria

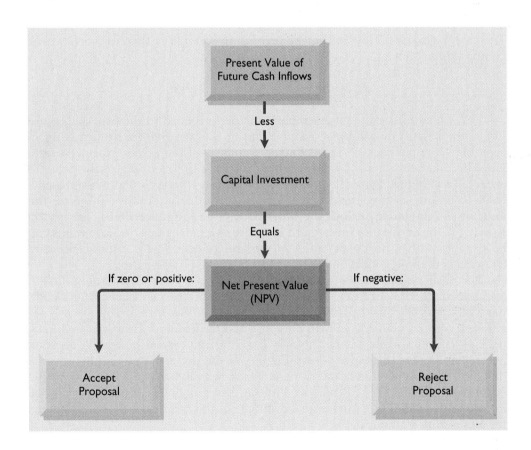

Helpful Hint Discounted future cash flows may not take into account all of the important considerations needed to make an informed capital budgeting decision. Other issues, for example, could include worker safety, product quality, and environmental impact. We look at these issues later.

When making a selection among acceptable proposals, **the higher the positive net present value, the more attractive the investment.** The application of this method to two cases is described in the next two sections. In each case, we will assume that the investment has no salvage value at the end of its useful life.

EQUAL ANNUAL CASH FLOWS

Stewart's annual cash inflows are $24,000. If we assume this amount **is uniform over the asset's useful life,** the present value of the annual cash flows can be computed by using the present value of an annuity of 1 for 10 periods (in Table 4, Appendix C). Assuming a discount rate of 12%, the present value of cash flows is computed as follows (rounded to the nearest dollar):

	Present Value at 12%
Discount factor for 10 periods	5.65022
Present value of cash flows:	
$24,000 × 5.65022	$135,605

Illustration 10-6 Present value of annual cash flows

Therefore, the analysis of the proposal by the net present value method is as follows:

	12%
Present value of cash flows	$135,605
Capital investment	130,000
Net present value	$ 5,605

Illustration 10-7 Computation of net present value—equal annual cash flows proposal

The proposed capital expenditure is acceptable at a required rate of return of 12% because the net present value is positive.

UNEQUAL ANNUAL CASH FLOWS

When annual cash flows are unequal, it is not possible to use annuity tables to calculate their present value. Instead, tables showing the **present value of a single future amount must be applied to each annual cash flow.** To illustrate, assume that the management at Stewart Soup expects the same aggregate annual cash flows ($240,000) but a declining market demand for the new product over the life of the equipment. The present value of the annual cash flows is calculated as follows, using Table 3 in Appendix C:

> **Helpful Hint** The ABC Co. expects equal cash flows over an asset's 5-year useful life. What discount factor should be used in determining present values if management wants (1) a 12% return or (2) a 15% return? Answer: Using Table 4, the factors are (1) 3.60478 and (2) 3.35216.

Year	Assumed Annual Cash Flows	Discount Factor 12%	Present Value 12%
	(1)	(2)	(1) × (2)
1	$ 34,000	.89286	$ 30,357
2	30,000	.79719	23,916
3	27,000	.71178	19,218
4	25,000	.63552	15,888
5	24,000	.56743	13,618
6	22,000	.50663	11,146
7	21,000	.45235	9,499
8	20,000	.40388	8,078
9	19,000	.36061	6,852
10	18,000	.32197	5,795
	$240,000		$144,367

Illustration 10-8 Computation of present value of unequal annual cash flows

Therefore, the analysis of the proposal by the net present value method is as follows:

Illustration 10-9
Computation of net
present value—unequal
annual cash flows
proposal

	12%
Present value of cash flows	$144,367
Capital investment	130,000
Net present value	**$ 14,367**

In this example, the present value of the cash flows is greater than the $130,000 capital investment. Thus, the project is acceptable at a 12% required rate of return. The difference between the present values using the 12% rate under equal cash flows ($135,605) and unequal cash flows ($144,367) is due to the pattern of the flows. Since more money is received sooner under this particular uneven cash flow scenario, its present value is greater.

CHOOSING A DISCOUNT RATE

Now that you understand how the net present value method is applied, it is logical to turn to a related question: How is a discount rate determined in real capital budgeting decisions? In most instances a company uses a discount rate equal to its cost of capital—that is, the rate that it must pay to obtain funds from creditors and stockholders. The cost of capital is a weighted average of the rates paid on borrowed funds as well as on funds provided by investors in the company's common stock and preferred stock. If a project is believed to be of higher risk than the company's usual line of business, the discount rate should be increased. That is, the discount rate has two elements, a cost of capital element and a risk element. Often companies assume the risk element is equal to zero.

Using an incorrect discount rate can lead to incorrect capital budgeting decisions. Consider again the Stewart Soup example in Illustration 10-7, where we used a discount rate of 12%. Suppose that this discount rate does not take into account the fact that this project is riskier than most of the company's investments, and that a more appropriate discount rate, given the risk, would be 15%. Illustration 10-10 compares the net present values at the two rates. At the higher—and more appropriate—discount rate of 15%, the net present value is negative, and the company should reject the project.

Illustration 10-10
Comparison of net
present values at different
discount rates

	Present Values at Different Discount Rates	
	12%	15%
Discount factor for 10 periods	5.65022	5.01877
Present value of cash flows:		
$24,000 × 5.65022	$135,605	
$24,000 × 5.01877		$120,450
Capital investment	130,000	130,000
Positive (negative) net present value	$ 5,605	$ (9,550)

The discount rate is often referred to by alternative names, including the **hurdle rate,** the **required rate of return,** and the **cutoff rate.** Determination of the cost of capital varies somewhat depending on whether the entity is a for profit or not-for-profit enterprise. Calculation of the cost of capital is discussed more fully in advanced accounting and finance courses.

SIMPLIFYING ASSUMPTIONS

In our examples of the net present value method we have made a number of simplifying assumptions:

* *All cash flows come at the end of each year.* In reality, cash flows will come at uneven intervals throughout the year. However, it is far simpler to assume that all cash flows come at the end (or in some cases the beginning) of the year. In fact, this assumption is frequently made in practice.
* *All cash flows are immediately reinvested in another project that has a similar return.* In most capital budgeting situations cash flows are received during each year of a project's life. In order to determine the return on the investment, some assumption must be made about how the cash flows are reinvested in the year that they are received. It is customary to assume that cash flows received are reinvested in some other project of similar return until the end of the project's life.
* *All cash flows can be predicted with certainty.* The outcomes of business investments are full of uncertainty, as the Campbell Soup story shows. There is no way of knowing how popular a new product will be, how long a new machine will last, or what competitors' reactions might be to changes in your product. But, in order to make investment decisions, analysts must estimate future outcomes. In this chapter we have assumed that future amounts are known with certainty.[1] In reality, little is known with certainty. More advanced capital budgeting techniques deal with uncertainty by considering the probability that various outcomes will occur.

BEFORE YOU GO ON . . .

● Review It

1. What is the cash payback technique? What are its strengths and weaknesses?
2. What is the net present value decision rule to determine whether a project is acceptable?
3. What are common assumptions made in capital budgeting decisions?

● Do It

Watertown Paper Corporation is considering adding another machine for the manufacture of corrugated cardboard. The machine would cost $800,000, have an estimated life of 7 years, and a salvage value of $40,000. It is estimated that annual cash inflows would increase by $400,000 and that annual cash outflows would increase by $190,000. Management believes a discount rate of 9% is appropriate. Using the net present value technique, should the project be accepted?

Reasoning: The net present value technique calculates the difference between the present value of future cash flows and the initial investment. If the net present value is positive, the project should be accepted.

---
[1]One exception is a brief discussion of sensitivity analysis later in the chapter.

Solution:

Estimated annual cash inflows	$400,000
Estimated annual cash outflows	190,000
Net annual cash inflow	$210,000

	Cash Flows	×	9% Discount Factor	=	Present Value
Present value of net annual cash flow	$210,000	×	5.03295[a]	=	$1,056,920
Present value of salvage value	$ 40,000	×	.54703[b]	=	21,881
Present value of cash flows					1,078,801
Capital investment					800,000
Net present value					$ 278,801

[a]Table 4, Appendix C.

[b]Table 3, Appendix C.

Since the net present value is positive, the project is acceptable.

Related exercise material: BE10-3, BE10-4, BE10-5, E10-1, E10-2, and E10-3.

COMPREHENSIVE EXAMPLE

Best Taste Foods is considering investing in new equipment to produce fat-free snack foods. Management believes that although demand for fat-free foods has leveled off, fat-free foods are here to stay. The following estimated cost flows, cost of capital, and cash flows were determined in consultation with the marketing, production, and finance departments:

Illustration 10-11
Investment information for Best Taste Foods example

Initial investment	$1,000,000
Cost of equipment overhaul in 5 years	$ 200,000
Salvage value of equipment in 10 years	$ 20,000
Cost of capital	15%
Estimated annual cash flows:	
Cash inflows received from sales	$500,000
Cash outflows for cost of goods sold	$200,000
Maintenance costs	$ 30,000
Other direct operating costs	$ 40,000

As indicated in Illustration 10-11, we are using cash flows in our analysis, not accrual revenues and expenses. Thus, for example, the direct operating costs would not include depreciation expense, since depreciation expense does not use cash. Illustration 10-12 presents the computation of the net annual cash inflows of this project.

Illustration 10-12
Computation of net annual cash inflow

Cash inflows received from sales	$500,000
Cash outflows for cost of goods sold	(200,000)
Maintenance costs	(30,000)
Other direct operating costs	(40,000)
Net annual cash inflow	$230,000

The computation of the net present value is shown in Illustration 10-13:

Event	Time Period	Cash Flow	×	15% Discount Factor	=	Present Value
Equipment purchase	0	$1,000,000		1.00000		$(1,000,000)
Equipment overhaul	5	200,000		.49718		(99,436)
Net annual cash inflows	1–10	230,000		5.01877		1,154,317
Salvage value	10	20,000		.24719		4,944
Net present value						$ 59,825

Illustration 10-13
Computation of net present value for Best Taste Foods investment

Because the net present value of the project is positive, the project should be accepted.

DECISION TOOLKIT

Decision Checkpoints	Info Needed for Decision	Tool to Use for Decision	How to Evaluate Results
Should the company invest in a proposed project?	Cash flow estimates, discount rate	Net present value = Present value of future cash flows less capital investment	The investment is financially acceptable if net present value is positive.

ADDITIONAL CONSIDERATIONS

Now that you understand how the net present value method works, we can add some "additional wrinkles." Specifically, these are: the impact of intangible benefits, a way to compare mutually exclusive projects, refinements that take into account the existence of risk, and the need to conduct post-audits of investment projects.

INTANGIBLE BENEFITS

The NPV evaluation techniques employed thus far rely on tangible, relatively easily quantified costs and benefits. Some investment projects, especially high-tech projects, fail to make it through initial capital budget screens because only the project's "tangible" benefits are considered. By ignoring intangible benefits, such as increased quality or safety or employee loyalty, capital budgeting techniques might incorrectly eliminate projects that could be financially beneficial to the company.

To avoid rejecting projects that actually should be accepted, two possible approaches are suggested:

1. Calculate net present value ignoring intangible benefits, and then, if the NPV is negative, ask whether the intangible benefits are worth at least the amount of the negative NPV.
2. Project rough, conservative estimates of the value of the intangible benefits, and incorporate these values into the NPV calculation.

STUDY OBJECTIVE 4
Identify the challenges presented by intangible benefits in capital budgeting.

Example

Assume that Berg Company is considering the purchase of a new mechanical robot to be used for soldering electrical connections. The estimates related to this proposed purchase are shown in Illustration 10-14.

Illustration 10-14
Investment information for
Berg Company example

Initial investment	$200,000			
Annual cash inflows	$ 50,000			
Annual cash outflows	20,000			
Net annual cash inflows	$ 30,000			
Estimated life of equipment	10 years			
Discount rate	12%			

	Cash Flows	×	12% Discount Factor	=	Present Value
Present value of cash flows	$30,000	×	5.65022	=	$ 169,507
Initial investment					200,000
Net present value					$(30,493)

Based on the negative net present value of $30,493, the proposed project is not acceptable. This calculation, however, ignores important information. First, the company's engineers believe that purchasing this machine will dramatically improve the electrical connections in the company's products. As a result, future warranty costs will be reduced. Also, the company believes that higher quality will translate into higher future sales. Finally, the new machine will be much safer than the previous one.

This new information can be incorporated into the capital budgeting decision in the two ways listed earlier: First, one might simply ask whether the reduced warranty costs, increased sales, and improved safety benefits have an estimated total present value to the company of at least $30,493. If yes, then the project is acceptable. Alternatively, an estimate of the annual cash flows of these benefits can be made. In our initial calculation, each of these benefits was assumed to have a value of zero. It seems likely that their actual values are much higher than zero. Given the difficulty of estimating these benefits, however, conservative values should be assigned to them. If, after using conservative estimates, the net present value is positive, the project should be accepted.

To illustrate, assume that Berg estimates a sales increase of $10,000 annually as a result of an increase in perceived quality. In addition, the company estimates that cost outflows would be reduced by $5,000 as a result of lower warranty claims, reduced injury claims, and missed work. Consideration of the intangible benefits results in the following revised net present value calculation:

Illustration 10-15
Revised investment
information for Berg
Company example, including intangible benefits

Initial investment	$200,000			
Annual cash inflows (revised)	$ 60,000			
Annual cash outflows (revised)	15,000			
Net annual cash inflow	$ 45,000			
Estimated life of equipment	10 years			
Discount rate	12%			

	Cash Flows	×	12% Discount Factor	=	Present Value
Present value of cash flows	$45,000	×	5.65022	=	$254,260
Initial investment					200,000
Net present value					$ 54,260

Using these conservative estimates of the value of the additional benefits, it appears that the project should be accepted.

MUTUALLY EXCLUSIVE PROJECTS

In theory, all projects with positive NPVs should be accepted. However, companies rarely are able to adopt all positive-NPV proposals. First, proposals often are **mutually exclusive,** meaning that if the company adopts one proposal, it would be impossible also to adopt the other proposal. For example, a company may be considering the purchase of a new packaging machine and is looking at various brands and models of packaging machines. Because only one packaging machine is needed, once the company has determined which brand and model to purchase, the others will not be purchased—even though they may also have positive net present values.

Even in instances where projects are not mutually exclusive, managers often must choose between various positive-NPV projects because of limited resources. For example, the company might have ideas for two new lines of business, each of which has a projected positive net present value. However, if both of these proposals require skilled personnel, and the company determines that it will not be able to find enough skilled personnel to staff both projects, then management will have to choose the project it thinks is a better option.

When choosing between alternative proposals, it is tempting simply to choose the project with the higher NPV. Consider the following example of two mutually exclusive projects, each assumed to have a 10-year life and a 12% discount rate:

	Project A	Project B
Initial investment	$40,000	$90,000
Net annual cash inflows	10,000	19,000
Salvage value	5,000	10,000
Net present value	18,112	20,574

Illustration 10-16
Investment information for mutually exclusive projects

Project B has the higher NPV, and so it would seem that the company should adopt Project B. Note, however, that Project B also requires more than twice the original investment of Project A. In choosing between the two projects, the company should also include in its calculations the amount of the original investment.

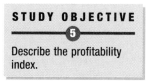

STUDY OBJECTIVE
5
Describe the profitability index.

One relatively simple method of comparing alternative projects that takes into account both the size of the original investment and the discounted cash flows is the profitability index. The profitability index is calculated by dividing the present value of cash flows that occur after the initial investment by the initial investment.

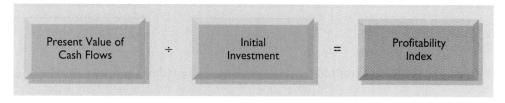

Illustration 10-17
Formula for profitability index

The profitability index allows comparison of the relative desirability of projects that require differing initial investments. Note that any project with a positive NPV will have a profitability index above 1. Applying the profitability index to the preceding example, we get the following present values:

Illustration 10-18
Revised investment
information for mutually
exclusive projects

	Project A	Project B
Initial investment	$40,000	$ 90,000
Net annual cash inflow	10,000	19,000
Present value of cash flows		
($10,000 × 5.65022) + ($5,000 × .32197)	58,112	
($19,000 × 5.65022) + ($10,000 × .32197)		110,574

The profitability index for the two projects is calculated as shown below:

Illustration 10-19
Calculation of profitability
index

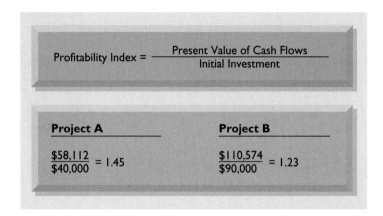

$$\text{Profitability Index} = \frac{\text{Present Value of Cash Flows}}{\text{Initial Investment}}$$

Project A

$$\frac{\$58,112}{\$40,000} = 1.45$$

Project B

$$\frac{\$110,574}{\$90,000} = 1.23$$

In this case the profitability index of Project A exceeds that of Project B. Thus, Project A is more desirable. Again, if these were not mutually exclusive projects, and if resources were not limited, then the company should invest in both projects, since both have positive NPVs. Additional considerations related to preference decisions are discussed in more advanced courses.

DECISION TOOLKIT

Decision Checkpoints	Info Needed for Decision	Tool to Use for Decision	How to Evaluate Results
Which investment proposal should a company accept?	Estimated cash flows and discount rate for each proposal	Profitability index = $\dfrac{\text{Present value of future cash flows}}{\text{Initial investment}}$	The investment proposal with the highest profitability index should be accepted.

RISK ANALYSIS

A simplifying assumption made by many financial analysts is that projected results are known with certainty. In reality, projected results are only estimates based upon the forecaster's belief as to the most probable outcome. One approach for dealing with uncertainty is **sensitivity analysis.** Sensitivity analysis uses a number of outcome estimates to get a sense of the variability among potential returns. An example of sensitivity analysis was presented in Illustration 10-10, where we illustrated the impact on net present value of different discount rate assumptions. A higher-risk project would be evaluated using a higher discount rate. Similarly, to take into account that more distant cash flows are often more uncertain, a higher discount rate can be used to discount more distant cash flows. Other techniques to address uncertainty are discussed in advanced courses.

POST-AUDIT OF INVESTMENT PROJECTS

Any well-run organization should perform an evaluation, called a post-audit, of its investment projects after their completion. A post-audit is a thorough evaluation of how well a project's actual performance matches the projections made when the project was proposed. An example of a post-audit is seen in the *Feature Story* about Campbell Soup. The original decision to invest in the Intelligent Quisine line was made based on management's best estimates of future cash flows. During the development phase of the project an outside consulting firm was hired to evaluate the project's potential for success. Because actual results during the initial years were far below the estimated results, and because the future also did not look promising, the project was terminated.

Performing a post-audit is important for a variety of reasons. First, if managers know that their estimates will be compared to actual results they will be more likely to submit reasonable and accurate data when they make investment proposals—rather than submitting overly optimistic estimates in an effort to get pet projects approved. Second, as seen in the case of Campbell Soup, a post-audit provides a formal mechanism by which the company can determine whether existing projects should be supported or terminated. Third, post-audits improve the development of future investment proposals because, by evaluating their past successes and failures, managers improve their estimation techniques.

A post-audit involves the same evaluation techniques that were used in making the original capital budgeting decision—for example, use of the net present value method. The difference is that, in the post-audit, actual figures are inserted where known, and estimation of future amounts is revised based on new information. The managers responsible for the estimates used in the original proposal must explain the reasons for any significant differences between their estimates and actual results.

Post-audits are not foolproof. In the case of Campbell Soup, critics of the company suggested that the company was too quick to abandon the project. Industry analysts suggested that with more time and more advertising expenditures, the company might have enjoyed a success.

> **STUDY OBJECTIVE**
> **6**
> Indicate the benefits of performing a post-audit.

BUSINESS INSIGHT
Management Perspective

Inaccurate trend forecasting and market positioning are more detrimental to a budget than using the wrong discount rate. Ampex patented the VCR, but failed to see its market potential. Westinghouse made the same mistake with flat-screen video display. More often, companies adopt projects or businesses only to discontinue them in response to market changes. Texas Instruments has just announced it will stop manufacturing computer chips, after investing to become one of the world's leading suppliers. The company has dropped out of some 12 business lines in recent years.

Source: World Research Advisory Inc.; London; August 1998; page 4.

OTHER CAPITAL BUDGETING TECHNIQUES

Some companies use capital budgeting techniques other than or in addition to the cash payback and net present value methods. In this section we will briefly discuss these other approaches.

INTERNAL RATE OF RETURN METHOD

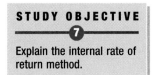

The **internal rate of return method** differs from the net present value method in that it results in finding the **interest yield of the potential investment.** The **internal rate of return** is the rate that will cause the present value of the proposed capital expenditure to equal the present value of the expected annual cash inflows (that is, the NPV equals zero). Note that because it recognizes the time value of money, the internal rate of return method is, like the NPV method, a discounted cash flow technique.

Suppose that Tampa Company is considering a new project with an 8-year estimated life, an initial cost of $249,000, and a net annual cash inflow of $45,000. When the net annual cash inflow is assumed to be equal each year, determining the internal rate of return involves three steps.

Step 1. Compute the internal rate of return factor. The formula for this factor is:

Illustration 10-20
Formula for internal rate of return factor

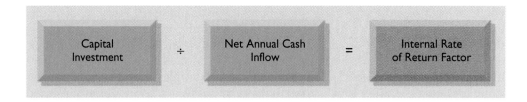

Using the Tampa Company example, the computation of the internal rate of return factor, assuming an equal net annual cash inflow is:

$$\$249{,}000 \div \$45{,}000 = 5.5333^2$$

Step 2. Use the factor and the present value of an annuity of 1 table to find the internal rate of return. Table 4 of Appendix C is used in this step. The internal rate of return is found by locating the discount factor in the table that is closest to the internal rate of return factor for the time period covered by the net annual cash inflow.

For Tampa, the net annual cash inflow is expected to continue for 8 years. Thus, it is necessary to read across the period-8 row in Table 4 to find the discount factor that is closest in value to the internal rate of return factor. Row 8 is reproduced below for your convenience.

TABLE 4   Present Value of an Annuity of 1

(n) Periods	5%	6%	8%	9%	10%	11%	12%	15%
8	6.46321	6.20979	5.74664	5.53482	5.33493	5.14612	4.96764	**4.48732**

---

[2]When the net annual cash inflow is equal, the internal rate of return factor is the same as the cash payback period.

In this case, the closest discount factor to 5.53333 is 5.53482, which represents an interest rate of approximately 9%. The approximate rate can be determined by interpolation, but since we are using estimated annual cash inflows, such precision is seldom required.

It is important to note that **steps 1 and 2 assume that net annual cash inflows would be equal.** If they are not assumed to be equal, then the internal rate of return must be calculated differently. This alternative is based on the fact that the internal rate of return is the discount rate that will result in a net present value of zero. To determine this rate, one must experiment with various discount rates to arrive at the rate that results in a zero net present value.

Step 3. Compare the internal rate of return to management's required minimum rate of return. The decision rule, therefore, is: **Accept the project when the internal rate of return is equal to or greater than the required rate of return (hurdle rate), and reject the project when the internal rate of return is less than the required rate.** These relationships are shown graphically in Illustration 10-21. Assuming the minimum required rate of return is 8% for Tampa Company, the project is acceptable because the 9% internal rate of return is greater than the required rate.

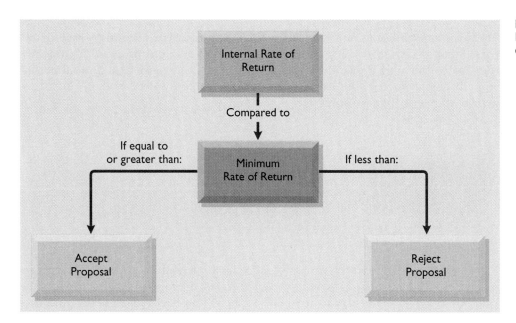

Illustration 10-21
Internal rate of return
decision criteria

The internal rate of return method is widely used in practice. Most managers find the internal rate of return easy to interpret.

DECISION TOOLKIT

Decision Checkpoints	Info Needed for Decision	Tool to Use for Decision	How to Evaluate Results
Should the company invest in a proposed project?	Estimated cash flows and the required rate of return (hurdle rate)	Internal rate of return = Interest rate that results in a net present value of zero	If the internal rate of return exceeds the specified discount rate (hurdle rate) for the project, then the project is financially acceptable.

COMPARING DISCOUNTED CASH FLOW METHODS

A comparison of the two discounted cash flow methods—net present value and internal rate of return—is presented in Illustration 10-22. When properly used, either method will provide management with relevant quantitative data for making capital budgeting decisions.

Illustration 10-22
Comparison of discounted cash flow methods

	Net Present Value	**Internal Rate of Return**
1. Objective	Compute net present value (a dollar amount).	Compute internal rate of return (a percentage).
2. Decision rule	If net present value is zero or positive, accept the proposal; if net present value is negative, reject the proposal.	If internal rate of return is equal to or greater than the minimum required rate of return, accept the proposal; if internal rate of return is less than the minimum rate, reject the proposal.

ANNUAL RATE OF RETURN METHOD

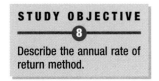

STUDY OBJECTIVE
8
Describe the annual rate of return method.

The final capital budgeting technique we will look at is the **annual rate of return method,** which is based directly on accrual accounting data. It indicates **the profitability of a capital expenditure** by dividing expected annual net income by the average investment. The formula for computing annual rate of return is shown in Illustration 10-23.

Illustration 10-23
Annual rate of return formula

Expected Annual Net Income ÷ Average Investment = Annual Rate of Return

Assume that Reno Company is considering an investment of $130,000 in new equipment. The new equipment is expected to last 5 years and have zero salvage value at the end of its useful life. The straight-line method of depreciation is used for accounting purposes. The expected annual revenues and costs of the new product that will be produced from the investment are:

Illustration 10-24
Estimated annual net income from Reno Company's capital expenditure

Sales		$200,000
Less: Costs and expenses		
Manufacturing costs (exclusive of depreciation)	$132,000	
Depreciation expense ($130,000 ÷ 5)	26,000	
Selling and administrative expenses	22,000	180,000
Income before income taxes		20,000
Income tax expense		7,000
Net income		$ 13,000

Reno's expected annual net income is $13,000. Average investment is derived from the following formula:

$$\text{Average investment} = \frac{\text{Original investment} + \text{Investment at end of useful life}}{2}$$

Illustration 10-25
Formula for computing
average investment

The investment at the end of useful life is equal to the asset's salvage value, if any. For Reno, average investment is $65,000 [($130,000 + $0) ÷ 2]. The expected annual rate of return for Reno's investment in new equipment is therefore 20%, computed as follows:

$$\$13,000 \div \$65,000 = 20\%$$

The annual rate of return is then compared with management's required minimum rate of return for investments of similar risk. The minimum rate of return (the hurdle rate or cutoff rate) is generally based on the company's cost of capital. The decision rule is: **A project is acceptable if its rate of return is greater than management's minimum rate of return; it is unacceptable when the reverse is true.** When the rate of return technique is used in deciding among several acceptable projects, **the higher the rate of return for a given risk, the more attractive the investment.**

The principal advantages of this method are the simplicity of its calculation and management's familiarity with the accounting terms used in the computation. A major limitation of the annual rate of return method is that it does not consider the time value of money. For example, no consideration is given as to whether earnings from the investment will occur early or late in the life of the investment. As explained in Appendix C, recognition of the time value of money can make a significant difference between the future value and the discounted present value of an investment. A second disadvantage is that this method relies on accrual accounting numbers rather than actual cash flows.

Helpful Hint A capital budgeting decision based on only one technique may be misleading. It is often wise to analyze the situation from a number of different perspectives.

BEFORE YOU GO ON . . .

● **Review It**

1. When is a proposal acceptable under (a) the net present value method and (b) the internal rate of return method?
2. How does the internal rate of return method differ from the net present value method?
3. What is the formula for and the decision rule in using the annual rate of return method? What are the drawbacks to the annual rate of return method?

THE
NAVIGATOR

USING THE DECISION TOOLKIT

Campbell Soup is considering expanding its international presence. It sells 38% of the soup consumed in the United States, but only 2% of soup worldwide. Thus the company believes that it has great potential for international sales. In 1997, 20% of Campbell's sales were in foreign markets (and nearly all of that was in Europe). Its goal is that by the year 2000, 30% of its sales will be in foreign markets. In order to accomplish this goal, the company will have to invest heavily. In recent years it has spent between $300 and $400 million on capital expenditures. Suppose that Campbell is interested in expanding its South American presence by building a new production facility. After considering tax, marketing, labor, transportation, and political issues Campbell has determined that the most desirable location is either in Buenos Aires or Rio de Janeiro. The following estimates have been provided (all amounts are stated in U.S. dollars).

	Buenos Aires	Rio de Janeiro
Initial investment	$2,500,000	$1,400,000
Estimated useful life	20 years	20 years
Annual revenues (accrual)	$ 500,000	$ 380,000
Annual expenses (accrual)	$ 200,000	$ 180,000
Annual cash inflows	$ 550,000	$ 430,000
Annual cash outflows	$ 222,250	$ 206,350
Estimated salvage value	$ 500,000	$0
Discount rate	9%	9%

Instructions

Evaluate each of these mutually exclusive proposals employing (1) cash payback, (2) net present value, (3) the profitability index, (4) the internal rate of return, and (5) annual rate of return. Discuss the implications of your findings.

Solution

	Buenos Aires	Rio de Janeiro
(1) Cash payback	$\dfrac{\$2,500,000}{\$327,750} = 7.63$ years	$\dfrac{\$1,400,000}{\$223,650} = 6.26$ years

(2) Net present value

Present value of cash flows

Buenos Aires	Rio de Janeiro
$327,750 × 9.12855 = $2,991,882	$223,650 × 9.12855 = $2,041,600
$500,000 × 0.17843 = 89,215	
3,081,097	
Less: Initial investment 2,500,000	1,400,000
Net present value $ 581,097	$ 641,600

(3) Profitability index	$\dfrac{\$3,081,097}{\$2,500,000} = 1.23$	$\dfrac{\$2,041,600}{\$1,400,000} = 1.46$

(4) Internal rate of return: The internal rate of return can be approximated by experimenting with different discount rates to see which one comes the closest to resulting in a net present value of zero. Doing this, we find that Buenos Aires has an internal rate of return of approximately 12%, while the internal rate of return of the Rio de Janeiro location is approximately 15% as shown below. Rio, therefore, is preferable.

Internal rate of return

Cash Flows	×	12% Discount Factor	=	Present Value		Cash Flows	×	15% Discount Factor	=	Present Value
$327,750 ×		7.46944	=	$2,448,109		$223,650 ×		6.25933	=	$1,399,899
$500,000 ×		0.10367	=	51,835						
				$2,499,944						
Less: Capital investment				2,500,000						1,400,000
Net present value				$ (56)						$ (101)

(5) Annual rate of return

Average investment

$$\frac{(\$2,500,000 + \$500,000)}{2} = \$1,500,000 \qquad \frac{(\$1,400,000 + \$0)}{2} = \$700,000$$

Annual rate of return $\dfrac{\$300,000}{\$1,500,000} = .20 = 20\%$ $\dfrac{\$200,000}{\$700,000} = .286 = 28.6\%$

Summary: Although the annual rate of return is higher for Rio de Janeiro, this method has the disadvantage of ignoring time value of money, as well as using accrual numbers rather than cash flows. The cash payback of Rio de Janeiro is also higher, but this method also ignores the time value of money. Thus, while these two methods can be used for a quick assessment, neither should be relied upon as the sole evaluation tool.

From the net present value calculation it would appear that the two projects are nearly identical in their acceptability. However, the profitability index indicates that the Rio de Janeiro investment is far more desirable because it generates its cash flows with a much smaller initial investment. A similar result is found by using the internal rate of return. Overall, assuming that the company will invest in only one project, it would appear that the Rio de Janeiro project should be chosen.

THE NAVIGATOR

SUMMARY OF STUDY OBJECTIVES

❶ Discuss the capital budgeting evaluation process, and explain what inputs are used in capital budgeting. Project proposals are gathered from each department and submitted to a capital budget committee, which screens the proposals and recommends worthy projects. Company officers decide which projects to fund, and the board of directors approves the capital budget. In capital budgeting, estimated cash inflows and outflows, rather than accrual-accounting numbers, are the generally preferred inputs.

❷ Describe the cash payback technique. The cash payback technique identifies the time period to recover the cost of the investment. The formula is: Cost of capital expenditure divided by estimated net annual cash inflow equals cash payback period.

❸ Explain the net present value method. Under the net present value method, the present value of future cash inflows is compared with the capital investment to determine net present value. The decision rule is: Accept the project if net present value is zero or positive; reject the project if net present value is negative.

❹ Identify the challenges presented by intangible benefits in capital budgeting. Intangible benefits are difficult to quantify, and thus are often ignored in capital budgeting decisions. This can result in incorrectly rejecting some projects. One method for considering intangible benefits is to calculate the net present value, ignoring intangible benefits, and if the resulting net present value is below zero, evaluate whether the benefits are worth at least the amount of the negative net present value. Alternatively, intangible benefits can be incorporated into the NPV calculation, using conservative estimates of their value.

❺ Describe the profitability index. The profitability index is a tool for comparing the relative merits of two alternative capital investment opportunities. It is computed by dividing the present value of future cash flows by the initial investment. The higher the index, the more desirable the project.

❻ Indicate the benefits of performing a post-audit. A post-audit is an evaluation of a capital investment project's actual performance. Post-audits create an incentive for managers to make accurate estimates, since managers know that their results will be evaluated. Post-audits also are useful for determining whether a project should be continued, expanded, or terminated. Finally, post-audits provide feedback that is useful for improving estimation techniques.

❼ Explain the internal rate of return method. The objective of the internal rate of return method is to find the interest yield of the potential investment, which is expressed as a percentage rate. The decision rule is: Accept the project when the internal rate of return is equal to or greater than the required rate of return; reject the project when the internal rate of return is less than the required rate.

❽ Describe the annual rate of return method. The annual rate of return uses accounting data to indicate the profitability of a capital investment. It is obtained by dividing the expected annual net income by the amount of the average investment. The higher the rate of return, the more attractive the investment.

THE NAVIGATOR

DECISION TOOLKIT—A SUMMARY

Decision Checkpoints	Info Needed for Decision	Tool to Use for Decision	How to Evaluate Results
Should the company invest in a proposed project?	Cash flow estimates, discount rate	Net present value = Present value of future cash flows less capital investment	The investment is financially acceptable if net present value is positive.
Which investment proposal should a company accept?	Estimated cash flows and discount rate for each proposal	Profitability index = $\dfrac{\text{Present value of future cash flows}}{\text{initial investment}}$	The investment proposal with the highest profitability index should be accepted.
Should the company invest in a proposed project?	Estimated cash flows and the required rate of return (hurdle rate)	Internal rate of return = Interest rate that results in a net present value of zero	If the internal rate of return exceeds the specified discount rate (hurdle rate) for the project, then the project is financially acceptable.

GLOSSARY

Annual rate of return method The determination of the profitability of a capital expenditure by dividing expected annual net income by the average investment. (p. 392)

Capital budgeting The process of making capital expenditure decisions in business. (p. 376)

Cash payback technique A capital budgeting technique that identifies the time period required to recover the cost of a capital investment from the annual cash inflow produced by the investment. (p. 379)

Cost of capital The average rate of return that the firm must pay to obtain borrowed and equity funds. (p. 382)

Discounted cash flow technique A capital budgeting technique that considers both the estimated total cash inflows from the investment and the time value of money. (p. 379)

Internal rate of return method A method used in capital budgeting that results in finding the interest yield of the potential investment. (p. 390)

Net present value method A method used in capital budgeting in which cash inflows are discounted to their present value and then compared to the capital outlay required by the investment. (p. 380)

Post-audit A thorough evaluation of how well a project's actual performance matches the projections made when the project was proposed. (p. 389).

Profitability index A method of comparing alternative projects that takes into account both the size of the investment and its discounted future cash flows. It is computed by dividing the present value of net future cash flows by the initial investment. (p. 387)

DEMONSTRATION PROBLEM

Sierra Company is considering a long-term capital investment project called ZIP. ZIP will require an investment of $120,000, and it will have a useful life of 4 years. Annual net income is expected to be: Year 1, $12,000; Year 2, $10,000; Year 3, $8,000; and Year 4, $6,000. Depreciation is computed by the straight-line method with no salvage value. The company's cost of capital is 12%. (*Hint:* Assume cash flows can be computed by adding back depreciation expense.)

Instructions

(Round all computations to two decimal places.)
(a) Compute the cash payback period for the project. (Round to two decimals.)
(b) Compute the net present value for the project. (Round to nearest dollar.)
(c) Compute the annual rate of return for the project.
(d) Should the project be accepted? Why?

Solution to Demonstration Problem

(a) $120,000 ÷ $39,000 ($9,000 + $30,000) = 3.08 years
(b)

Year	Discount Factor	Cash Inflow	Present Value
1	.89286	$42,000	$ 37,500
2	.79719	40,000	31,888
3	.71178	38,000	27,048
4	.63552	36,000	22,879
			119,315
	Capital investment		120,000
	Negative net present value		$ (685)

(c) $9,000 ($36,000 ÷ 4) ÷ $60,000 ($120,000 ÷ 2) = 15%

(d) The annual rate of return of 15% is good. However, the cash payback period is 77% of the project's useful life, and net present value is negative. The recommendation is to reject the project.

Problem-Solving Strategies

1. The formula for the cash payback method is cost of the investment divided by annual cash inflows.
2. Annual cash inflow equals annual net income plus annual depreciation expense.
3. The formula for annual rate of return is expected annual net income divided by average investment.
4. Be careful to use the correct discount factor in using the net present value method.

THE
NAVIGATOR

SELF-STUDY QUESTIONS

Answers are at the end of the chapter.

(SO 1) 1. Which of the following is *not* an example of a capital budgeting decision?
(a) Decision to build a new plant
(b) Decision to renovate an existing facility
(c) Decision to buy a piece of machinery
(d) All of these are capital budgeting decisions.

(SO 1) 2. What is the order of involvement of the following parties in the capital-budgeting authorization process?
(a) Plant managers, officers, capital budget committee, board of directors
(b) Board of directors, plant managers, officers, capital budget committee
(c) Plant managers, capital budget committee, officers, board of directors
(d) Officers, plant managers, capital budget committee, board of directors

(SO 2) 3. What is a weakness of the cash payback approach?
(a) It uses accrual based accounting numbers.
(b) It ignores the time value of money.
(c) It ignores the useful life of alternative projects.
(d) Both (b) and (c) are true.

(SO 3) 4. Which is a true statement regarding using a higher discount rate to calculate the net present value of a project?
(a) It will make it less likely that the project will be accepted.
(b) It will make it more likely that the project will be accepted.
(c) It is appropriate to use a higher rate if the project is perceived as being less risky than other projects being considered.
(d) It is appropriate to use a higher rate if the project will have a short useful life relative to other projects being considered.

(SO 3) 5. A positive net present value means that the:
(a) project's rate of return is less than the cutoff rate.
(b) project's rate of return exceeds the required rate of return.
(c) project's rate of return equals the required rate of return.
(d) project is unacceptable.

(SO 3) 6. Which of the following is *not* an alternative name for the discount rate?
(a) Hurdle rate
(b) Required rate of return

(c) Cutoff rate

(d) All of these are alternative names for the discount rate.

(SO 4) 7. If a project has intangible benefits whose value is hard to estimate, the best thing to do is:
(a) ignore these benefits, since any estimate of their value will most likely be wrong.
(b) include a conservative estimate of their value.
(c) ignore their value in your initial net present value calculation, but then estimate whether their potential value is worth at least the amount of the net present value deficiency.
(d) either (b) or (c) is correct.

(SO 6) 8. A post-audit of an investment project should be performed:
(a) on all significant capital expenditure projects.
(b) on all projects that management feels might be financial failures.

(c) on randomly selected projects.

(d) only on projects that enjoy tremendous success.

9. A project should be accepted if its internal rate   (SO 7)
of return exceeds:
(a) zero.
(b) the rate of return on a government bond.
(c) the company's required rate of return.
(d) the rate the company pays on borrowed funds.

10. Which of the following is *incorrect* about the   (SO 8)
annual rate of return technique?
(a) The calculation is simple.
(b) The accounting terms used are familiar to management.
(c) The timing of the cash inflows is not considered.
(d) The time value of money is considered.

THE NAVIGATOR

Questions

1. Describe the process a company may use in screening and approving the capital expenditure budget.

2. What are the advantages and disadvantages of the cash payback technique?

3. Pete Henning claims the formula for the cash payback technique is the same as the formula for the annual rate of return technique. Is Pete correct? What is the formula for the cash payback technique?

4. Two types of present value tables may be used with the discounted cash flow technique. Identify the tables and the circumstance(s) when each table should be used.

5. What is the decision rule under the net present value method?

6. Discuss the factors that determine the appropriate discount rate to use when calculating the net present value.

7. What simplifying assumptions were made in the chapter regarding calculation of net present value?

8. What are some examples of potential intangible benefits of investment proposals? Why do these intangible benefits complicate the capital budget evaluation process? What might happen if intangible benefits are ignored in a capital budget decision?

9. What steps can be taken to incorporate intangible benefits into the capital budget evaluation process?

10. What advantages does the profitability index provide over direct comparison of net present value when comparing two projects?

11. What is a post-audit? What are the potential benefits of a post-audit?

12. Identify the steps required in using the internal rate of return method.

13. Cheryl Munns Company uses the internal rate of return method. What is the decision rule for this method?

14. What are the strengths of the annual rate of return approach? What are its weaknesses?

15. Your classmate, Jana Kingston, is confused about the factors that are included in the annual rate of return technique. What is the formula for this technique?

16. Ernie Lobb is trying to understand the term "cost of capital." Define the term and indicate its relevance to the decision rule under the annual rate of return technique.

Brief Exercises

Compute the cash payback period for a capital investment.

(SO 2)

BE10-1 Mouser Company is considering purchasing new equipment for $400,000. It is expected that the equipment will produce annual net income of $10,000 over its 10-year useful life. Annual depreciation will be $40,000. Compute the payback period.

BE10-2 Weng Company accumulates the following data concerning a proposed capital investment: cash cost $225,000, annual cash inflow $40,000, present value of cash inflows for 10 years 5.65 (rounded). Determine the net present value, and indicate whether the investment should be made.

Compute net present value of an investment.
(SO 3)

BE10-3 Tracy Corporation, an amusement park, is considering a capital investment in a new exhibit. The exhibit would cost $140,000 and have an estimated useful life of 5 years. It will be sold for $75,000 at that time. It will be expected to increase net annual cash inflows by $25,000. The total expected life of the equipment is 10 years, with a salvage value of zero. (Amusement parks need to rotate exhibits to keep people interested.) The company's borrowing rate is 6%. Its cost of capital is 8%. Calculate the net present value of this project to the company.

Compute net present value of an investment.
(SO 3)

BE10-4 Lindy Bottling Corporation is considering the purchase of a new bottling machine. The machine would cost $200,000 and has an estimated useful life of 8 years with zero salvage value. Management estimates that the new bottling machine will provide net annual cash inflows of $33,000. Management also believes that the new bottling machine will save the company money because it is expected to be more reliable than other machines, and thus will reduce downtime. How much would the reduction in downtime have to be worth in order for the project to be acceptable? Assume a discount rate of 10%. (*Hint:* Calculate the net present value.)

Compute net present value of an investment.
(SO 3)

BE10-5 Sondhi Company is considering two different, mutually exclusive capital expenditure proposals. Project A will cost $220,000, has an expected useful life of 10 years, a salvage value of zero, and is expected to increase net cash inflows by $40,000. Project B will cost $395,000, has an expected useful life of 10 years, a salvage value of zero, and is expected to increase cash flows by $70,000. A discount rate of 8% is appropriate for both projects. Compute the net present value and profitability index of each project. Which project should be accepted?

Compute net present value and profitability index.
(SO 3, 5)

BE10-6 Fried Company is performing a post-audit of a project completed one year ago. The initial estimates were that the project would cost $250,000, would have a useful life of 9 years, zero salvage value, and would result in net cash inflows of $45,000 per year. Now that the investment has been in operation for 1 year, revised figures indicate that it actually cost $290,000, will have a useful life of 12 years, and will produce net cash inflows of $37,000 per year. Evaluate the success of the project. Assume a discount rate of 9%.

Perform a post-audit.
(SO 6)

BE10-7 Dobbs Company is evaluating the purchase of a rebuilt spot-welding machine to be used in the manufacture of a new product. The machine will cost $150,000, has an estimated useful life of 10 years, a salvage value of zero, and will increase net annual cash inflows by $22,350. What is its approximate internal rate of return?

Calculate internal rate of return.
(SO 7)

BE10-8 Smith Corporation is considering investing in a new facility. The estimated cost of the facility is $2,008,000. It will be used for 15 years, then sold for $700,000. The facility will generate annual cash inflows of $400,000 and will need new annual cash outflows of $158,000. The company has a hurdle rate of 7%. Calculate the internal rate of return on this project, and discuss whether the project should be accepted.

Calculate internal rate of return.
(SO 7)

BE10-9 Marais Oil Company is considering investing in a new oil well. It is expected that the oil well will increase annual revenues by $100,000 and will increase annual expenses by $80,000 including depreciation. The oil well will cost $410,000 and will have a $10,000 salvage value at the end of its 10-year useful life. Calculate the annual rate of return.

Compute annual rate of return.
(SO 8)

EXERCISES

E10-1 Hong Corporation is considering purchasing a new delivery truck. The truck has many advantages over the company's current truck (not the least of which is that it runs). The new truck would cost $57,000. Because of the increased capacity, reduced maintenance costs, and increased fuel economy, the new truck is expected to generate cost savings of $8,000. At the end of 8 years the company will sell the truck for an estimated $35,000. Traditionally the company has used a rule of thumb that a proposal should not

Compute cash payback and net present value.
(SO 2, 3)

be accepted unless it has a payback period that is less than 50% of the asset's estimated useful life. Tom Smith, a new manager, has suggested that the company should not rely solely on the payback approach, but should also employ the net present value method when evaluating new projects. The company's cost of capital is 8%.

Instructions
(a) Compute the cash payback period and net present value of the proposed investment.
(b) Does the project meet the company's cash payback criteria? Does it meet the net present value criteria for acceptance? Discuss your results.

Compute cash payback period and net present value.

(SO 2, 3)

E10-2   Jimmy Smits Manufacturing Company is considering three new projects, each requiring an equipment investment of $22,000. Each project will last for 3 years and produce the following cash inflows:

Year	AA	BB	CC
1	$ 7,500	$ 9,500	$13,000
2	9,000	9,500	9,000
3	15,000	9,500	11,000
Total	$31,500	$28,500	$33,000

The equipment's salvage value is zero, and Smits uses straight-line depreciation. Smits will not accept any project with a payback period over 2 years. Smits's minimum required rate of return is 15%.

Instructions
(a) Compute each project's payback period, indicating the most desirable project and the least desirable project using this method. (Round to two decimals.)
(b) Compute the net present value of each project. Does your evaluation change? (Round to nearest dollar.)

Compute net present value and profitability index.

(SO 3, 5)

E10-3   CompKare Corp. is considering purchasing one of two new diagnostic machines. Both machines would make it possible for the company to bid on jobs that it currently isn't equipped to do. Estimates regarding each machine are provided below.

	Machine A	Machine B
Original cost	$80,000	$180,000
Estimated life	8 years	8 years
Salvage value	–0–	–0–
Estimated annual cash inflows	$20,000	$35,000
Estimated annual cash outflows	$ 4,000	$ 8,000

Instructions
Calculate the net present value and profitability index of each machine. Assume a 9% discount rate. Which machine should be purchased?

Determine internal rate of return.

(SO 7)

E10-4   Lubar Corporation is involved in the business of injection molding of plastics. It is considering the purchase of a new computer-aided design and manufacturing machine for $500,000. The company believes that with this new machine it will improve productivity and increase quality, resulting in an annual increase in net cash flows of $74,500 for the next 10 years. Management requires a 9% rate of return on all new investments.

Instructions
Calculate the internal rate of return on this new machine. Should the investment be accepted?

Determine internal rate of return.

(SO 7)

E10-5   Novak Company is considering three capital expenditure projects. Relevant data for the projects are as follows:

Project	Investment	Annual Income	Life of Project
22A	$240,000	$15,000	6 years
23A	270,000	26,400	9 years
24A	288,000	22,000	8 years

Annual income is constant over the life of the project. Each project is expected to have zero salvage value at the end of the project. Novak Company uses the straight-line method of depreciation.

Instructions
(a) Determine the internal rate of return for each project. Round the internal rate of return factor to three decimals.
(b) If Novak Company's minimum required rate of return is 12%, which projects are acceptable?

E10-6 Kost Kutters is considering opening a new hair salon in Crewcutville. The cost of building a new salon is $200,000. A new salon will normally generate annual revenues of $80,000, with annual expenses of $50,000. At the end of 15 years the salon will have a salvage value of $50,000.

Calculate annual rate of return.
(SO 8)

Instructions
Calculate the annual rate of return on the project.

E10-7 Wamser Service Center just purchased an automobile hoist for $13,000. The hoist has a 5-year life and an estimated salvage value of $940. Installation costs and freight charges were $2,900 and $740, respectively. Wamser uses straight-line depreciation.

The new hoist will be used to replace mufflers and tires on automobiles. Wamser estimates that the new hoist will enable his mechanics to replace four extra mufflers per week. Each muffler sells for $65 installed. The cost of a muffler is $35 and the labor cost to install a muffler is $10.

Compute cash payback period and annual rate of return.
(SO 2, 8)

Instructions
(a) Compute the payback period for the new hoist.
(b) Compute the annual rate of return for the new hoist. (Round to one decimal.)

E10-8 Silva Company is considering a capital investment of $150,000 in additional productive facilities. The new machinery is expected to have a useful life of 5 years with no salvage value. Depreciation is by the straight-line method. During the life of the investment, annual net income and cash inflows are expected to be $18,000 and $48,000 respectively. Silva has a 15% cost of capital rate which is the minimum acceptable rate of return on the investment.

Compute annual rate of return, cash payback period, and net present value.
(SO 2, 3, 8)

Instructions
(Round to two decimals.)
(a) Compute (1) the cash payback period and (2) the annual rate of return on the proposed capital expenditure.
(b) Using the discounted cash flow technique, compute the net present value.

PROBLEMS: SET A

P10-1A The Vera and Tucker partnership is considering three long-term capital investment proposals. Each investment has a useful life of 5 years. Relevant data on each project are as follows:

Compute rate of return, cash payback, and net present value.
(SO 2, 3, 8)

	Project Tic	Project Tac	Project Toe
Capital investment	$150,000	$160,000	$200,000
Annual net income:			
Year 1	13,000	18,000	27,000
2	13,000	17,000	22,000
3	13,000	16,000	21,000
4	13,000	12,000	18,000
5	13,000	9,000	12,000
Total	$ 65,000	$ 72,000	$100,000

Depreciation is computed by the straight-line method with no salvage value. The company's cost of capital is 15%.

Instructions

(a) Compute the cash payback period for each project. (Round to two decimals.)
(b) Compute the net present value for each project. (Round to nearest dollar.)
(c) Compute the annual rate of return for each project. (Round to two decimals.)
(d) Rank the projects on each of the foregoing bases. Which project do you recommend?

Compute annual rate of return, cash payback, and net present value.

(SO 1, 2, 3, 8)

P10-2A Jill Kobe is an accounting major at a midwestern state university located approximately 60 miles from a major city. Many of the students attending the university are from the metropolitan area and visit their homes regularly on the weekends. Jill, an entrepreneur at heart, realizes that few good commuting alternatives are available for students doing weekend travel. She believes that a weekend commuting service could be organized and run profitably from several suburban and downtown shopping mall locations. Jill has gathered the following investment information:

1. Six used vans would cost a total of $69,000 to purchase and would have a 3-year useful life with negligible salvage value. Jill plans to use straight-line depreciation.
2. Ten drivers would have to be employed at a total payroll expense of $48,000.
3. Other annual out of pocket expenses associated with running the commuter service would include Gasoline $12,000, Maintenance $2,800, Repairs $3,500, Insurance $3,200, Advertising $1,500.
4. Jill has visited several financial institutions to discuss funding for her new venture. The best interest rate she has been able to negotiate is 12%. Use this rate for cost of capital.
5. Jill expects each van to make nine round trips weekly and carry an average of five students each trip. The service is expected to operate 30 weeks each year, and each student will be charged $12.00 for a round-trip ticket.

Instructions

(a) Determine the annual (1) net income and (2) cash inflow for the commuter service.
(b) Compute (1) the cash payback period and (2) the annual rate of return. (Round to two decimals.)
(c) Compute the net present value of the commuter service. (Round to the nearest dollar.)
(d) ▭▭▭▭▶ What should Jill conclude from these computations?

Compute net present value, profitability index, and internal rate of return.

(SO 3, 5, 7)

P10-3A Lake Bluff Clinic is considering investing in new heart monitoring equipment. It has two options: Option A would have an initial lower cost but would require a significant expenditure for rebuilding after 4 years. Option B would require no rebuilding expenditure, but its maintenance costs would be higher. Since the option B machine is of initial higher quality, it is expected to have a salvage value at the end of its useful life. The following estimates were made of the cash flows:

	Option A	Option B
Initial cost	$135,000	$203,000
Annual cash inflows	$ 70,000	$ 70,000
Annual cash outflows	$ 39,200	$ 30,000
Cost to rebuild (end of year 4)	$ 50,000	$ 0
Salvage value	$ 0	$ 10,000
Estimated useful life	8 years	8 years

The company's cost of capital is 8%.

Instructions

(a) Compute the (1) net present value, (2) profitability index, and (3) internal rate of return for each option.
(b) Which option should be accepted? (*Hint:* To solve for internal rate of return, experiment with alternative discount rates to arrive at a net present value of zero.)

Compute net present value considering intangible benefits.

(SO 3, 4)

P10-4A The Fredonia Car Clinic is considering the purchase of a new tow truck. The garage doesn't currently have a tow truck, and the $55,000 price tag for a new truck would represent a major expenditure for the garage. Joe Bare, owner of the garage, has compiled the following estimates in trying to determine whether the tow truck should be purchased:

Initial cost	$55,000
Estimated useful life	8 years
Annual cash inflows from towing	$ 6,000
Overhaul costs (end of year 4)	$ 4,000
Salvage value	$15,000

Joe's good friend, Steve Large, stopped by. He is trying to convince Joe that the tow truck will have other benefits that Joe hasn't even considered. First, he says, cars that need towing need to be fixed. Thus, when Joe tows them to his facility his repair revenues will increase. Second, he notes that the tow truck could have a plow mounted on it, thus saving Joe the cost of plowing his parking lot. (Steve will give him a used plow blade for free if Joe will plow Steve's driveway.) Third, he notes that the truck will generate goodwill; that is, people who are rescued by Joe and his tow truck will feel grateful and might be more inclined to used his service station in the future, or buy gas there. Fourth, the tow truck will have "Fredonia Car Clinic" on its doors, hood, and back tailgate—a form of free advertising wherever the tow truck goes.

Steve estimates that, at a minimum, these benefits would be worth the following:

Additional annual net cash inflows from repair work	$5,000
Annual savings from plowing	500
Additional annual net cash inflows from customer "goodwill"	1,000
Additional annual net cash inflows resulting from free advertising	500

The company's cost of capital is 9%.

Instructions
(a) Calculate the net present value, ignoring the additional benefits described by Steve. Should the tow truck be purchased?
(b) Calculate the net present value, incorporating the additional benefits suggested by Steve. Should the tow truck be purchased?
(c) Suppose Steve has been overly optimistic in his assessment of the value of the additional benefits (perhaps because he wants his driveway plowed). At a minimum, how much would the additional benefits have to be worth in order for the project to be accepted?

P10-5A Thumper Corp. is thinking about opening a soccer camp in northern California. In order to start the camp, the company would need to purchase land, build four soccer fields, and a dormitory-type sleeping and dining facility to house 150 soccer players. Each year the camp would be run for 8 sessions of 1 week each. The company would hire college soccer players as coaches. The camp attendees would be male and female soccer players age 12–18. Property values in northern California have enjoyed a steady increase in value. It is expected that after using the facility for 20 years, Thumper can sell the property for more than it was originally purchased for. The following amounts have been estimated:

Compute net present value and internal rate of return with sensitivity analysis.
(SO 3, 7)

Cost of land	$ 200,000
Cost to build dorm and dining facility	$ 500,000
Annual cash inflows assuming 150 players and 8 weeks	$ 960,000
Annual cash outflows	$ 860,000
Estimated useful life	20 years
Salvage value	$1,500,000
Discount rate	9%

Instructions
(a) Calculate the net present value of the project.
(b) To gauge the sensitivity of the project to these estimates, assume that if only 130 campers attend each week, revenues will be $800,000 and expenses will be $780,000. What is the net present value using these alternative estimates? Discuss your findings.
(c) Assuming the original facts, what is the net present value if the project is actually riskier than first assumed, and a 12% discount rate is more appropriate?
(d) Assume that during the first 5 years the annual net cash flows each year were only $13,600. At the end of the fifth year the company is running low on cash, so man-

agement decides to sell the property for $1,150,000. What was the actual internal rate of return on the project? Explain how this return was possible given that the camp did not appear to be successful.

PROBLEMS: SET B

Compute rate of return, cash payback, and net present value.

(SO 2, 3, 8)

P10-1B The partnership of Malle and Stine is considering three long-term capital investment proposals. Relevant data on each project are as follows:

	Project		
	Brown	**Red**	**Yellow**
Capital investment	$180,000	$220,000	$250,000
Annual net income:			
Year 1	25,000	20,000	31,000
2	16,000	20,000	24,000
3	13,000	20,000	23,000
4	10,000	20,000	22,000
5	8,000	20,000	20,000
Total	$ 72,000	$100,000	$120,000

Salvage value is expected to be zero at the end of each project. Depreciation is computed by the straight-line method. The company's minimum rate of return is the company's cost of capital which is 12%.

Instructions
(a) Compute the cash payback period for each project. (Round to two decimals.)
(b) Compute the net present value for each project. (Round to nearest dollar.)
(c) Compute the average annual rate of return for each project. (Round to two decimals.)
(d) Rank the projects on each of the foregoing bases. What project do you recommend?

Compute annual rate of return, cash payback, and net present value.

(SO 1, 2, 3, 8)

P10-2B Tammy Yewell is managing director of the Village Day Care Center. Village is currently set up as a full-time child care facility for children between the ages of 12 months and 6 years. Tammy is trying to determine whether the center should expand its facilities to incorporate a newborn care room for infants between the ages of 6 weeks and 12 months. The necessary space already exists. An investment of $25,000 would be needed, however, to purchase cribs, high chairs, etc. The equipment purchased for the room would have a 5-year useful life with zero salvage value.

The newborn nursery would be staffed to handle 12 infants on a full-time basis. The parents of each infant would be charged $150 weekly, and the facility would operate 52 weeks of the year. Staffing the nursery would require two full-time specialists and five part-time assistants at an annual cost of $74,000. Food, diapers, and other miscellaneous supplies are expected to total $12,500 annually.

Instructions
(a) Determine (1) annual net income and (2) cash inflow for the new nursery.
(b) Compute (1) the cash payback period for the new nursery and (2) the annual rate of return. (Round to two decimals.)
(c) Compute the net present value of incorporating a newborn care room (round to the nearest dollar).
(d) ▭▭▭➤ What should Tammy conclude from these computations?

Compute net present value, profitability index, and internal rate of return.

(SO 3, 5, 7)

P10-3B Heartland Soil Testing is considering investing in a new testing device. It has two options: Option A would have an initial lower cost but would require a significant expenditure for rebuilding after 4 years. Option B would require no rebuilding expenditure, but its maintenance costs would be higher. Since the option B machine is of initial higher quality, it is expected to have a salvage value at the end of its useful life. The following estimates were provided:

	Option A	**Option B**
Initial cost	$ 91,600	$186,000
Annual cash inflows	$180,000	$140,000

Annual cash outflows	$159,000	$105,000
Cost to rebuild (end of year 4)	$ 25,000	$ 0
Salvage value	$ 0	$ 30,000
Estimated useful life	8 years	8 years

The company's cost of capital is 8%.

Instructions

(a) Compute the (1) net present value, (2) profitability index, and (3) internal rate of return for each option.

(b) Which option should be accepted? (*Hint:* To solve for internal rate of return, experiment with alternative discount rates to arrive at a net present value of zero.)

P10-4B The Cedar Grove Sanitation Company is considering the purchase of a garbage truck. The $95,000 price tag for a new truck would represent a major expenditure for the company. Bob Sims, owner of the company, has compiled the following estimates in trying to determine whether the garbage truck should be purchased:

Compute net present value considering intangible benefits.
(SO 3, 4)

Initial cost	$70,000
Estimated useful life	10 years
Annual net cash flows	$ 9,000
Overhaul costs (end of year 5)	$ 6,000
Salvage value	$25,000

One of the company's employees is trying to convince Bob that the truck has other merits that haven't been considered in the initial estimates. First, the new truck will be more efficient, with lower maintenance and operating costs. Second, the new truck will be safer. Third, the new truck has the ability to handle recycled materials at the same time as trash, thus offering a new revenue source. Estimates of the minimum value of these benefits are the following:

Annual savings from reduced operating costs	$ 700
Annual savings from reduced maintenance costs	1,600
Additional annual net cash savings from reduced employee absence	1,300
Additional annual net cash inflows from recycling	500

The company's cost of capital is 10%.

Instructions

(a) Calculate the net present value, ignoring the additional benefits. Should the truck be purchased?

(b) Calculate the net present value, incorporating the additional benefits. Should the tow truck be purchased?

(c) Suppose management has been overly optimistic in the assessment of the value of the additional benefits. At a minimum, how much would the additional benefits have to be worth in order for the project to be accepted?

P10-5B Conrad Corp. is thinking about opening an ice hockey camp in Colorado. In order to start the camp the company would need to purchase land, build two ice rinks, and a dormitory-type sleeping and dining facility to house 200 players. Each year the camp would be run for 8 sessions of 1 week each. The company would hire college hockey players as coaches. The camp attendees would be male and female hockey players age 12–18. Property values in Colorado have enjoyed a steady increase in recent years. Conrad Corp. expects that after using the facility for 15 years, the rinks will have to be dismantled, but the land and buildings will be worth more than they were originally purchased for. The following amounts have been estimated:

Compute net present value and internal rate of return with sensitivity analysis.
(SO 3, 4, 7)

Cost of land	$ 100,000
Cost to build dorm and dining hall	$ 500,000
Annual cash inflows assuming 200 players and 8 weeks	$ 920,000
Annual cash outflows	$ 750,000
Estimated useful life	15 years
Salvage value	$1,200,000
Discount rate	10%

Instructions
(a) Calculate the net present value of the project.
(b) To gauge the sensitivity of the project to these estimates, assume that if only 170 campers attend each week, revenues will be $700,000 and expenses will be $680,000. What is the net present value using these alternative estimates? Discuss your findings.
(c) Assuming the original facts, what is the net present value if the project is actually riskier than first assumed, and a 15% discount rate is more appropriate?
(d) Assume that during the first 6 years the annual net cash flows each year were only $11,000. At the end of the sixth year the company is running low on cash, so management decides to sell the property for $1,035,000. What was the actual internal rate of return on the project? Explain how this return was possible given that the camp did not appear to be successful.

BROADENING YOUR PERSPECTIVE

GROUP DECISION CASE

BYP10-1 Sanchez Company is considering the purchase of a new machine. The invoice price of the machine is $115,000, freight charges are estimated to be $4,000, and installation costs are expected to be $6,000. Salvage value of the new equipment is expected to be zero after a useful life of 4 years. Existing equipment could be retained and used for an additional 4 years if the new machine is not purchased. At that time, the salvage value of the equipment would be zero. If the new machine is purchased now, the existing machine would have to be scrapped. Sanchez's accountant, Diane Gallup, has accumulated the following data regarding annual sales and expenses with and without the new machine:

1. Without the new machine, Sanchez can sell 11,000 units of product annually at a per unit selling price of $100. If the new unit is purchased, the number of units produced and sold would increase by 20%, and the selling price would remain the same.
2. The new machine is faster than the old machine, and it is more efficient in its usage of materials. With the old machine the gross profit rate will be 27.5% of sales, whereas the rate will be 29% of sales with the new machine.
3. Annual selling expenses are $180,000 with the current equipment. Because the new equipment would produce a greater number of units to be sold, annual selling expenses are expected to increase by 10% if it is purchased.
4. Annual administrative expenses are expected to be $100,000 with the old machine, and $113,000 with the new machine.
5. The current book value of the existing machine is $36,000. Sanchez uses straight-line depreciation.
6. Sanchez's management wants a minimum rate of return of 15% on its investment and a payback period of no more than 3 years.

Instructions
With the class divided into groups, answer the following (ignore income tax effects):
(a) Calculate the annual rate of return for the new machine. (Round to two decimals.)
(b) Compute the payback period for the new machine. (Round to two decimals.)
(c) Compute the net present value of the new machine. (Round to the nearest dollar.)
(d) On the basis of the foregoing data, would you recommend that Sanchez buy the machine? Why?

MANAGERIAL ANALYSIS

BYP10-2 Streamline Skateboards is considering building a new plant. Robert Optimist, the company's marketing manager, is an enthusiastic supporter of the new plant. Roberta Wunderland, the company's chief financial officer, is not so sure that the plant is a good idea. Currently the company purchases its skateboards from foreign manufacturers. The following figures were estimated regarding the construction of a new plant.

Cost of plant	$4,500,000
Annual cash inflows	4,000,000
Annual cash outflows	3,500,000
Estimated useful life	15 years
Salvage value	$2,000,000
Discount rate	12%

Robert Optimist believes that these figures understate the true potential value of the plant. He suggests that by manufacturing its own skateboards the company will benefit from a "buy American" patriotism that he believes is common among skateboarders. He also notes that the firm has had numerous quality problems with the skateboards manufactured by its suppliers. He suggests that the inconsistent quality has resulted in lost sales, increased warranty claims, and some costly lawsuits. Overall, he believes sales will be $200,000 higher each year than projected above, and that the savings from lower warranty costs and legal costs will be $100,000 per year. He also believes that the project is not as risky as assumed above, and that an 8% discount rate is more reasonable.

Instructions
Answer each of the following questions:
(a) Compute the net present value of the project based on the original projections.
(b) Compute the net present value incorporating Robert's estimates of the value of the intangible benefits, but still using the 12% discount rate.
(c) Compute the net present value using the original estimates, but employing the 8% discount rate that Robert suggests is more appropriate.
(d) Comment on your findings.

REAL-WORLD FOCUS

TECUMSEH PRODUCTS COMPANY

BYP10-3 Tecumseh Products Company has its headquarters in Tecumseh, Michigan. It describes itself as "a global multinational corporation producing mechanical and electrical components essential to industries creating end-products for health, comfort, and convenience."

The following was excerpted from the management discussion and analysis section of the company's 1997 annual report.

TECUMSEH PRODUCTS COMPANY
Management Discussion and Analysis

The company has invested approximately $50 million in a scroll compressor manufacturing facility in Tecumseh, Michigan. After experiencing setbacks in developing a commercially acceptable scroll compressor, the Company is currently testing a new generation of scroll product. The Company is unable to predict when or if it will offer a scroll compressor for commercial sale, but it does anticipate that reaching volume production will require a significant additional investment. Given such additional investment and current market conditions, management is currently reviewing its options with respect to scroll product improvement, cost reductions, joint ventures and alternative new products.

Instructions
Discuss issues the company should consider and techniques the company should employ to determine whether to continue pursuing this project.

COMMUNICATION ACTIVITY

BYP10-4 Refer back to Exercise 10-7 to address the following:

Instructions
Prepare a memo to Mary Ann Griffin, your supervisor. Show your calculations from E10-7, (a) and (b). In one or two paragraphs, discuss important nonfinancial considerations. Make any assumptions you believe to be necessary. Make a recommendation based on your analysis.

RESEARCH ASSIGNMENT

BYP10-5 The April 21, 1997, issue of *Forbes* includes an article by Toni Mack entitled, "The Tiger Is on the Prowl."

Instructions
Read the article and answer the following questions:
(a) What have been the relative capital spending practices of Royal Dutch Shell versus Mobil Corp. versus Exxon?
(b) What has been "the religion" (business objective) of Exxon's headquarters since 1983?
(c) What was Exxon's capital budget in 1994 and 1995? What is Exxon's capital budget expected to swell to in 2 or 3 years?
(d) Did Exxon's capital spending strategy pay off during the past 15 years?

ETHICS CASE

BYP10-6 Bristle Brush Company operates in a state where corporate taxes and workmen's compensation insurance rates have recently doubled. Bristle's president has just assigned you the task of preparing an economic analysis and making a recommendation relative to moving the company's entire operation to Missouri. The president is slightly in favor of such a move because Missouri is his boyhood home and he also owns a fishing lodge there.

You have just completed building your dream house, moved in, and sodded the lawn. Your children are all doing well in school and sports and, along with your spouse, want no part of a move to Missouri. If the company does move, so will you because the town is a one-industry community and you and your spouse will have to move to have employment. Moving when everyone else does will cause you to take a big loss on the sale of your house. The same hardships will be suffered by your coworkers, and the town will be devastated.

In compiling the costs of moving versus not moving, you have latitude in the assumptions you make, the estimates you compute, and the discount rates and time periods you project. You are in a position to influence the decision singlehandedly.

Instructions
(a) Who are the stakeholders in this situation?
(b) What are the ethical issues in this situation?
(c) What would you do in this situation?

SURFING THE NET

BYP10-7 Campbell Soup Company is an international provider of soup products. Management is very interested in continuing to grow the company in its core business, while "spinning off" those businesses that are not part of its core operation.

Address: http://www.campbellsoups.com

Steps:
1. Go to the home page of Campbell Soup Company at the address shown above.
2. Choose the current annual report.

Instructions
Review the financial statements and management's discussion and analysis, and answer the following questions:
(a) What was the total amount of capital expenditures in the current year, and how does this amount compare with the previous year? If next year's projected expenditures are presented, provide this amount also.
(b) What interest rate did the company pay on new borrowings in the current year?
(c) Assume that this year's capital expenditures are expected to increase cash flows by $54 million. What is the expected internal rate of return (IRR) for these capital expenditures? (Assume a 10-year period for the cash flows.)

Answers to Self-Study Questions
1. d   2. c   3. d   4. a   5. b   6. d   7. d   8. a   9. c   10. d

 Remember to go back to the Navigator box on the chapter-opening page and check off your completed work.

CHAPTER 11

Statement of Cash Flows

STUDY OBJECTIVES

After studying this chapter, you should be able to:

① Indicate the primary purpose of the statement of cash flows.

② Distinguish among operating, investing, and financing activities.

③ Explain the impact of the product life cycle on a company's cash flows.

④ Prepare a statement of cash flows using one of two approaches: (a) the indirect method or (b) the direct method.

⑤ Use the statement of cash flows to evaluate a company.

THE NAVIGATOR

FEATURE STORY

I've Got Fourteen Billion Dollars Burning a Hole in My Pocket!

Imagine starting a company in a brand new industry and growing it into one of the biggest companies in the world—in just 23 years. Imagine you are one of the richest people on the planet at age 42. Now wake up! Bill Gates, founder of software maker Microsoft Corporation, accomplished all of this and more between 1975 and 1998. It all started with MS-DOS, a software package that Gates bought from a Seattle-based programmer for $50,000. Then MS-DOS was adopted by IBM as *the* operating system for all of its personal computers. Translation: Every IBM and IBM-compatible computer *in the*

world needed a copy of MS-DOS to run. The rest is history.

Although MS-DOS got the Microsoft ball rolling, in an environment that changes as fast as the computer industry, it takes continual new products to survive and thrive. To develop new products it takes cash—lots and lots of cash. And to have lots and lots of cash when you are a young company requires great cash management and careful attention to cash flows. During its early years, in order to ensure that it had enough cash to meet its needs, Microsoft employed many cash management techniques. For example, all of its employees received stock options, rather than cash, as a portion of their compensation. Stock options become valuable if Microsoft's stock price increases. By some estimates,

more than 1,000 Microsoft employees have become millionaires because of these options. These and other cash management practices enabled Microsoft to build up a "war chest" of cash and short-term investments. Its 1998 statement of cash flows reported cash provided by operations of approximately $7 billion. At its fiscal year end of June 30, 1998, cash and short-term investments amounted to nearly $14 billion—65% of its total assets. At December 31, 1998, this amount had grown to nearly $19 billion. This might sound excessive, but it means that Microsoft can move quickly when it needs to—and in the computer industry speed is everything.

THE NAVIGATOR

On the World Wide Web
Microsoft: http://www.microsoft.com

THE NAVIGATOR ✔

- Scan *Study Objectives* ☐
- Read *Feature Story* ☐
- Read *Preview* ☐
- Read text and answer *Before You Go On*
  p. 416 ☐   p. 420 ☐   p. 430 ☐
  p. 443 ☐   p. 452 ☐
- Work *Using the Decision Toolkit* ☐
- Review *Summary of Study Objectives* ☐
- Work *Demonstration Problem* ☐
- Answer *Self-Study Questions* ☐
- Complete assignments ☐

The balance sheet, income statement, and retained earnings statement do not always show the whole picture of the financial condition of a company or institution. In fact, looking at these three financial statements of some well-known companies, a thoughtful investor might ask questions like these: How did Eastman Kodak finance cash dividends of $649 million in a year in which it earned only $17 million? How could Delta Air Lines purchase new planes that cost $900 million in a year in which it reported a net loss of $86 million? How did Kohlberg Kravis and Roberts finance its record-shattering $25 billion purchase of RJR Nabisco? Answers to these and similar questions can be found in this chapter, which presents the statement of cash flows.

The content and organization of this chapter are as follows:

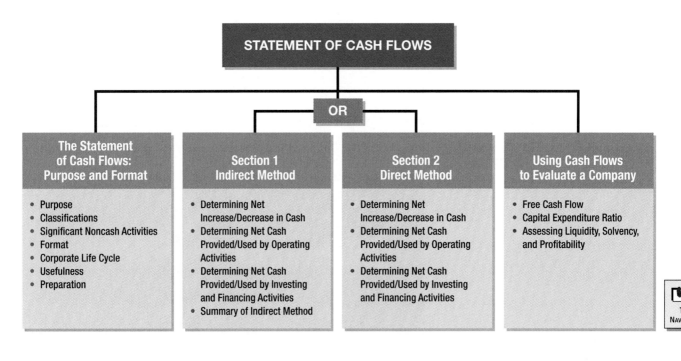

STATEMENT OF CASH FLOWS

OR

The Statement of Cash Flows: Purpose and Format
- Purpose
- Classifications
- Significant Noncash Activities
- Format
- Corporate Life Cycle
- Usefulness
- Preparation

Section 1 Indirect Method
- Determining Net Increase/Decrease in Cash
- Determining Net Cash Provided/Used by Operating Activities
- Determining Net Cash Provided/Used by Investing and Financing Activities
- Summary of Indirect Method

Section 2 Direct Method
- Determining Net Increase/Decrease in Cash
- Determining Net Cash Provided/Used by Operating Activities
- Determining Net Cash Provided/Used by Investing and Financing Activities

Using Cash Flows to Evaluate a Company
- Free Cash Flow
- Capital Expenditure Ratio
- Assessing Liquidity, Solvency, and Profitability

THE NAVIGATOR

THE STATEMENT OF CASH FLOWS: PURPOSE AND FORMAT

The basic financial statements we have presented so far provide only limited information about a company's cash flows (cash receipts and cash payments). For example, comparative balance sheets show the increase in property, plant, and equipment during the year, but they do not show how the additions were financed or paid for. The income statement shows net income, but it does not indicate the amount of cash generated by operating activities. Similarly, the retained earnings statement shows cash dividends declared but not the cash dividends paid during the year. None of these statements presents a detailed summary of the **net change in cash** as a result of operating, investing, and financing activities during the period.

Helpful Hint Recall that the retained earnings statement is often presented in the statement of stockholders' equity.

STUDY OBJECTIVE
——●——
Indicate the primary purpose of the statement of cash flows.

PURPOSE OF THE STATEMENT OF CASH FLOWS

The primary purpose of the statement of cash flows is to provide information about cash receipts, cash payments, and the net change in cash resulting from the operating, investing, and financing activities of a company during the period. These activities involving cash are reported in a format that reconciles the beginning and ending cash balances.

Reporting the causes of changes in cash is useful because investors, creditors, and other interested parties want to know what is happening to a company's most liquid resource, its cash. As the opening story about Microsoft demonstrates, to understand a company's financial position it is essential to understand its cash flows. The statement of cash flows provides answers to these important questions about an enterprise:

Where did the cash come from during the period?

What was the cash used for during the period?

What was the change in the cash balance during the period?

The answers provide important clues about whether a dynamic company like Microsoft will be able to continue to thrive and invest in new ideas. The statement of cash flows also provides clues about whether a struggling company will survive or perish.

CLASSIFICATION OF CASH FLOWS

The statement of cash flows classifies cash receipts and cash payments into operating, investing, and financing activities. Transactions within each activity are as follows:

STUDY OBJECTIVE
2
Distinguish among operating, investing, and financing activities.

1. **Operating activities** include the cash effects of transactions that create revenues and expenses and thus enter into the determination of net income.

2. **Investing activities** include (a) purchasing and disposing of investments and productive long-lived assets using cash and (b) lending money and collecting the loans.

3. **Financing activities** include (a) obtaining cash from issuing debt and repaying the amounts borrowed and (b) obtaining cash from stockholders and paying them dividends.

Operating activities is the most important category because it shows the cash provided or used by company operations. This source of cash is generally considered to be the best measure of whether a company can generate sufficient cash to continue as a going concern and to expand. Illustration 11-1 (page 414) lists typical cash receipts and cash payments within each of the three activities.

Helpful Hint You determine what classification a transaction is by looking to see if it is in the list of investing activities or financing activities. If it is in neither of these lists, it is an operating activity.

As you can see, some cash flows relating to investing or financing activities are classified as operating activities. For example, receipts of investment revenue (interest and dividends) and payments of interest to lenders are classified as operating activities because these items are reported in the income statement.

Note that, generally, (1) operating activities involve income determination (income statement) items, (2) investing activities involve cash flows resulting from changes in investments and long-term asset items, and (3) financing activities involve cash flows resulting from changes in long-term liability and stockholders' equity items.

SIGNIFICANT NONCASH ACTIVITIES

Not all of a company's significant activities involve cash. Here are four examples of significant noncash activities:

1. Issuance of common stock to purchase assets
2. Conversion of bonds into common stock
3. Issuance of debt to purchase assets
4. Exchanges of plant assets

Types of Cash Inflows and Outflows

Operating activities

Cash inflows:

From sale of goods or services

From returns on loans (interest received) and on equity securities (dividends received)

Cash outflows:

To suppliers for inventory

To employees for services

To government for taxes

To lenders for interest

To others for expenses

Investing activities

Cash inflows:

From sale of property, plant, and equipment

From sale of debt or equity securities of other entities

From collection of principal on loans to other entities

Cash outflows:

To purchase property, plant, and equipment

To purchase debt or equity securities of other entities

To make loans to other entities

Financing activities

Cash inflows:

From sale of equity securities (company's own stock)

From issuance of debt (bonds and notes)

Cash outflows:

To stockholders as dividends

To redeem long-term debt or reacquire capital stock

Helpful Hint Operating activities generally relate to changes in current assets and current liabilities. Investing activities generally relate to changes in investments and noncurrent assets. Financing activities relate to changes in noncurrent liabilities and stockholders' equity accounts.

Helpful Hint Do not include noncash investing and financing activities in the body of the statement of cash flows. Report this information in a separate schedule at the bottom of the statement

Significant financing and investing activities that do not affect cash are not reported in the body of the statement of cash flows. However, these activities are reported either in a separate schedule at the bottom of the statement of cash flows or in a separate note or supplementary schedule to the financial statements.

The reporting of these activities in a separate note or supplementary schedule satisfies the **full disclosure principle** because it identifies significant noncash investing and financing activities of the enterprise. In doing homework assignments you should present significant noncash investing and financing activities in a separate schedule at the bottom of the statement of cash flows. (See the lower section of Illustration 11-2 for an example.)

FORMAT OF THE STATEMENT OF CASH FLOWS

The three activities discussed above—operating, investing, and financing—plus the significant noncash investing and financing activities make up the general format of the statement of cash flows. A widely used form of the statement of cash flows is shown in Illustration 11-2.

As illustrated, the section of cash flows from operating activities always appears first, followed by the investing activities and the financing activities sections. Also, **the individual inflows and outflows from investing and financ-**

COMPANY NAME
Statement of Cash Flows
Period Covered

Cash flows from operating activities		
(List of individual items)	XX	
Net cash provided (used) by operating activities		XXX
Cash flows from investing activities		
(List of individual inflows and outflows)	XX	
Net cash provided (used) by investing activities		XXX
Cash flows from financing activities		
(List of individual inflows and outflows)	XX	
Net cash provided (used) by financing activities		XXX
Net increase (decrease) in cash		XXX
Cash at beginning of period		XXX
Cash at end of period		XXX
Noncash investing and financing activities		
(List of individual noncash transactions)		XXX

Illustration 11-2 Format of statement of cash flows

Helpful Hint Indicate the classification in the statement of cash flows for each of the following: (1) Proceeds from the sale of an investment. (2) Disbursement for the purchase of treasury stock. (3) Loan to another corporation. (4) Proceeds from an insurance policy because a building was destroyed by fire. (5) Proceeds from winning a lawsuit. (6) Receipt of interest from an investment in bonds. (7) Payment of dividends. (8) Sale of merchandise for cash.
Answers:
(1) Investing   (2) Financing
(3) Investing   (4) Investing
(5) Operating   (6) Operating
(7) Financing   (8) Operating

ing activities are reported separately. Thus, the cash outflow for the purchase of property, plant, and equipment is reported separately from the cash inflow from the sale of property, plant, and equipment. Similarly, the cash inflow from the issuance of debt securities is reported separately from the cash outflow for the retirement of debt. If a company did not report the inflows and outflows separately, it would obscure the investing and financing activities of the enterprise and thus make it more difficult for the user to assess future cash flows.

The reported operating, investing, and financing activities result in net cash either **provided or used** by each activity. The net cash provided or used by each activity is totaled to show the net increase (decrease) in cash for the period. The net increase (decrease) in cash for the period is then added to or subtracted from the beginning-of-period cash balance to obtain the end-of-period cash balance. Finally, any significant noncash investing and financing activities are reported in a separate schedule at the bottom of the statement.

BUSINESS INSIGHT
Investor Perspective

Net income is not the same as net cash generated by operations. The differences are illustrated by the following results from recent annual reports for the same fiscal year ($ in millions):

Company	Net Income	Net Cash Provided by Operations
Kmart Corporation	$ 296	$ 76
Wal-Mart Stores, Inc.	2,681	2,906
Woolworth Corporation	47	(340)
J.C. Penney Company, Inc.	1,057	738
Sears Roebuck & Co.	1,454	1,930
The May Department Stores Company	782	999

Note the wide disparity among these companies that all engaged in similar types of retail merchandising.

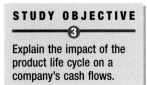

BEFORE YOU GO ON . . .

● **Review It**

1. What is the primary purpose of a statement of cash flows?
2. What are the major classifications of cash flows on the statement of cash flows?
3. What are some examples of significant noncash activities?

THE CORPORATE LIFE CYCLE

STUDY OBJECTIVE

3

Explain the impact of the product life cycle on a company's cash flows.

All products go through a series of phases called the **product life cycle.** The phases (in order of their occurrence) are often referred to as the **introductory phase, growth phase, maturity phase,** and **decline phase.** The introductory phase occurs when the company is purchasing fixed assets and beginning to produce and sell. During the growth phase, the company is striving to expand its production and sales. In the maturity phase, sales and production level off. And during the decline phase, sales of the product fall due to a weakening in consumer demand.

If a company had only one product and that product was, for example, nearing the end of its salable life, we would say that the company was in the decline phase. Companies generally have more than one product, however, and not all of a company's products are in the same phase of the product life cycle at the same time. We can still characterize a company as being in one of the four phases because the majority of its products are in a particular phase.

Illustration 11-3 shows that the phase a company is in affects its cash flows. In the **introductory stage,** we expect that the company will be spending considerable amounts to purchase productive assets, but it will not be generating much (if any) cash from operations. To support its asset purchases it may have to issue stock or debt. Thus, we expect cash from operations to be negative, cash from investing to be negative, and cash from financing to be positive.

Illustration 11-3 Impact of product life cycle on cash flows

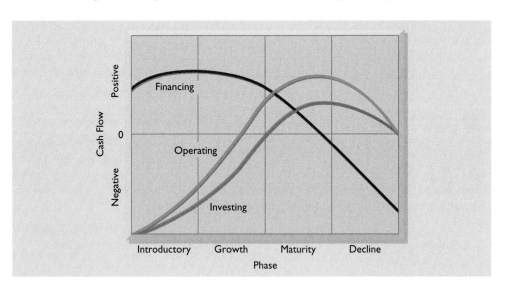

During the **growth phase,** we expect to see the company start to generate small amounts of cash from operations. Cash from operations continues to be less than net income during this phase, though, because inventory must be purchased for future projected sales. Since those sales are projected to be increasing, the size of inventory purchases must increase. Thus, less inventory will be expensed on an accrual basis than purchased on a cash basis in the growth phase.

Also, collections on accounts receivable will lag behind sales, and because sales are growing, accrual sales during a period will exceed cash collections during that period. Cash needed for asset acquisitions will continue to exceed cash provided by operations, requiring that the company make up the deficiency by issuing new stock or debt. Thus, the company continues to show negative cash from investing and positive cash from financing in the growth phase.

During the **maturity phase,** cash from operations and net income are approximately the same. Cash generated from operations exceeds investing needs. Thus, in the maturity phase the company can actually start to retire debt or buy back stock.

Finally, during the **decline phase,** cash from operations decreases. Cash from investing might actually become positive as the firm sells off excess assets, and cash from financing may be negative as the company buys back stock and retires debt.

Consider Microsoft: During its early years it had significant product development costs with little revenue. Microsoft was lucky in that its agreement with IBM to provide the operating system for IBM PCs gave it an early steady source of cash to support growth. As noted earlier, one way it conserved cash was to pay employees with stock options rather than cash. Today Microsoft could best be characterized as being between the growth and maturity phases. It continues to spend considerable amounts on research and development and investment in new assets. For the last 3 years, however, its cash from operations has exceeded its net income. Cash from operations also exceeds cash used for investing, and common stock repurchased exceeds common stock issued. For Microsoft, as for any large company, the challenge is to maintain its growth. In the software industry, where products become obsolete very quickly, the challenge is particularly great.

BUSINESS INSIGHT
Investor Perspective

Listed here are the net income, and cash from operations, investing, and financing during a recent year for some of the companies that we have discussed in previous chapters. The final column suggests their likely phase in the life cycle based on these figures.

Company ($ in millions)	Net Income	Cash Provided by Operations	Cash Provided (Used) by Investing	Cash Provided (Used) by Financing	Likely Phase in Life Cycle
Netscape	$ (3)	$ 15	$ (140)	$ 168	Introductory
Iomega	8.5	(27)	(43)	54	Introductory
Caterpillar	1,136	2,190	(1,749)	(208)	Maturity
McDonnell Douglas	(416)	869	(213)	(280)	Early Decline
Kellogg	490	1,041	(309)	(759)	Late Maturity
Southwest Airlines	183	456	(729)	415	Early Maturity
Starbucks	42	137	(211)	180	Growth

USEFULNESS OF THE STATEMENT OF CASH FLOWS

Many investors believe that "Cash is cash and everything else is accounting"; that is, cash flow is less susceptible to management manipulation and fraud than traditional accounting measures such as net income. Although we suggest that reliance on cash flows to the exclusion of accrual accounting is inappropriate, comparing cash from operations to net income can reveal important information about the "quality" of reported net income—that is, the extent to which net income provides a good measure of actual performance.

The information in a statement of cash flows should help investors, creditors, and others evaluate these aspects of the firm's financial position:

1. **The entity's ability to generate future cash flows.** By examining relationships between such items as sales and net cash provided by operating activities, or cash provided by operations and increases or decreases in cash, investors and others can predict the amounts, timing, and uncertainty of future cash flows better than from accrual-based data.

2. **The entity's ability to pay dividends and meet obligations.** Simply put, if a company does not have adequate cash, it cannot pay employees, settle debts, or pay dividends. Employees, creditors, stockholders, and customers should be particularly interested in this statement because it alone shows the flows of cash in a business.

3. **The reasons for the difference between net income and net cash provided (used) by operating activities.** Net income is important because it provides information on the success or failure of a business enterprise. However, some are critical of accrual basis net income because it requires many estimates; as a result, the reliability of the number is often challenged. Such is not the case with cash. Thus, many readers of the financial statements want to know the reasons for the difference between net income and net cash provided by operating activities. Then they can assess for themselves the reliability of the income number.

4. **The cash investing and financing transactions during the period.** By examining a company's investing activities and financing transactions, a financial statement reader can better understand *why* assets and liabilities increased or decreased during the period.

Helpful Hint Income from operations and cash flow from operating activities are different. Income from operations is based on accrual accounting; cash flow from operating activities is prepared on a cash basis.

In summary, the information in the statement of cash flows is useful in answering the following questions:

How did cash increase when there was a net loss for the period?
How were the proceeds of the bond issue used?
How was the expansion in the plant and equipment financed?
Why were dividends not increased?
How was the retirement of debt accomplished?
How much money was borrowed during the year?
Is cash flow greater or less than net income?

BUSINESS INSIGHT
Investor Perspective

Cash flow is also sometimes used to determine the price of a company. Page Net, a company in the telephone beeper business, had an initial public offering (IPO) in which $590 million of stock was sold. In December 1993 the stock had a market value of $1.5 billion, yet Page Net reported losses in every quarter since it went public. Its cash flow the year before the IPO was $39 million, $57 million in the IPO year, $75 million in 1992, and approximately $99 million in 1993. As one expert noted, "It is a classic example of a company valued by cash flow."

PREPARING THE STATEMENT OF CASH FLOWS

The statement of cash flows is prepared differently from the other basic financial statements. First, it is not prepared from an adjusted trial balance. Because the statement requires detailed information concerning the changes in account balances that occurred between two periods of time, an adjusted trial balance does not provide the data necessary for the statement. Second, the statement of cash flows deals with cash receipts and payments. As a result, **the accrual concept is not used in the preparation of a statement of cash flows.**

The information to prepare this statement usually comes from three sources:

1. **Comparative balance sheet.** Information in this statement indicates the amount of the changes in assets, liabilities, and stockholders' equities from the beginning to the end of the period.
2. **Current income statement.** Information in this statement helps the reader determine the amount of cash provided or used by operations during the period.
3. **Additional information.** Additional information includes transaction data that are needed to determine how cash was provided or used during the period.

Preparing the statement of cash flows from these data sources involves the three major steps explained in Illustration 11-4. First, to see where you are headed, start by identifying the change in cash during the period. Has cash increased or decreased during the year? Second, determine the net cash provided/used by operating activities. Third, determine the net cash provided/used by investing and financing activities.

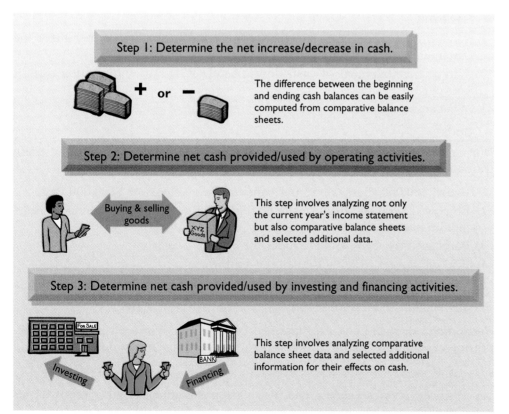

Illustration 11-4 Three major steps in preparing the statement of cash flows

Step 1: Determine the net increase/decrease in cash.

The difference between the beginning and ending cash balances can be easily computed from comparative balance sheets.

Step 2: Determine net cash provided/used by operating activities.

Buying & selling goods

This step involves analyzing not only the current year's income statement but also comparative balance sheets and selected additional data.

Step 3: Determine net cash provided/used by investing and financing activities.

Investing   Financing

This step involves analyzing comparative balance sheet data and selected additional information for their effects on cash.

🌐 **International Note**

International accounting requirements are quite similar with regard to the cash flow statement. Here are some interesting exceptions: In Japan operating and investing activities are combined, in Australia the direct method is mandatory, and in Spain the indirect method is mandatory. Also, in a number of European and Scandinavian countries a cash flow statement is not required at all, although in practice most publicly traded companies provide one.

Indirect and Direct Methods

In order to determine the cash provided/used by operating activities, **net income must be converted from an accrual basis to a cash basis.** This conversion may be done by either of two methods: indirect or direct. **Both methods arrive at the same total amount** for "Net cash provided by operating activities," but they differ in disclosing the items that make up the total amount. Note that the two different methods affect only the operating activities section; the investing activities and financing activities sections **are not affected by the choice of method.**

The indirect method is used extensively in practice—over 98% of companies in a recent survey.[1] Companies favor the indirect method for three reasons: (1) It is easier to prepare, (2) it focuses on the differences between net income and net cash flow from operating activities, and (3) it tends to reveal less company information to competitors.

Others, however, favor the direct method, which is more consistent with the objective of a statement of cash flows because it shows operating cash receipts and payments. The FASB has expressed a preference for the direct method but allows the use of either method. However, when the direct method is used, the net cash flow from operating activities as computed using the indirect method must also be reported in a separate schedule.

On the following pages, in two separate sections, we describe the use of the two methods. Section 1 illustrates the indirect method, and Section 2 illustrates the direct method. These sections are independent of each other; *only one or the other* need be covered in order to understand and prepare the statement of cash flows. When you have finished the section assigned by your instructor, turn to the next topic on page 446—"Using Cash Flows to Evaluate a Company."

BEFORE YOU GO ON . . .

● **Review It**

1. What are the phases of the product life cycle, and how do they affect the statement of cash flows?
2. Why is the statement of cash flows useful? What key information does it convey?
3. What are the three major steps in the preparation of a statement of cash flows?

● **Do It**

During the first week of its existence, Sandwich Molding Company had these transactions:

1. Issued 100,000 shares of $5 par value common stock for $800,000 cash.
2. Borrowed $200,000 from Castle National Bank, signing a 5-year note bearing 8% interest.
3. Purchased two semi-trailer trucks for $170,000 cash.
4. Paid employees $12,000 for salaries and wages.
5. Collected $20,000 cash for services rendered.

Classify each of these transactions by type of cash flow activity.

Reasoning: All cash flows are classified into three activities for purposes of reporting cash inflows and outflows: operating activities, investing activities, and

---

[1] *Accounting Trends and Techniques—1998* (New York: American Institute of Certified Public Accountants, 1998).

financing activities. Operating activities include the cash effects of transactions that create revenues and expenses and thus enter into the determination of net income. Investing activities include (a) purchasing and disposing of investments and productive long-lived assets using cash and (b) lending money and collecting the loans. Financing activities include (a) obtaining cash from issuing debt and repaying the amounts borrowed and (b) obtaining cash from stockholders and providing them with a return on their investment.

Solution:

1. Financing activity
2. Financing activity
3. Investing activity
4. Operating activity
5. Operating activity

Related exercise material: BE11-4, E11-3.

THE
NAVIGATOR

SECTION 1

STATEMENT OF CASH FLOWS— INDIRECT METHOD

To explain and illustrate the indirect method, we will use the transactions of Computer Services Company for two years: 1999 and 2000. Annual statements of cash flows will be prepared. Basic transactions will be used in the first year with additional transactions in the second year.

STUDY OBJECTIVE
4a
Prepare a statement of cash flows using the indirect method.

FIRST YEAR OF OPERATIONS—1999

Computer Services Company started on January 1, 1999, when it issued 50,000 shares of $1 par value common stock for $50,000 cash. The company rented its office space and furniture and performed consulting services throughout the first year. The comparative balance sheet for the beginning and end of 1999, showing increases or decreases, appears in Illustration 11-5.

Illustration 11-5 Comparative balance sheet, 1999, with increases and decreases

COMPUTER SERVICES COMPANY Comparative Balance Sheet December 31			
Assets	Dec. 31, 1999	Jan. 1, 1999	Change Increase/Decrease
Cash	$34,000	$-0-	$34,000 increase
Accounts receivable	30,000	-0-	30,000 increase
Equipment	10,000	-0-	10,000 increase
Total	$74,000	$-0-	
Liabilities and Stockholders' Equity			
Accounts payable	$ 4,000	$-0-	$ 4,000 increase
Common stock	50,000	-0-	50,000 increase
Retained earnings	20,000	-0-	20,000 increase
Total	$74,000	$-0-	

Helpful Hint Note that although each of the balance sheet items increased, their individual effects are not the same. Some of these increases are cash inflows, and some are cash outflows.

The income statement and additional information for Computer Services Company are shown in Illustration 11-6.

Illustration 11-6 Income statement and additional information, 1999

COMPUTER SERVICES COMPANY	
Income Statement	
For the Year Ended December 31, 1999	
Revenues	$85,000
Operating expenses	40,000
Income before income taxes	45,000
Income tax expense	10,000
Net income	$35,000

Additional information:
(a) Examination of selected data indicates that a dividend of $15,000 was declared and paid during the year.
(b) The equipment was purchased at the end of 1999. No depreciation was taken in 1999.

DETERMINING THE NET INCREASE/DECREASE IN CASH (STEP 1)

Helpful Hint You may wish to insert the beginning and ending cash balances and the increase/decrease in cash necessitated by these balances immediately into the statement of cash flows. The net increase/decrease is the target amount. The net cash flows from the three activities must equal the target amount.

To prepare a statement of cash flows, the first step is to **determine the net increase or decrease in cash.** This is a simple computation. For example, Computer Services Company had no cash on hand at the beginning of 1999, but had $34,000 on hand at the end of the year. Thus, the change in cash for 1999 was an increase of $34,000.

DETERMINING NET CASH PROVIDED/USED BY OPERATING ACTIVITIES (STEP 2)

To determine net cash provided by operating activities under the indirect method, **net income is adjusted for items that did not affect cash.** A useful starting point in determining net cash provided by operating activities is to understand **why** net income must be converted. Under generally accepted accounting principles, most companies use the accrual basis of accounting. As you have learned, this basis requires that revenue be recorded when earned and that expenses be recorded when incurred. Earned revenues may include credit sales that have not been collected in cash, and expenses incurred may include costs that have not been paid in cash. Under the accrual basis of accounting, net income does not indicate the net cash provided by operating activities. Therefore, under the indirect method, net income must be adjusted to convert certain items to the cash basis.

The indirect method (or reconciliation method) starts with net income and converts it to net cash provided by operating activities. In other words, **the indirect method adjusts net income for items that affected reported net income but did not affect cash,** as shown in Illustration 11-7. That is, noncash charges in the income statement are added back to net income and noncash credits are deducted, to compute net cash provided by operating activities.

A useful starting point in identifying the adjustments to net income is the current asset and current liability accounts other than cash. Those accounts—receivables, payables, prepayments, and inventories—should be analyzed for their effects on cash. We do that next for various accounts.

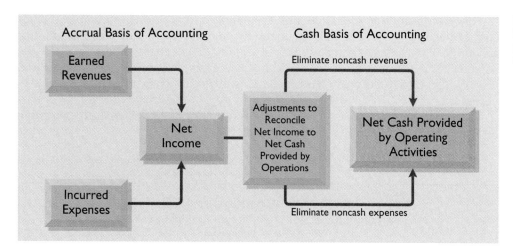

Illustration 11-7 Net income versus net cash provided by operating activities

Increase in Accounts Receivable. When accounts receivable increase during the year, revenues on an accrual basis are higher than revenues on a cash basis. In other words, operations of the period led to revenues, **but not all of these revenues resulted in an increase in cash;** some of the revenues resulted in an increase in accounts receivable.

For example, Computer Services Company, in its first year of operations, had revenues of $85,000 but collected only $55,000 in cash. Thus, on an accrual basis revenue was $85,000, but on a cash basis we would record only the $55,000 received during the period. Illustration 11-8 shows that, to convert net income to net cash provided by operating activities, the increase of $30,000 in accounts receivable must be deducted from net income.

ACCOUNTS RECEIVABLE			
Jan. 1 Balance	0	**Receipts from customers**	**55,000**
Revenues	**85,000**		
Dec. 31 Balance	30,000		

Illustration 11-8 Analysis of accounts receivable

Increase in Accounts Payable. In the first year, operating expenses incurred on account were credited to Accounts Payable. When accounts payable increase during the year, operating expenses on an accrual basis are higher than they are on a cash basis. For Computer Services Company, operating expenses reported in the income statement were $40,000. However, since Accounts Payable increased $4,000, only $36,000 ($40,000 − $4,000) of the expenses were paid in cash. To convert net income to net cash provided by operating activities, the increase of $4,000 in accounts payable must be added to net income.

The T account analysis in Illustration 11-9 also indicates that payments to creditors are less than operating expenses.

ACCOUNTS PAYABLE			
Payments to creditors	**36,000**	Jan. 1 Balances	0
		Operating expenses	**40,000**
		Dec. 31 Balance	4,000

Illustration 11-9 Analysis of accounts payable

For Computer Services Company, the changes in accounts receivable and accounts payable were the only changes in current asset and current liability accounts. This means that any other revenues or expenses reported in the income statement were received or paid in cash. Thus, Computer Services' income tax expense of $10,000 was paid in cash, and no adjustment of net income is necessary.

The operating activities section of the statement of cash flows for Computer Services Company is shown in Illustration 11-10.

Illustration 11-10 Operating activities section, 1999—indirect method

COMPUTER SERVICES COMPANY		
Partial Statement of Cash Flows—Indirect Method		
For the Year Ended December 31, 1999		
Cash flows from operating activities		
Net income		$35,000
Adjustments to reconcile net income to net cash provided by operating activities:		
Increase in accounts receivable	$(30,000)	
Increase in accounts payable	4,000	(26,000)
Net cash provided by operating activities		**$ 9,000**

DETERMINING NET CASH PROVIDED/USED BY INVESTING AND FINANCING ACTIVITIES (STEP 3)

The third and final step in preparing the statement of cash flows begins with a study of the balance sheet to determine changes in noncurrent accounts. The changes in each noncurrent account are then analyzed using selected transaction data to determine the effect, if any, the changes had on cash.

For Computer Services Company, the three noncurrent accounts are Equipment, Common Stock, and Retained Earnings, and all three have increased during the year. What caused these increases? No transaction data are given for the increases in Equipment of $10,000 and Common Stock of $50,000. When other explanations are lacking, we assume that any differences involve cash. Thus, the increase in equipment is assumed to be a purchase of equipment for $10,000 cash. This purchase is reported as a cash outflow in the investing activities section. The increase in common stock is assumed to result from the issuance of common stock for $50,000 cash. It is reported as an inflow of cash in the financing activities section of the statement of cash flows. In doing your homework, assume that **any unexplained differences in noncurrent accounts involve cash.**

The reasons for the net increase of $20,000 in the Retained Earnings account are determined by analysis. First, net income increased retained earnings by $35,000. Second, the additional information provided below the income statement in Illustration 11-6 indicates that a cash dividend of $15,000 was declared and paid. The $35,000 increase due to net income is reported in the operating activities section. The cash dividend paid is reported in the financing activities section.

This analysis can also be made directly from the Retained Earnings account in the ledger of Computer Services Company as shown in Illustration 11-11.

The $20,000 increase in Retained Earnings in 1997 is a **net** change. When a net change in a noncurrent balance sheet account has occurred during the

RETAINED EARNINGS				
Dec. 31 Cash dividend	15,000	Jan. 1	Balance	0
		Dec. 31	Net income	35,000
		Dec. 31	Balance	20,000

Illustration 11-11 Analysis of retained earnings

year, it generally is necessary to report the causes of the net change separately in the statement of cash flows.

STATEMENT OF CASH FLOWS—1999

Having completed the three steps above, we can prepare the statement of cash flows by the indirect method. The statement starts with the operating activities section, followed by the investing activities section, and then the financing activities section. The 1999 statement of cash flows for Computer Services is shown in Illustration 11-12.

Illustration 11-12 Statement of cash flows, 1999—indirect method

COMPUTER SERVICES COMPANY
Statement of Cash Flows—Indirect Method
For the Year Ended December 31, 1999

Cash flows from operating activities		
Net income		$35,000
Adjustments to reconcile net income to net cash provided by operating activities:		
Increase in accounts receivable	$(30,000)	
Increase in accounts payable	4,000	(26,000)
Net cash provided by operating activities		9,000
Cash flows from investing activities		
Purchase of equipment	(10,000)	
Net cash used by investing activities		(10,000)
Cash flows from financing activities		
Issuance of common stock	50,000	
Payment of cash dividends	(15,000)	
Net cash provided by financing activities		35,000
Net increase in cash		34,000
Cash at beginning of period		0
Cash at end of period		$34,000

Computer Services Company's statement of cash flows for 1999 shows that operating activities **provided** $9,000 cash; investing activities **used** $10,000 cash; and financing activities **provided** $35,000 cash. The increase in cash of $34,000 reported in the statement of cash flows agrees with the increase of $34,000 shown as the change in the cash account in the comparative balance sheet.

SECOND YEAR OF OPERATIONS—2000

Presented in Illustrations 11-13 and 11-14 is information related to the second year of operations for Computer Services Company.

Illustration 11-13 Comparative balance sheet, 2000, with increases and decreases

COMPUTER SERVICES COMPANY
Comparative Balance Sheet
December 31

Assets	2000	1999	Change Increase/Decrease
Cash	$ 56,000	$34,000	$ 22,000 increase
Accounts receivable	20,000	30,000	10,000 decrease
Prepaid expenses	4,000	0	4,000 increase
Land	130,000	0	130,000 increase
Building	160,000	0	160,000 increase
Accumulated depreciation—building	(11,000)	0	11,000 increase
Equipment	27,000	10,000	17,000 increase
Accumulated depreciation—equipment	(3,000)	0	3,000 increase
Total	$383,000	$74,000	
Liabilities and Stockholders' Equity			
Accounts payable	$ 59,000	$ 4,000	$ 55,000 increase
Bonds payable	130,000	0	130,000 increase
Common stock	50,000	50,000	0
Retained earnings	144,000	20,000	124,000 increase
Total	$383,000	$74,000	

Illustration 11-14 Income statement and additional information, 2000

COMPUTER SERVICES COMPANY
Income Statement
For the Year Ended December 31, 2000

Revenues		$507,000
Operating expenses (excluding depreciation)	$261,000	
Depreciation expense	15,000	
Loss on sale of equipment	3,000	279,000
Income from operations		228,000
Income tax expense		89,000
Net income		$139,000

Additional information:
(a) In 2000 the company declared and paid a $15,000 cash dividend.
(b) The company obtained land through the issuance of $130,000 of long-term bonds.
(c) An office building costing $160,000 was purchased for cash; equipment costing $25,000 was also purchased for cash.
(d) During 2000 the company sold equipment with a book value of $7,000 (cost $8,000 less accumulated depreciation $1,000) for $4,000 cash.

DETERMINING THE NET INCREASE/DECREASE IN CASH (STEP 1)

To prepare a statement of cash flows from this information, the first step is to **determine the net increase or decrease in cash.** As indicated from the information presented, cash increased $22,000 ($56,000 − $34,000).

DETERMINING NET CASH PROVIDED/USED BY OPERATING ACTIVITIES (STEP 2)

As in step 2 in 1999, net income on an accrual basis must be adjusted to arrive at net cash provided/used by operating activities. Explanations for the adjustments to net income for Computer Services Company in 2000 are as follows:

Decrease in Accounts Receivable. Accounts receivable decreases during the period because cash receipts are higher than revenues reported on an accrual basis. To convert net income to net cash provided by operating activities, the decrease of $10,000 in accounts receivable must be added to net income.

Increase in Prepaid Expenses. Prepaid expenses increase during a period because cash paid for expenses is greater than expenses reported on an accrual basis. Cash payments have been made in the current period, but expenses (as charges to the income statement) have been deferred to future periods. To convert net income to net cash provided by operating activities, the increase of $4,000 in prepaid expenses must be deducted from net income. An increase in prepaid expenses results in a decrease in cash during the period.

Increase in Accounts Payable. Like the increase in 1999, the 2000 increase of $55,000 in accounts payable must be added to net income to convert to net cash provided by operating activities.

Depreciation Expense. During 2000 Computer Services Company reported depreciation expense of $15,000. Of this amount, $11,000 related to the building and $4,000 to the equipment. These two amounts were determined by analyzing the accumulated depreciation accounts as follows.

Increase in Accumulated Depreciation—Building. As shown in Illustration 11-13, this accumulated depreciation increased $11,000. This change represents the depreciation expense on the building for the year. **Because depreciation expense is a noncash charge, it is added back to net income** in order to arrive at net cash provided by operating activities.

Increase in Accumulated Depreciation—Equipment. The increase in the Accumulated Depreciation—Equipment account was $3,000. This amount does not represent the total depreciation expense for the year, though, because the additional information indicates that this account was decreased (debited $1,000) as a result of the sale of some equipment. Thus, depreciation expense for 2000 was $4,000 ($3,000 + $1,000). This amount is **added to net income** to determine net cash provided by operating activities. The T account in Illustration 11-15 provides information about the changes that occurred in this account in 2000.

> **Helpful Hint** Whether the indirect or direct method (Section 2) is used, net cash provided by operating activities will be the same.

> **Helpful Hint** Depreciation is similar to any other expense in that it reduces net income. It differs in that it does not involve a current cash outflow; that is why it must be added back to net income to arrive at cash provided by operations.

ACCUMULATED DEPRECIATION—EQUIPMENT			
Accumulated depreciation on equipment sold	1,000	Jan. 1 Balance	0
		Depreciation expense	**4,000**
		Dec. 31 Balance	3,000

Illustration 11-15
Analysis of accumulated depreciation—equipment

Depreciation expense of $11,000 on the building plus depreciation expense of $4,000 on the equipment equals the depreciation expense of $15,000 reported on the income statement.

Other charges to expense **that do not require the use of cash,** such as the amortization of intangible assets, are treated in the same manner as depreciation. Depreciation and similar noncash charges are frequently listed in the statement of cash flows as the first adjustments to net income.

Loss on Sale of Equipment. On the income statement, Computer Services Company reported a $3,000 loss on the sale of equipment (book value $7,000 less cash proceeds $4,000). The loss reduced net income but **did not reduce cash.** Thus, the loss is **added to net income** in determining net cash provided by operating activities.[2]

As a result of the previous adjustments, net cash provided by operating activities is $218,000, as computed in Illustration 11-16.

Illustration 11-16 Operating activities section, 2000—indirect method

Helpful Hint By custom we use the label "depreciation expense," even though the expense causes an *increase* in accumulated depreciation and could also be described as "increase in accumulated depreciation."

COMPUTER SERVICES COMPANY Partial Statement of Cash Flows—Indirect Method For the Year Ended December 31, 2000		
Cash flows from operating activities		
Net income		$139,000
Adjustments to reconcile net income to net cash		
provided by operating activities:		
Depreciation expense	$15,000	
Loss on sale of equipment	3,000	
Decrease in accounts receivable	10,000	
Increase in prepaid expenses	(4,000)	
Increase in accounts payable	55,000	79,000
Net cash provided by operating activities		**$218,000**

DETERMINING NET CASH PROVIDED/USED BY INVESTING AND FINANCING ACTIVITIES (STEP 3)

After the determination of net cash provided by operating activities, the final step involves analyzing the remaining changes in balance sheet accounts to determine net cash provided/used by investing and financing activities.

Increase in Land. As indicated from the change in the land account, land of $130,000 was purchased through the issuance of long-term bonds. Although the issuance of bonds payable for land has no effect on cash, it is a significant noncash investing and financing activity that merits disclosure. As indicated earlier, these activities are disclosed in a separate schedule at the bottom of the statement of cash flows.

Increase in Building. As indicated in the additional information, an office building was acquired using cash of $160,000. This transaction is a cash outflow reported in the investing activities section.

Increase in Equipment. The equipment account increased $17,000. Based on the additional information, this was a net increase that resulted from two transactions: (1) a purchase of equipment for $25,000 and (2) the sale of equipment costing $8,000 for $4,000. These transactions are classified as investing activities, and each transaction should be reported separately. Thus, the purchase of equipment should be reported as an outflow of cash for $25,000, and the sale should be reported as an inflow of cash for $4,000. The T account in Illustration 11-17 shows the reasons for the change in this account during the year.

---

[2]If a gain on sale occurs, a different situation results: To allow a gain to flow through to net cash provided by operating activities would be double-counting the gain—once in net income and again in the investing activities section as part of the cash proceeds from sale. As a result, a gain is deducted from net income in reporting net cash provided by operating activities.

EQUIPMENT			
Jan. 1 Balance	10,000	Cost of equipment sold	8,000
Purchase of equipment	25,000		
Dec. 31 Balance	27,000		

Illustration 11-17
Analysis of equipment

Increase in Bonds Payable. The Bonds Payable account increased $130,000. As shown in the additional information, land was acquired through the issuance of these bonds. As indicated earlier, this noncash transaction is reported in a separate schedule at the bottom of the statement.

Helpful Hint When stocks or bonds are issued for cash, it is the amount of the issuance price (proceeds) that appears on the statement of cash flows as a financing inflow—rather than the par value of the stocks or face value of bonds.

Increase in Retained Earnings. Retained Earnings increased $124,000 during the year. This increase can be explained by two factors: (1) Net income of $139,000 increased Retained Earnings and (2) dividends of $15,000 decreased Retained Earnings. Net income is converted to net cash provided by operating activities in the operating activities section. Payment of the dividends is a **cash outflow that is reported as a financing activity.**

Helpful Hint It is the *payment* of dividends, not the declaration, that appears on the statement of cash flows.

STATEMENT OF CASH FLOWS—2000

Combining the previous items, we obtain a statement of cash flows for 2000 for Computer Services Company as presented in Illustration 11-18.

Illustration 11-18 Statement of cash flows, 2000—indirect method

COMPUTER SERVICES COMPANY
Statement of Cash Flows—Indirect Method
For the Year Ended December 31, 2000

Cash flows from operating activities		
Net income		$139,000
Adjustments to reconcile net income to net cash		
provided by operating activities:		
Depreciation expense	$ 15,000	
Loss on sale of equipment	3,000	
Decrease in accounts receivable	10,000	
Increase in prepaid expenses	(4,000)	
Increase in accounts payable	55,000	79,000
Net cash provided by operating activities		218,000
Cash flows from investing activities		
Purchase of building	(160,000)	
Purchase of equipment	(25,000)	
Sale of equipment	4,000	
Net cash used by investing activities		(181,000)
Cash flows from financing activities		
Payment of cash dividends	(15,000)	
Net cash used by financing activities		(15,000)
Net increase in cash		22,000
Cash at beginning of period		34,000
Cash at end of period		$ 56,000
Noncash investing and financing activities		
Issuance of bonds payable to purchase land		$130,000

Helpful Hint Note that in the investing and financing activities sections, positive numbers indicate cash inflows (receipts) and negative numbers indicate cash outflows (payments).

SUMMARY OF CONVERSION TO NET CASH PROVIDED BY OPERATING ACTIVITIES — INDIRECT METHOD

As shown in the previous illustrations, the statement of cash flows prepared by the indirect method starts with net income and adds or deducts items not affecting cash, to arrive at net cash provided by operating activities. The additions and deductions consist of (1) changes in specific current assets and current liabilities and (2) noncash charges reported in the income statement. A summary of the adjustments for current assets and current liabilities is provided in Illustration 11-19.

Illustration 11-19
Adjustments for current assets and current liabilities

Current Assets and Current Liabilities	Adjustments to Convert Net Income to Net Cash Provided by Operating Activities	
	Add to Net Income	Deduct from Net Income
Accounts receivable	Decrease	Increase
Inventory	Decrease	Increase
Prepaid expenses	Decrease	Increase
Accounts payable	Increase	Decrease
Accrued expenses payable	Increase	Decrease

Adjustments for the noncash charges reported in the income statement are made as shown in Illustration 11-20.

Illustration 11-20
Adjustments for noncash charges

Noncash Charges	Adjustments to Convert Net Income to Net Cash Provided by Operating Activities
Depreciation expense	Add
Patent amortization expense	Add
Loss on sale of asset	Add

BEFORE YOU GO ON . . .

● **Review It**

1. What is the format of the operating activities section of the statement of cash flows using the indirect method?
2. Where is depreciation expense shown on a statement of cash flows using the indirect method?
3. Where are significant noncash investing and financing activities shown in a statement of cash flows? Give some examples.

● **Do It**

The following information relates to Reynolds Company. Use it to prepare a statement of cash flows using the indirect method.

REYNOLDS COMPANY
Comparative Balance Sheet
December 31

Assets	2000	1999	Change Increase/Decrease
Cash	$ 54,000	$ 37,000	$ 17,000 increase
Accounts receivable	68,000	26,000	42,000 increase
Inventories	54,000	0	54,000 increase
Prepaid expenses	4,000	6,000	2,000 decrease
Land	45,000	70,000	25,000 decrease
Buildings	200,000	200,000	0
Accumulated depreciation—buildings	(21,000)	(11,000)	10,000 increase
Equipment	193,000	68,000	125,000 increase
Accumulated depreciation—equipment	(28,000)	(10,000)	18,000 increase
Totals	$569,000	$386,000	
Liabilities and Stockholders' Equity			
Accounts payable	$ 23,000	$ 40,000	$ 17,000 decrease
Accrued expenses payable	10,000	0	10,000 increase
Bonds payable	110,000	150,000	40,000 decrease
Common stock ($1 par)	220,000	60,000	160,000 increase
Retained earnings	206,000	136,000	70,000 increase
Total	$569,000	$386,000	

REYNOLDS COMPANY
Income Statement
For the Year Ended December 31, 2000

Revenues		$890,000
Cost of goods sold	$465,000	
Operating expenses	221,000	
Interest expense	12,000	
Loss on sale of equipment	2,000	700,000
Income from operations		190,000
Income tax expense		65,000
Net income		$125,000

Additional information:
(a) Operating expenses include depreciation expense of $33,000.
(b) Land was sold at its book value for cash.
(c) Cash dividends of $55,000 were declared and paid in 2000.
(d) Interest expense of $12,000 was paid in cash.
(e) Equipment with a cost of $166,000 was purchased for cash. Equipment with a cost of $41,000 and a book value of $36,000 was sold for $34,000 cash.
(f) Bonds of $10,000 were redeemed at their book value for cash; bonds of $30,000 were converted into common stock.
(g) Common stock ($1 par) of $130,000 was issued for cash.
(h) Accounts payable pertain to merchandise suppliers.

Reasoning: The balance sheet and the income statement are prepared from an adjusted trial balance of the general ledger. The statement of cash flows is prepared from an analysis of the content and changes in the balance sheet and the income statement.

Helpful Hint To prepare the statement of cash flows:

1. Determine the net increase/decrease in cash.
2. Determine net cash provided/used by operating activities.
3. Determine net cash provided/used by investing and financing activities.
4. Operating activities generally relate to changes in current assets and current liabilities.
5. Investing activities generally relate to changes in noncurrent assets.
6. Financing activities generally relate to changes in noncurrent liabilities and stockholders' equity accounts.

Solution:

REYNOLDS COMPANY
Statement of Cash Flows—Indirect Method
For the Year Ended December 31, 2000

Cash flows from operating activities		
Net income		$125,000
Adjustments to reconcile net income to net cash		
provided by operating activities:		
Depreciation expense	$ 33,000	
Increase in accounts receivable	(42,000)	
Increase in inventories	(54,000)	
Decrease in prepaid expenses	2,000	
Decrease in accounts payable	(17,000)	
Increase in accrued expenses payable	10,000	
Loss on sale of equipment	2,000	(66,000)
Net cash provided by operating activities		59,000
Cash flows from investing activities		
Sale of land	25,000	
Sale of equipment	34,000	
Purchase of equipment	(166,000)	
Net cash used by investing activities		(107,000)
Cash flows from financing activities		
Redemption of bonds	(10,000)	
Sale of common stock	130,000	
Payment of dividends	(55,000)	
Net cash provided by financing activities		65,000
Net increase in cash		17,000
Cash at beginning of period		37,000
Cash at end of period		$ 54,000
Noncash investing and financing activities		
Conversion of bonds into common stock		$ 30,000

THE NAVIGATOR

Related exercise material: BE11-1, BE11-2, BE11-5, BE11-8, BE11-10, E11-2, E11-4, E11-5, E11-6.

Note: This concludes Section 1 on preparation of the statement of cash flows using the indirect method. Unless your instructor assigns Section 2, you should turn to the concluding section of the chapter, "Using Cash Flows to Evaluate a Company," on page 446.

SECTION 2

STATEMENT OF CASH FLOWS— DIRECT METHOD

To explain and illustrate the direct method, we will use the transactions of Juarez Company for two years: 1999 and 2000. Annual statements of cash flow will be prepared. Basic transactions will be used in the first year with additional transactions in the second year.

FIRST YEAR OF OPERATIONS—1999

Juarez Company began business on January 1, 1999, when it issued 300,000 shares of $1 par value common stock for $300,000 cash. The company rented office and sales space along with equipment. The comparative balance sheet at the beginning and end of 1999 and the changes in each account are shown in Illustration 11-21. The income statement and additional information for Juarez Company are shown in Illustration 11-22 on page 434.

> **STUDY OBJECTIVE**
> ——— 4b ———
> Prepare a statement of cash flows using the direct method.

JUAREZ COMPANY
Comparative Balance Sheet
December 31

Assets	Dec. 31, 1999	Jan. 1, 1999	Change Increase/Decrease
Cash	$159,000	$-0-	$159,000 increase
Accounts receivable	15,000	-0-	15,000 increase
Inventory	160,000	-0-	160,000 increase
Prepaid expenses	8,000	-0-	8,000 increase
Land	80,000	-0-	80,000 increase
Total	$422,000	$-0-	
Liabilities and Stockholders' Equity			
Accounts payable	$ 60,000	$-0-	$ 60,000 increase
Accrued expenses payable	20,000	-0-	20,000 increase
Common stock	300,000	-0-	300,000 increase
Retained earnings	42,000	-0-	42,000 increase
Total	$422,000	$-0-	

Illustration 11-21   Comparative balance sheet, 1999, with increases and decreases

The three steps cited in Illustration 11-4 on page 419 for preparing the statement of cash flows are used in the direct method.

DETERMINING THE NET INCREASE/DECREASE IN CASH (STEP 1)

The comparative balance sheet for Juarez Company shows a zero cash balance at January 1, 1999, and a cash balance of $159,000 at December 31, 1999. Therefore, the change in cash for 1999 was a net increase of $159,000.

Illustration 11-22
Income statement and
additional information,
1999

JUAREZ COMPANY
Income Statement
For the Year Ended December 31, 1999

Revenues from sales	$780,000
Cost of goods sold	450,000
Gross profit	330,000
Operating expenses	170,000
Income before income taxes	160,000
Income tax expense	48,000
Net income	$112,000

Additional information:
(a) Dividends of $70,000 were declared and paid in cash.
(b) The accounts payable increase resulted from the purchase of merchandise.

DETERMINING NET CASH PROVIDED/USED BY OPERATING ACTIVITIES (STEP 2)

Under the direct method, net cash provided by operating activities is computed by **adjusting each item in the income statement** from the accrual basis to the cash basis. To simplify and condense the operating activities section, **only major classes of operating cash receipts and cash payments are reported.** The difference between these major classes of cash receipts and cash payments is the net cash provided by operating activities, as shown in Illustration 11-23.

Illustration 11-23 Major
classes of cash receipts
and payments

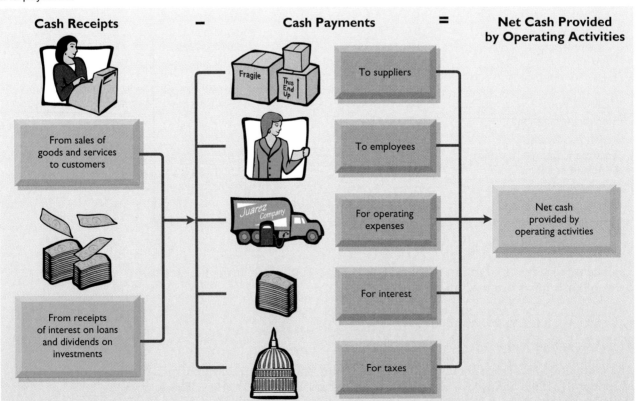

An efficient way to apply the direct method is to analyze the revenues and expenses reported in the income statement in the order in which they are listed and then determine cash receipts and cash payments related to these revenues and expenses. The direct method adjustments for Juarez Company in 1999 to determine net cash provided by operating activities are presented in the following sections.

Cash Receipts from Customers.   The income statement for Juarez Company reported revenues from customers of $780,000. To determine cash receipts from customers, it is necessary to consider the change in accounts receivable during the year. When accounts receivable increase during the year, revenues on an accrual basis are higher than cash receipts from customers. In other words, operations led to increased revenues, but not all of these revenues resulted in cash receipts. To determine the amount of cash receipts, the increase in accounts receivable is deducted from sales revenues. Conversely, a decrease in accounts receivable is added to sales revenues because cash receipts from customers then exceed sales revenues.

For Juarez Company accounts receivable increased $15,000. Thus, cash receipts from customers were $765,000, computed as shown in Illustration 11-24.

Revenues from sales	$ 780,000
Deduct: Increase in accounts receivable	15,000
Cash receipts from customers	**$765,000**

Illustration 11-24   Computation of cash receipts from customers

Cash receipts from customers may also be determined from an analysis of the Accounts Receivable account, as shown in Illustration 11-25.

ACCOUNTS RECEIVABLE			
Jan. 1 Balance	0	**Receipts from customers**	**765,000**
Revenues from sales	780,000		
Dec. 31 Balance	15,000		

Illustration 11-25   Analysis of accounts receivable

Helpful Hint The T account shows that revenue less increase in receivables equals cash receipts.

The relationships among cash receipts from customers, revenues from sales, and changes in accounts receivable are shown in Illustration 11-26.

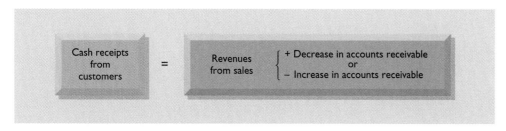

Illustration 11-26
Formula to compute cash receipts from customers—direct method

Cash Payments to Suppliers.   Juarez Company reported cost of goods sold on its income statement of $450,000. To determine cash payments to suppliers, it is first necessary to find purchases for the year. To find purchases, cost of goods sold is adjusted for the change in inventory. When inventory increases during the year, it means that purchases this year exceed cost of goods sold. As a result, the increase in inventory is added to cost of goods sold to arrive at purchases.

In 1999 Juarez Company's inventory increased $160,000. Purchases, therefore, are computed as shown in Illustration 11-27.

Illustration 11-27
Computation of
purchases

Cost of goods sold	$ 450,000
Add: Increase in inventory	160,000
Purchases	**$610,000**

After purchases are computed, cash payments to suppliers are determined by adjusting purchases for the change in accounts payable. When accounts payable increase during the year, purchases on an accrual basis are higher than they are on a cash basis. As a result, an increase in accounts payable is deducted from purchases to arrive at cash payments to suppliers. Conversely, a decrease in accounts payable is added to purchases because cash payments to suppliers exceed purchases. Cash payments to suppliers were $550,000, computed as in Illustration 11-28.

Illustration 11-28
Computation of cash
payments to suppliers

Purchases	$ 610,000
Deduct: Increase in accounts payable	60,000
Cash payments to suppliers	**$550,000**

Cash payments to suppliers may also be determined from an analysis of the Accounts Payable account, as shown in Illustration 11-29.

Illustration 11-29   Analysis of accounts payable

Helpful Hint The T account shows that purchases less increase in accounts payable equals payments to suppliers.

ACCOUNTS PAYABLE			
Payments to suppliers	550,000	Jan. 1 Balance	0
		Purchases	610,000
		Dec. 31 Balance	60,000

The relationship between cash payments to suppliers, cost of goods sold, changes in inventory, and changes in accounts payable is shown in the formula in Illustration 11-30.

Illustration 11-30   Formula to compute cash payments to suppliers—direct method

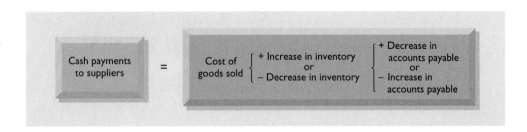

Cash Payments for Operating Expenses.   Operating expenses of $170,000 were reported on Juarez Company's income statement. To determine the cash paid for operating expenses, this amount must be adjusted for any changes in prepaid expenses and accrued expenses payable. For example, when prepaid expenses increased $8,000 during the year, cash paid for operating expenses was $8,000 higher than operating expenses reported on the income statement. To convert operating expenses to cash payments for operating expenses, the increase of $8,000 must be added to operating expenses. Conversely, if prepaid expenses decrease during the year, the decrease must be deducted from operating expenses.

Operating expenses must also be adjusted for changes in accrued expenses payable. When accrued expenses payable increase during the year, operating expenses on an accrual basis are higher than they are on a cash basis. As a result, an increase in accrued expenses payable is deducted from operating expenses to arrive at cash payments for operating expenses. Conversely, a decrease in accrued expenses payable is added to operating expenses because cash payments exceed operating expenses.

Juarez Company's cash payments for operating expenses were $158,000, computed as shown in Illustration 11-31.

Operating expenses	$ 170,000
Add: Increase in prepaid expenses	8,000
Deduct: Increase in accrued expenses payable	(20,000)
Cash payments for operating expenses	**$158,000**

Helpful Hint Decrease in accounts receivable: Indicates that cash collections were greater than sales. **Increase in accounts receivable:** Indicates that sales were greater than cash collections. **Increase in prepaid expenses:** Indicates that the amount paid for the prepayments exceeded the amount that was recorded as an expense. **Decrease in prepaid expenses:** Indicates that the amount recorded as an expense exceeded the amount of cash paid for the prepayments. **Increase in accounts payable:** Indicates that expenses incurred exceed the cash paid for expenses that period.

Illustration 11-31
Computation of cash payments for operating expenses

The relationships among cash payments for operating expenses, changes in prepaid expenses, and changes in accrued expenses payable are shown in the formula in Illustration 11-32.

Illustration 11-32 Formula to compute cash payments for operating expenses—direct method

Cash Payments for Income Taxes. The income statement for Juarez Company shows income tax expense of $48,000. This amount equals the cash paid because the comparative balance sheet indicates no income taxes payable at either the beginning or end of the year.

All of the revenues and expenses in the 1999 income statement have now been adjusted to a cash basis. The operating activities section of the statement of cash flows is presented in Illustration 11-33.

Illustration 11-33
Operating activities section—direct method

JUAREZ COMPANY Partial Statement of Cash Flows—Direct Method For the Year Ended December 31, 1999		
Cash flows from operating activities		
Cash receipts from customers		$765,000
Cash payments:		
To suppliers	$550,000	
For operating expenses	158,000	
For income taxes	48,000	756,000
Net cash provided by operating activities		**$ 9,000**

DETERMINING NET CASH PROVIDED/USED BY INVESTING AND FINANCING ACTIVITIES (STEP 3)

Preparing the investing and financing activities sections of the statement of cash flows begins with a determination of the changes in noncurrent accounts reported in the comparative balance sheet. The change in each account is then analyzed using the additional information to determine the effect, if any, the change had on cash.

Increase in Land. No additional information is given for the increase in land. In such case, you should assume that the increase affected cash. You should make the same assumption in doing homework problems when the cause of a change in a noncurrent account is not explained. The purchase of land is an investing activity. Thus, an outflow of cash of $80,000 for the purchase of land should be reported in the investing activities section.

Increase in Common Stock. As indicated earlier, 300,000 shares of $1 par value stock were sold for $300,000 cash. The issuance of common stock is a financing activity. Thus, a cash inflow of $300,000 from the issuance of common stock is reported in the financing activities section.

Helpful Hint It is the *payment* of dividends, not the declaration, that appears on the cash flow statement.

Increase in Retained Earnings. For the Retained Earnings account, the reasons for the net increase of $42,000 are determined by analysis. First, net income increased retained earnings by $112,000. Second, the additional information indicates that a cash dividend of $70,000 was declared and paid. The adjustment of revenues and expenses to arrive at net cash provided by operations was done in step 2 earlier. The cash dividend paid is reported as an outflow of cash in the financing activities section.

This analysis can also be made directly from the Retained Earnings account in the ledger of Juarez Company, as shown in Illustration 11-34.

Illustration 11-34 Analysis of retained earnings

RETAINED EARNINGS			
Dec. 31 Cash dividend	70,000	Jan. 1 Balance	0
		Dec. 31 Net income	112,000
		Dec. 31 Balance	42,000

The $42,000 increase in Retained Earnings in 1999 is a net change. When a net change in a noncurrent balance sheet account has occurred during the year, it generally is necessary to report the individual items that cause the net change.

STATEMENT OF CASH FLOWS—1999

The statement of cash flows can now be prepared. The operating activities section is reported first, followed by the investing and financing activities sections. The statement of cash flows for Juarez Company for 1999 is presented in Illustration 11-35.

The statement of cash flows shows that operating activities **provided** $9,000 of the net increase in cash of $159,000. Financing activities **provided** $230,000 of cash, and investing activities **used** $80,000 of cash. The net increase in cash for the year of $159,000 agrees with the $159,000 increase in cash reported in the comparative balance sheet.

Illustration 11-35
Statement of cash flows, 1999—direct method

JUAREZ COMPANY
Statement of Cash Flows—Direct Method
For the Year Ended December 31, 1999

Cash flows from operating activities		
Cash receipts from customers		$765,000
Cash payments:		
To suppliers	$550,000	
For operating expenses	158,000	
For income taxes	48,000	756,000
Net cash provided by operating activities		9,000
Cash flows from investing activities		
Purchase of land	(80,000)	
Net cash used by investing activities		(80,000)
Cash flows from financing activities		
Issuance of common stock	300,000	
Payment of cash dividend	(70,000)	
Net cash provided by financing activities		230,000
Net increase in cash		159,000
Cash at beginning of period		0
Cash at end of period		$159,000

Helpful Hint Note that in the investing and financing activities sections, positive numbers indicate cash inflows (receipts) and negative numbers indicate cash outflows (payments).

SECOND YEAR OF OPERATIONS—2000

Illustrations 11-36 and 11-37 present the comparative balance sheet, the income statement, and additional information pertaining to the second year of operations for Juarez Company.

Illustration 11-36 Comparative balance sheet, 2000, with increases and decreases

JUAREZ COMPANY
Comparative Balance Sheet
December 31

Assets	2000	1999	Change Increase/Decrease
Cash	$191,000	$159,000	$ 32,000 increase
Accounts receivable	12,000	15,000	3,000 decrease
Inventory	130,000	160,000	30,000 decrease
Prepaid expenses	6,000	8,000	2,000 decrease
Land	180,000	80,000	100,000 increase
Equipment	160,000	0	160,000 increase
Accumulated depreciation—equipment	(16,000)	0	16,000 increase
Total	$663,000	$422,000	
Liabilities and Stockholders' Equity			
Accounts payable	$ 52,000	$ 60,000	$ 8,000 decrease
Accrued expenses payable	15,000	20,000	5,000 decrease
Income taxes payable	12,000	0	12,000 increase
Bonds payable	90,000	0	90,000 increase
Common stock	400,000	300,000	100,000 increase
Retained earnings	94,000	42,000	52,000 increase
Total	$663,000	$422,000	

Illustration 11-37
Income statement and
additional information,
2000

JUAREZ COMPANY
Income Statement
For the Year Ended December 31, 2000

Revenues from sales		$975,000
Cost of goods sold	$660,000	
Operating expenses (excluding depreciation)	176,000	
Depreciation expense	18,000	
Loss on sale of store equipment	1,000	855,000
Income before income taxes		120,000
Income tax expense		36,000
Net income		$ 84,000

Additional information:
(a) In 2000 the company declared and paid a $32,000 cash dividend.
(b) Bonds were issued at face value for $90,000 in cash.
(c) Equipment costing $180,000 was purchased for cash.
(d) Equipment costing $20,000 was sold for $17,000 cash when the book value of
   the equipment was $18,000.
(e) Common stock of $100,000 was issued to acquire land.

DETERMINING THE NET INCREASE/DECREASE IN CASH (STEP 1)

The comparative balance sheet shows a beginning cash balance of $159,000 and an ending cash balance of $191,000. Thus, there was a net increase in cash in 2000 of $32,000.

DETERMINING NET CASH PROVIDED/USED BY OPERATING ACTIVITIES (STEP 2)

Cash Receipts from Customers.   Revenues from sales were $975,000. Since accounts receivable decreased $3,000, cash receipts from customers were greater than sales revenues. Cash receipts from customers were $978,000, computed as shown in Illustration 11-38.

Illustration 11-38
Computation of cash
receipts from customers

Revenues from sales	$ 975,000
Add: Decrease in accounts receivable	3,000
Cash receipts from customers	**$978,000**

Cash Payments to Suppliers.   The conversion of cost of goods sold to purchases and purchases to cash payments to suppliers is similar to the computations made in 1999. For 2000 purchases are computed using cost of goods sold of $660,000 from the income statement and the decrease in inventory of $30,000 from the comparative balance sheet. Purchases are then adjusted by the decrease in accounts payable of $8,000. Cash payments to suppliers were $638,000, computed as in Illustration 11-39.

Illustration 11-39
Computation of cash
payments to suppliers

Cost of goods sold	$ 660,000
Deduct: Decrease in inventory	30,000
Purchases	630,000
Add: Decrease in accounts payable	8,000
Cash payments to suppliers	**$638,000**

Cash Payments for Operating Expenses. Operating expenses (exclusive of depreciation expense) for 2000 were reported at $176,000. This amount is then adjusted for changes in prepaid expenses and accrued expenses payable to arrive at cash payments for operating expenses.

As indicated from the comparative balance sheet, prepaid expenses decreased $2,000 during the year. This means that $2,000 was allocated to operating expenses (thereby increasing operating expenses), but cash payments did not increase by that amount. To arrive at cash payments for operating expenses, the decrease in prepaid expenses is deducted from operating expenses.

Accrued expenses payable decreased $5,000 during the period. As a result, cash payments were higher by $5,000 than the amount reported for operating expenses. The decrease in accrued expenses payable is added to operating expenses. Cash payments for operating expenses were $179,000, computed as shown in Illustration 11-40.

Operating expenses, exclusive of depreciation	$ 176,000	
Deduct: Decrease in prepaid expenses	(2,000)	
Add: Decrease in accrued expenses payable	5,000	
Cash payments for operating expenses	**$179,000**	

Illustration 11-40
Computation of cash payments for operating expenses

Depreciation Expense and Loss on Sale of Equipment. Operating expenses are shown exclusive of depreciation. Depreciation expense in 2000 was $18,000. Depreciation expense is not shown on a statement of cash flows under the direct method because it is a noncash charge. If the amount for operating expenses includes depreciation expense, operating expenses must be reduced by the amount of depreciation to determine cash payments for operating expenses.

The loss on sale of store equipment of $1,000 is also a noncash charge. The loss on sale of equipment reduces net income, but it does not reduce cash. Thus, the loss on sale of equipment is not reported on a statement of cash flows prepared using the direct method.

Other charges to expense that do not require the use of cash, such as the amortization of intangible assets and depletion expense, are treated in the same manner as depreciation.

Cash Payments for Income Taxes. Income tax expense reported on the income statement was $36,000. Income taxes payable, however, increased $12,000, which means that $12,000 of the income taxes have not been paid. As a result, income taxes paid were less than income taxes reported on the income statement. Cash payments for income taxes were therefore $24,000, as shown in Illustration 11-41.

Income tax expense	$ 36,000	
Deduct: Increase in income taxes payable	12,000	
Cash payments for income taxes	**$24,000**	

Illustration 11-41
Computation of cash payments for income taxes

The relationship among cash payments for income taxes, income tax expense, and changes in income taxes payable are shown in the formula in Illustration 11-42.

Illustration 11-42 Formula to compute cash payments for income taxes—direct method

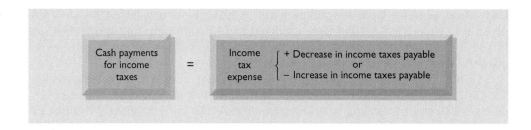

DETERMINING NET CASH PROVIDED/USED BY INVESTING AND FINANCING ACTIVITIES (STEP 3)

Increase in Land. Land increased $100,000. The additional information indicates that common stock was issued to purchase the land. Although the issuance of common stock for land has no effect on cash, it is a **significant noncash investing and financing transaction.** This transaction requires disclosure in a separate schedule at the bottom of the statement of cash flows.

Increase in Equipment. The comparative balance sheet shows that equipment increased $160,000 in 2000. The additional information in Illustration 11-37 indicates that the increase resulted from two investing transactions: (1) Equipment costing $180,000 was purchased for cash, and (2) equipment costing $20,000 was sold for $17,000 cash when its book value was $18,000. The relevant data for the statement of cash flows are the cash paid for the purchase and the cash proceeds from the sale. For Juarez Company the investing activities section will show: Purchase of equipment $180,000 as an outflow of cash, and sale of equipment $17,000 as an inflow of cash. The two amounts **should not be netted; both flows should be shown.**

The analysis of the changes in equipment should include the related Accumulated Depreciation account. These two accounts for Juarez Company are shown in Illustration 11-43.

Illustration 11-43 Analysis of equipment and related accumulated depreciation

EQUIPMENT				
Jan. 1	Balance	0	Cost of equipment sold	20,000
	Cash purchase	180,000		
Dec. 31	Balance	160,000		

ACCUMULATED DEPRECIATION—EQUIPMENT				
Sale of equipment	2,000	Jan. 1	Balance	0
			Depreciation expense	18,000
		Dec. 31	Balance	16,000

Increase in Bonds Payable. Bonds Payable increased $90,000. The additional information in Illustration 11-37 indicates that bonds with a face value of $90,000 were issued for $90,000 cash. The issuance of bonds is a financing activity. For Juarez Company, there is an inflow of cash of $90,000 from the issuance of bonds payable.

Increase in Common Stock. The Common Stock account increased $100,000. As indicated in the additional information, land was acquired from the issuance of common stock. This transaction is a **significant noncash investing and financing transaction** that should be reported in a separate schedule at the bottom of the statement.

Increase in Retained Earnings. The net increase in Retained Earnings of $52,000 resulted from net income of $84,000 and the declaration and payment of a cash dividend of $32,000. **Net income is not reported in the statement of cash flows under the direct method.** Cash dividends paid of $32,000 are reported in the financing activities section as an outflow of cash.

STATEMENT OF CASH FLOWS—2000

The statement of cash flows for Juarez Company is shown in Illustration 11-44.

Illustration 11-44   Statement of cash flows, 2000—direct method

JUAREZ COMPANY Statement of Cash Flows—Direct Method For the Year Ended December 31, 2000		
Cash flows from operating activities		
Cash receipts from customers		$978,000
Cash payments:		
To suppliers	$638,000	
For operating expenses	179,000	
For income taxes	24,000	841,000
Net cash provided by operating activities		137,000
Cash flows from investing activities		
Purchase of equipment	(180,000)	
Sale of equipment	17,000	
Net cash used by investing activities		(163,000)
Cash flows from financing activities		
Issuance of bonds payable	90,000	
Payment of cash dividends	(32,000)	
Net cash provided by financing activities		58,000
Net increase in cash		32,000
Cash at beginning of period		159,000
Cash at end of period		$191,000
Noncash investing and financing activities		
Issuance of common stock to purchase land		$100,000

BEFORE YOU GO ON . . .

● **Review It**

1. What is the format of the operating activities section of the statement of cash flows using the direct method?
2. Where is depreciation expense shown on a statement of cash flows using the direct method?
3. Where are significant noncash investing and financing activities shown on a statement of cash flows? Give some examples.

● **Do It**

The following information relates to Reynolds Company. Use it to prepare a statement of cash flows using the direct method.

REYNOLDS COMPANY
Comparative Balance Sheet
December 31

Assets	2000	1999	Change Increase/Decrease
Cash	$ 54,000	$ 37,000	$ 17,000 increase
Accounts receivable	68,000	26,000	42,000 increase
Inventories	54,000	0	54,000 increase
Prepaid expenses	4,000	6,000	2,000 decrease
Land	45,000	70,000	25,000 decrease
Buildings	200,000	200,000	0
Accumulated depreciation—buildings	(21,000)	(11,000)	10,000 increase
Equipment	193,000	68,000	125,000 increase
Accumulated depreciation—equipment	(28,000)	(10,000)	18,000 increase
Totals	$569,000	$386,000	

Liabilities and Stockholders' Equity			
Accounts payable	$ 23,000	$ 40,000	$ 17,000 decrease
Accrued expenses payable	10,000	0	10,000 increase
Bonds payable	110,000	150,000	40,000 decrease
Common stock ($1 par)	220,000	60,000	160,000 increase
Retained earnings	206,000	136,000	70,000 increase
Total	$569,000	$386,000	

REYNOLDS COMPANY
Income Statement
For the Year Ended December 31, 2000

Revenues		$890,000
Cost of goods sold	$465,000	
Operating expenses	221,000	
Interest expense	12,000	
Loss on sale of equipment	2,000	700,000
Income from operations		190,000
Income tax expense		65,000
Net income		$125,000

Additional information:
(a) Operating expenses include depreciation expense of $33,000.
(b) Land was sold at its book value for cash.
(c) Cash dividends of $55,000 were declared and paid in 2000.
(d) Interest expense of $12,000 was paid in cash.
(e) Equipment with a cost of $166,000 was purchased for cash. Equipment with a cost of $41,000 and a book value of $36,000 was sold for $34,000 cash.
(f) Bonds of $10,000 were redeemed at their book value for cash; bonds of $30,000 were converted into common stock.
(g) Common stock ($1 par) of $130,000 was issued for cash.
(h) Accounts payable pertain to merchandise suppliers.

Reasoning: The direct method reports cash receipts less cash payments to arrive at net cash provided by operating activities.

Solution:

REYNOLDS COMPANY
Statement of Cash Flows—Direct Method
For the Year Ended December 31, 2000

Cash flows from operating activities		
Cash receipts from customers		$848,000^a
Cash payments:		
To suppliers	$536,000^b	
For operating expenses	176,000^c	
For interest expense	12,000	
For income taxes	65,000	789,000
Net cash provided by operating activities		59,000
Cash flows from investing activities		
Sale of land	25,000	
Sale of equipment	34,000	
Purchase of equipment	(166,000)	
Net cash used by investing activities		(107,000)
Cash flows from financing activities		
Redemption of bonds	(10,000)	
Sale of common stock	130,000	
Payment of dividends	(55,000)	
Net cash provided by financing activities		65,000
Net increase in cash		17,000
Cash at beginning of period		37,000
Cash at end of period		$ 54,000
Noncash investing and financing activities		
Conversion of bonds into common stock		$ 30,000

Computations:
^{a}$848,000 = $890,000 − $42,000
^{b}$536,000 = $465,000 + $54,000 + $17,000
^{c}$176,000 = $221,000 − $33,000 − $2,000 − $10,000
Technically, an additional schedule reconciling net income to net cash provided by operating activities should be presented as part of the statement of cash flows when using the direct method.

Helpful Hint To prepare the statement of cash flows:

1. Determine the net increase/decrease in cash.
2. Determine net cash provided/used by operating activities.
3. Determine net cash provided/used by investing and financing activities.
4. Operating activities generally relate to changes in current assets and current liabilities.
5. Investing activities generally relate to changes in noncurrent assets.
6. Financing activities generally relate to changes in noncurrent liabilities and stockholders' equity accounts.

Related exercise material: BE11-7, BE11-9, E11-8, E11-9, E11-10, E11-11.

THE NAVIGATOR

Note: This concludes Section 2 on preparation of the statement of cash flows using the direct method. You should now turn to the next—and concluding—section of the chapter, "Using Cash Flows to Evaluate a Company."

*U*SING CASH FLOWS TO EVALUATE A COMPANY

Traditionally, the ratios most commonly used by investors and creditors have been based on accrual accounting. In this chapter we introduce you to some cash-based ratios that are gaining increased acceptance among analysts.

FREE CASH FLOW

In the statement of cash flows, cash provided by operating activities is intended to indicate the cash-generating capability of the company. Analysts have noted, however, that **net cash provided by operating activities fails to take into account that a company must invest in new fixed assets** just to maintain its current level of operations, and it must at least **maintain dividends at current levels** to satisfy investors. Free cash flow is the term used to describe the cash remaining from operations after adjustment for capital expenditures and dividends.

Consider the following example: Suppose that MPC produced and sold 10,000 personal computers this year. It reported net cash provided by operating activities of $100,000. In order to maintain production at 10,000 computers, MPC invested $20,000 in equipment. It chose to pay no dividends. Its free cash flow was then $80,000 ($100,000 − $20,000). The company could use this $80,000 either to purchase new assets to expand the business or to pay an $80,000 dividend and continue to produce 10,000 computers. Unfortunately, companies do not typically disclose what portion of their expenditures on fixed assets during the year was for maintaining current production levels, and what portion was for expanding production. Thus, analysts often estimate this amount by using the reported expenditures for the purchase of new fixed assets shown in the investing section of the statement of cash flows. In practice, free cash flow is often calculated with the formula in Illustration 11-45. Alternative definitions also exist.

Illustration 11-45
Free cash flow

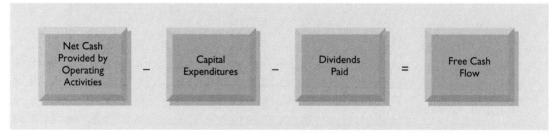

Illustration 11-46 provides basic information excerpted from the 1998 statement of cash flows of Microsoft Corporation.

Illustration 11-46
Microsoft cash flow information ($ in millions)

MICROSOFT CORPORATION Partial Statement of Cash Flows 1998		
Net cash provided by operating activities		$6,880
Cash flows from investing activities		
Additions to property, plant, and equipment	$ (656)	
Other assets	(190)	
Short-term investments	(6,426)	
Net cash used by investing activities		(7,272)
Net cash provided by financing activities		554

Microsoft's free cash flow (again noting that we do not have details to differentiate between amounts spent to maintain the current level of operations and amounts spent to expand production) is calculated as shown below in Illustration 11-47.

Net cash provided by operating activities	$6,880
Less: Expenditures on property, plant, and equipment	(656)
Dividends paid	0
Free cash flow	$6,224

Illustration 11-47 Calculation of Microsoft's free cash flow ($ in millions)

This is a tremendous amount of cash generated in a single year. It is available for the acquisition of new assets, the retirement of stock or debt, or the payment of dividends. Microsoft chose to invest its free cash flow in securities. It should also be noted that this amount is considerably more than Microsoft's reported income for 1998 of $4,490 million.

Oracle Corporation is the world's largest seller of database software and information management services. Like Microsoft, its success depends on continuing to improve its existing products while developing new products to keep pace with rapid changes in technology. Oracle's free cash flow for 1998 was $1,943 million. Thus, relative to a major competitor, Microsoft's free cash flow is also impressive.

DECISION TOOLKIT

Decision Checkpoints	Info Needed for Decision	Tool to Use for Decision	How to Evaluate Results
How much cash did the company generate to either expand operations or pay dividends?	Net cash provided by operating activities, cash spent on fixed assets, and cash dividends. (Ideally, the measure would use cash spent to maintain the current level of operations, but that is rarely available.)	$$\text{Free cash flow} = \substack{\text{Net cash} \\ \text{provided by} \\ \text{operating} \\ \text{activities}} - \substack{\text{Capital} \\ \text{expenditures}} - \substack{\text{Dividends} \\ \text{paid}}$$	Significant free cash flow indicates greater potential to finance new investment and pay additional dividends.

BUSINESS INSIGHT
Investor Perspective

Managers in some industries have long suggested that accrual-based income measures understate the true long-term potential of their companies because of what they suggest are excessive depreciation charges. For example, cable companies frequently suggested that, once they had installed a cable, it would require minimal maintenance and would guarantee the company returns for a long time to come. As a consequence, cable companies, which reported strong operating cash flows but low net income, had high stock prices because investors focused more on their cash flows from operations than on their net income. A recent *Wall Street Journal* article suggested, however, that investors have grown impatient with the cable companies and have lost faith in cash flow from operations as an indicator of cable performance. As it turns out, cable companies have had to make many expensive upgrades to previously installed cable systems. Today, after cable stock prices have fallen dramatically, cable industry analysts emphasize that either free cash flows or net income is a better indicator of a cable TV company's long-term potential than cash provided by operating activities.

Source: Susan Pulliam and Mark Robichaux, "Heard on the Street: Cash Flow Stops Propping Cable Stock," *The Wall Street Journal,* January 9, 1997, p. C1.

CAPITAL EXPENDITURE RATIO

Another indicator of a company's ability to generate sufficient cash to finance the purchase of new fixed assets is the capital expenditure ratio: net cash provided by operating activities divided by capital expenditures. This measure is similar to free cash flow, except that free cash flow reveals the amount of cash available for discretionary use by management, whereas the capital expenditure ratio provides a *relative measure* of cash provided by operations compared to cash used for the purchase of productive assets. Amounts spent on capital expenditures are listed in the investing activities section of the statement of cash flows. Using the Microsoft information in Illustration 11-46, we can calculate its capital expenditure ratio as shown in Illustration 11-48.

Illustration 11-48 Capital expenditure ratio for Microsoft ($ in millions)

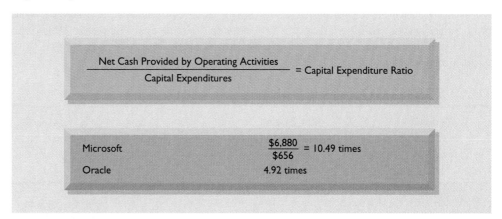

$$\frac{\text{Net Cash Provided by Operating Activities}}{\text{Capital Expenditures}} = \text{Capital Expenditure Ratio}$$

Microsoft $\dfrac{\$6,880}{\$656} = 10.49$ times

Oracle   4.92 times

Microsoft's ratio of 10.49 times suggests that it could have purchased ten times as much property, plant, and equipment as it did *without requiring any additional outside financing.* In comparison, Oracle's capital expenditure ratio for 1998 was 4.9 times. This provides additional evidence of Microsoft's superior cash-generating capability. This ratio will vary across industries depending on the capital intensity of the industry. That is, we would expect a manufacturing company to have a lower ratio (because it has higher capital expenditures) than a software company, which spends less of its money on fixed assets and more on "intellectual" capital. This difference is evident in the Using the Decision Toolkit exercise at the end of this chapter where we evaluate two computer chip manufacturers.

DECISION TOOLKIT

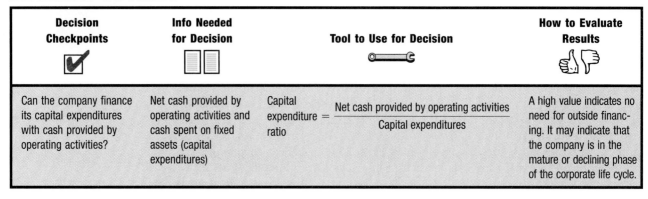

Decision Checkpoints	Info Needed for Decision	Tool to Use for Decision	How to Evaluate Results
Can the company finance its capital expenditures with cash provided by operating activities?	Net cash provided by operating activities and cash spent on fixed assets (capital expenditures)	Capital expenditure ratio = $\dfrac{\text{Net cash provided by operating activities}}{\text{Capital expenditures}}$	A high value indicates no need for outside financing. It may indicate that the company is in the mature or declining phase of the corporate life cycle.

ASSESSING LIQUIDITY, SOLVENCY, AND PROFITABILITY USING CASH FLOWS

Previous chapters have presented ratios used to analyze a company's liquidity, solvency, and profitability. Those ratios used accrual-based numbers from the income statement and balance sheet. Now we introduce ratios that are *cash-based* rather than accrual-based; that is, instead of using numbers from the income statement, these ratios use numbers from the statement of cash flows.

As discussed earlier, many analysts are critical of accrual-based numbers because they feel that the adjustment process allows too much management discretion. These analysts like to supplement accrual-based analysis with measures that use the cash flow statement. One disadvantage of these measures is that, unlike the more commonly employed accrual-based measures, there are no readily available published industry averages for comparison. In the following discussion we use cash flow-based ratios to analyze Microsoft. In addition to the cash flow information provided in Illustration 11-46, we need the following information related to Microsoft in Illustration 11-49.

($ in millions)	1998	1997
Current liabilities	$ 5,730	$ 3,610
Total liabilities	5,730	3,610
Sales	14,484	11,358

Illustration 11-49 Additional Microsoft data

Helpful Hint Note that Microsoft has no long-term debt.

Liquidity

Liquidity is the ability of a business to meet its immediate obligations. You learned that one measure of liquidity is the *current ratio*: current assets divided by current liabilities. A disadvantage of the current ratio is that it uses year-end balances of current asset and current liability accounts, and these year-end balances may not be representative of the company's position during most of the year.

A ratio that partially corrects this problem is the current cash debt coverage ratio: net cash provided by operating activities divided by average current liabilities. Because net cash provided by operating activities involves the entire year rather than a balance at one point in time, it is often considered a better representation of liquidity on the average day. The ratio is calculated as shown in Illustration 11-50, with the ratio computed for Microsoft Corporation and comparative numbers given for Oracle. We have also provided each company's current ratio for comparative purposes.

Illustration 11-50 Current cash debt coverage ratio

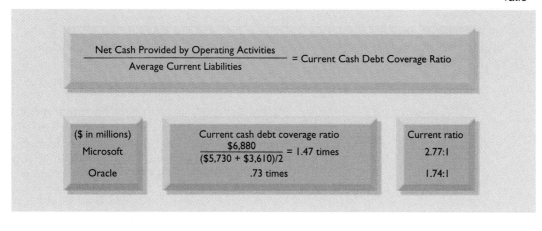

Microsoft's net cash provided by operating activities is nearly one and one half times its average current liabilities. Oracle's ratio of .73 times, though not a cause for concern, is substantially lower than that of Microsoft. Keep in mind that Microsoft's cash position of nearly $14 billion is extraordinary. For example, many companies now have current ratios in the range of 1.0. By this standard, Oracle's current ratio of 1.74:1 is respectable, but Microsoft's current ratio of 2.77:1 is quite high.

DECISION TOOLKIT

Decision Checkpoints	Info Needed for Decision	Tool to Use for Decision	How to Evaluate Results
Is the company generating sufficient cash provided by operating activities to meet its current obligations?	Net cash provided by operating activities and average current liabilities	Current cash debt coverage ratio $= \dfrac{\text{Net cash provided by operating activities}}{\text{Average current liabilities}}$	A high value suggests good liquidity. Since the numerator contains a "flow" measure, it provides a good supplement to the current ratio.

Solvency

Solvency is the ability of a company to survive over the long term. A measure of solvency that uses cash figures is the **cash debt coverage ratio:** the ratio of net cash provided by operating activities to total debt as represented by average total liabilities. This ratio indicates a company's ability to repay its liabilities from cash generated from operations—that is, without having to liquidate productive assets such as property, plant, and equipment. The cash debt coverage ratios for Microsoft and Oracle for 1998 are given in Illustration 11-51. The debt to total assets ratios for each company are also provided for comparative purposes.

Illustration 11-51 Cash debt coverage ratio

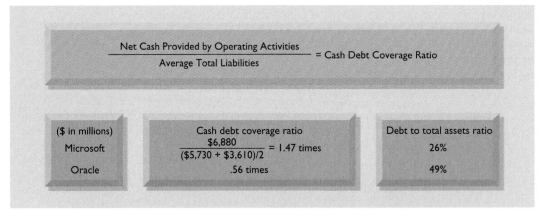

Microsoft has no long-term obligations; thus, its cash debt coverage ratio is identical to its current cash debt coverage ratio. Obviously, Microsoft is very solvent. On the other hand, Oracle has some long-term debt, and its cash debt coverage ratio suggests that its long-term financial health needs closer monitoring than that of Microsoft. However, neither the cash nor accrual measures suggest any real cause for concern for either company.

DECISION TOOLKIT

Decision Checkpoints	Info Needed for Decision	Tool to Use for Decision	How to Evaluate Results
Is the company generating sufficient cash provided by operating activities to meet its long-term obligations?	Net cash provided by operating activities and average total liabilities	Cash debt coverage ratio $= \dfrac{\text{Net cash provided by operating activities}}{\text{Average total liabilities}}$	A high value suggests the company is solvent; that is, it will meet its obligations in the long term.

Profitability

Profitability refers to a company's ability to generate a reasonable return. In Chapter 12 accrual-based ratios that measure profitability are discussed, such as gross profit rate, profit margin, and return on assets. In measures of profitability the potential differences between cash accounting and accrual accounting are most pronounced. Although some differences are expected because of the difference in the timing of revenue and expense recognition under cash versus accrual accounting, significant differences should be investigated. A cash-based measure of performance is the cash return on sales ratio.

The **cash return on sales ratio** is cash provided by operating activities divided by net sales. This ratio indicates the company's ability to turn sales into dollars for the firm. A low cash return on sales ratio should be investigated because it might indicate that the firm is recognizing sales that are not really sales—that is, sales it will never collect. The cash return on sales ratios for Microsoft and Oracle for 1998 are presented in Illustration 11-52.

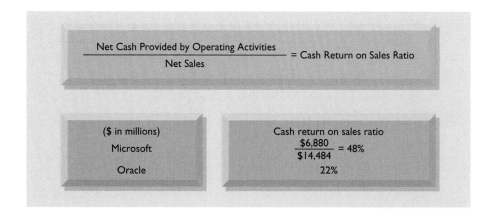

Illustration 11-52 Cash return on sales ratio

Oracle's cash return on sales ratio of 22% is substantially less than Microsoft's at 48%. It indicates that Microsoft is more efficient in turning sales into cash. Yet Oracle's cash return on sales ratio is quite respectable.

DECISION TOOLKIT

Decision Checkpoints ✔	Info Needed for Decision 📄📄	Tool to Use for Decision ⚬━━⚬	How to Evaluate Results 👍👎
Are differences between cash and accrual accounting reasonable?	Net cash provided by operating activities and sales.	$\text{Cash return on sales ratio} = \dfrac{\text{Net cash provided by operating activities}}{\text{Net sales}}$	Cash return on sales ratio should be compared to other companies', and significant differences over a series of years should be investigated.

BUSINESS INSIGHT
Management Perspective

A recent *Wall Street Journal* article noted that while Microsoft's cash position is enviable, it does present some challenges; management can't find enough ways to spend the cash. For example, unlike computer chip manufacturer Intel Corporation (another huge generator of cash), Microsoft has few manufacturing costs, so it cannot spend huge sums on new plant and equipment. Microsoft's management would like to purchase other major software companies, but the federal government won't let it, for fear that it will reduce competition. (For example, the Justice Department blocked Microsoft's proposed purchase of software maker Intuit.) Instead, Microsoft is constrained to purchasing small software makers with promising new products. Ironically, even this does not use much of its cash because, first of all, the companies are small, and second, the owners of these small companies prefer to be paid with Microsoft stock rather than cash.

Microsoft's huge holdings of liquid assets could eventually hurt its stock performance. Liquid assets typically provide about a 5% return, whereas Microsoft investors are accustomed to 30% returns. If Microsoft's performance starts to decline because it can't find enough good investment projects, it should distribute cash to its shareholders in the form of dividends. One big problem: Bill Gates owns 24% of Microsoft, and the last thing he wants to do is pay personal income tax on billions of dollars of dividend income. In the early years Microsoft did not pay dividends because it wanted to conserve cash. Today it is drowning in cash but still can't pay a dividend.

Source: David Bank, "Microsoft's Problem Is What Many Firms Just Wish They Had," *The Wall Street Journal,* January 17, 1997, p. A9.

BEFORE YOU GO ON . . .

● **Review It**

1. What is the difference between cash from operating activities and free cash flow?
2. What does it mean if a company has negative free cash flow?
3. Why might an analyst want to supplement accrual-based ratios with cash-based ratios? What are some cash-based ratios?

THE NAVIGATOR

USING THE DECISION TOOLKIT

Intel Corporation is the leading producer of computer chips for personal computers. It makes the hugely successful Pentium chip. Its primary competitor is AMD (formerly Advanced Micro Devices). The two are vicious competitors, with frequent lawsuits filed between them.

Instructions

Calculate the following cash-based measures for Intel, and compare them with those provided here for AMD. Financial statement data for Intel are also provided.

1. Free cash flow

2. Capital expenditure ratio

3. Current cash debt coverage ratio

4. Cash debt coverage ratio

5. Cash return on sales ratio

INTEL CORPORATION
Balance Sheet
December 31, 1997 and 1996
(in millions)

	1997	1996
Assets		
Current assets	$15,867	$13,684
Property, plant, and equipment	10,666	8,487
Long-term investments	1,839	1,353
Other assets	508	211
Total assets	$28,880	$23,735
Liabilities and Stockholders' Equity		
Current liabilities	$ 6,020	$ 4,863
Long-term debt	448	728
Other liabilities	1,076	997
Total liabilities	7,544	6,588
Stockholders' equity	21,336	17,147
Total liabilities and stockholders' equity	$28,880	$23,735

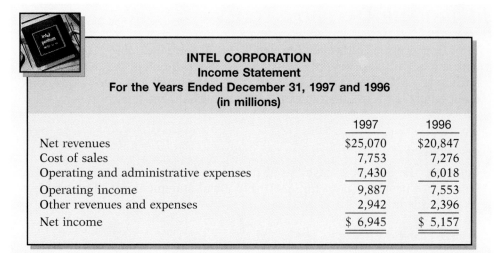

INTEL CORPORATION
Income Statement
For the Years Ended December 31, 1997 and 1996
(in millions)

	1997	1996
Net revenues	$25,070	$20,847
Cost of sales	7,753	7,276
Operating and administrative expenses	7,430	6,018
Operating income	9,887	7,553
Other revenues and expenses	2,942	2,396
Net income	$ 6,945	$ 5,157

INTEL CORPORATION
Statement of Cash Flows
For the Years Ended December 31, 1997 and 1996
(in millions)

	1997	1996
Net cash provided by operating activities	$10,008	$8,743
Net cash used for investing activities (see note 1)	(6,859)	(5,268)
Net cash used for financing activities	(3,212)	(773)
Net increase (decrease) in cash and cash equivalents	$ (63)	$2,702

Note 1. Cash spent on property, plant, and equipment in 1997 was $4,501. Cash paid for dividends was $180.

Here are the comparative data for AMD:

1. Free cash flow   ($286 million)
2. Capital expenditure ratio   .58 times
3. Current cash debt coverage ratio   .61 times
4. Cash debt coverage ratio   .31 times
5. Cash return on sales ratio   17%

Solution

1. Intel's free cash flow is $5,327 million ($10,008 − $4,501 − $180), and AMD's is actually a negative $286 million. This gives Intel an advantage in ability to move quickly to invest in new projects. AMD's weak ratios are a result of having only a break-even year profitwise.

2. Intel's capital expenditure ratio is 2.22 times ($10,008 ÷ $4,501), and AMD's is .58 times. This is a useful supplement to the free cash flow measure. It shows that, even though Intel appears to have considerably more ability to generate cash for capital expenditure, its cash-generating ability relative to its expenditures is not that much greater than AMD's. Note that Intel's free cash flow is nearly as great as Microsoft's. Intel's capital expenditure ratio, however, is considerably less than Microsoft's, 2.22 times versus 10.49 times, but it should be since manufacturing computer chips is very capital intensive compared to producing software.

3. The current cash debt coverage ratio for Intel is calculated as:

$$\frac{\$10,008}{(\$6,020 + \$4,863)/2} = 1.84 \text{ times}$$

   Compared to AMD's value of .61 times, Intel appears to be significantly more liquid.

4. The cash debt coverage ratio for Intel is calculated as:

$$\frac{\$10,008}{(\$7,544 + \$6,588)/2} = 1.42 \text{ times}$$

   Compared to AMD's value of .31 times, Intel appears to be considerably more solvent.

5. The cash return on sales ratio for Intel is calculated as:

$$\frac{\$10,008}{\$25,000} = 40\%$$

   AMD's cash return on sales ratio is 17%. Thus, Intel again has the better ability to generate cash from sales.

THE NAVIGATOR

SUMMARY OF STUDY OBJECTIVES

1 *Indicate the primary purpose of the statement of cash flows.* The statement of cash flows provides information about the cash receipts and cash payments of an entity during a period. A secondary objective is to provide information about the operating, investing, and financing activities of the entity during the period.

2 *Distinguish among operating, investing, and financing activities.* Operating activities include the cash effects of transactions that enter into the determination of net income. Investing activities involve cash flows resulting from changes in investments and long-term asset items. Financing activities involve cash flows resulting from changes in long-term liability and stockholders' equity items.

3 *Explain the impact of the product life cycle on a company's cash flows.* During the introductory stage, cash provided by operating activities and cash from investing are negative, whereas cash from financing is positive. During the growth stage, cash provided by operating activities becomes positive. During the maturity stage, cash provided by operating activities exceeds investing needs, so the company begins to retire debt. During the decline stage, cash provided by operating activities is reduced, cash from investing becomes positive, and cash from financing becomes more negative.

4a *Prepare a statement of cash flows using the indirect method.* The preparation of a statement of cash flows involves three major steps: (a) determine the net increase or decrease in cash, (b) determine net cash provided (used) by operating activities, and (c) determine

net cash provided (used) by investing and financing activities. Under the indirect method, accrual-basis net income is adjusted to net cash provided by operating activities.

4b *Prepare a statement of cash flows using the direct method.* The preparation of the statement of cash flows involves three major steps: (a) determine the net increase or decrease in cash, (b) determine net cash provided (used) by operating activities, and (c) determine net cash provided (used) by investing and financing activities. The direct method reports cash receipts less cash payments to arrive at net cash provided by operating activities.

5 *Use the statement of cash flows to evaluate a company.* A number of measures can be derived by using information from the statement of cash flows as well as the other required financial statements. Free cash flow indicates the amount of cash a company generated during the current year that is available for the payment of dividends or for expansion. The capital expenditure ratio, cash provided by operating activities divided by capital expenditures, complements free cash flow by giving a relative indicator of the sufficiency of cash from operations to fund capital expenditures. Liquidity can be measured with the current cash debt coverage ratio (cash provided by operating activities divided by average current liabilities), solvency by the cash debt coverage ratio (cash provided by operating activities divided by average total liabilities), and profitability by the cash return on sales ratio (cash provided by operating activities divided by sales).

THE NAVIGATOR

DECISION TOOLKIT—A SUMMARY

Decision Checkpoints	Info Needed for Decision	Tool to Use for Decision	How to Evaluate Results
How much cash did the company generate to either expand operations or pay dividends?	Net cash provided by operating activities, cash spent on fixed assets, and cash dividends. (Ideally, the measure would use cash spent to maintain the current level of operations, but that is rarely available).	$\text{Free cash flow} = \text{Net cash provided by operating activities} - \text{Capital expenditures} - \text{Dividends paid}$	Significant free cash flow indicates greater potential to finance new investment and pay additional dividends.
Can the company finance its capital expenditures with cash provided by operating activities?	Net cash provided by operating activities and cash spent on fixed assets (capital expenditures).	$\text{Capital expenditure ratio} = \dfrac{\text{Net cash provided by operating activities}}{\text{Capital expenditures}}$	A high value indicates no need for outside financing. It may indicate that the company is in the mature or declining phase of the corporate life cycle.
Is the company generating sufficient cash provided by operating activities to meet its current obligations?	Net cash provided by operating activities and average current liabilities	$\text{Current cash debt coverage ratio} = \dfrac{\text{Net cash provided by operating activities}}{\text{Average current liabilities}}$	A high value suggests good liquidity. Since the numerator contains a "flow" measure, it provides a good supplement to the current ratio.
Is the company generating sufficient cash provided by operating activities to meet its long-term obligations?	Net cash provided by operating activities and average total liabilities	$\text{Cash debt coverage ratio} = \dfrac{\text{Net cash provided by operating activities}}{\text{Average total liabilities}}$	A high value suggests the company is solvent; that is, it will meet its obligations in the long term.
Are differences between cash and accrual accounting reasonable?	Net cash provided by operating activities and sales.	$\text{Cash return on sales ratio} = \dfrac{\text{Net cash provided by operating activities}}{\text{Net sales}}$	Cash return on sales ratio should be compared to other companies', and significant differences over a series of years should be investigated.

GLOSSARY

Capital expenditure ratio A cash-basis ratio that indicates the extent to which cash provided by operating activities was sufficient to fund capital expenditure (fixed asset) purchases during the year. (p. 448)

Cash debt coverage ratio A cash-basis ratio used to evaluate solvency, calculated as net cash provided by operating activities divided by average total liabilities. (p. 450)

Cash return on sales ratio A cash-basis ratio used to evaluate profitability, calculated as net cash provided by operating activities divided by net sales. (p. 451)

Current cash debt coverage ratio A cash-basis ratio used to evaluate liquidity, calculated as net cash provided by operating activities divided by average current liabilities. (p. 449)

Direct method A method of determining net cash provided by operating activities by adjusting each item in the income statement from the accrual basis to the cash basis. (p. 434)

Financing activities Cash flow activities that include (a) obtaining cash from issuing debt and repaying the amounts borrowed and (b) obtaining cash from stockholders and providing them with a return on their investment. (p. 413)

Free cash flow Cash provided by operating activities adjusted for a charge for investments made to maintain the current level of operations. (p. 446)

Indirect method A method of preparing a statement of cash flows in which net income is adjusted for items that do not affect cash, to determine net cash provided by operating activities. (p. 422)

Investing activities Cash flow activities that include (a) purchasing and disposing of investments and productive

long-lived assets using cash and (b) lending money and collecting on those loans. (p. 413)

Operating activities Cash flow activities that include the cash effects of transactions that create revenues and expenses and thus enter into the determination of net income. (p. 413)

Statement of cash flows A basic financial statement that provides information about the cash receipts and cash payments of an entity during a period, classified as operating, investing, and financing activities, in a format that reconciles the beginning and ending cash balances. (p. 412)

DEMONSTRATION PROBLEM

The income statement for John Kosinski Manufacturing Company contains the following condensed information:

JOHN KOSINSKI MANUFACTURING COMPANY
Income Statement
For the Year Ended December 31, 1999

Revenues		$6,583,000
Operating expenses, excluding depreciation	$4,920,000	
Depreciation expense	880,000	5,800,000
Income before income taxes		783,000
Income tax expense		353,000
Net income		$ 430,000

Included in operating expenses is a $24,000 loss resulting from the sale of machinery for $270,000 cash. Machinery was purchased at a cost of $750,000. The following balances are reported on Kosinski's comparative balance sheet at December 31:

	1999	1998
Cash	$672,000	$130,000
Accounts receivable	775,000	610,000
Inventories	834,000	867,000
Accounts payable	521,000	501,000

Income tax expense of $353,000 represents the amount paid in 1999. Dividends declared and paid in 1999 totaled $200,000.

Instructions

(a) Prepare the statement of cash flows using the indirect method.
(b) Prepare the statement of cash flows using the direct method.

Solution to Demonstration Problem

(a) **JOHN KOSINSKI MANUFACTURING COMPANY**
Statement of Cash Flows—Indirect Method
For the Year Ended December 31, 1999

Cash flows from operating activities		
Net income		$ 430,000
Adjustments to reconcile net income to net cash		
provided by operating activities:		
Depreciation expense	$880,000	
Loss on sale of machinery	24,000	
Increase in accounts receivable	(165,000)	

Problem-Solving Strategy

This demonstration problem illustrates both the direct and indirect methods using the same basic data. Note the similarities and the differences between the two methods. Both methods report the same information in the investing and financing activities sections. The cash flow from operating activities section reports different information, but the amount — net cash provided by operating activities—is the same for both methods.

Decrease in inventories	33,000	
Increase in accounts payable	20,000	792,000
Net cash provided by operating activities		1,222,000
Cash flows from investing activities		
Sale of machinery	270,000	
Purchase of machinery	(750,000)	
Net cash used by investing activities		(480,000)
Cash flows from financing activities		
Payment of cash dividends	(200,000)	
Net cash used by financing activities		(200,000)
Net increase in cash		542,000
Cash at beginning of period		130,000
Cash at end of period		$672,000

(b)
JOHN KOSINSKI MANUFACTURING COMPANY
Statement of Cash Flows—Direct Method
For the Year Ended December 31, 1999

Cash flows from operating activities		
Cash collections from customers		$6,418,000*
Cash payments for operating expenses		4,843,000**
		1,575,000
Cash payment for income taxes		353,000
Net cash provided by operating activities		1,222,000
Cash flows from investing activities		
Sale of machinery	$270,000	
Purchase of machinery	(750,000)	
Net cash used by investing activities		(480,000)
Cash flows from financing activities		
Payment of cash dividends	(200,000)	
Net cash used by financing activities		(200,000)
Net increase in cash		542,000
Cash at beginning of period		130,000
Cash at end of period		$ 672,000

Direct Method Computations:

*Computation of cash collections from customers:

Revenues per the income statement	$6,583,000
Less increase in accounts receivable	165,000
Cash collections from customers	$6,418,000

**Computation of cash payments for operating expenses:

Operating expenses per the income statement	$4,920,000
Deduct loss from sale of machinery	(24,000)
Deduct decrease in inventories	(33,000)
Deduct increase in accounts payable	(20,000)
Cash payments for operating expenses	$4,843,000

THE
NAVIGATOR

SELF-STUDY QUESTIONS

Answers are at the end of the chapter.

(SO 1)   1. Which of the following is *incorrect* about the statement of cash flows?
(a) It is a fourth basic financial statement.

(b) It provides information about cash receipts and cash payments of an entity during a period.

(c) It reconciles the ending cash account balance to the balance per the bank statement.

(d) It provides information about the operating, investing, and financing activities of the business.

(SO 2) 2. The statement of cash flows classifies cash receipts and cash payments by these activities:
(a) operating and nonoperating.
(b) investing, financing, and operating.
(c) financing, operating, and nonoperating.
(d) investing, financing, and nonoperating.

(SO 2) 3. Which is an example of a cash flow from an operating activity?
(a) Payment of cash to lenders for interest
(b) Receipt of cash from the sale of capital stock
(c) Payment of cash dividends to the company's stockholders
(d) None of the above

(SO 2) 4. Which is an example of a cash flow from an investing activity?
(a) Receipt of cash from the issuance of bonds payable
(b) Payment of cash to repurchase outstanding capital stock
(c) Receipt of cash from the sale of equipment
(d) Payment of cash to suppliers for inventory

(SO 2) 5. Cash dividends paid to stockholders are classified on the statement of cash flows as:
(a) operating activities.
(b) investing activities.
(c) a combination of (a) and (b).
(d) financing activities.

(SO 2) 6. Which is an example of a cash flow from a financing activity?
(a) Receipt of cash from sale of land
(b) Issuance of debt for cash
(c) Purchase of equipment for cash
(d) None of the above

(SO 2) 7. Which of the following is *incorrect* about the statement of cash flows?
(a) The direct method may be used to report cash provided by operations.
(b) The statement shows the cash provided (used) for three categories of activity.
(c) The operating section is the last section of the statement.
(d) The indirect method may be used to report cash provided by operations.

(SO 3) 8. During the introductory phase of a company's life cycle, one would normally expect to see:
(a) negative cash from operations, negative cash from investing, and positive cash from financing.
(b) negative cash from operations, positive cash from investing, and positive cash from financing.

(c) positive cash from operations, negative cash from investing, and negative cash from financing.
(d) positive cash from operations, negative cash from investing, and positive cash from financing.

Questions 9 and 10 apply only to the indirect method.

(SO 4a) 9. Net income is $132,000, accounts payable increased $10,000 during the year, inventory decreased $6,000 during the year, and accounts receivable increased $12,000 during the year. Under the indirect method, what is net cash provided by operations?
(a) $102,000   (c) $124,000
(b) $112,000   (d) $136,000

(SO 4a) 10. Noncash charges that are added back to net income in determining cash provided by operations under the indirect method do *not* include:
(a) depreciation expense.
(b) an increase in inventory.
(c) amortization expense.
(d) loss on sale of equipment.

Questions 11 and 12 apply only to the direct method.

(SO 4b) 11. The beginning balance in accounts receivable is $44,000, the ending balance is $42,000, and sales during the period are $129,000. What are cash receipts from customers?
(a) $127,000   (c) $131,000
(b) $129,000   (d) $141,000

(SO 4b) 12. Which of the following items is reported on a cash flow statement prepared by the direct method?
(a) Loss on sale of building
(b) Increase in accounts receivable
(c) Depreciation expense
(d) Cash payments to suppliers

(SO 5) 13. The statement of cash flows should *not* be used to evaluate an entity's ability to:
(a) earn net income.
(b) generate future cash flows.
(c) pay dividends.
(d) meet obligations.

(SO 5) 14. Free cash flow provides an indication of a company's ability to:
(a) generate net income.
(b) generate cash to pay dividends.
(c) generate cash to invest in new capital expenditures.
(d) both (b) and (c).

(SO 5) 15. Which of the following ratios provides a useful comparison to the profit margin ratio?
(a) Capital expenditure ratio
(b) Cash return on sales ratio
(c) Cash debt coverage ratio
(d) Current cash debt coverage ratio

THE
NAVIGATOR

QUESTIONS

1. (a) What is a statement of cash flows?
   (b) Alice Weiseman maintains that the statement of cash flows is an optional financial statement. Do you agree? Explain.

2. What questions about cash are answered by the statement of cash flows?

3. Distinguish among the three activities reported in the statement of cash flows.

4. (a) What are the major sources (inflows) of cash in a statement of cash flows?
   (b) What are the major uses (outflows) of cash?

5. Why is it important to disclose certain noncash transactions? How should they be disclosed?

6. Wilma Flintstone and Barny Kublestone were discussing the format of the statement of cash flows of Rock Candy Co. At the bottom of Rock Candy's statement of cash flows was a separate section entitled "Noncash investing and financing activities." Give three examples of significant noncash transactions that would be reported in this section.

7. Why is it necessary to use comparative balance sheets, a current income statement, and certain transaction data in preparing a statement of cash flows?

8. (a) What are the phases of the corporate life cycle?
   (b) What effect does each phase have on the numbers reported in a statement of cash flows?

9. Contrast the advantages and disadvantages of the direct and indirect methods of preparing the statement of cash flows. Are both methods acceptable? Which method is preferred by the FASB? Which method is more popular?

10. When the total cash inflows exceed the total cash outflows in the statement of cash flows, how and where is this excess identified?

11. Describe the indirect method for determining net cash provided (used) by operating activities.

12. Why is it necessary to convert accrual-based net income to cash-basis income when preparing a statement of cash flows?

13. The president of Aerosmith Company is puzzled. During the last year, the company experienced a net loss of $800,000, yet its cash increased $300,000 during the same period of time. Explain to the president how this could occur.

14. Identify five items that are adjustments to convert net income to net cash provided by operating activities under the indirect method.

15. Why and how is depreciation expense reported in a statement prepared using the indirect method?

16. Why is the statement of cash flows useful?

17. During 1999 Johnny Carson Company converted $1,700,000 of its total $2,000,000 of bonds payable into common stock. Indicate how the transaction would be reported on a statement of cash flows, if at all.

18. Describe the direct method for determining net cash provided by operating activities.

19. Give the formulas under the direct method for computing (a) cash receipts from customers and (b) cash payments to suppliers.

20. Cindy Crawford Inc. reported sales of $2 million for 1999. Accounts receivable decreased $100,000 and accounts payable increased $300,000. Compute cash receipts from customers, assuming that the receivable and payable transactions related to operations.

21. In the direct method, why is depreciation expense not reported in the cash flows from operating activities section?

22. Give an example of one accrual-based ratio and one cash-based ratio to measure these characteristics of a company:
    (a) Liquidity
    (b) Solvency
    (c) Profitability

BRIEF EXERCISES

Compute cash provided by operating activities—indirect method.
(SO 4a)

BE11-1 Crystal, Inc., reported net income of $2.5 million in 1999. Depreciation for the year was $260,000, accounts receivable decreased $350,000, and accounts payable decreased $310,000. Compute net cash provided by operating activities using the indirect approach.

Compute cash provided by operating activities—indirect method.
(SO 4a)

BE11-2 The net income for Sterling Engineering Co. for 1999 was $280,000. For 1999 depreciation on plant assets was $60,000, and the company incurred a loss on sale of plant assets of $9,000. Compute net cash provided by operating activities under the indirect method.

Indicate statement presentation of selected transactions.
(SO 2)

BE11-3 Each of these items must be considered in preparing a statement of cash flows for Murphy Co. for the year ended December 31, 1999. For each item, state how it should be shown in the statement of cash flows for 1999.

(a) Issued bonds for $200,000 cash
(b) Purchased equipment for $150,000 cash
(c) Sold land costing $20,000 for $20,000 cash
(d) Declared and paid a $50,000 cash dividend

BE11-4
(a) Why is cash from operations likely to be lower than reported net income during the growth phase?
(b) Why is cash from investing often positive during the late maturity phase and during the decline phase?

Answer questions related to the phases of product life cycle.
(SO 3)

BE11-5   The comparative balance sheet for Rolex Company shows these changes in non-cash current asset accounts: accounts receivable decrease $80,000, prepaid expenses increase $12,000, and inventories increase $30,000. Compute net cash provided by operating activities using the indirect method assuming that net income is $200,000.

Compute net cash provided by operating activities—indirect method.
(SO 4a)

BE11-6   Classify each item as an operating, investing, or financing activity. Assume all items involve cash unless there is information to the contrary.
(a) Purchase of equipment   (d) Depreciation
(b) Sale of building   (e) Payment of dividends
(c) Redemption of bonds   (f) Issuance of capital stock

Classify items by activities.
(SO 2)

BE11-7   Billy Idol Corporation has accounts receivable of $14,000 at January 1, 1999, and $24,000 at December 31, 1999. Sales revenues were $480,000 for the year 1999. What is the amount of cash receipts from customers in 1999?

Compute receipts from customers—direct method.
(SO 4b)

BE11-8   Depeche Mode Corporation reported income taxes of $70,000 on its 1999 income statement and income taxes payable of $12,000 at December 31, 1998, and $9,000 at December 31, 1999. What amount of cash payments were made for income taxes during 1999?

Compute cash payments for income taxes—indirect method.
(SO 4a)

BE11-9   Excel Corporation reports operating expenses of $90,000 excluding depreciation expense of $15,000 for 1999. During the year prepaid expenses decreased $6,600 and accrued expenses payable increased $4,400. Compute the cash payments for operating expenses in 1999.

Compute cash payments for operating expenses—direct method.
(SO 4b)

BE11-10   The T accounts for Equipment and the related Accumulated Depreciation for Cindy Trevis Company at the end of 1999 are shown here:

Determine cash received from sale of equipment.
(SO 4)

Equipment					Accumulated Depreciation			
Beg. bal.	80,000	Disposals	22,000		Disposals	5,500	Beg. bal.	44,500
Acquisitions	41,600						Depr.	12,000
End. bal.	99,600						End. bal.	51,000

In addition, Cindy Trevis Company's income statement reported a loss on the sale of equipment of $6,700. What amount was reported on the statement of cash flows as "cash flow from sale of equipment"?

BE11-11   The following T account is a summary of the cash account of Anita Baker Company:

Identify financing activity transactions.
(SO 2)

Cash (Summary Form)

Balance, Jan. 1	8,000		
Receipts from customers	364,000	Payments for goods	200,000
Dividends on stock investments	6,000	Payments for operating expenses	140,000
Proceeds from sale of equipment	36,000	Interest paid	10,000
Proceeds from issuance of		Taxes paid	8,000
bonds payable	100,000	Dividends paid	40,000
Balance, Dec. 31	116,000		

What amount of net cash provided (used) by financing activities should be reported in the statement of cash flows?

Calculate cash-based ratios.
(SO 5)

BE11-12 Mary Jo Corporation reported cash from operations of $300,000, cash used in investing of $250,000, and cash from financing of $70,000. In addition, cash spent for fixed assets during the period was $200,000. Average current liabilities were $150,000 and average total liabilities were $225,000. No dividends were paid. Calculate these values:
(a) Free cash flow
(b) Capital expenditure ratio
(c) Current cash debt coverage ratio

EXERCISES

Classify transactions by type of activity.
(SO 2)

E11-1 Li Eng Corporation had these transactions during 1999:
(a) Purchased a machine for $30,000, giving a long-term note in exchange.
(b) Issued $50,000 par value common stock for cash.
(c) Collected $16,000 of accounts receivable.
(d) Declared and paid a cash dividend of $25,000.
(e) Sold a long-term investment with a cost of $15,000 for $15,000 cash.
(f) Issued $200,000 par value common stock upon conversion of bonds having a face value of $200,000.
(g) Paid $18,000 on accounts payable.

Instructions
Analyze the transactions and indicate whether each transaction resulted in a cash flow from operating activities, investing activities, financing activities, or noncash investing and financing activities.

Prepare the operating activities section—indirect method.
(SO 4a)

E11-2 Joe Pesci Company reported net income of $195,000 for 1999. Pesci also reported depreciation expense of $35,000 and a loss of $5,000 on the sale of equipment. The comparative balance sheet shows an increase in accounts receivable of $15,000 for the year, an $8,000 increase in accounts payable, and a $4,000 decrease in prepaid expenses.

Instructions
Prepare the operating activities section of the statement of cash flows for 1999. Use the indirect method.

Identify phases of product life cycle.
(SO 3)

E11-3 The information in the table is from the statement of cash flows for a company at four different points in time (A, B, C, and D). Negative values are presented in parentheses.

	Point in Time			
	A	**B**	**C**	**D**
Cash provided by operations	$100,000	$ 30,000	($ 60,000)	($ 10,000)
Cash provided by investing	30,000	25,000	(100,000)	(40,000)
Cash provided by financing	(50,000)	(110,000)	70,000	120,000
Net income	100,000	10,000	(40,000)	(5,000)

Instructions
For each point in time, state whether the company is most likely characterized as being in the introductory phase, growth phase, maturity phase, or decline phase. In each case explain your choice.

Prepare the operating activities section—indirect method.
(SO 4a)

E11-4 The current sections of Barth Inc.'s balance sheets at December 31, 1998 and 1999, are presented here:

	1999	1998
Current assets		
Cash	$105,000	$ 99,000
Accounts receivable	110,000	89,000
Inventory	171,000	186,000
Prepaid expenses	27,000	32,000
Total current assets	$413,000	$406,000

Current liabilities		
Accrued expenses payable	$ 15,000	$ 5,000
Accounts payable	85,000	92,000
Total current liabilities	$100,000	$ 97,000

Barth's net income for 1999 was $122,000. Depreciation expense was $24,000.

Instructions
Prepare the net cash provided by operating activities section of Barth Inc.'s statement of cash flows for the year ended December 31, 1999, using the indirect method.

E11-5   These three accounts appear in the general ledger of Roberta Dupre Corp. during 1999:

Prepare partial statement of cash flows—indirect method.

(SO 4a)

Equipment

Date		Debit	Credit	Balance
Jan. 1	Balance			160,000
July 31	Purchase of equipment	70,000		230,000
Sept. 2	Cost of equipment constructed	53,000		283,000
Nov. 10	Cost of equipment sold		45,000	238,000

Accumulated Depreciation—Equipment

Date		Debit	Credit	Balance
Jan. 1	Balance			71,000
Nov. 10	Accumulated depreciation on equipment sold	30,000		41,000
Dec. 31	Depreciation for year		24,000	65,000

Retained Earnings

Date		Debit	Credit	Balance
Jan. 1	Balance			105,000
Aug. 23	Dividends (cash)	14,000		91,000
Dec. 31	Net income		47,000	138,000

Instructions
From the postings in the accounts, indicate how the information is reported on a statement of cash flows using the indirect method. The loss on sale of equipment was $6,000. [*Hint:*   Purchase of equipment is reported in the investing activities section as a decrease in cash of $70,000.]

E11-6   Here is a comparative balance sheet for Oprah Winfrey Company:

Prepare a statement of cash flows—indirect method, and compute cash-based ratios.

(SO 4a, 5)

OPRAH WINFREY COMPANY
Comparative Balance Sheet
December 31

Assets	1999	1998
Cash	$ 63,000	$ 22,000
Accounts receivable	85,000	76,000
Inventories	180,000	189,000
Land	75,000	100,000
Equipment	260,000	200,000
Accumulated depreciation	(66,000)	(42,000)
Total	$597,000	$545,000

Liabilities and Stockholders' Equity	1999	1998
Accounts payable	$ 34,000	$ 47,000
Bonds payable	150,000	200,000
Common stock ($1 par)	214,000	164,000
Retained earnings	199,000	134,000
Total	$597,000	$545,000

Additional information:
1. Net income for 1999 was $105,000.
2. Cash dividends of $40,000 were declared and paid.
3. Bonds payable amounting to $50,000 were redeemed for cash $50,000.
4. Common stock was issued for $50,000 cash.
5. Sales for 1999 were $978,000.

Instructions
(a) Prepare a statement of cash flows for 1999 using the indirect method.
(b) Compute these cash-basis ratios:
   (1) Current cash debt coverage
   (2) Cash return on sales
   (3) Cash debt coverage

Classify transactions by type of activity.

(SO 2)

E11-7 An analysis of comparative balance sheets, the current year's income statement, and the general ledger accounts of Pierce Brosnan Corp. uncovered the following items. Assume all items involve cash unless there is information to the contrary.
(a) Purchase of land
(b) Payment of dividends
(c) Sale of building at book value
(d) Exchange of land for patent
(e) Depreciation
(f) Redemption of bonds
(g) Receipt of interest on notes receivable
(h) Issuance of capital stock
(i) Amortization of patent
(j) Issuance of bonds for land
(k) Payment of interest on notes payable
(l) Conversion of bonds into common stock
(m) Loss on sale of land
(n) Receipt of dividends on investment in stock

Instructions
Indicate how each item should be classified in the statement of cash flows using these four major classifications: operating activity (indirect method), investing activity, financing activity, and significant noncash investing and financing activity.

Compute cash provided by operating activities—direct method.

(SO 4b)

E11-8 Kelly McGillis Company completed its first year of operations on December 31, 1999. Its initial income statement showed that Kelly McGillis had revenues of $157,000 and operating expenses of $78,000. Accounts receivable and accounts payable at year end were $42,000 and $33,000, respectively. Assume that accounts payable related to operating expenses. Ignore income taxes.

Instructions
Compute net cash provided by operating activities using the direct method.

Compute cash payments— direct method.

(SO 4b)

E11-9 The income statement for Garcia Company shows cost of goods sold $355,000 and operating expenses (exclusive of depreciation) $230,000. The comparative balance sheet for the year shows that inventory increased $6,000, prepaid expenses decreased $6,000, accounts payable (merchandise suppliers) decreased $8,000, and accrued expenses payable increased $8,000.

Instructions
Using the direct method, compute (a) cash payments to suppliers and (b) cash payments for operating expenses.

Compute cash flow from operating activities—direct method.

(SO 4b)

E11-10 The 1999 accounting records of Flypaper Airlines reveal these transactions and events:

Payment of interest	$ 6,000	Collection of accounts receivable	$180,000
Cash sales	48,000	Payment of salaries and wages	68,000
Receipt of dividend revenue	14,000	Depreciation expense	16,000
Payment of income taxes	16,000	Proceeds from sale of aircraft	812,000
Net income	38,000	Purchase of equipment for cash	22,000
Payment of accounts payable		Loss on sale of aircraft	3,000
for merchandise	90,000	Payment of dividends	14,000
Payment for land	74,000	Payment of operating expenses	20,000

Instructions
Prepare the cash flows from operating activities section using the direct method. (Not all of the items will be used.)

(SO 4b)
E11-11 The following information is taken from the 1999 general ledger of Joan Robinson Company:

Calculate cash flows—direct method.

Rent	Rent expense	$ 31,000
	Prepaid rent, January 1	5,900
	Prepaid rent, December 31	3,000
Salaries	Salaries expense	$ 54,000
	Salaries payable, January 1	5,000
	Salaries payable, December 31	8,000
Sales	Revenue from sales	$180,000
	Accounts receivable, January 1	12,000
	Accounts receivable, December 31	9,000

Instructions
In each case, compute the amount that should be reported in the operating activities section of the statement of cash flows under the direct method.

E11-12 Presented here is information for two companies in the same industry: Rita Corporation and Les Corporation:

Compare two companies by using cash-based ratios.
(SO 5)

	Rita Corporation	Les Corporation
Cash provided by operations	$200,000	$200,000
Average current liabilities	50,000	100,000
Average total liabilities	200,000	250,000
Net income	200,000	200,000
Sales	400,000	800,000

Instructions
Using the cash-based ratios presented in this chapter, compare the (a) liquidity, (b) solvency, and (c) profitability of the two companies.

PROBLEMS: SET A

P11-1A The income statement of Breckenridge Company is presented here:

Prepare the operating activities section—indirect method.
(SO 4a)

BRECKENRIDGE COMPANY
Income Statement
For the Year Ended November 30, 1999

Sales		$6,900,000
Cost of goods sold		
Beginning inventory	$1,900,000	
Purchases	4,400,000	
Goods available for sale	6,300,000	
Ending inventory	1,600,000	
Total cost of goods sold		4,700,000
Gross profit		2,200,000
Operating expenses		
Selling expenses	450,000	
Administrative expenses	700,000	1,150,000
Net income		$1,050,000

Additional information:
1. Accounts receivable decreased $300,000 during the year.
2. Prepaid expenses increased $150,000 during the year.
3. Accounts payable to suppliers of merchandise decreased $300,000 during the year.
4. Accrued expenses payable decreased $100,000 during the year.
5. Administrative expenses include depreciation expense of $60,000.

Instructions
Prepare the operating activities section of the statement of cash flows for the year ended November 30, 1999, for Breckenridge Company, using the indirect method.

Prepare the operating activities section—direct method.
(SO 4b)

P11-2A Data for Breckenridge Company are presented in P11-1A.

Instructions
Prepare the operating activities section of the statement of cash flows using the direct method.

Prepare the operating activities section—direct method.
(SO 4b)

P11-3A Vail Company's income statement contained the condensed information below:

VAIL COMPANY
Income Statement
For the Year Ended December 31, 1999

Revenues		$840,000
Operating expenses, excluding depreciation	$624,000	
Depreciation expense	60,000	
Loss on sale of equipment	26,000	710,000
Income before income taxes		130,000
Income tax expense		40,000
Net income		$ 90,000

Vail's balance sheet contained these comparative data at December 31:

	1999	1998
Accounts receivable	$47,000	$55,000
Accounts payable	41,000	33,000
Income taxes payable	4,000	9,000

Accounts payable pertain to operating expenses.

Instructions
Prepare the operating activities section of the statement of cash flows using the direct method.

Prepare the operating activities section—indirect method.
(SO 4a)

P11-4A Data for Vail Company are presented in P11-3A.

Instructions
Prepare the operating activities section of the statement of cash flows using the indirect method.

Prepare a statement of cash flows—indirect method, and compute cash-based ratios.
(SO 4a, 5)

P11-5A These are the financial statements of Patrick Swayze Company:

PATRICK SWAYZE COMPANY
Comparative Balance Sheet
December 31

Assets	1999	1998
Cash	$ 29,000	$ 13,000
Accounts receivable	28,000	14,000
Merchandise inventory	25,000	35,000
Property, plant, and equipment	60,000	78,000
Accumulated depreciation	(20,000)	(24,000)
Total	$122,000	$116,000

Liabilities and Stockholders' Equity	1999	1998
Accounts payable	$ 29,000	$ 23,000
Income taxes payable	5,000	8,000
Bonds payable	27,000	33,000
Common stock	18,000	14,000
Retained earnings	43,000	38,000
Total	$122,000	$116,000

PATRICK SWAYZE COMPANY
Income Statement
For the Year Ended December 31, 1999

Sales		$220,000
Cost of goods sold		180,000
Gross profit		40,000
Selling expenses	$18,000	
Administrative expenses	6,000	24,000
Income from operations		16,000
Interest expense		2,000
Income before income taxes		14,000
Income tax expense		4,000
Net income		$ 10,000

The following additional data were provided:
1. Dividends declared and paid were $5,000.
2. During the year equipment was sold for $8,500 cash. This equipment cost $18,000 originally and had a book value of $8,500 at the time of sale.
3. All depreciation expense is in the selling expense category.
4. All sales and purchases are on account.

Instructions
(a) Prepare a statement of cash flows using the indirect method.
(b) Compute these cash-basis measures:
   (1) Current cash debt coverage ratio
   (2) Cash return on sales ratio
   (3) Cash debt coverage ratio
   (4) Free cash flow

P11-6A   Data for Patrick Swayze Company are presented in P11-5A. Further analysis reveals the following:
1. Accounts payable pertain to merchandise suppliers.
2. All operating expenses except for depreciation were paid in cash.

Prepare a statement of cash flows—direct method, and compute cash-based ratios.

(SO 4b, 5)

Instructions
(a) Prepare a statement of cash flows for Patrick Swayze Company using the direct method.
(b) Compute these cash-basis measures:
   (1) Current cash debt coverage ratio
   (2) Cash return on sales ratio
   (3) Cash debt coverage ratio
   (4) Free cash flow

P11-7A   Condensed financial data of Fern Galenti, Inc., follow.

Prepare a statement of cash flows—indirect method.

(SO 4a)

FERN GALENTI, INC.
Comparative Balance Sheet
December 31

Assets	1999	1998
Cash	$ 97,800	$ 38,400
Accounts receivable	90,800	33,000
Inventories	112,500	102,850
Prepaid expenses	18,400	16,000
Investments	108,000	94,000
Plant assets	270,000	242,500
Accumulated depreciation	(50,000)	(52,000)
Total	$647,500	$474,750

Liabilities and Stockholders' Equity

Accounts payable	$ 92,000	$ 67,300
Accrued expenses payable	16,500	17,000
Bonds payable	85,000	110,000
Common stock	220,000	175,000
Retained earnings	234,000	105,450
Total	$647,500	$474,750

FERN GALENTI, INC.
Income Statement Data
For the Year Ended December 31, 1999

Sales		$342,780
Less:		
Cost of goods sold	$115,460	
Operating expenses, excluding depreciation	12,410	
Depreciation expense	46,500	
Income taxes	7,280	
Interest expense	2,730	
Loss on sale of plant assets	7,500	191,880
Net income		$150,900

Additional information:
1. New plant assets costing $85,000 were purchased for cash during the year.
2. Old plant assets having an original cost of $57,500 were sold for $1,500 cash.
3. Bonds matured and were paid off at face value for cash.
4. A cash dividend of $22,350 was declared and paid during the year.

Instructions
Prepare a statement of cash flows using the indirect method.

Prepare a statement of cash flows—direct method.

(SO 4b)

P11-8A Data for Fern Galenti, Inc., are presented in P11-7A. Further analysis reveals that accounts payable pertain to merchandise creditors.

Instructions
Prepare a statement of cash flows for Fern Galenti, Inc., using the direct method.

Prepare a statement of cash flows—indirect method.

(SO 4a)

P11-9A This comparative balance sheet is for Cousin Tommy's Toy Company as of December 31:

COUSIN TOMMY'S TOY COMPANY
Comparative Balance Sheet
December 31

Assets	1999	1998
Cash	$ 41,000	$ 45,000
Accounts receivable	47,500	52,000
Inventory	151,450	142,000
Prepaid expenses	16,780	21,000
Land	100,000	130,000
Equipment	228,000	155,000
Accumulated depreciation—equipment	(45,000)	(35,000)
Building	200,000	200,000
Accumulated depreciation—building	(60,000)	(40,000)
Total	$679,730	$670,000

Liabilities and Stockholders' Equity		
Accounts payable	$ 43,730	$ 40,000
Bonds payable	250,000	300,000
Common stock, $1 par	200,000	150,000
Retained earnings	186,000	180,000
Total	$679,730	$670,000

Additional information:
1. Operating expenses include depreciation expense of $42,000 and charges from prepaid expenses of $4,220.
2. Land was sold for cash at book value.
3. Cash dividends of $32,000 were paid.
4. Net income for 1999 was $38,000.
5. Equipment was purchased for $95,000 cash. In addition, equipment costing $22,000 with a book value of $10,000 was sold for $8,100 cash.
6. Bonds were converted at face value by issuing 50,000 shares of $1 par value common stock.

Instructions
Prepare a statement of cash flows for the year ended December 31, 1999, using the indirect method.

PROBLEMS: SET B

P11-1B The income statement of Tina Maria Company is presented here:

Prepare the operating activities section—indirect method.
(SO 4a)

TINA MARIA COMPANY
Income Statement
For the Year Ended December 31, 1999

Sales		$7,100,000
Cost of goods sold		
Beginning inventory	$1,700,000	
Purchases	5,430,000	
Goods available for sale	7,130,000	
Ending inventory	1,920,000	
Total cost of goods sold		5,210,000
Gross profit		1,890,000
Operating expenses		
Selling expenses	400,000	
Administrative expense	525,000	
Depreciation expense	75,000	
Amortization expense	30,000	1,030,000
Net income		$ 860,000

Additional information:
1. Accounts receivable increased $510,000 during the year.
2. Prepaid expenses increased $170,000 during the year.
3. Accounts payable to merchandise suppliers increased $50,000 during the year.
4. Accrued expenses payable decreased $180,000 during the year.

Instructions
Prepare the operating activities section of the statement of cash flows for the year ended December 31, 1999, for Tina Maria Company, using the indirect method.

P11-2B Data for Tina Maria Company are presented in P11-1B.

Prepare the operating activities section—direct method.
(SO 4b)

Instructions
Prepare the operating activities section of the statement of cash flows using the direct method.

P11-3B The income statement of Hanalei International Inc. reported the following condensed information:

Prepare the operating activities section—direct method.

(SO 4b)

HANALEI INTERNATIONAL INC.
Income Statement
For the Year Ended December 31, 1999

Revenues	$430,000
Operating expenses	280,000
Income from operations	150,000
Income tax expense	47,000
Net income	$103,000

Hanalei's balance sheet contained these comparative data at December 31:

	1999	1998
Accounts receivable	$50,000	$40,000
Accounts payable	30,000	41,000
Income taxes payable	6,000	4,000

Hanalei has no depreciable assets. Accounts payable pertain to operating expenses.

Instructions
Prepare the operating activities section of the statement of cash flows using the direct method.

Prepare the operating activities section—indirect method.

(SO 4a)

P11-4B Data for Hanalei International Inc. are presented in P11-3B.

Instructions
Prepare the operating activities section of the statement of cash flows using the indirect method.

Prepare a statement of cash flows—indirect method, and compute cash-based ratios.

(SO 4a, 5)

P11-5B Here are the financial statements of Sean Seymor Company:

SEAN SEYMOR COMPANY
Comparative Balance Sheet
December 31

Assets		1999		1998
Cash		$ 26,000		$ 13,000
Accounts receivable		18,000		14,000
Merchandise inventory		38,000		35,000
Property, plant, and equipment	$70,000		$78,000	
Less accumulated depreciation	(30,000)	40,000	(24,000)	54,000
Total		$122,000		$116,000
Liabilities and Stockholders' Equity				
Accounts payable		$ 29,000		$ 33,000
Income taxes payable		15,000		20,000
Bonds payable		20,000		10,000
Common stock		25,000		25,000
Retained earnings		33,000		28,000
Total		$122,000		$116,000

SEAN SEYMOR COMPANY
Income Statement
For the Year Ended December 31, 1999

Sales	$240,000
Cost of goods sold	180,000
Gross profit	60,000

Selling expenses	$28,000	
Administrative expenses	6,000	34,000
Income from operations		26,000
Interest expense		2,000
Income before income taxes		24,000
Income tax expense		7,000
Net income		$ 17,000

The following additional data were provided:
1. Dividends of $12,000 were declared and paid.
2. During the year equipment was sold for $10,000 cash. This equipment cost $15,000 originally and had a book value of $10,000 at the time of sale.
3. All depreciation expense, $11,000, is in the selling expense category.
4. All sales and purchases are on account.
5. Additional equipment was purchased for $7,000 cash.

Instructions
(a) Prepare a statement of cash flows using the indirect method.
(b) Compute these cash-basis measures:
   (1) Current cash debt coverage ratio
   (2) Cash return on sales ratio
   (3) Cash debt coverage ratio
   (4) Free cash flow

P11-6B Data for the Sean Seymor Company are presented in P11-5B. Further analysis reveals the following:
1. Accounts payable pertains to merchandise creditors.
2. All operating expenses except for depreciation are paid in cash.

Prepare a statement of cash flows—direct method, and compute cash-based ratios.
(SO 4b, 5)

Instructions
(a) Prepare a statement of cash flows using the direct method.
(b) Compute these cash-basis measures:
   (1) Current cash debt coverage ratio
   (2) Cash return on sales ratio
   (3) Cash debt coverage ratio
   (4) Free cash flow

P11-7B Condensed financial data of Norway Company follow.

Prepare a statement of cash flows—indirect method.
(SO 4a)

NORWAY COMPANY
Comparative Balance Sheet
December 31

Assets	1999	1998
Cash	$ 96,700	$ 47,250
Accounts receivable	86,800	57,000
Inventories	121,900	102,650
Investments	84,500	87,000
Plant assets	250,000	205,000
Accumulated depreciation	(49,500)	(40,000)
Total	$590,400	$458,900

Liabilities and Stockholders' Equity		
Accounts payable	$ 52,700	$ 48,280
Accrued expenses payable	12,100	18,830
Bonds payable	100,000	70,000
Common stock	250,000	200,000
Retained earnings	175,600	121,790
Total	$590,400	$458,900

NORWAY COMPANY
Income Statement Data
For the Year Ended December 31, 1999

Sales		$297,500
Gain on sale of plant assets		8,750
		306,250
Less:		
Cost of goods sold	$99,460	
Operating expenses, excluding depreciation expense	14,670	
Depreciation expense	49,700	
Income taxes	7,270	
Interest expense	2,940	174,040
Net income		$132,210

Additional information:
1. New plant assets costing $92,000 were purchased for cash during the year.
2. Investments were sold at cost.
3. Plant assets costing $47,000 were sold for $15,550, resulting in a gain of $8,750.
4. A cash dividend of $78,400 was declared and paid during the year.

Instructions
Prepare a statement of cash flows using the indirect method.

Prepare a statement of cash flows—direct method.
(SO 4b)

P11-8B Data for Norway Company are presented in P11-7B. Further analysis reveals that accounts payable pertain to merchandise creditors.

Instructions
Prepare a statement of cash flows for Norway Company using the direct method.

Prepare a statement of cash flows—indirect method.
(SO 4a)

P11-9B Presented here is the comparative balance sheet for Cortina Company at December 31:

CORTINA COMPANY
Comparative Balance Sheet
December 31

Assets	1999	1998
Cash	$ 40,000	$ 57,000
Accounts receivable	77,000	64,000
Inventory	132,000	140,000
Prepaid expenses	12,140	16,540
Land	125,000	150,000
Equipment	200,000	175,000
Accumulated depreciation—equipment	(60,000)	(42,000)
Building	250,000	250,000
Accumulated depreciation—building	(75,000)	(50,000)
Total	$701,140	$760,540
Liabilities and Stockholders' Equity		
Accounts payable	$ 33,000	$ 45,000
Bonds payable	235,000	265,000
Common stock, $1 par	280,000	250,000
Retained earnings	153,140	200,540
Total	$701,140	$760,540

Additional information:
1. Operating expenses include depreciation expense $70,000 and charges from prepaid expenses of $4,400.
2. Land was sold for cash at cost.
3. Cash dividends of $74,290 were paid.

4. Net income for 1999 was $26,890.
5. Equipment was purchased for $65,000 cash. In addition, equipment costing $40,000 with a book value of $13,000 was sold for $14,000 cash.
6. Bonds were converted at face value by issuing 30,000 shares of $1 par value common stock.

Instructions
Prepare a statement of cash flows for 1999 using the indirect method.

BROADENING YOUR PERSPECTIVE

*F*INANCIAL REPORTING PROBLEM

STARBUCKS CORPORATION

Instructions
BYP11-1 Refer to the financial statements of Starbucks presented in Appendix A. Answer these questions:
(a) What was the amount of net cash provided by operating activities for the year ended September 29, 1996? For the year ended October 1, 1995? What were the primary causes of any significant changes in cash from operations between 1995 and 1996?
(b) What was the amount of increase or decrease in cash and cash equivalents for the year ended September 29, 1996? For the year ended October 1, 1995?
(c) Which method of computing net cash provided by operating activities does Starbucks use?
(d) From your analysis of the 1996 statement of cash flows, was the change in accounts and notes receivable a decrease or an increase? Was the change in inventories a decrease or an increase? Was the change in accounts payable a decrease or an increase?
(e) What was the total (net) cash used for investing activities for 1996?
(f) What was the amount of interest paid in 1996? What was the amount of income taxes paid in 1996?
(g) What significant noncash financing and investing activities did Starbucks complete in 1996?

*C*OMPARATIVE ANALYSIS PROBLEM

STARBUCKS VS. GREEN MOUNTAIN COFFEE

BYP11-2 The financial statements of Green Mountain Coffee are presented in Appendix B, following the financial statements for Starbucks in Appendix A.

Instructions
(a) Based on the information in these financial statements, compute these 1996 ratios for each company:
   (1) Current cash debt coverage
   (2) Cash return on sales
   (3) Cash debt coverage
(b) What conclusions concerning the management of cash can be drawn from these data?

*I*NTERPRETING FINANCIAL STATEMENTS

MATTEL CORPORATION

BYP11-3 Mattel Corporation makes toys—some very famous toys. Among these are Barbie, Fisher-Price, Disney toys (such as Pocahontas), and Hot Wheels cars. In 1994 the company had a great year; in fact, at that point it was the best year in its history. A review of the company's balance sheet, however, reveals that the company's cash dropped from $506 million to $239 million. This drop of $267 million represented a 53% decrease in cash. The following additional information was also available from Mattel's financial statements:

	1994	1993
Cash	$ 237,002	$ 506,113
Marketable securities	20,581	17,468
Accounts receivable, net	762,024	580,313
Inventories	339,143	219,993
Prepaid expenses and other current assets	182,675	146,863
Total current assets	1,543,523	1,470,750
Total current liabilities	915,881	783,329
Cash provided (used) by operations	343,439	303,344
Cash provided (used) by investing	(526,497)	(88,804)
Cash provided (used) by financing	(86,053)	(16,369)

Instructions

(a) Discuss whether Mattel has suffered a significant reduction in its liquidity as a result of this decline in cash on hand. Use the current ratio and the current cash debt coverage ratio to support your position. [*Note:* Assume that current liabilities at December 31, 1992, were $529,389.]

(b) Using the data provided, explain why cash declined, and discuss whether this should be a concern to the company and its investors.

VERMONT TEDDY BEAR CO.

BYP11-4 Founded in the early 1980s, Vermont Teddy Bear Co. designs and manufactures American-made teddy bears and markets them primarily as gifts called Bear-Grams or Teddy Bear-Grams. Bear-Grams are personalized teddy bears delivered directly to the recipient for special occasions such as birthdays and anniversaries. The Shelburne, Vermont, company's primary markets are New York, Boston, and Chicago. Sales jumped dramatically in recent years, exceeding 50% increases for several consecutive years prior to 1994. Such dramatic growth has significant implications for cash flows. Here are the company's cash flow statements for 1993 and 1994:

VERMONT TEDDY BEAR CO.
Comparative Statement of Cash Flows
For the Year Ended December 31

	1994	1993
Cash flows from operating activities		
Net income	$ 17,523	$ 838,955
Adjustments to reconcile net income to net cash provided by operating activities		
Deferred income taxes	(69,524)	(146,590)
Depreciation and amortization	316,416	181,348
Changes in assets and liabilities:		
Accounts receivable, trade	(38,267)	(25,947)
Inventories	(1,599,014)	(1,289,293)
Prepaid and other current assets	(444,794)	(113,205)
Deposit and other assets	(24,240)	(83,044)
Accounts payable	2,017,059	(284,567)
Accrued expenses	61,321	170,755
Accrued interest payable, debentures	—	(58,219)
Other	—	(8,960)
Income taxes payable	—	117,810
Net cash provided by (used for) operating activities	236,480	(700,957)
Net cash used for investing activities	(2,102,892)	(4,422,953)

Net cash provided by (used for) financing activities	(315,353)	9,685,435
Net change in cash and cash equivalents	($2,181,765)	$ 4,561,525
Other information		
Current liabilities	$ 4,055,465	$ 1,995,600
Total liabilities	4,620,085	2,184,386
Net sales	20,560,566	17,025,856

Instructions

(a) Note that net income in 1994 was only $17,523 compared to 1993 income of $838,955, but cash flow from operations was $236,480 in 1994 and a negative $700,957 in 1993. Explain the causes of this apparent paradox.

(b) Evaluate Vermont Teddy Bear's liquidity, solvency, and profitability for 1994 using cash flow-based ratios.

GROUP DECISION CASE

BYP11-5 Greg Rhoda and Debra Sondgeroth are examining the following statement of cash flows for K.K. Bean Trading Company for the year ended January 31, 1999:

K.K. BEAN TRADING COMPANY
Statement of Cash Flows
For the Year Ended January 31, 1999

Sources of cash	
From sales of merchandise	$370,000
From sale of capital stock	420,000
From sale of investment (purchased below)	80,000
From depreciation	55,000
From issuance of note for truck	20,000
From interest on investments	6,000
Total sources of cash	951,000
Uses of cash	
For purchase of fixtures and equipment	340,000
For merchandise purchased for resale	258,000
For operating expenses (including depreciation)	160,000
For purchase of investment	75,000
For purchase of truck by issuance of note	20,000
For purchase of treasury stock	10,000
For interest on note payable	3,000
Total uses of cash	866,000
Net increase in cash	$ 85,000

Greg claims that K.K. Bean's statement of cash flows is an excellent portrayal of a superb first year with cash increasing $85,000. Debra replies that it was not a superb first year—but, rather, that the year was an operating failure, that the statement is presented incorrectly, and that $85,000 is not the actual increase in cash. The cash balance at the beginning of the year was $140,000.

Instructions

With the class divided into groups, answer the following:

(a) With whom do you agree, Greg or Debra? Explain your position.

(b) Using the data provided, prepare a statement of cash flows in proper form using the indirect method. The only noncash items in the income statement are depreciation and the gain from the sale of the investment.

REAL-WORLD FOCUS

PRAXAIR INCORPORATED

BYP11-6 *Praxair Incorporated* was founded in 1907 as Linde-Air Products Company and was a pioneer in separating oxygen from air. It was purchased and run as a subsidiary of Union Carbide. In 1992 Praxair became an independent public company. Today the company is one of the top three largest suppliers of industrial gases worldwide. Praxair has operations in all regions of the world, with a majority of its sales occurring outside of the United States.

The following management discussion was included in Praxair's 1994 annual report:

PRAXAIR
Management Discussion and Analysis

Liquidity, Capital Resources, and Other Financial Data: In 1994 Praxair changed its presentation of the Statement of Cash Flows to the direct method to report major classes of cash receipts and payments from operations. Praxair believes the direct method more clearly presents its operating cash flows. Prior years' cash flow information has been reclassified to conform to the current year presentation.

Instructions
(a) What method has Praxair changed from?
(b) What will the newly prepared cash flow statement show that the former one did not?
(c) Will the cash flows from investing and financing appear any differently under the new method of preparation than they did under the old method?

COMMUNICATION ACTIVITY

BYP11-7 Arnold Byte, the owner-president of Computer Services Company, is unfamiliar with the statement of cash flows that you, as his accountant, prepared. He asks for further explanation.

Instructions
Write him a brief memo explaining the form and content of the statement of cash flows as shown in Illustration 11-12.

RESEARCH ASSIGNMENT

BYP11-8 The March 25, 1996, issue of *Barron's* includes an article by Harry B. Ernst and Jeffrey D. Fotta entitled "Weary Bull."

Instructions
Read the article and answer these questions:
(a) The article describes a cash flow-based model used by investors. Identify the model and briefly describe its purpose.
(b) How does the model classify a firm's cash flows?
(c) Identify one way in which the cash flow classifications described in the article differ from those under GAAP.
(d) How can the model be used to predict stock prices?

ETHICS CASE

BYP11-9   Puebla Corporation is a medium-sized wholesaler of automotive parts. It has ten stockholders who have been paid a total of $1 million in cash dividends for 8 consecutive years. The board of director's policy requires that in order for this dividend to be declared, net cash provided by operating activities as reported in Puebla's current year's statement of cash flows must exceed $1 million. President and CEO Phil Monat's job is secure so long as he produces annual operating cash flows to support the usual dividend.

At the end of the current year, controller Rick Rodgers presents president Monat with some disappointing news: The net cash provided by operating activities is calculated by the indirect method to be only $970,000. The president says to Rick, "We must get that amount above $1 million. Isn't there some way to increase operating cash flow by another $30,000?" Rick answers, "These figures were prepared by my assistant. I'll go back to my office and see what I can do." The president replies, "I know you won't let me down, Rick."

Upon close scrutiny of the statement of cash flows, Rick concludes that he can get the operating cash flows above $1 million by reclassifying a $60,000, 2-year note payable listed in the financing activities section as "Proceeds from bank loan—$60,000." He will report the note instead as "Increase in payables—$60,000" and treat it as an adjustment of net income in the operating activities section. He returns to the president, saying, "You can tell the board to declare their usual dividend. Our net cash flow provided by operating activities is $1,030,000." "Good man, Rick! I knew I could count on you," exults the president.

Instructions
(a) Who are the stakeholders in this situation?
(b) Was there anything unethical about the president's actions? Was there anything unethical about the controller's actions?
(c) Are the board members or anyone else likely to discover the misclassification?

SURFING THE NET

BYP11-10   *Purpose:*   Locating SEC filing in Edgar Database.

Address: http://www.sec.gov/index.html

Steps:
1. From the SEC homepage, choose **Edgar Database.**
2. Choose **Search the Edgar Database.**
3. Choose **Current Event Analysis.**
4. Select a company from the Edgar Daily Report.

Instructions
Answer the following questions:
(a) What form type did you retrieve?
(b) What is the company's name?
(c) What is the Standard Industrial Classification?
(d) What period does this report cover?
(e) In what state or jurisdiction is the organization?

BYP11-11   *Purpose:*   Use the Internet to view SEC filings.

Address: http://www.yahoo.com

Steps:
1. From the Yahoo homepage, choose **Stock Quotes.**
2. Enter stock symbol or use "Symbol Lookup."
3. Choose **Get Quotes.**

Instructions

Answer the following questions:

(a) What company did you select?

(b) What is its stock symbol?

(c) What was the stock's trading range for the day?

(d) What was the stock's trading range for the year?

Answers to Self-Study Questions

1. c   2. b   3. a   4. c   5. d   6. b   7. c   8. a   9. d   10. b
11. c   12. d   13. a   14. d   15. b

 Remember to go back to the Navigator box on the chapter-opening page and check off your completed work.

CHAPTER 12

Financial Statement Analysis

CLASS A
COMMON STOC
PAR VALUE
$1 PER SHARE

NUMBER

A

CUSIP 968223

STUDY OBJECTIVES

After studying this chapter, you should be able to:

1. Understand the concept of earning power and indicate how irregular items are presented.

2. Discuss the need for comparative analysis and identify the tools of financial statement analysis.

3. Explain and apply horizontal analysis.

4. Describe and apply vertical analysis.

5. Identify and compute ratios and describe their purpose and use in analyzing a firm's liquidity, solvency, and profitability.

6. Discuss the limitations of financial statement analysis.

THE
NAVIGATOR

FEATURE STORY

Just Fooling Around?

The information superhighway added a new lane recently when two brothers, Tom and David Gardner, created an online investor service called the Motley Fool. The name comes from Shakespeare's *As You Like It*. The fool in Shakespeare's plays was the only one who could speak unpleasant truths to kings and queens without being killed. Tom and David view themselves as 20th-century "fools," revealing the "truths" of Wall Street to the small investor, who they feel has been taken advantage of by Wall Street insiders. They provide a bulletin board service where America Online subscribers can exchange information and insights about companies that may be of interest to investors.

One company, Iomega, has captured the interest of Motley

Fool subscribers more than all others. Iomega makes a new kind of computer disk drive called a Zip drive. In less than one year, Iomega's stock price soared by a multiple of 16; that is, a $1,000 investment was suddenly worth $16,000! Many people suggest that this tremendous run-up in price (one of the highest increases experienced by any U.S. company during that period) was caused by the attention the stock received on the Motley Fool bulletin board. Supporters of the Motley Fool say that this is an example of how the Internet can be used by small investors to make the kind of returns that the "big guys" make. Participants share any information they can find about the company and its product: Are Zip drive users happy with the product? How quickly are Zip drives moving off store

shelves? How full is the employee parking lot at Iomega on Sundays?

Critics, however, contend that the bulletin board is merely a high-tech rumor mill that has built a speculative house of cards. One potentially troubling aspect of the bulletin board is that participants on the board don't have to give their identities. Consequently, there is little to stop people from putting misinformation on the board to influence the price in the direction they desire.

As information services such as Motley Fool proliferate, gathering information will become easier, and evaluating it will become the harder task.

THE
NAVIGATOR

On the World Wide Web:
http://www.fool.com

THE NAVIGATOR ✔

- ■ Scan *Study Objectives* ☐
- ■ Read *Feature Story* ☐
- ■ Read *Preview* ☐
- ■ Read text and answer *Before You Go On*
  p. 489 ☐   p. 495 ☐   p. 509 ☐
  p. 510 ☐
- ■ Work *Using the Decision Toolkit* ☐
- ■ Review *Summary of Study Objectives* ☐
- ■ Work *Demonstration Problem* ☐
- ■ Answer *Self-Study Questions* ☐
- ■ Complete assignments ☐

If you are thinking of purchasing Iomega Corporation stock, or the stock of any company, how can you determine the worth of the stock? How can you determine the company's financial soundness or its profitability? How does Iomega compare financially with other companies in the high-tech industry of computer disk-drive manufacturers? To answer these types of questions, it is helpful for you to understand how to analyze financial statement information.

Financial statement analysis, the topic of this chapter, enhances the usefulness of published financial statements in making decisions about a company. To provide realism throughout this chapter and let you work with a familiar company, we will analyze the financial statements of Kellogg Company—the world's leading producer of ready-to-eat cereal products. The content and organization of this chapter are shown below:

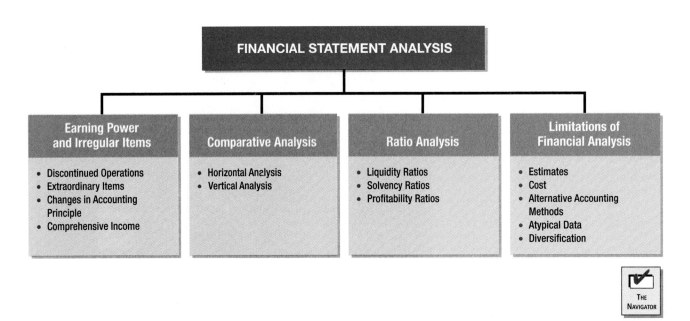

FINANCIAL STATEMENT ANALYSIS

Earning Power and Irregular Items
- Discontinued Operations
- Extraordinary Items
- Changes in Accounting Principle
- Comprehensive Income

Comparative Analysis
- Horizontal Analysis
- Vertical Analysis

Ratio Analysis
- Liquidity Ratios
- Solvency Ratios
- Profitability Ratios

Limitations of Financial Analysis
- Estimates
- Cost
- Alternative Accounting Methods
- Atypical Data
- Diversification

THE NAVIGATOR

EARNING POWER AND IRREGULAR ITEMS

STUDY OBJECTIVE

①

Understand the concept of earning power and indicate how irregular items are presented.

Ultimately, the value of a company is a function of its future cash flows. When analysts use this year's net income to estimate future cash flows, they must make sure that this year's net income does not include irregular revenues, expenses, gains, or losses. Net income adjusted for irregular items is referred to as **earning power. Earning power is the most likely level of income to be obtained in the future—that is, to the extent this year's net income is a good predictor of future years' net income.** Earning power differs from actual net income by the amount of irregular revenues, expenses, gains, and losses included in this year's net income.

Users are interested in earning power because it helps them derive an estimate of future earnings without the "noise" of irregular items. For example, suppose Rye Corporation reports that this year's net income is $500,000 but included in that amount is a once-in-a-lifetime gain of $400,000. In estimating next year's net income for Rye Corporation, we would likely ignore this $400,000 gain and estimate that next year's net income will be in the neighborhood of $100,000.

That is, based on this year's results, the company's earning power is roughly $100,000. Therefore, identifying irregular items has important implications for using reported earnings as an input in estimating a company's value.

As an aid in the determination of earning power (or regular income), irregular items are identified by type on the income statement. Three types of irregular items are reported:

1. Discontinued operations
2. Extraordinary items
3. Changes in accounting principle

All these irregular items are reported net of income taxes; that is, the applicable income tax expense or tax savings is shown for income before income taxes and for each of the listed irregular items. The general concept is "Let the tax follow income or loss."

DISCONTINUED OPERATIONS

To downsize its operations, General Dynamics Corp. sold its missile business to Hughes Aircraft Co. for $450 million. In its income statement, General Dynamics was required to report the sale in a separate section entitled "Discontinued operations." **Discontinued operations** refer to the disposal of a significant segment of a business, such as the elimination of a major class of customers or an entire activity. Thus, the decision by Singer Co. to end its manufacture and sale of computers and the decision to close all overseas offices and terminate all foreign sales were both reported as discontinued operations. The phasing out of a model or part of a line of business, however, is *not* considered to be a disposal of a segment.

When the disposal of a significant segment occurs, the income statement should report both income from continuing operations and income (or loss) from discontinued operations. **The income (loss) from discontinued operations consists of the income (loss) from operations and the gain (loss) on disposal of the segment.** To illustrate, assume that Rozek Inc. has revenues of $2.5 million and expenses of $1.7 million from continuing operations in 1999. The company therefore has income before income taxes of $800,000. During 1999 the company discontinued and sold its unprofitable chemical division. The loss in 1999 from chemical operations (net of $60,000 taxes) was $140,000, and the loss on disposal of the chemical division (net of $30,000 taxes) was $70,000. Assuming a 30% tax rate on income before income taxes, we show the income statement presentation in Illustration 12-1.

Illustration 12-1 Statement presentation of discontinued operations

ROZEK INC. Partial Income Statement For the Year Ended December 31, 1999		
Income before income taxes		$800,000
Income tax expense		240,000
Income from continuing operations		560,000
Discontinued operations		
Loss from operations of chemical division, net of $60,000 income tax saving	$140,000	
Loss from disposal of chemical division, net of $30,000 income tax saving	70,000	210,000
Net income		$350,000

Note that the caption "Income from continuing operations" is used and the section "Discontinued operations" is added. **Within the new section, both the operating loss and the loss on disposal are reported net of applicable income taxes.** This presentation clearly indicates the separate effects of continuing operations and discontinued operations on net income.

Besides being the world's leading cereal maker, Kellogg Company also manufactures toaster pastries, frozen waffles, cereal bars, and other convenience foods. Kellogg's products are manufactured in 20 countries on six continents and distributed in nearly 160 countries. In 1997 Kellogg did not report any discontinued operations.

DECISION TOOLKIT

Decision Checkpoints	Info Needed for Decision	Tool to Use for Decision	How to Evaluate Results
Has the company sold any major lines of business?	Discontinued operations section of income statement	Items reported in this section indicate that the company has discontinued a major line of business.	If a major business line has been discontinued, its results in the current period should not be included in estimates of future net income.

EXTRAORDINARY ITEMS

Extraordinary items are events and transactions that meet two conditions: They are **unusual in nature** and **infrequent in occurrence.** To be considered *unusual,* the item should be abnormal and only incidentally related to the usual activities of the business. To be regarded as *infrequent,* the event or transaction should not be reasonably expected to recur in the foreseeable future. Both criteria must be evaluated in terms of the environment in which the entity operates. Thus, Weyerhaeuser Co. reported the $36 million in damages to its timberland caused by the eruption of Mount St. Helens as an extraordinary item because the event was both unusual and infrequent. In contrast, Florida Citrus Company does not report frost damage to its citrus crop as an extraordinary item because frost damage is not viewed as infrequent. Illustration 12-2 shows the appropriate classification of extraordinary and ordinary items.

Helpful Hint Ordinary gains and losses are reported at pretax amounts in arriving at income before income taxes.

Extraordinary items are reported net of taxes in a separate section of the income statement immediately below discontinued operations. To illustrate, assume that in 1999 a revolutionary foreign government expropriated property held as an investment by Rozek Inc. If the loss is $70,000 before applicable income taxes of $21,000, the income statement presentation will show a deduction of $49,000, as in Illustration 12-3.

As illustrated, the caption "Income before extraordinary item" is added immediately before the listing of extraordinary items. This presentation clearly indicates the effect of the extraordinary item on net income. If there were no discontinued operations, the third line of the income statement in Illustration 12-3 would be "Income before extraordinary item."

If a transaction or event meets one, but not both, of the criteria for an extraordinary item, it should be reported in a separate line item in the upper half of the income statement, rather than being reported in the bottom half as an extraordinary item. Usually these items are reported under either "Other revenues and gains" or "Other expenses and losses" at their gross amount (not net of tax).

Extraordinary items

1. Effects of major casualties (acts of God), if rare in the area.

2. Expropriation (takeover) of property by a foreign government.

3. Effects of a newly enacted law or regulation, such as a condemnation action.

Ordinary items

1. Effects of major casualties (acts of God), frequent in the area.

2. Write-down of inventories or write-off of receivables.

3. Losses attributable to labor strikes.

4. Gains or losses from sales of property, plant, or equipment.

Illustration 12-2 Classification of extraordinary and ordinary items

This is true, for example, of gains (losses) resulting from the sale of property, plant, and equipment.

Kellogg did not report any extraordinary items in its 1996 or 1997 income statements. It did, however, incur significant charges as the result of "restructuring" efforts to reduce costs. These restructuring charges did not meet the criteria required for extraordinary item classification. Instead, Kellogg reported them as "Nonrecurring charges"—of $136.1 million in 1996 and $184.1 million

Illustration 12-3 Statement presentation of extraordinary items

ROZEK INC. Partial Income Statement For the Year Ended December 31, 1999		
Income before income taxes		$800,000
Income tax expense		240,000
Income from continuing operations		560,000
Discontinued operations		
Loss from operations of chemical division, net of $60,000 income tax saving	$140,000	
Loss from disposal of chemical division, net of $30,000 income tax saving	70,000	210,000
Income before extraordinary item		350,000
Extraordinary item		
Expropriation of investment, net of $21,000 income tax saving		49,000
Net income		$301,000

in 1997—in the upper half (income from operations section) of its income statement. The title "nonrecurring" suggests that the charges occur infrequently. In analyzing Kellogg's results, we must decide whether to use its income as reported, or instead to assume that these charges are, in fact, not representative of the company's future earning power. If we assume they are not representative of the company's earning power, we would add them back to net income (after consideration of their tax impact) to estimate next year's income. Since further investigation reveals that the company had similar "nonrecurring charges" in 1995 ($421.8 million), we have concluded that these charges are not as "infrequent" as the name "nonrecurring" might imply. Therefore, we use net income as it was reported by the company for all subsequent analysis.

DECISION TOOLKIT

Decision Checkpoints	Info Needed for Decision	Tool to Use for Decision	How to Evaluate Results
Has the company experienced any extraordinary events or transactions?	Extraordinary item section of income statement	Items reported in this section indicate that the company experienced an event that was both unusual and infrequent.	These items should usually be ignored in estimating future net income.

BUSINESS INSIGHT
Management Perspective

In the recession of the early 1990s, many companies closed some of their plants and reduced the size of their work force. The costs incurred in these activities, called plant restructuring costs, are reported as Other Expenses and Losses in the income statement. These costs are not considered to be an extraordinary item because plant closings are neither unusual nor infrequent in many industries. Plant restructuring costs often have a significant effect on net income, as illustrated by the following cases:

Union Pacific Corp. $585 million after-tax charge, of which $492 million applies to the disposal of 7,100 miles of the Union Pacific Railroad.

Borden, Inc. $71.6 million before-tax charge for business reorganization costs as well as severance, relocation, and other employee-related expenses.

CHANGES IN ACCOUNTING PRINCIPLE

For ease of comparison, financial statements are expected to be prepared on a basis **consistent** with that used for the preceding period. That is, where a choice of accounting principles is available, the principle initially chosen should be applied consistently from period to period. A change in accounting principle occurs when the principle used in the current year is different from the one used in the preceding year. A change is permitted, when (1) management can show that the new principle is preferable to the old principle and (2) the effects of the change are clearly disclosed in the income statement. Two examples are a change in depreciation methods (such as declining-balance to straight-line) and a change in inventory costing methods (such as FIFO to average cost). The effect of a change in an accounting principle on net income can be significant. When U.S. West, one of the six regional Bell telephone companies, changed the depreciation method for its telecommunications equipment, it posted a $3.2 billion loss (net of tax).

Sometimes a change in accounting principle is mandated by the Financial Accounting Standards Board (FASB). An example is the change in accounting for costs of business process engineering activities. In its 1997 income statement, Kellogg Company reported a charge of $18 million, net of income taxes of $7.7 million, under "Cumulative effect of accounting change." An accompanying note explained that the charge resulted from adopting the new standard for its previously capitalized costs associated with business process engineering activities that were part of Kellogg's information technology project; these costs must now be expensed as incurred.

A change in an accounting principle affects reporting in two ways:

1. The new principle should be used in reporting the results of operations of the current year.
2. The cumulative effect of the change on all prior-year income statements should be disclosed net of applicable taxes in a special section immediately preceding Net Income.

To illustrate, we will assume that at the beginning of 1999, Rozek Inc. changes from the straight-line method to the declining-balance method for equipment purchased on January 1, 1996. The cumulative effect on prior-year income statements (statements for 1996–1998) is to increase depreciation expense and decrease income before income taxes by $24,000. If there is a 30% tax rate, the net-of-tax effect of the change is $16,800 ($24,000 × 70%). The income statement presentation is shown in Illustration 12-4.

ROZEK INC.
Partial Income Statement
For the Year Ended December 31, 1999

Income before income taxes		$800,000
Income tax expense		240,000
Income from continuing operations		560,000
Discontinued operations		
Loss from operations of chemical division, net of $60,000 income tax saving	$140,000	
Loss from disposal of chemical division, net of $30,000 income tax saving	70,000	210,000
Income before extraordinary item and cumulative effect of change in accounting principle		350,000
Extraordinary item		
Expropriation of investment, net of $21,000 income tax saving		49,000
Cumulative effect of change in accounting principle		
Effect on prior years of change in depreciation method, net of $7,200 income tax saving		16,800
Net income		$284,200

Illustration 12-4 Statement presentation of a change in accounting principle

The income statement for Rozek will also show depreciation expense for the current year. The amount is based on the new depreciation method. In this case the caption "Income before extraordinary item and cumulative effect of change in accounting principle" is inserted immediately following the section on discontinued operations. This presentation clearly indicates the cumulative effect of the change on prior years' income. If a company has neither discontinued operations nor extraordinary items, the caption "Income before cumulative effect of change in accounting principle" is used in place of "Income from continuing operations."

Helpful Hint A complete income statement showing all material items not typical of regular operations is presented in the Demonstration Problem on page 516.

In summary, in evaluating a company, it generally makes sense to eliminate all irregular items in estimating future earning power. In some cases you must even decide whether certain information reported in the top half of the income statement should be ignored for analysis purposes, such as Kellogg's "nonrecurring" items.

DECISION TOOLKIT

Decision Checkpoints	Info Needed for Decision	Tool to Use for Decision	How to Evaluate Results
Has the company changed any of its accounting policies?	Cumulative effect of change in accounting principle section of income statement	Items reported in this section indicate that the company has changed an accounting policy during the current year.	The cumulative effect should be ignored in estimating the future net income.

COMPREHENSIVE INCOME

Most revenues, expenses, gains, and losses recognized during the period are included in income. However, over time, specific exceptions to this general practice have developed so that certain items now bypass income and are reported directly in stockholders' equity. For example, unrealized gains and losses on available-for-sale securities are not included in income, but rather are reported in the balance sheet as adjustments to stockholders' equity.

Why are these gains and losses on available-for-sale securities excluded from net income? They are excluded to reduce the volatility of net income due to fluctuations in fair value. They are disclosed separately in the balance sheet as adjustments to stockholders' equity to inform the financial statement user of the gain or loss that would be incurred if the securities were sold at fair value.

Many analysts have expressed concern that the number of items that bypass the income statement has increased significantly. They feel that this has reduced the usefulness of the income statement. To address this concern, the FASB now requires that, in addition to reporting net income, a company must also report comprehensive income. **Comprehensive income** includes all changes in stockholders' equity during a period except those resulting from investments by stockholders and distributions to stockholders. A number of alternative formats for reporting comprehensive income are allowed. These formats are discussed in advanced accounting courses.

● **Review It**

1. What is earning power?
2. What are irregular items and what effect might they have on the estimation of future earnings and future cash flows?
3. What is comprehensive income?

COMPARATIVE ANALYSIS

Every item reported in a financial statement has significance: Its inclusion indicates that the item exists at a given time and in a certain quantity. For example, if Iomega Corporation reports $243.8 million on its balance sheet as cash, we know that Iomega did have cash and that the quantity was $243.8 million. But whether that represents an increase over prior years, or whether it is adequate in relation to the company's needs, cannot be determined from the amount alone. The amount must be compared with other financial data to provide more information.

Three types of comparisons increase the decision usefulness of financial information:

STUDY OBJECTIVE
❷
Discuss the need for comparative analysis and identify the tools of financial statement analysis.

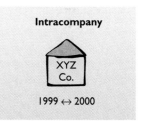

1. **Intracompany basis.**   Comparisons within a company are often useful to detect changes in financial relationships and significant trends. For example, a comparison of Iomega's current year's cash amount with the prior year's cash amount shows either an increase or a decrease. Likewise, a comparison of Iomega's year-end cash amount with the amount of its total assets at year-end shows the proportion of total assets in the form of cash.
2. **Industry averages.**   Comparisons with industry averages provide information about a company's relative position within the industry. For example, Iomega's financial data can be compared with the averages for its industry compiled by financial ratings organizations such as Dun & Bradstreet, Moody's, and Standard & Poor's.
3. **Intercompany basis.**   Comparisons with other companies provide insight into a company's competitive position. For example, Iomega's total sales for the year can be compared with the total sales of its competitors in the computer hard-drive and storage solutions industry, such as IBM and Nomai.

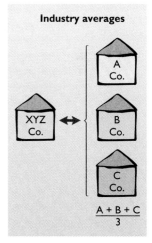

Three basic tools are used in financial statement analysis to highlight the significance of financial statement data:

1. Horizontal analysis
2. Vertical analysis
3. Ratio analysis

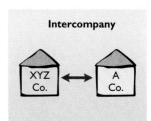

HORIZONTAL ANALYSIS

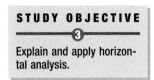

STUDY OBJECTIVE

❸

Explain and apply horizontal analysis.

Horizontal analysis is a technique for evaluating a series of financial statement data over a period of time. Its purpose is to determine the increase or decrease that has taken place, expressed as either an amount or a percentage. For example, here are the recent net sales figures (in millions) of Kellogg Company:

1997	1996	1995	1994	1993
$6,830.1	$6,676.6	$7,003.7	$6,562.0	$6,295.4

Alternative Terminology Horizontal analysis is also often referred to as **trend analysis.**

If we assume that 1993 is the base year, we can measure all percentage increases or decreases from this base-period amount with the formula shown in Illustration 12-5.

Illustration 12-5
Horizontal analysis computation of changes since base period

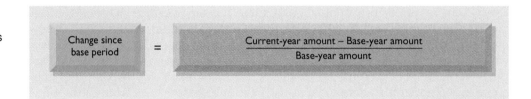

For example, we can determine that net sales for Kellogg Company increased approximately 4.2% [($6,562.0 − $6,295.4)/$6,295.4] from 1993 to 1994. Similarly, we can also determine that net sales increased by almost 8.5% [($6,830.1 − $6,295.4)/$6,295.4] from 1993 to 1997. The percentage of the base period for each of the 5 years, assuming 1993 as the base period, is shown in Illustration 12-6.

Illustration 12-6
Horizontal analysis of net sales

KELLOGG COMPANY
Net Sales (in millions)
Base Period 1993

1997	1996	1995	1994	1993
$6,830.1	$6,676.6	$7,003.7	$6,562.0	$6,295.4
108.5%	106.1%	111.3%	104.2%	100%

To further illustrate horizontal analysis, we use the financial statements of Kellogg Company. Its 2-year condensed balance sheets for 1997 and 1996 showing dollar and percentage changes are presented in Illustration 12-7.

The comparative balance sheet shows that a number of changes occurred in Kellogg's financial position from 1996 to 1997. In the assets section, current assets decreased $60.9 million, or 4.0% ($60.9 ÷ $1,528.6), plant assets (net) decreased $159.6, or 5.4%, and other assets increased 8.2% ($48.1 ÷ $588.5). In the liabilities section, current liabilities decreased $541.7, or 24.6%, while long-term liabilities increased $654.2, or 41.7%. In the stockholders' equity section, we find that retained earnings decreased $3,025.5, or 75.9%. The decrease in retained earnings and treasury stock is due to a retirement of a significant number of shares (105.3 million) of treasury stock.

Presented in Illustration 12-8 is a 2-year comparative income statement of Kellogg Company for 1997 and 1996 in a condensed format.

Illustration 12-7
Horizontal analysis
of a balance sheet

KELLOGG COMPANY, INC.
Condensed Balance Sheets
December 31
(in millions)

	1997	1996	Increase (Decrease) during 1997 Amount	Percent
Assets				
Current assets	$1,467.7	$1,528.6	$ (60.9)	**(4.0)**%
Plant assets (net)	2,773.3	2,932.9	(159.6)	**(5.4)**
Other assets	636.6	588.5	48.1	8.2
Total assets	$4,877.6	$5,050.0	$ (172.4)	**(3.4)**
Liabilities and Stockholders' Equity				
Current liabilities	$1,657.3	$2,199.0	$ (541.7)	**(24.6)**
Long-term liabilities	2,222.8	1,568.6	654.2	**41.7**
Total liabilities	3,880.1	3,767.6	112.5	**3.0**
Stockholders' equity				
Common stock	196.3	201.8	(5.5)	**(2.7)**
Retained earnings and other	958.5	3,984.0	(3,025.5)	**(76.0)**
Treasury stock (cost)	(157.3)	(2,903.4)	2,746.1	**(94.6)**
Total stockholders' equity	997.5	1,282.4	(284.9)	**(22.2)**
Total liabilities and stockholders' equity	$4,877.6	$5,050.0	$ (172.4)	**(3.4)**%

Helpful Hint It is difficult to comprehend the significance of a change when only the dollar amount of change is examined. When the change is expressed in percentage form, it is easier to grasp the true magnitude of the change.

Illustration 12-8
Horizontal analysis of an income statement

KELLOGG COMPANY, INC.
Condensed Income Statement
For the Years Ended December 31
(in millions)

	1997	1996	Increase (Decrease) during 1997 Amount	Percent
Net sales	$6,830.1	$6,676.6	$153.5	2.3%
Cost of goods sold	3,270.1	3,122.9	147.2	4.7
Gross profit	3,560.0	3,553.7	6.3	0.2
Selling and administrative expenses	2,366.8	2,458.7	(91.9)	(3.7)
Nonrecurring charges	184.1	136.1	48.0	35.3
Income from operations	1,009.1	958.9	50.2	5.2
Interest expense	108.3	65.6	42.7	65.1
Other income (expense), net	3.7	(33.4)	(37.1)	—
Income before income taxes and cumulative effect of accounting change	904.5	859.9	44.6	5.2
Income taxes	340.5	328.9	11.6	3.5
Income before cumulative effect of accounting change	564.0	531.0	33.0	6.2
Cumulative effect of accounting change (net)	(18.0)	—	(18.0)	—
Net income	$ 546.0	$ 531.0	$ 15.0	2.8%

Helpful Hint Note that, in a horizontal analysis, while the *Amount* column is additive (the total is $15 million), the *Percent* column is not additive (2.8% is **not** a total).

Helpful Hint When using horizontal analysis, both dollar amount changes and percentage changes need to be examined. It is not necessarily bad if a company's earnings are growing at a declining rate. The **amount** of increase may be the same as or more than the base year, but the **percentage** change may be less because the base is greater each year.

Horizontal analysis of the income statements shows these changes:

Net sales increased $153.5, or 2.3% ($153.5 ÷ $6,676.6).

Cost of goods sold increased $147.2, or 4.7% ($147.2 ÷ $3,122.9).

Selling and administrative expenses decreased $91.9, or 3.7% ($91.9 ÷ $2,458.7).

Overall, gross profit increased $6.3 million or less than 1% and net income increased 2.8%. The increase in net income can be primarily attributed to the $91.9 million or 3.7% decrease from 1996 to 1997 in selling and administrative expenses.

The measurement of changes from period to period in percentages is relatively straightforward and quite useful. However, complications can result in making the computations. If an item has no value in a base year or preceding year and a value in the next year, no percentage change can be computed. And if a negative amount appears in the base or preceding period and a positive amount exists the following year, or vice versa, no percentage change can be computed. For example, no percentage could be calculated for the cumulative effect in Kellogg's condensed income statement.

DECISION TOOLKIT

Decision Checkpoints	Info Needed for Decision	Tool to Use for Decision	How to Evaluate Results
How do the company's financial position and operating results compare with those of previous period?	Income statement and balance sheet	Comparative financial statements should be prepared over at least 2 years, with the first year reported being the base year. Changes in each line item relative to the base year should be presented both by amount and by percentage. This is called horizontal analysis.	Significant changes should be investigated to determine the reason for the change.

VERTICAL ANALYSIS

STUDY OBJECTIVE

4

Describe and apply vertical analysis.

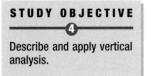

Alternative Terminology Vertical analysis is sometimes referred to as **common-size analysis.**

Vertical analysis is a technique for evaluating financial statement data that expresses each item in a financial statement as a percent of a base amount. For example, on a balance sheet we might say that current assets are 22% of total assets (total assets being the base amount). Or on an income statement we might say that selling expenses are 16% of net sales (net sales being the base amount).

Presented in Illustration 12-9 is the comparative balance sheet of Kellogg for 1997 and 1996, analyzed vertically. The base for the asset items is **total assets,** and the base for the liability and stockholders' equity items is **total liabilities and stockholders' equity.**

In addition to showing the relative size of each category on the balance sheet, vertical analysis may show the percentage change in the individual asset, liability, and stockholders' equity items. In this case, current assets decreased $60.9 million from 1996 to 1997, decreasing slightly from 30.3% to 30.1% of total assets. Plant assets (net) decreased from 58.0% to 56.9% of total assets. Current liabilities decreased $541.7 million from 43.5% to 34.0% while long-term liabil-

Illustration 12-9
Vertical analysis of a
balance sheet

KELLOGG COMPANY, INC.
Condensed Balance Sheet
December 31
(in millions)

	1997		1996	
	Amount	Percent	Amount	Percent
Assets				
Current assets	$1,467.7	30.1%	$1,528.6	30.3%
Plant assets (net)	2,773.3	56.9	2,932.9	58.0
Other assets	636.6	13.0	588.5	11.7
Total assets	$4,877.6	100.0%	$5,050.0	100.0%
Liabilities and Stockholders' Equity				
Current liabilities	$1,657.3	34.0%	$2,199.0	43.5%
Long-term liabilities	2,222.8	45.6	1,568.6	31.1
Total liabilities	3,880.1	79.6	3,767.6	74.6
Stockholders' equity				
Common stock	196.3	4.0	201.8	4.0
Retained earnings and other	958.5	19.6	3,984.0	78.9
Treasury stock (cost)	(157.3)	(3.2)	(2,903.4)	(57.5)
Total stockholders' equity	997.5	20.4	1,282.4	25.4
Total liabilities and stockholders' equity	$4,877.6	100.0%	$5,050.0	100.0%

Illustration 12-10
Vertical analysis of
an income statement

KELLOGG COMPANY, INC.
Condensed Income Statement
For the Years Ended December 31
(in millions)

	1997		1996	
	Amount	Percent	Amount	Percent
Net sales	$6,830.1	100.0%	$6,676.6	100.0%
Cost of goods sold	3,270.1	47.9	3,122.9	46.8
Gross profit	3,560.0	52.1	3,553.7	53.2
Selling and administrative expenses	2,366.8	34.6	2,458.7	36.8
Nonrecurring charges	184.1	2.7	136.1	2.0
Income from operations	1,009.1	14.8	958.9	14.4
Interest expense	108.3	1.6	65.6	1.0
Other income (expense), net	3.7	.1	33.4	(.5)
Income before income taxes and cumulative effect of accounting change	904.5	13.3	859.9	12.9
Income taxes	340.5	5.0	328.9	4.9
Income before cumulative effect of accounting change	564.0	8.3	531.0	8.0
Cumulative effect of accounting change (net)	(18.0)	.3	—	—
Net income	$ 546.0	8.0%	$ 531.0	8.0%

ities increased $654.2 million from 31.1% to 45.6% of total liabilities and stock-holders' equity. Significantly, during the same year, stockholders' equity decreased by $284.9 million from 25.4% to 20.4%. Thus, the company shifted toward a heavier reliance on debt financing both by using more long-term debt and by reducing the amount of outstanding equity.

Vertical analysis of the comparative income statements of Kellogg, shown in Illustration 12-10 on page 493, reveals that cost of goods sold **as a percentage of net sales** increased 1.1% (from 46.8% to 47.9%) while selling and administrative expenses decreased 2.2% (from 36.8% to 34.6%). Even with these changes, net income as a percent of net sales remained the same, yet net income actually increased $15 million.

An associated benefit of vertical analysis is that it enables you to compare companies of different sizes. For example, one of Kellogg's main competitors is General Mills, Inc. Using vertical analysis, we can more meaningfully compare the condensed income statements of Kellogg and General Mills, as shown in Illustration 12-11.

Although Kellogg's net sales are $1,220.8 million (22%) greater than the net sales of General Mills, vertical analysis eliminates this difference. Kellogg's gross profit is 52.1% as a percentage of net sales versus 58.5% for General Mills. This is due to Kellogg's cost of goods sold being 6.4% higher (47.9% to 41.5%) than that of General Mills. Yet net income as a percent of sales is very close—8% for Kellogg and 7.9% for General Mills. Kellogg achieves this in spite of its lower gross profit percentage because its selling and administrative expenses are 8.6% lower than General Mills' (34.6% to 43.2%).

Illustration 12-11 Inter-company comparison by vertical analysis

CONDENSED INCOME STATEMENTS **For the Year Ended December 31, 1997** **(in millions)**				
	Kellogg Company, Inc.		General Mills, Inc.	
	Amount	Percent	Amount	Percent
Net sales	$6,830.1	100.0%	$5,609.3	100.0%
Cost of goods sold	3,270.1	47.9	2,328.4	41.5
Gross profit	3,560.0	52.1	3,280.9	58.5
Selling and administrative expenses	2,366.8	34.6	2,422.0	43.2
Nonrecurring (charges) gains	184.1	2.7	48.4	.9
Income from operations	1,009.1	14.8	810.5	14.4
Interest expense	108.3	1.6	100.5	1.8
Other income (expense), net	3.7	.1	(6.3)	(.1)
Income before income taxes and cumulative effect of accounting change	904.5	13.3	703.7	12.5
Income taxes	340.5	5.0	258.3	4.6
Income before cumulative effect of accounting change	564.0	8.3	445.4	7.9
Cumulative effect of accounting change (net)	(18.0)	.3	—	—
Net income	$ 546.00	8.0%	$ 445.4	7.9%

DECISION TOOLKIT

Decision Checkpoints	Info Needed for Decision	Tool to Use for Decision	How to Evaluate Results
How do the relationships between items in this year's financial statements compare with those of last year or those of competitors?	Income statement and balance sheet	Each line item on the income statement should be presented as a percentage of net sales, and each line item on the balance sheet should be presented as a percentage of total assets or total liabilities and stockholders' equity. These percentages should be investigated for differences either across years in the same company or in the same year across different companies. This is called vertical analysis.	Any differences either across years or between companies should be investigated to determine the cause.

BEFORE YOU GO ON . . .

● **Review It**

1. What different bases can be used to compare financial information?
2. What is horizontal analysis?
3. What is vertical analysis?

THE
NAVIGATOR

RATIO ANALYSIS

In this section we provide a comprehensive coverage of financial ratios, discuss some important relationships among the ratios, and focus on their interpretation.

For analysis of the primary financial statements, ratios can be classified into three types:

STUDY OBJECTIVE
⑤
Identify and compute ratios and describe their purpose and use in analyzing a firm's liquidity, solvency, and profitability.

1. Liquidity ratios: measures of the short-term ability of the company to pay its maturing obligations and to meet unexpected needs for cash
2. Solvency ratios: measures of the ability of the company to survive over a long period of time
3. Profitability ratios: measures of the income or operating success of a company for a given period of time

As a tool of analysis, ratios can provide clues to underlying conditions that may not be apparent from an inspection of the individual components of a particular ratio. But a single ratio by itself is not very meaningful. Accordingly, in this discussion we use the following comparisons:

1. **Intracompany comparisons** covering 2 years for Kellogg Company (using comparative financial information from Illustrations 12-9 and 12-10).
2. **Intercompany comparisons** using General Mills, Inc., as one of Kellogg's principal competitors.

3. **Industry average comparisons** based on Robert Morris Associates median ratios for manufacturers of flour and other grain mill products and comparisons with other sources. For some of the ratios that we use, industry comparisons are not available. (These are denoted "na.")

LIQUIDITY RATIOS

Liquidity ratios measure the short-term ability of the enterprise to pay its maturing obligations and to meet unexpected needs for cash. Short-term creditors such as bankers and suppliers are particularly interested in assessing liquidity. The measures that can be used to determine the enterprise's short-term debt-paying ability are the current ratio, the acid-test ratio, the current cash debt coverage ratio, the receivables turnover ratio, the average collection period, the inventory turnover ratio, and average days in inventory.

1. **Current ratio.** The current ratio expresses the relationship of current assets to current liabilities, computed by dividing current assets by current liabilities. It is widely used for evaluating a company's liquidity and short-term debt-paying ability. The 1997 and 1996 current ratios for Kellogg and comparative data are shown in Illustration 12-12.

Illustration 12-12
Current ratio

Ratio	Formula	Indicates:	Kellogg 1997	Kellogg 1996	General Mills 1997	Industry 1997
Current ratio	Current assets / Current liabilities	Short-term debt-paying ability	.89	.70	.78	1.0

What do the measures actually mean? The 1997 ratio of .89 means that for every dollar of current liabilities, Kellogg has $.89 of current assets. We sometimes state such ratios as .89:1 to reinforce this interpretation. Kellogg's current ratio—and therefore its liquidity—increased in 1997. In both 1997 and 1996 Kellogg's current ratio was below the industry average, although not much different than General Mills'.

The current ratio is only one measure of liquidity. It does not take into account the composition of the current assets. For example, a satisfactory current ratio does not disclose that a portion of the current assets may be tied up in slow-moving inventory. A dollar of cash is more readily available to pay the bills than is a dollar's worth of slow-moving inventory. These weaknesses are addressed by the next ratio.

BUSINESS INSIGHT
Investor Perspective

The apparent simplicity of the current ratio can have real-world limitations because adding equal amounts to both the numerator and the denominator causes the ratio to decrease. Assume, for example, that a company has $2,000,000 of current assets and $1,000,000 of current liabilities; its current ratio is 2:1. If it purchases $1,000,000 of inventory on account, it will have $3,000,000 of current assets and $2,000,000 of current liabilities; its current ratio decreases to 1.5:1. If, instead, the company pays off $500,000 of its current liabilities, it will have $1,500,000 of current assets and $500,000 of current liabilities; its current ratio increases to 3:1. Thus, any trend analysis should be done with care because the ratio is susceptible to quick changes and is easily influenced by management.

2. **Acid-test ratio.** The acid-test or quick ratio is a measure of a company's immediate short-term liquidity. It is computed by dividing the sum of cash, marketable securities, and net receivables by current liabilities. Thus, it is an important complement to the current ratio. Note that it does not include inventory or prepaid expenses. Cash, marketable securities (short-term), and receivables (net) are highly liquid compared with inventory and prepaid expenses. The inventory may not be readily salable, and the prepaid expenses may not be transferable to others. The acid-test ratio for Kellogg is shown in Illustration 12-13.

Illustration 12-13
Acid-test ratio

Ratio	Formula	Indicates:	Kellogg 1997	Kellogg 1996	General Mills 1997	Industry 1997
Acid-test or quick ratio	$\dfrac{\text{Cash} + \text{Marketable securities} + \text{Net receivables}}{\text{Current liabilities}}$	Immediate short-term liquidity	.46	.38	.33	.40

The 1997 and 1996 acid-test ratios for Kellogg again suggest that its liquidity rose during that time. Is Kellogg's 1997 acid-test ratio of .46:1 adequate? When compared with the industry average of .40:1 and Quaker Oats' .33:1, Kellogg's acid-test ratio does seem adequate.

3. **Current cash debt coverage ratio.** A disadvantage of the current and acid-test ratios is that they use year-end balances of current asset and current liability accounts. These year-end balances may not be representative of the company's current position during most of the year. A ratio that partially corrects for this problem is the ratio of net cash provided by operating activities to average current liabilities, called the **current cash debt coverage ratio.** Because it uses net cash provided by operating activities rather than a balance at one point in time, it may provide a better representation of liquidity. Kellogg's current cash debt coverage ratio is shown in Illustration 12-14.

Illustration 12-14
Current cash debt coverage ratio

Ratio	Formula	Indicates:	Kellogg 1997	Kellogg 1996	General Mills 1997	Industry 1997
Current cash debt coverage ratio	$\dfrac{\text{Net cash provided by operating activities}}{\text{Average current liabilities}}$	Short-term debt-paying ability (cash basis)	.46	.41	.47	na

Like the previous measures of liquidity, this ratio increased slightly in 1997 for Kellogg. Is the coverage adequate? Probably so. Kellogg's operating cash flow coverage of average current liabilities is nearly the same as General Mills'. No industry comparison is available.

4. **Receivables turnover ratio.** Liquidity may be measured by how quickly certain assets can be converted to cash. Low values of the previous ratios can sometimes be compensated for if some of the company's current assets are highly liquid. How liquid, for example, are the receivables? The ratio used to assess the liquidity of the receivables is the **receivables turnover ratio,** which measures the number of times, on average, receivables are col-

lected during the period. The receivables turnover ratio is computed by dividing net credit sales (net sales less cash sales) by average net receivables during the year. The receivables turnover ratio for Kellogg is shown in Illustration 12-15.

Illustration 12-15
Receivables turnover ratio

Ratio	Formula	Indicates:	Kellogg 1997	Kellogg 1996	General Mills 1997	Industry 1997
Receivables turnover ratio	Net credit sales / Average net receivables	Liquidity of receivables	11.6	11.3	14.8	11.7

If we assume that all sales are credit sales, the receivables turnover ratio for Kellogg rose slightly in 1997. The turnover of 11.6 times compares favorably with the industry median of 11.7, even though it is well below that of 14.8 times for Quaker Oats.

BUSINESS INSIGHT
Investor Perspective

In some cases, the receivables turnover ratio may be misleading. Some companies, especially large retail chains, encourage credit and revolving charge sales, and they slow collections in order to earn a healthy return on the outstanding receivables in the form of interest at rates of 18% to 22%. In general, however, the faster the turnover, the greater the reliance that can be placed on the current and acid-test ratios for assessing liquidity.

5. **Average collection period.** A popular variant of the receivables turnover ratio converts it into an average collection period in days. This is done by dividing the receivables turnover ratio into 365 days. The average collection period for Kellogg is shown in Illustration 12-16.

Illustration 12-16
Average collection period

Ratio	Formula	Indicates:	Kellogg 1997	Kellogg 1996	General Mills 1997	Industry 1997
Average collection period	365 days / Receivables turnover ratio	Liquidity of receivables and collection success	31.5	32.3	24.6	31.2

Kellogg's 1997 receivables turnover of 11.6 times is divided into 365 days to obtain approximately 31.5 days. This means that the average collection period for receivables is $31^{1}/_{2}$ days, or approximately every four and one-half weeks. Analysts frequently use the average collection period to assess the effectiveness of a company's credit and collection policies. The general rule is that the collection period should not greatly exceed the credit term period (i.e., the time allowed for payment). It is interesting to note that General Mills' average collection period is significantly shorter than those of Kellogg and the industry. This difference may be due to more aggressive collection practices, but it is more likely due to a difference in credit terms granted. General Mills might grant more generous discounts for early payment than others in the industry.

6. **Inventory turnover ratio.** The inventory turnover ratio measures the number of times on average the inventory is sold during the period. Its purpose is to measure the liquidity of the inventory. The inventory turnover ratio is computed by dividing the cost of goods sold by the average inventory during the period. Unless seasonal factors are significant, average inventory can be computed from the beginning and ending inventory balances. Kellogg's inventory turnover ratio is shown in Illustration 12-17.

Illustration 12-17
Inventory turnover ratio

Ratio	Formula	Indicates:	Kellogg 1997	Kellogg 1996	General Mills 1997	Industry 1997
Inventory turnover ratio	Cost of goods sold / Average inventory	Liquidity of inventory	7.6	7.9	6.1	7.5

Kellogg's inventory turnover ratio declined slightly in 1997. The turnover ratio of 7.6 times is slightly higher than the industry average of 7.5 and higher than General Mills' 6.1. Generally, the faster the inventory turnover, the less cash is tied up in inventory and the less the chance of inventory becoming obsolete. Of course, a downside of high inventory turnover is that the company can run out of inventory when it is needed.

7. **Average days in inventory.** A variant of the inventory turnover ratio is the average days in inventory, which measures the average number of days it takes to sell the inventory. The average days in inventory for Kellogg is shown in Illustration 12-18.

Illustration 12-18
Average days in inventory

Ratio	Formula	Indicates:	Kellogg 1997	Kellogg 1996	General Mills 1997	Industry 1997
Average days in inventory	365 days / Inventory turnover ratio	Liquidity of inventory and inventory management	48.0	46.2	59.8	48.7

Kellogg's 1997 inventory turnover ratio of 7.6 divided into 365 is approximately 48 days. An average selling time of 48 days is roughly the same as the industry average but significantly better than that of General Mills. Some of this difference might be explained by differences in product lines across the two companies, although in many ways the types of products of these two companies are quite similar.

Inventory turnover ratios vary considerably among industries. For example, grocery store chains have a turnover of 10 times and an average selling period of 37 days. In contrast, jewelry stores have an average turnover of 1.3 times and an average selling period of 281 days. Within a company there may be significant differences in inventory turnover among different types of products. Thus, in a grocery store the turnover of perishable items such as produce, meats, and dairy products is faster than the turnover of soaps and detergents.

To conclude, most of these liquidity measures suggest that Kellogg's liquidity rose during 1997. And, its liquidity appears acceptable when compared both to that of General Mills and to the industry as a whole.

SOLVENCY RATIOS

Solvency ratios measure the ability of the enterprise to survive over a long period of time. Long-term creditors and stockholders are interested in a company's long-run solvency, particularly its ability to pay interest as it comes due and to repay the face value of the debt at maturity. The debt to total assets ratio, the times interest earned ratio, and the cash debt coverage ratio provide information about debt-paying ability. In addition, free cash flow provides information about the company's solvency and its ability to pay additional dividends or invest in new projects.

8. **Debt to total assets ratio.** The debt to total assets ratio measures the percentage of the total assets provided by creditors. It is computed by dividing total debt (both current and long-term liabilities) by total assets. This ratio indicates the degree of leveraging; it provides some indication of the company's ability to withstand losses without impairing the interests of its creditors. The higher the percentage of debt to total assets, the greater the risk that the company may be unable to meet its maturing obligations. The lower the ratio, the more equity "buffer" is available to creditors if the company becomes insolvent. Thus, from the creditors' point of view, a low ratio of debt to total assets is usually desirable. Kellogg's debt to total assets ratio is shown in Illustration 12-19.

Illustration 12-19   Debt to total assets ratio

Ratio	Formula	Indicates:	Kellogg 1997	Kellogg 1996	General Mills 1997	Industry 1997
Debt to total assets ratio	Total debt / Total assets	Percentage of total assets provided by creditors	.80	.75	.87	.68

Kellogg's 1997 ratio of .80 means that creditors have provided financing sufficient to cover 80% of the company's total assets. Alternatively, it says that Kellogg would have to liquidate 80% of its assets at their book value in order to pay off all of its debts. Kellogg's 80% is above the industry average of 68% but below the 87% ratio of General Mills. Kellogg's solvency declined during the year. In that time, Kellogg's use of debt financing changed. First, Kellogg decreased its use of short-term debt. Second, it significantly increased its use of long-term debt. And third, it retired a considerable number of shares of its own stock. These factors reduced its solvency.

The adequacy of this ratio is often judged in light of the company's earnings. Generally, companies with relatively stable earnings, such as public utilities, have higher debt to total assets ratios than cyclical companies with widely fluctuating earnings, such as many high-tech companies.

Another ratio with a similar meaning is the **debt to equity ratio.** It shows the relative use of borrowed funds (total liabilities) compared with resources invested by the owners. Because this ratio can be computed in several ways, care should be taken when making comparisons. Debt may be defined to include only the noncurrent portion of liabilities, and intangible assets may be excluded from stockholders' equity (which would equal tangible net worth). If debt and assets are defined as above (all liabilities and all assets), then when the debt to total assets ratio equals 50%, the debt to equity ratio is 1:1.

9. **Times interest earned ratio.** The times interest earned ratio (also called interest coverage) indicates the company's ability to meet interest payments as they come due. It is computed by dividing income before interest expense and income taxes by interest expense. Note that this ratio uses income before interest expense and income taxes because this amount represents what is available to cover interest. Kellogg's times interest earned ratio is shown in Illustration 12-20.

Illustration 12-20 Times interest earned ratio

Ratio	Formula	Indicates:	Kellogg 1997	Kellogg 1996	General Mills 1997	Industry 1997
Times interest earned ratio	Income before interest expense and income taxes / Interest expense	Ability to meet interest payments as they come due	9.2	14.1	8.0	2.8

For Kellogg the 1997 coverage was 9.2, which indicates that income before interest and taxes was 9.2 times the amount needed for interest expense. This was a bit higher than the rate for General Mills and over three times the average rate for the industry. Thus, although its long-term debt increased over 40% in 1997 and the debt to assets ratio suggests that Kellogg relies heavily on debt financing, the times interest earned ratio suggests that the company can easily service its debt.

10. **Cash debt coverage ratio.** The ratio of net cash provided by operating activities to average total liabilities, called the cash debt coverage ratio, is a cash-basis measure of solvency. This ratio indicates a company's ability to repay its liabilities from cash generated from operating activities without having to liquidate the assets used in its operations. Illustration 12-21 shows Kellogg's cash debt coverage ratio.

Illustration 12-21 Cash debt coverage ratio

Ratio	Formula	Indicates:	Kellogg 1997	Kellogg 1996	General Mills 1997	Industry 1997
Cash debt coverage ratio	Net cash provided by operating activities / Average total liabilities	Long-term debt-paying ability (cash basis)	.23	.22	.18	na

An industry average for this measure is not available, but Kellogg's .23 exceeded General Mills' .18, and it did increase slightly from .22 in 1996. One way of interpreting this ratio is to say that net cash generated from 1 year of operations would be sufficient to pay off 23% of Kellogg's total liabilities. If 23% of this year's liabilities were retired each year, it would take over 4 years to retire all of its debt, whereas it would take General Mills more than $5\frac{1}{2}$ years to do so.

11. **Free cash flow.** One indication of a company's solvency, as well as of its ability to pay dividends or expand operations, is the amount of excess cash it generated after investing to maintain its current productive capacity and paying dividends. This measure, discussed in Chapter 11, and is referred

to as free cash flow. For example, if you generate $100,000 of cash from operations but you spend $30,000 to maintain and replace your productive facilities at their current levels and pay $10,000 in dividends, you have $60,000 to use either to expand operations or to pay additional dividends.

As a practical matter, companies do not disclose what percentage of their capital expenditures was made to maintain existing production and what percentage was made to expand operations. Thus, external users normally calculate free cash flow by simply subtracting expenditures made for property, plant, and equipment (fixed assets) from cash from operations. Kellogg's free cash flow is shown in Illustration 12-22.

Illustration 12-22
Free cash flow

Ratio	Formula			Indicates:	Kellogg 1997	Kellogg 1996	General Mills 1997	Industry 1997
Free cash flow	Net cash provided by operating activities	− Capital expenditures	− Dividends paid	Cash available for paying dividends or expanding operations	$207.3 (in millions)	$60.5	$104.1 (in millions)	na

Kellogg's free cash flow increased considerably from 1996 to 1997. Its 1997 free cash flow of $207 million is nearly double that of General Mills' $104.1 million. Kellogg has chosen to use a large portion of its free cash flow each year to repurchase its own stock.

PROFITABILITY RATIOS

Profitability ratios measure the income or operating success of a company for a given period of time. A company's income, or the lack of it, affects its ability to obtain debt and equity financing, its liquidity position, and its ability to grow. As a consequence, creditors and investors alike are interested in evaluating profitability. Profitability is frequently used as the ultimate test of management's operating effectiveness. Some commonly used measures of profitability are discussed in the following pages.

The relationships among these profitability measures are very important. Understanding them can help management determine where to focus its efforts to improve a company's profitability. Illustration 12-23 diagrams these relationships. Our discussion of Kellogg's profitability is structured around this diagram.

Illustration 12-23
Relationships among profitability measures

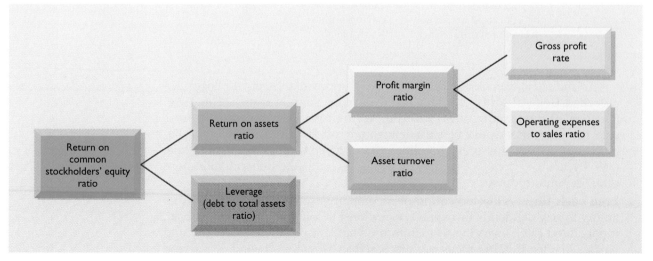

12. **Return on common stockholders' equity ratio.** A widely used measure of profitability from the common stockholder's viewpoint is the return on common stockholders' equity ratio (ROE). This ratio shows how many dollars of net income were earned for each dollar invested by the owners. It is computed by dividing net income minus any preferred stock dividends— that is, income available to common stockholders—by average common stockholders' equity. The return on common stockholders' equity for Kellogg is shown in Illustration 12-24.

Illustration 12-24
Return on common stockholders' equity ratio

Ratio	Formula	Indicates:	Kellogg 1997	Kellogg 1996	General Mills 1997	Industry 1997
Return on common stockholders' equity ratio	Income available to common stockholders / Average common stockholders' equity	Profitability of common stockholders' investment	.48	.37	1.11	.19

Kellogg's 1997 rate of return on common stockholders' equity is unusually high at 48%, considering an industry average of 19%. But, it is dwarfed by the incredible 111% rate of return earned by General Mills, which is partly a result of its high debt to equity leverage.

13. **Return on assets ratio.** The return on common stockholders' equity ratio is affected by two factors: the return on assets ratio (ROA) and the degree of leverage. The return on assets ratio measures the overall profitability of assets in terms of the rate earned on each dollar invested in assets. It is computed by dividing net income by average total assets. Kellogg's return on assets ratio is shown in Illustration 12-25.

Illustration 12-25
Return on assets ratio

Ratio	Formula	Indicates:	Kellogg 1997	Kellogg 1996	General Mills 1997	Industry 1997
Return on assets ratio	Net income / Average total assets	Overall profitability of assets	.11	.11	.12	.14

Kellogg had an 11% return on assets in both 1997 and 1996. This ROA is below the industry average and below General Mills'.

Note that Kellogg's rate of return on stockholders' equity (48%) is substantially higher than its rate of return on assets (11%). The reason is that Kellogg has made effective use of **leverage.** Leveraging or trading on the equity at a gain means that the company has borrowed money by issuing bonds or notes at a lower rate of interest than it is able to earn by using the borrowed money. Leverage is simply trying to use money supplied by nonowners to increase the return to owners. A comparison of the rate of return on assets with the rate of interest paid for borrowed money indicates the profitability of trading on the equity. If you borrow money at 8% and your rate of return on assets is 11%, you are trading on the equity at a gain. Note, however, that trading on the equity is a two-way street; for example, if you borrow money at 11% and earn only 8% on it, you are trading on the equity at a loss. Kellogg earns more on its borrowed funds than it has to pay in interest. The notes to Kellogg's financial statements disclose that it pays interest rates of between 5% and 8% on outstanding debts, yet, as noted above, it earns 11% on each dollar invested in assets. Thus, the return to stockholders exceeds the return on the assets because of the positive benefit of leverage. Recall from our earlier discussion that Kellogg's percentage of debt financing as measured by the ratio of debt to total assets (or debt to equity) increased in 1997. It appears that Kellogg's increase in return on stockholders' equity was largely a function of increased leverage.

14. **Profit margin ratio.** The return on assets ratio is affected by two factors, the first of which is the profit margin ratio. The profit margin ratio, or rate of return on sales, is a measure of the percentage of each dollar of sales that results in net income. It is computed by dividing net income by net sales for the period. Kellogg's profit margin ratio is shown in Illustration 12-26.

Illustration 12-26 Profit margin ratio

Ratio	Formula	Indicates:	Kellogg 1997	Kellogg 1996	General Mills 1997	Industry 1997
Profit margin ratio	Net income / Net sales	Net income generated by each dollar of sales	.08	.08	.08	.04

Kellogg experienced no change in its profit margin ratio from 1996 to 1997. Its profit margin ratio is high in comparison with the industry average of 4% and equal to General Mills' 8%.

High-volume (high inventory turnover) enterprises such as grocery stores and pharmacy chains generally experience low profit margins, whereas low-volume enterprises such as jewelry stores and airplane manufacturers have high profit margins.

15. **Asset turnover ratio.** The other factor that affects the return on assets ratio is the asset turnover ratio. The asset turnover ratio measures how efficiently a company uses its assets to generate sales. It is determined by dividing net sales by average total assets for the period. The resulting number shows the dollar of sales produced by each dollar invested in assets. Illustration 12-27 shows the asset turnover ratio for Kellogg.

Illustration 12-27 Asset turnover ratio

Ratio	Formula	Indicates:	Kellogg 1997	Kellogg 1996	General Mills 1997	Industry 1997
Asset turnover ratio	Net sales / Average total assets	How efficiently assets are used to generate sales	1.38	1.41	1.55	1.5

The asset turnover ratio shows that Kellogg generated sales of $1.38 in 1997 for each dollar it had invested in assets. The ratio declined a bit from 1996 to 1997. Kellogg's asset turnover ratio is slightly below the industry average of 1.5 times and also below General Mills' ratio of 1.55.

Asset turnover ratios vary considerably among industries. For example, a large utility company like Union Electric Company (St. Louis) has a low turnover ratio of .36, whereas the large grocery chain Great Atlantic and Pacific Tea (A&P) has a high turnover ratio of 3.8.

Summarizing Kellogg's profitability, its return on assets ratio remained unchanged from 1996 to 1997 at 11%. Underlying this stability was a continued 8% profitability on each dollar of sales, as measured by the profit margin ratio, along with stability in the sales-generating efficiency of its assets, as measured by the asset turnover ratio. The combined effects of profit margin and asset turnover on return on assets for Kellogg can be analyzed as shown in Illustration 12-28.

Illustration 12-28
Composition of return on assets ratio

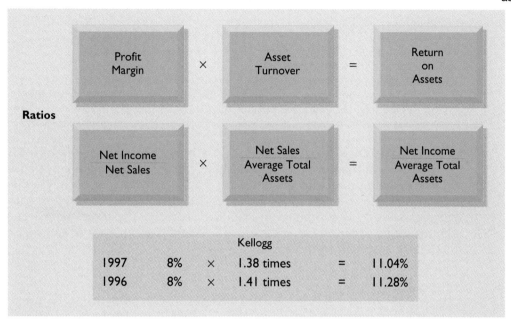

16. **Gross profit rate.**   Two factors strongly influence the profit margin ratio. One is the gross profit rate. The gross profit rate is determined by dividing gross profit (net sales less cost of goods sold) by net sales. This rate indicates a company's ability to maintain an adequate selling price above its costs. As an industry becomes more competitive, this ratio declines. For example, in the early years of the personal computer industry, gross profit rates were quite high. Today, because of dramatically increased competition and a belief that most brands of personal computers are similar in quality, gross profit rates have become relatively thin. Gross profit rates should be closely monitored over time. Illustration 12-29 shows Kellogg's gross profit rate.

Illustration 12-29
Gross profit rate

Ratio	Formula	Indicates:	Kellogg 1997	Kellogg 1996	General Mills 1997	Industry 1997
Gross profit rate	Gross profit / Net sales	Margin between selling price and cost of goods sold	.52	.53	.59	na

Kellogg's gross profit rate declined somewhat from 1996 to 1997 in the face of cuts in the selling price of cereal by many of its competitors. Much can be learned about the reasons for Kellogg's reduced profitability by reading its annual report. Consider the excerpt in Illustration 12-30 (at the top of the next page).

Illustration 12-30
Kellogg's management
discussion and analysis

KELLOGG COMPANY, INC.
Management Discussion and Analysis

1997 compared to 1996 Excluding non-recurring charges and other unusual items, the Company reported 1997 earnings per share of $1.70, an 11% increase over the prior-year results of $1.53. The year-over-year increase in earnings per share of $.17 resulted from $.12 of business growth, $.03 of common stock repurchases, and $.04 of favorable tax rate movements, partially offset by $.02 of unfavorable foreign currency movements. The business growth was principally attributable to cereal volume growth in the Company's U.S. and Latin American markets, continued double-digit growth in other convenience foods volume, and reductions in manufacturing and marketing costs.

Gross margin performance for 1997 benefited from volume increases and year-over-year operational cost savings. However, these favorable factors were outweighed by the negative impact of prior-year pricing actions.

17. **Operating expenses to sales ratio.** This is the other factor that directly affects the profit margin ratio. Management can influence a company's profitability by maintaining adequate prices, cutting expenses, or both. The operating expenses to sales ratio measures the costs incurred to support each dollar of sales. It is computed by dividing operating expenses (selling and administrative expenses) by net sales. The operating expenses to sales ratio for Kellogg is shown in Illustration 12-31.

Illustration 12-31
Operating expenses to
sales ratio

Ratio	Formula	Indicates:	Kellogg 1997	Kellogg 1996	General Mills 1997	Industry 1997
Operating expenses to sales ratio	Operating expenses / Net sales	The costs incurred to support each dollar of sales	.35	.37	.43	na

Kellogg's operating expenses (selling, general, and administrative expenses) decreased both in amount and as a percentage of net sales (from 37% in 1996 to 35% in 1997). Kellogg management commented on this cost reduction as follows: "The improvement in selling, general, and administrative (SGA%) primarily reflects reduced promotional spending in the U.S. market, in line with the Company's integrated pricing strategy."

18. **Cash return on sales ratio.** The profit margin ratio discussed earlier is an accrual-based ratio using net income as a numerator. The cash-basis counterpart to that ratio is the cash return on sales ratio, which uses net cash provided by operating activities as the numerator and net sales as the denominator. The difference between these two ratios should be explainable as differences between accrual accounting and cash-basis accounting, such as differences in the timing of revenue and expense recognition. The cash return on sales ratio for Kellogg is shown in Illustration 12-32.

Illustration 12-32 Cash
return on sales ratio

Ratio	Formula	Indicates:	Kellogg 1997	Kellogg 1996	General Mills 1997	Industry 1997
Cash return on sales ratio	Net cash provided by operating activities / Net sales	Net cash flow generated by each dollar of sales	.13	.11	.11	na

19. **Earnings per share (EPS).** Stockholders usually think in terms of the number of shares they own or plan to buy or sell. Expressing net income earned on a per share basis provides a useful perspective for determining profitability. Earnings per share is a measure of the net income earned on each share of common stock. It is computed by dividing net income by the number of weighted average common shares outstanding during the year. When we use "net income per share" or "earnings per share," it refers to the amount of net income applicable to each share of *common stock*. Therefore, when we compute earnings per share, if there are preferred dividends declared for the period, they must be deducted from net income to arrive at income available to the common stockholders. Kellogg's earnings per share is shown in Illustration 12-33.

Illustration 12-33
Earnings per share

Ratio	Formula	Indicates:	Kellogg 1997	Kellogg 1996	General Mills 1997	Industry 1997
Earnings per share (EPS)	Income available to common stockholders / Average number of outstanding common shares	Net income earned on each share of common stock	$1.32	$1.25	$2.82	na

Note that no industry average is presented in Illustration 12-33. Industry data for earnings per share are not reported, and in fact the Kellogg and General Mills ratios should not be compared. Such comparisons are not meaningful because of the wide variations in the number of shares of outstanding stock among companies. Kellogg's earnings per share increased 7 cents per share in 1997. This represents a 5.6% increase over the 1996 EPS of $1.25.

20. **Price-earnings ratio.** The price-earnings ratio is an oft-quoted statistic that measures the ratio of the market price of each share of common stock to the earnings per share. The price-earnings (P-E) ratio is a reflection of investors' assessments of a company's future earnings. It is computed by dividing the market price per share of the stock by earnings per share. Kellogg's price-earnings ratio is shown in Illustration 12-34.

Illustration 12-34
Price-earnings ratio

Ratio	Formula	Indicates:	Kellogg 1997	Kellogg 1996	General Mills 1997	Industry 1997
Price-earnings ratio	Stock price / Earnings per share	Relationship between market price per share and earnings per share	38	31	23	19

At the end of 1997 and 1996 the market price of Kellogg's stock was $49\frac{5}{8}$ and $38\frac{3}{4}$, respectively. General Mills' stock was selling for $64\frac{1}{4}$ at the end of 1997.

At December 31, 1997, each share of Kellogg's stock sold for 38 times the amount that was earned on each share. Kellogg's price-earnings ratio is significantly higher than the industry average of 19 times and higher than its previous year's ratio of 31. General Mills' ratio of 23 times, although below Kellogg's, is higher than the industry average. These higher P-E ratios suggest that the market is more optimistic about Kellogg and General Mills than about the other companies in the industry. However, it might also signal that their stock is overpriced. The average price-earnings ratio for the stocks that constitute the Standard and Poor's Composite 1,500 Company Index in December 1998 was an unusually high 22 times.

21. **Payout ratio.** The payout ratio measures the percentage of earnings distributed in the form of cash dividends. It is computed by dividing cash dividends paid on common stock by net income. Companies that have high growth rates are characterized by low payout ratios because they reinvest most of their net income in the business. The payout ratio for Kellogg is shown in Illustration 12-35.

Illustration 12-35
Payout ratio

Ratio	Formula	Indicates:	Kellogg 1997	Kellogg 1996	General Mills 1997	Industry 1997
Payout ratio	Cash dividends / Net income	Percentage of earnings distributed in the form of cash dividends	.66	.65	.72	.38

The 1997 and 1996 payout ratios for Kellogg are comparatively high when compared with the industry average of .38 but are even less than that of General Mills.

Management has some control over the amount of dividends paid each year, and companies are generally reluctant to reduce a dividend below the amount paid in a previous year. Therefore, the payout ratio will actually increase if a company's net income declines but the company keeps its total dividend payment the same. Of course, unless the company returns to its previous level of profitability, maintaining this higher dividend payout ratio is probably not possible over the long run. Before drawing any conclusions regarding Kellogg's dividend payout ratio, we should calculate this ratio over a longer period of time to evaluate any trends, and also try to find out whether management's philosophy regarding dividends has changed recently. The "selected financial data" section of Kellogg's Management Discussion and Analysis shows that over a 10-year period earnings per share have grown 5% per year, while dividends per share have grown 11% per year. Unless earnings growth improves, this rapid dividend growth is probably not sustainable over the long term.

BUSINESS INSIGHT
Management Perspective

Generally, companies with stable earnings have high payout ratios. For example, a utility such as Potomac Electric Company had an 86% payout ratio over a recent 5-year period, and Amoco Corporation had a 63% payout ratio over the same period. Conversely, companies that are expanding rapidly, such as Toys 'R' Us and Microsoft, have never paid a cash dividend.

In terms of the types of financial information available and the ratios used by various industries, what can be practically covered in this textbook gives you only the "Titanic approach": You are seeing only the tip of the iceberg compared to the vast databases and types of ratio analysis that are available on computers. The availability of information is not a problem. The real trick is to be discriminating enough to perform relevant analysis and select pertinent comparative data.

BEFORE YOU GO ON . . .

● Review It

1. What are liquidity ratios? Explain the current ratio, acid-test ratio, receivables turnover ratio, inventory turnover ratio, and current cash debt coverage ratio.
2. What are solvency ratios? Explain the debt to total assets ratio, the times interest earned ratio, and the cash debt coverage ratio.
3. What are profitability ratios? Explain the return on common stockholders' equity ratio, return on assets ratio, asset turnover ratio, cash return on sales, earnings per share, price-earnings ratio, and payout ratio.

THE
NAVIGATOR

LIMITATIONS OF FINANCIAL ANALYSIS

Significant business decisions are frequently made using one or more of the three analytical tools presented in this chapter: horizontal, vertical, and ratio analysis. You should be aware of some of the limitations of these tools and of the financial statements on which they are based.

STUDY OBJECTIVE
6
Discuss the limitations
of financial statement
analysis.

ESTIMATES

Financial statements contain numerous estimates. Estimates are used, for example, in determining the allowance for uncollectible receivables, periodic depreciation, the costs of warranties, and contingent losses. To the extent that these estimates are inaccurate, the financial ratios and percentages are also inaccurate.

COST

Traditional financial statements are based on cost and are not adjusted for price-level changes. Comparisons of unadjusted financial data from different periods may be rendered invalid by significant inflation or deflation. For example, a 5-year comparison of Kellogg's revenues shows a growth of 8%. But if, for example, the general price level also increased by 8%, the company's real growth would be zero. Also, some assets such as property, plant, and equipment might be many years old. The historical cost at which they are shown on the balance sheet might be significantly lower than what they could currently be sold for.

ALTERNATIVE ACCOUNTING METHODS

Variations among companies in the application of generally accepted accounting principles may hamper comparability. For example, one company may use the FIFO method of inventory costing, while another company in the same industry may use LIFO. If inventory is a significant asset to both companies, it is unlikely that their current ratios are comparable. For example, if General Motors Corporation had used FIFO instead of LIFO in valuing its inventories, its inventories would have been 26% higher, which significantly affects the current ratio (and other ratios as well).

In addition to differences in inventory costing methods, differences also exist in reporting such items as depreciation, depletion, and amortization. Although these differences in accounting methods might be detectable from reading the notes to the financial statements, adjusting the financial data to compensate for the different methods is difficult, if not impossible, in some cases.

ATYPICAL DATA

Fiscal year-end data may not be typical of a company's financial condition during the year. Firms frequently establish a fiscal year-end that coincides with the low point in their operating activity or inventory levels. Therefore, certain account balances (cash, receivables, payables, and inventories) may not be representative of the balances in the accounts during the year.

DIVERSIFICATION

Diversification in American industry also limits the usefulness of financial analysis. Many firms today are so diversified that they cannot be classified by industry. Others appear to be comparable but are not. You might think that PepsiCo, Inc., and Coca-Cola Company would be comparable as soft drink industry competitors. But are they comparable when until recently, PepsiCo, in addition to producing Pepsi-Cola, owned Pizza Hut, Kentucky Fried Chicken, Taco Bell, and Frito-Lay; and Coca-Cola, in addition to producing Coke, owns Hi-C (fruit drinks), Minute Maid (frozen juice concentrate), and Columbia Pictures (motion pictures, TV shows, and commercials)? Or, we might like to compare Kellogg to RJR Nabisco, one of its biggest competitors. But since RJR Nabisco generates a significant portion of its profits from cigarette sales, and a lot of the rest of its profits from nongrain-related products, comparisons are difficult. As a consequence, deciding what industry a company is in is actually one of the main challenges to effective evaluation of its results.

When companies have significant operations in different lines of business, they are required to report additional disclosures in a segmental data note to their financial statements. Segmental data include total sales, total identifiable assets, operating profit, depreciation expense, and capital expenditures by business segment. Many analysts say that the segmental information is the most important data in the financial statements because, without it, comparison of diversified companies is very difficult.

DECISION TOOLKIT

Decision Checkpoints	Info Needed for Decision	Tool to Use for Decision	How to Evaluate Results
Are efforts to evaluate the company significantly hampered by any of the common limitations of financial analysis?	Financial statements as well as a general understanding of the company and its business	The primary limitations of financial analysis are estimates, cost, alternative accounting methods, atypical data, and diversification.	If any of these factors is significant, the analysis should be relied upon with caution.

BEFORE YOU GO ON . . .

● **Review It**

1. What are some of the limitations of financial analysis?
2. What are the required disclosures in segmental data notes?

THE NAVIGATOR

USING THE DECISION TOOLKIT

In analyzing a company, you should always investigate a number of years in order to determine whether the condition and performance of the company are changing. The condensed financial statements of Kellogg Company for 1994 and 1993 are presented here:

KELLOGG COMPANY, INC.
Balance Sheet
December 31
(in millions)

	1994	1993
Assets		
Current assets		
Cash and short-term investments	$ 266.3	$ 98.1
Accounts receivable (net)	564.5	536.8
Inventories	396.3	403.1
Prepaid expenses and other current assets	206.4	207.1
Total current assets	1,433.5	1,245.1
Property, plant, and equipment (net)	2,892.8	2,768.4
Intangibles and other assets	141.0	223.6
Total assets	$4,467.3	$4,237.1
Liabilities and Stockholders' Equity		
Current liabilities	$1,185.2	$1,214.6
Long-term liabilities	1,474.6	1,309.1
Stockholders' equity—common	1,807.5	1,713.4
Total liabilities and stockholders' equity	$4,467.3	$4,237.1

KELLOGG COMPANY, INC.
Income Statement
For the Years Ended December 31
(in millions)

	1994	1993
Revenues	$6,562.0	$6,295.4
Costs and expenses		
Cost of goods sold	2,950.7	2,989.0
Selling and administrative expenses	2,448.7	2,237.5
Interest expense	32.6	34.8
Total costs and expenses	5,432.0	5,261.3
Income before income taxes	1,130.0	1,034.1
Income tax expense	424.6	353.4
Net income	$ 705.4	$ 680.7

Instructions

Compute the following ratios for Kellogg for 1994 and 1993 and comment on each relative to the amounts reported in the chapter.

1. Liquidity:
   (a) Current ratio
   (b) Inventory turnover ratio (Inventory on December 31, 1992, was $416.4 million.)
2. Solvency:
   (a) Debt to total assets ratio
   (b) Times interest earned ratio
3. Profitability:
   (a) Return on common stockholders' equity ratio (Equity on December 31, 1992, was $1,945.2 million.)
   (b) Return on assets ratio (Assets on December 31, 1992, were $4,015.0 million.)
   (c) Profit margin ratio

Solution

1. Liquidity
   (a) Current ratio:

   1994: $\dfrac{\$1,433.5}{\$1,185.2} = 1.2{:}1$

   1994: $\dfrac{\$1,245.1}{\$1,214.6} = 1.0{:}1$

   (b) Inventory turnover ratio:

   1994: $\dfrac{\$2,950.7}{(\$396.3 + \$403.1)/2} = 7.4 \text{ times}$

   1993: $\dfrac{\$2,989.0}{(\$403.1 + \$416.4)/2} = 7.3 \text{ times}$

In the chapter we noted that Kellogg's liquidity as measured by the current ratio increased sharply in 1997 due to a large decrease in current liabilities. Its current ratio in both 1994 and 1993 was at or above the 1997 industry average. The inventory turnover ratio in 1997 is better than it was in either 1994 or 1993. The faster that inventory turns, the more liquid it is; that is, the company can accept a lower current ratio if it can turn its inventory (and receivables) more quickly.

2. Solvency
   (a) Debt to total assets ratio:

   1994: $\dfrac{\$2.659.8}{\$4,467.3} = 60\%$

   1993: $\dfrac{\$2,523.7}{\$4,237.1} = 60\%$

   (b) Times interest earned ratio:

   1994: $\dfrac{\$705.4 + \$424.6 + \$32.6}{\$32.6} = 35.7 \text{ times}$

   1993: $\dfrac{\$680.7 + \$353.4 + \$34.8}{\$34.8} = 30.7 \text{ times}$

Kellogg's solvency as measured by the debt to total assets ratio declined in 1996 and 1997 relative to its level in 1994 and 1993. However, we can see from the 1994 and 1993 measures that the high times interest earned ratio that we observed in 1996 and 1997 was not unusual for Kellogg, but instead is about the normal measure. This consistently high times interest earned measure gives us confidence that Kellogg can meet its debt payments when due.

3. Profitability

   (a) Return on common stockholders' equity ratio:

$$1994: \quad \frac{\$705.4}{(\$1,807.5 + \$1,713.4)/2} = 40\%$$

$$1993: \quad \frac{\$680.7}{(\$1,713.4 + \$1,945.2)/2} = 37\%$$

   (b) Return on assets ratio:

$$1994: \quad \frac{\$705.4}{(\$4,467.3 + \$4,237.1)/2} = 16\%$$

$$1993: \quad \frac{\$608.7}{(\$4,237.1 + \$4,015.0)/2} = 16\%$$

   (c) Profit margin ratio:

$$1994: \quad \frac{\$705.4}{\$6,562.0} = 11\%$$

$$1993: \quad \frac{\$680.7}{\$6,295.4} = 11\%$$

We noted in the chapter that Kellogg's return on common stockholders' equity ratio was unusually high. We suggested that in 1997 Kellogg reached this high measure by increasing its leverage—that is, by trading on the equity. Note that its return on common stockholders' equity ratio was also very high back in 1994 and 1993. However, then it had much higher profit margin and return on assets ratios. By increasing its leverage, Kellogg has been able to maintain a high return on common stockholders' equity ratio, but, as we noted in the chapter, higher leverage means higher risk. That is, with higher leverage, if the company's sales turn sour, its profitability could really be hurt.

THE NAVIGATOR

SUMMARY OF STUDY OBJECTIVES

❶ Understand the concept of earning power and indicate how irregular items are presented. Earning power refers to a company's ability to sustain its profits from operations. Irregular items—discontinued operations, extraordinary items, and changes in accounting principles—are presented on the income statement net of tax below "Income from continuing operations" to highlight their unusual nature.

❷ Discuss the need for comparative analysis and identify the tools of financial statement analysis. Comparative analysis is performed to evaluate a firm's short-term liquidity, profitability, and long-term solvency. Comparisons can detect changes in financial relationships and significant trends and provide insight into a company's competitive position and relative position in its industry. Financial statements may be analyzed horizontally, vertically, and with ratios.

❸ Explain and apply horizontal analysis. Horizontal analysis is a technique for evaluating a series of data over a period of time to determine the increase or decrease that has taken place, expressed as either an amount or a percentage.

❹ Describe and apply vertical analysis. Vertical analysis is a technique that expresses each item in a financial statement as a percentage of a relevant total or a base amount.

❺ Identify and compute ratios and describe their purpose and use in analyzing a firm's liquidity, solvency, and profitability. Financial ratios are provided in Illustrations 12-12 through 12-18 (liquidity), Illustrations 12-19 through 12-22 (solvency), and Illustrations 12-24 through 12-29, and 12-31 through 12-35 (profitability).

❻ Discuss the limitations of financial statement analysis. The usefulness of analytical tools is limited by the use of estimates, the cost basis, the application of alternative accounting methods, atypical data at year-end, and the diversification of companies.

THE NAVIGATOR

DECISION TOOLKIT—A SUMMARY

Decision Checkpoints	Info Needed for Decision	Tool to Use for Decision	How to Evaluate Results
Has the company sold any major lines of business?	Discontinued operations section of income statement	Items reported in this section indicate that the company has discontinued a major line of business.	If a major business line has been discontinued, its results in the current period should not be included in estimates of future net income.
Has the company experienced any extraordinary events or transactions?	Extraordinary item section of income statement	Items reported in this section indicate that the company experienced an event that was both unusual and infrequent.	These items should usually be ignored in estimating future net income.
Has the company changed any of its accounting policies?	Cumulative effect of change in accounting principle section of income statement	Items reported in this section indicate that the company has changed an accounting policy during the current year.	The cumulative effect should be ignored in estimating the future net income.
How do the company's financial position and operating results compare with those of previous period?	Income statement and balance sheet	Comparative financial statements should be prepared over at least 2 years, with the first year reported being the base year. Changes in each line item relative to the base year should be presented both by amount and by percentage. This is called horizontal analysis.	Significant changes should be investigated to determine the reason for the change.
How do the relationships between items in this year's financial statements compare with those of last year or those of competitors?	Income statement and balance sheet	Each line item on the income statement should be presented as a percentage of net sales, and each line item on the balance sheet should be presented as a percentage of total assets or total liabilities and stockholders' equity. These percentages should be investigated for differences either across years in the same company or in the same year across different companies. This is called vertical analysis.	Any differences either across years or between companies should be investigated to determine the cause.
Are efforts to evaluate the company significantly hampered by any of the common limitations of financial analysis?	Financial statements as well as a general understanding of the company and its business	The primary limitations of financial analysis are estimates, cost, alternative accounting methods, atypical data, and diversification.	If any of these factors is significant, the analysis should be relied upon with caution.

GLOSSARY

Acid-test (quick) ratio A measure of a company's immediate short-term liquidity, computed as the sum of cash, marketable securities, and net receivables divided by current liabilities. (p. 497)

Asset turnover ratio A measure of how efficiently a company uses its assets to generate sales, computed as net sales divided by average total assets. (p. 504)

Average collection period The average number of days that receivables are outstanding, calculated as receivables turnover divided into 365 days. (p. 498)

Average days in inventory A measure of the average number of days it takes to sell the inventory, computed as inventory turnover divided into 365 days. (p. 499)

Cash debt coverage ratio A cash-basis measure used to evaluate solvency, computed as cash from operations divided by average total liabilities. (p. 501)

Cash return on sales ratio The cash-basis measure of net income generated by each dollar of sales, computed as net cash from operations divided by net sales. (p. 506)

Change in accounting principle Use of an accounting principle in the current year different from the one used in the preceding year. (p. 486)

Comprehensive income Includes all changes in stockholders' equity during a period except those resulting from investments by stockholders and distributions to stockholders. (p. 488)

Current cash debt coverage ratio A cash-basis measure of short-term debt-paying ability, computed as cash from operations divided by average current liabilities. (p. 497)

Current ratio A measure that expresses the relationship of current assets to current liabilities, calculated as current assets divided by current liabilities. (p. 496)

Debt to total assets ratio A measure of the percentage of total assets provided by creditors, computed as total debt divided by total assets. (p. 500)

Discontinued operations The disposal of a significant segment of a business. (p. 483)

Earnings per share The net income earned by each share of common stock, computed as net income divided by the weighted average common shares outstanding. (p. 507)

Extraordinary items Events and transactions that meet two conditions: (1) unusual in nature and (2) infrequent in occurrence. (p. 484)

Free cash flow The amount of cash from operations available for paying dividends or expanding operations after spending enough cash to maintain operations at their current level. (p. 502)

Gross profit rate An indicator of a company's ability to maintain an adequate selling price of goods above their cost, computed as gross profit divided by net sales. (p. 505)

Horizontal analysis A technique for evaluating a series of financial statement data over a period of time to determine the increase (decrease) that has taken place, expressed as either an amount or a percentage. (p. 490)

Inventory turnover ratio A measure of the liquidity of inventory, computed as cost of goods sold divided by average inventory. (p. 499)

Leveraging Borrowing money at a lower rate of interest than can be earned by using the borrowed money; also referred to as trading on the equity. (p. 503)

Liquidity ratios Measures of the short-term ability of the enterprise to pay its maturing obligations and to meet unexpected needs for cash. (p. 495)

Operating expenses to sales ratio A measure of the costs incurred to support each dollar of sales, computed as operating expenses divided by net sales. (p. 506)

Payout ratio A measure of the percentage of earnings distributed in the form of cash dividends, calculated as cash dividends divided by net income. (p. 508)

Price-earnings ratio A comparison of the market price of each share of common stock to the earnings per share, computed as the market price of the stock divided by earnings per share. (p. 507)

Profit margin ratio A measure of the net income generated by each dollar of sales, computed as net income divided by net sales. (p. 504)

Profitability ratios Measures of the income or operating success of an enterprise for a given period of time. (p. 495)

Quick ratio Another name for the acid-test ratio. (p. 497)

Receivables turnover ratio A measure of the liquidity of receivables, computed as net credit sales divided by average net receivables. (p. 497)

Return on assets ratio (ROA) An overall measure of profitability, calculated as net income divided by average total assets. (p. 503)

Return on common stockholders' equity ratio A measure of the dollars of net income earned for each dollar invested by the owners, computed as income available to common stockholders divided by average common stockholders' equity. (p. 503)

Segmental data A required note disclosure for diversified companies in which the company reports sales, operating profit, identifiable assets, depreciation expense, and capital expenditures by major business segment. (p. 510)

Solvency ratios Measures of the ability of the enterprise to survive over a long period of time. (p. 495)

Times interest earned ratio A measure of a company's ability to meet interest payments as they come due, calculated as income before interest expense and income taxes divided by interest expense. (p. 501)

Trading on the equity Same as leveraging. (p. 503)

Vertical analysis A technique for evaluating financial statement data that expresses each item in a financial statement as a percent of a base amount. (p. 492)

DEMONSTRATION PROBLEM

The events and transactions of Dever Corporation for the year ending December 31, 1999, resulted in these data:

Cost of goods sold	$2,600,000
Net sales	4,400,000
Other expenses and losses	9,600
Other revenues and gains	5,600
Selling and administrative expenses	1,100,000
Income from operations of plastics division	70,000
Gain on sale of plastics division	500,000
Loss from tornado disaster (extraordinary loss)	600,000
Cumulative effect of changing from straight-line depreciation to double-declining-balance (increase in depreciation expense)	300,000

Analysis reveals:

1. All items are before the applicable income tax rate of 30%.
2. The plastics division was sold on July 1.
3. All operating data for the plastics division have been segregated.

Instructions

Prepare an income statement for the year, excluding the presentation of earnings per share.

Problem-Solving Strategies

1. Remember that material items not typical of operations are reported in separate sections net of taxes.

2. Income taxes should be associated with the item that affects the taxes.

3. A corporation income statement has income tax expense when there is income before income tax.

4. All data presented in determining income before income taxes are the same as for unincorporated companies.

Solution to Demonstration Problem

DEVER CORPORATION
Income Statement
For the Year Ended December 31, 1999

Net sales		$4,400,000
Cost of goods sold		2,600,000
Gross profit		1,800,000
Selling and administrative expenses		1,100,000
Income from operations		700,000
Other revenues and gains	$ 5,600	
Other expenses and losses	9,600	4,000
Income before income taxes		696,000
Income tax expense ($696,000 × 30%)		208,800
Income from continuing operations		487,200
Discontinued operations		
Income from operations of plastics division, net of $21,000 income taxes ($70,000 × 30%)	49,000	
Gain on sale of plastics division, net of $150,000 income taxes ($500,000 × 30%)	350,000	399,000
Income before extraordinary item and cumulative effect of change in accounting principle		886,200
Extraordinary item		
Tornado loss, net of income tax saving $180,000 ($600,000 × 30%)		420,000
Cumulative effect of change in accounting principle		
Effect on prior years of change in depreciation method, net of $90,000 income tax saving ($300,000 × 30%)		210,000
Net income		$ 256,200

THE NAVIGATOR

SELF-STUDY QUESTIONS

Answers are at the end of the chapter.

(SO 1)   1. In reporting discontinued operations, the income statement should show in a special section:
   (a) gains and losses on the disposal of the discontinued segment.
   (b) gains and losses from operations of the discontinued segment.
   (c) Neither (a) nor (b)
   (d) Both (a) and (b)

(SO 1)   2. The Candy Stick Corporation has income before taxes of $400,000 and an extraordinary loss of $100,000. If the income tax rate is 25% on all items, the income statement should show income before extraordinary items, and extraordinary items, respectively, of
   (a) $325,000 and $100,000.
   (b) $325,000 and $75,000.
   (c) $300,000 and $100,000.
   (d) $300,000 and $75,000.

(SO 2)   3. Comparisons of data within a company are an example of the following comparative basis:
   (a) industry averages.
   (b) intracompany.
   (c) intercompany.
   (d) Both (b) and (c)

(SO 4)   4. In horizontal analysis, each item is expressed as a percentage of the:
   (a) net income amount.
   (b) stockholders' equity amount.
   (c) total assets amount.
   (d) base-year amount.

(SO 4)   5. In vertical analysis, the base amount for depreciation expense is generally:
   (a) net sales.
   (b) depreciation expense in a previous year.
   (c) gross profit.
   (d) fixed assets.

(SO 4)   6. The following schedule is a display of what type of analysis?

	Amount	Percent
Current assets	$200,000	25%
Property, plant, and equipment	600,000	75%
Total assets	$800,000	

   (a) Horizontal analysis
   (b) Differential analysis
   (c) Vertical analysis
   (d) Ratio analysis

(SO 3)   7. Leland Corporation reported net sales of $300,000, $330,000, and $360,000 in the years 1997, 1998, and 1999, respectively. If 1997 is the base year, what is the trend percentage for 1999?
   (a) 77%
   (b) 108%
   (c) 120%
   (d) 130%

(SO 5)   8. Which measure is an evaluation of a firm's ability to pay current liabilities?
   (a) Acid-test ratio
   (b) Current ratio
   (c) Both (a) and (b)
   (d) None of the above

(SO 5)   9. Which measure is useful in evaluating the efficiency in managing inventories?
   (a) Inventory turnover ratio
   (b) Average days in inventory
   (c) Both (a) and (b)
   (d) None of the above

(SO 5) 10. Which of these is *not* a liquidity ratio?
   (a) Current ratio
   (b) Asset turnover ratio
   (c) Inventory turnover ratio
   (d) Receivables turnover ratio

(SO 5) 11. Plano Corporation reported net income $24,000; net sales $400,000; and average assets $600,000 for 1999. What is the 1999 profit margin?
   (a) 6%
   (b) 12%
   (c) 40%
   (d) 200%

(SO 6) 12. Which of the following is generally *not* considered to be a limitation of financial analysis?
   (a) Use of ratio analysis
   (b) Use of estimates
   (c) Use of cost
   (d) Use of alternative accounting methods

THE
NAVIGATOR

QUESTIONS

1. Explain earning power. What relationship does this concept have to the treatment of irregular items on the income statement? *Regular income*

2. Indicate which of the following items would be reported as an extraordinary item on Fine & Fancy Food Corporation's income statement.
   (a) Loss from damages caused by a volcano eruption
   (b) Loss from the sale of temporary investments *—or*
   (c) Loss attributable to a labor strike *— or*
   (d) Loss caused when the Food and Drug Administration prohibited the manufacture and sale of a product line *—ex or*
   (e) Loss of inventory from flood damage because a warehouse is located on a flood plain that floods every 5 to 10 years *Ord.*
   (f) Loss on the write-down of outdated inventory *o*
   (g) Loss from a foreign government's expropriation of a production facility *— exord*
   (h) Loss from damage to a warehouse in southern California from a minor earthquake *— exord*

3. Iron Ingots Inc. reported 1998 earnings per share of $3.26 and had no extraordinary items. In 1999 earnings per share on income before extraordinary items was $2.99, and earnings per share on net income was $3.49. Do you consider this trend to be favorable? Why or why not?

4. Rodger Robotics Inc. has been in operation for 3 years. All of its manufacturing equipment, which has a useful life of 10 to 12 years, has been depreciated on a straight-line basis. During the fourth year, Rodger Robotics changes to an accelerated depreciation method for all of its equipment.
   (a) Will Rodger Robotics post a gain or a loss on this change?
   (b) How will this change be reported?

5. (a) Tia Kim believes that the analysis of financial statements is directed at two characteristics of a company: liquidity and profitability. Is Tia correct? Explain.
   (b) Are short-term creditors, long-term creditors, and stockholders interested in primarily the same characteristics of a company? Explain.

6. (a) Distinguish among the following bases of comparison: intracompany, industry averages, and intercompany.
   (b) Give the principal value of using each of the three bases of comparison.

7. Two popular methods of financial statement analysis are horizontal analysis and vertical analysis. Explain the difference between these two methods.

8. (a) If Roe Company had net income of $540,000 in 1998 and it experienced a 24.5% increase in net income for 1999, what is its net income for 1999?

   (b) If six cents of every dollar of Roe's revenue is net income in 1998, what is the dollar amount of 1998 revenue?

9. Name the major ratios useful in assessing (a) liquidity and (b) solvency.

10. Tony Robins is puzzled. His company had a profit margin of 10% in 1999. He feels that this is an indication that the company is doing well. Joan Graham, his accountant, says that more information is needed to determine the firm's financial well-being. Who is correct? Why?

11. What does each type of ratio measure?
    (a) Liquidity ratios
    (b) Solvency ratios
    (c) Profitability ratios

12. What is the difference between the current ratio and the acid-test ratio?

13. Gerry Bullock Company, a retail store, has a receivables turnover ratio of 4.5 times. The industry average is 12.5 times. Does Bullock have a collection problem with its receivables?

14. Which ratios should be used to help answer each of these questions?
    (a) How efficient is a company in using its assets to produce sales?
    (b) How near to sale is the inventory on hand?
    (c) How many dollars of net income were earned for each dollar invested by the owners?
    (d) How able is a company to meet interest charges as they fall due?

15. The price-earnings ratio of McDonnell Douglas (aircraft builder) was 5, and the price-earnings ratio of Microsoft (computer software) was 43. Which company did the stock market favor? Explain.

16. What is the formula for computing the payout ratio? Do you expect this ratio to be high or low for a growth company?

17. Holding all other factors constant, indicate whether each of the following changes generally signals good or bad news about a company:
    (a) Increase in profit margin ratio
    (b) Decrease in inventory turnover ratio
    (c) Increase in current ratio
    (d) Decrease in earnings per share
    (e) Increase in price-earnings ratio
    (f) Increase in debt to total assets ratio
    (g) Decrease in times interest earned ratio

18. The return on assets for Windsor Corporation is 7.6%. During the same year Windsor's return on common stockholders' equity is 12.8%. What is the explanation for the difference in the two rates?

19. Which two ratios do you think should be of greatest interest in each of these cases:
    (a) A pension fund considering the purchase of 20-year bonds

(b) A bank contemplating a short-term loan

(c) A common stockholder

20. (a) What is meant by trading on the equity?

(b) How would you determine the profitability of trading on the equity?

21. Khris Inc. has net income of $270,000, weighted average shares of common stock outstanding of 50,000 and preferred dividends for the period of $40,000. What is Khris's earnings per share of common stock? Phil Remmers, the president of Khris Inc., believes that the computed EPS of the company is high. Comment.

22. Identify and briefly explain five limitations of financial analysis.

23. Explain how the choice of one of the following accounting methods over the other raises or lowers a company's net income during a period of continuing inflation.

(a) Use of FIFO instead of LIFO for inventory costing

(b) Use of a 6-year life for machinery instead of a 9-year life

(c) Use of straight-line depreciation instead of accelerated declining-balance depreciation

BRIEF EXERCISES

BE12-1 On June 30 Osborn Corporation discontinued its operations in Mexico. During the year, the operating loss was $400,000 before taxes. On September 1 Osborn disposed of the Mexico facility at a pretax loss of $150,000. The applicable tax rate is 30%. Show the discontinued operations section of Osborn's income statement.

Prepare a discontinued operations section of an income statement.
(SO 1)

BE12-2 An inexperienced accountant for Lima Corporation showed the following in Lima's income statement: Income before income taxes, $300,000; Income tax expense, $72,000; Extraordinary loss from flood (before taxes), $60,000; and Net income, $168,000. The extraordinary loss and taxable income are both subject to a 30% tax rate. Prepare a corrected income statement beginning with "Income before income taxes."

Prepare a corrected income statement with an extraordinary item.
(SO 1)

BE12-3 On January 1, 1999, Shirli Inc. changed from the straight-line method of depreciation to the declining-balance method. The cumulative effect of the change was to increase the prior years' depreciation by $40,000 and 1999 depreciation by $8,000. Show the change in accounting principle section of the 1999 income statement, assuming the tax rate is 30%.

Prepare a change in accounting principles section of an income statement.
(SO 1)

BE12-4 Using these data from the comparative balance sheet of All-State Company, perform horizontal analysis.

Prepare horizontal analysis.
(SO 3)

	December 31, 1999	December 31, 1998
Accounts receivable	$ 600,000	$ 400,000
Inventory	780,000	600,000
Total assets	3,220,000	2,800,000

BE12-5 Using the data presented in BE12-4 for All-State Company, perform vertical analysis.

Prepare vertical analysis.
(SO 4)

BE12-6 Net income was $500,000 in 1997, $420,000 in 1998, and $504,000 in 1999. What is the percentage of change from (a) 1997 to 1998 and (b) 1998 to 1999? Is the change an increase or a decrease?

Calculate percentage of change.
(SO 3)

BE12-7 If Cavalier Company had net income of $672,300 in 1999 and it experienced a 25% increase in net income over 1998, what was its 1998 net income?

Calculate net income.
(SO 3)

BE12-8 Vertical analysis (common-size) percentages for Waubons Company's sales, cost of goods sold, and expenses are listed here:

Calculate change in net income.
(SO 4)

Vertical Analysis	1999	1998	1997
Sales	100.0%	100.0%	100.0%
Cost of goods sold	59.2	62.4	64.5
Expenses	25.0	26.6	29.5

Did Waubons' net income as a percent of sales increase, decrease, or remain unchanged over the 3-year period? Provide numerical support for your answer.

Calculate change in net income.
(SO 3)

BE12-9   Horizontal analysis (trend analysis) percentages for Tilden Company's sales, cost of goods sold, and expenses are listed here:

Horizontal Analysis	1999	1998	1997
Sales	96.2%	106.8%	100.0%
Cost of goods sold	102.0	97.0	100.0
Expenses	110.6	95.4	100.0

✏️➤ Explain whether Tilden's net income increased, decreased, or remained unchanged over the 3-year period.

Calculate liquidity ratios.
(SO 5)

BE12-10   These selected condensed data are taken from a recent balance sheet of Bob Evans Farms:

Cash	$ 8,241,000
Marketable securities	1,947,000
Accounts receivable	12,545,000
Inventories	14,814,000
Other current assets	5,371,000
Total current assets	$42,918,000
Total current liabilities	$44,844,000

What are the (a) current ratio and (b) acid-test ratio?

Evaluate collection of accounts receivable.
(SO 5)

BE12-11   The following data are taken from the financial statements of Diet-Mite Company:

	1999	1998
Accounts receivable (net), end of year	$ 560,000	$ 540,000
Net sales on account	5,500,000	4,100,000
Terms for all sales are 1/10, n/45.		

Compute for each year (a) the receivables turnover ratio and (b) the average collection period. What conclusions about the management of accounts receivable can be drawn from these data? At the end of 1997, accounts receivable (net) was $490,000.

Evaluate management of inventory.
(SO 5)

BE12-12   The following data were taken from the income statements of Linda Shumway Company:

	1999	1998
Sales	$6,420,000	$6,240,000
Beginning inventory	980,000	837,000
Purchases	4,640,000	4,661,000
Ending inventory	1,020,000	980,000

✏️➤ Compute for each year (a) the inventory turnover ratio and (b) the average days in inventory. What conclusions concerning the management of the inventory can be drawn from these data?

Calculate profitability ratios.
(SO 5)

BE12-13   Boston Patriots Corporation has net income of $15 million and net revenue of $100 million in 1999. Its assets were $12 million at the beginning of the year and $14 million at the end of the year. What are the Patriots' (a) asset turnover ratio and (b) profit margin ratio? (Round to two decimals.)

Calculate profitability ratios.
(SO 5)

BE12-14   Haymark Products Company has stockholders' equity of $400,000 and net income of $50,000. It has a payout ratio of 20% and a rate of return on assets of 16%. How much did Haymark Products pay in cash dividends, and what were its average assets?

Calculate cash-basis liquidity, profitability, and solvency ratios.
(SO 5)

BE12-15   Selected data taken from the 1999 financial statements of Shirley Denison Manufacturing Company are as follows:

Net sales for 1999	$6,860,000
Current liabilities, January 1, 1999	180,000
Current liabilities, December 31, 1999	240,000
Net cash provided by operating activities	760,000
Total liabilities, January 1, 1999	1,500,000
Total liabilities, December 31, 1999	1,300,000

Compute these ratios at December 31, 1999: (a) current cash debt coverage ratio, (b) cash return on sales ratio, and (c) cash debt coverage ratio.

EXERCISES

E12-1 The Davis Company has income from continuing operations of $240,000 for the year ended December 31, 1999. It also has the following items (before considering income taxes): (1) an extraordinary fire loss of $60,000, (2) a gain of $40,000 from the discontinuance of a division, which includes a $110,000 gain from the operation of the division and a $70,000 loss on its disposal, and (3) a cumulative change in accounting principle that resulted in an increase in the prior year's depreciation of $30,000. Assume all items are subject to income taxes at a 30% tax rate.

Prepare irregular items portion of an income statement.
(SO 1)

Instructions
Prepare Davis Company's income statement for 1999, beginning with "Income from continuing operations."

E12-2 *The Wall Street Journal* routinely publishes summaries of corporate quarterly and annual earnings reports in a feature called the "Earnings Digest." A typical "digest" report takes the following form:

Evaluate the effects of unusual or irregular items.
(SO 1, 5, 6)

ENERGY ENTERPRISES (A)

	Quarter ending July 31	
	1999	1998
Revenues	$2,049,000,000	$1,754,000,000
Net income	97,000,000	(a) 68,750,000
EPS: Net income	1.31	.93

	9 months ending July 31	
	1999	1998
Revenues	$5,578,500,000	$5,065,300,000
Extraordinary item	(b) 1,900,000	
Net income	102,700,000	(a) 33,250,000
EPS: Net income	1.39	.45

(a) Includes a net charge of $26,000,000 from loss on the sale of electrical equipment
(b) Extraordinary gain on Middle East property expropriation

The letter in parentheses following the company name indicates the exchange on which Energy Enterprises' stock is traded—in this case, the American Stock Exchange.

Instructions
Answer these questions:
(a) How was the loss on the electrical equipment reported on the income statement? Was it reported in the third quarter of 1998? How can you tell?
(b) Why did *The Wall Street Journal* list the extraordinary item separately?
(c) What is the extraordinary item? Was it included in income for the third quarter? How can you tell?
(d) Did Energy Enterprises have an operating loss in any quarter of 1998? Of 1999? How do you know?
(e) Approximately how many shares of stock were outstanding in 1999? Did the number of outstanding shares change from July 31, 1998, to July 31, 1999?
(f) As an investor, what numbers should you use to determine Energy Enterprises' profit margin ratio? Calculate the 9-month profit margin ratio for 1998 and 1999 that you consider most useful. Explain your decision.

Prepare horizontal analysis.
(SO 3)

E12-3 Here is financial information for Merchandise Inc.:

	December 31, 1999	December 31, 1998
Current assets	$120,000	$100,000
Plant assets (net)	400,000	330,000
Current liabilities	91,000	70,000
Long-term liabilities	144,000	95,000
Common stock, $1 par	150,000	115,000
Retained earnings	135,000	150,000

Instructions
Prepare a schedule showing a horizontal analysis for 1999 using 1998 as the base year.

Prepare vertical analysis.
(SO 4)

E12-4 Operating data for Fleetwood Corporation are presented here:

	1999	1998
Sales	$800,000	$600,000
Cost of goods sold	472,000	390,000
Selling expenses	120,000	72,000
Administrative expenses	80,000	54,000
Income tax expense	38,400	25,200
Net income	89,600	58,800

Instructions
Prepare a schedule showing a vertical analysis for 1999 and 1998.

Prepare horizontal and vertical analyses.
(SO 3, 4)

E12-5 The comparative balance sheets of Oklahoma Corporation are presented here:

OKLAHOMA CORPORATION
Comparative Balance Sheets
December 31

	1999	1998
Assets		
Current assets	$ 72,000	$ 80,000
Property, plant, and equipment (net)	99,000	90,000
Intangibles	24,000	40,000
Total assets	$195,000	$210,000
Liabilities and Stockholders' Equity		
Current liabilities	$ 40,800	$ 48,000
Long-term liabilities	138,000	150,000
Stockholders' equity	16,200	12,000
Total liabilities and stockholders' equity	$195,000	$210,000

Instructions
(a) Prepare a horizontal analysis of the balance sheet data for Oklahoma Corporation using 1998 as a base. (Show the amount of increase or decrease as well.)
(b) Prepare a vertical analysis of the balance sheet data for Oklahoma Corporation for 1999.

Prepare horizontal and vertical analyses.
(SO 3, 4)

E12-6 Here are the comparative income statements of Olympic Corporation:

OLYMPIC CORPORATION
Comparative Income Statements
For the Years Ended December 31

	1999	1998
Net sales	$550,000	$550,000
Cost of goods sold	440,000	450,000
Gross profit	$110,000	$100,000
Operating expenses	57,200	54,000
Net income	$ 52,800	$ 46,000

Instructions
(a) Prepare a horizontal analysis of the income statement data for Olympic Corporation using 1998 as a base. (Show the amounts of increase or decrease.)
(b) Prepare a vertical analysis of the income statement data for Olympic Corporation for both years.

E12-7 Nordstrom, Inc., operates department stores in numerous states. Selected financial statement data (in millions) for a recent year are presented here:

Compute liquidity ratios and compare results.
(SO 5)

	End of Year	Beginning of Year
Cash and cash equivalents	$ 33	$ 91
Receivables (net)	676	586
Merchandise inventory	628	586
Prepaid expenses	61	52
Total current assets	$1,398	$1,315
Total current liabilities	$ 690	$ 627

For the year, net sales were $3,894, cost of goods sold was $2,600, and cash from operations was $215.

Instructions
Compute the current ratio, acid-test ratio, current cash debt coverage ratio, receivables turnover ratio, average collection period, inventory turnover ratio, and average days in inventory at the end of the current year.

E12-8 Firpo Incorporated had the following transactions involving current assets and current liabilities during February 1999:

Perform current and acid-test ratio analysis.
(SO 5)

Feb.	3	Collected accounts receivable of $15,000.
	7	Purchased equipment for $25,000 cash.
	11	Paid $3,000 for a 3-year insurance policy.
	14	Paid accounts payable of $14,000.
	18	Declared cash dividends, $6,000.

Additional information:
1. As of February 1, 1999, current assets were $140,000 and current liabilities were $50,000.
2. As of February 1, 1999, current assets included $15,000 of inventory and $5,000 of prepaid expenses.

Instructions
(a) Compute the current ratio as of the beginning of the month and after each transaction.
(b) Compute the acid-test ratio as of the beginning of the month and after each transaction.

E12-9 Georgette Company has these comparative balance sheet data:

Compute selected ratios.
(SO 5)

GEORGETTE COMPANY
Balance Sheet
December 31

	1999	1998
Cash	$ 20,000	$ 30,000
Receivables (net)	65,000	60,000
Inventories	60,000	50,000
Plant assets (net)	200,000	180,000
	$345,000	$320,000
Accounts payable	$ 50,000	$ 60,000
Mortgage payable (15%)	100,000	100,000
Common stock, $10 par	140,000	120,000
Retained earnings	55,000	40,000
	$345,000	$320,000

Additional information for 1999:
1. Net income was $25,000.
2. Sales on account were $420,000. Sales returns and allowances amounted to $20,000.
3. Cost of goods sold was $198,000.
4. Net cash provided by operating activities was $44,000.

Instructions
Compute the following ratios at December 31, 1999:
(a) Current   (f) Average days in inventory
(b) Acid-test   (g) Cash return on sales
(c) Receivables turnover   (h) Cash debt coverage
(d) Average collection period   (i) Current cash debt coverage
(e) Inventory turnover

Compute selected ratios.
(SO 5)

E12-10 Selected comparative statement data for Mighty Products Company are presented here. All balance sheet data are as of December 31.

	1999	1998
Net sales	$800,000	$720,000
Cost of goods sold	480,000	40,000
Interest expense	7,000	5,000
Net income	56,000	42,000
Accounts receivable	120,000	100,000
Inventory	85,000	75,000
Total assets	600,000	500,000
Total common stockholders' equity	450,000	310,000
Cash provided by operating activities	40,000	32,000

Instructions
Compute the following ratios for 1999:
(a) Profit margin   (d) Return on common stockholders' equity
(b) Asset turnover   (e) Cash return on sales
(c) Return on assets   (f) Gross profit rate

Compute selected ratios.
(SO 5)

E12-11 Here is the income statement for Jean LeFay, Inc:

JEAN LEFAY, INC.
Income Statement
For the Year Ended December 31, 1999

Sales	$400,000
Cost of goods sold	230,000
Gross profit	170,000
Expenses (including $20,000 interest and $24,000 income taxes)	100,000
Net income	$ 70,000

Additional information:
1. Common stock outstanding January 1, 1999, was 30,000 shares. On July 1, 1999, 10,000 more shares were issued.
2. The market price of Jean LeFay, Inc., stock was $15 in 1999.
3. Cash dividends of $21,000 were paid, $5,000 of which were to preferred stockholders.
4. Net cash provided by operating activities $98,000.

Instructions
Compute the following measures for 1999:
(a) Earnings per share   (d) Times interest earned ratio
(b) Price-earnings ratio   (e) Cash return on sales ratio
(c) Payout ratio

Compute amounts from ratios.
(SO 5)

E12-12 Shaker Corporation experienced a fire on December 31, 1999, in which its financial records were partially destroyed. It has been able to salvage some of the records and has ascertained the following balances:

	December 31, 1999	December 31, 1998
Cash	$ 30,000	$ 10,000
Receivables (net)	72,500	126,000
Inventory	200,000	180,000
Accounts payable	50,000	90,000
Notes payable	30,000	60,000
Common stock, $100 par	400,000	400,000
Retained earnings	113,500	101,000

Additional information:
1. The inventory turnover is 3.6 times.
2. The return on common stockholders' equity is 22%. The company had no additional paid-in capital.
3. The receivables turnover is 9.4 times.
4. The return on assets is 20%.
5. Total assets at December 31, 1998, were $605,000.

Instructions
Compute the following for Shaker Corporation:
(a) Cost of goods sold for 1999
(b) Net sales for 1999
(c) Net income for 1999
(d) Total assets at December 31, 1999

PROBLEMS: SET A

P12-1A Here are comparative statement data for Chen Company and Couric Company, two competitors. All balance sheet data are as of December 31, 1999, and December 31, 1998.

Prepare vertical analysis and comment on profitability.
(SO 4, 5)

	Chen Company		Couric Company	
	1999	1998	1999	1998
Net sales	$1,549,035		$339,038	
Cost of goods sold	1,080,490		238,006	
Operating expenses	302,275		79,000	
Interest expense	6,800		1,252	
Income tax expense	47,840		7,740	
Current assets	325,975	$312,410	83,336	$ 79,467
Plant assets (net)	521,310	500,000	139,728	125,812
Current liabilities	66,325	75,815	35,348	30,281
Long-term liabilities	108,500	90,000	29,620	25,000
Common stock, $10 par	500,000	500,000	120,000	120,000
Retained earnings	172,460	146,595	38,096	29,998

Instructions
(a) Prepare a vertical analysis of the 1999 income statement data for Chen Company and Couric Company.
(b) Comment on the relative profitability of the companies by computing the return on assets and the return on common stockholders' equity ratios for both companies.

Compute ratios from balance sheet and income statement.
(SO 5)
P12-2A   The comparative statements of Magic Johnson Company are presented here:

MAGIC JOHNSON COMPANY
Income Statement
For the Years Ended December 31

	1999	1998
Net sales	$1,818,500	$1,750,500
Cost of goods sold	1,005,500	996,000
Gross profit	813,000	754,500
Selling and administrative expenses	506,000	479,000
Income from operations	307,000	275,500
Other expenses and losses		
Interest expense	18,000	19,000
Income before income taxes	289,000	256,500
Income tax expense	86,700	77,000
Net income	$ 202,300	$ 179,500

MAGIC JOHNSON COMPANY
Balance Sheet
December 31

	1999	1998
Assets		
Current assets		
Cash	$ 60,100	$ 64,200
Marketable securities	54,000	50,000
Accounts receivable (net)	107,800	102,800
Inventory	123,000	115,500
Total current assets	344,900	332,500
Plant assets (net)	625,300	520,300
Total assets	$970,200	$852,800
Liabilities and Stockholders' Equity		
Current liabilities		
Accounts payable	$150,000	$145,400
Income taxes payable	43,500	42,000
Total current liabilities	193,500	187,400
Bonds payable	210,000	200,000
Total liabilities	403,500	387,400
Stockholders' equity		
Common stock ($5 par)	280,000	300,000
Retained earnings	286,700	165,400
Total stockholders' equity	566,700	465,400
Total liabilities and stockholders' equity	$970,200	$852,800

On July 1, 1999, 4,000 shares were repurchased and canceled. All sales were on account. Net cash provided by operating activities for 1999 was $280,000.

Instructions
Compute the following ratios for 1999:
(a) Earnings per share   (c) Return on assets
(b) Return on common stockholders' equity   (d) Current

(e) Acid-test
(f) Receivables turnover
(g) Average collection period
(h) Inventory turnover
(i) Average days in inventory
(j) Times interest earned

(k) Asset turnover
(l) Debt to total assets
(m) Current cash debt coverage
(n) Cash return on sales
(o) Cash debt coverage

P12-3A   Condensed balance sheet and income statement data for Pitka Corporation are presented here:

Perform ratio analysis.
(SO 5)

PITKA CORPORATION
Balance Sheet
December 31

	1999	1998	1997
Cash	$ 25,000	$ 20,000	$ 18,000
Receivables (net)	50,000	45,000	48,000
Other current assets	90,000	85,000	64,000
Investments	75,000	70,000	45,000
Plant and equipment (net)	400,000	370,000	358,000
	$640,000	$590,000	$533,000
Current liabilities	$ 75,000	$ 80,000	$ 70,000
Long-term debt	80,000	85,000	50,000
Common stock, $10 par	340,000	300,000	300,000
Retained earnings	145,000	125,000	113,000
	$640,000	$590,000	$533,000

PITKA CORPORATION
Income Statement
For the Years Ended December 31

	1999	1998
Sales	$740,000	$700,000
Less: Sales returns and allowances	40,000	50,000
Net sales	700,000	650,000
Cost of goods sold	420,000	400,000
Gross profit	280,000	250,000
Operating expenses (including income taxes)	236,000	218,000
Net income	$ 44,000	$ 32,000

Additional information:
1. The market price of Pitka's common stock was $4.00, $5.00, and $7.95 for 1997, 1998, and 1999, respectively.
2. All dividends were paid in cash.
3. On July 1, 1998, 4,000 shares of common stock were issued.

Instructions
(a) Compute the following ratios for 1998 and 1999:
   (1) Profit margin   (5) Price-earnings
   (2) Gross profit   (6) Payout
   (3) Asset turnover   (7) Debt to total assets
   (4) Earnings per share
(b) ▦▦▦➤ Based on the ratios calculated, discuss briefly the improvement or lack thereof in the financial position and operating results from 1998 to 1999 of Pitka Corporation.

Compute ratios; comment on overall liquidity and profitability.

(SO 5)

P12-4A   This financial information is for Caroline Company:

CAROLINE COMPANY
Balance Sheet
December 31

	1999	1998
Assets		
Cash	$ 70,000	$ 65,000
Short-term investments	45,000	40,000
Receivables (net)	94,000	90,000
Inventories	130,000	125,000
Prepaid expenses	25,000	23,000
Land	130,000	130,000
Building and equipment (net)	190,000	175,000
Total assets	$684,000	$648,000
Liabilities and Stockholders' Equity		
Notes payable	$100,000	$100,000
Accounts payable	45,000	42,000
Accrued liabilities	40,000	40,000
Bonds payable, due 2000	150,000	150,000
Common stock, $10 par	200,000	200,000
Retained earnings	149,000	116,000
Total liabilities and stockholders' equity	$684,000	$648,000

CAROLINE COMPANY
Income Statement
For the Years Ended December 31

	1999	1998
Sales	$850,000	$790,000
Cost of goods sold	620,000	575,000
Gross profit	230,000	215,000
Operating expenses	194,000	180,000
Net income	$ 36,000	$ 35,000

Additional information:
1. Inventory at the beginning of 1998 was $115,000.
2. Receivables at the beginning of 1998 were $88,000.
3. Total assets at the beginning of 1998 were $630,000.
4. No common stock transactions occurred during 1998 or 1999.
5. All sales were on account.

Instructions
(a) Indicate, by using ratios, the change in liquidity and profitability of Caroline Company from 1998 to 1999. [*Note:*   Not all profitability ratios can be computed nor can cash-basis ratios be computed.]
(b) Given below are three independent situations and a ratio that may be affected. For each situation, compute the affected ratio (1) as of December 31, 1998, and (2) as of December 31, 1999, after giving effect to the situation. Net income for 1999 was $40,000. Total assets on December 31, 1999, were $700,000.

Situation	Ratio
1. 18,000 shares of common stock were sold at par on July 1, 1999.	Return on common stockholders' equity
2. All of the notes payable were paid in 1999.	Debt to total assets
3. The market price of common stock was $9 and $12.80 on December 31, 1998 and 1999, respectively.	Price-earnings

P12-5A Selected financial data of two intense competitors in a recent year are presented here (in millions):

Compute selected ratios, and compare liquidity, profitability, and solvency for two companies.
(SO 5)

	Kmart Corporation	Wal-Mart Stores, Inc.
	Income Statement Data for Year	
Net sales	$34,025	$82,494
Cost of goods sold	25,992	65,586
Selling and administrative expenses	7,701	12,858
Interest expense	494	706
Other income (net)	572	918
Income tax expense	114	1,581
Net income	$ 296	$ 2,681
	Balance Sheet Data (End of Year)	
Current assets	$ 9,187	$15,338
Property, plant, and equipment (net)	7,842	17,481
Total assets	$17,029	$32,819
Current liabilities	$ 5,626	$ 9,973
Long-term debt	5,371	10,120
Total stockholders' equity	6,032	12,726
Total liabilities and stockholders' equity	$17,029	$32,819
	Beginning-of-Year Balances	
Total assets	$17,504	$26,441
Total stockholders' equity	6,093	10,753
	Other Data	
Average net receivables	$ 1,570	$ 695
Average inventory	7,317	12,539
Net cash provided by operating activities	351	3,106

Instructions

(a) For each company, compute the following ratios:

(1) Current	(8) Return on assets
(2) Receivables turnover	(9) Return on common stockholders' equity
(3) Average collection period	(10) Debt to total assets
(4) Inventory turnover	(11) Times interest earned
(5) Average days in inventory	(12) Current cash debt coverage
(6) Profit margin	(13) Cash return on sales
(7) Asset turnover	(14) Cash debt coverage

(b) Compare the liquidity, solvency, and profitability of the two companies.

P12-6A The comparative statements of Ultra Vision Company are presented here:

Compute numerous ratios.
(SO 5)

ULTRA VISION COMPANY
Income Statement
For Years Ended December 31

	1999	1998
Net sales (all on account)	$600,000	$520,000
Expenses		
Cost of goods sold	415,000	354,000
Selling and administrative	120,800	114,800
Interest expense	7,200	6,000
Income tax expense	18,000	14,000
Total expenses	561,000	488,800
Net income	$ 39,000	$ 31,200

ULTRA VISION COMPANY
Balance Sheet
December 31

	1999	1998
Assets		
Current assets		
Cash	$ 21,000	$ 18,000
Marketable securities	18,000	15,000
Accounts receivable (net)	92,000	74,000
Inventory	84,000	70,000
Total current assets	215,000	177,000
Plant assets (net)	423,000	383,000
Total assets	$638,000	$560,000
Liabilities and Stockholders' Equity		
Current liabilities		
Accounts payable	$112,000	$110,000
Income taxes payable	23,000	20,000
Total current liabilities	135,000	130,000
Long-term liabilities		
Bonds payable	130,000	80,000
Total liabilities	265,000	210,000
Stockholders' equity		
Common stock ($5 par)	150,000	150,000
Retained earnings	223,000	200,000
Total stockholders' equity	373,000	350,000
Total liabilities and stockholders' equity	$638,000	$560,000

Additional data: The common stock recently sold at $19.50 per share.

Instructions
Compute the following ratios for 1999:

(a) Current	(i) Return on assets
(b) Acid-test	(j) Return on common stockholders' equity
(c) Receivables turnover	(k) Earnings per share
(d) Average collection period	(l) Price-earnings
(e) Inventory turnover	(m) Payout
(f) Average days in inventory	(n) Debt to total assets
(g) Profit margin	(o) Times interest earned
(h) Asset turnover	

Compute missing informa-
tion given a set of ratios.
(SO 5)

P12-7A   Presented here are an incomplete income statement and an incomplete comparative balance sheet of Vienna Corporation:

VIENNA CORPORATION
Income Statement
For the Year Ended December 31, 1999

Sales	$11,000,000
Cost of goods sold	?
Gross profit	?
Operating expenses	1,665,000
Income from operations	?
Other expenses and losses	
Interest expense	?
Income before income taxes	?
Income tax expense	560,000
Net income	$?

VIENNA CORPORATION
December 31
Balance Sheet

	1999	1998
Assets		
Current assets		
Cash	$ 450,000	$ 375,000
Accounts receivable (net)	?	950,000
Inventory	?	1,720,000
Total current assets	?	3,045,000
Plant assets (net)	4,620,000	3,955,000
Total assets	$?	$7,000,000
Liabilities and Stockholders' Equity		
Current liabilities	$?	$ 825,000
Long-term notes payable	?	2,800,000
Total liabilities	?	3,625,000
Common stock, $1 par	3,000,000	3,000,000
Retained earnings	400,000	375,000
Total stockholders' equity	3,400,000	3,375,000
Total liabilities and stockholders' equity	$?	$7,000,000

Additional information:
1. The receivables turnover for 1999 is 10 times.
2. All sales are on account.
3. The profit margin for 1999 is 14.5%.
4. Return on assets is 22% for 1999.
5. The current ratio on December 31, 1999, is 3:1.
6. The inventory turnover for 1999 is 4.8 times.

Instructions
Compute the missing information given the ratios. Show your computations. [*Note:* Start with one ratio and derive as much information as possible from it before trying another ratio. List all missing amounts under the ratio used to find the information.]

PROBLEMS: SET B

P12-1B Here are comparative statement data for Brooke Company and Shields Company, two competitors. All balance sheet data are as of December 31, 1999, and December 31, 1998.

Prepare vertical analysis and comment on profitability.
(SO 4, 5)

	Brooke Company		Shields Company	
	1999	**1998**	**1999**	**1998**
Net sales	$250,000		$1,200,000	
Cost of goods sold	160,000		720,000	
Operating expenses	51,000		252,000	
Interest expense	3,000		10,000	
Income tax expense	11,000		65,000	
Current assets	130,000	$110,000	700,000	$650,000
Plant assets (net)	305,000	270,000	800,000	750,000
Current liabilities	60,000	52,000	250,000	275,000
Long-term liabilities	50,000	68,000	200,000	150,000
Common stock	260,000	210,000	750,000	700,000
Retained earnings	65,000	50,000	300,000	275,000

Instructions

(a) Prepare a vertical analysis of the 1999 income statement data for Brooke Company and Shields Company.

(b) ▣▭▭▷ Comment on the relative profitability of the companies by computing the return on assets and the return on common stockholders' equity ratios for both companies.

Compute ratios from balance sheet and income statement.

(SO 5)

P12-2B   The comparative statements of Marti Rosen Company are presented here:

MARTI ROSEN COMPANY
Income Statement
For the Years Ended December 31

	1999	1998
Net sales	$660,000	$624,000
Cost of goods sold	440,000	405,600
Gross profit	220,000	218,400
Selling and administrative expense	143,880	149,760
Income from operations	76,120	68,640
Other expenses and losses		
Interest expense	7,920	7,200
Income before income taxes	68,200	61,440
Income tax expense	25,300	24,000
Net income	$ 42,900	$ 37,440

MARTI ROSEN COMPANY
Balance Sheet
December 31

	1999	1998
Assets		
Current assets		
Cash	$ 23,100	$ 21,600
Marketable securities	34,800	33,000
Accounts receivable (net)	106,200	93,800
Inventory	72,400	64,000
Total current assets	236,500	212,400
Plant assets (net)	465,300	459,600
Total assets	$701,800	$672,000
Liabilities and Stockholders' Equity		
Current liabilities		
Accounts payable	$134,200	$132,000
Income taxes payable	25,300	24,000
Total current liabilities	159,500	156,000
Bonds payable	132,000	120,000
Total liabilities	291,500	276,000
Stockholders' equity		
Common stock ($10 par)	140,000	150,000
Retained earnings	270,300	246,000
Total stockholders' equity	410,300	396,000
Total liabilities and stockholders' equity	$701,800	$672,000

On July 1, 1999, 1,000 shares were repurchased and canceled. All sales were on account. Net cash provided by operating activities was $36,000.

Instructions

Compute the following ratios for 1999:

(a) Earnings per share
(b) Return on common stockholders' equity
(c) Return on assets
(d) Current
(e) Acid-test
(f) Receivables turnover
(g) Average collection period
(h) Inventory turnover

(i) Average days in inventory
(j) Times interest earned
(k) Asset turnover
(l) Debt to total assets
(m) Current cash debt coverage
(n) Cash return on sales
(o) Cash debt coverage

P12-3B   These are condensed balance sheet and income statement data for Los Colinas Corporation:

Perform ratio analysis.
(SO 5)

LOS COLINAS CORPORATION
Balance Sheet
December 31

	1999	1998	1997
Cash	$ 40,000	$ 24,000	$ 20,000
Receivables (net)	70,000	45,000	48,000
Other current assets	80,000	75,000	62,000
Investments	90,000	70,000	50,000
Plant and equipment (net)	450,000	400,000	360,000
	$730,000	$614,000	$540,000
Current liabilities	$ 98,000	$ 75,000	$ 70,000
Long-term debt	97,000	75,000	65,000
Common stock, $10 par	400,000	340,000	300,000
Retained earnings	135,000	124,000	105,000
	$730,000	$614,000	$540,000

LOS COLINAS CORPORATION
Income Statement
For the Years Ended December 31

	1999	1998
Sales	$700,000	$750,000
Less: Sales returns and allowances	40,000	50,000
Net sales	660,000	700,000
Cost of goods sold	420,000	400,000
Gross profit	240,000	300,000
Operating expenses (including income taxes)	194,000	237,000
Net income	$ 46,000	$ 63,000

Additional information:
1. The market price of Los Colinas's common stock was $5.00, $4.50, and $2.30 for 1997, 1998, and 1999, respectively.
2. All dividends were paid in cash.
3. On July 1, 1998, 4,000 shares of common stock were issued, and on July 1, 1999, 6,000 shares were issued.

Instructions

(a) Compute the following ratios for 1998 and 1999:

(1) Profit margin
(2) Gross profit rate
(3) Asset turnover
(4) Earnings per share

(5) Price-earnings
(6) Payout
(7) Debt to total assets

(b) ▭▭▭▶ Based on the ratios calculated, discuss briefly the improvement or lack thereof in the financial position and operating results from 1998 to 1999 of Los Colinas Corporation.

Compute ratios; comment on overall liquidity and profitability.

(SO 5)

P12-4B Financial information for Star Track Company is presented here:

STAR TRACK COMPANY
Balance Sheet
December 31

	1999	1998
Assets		
Cash	$ 50,000	$ 42,000
Short-term investments	80,000	100,000
Receivables (net)	100,000	87,000
Inventories	440,000	400,000
Prepaid expenses	25,000	31,000
Land	75,000	75,000
Building and equipment (net)	570,000	500,000
Total assets	$1,340,000	$1,235,000
Liabilities and Stockholders' Equity		
Notes payable	$ 125,000	$ 125,000
Accounts payable	160,000	140,000
Accrued liabilities	50,000	50,000
Bonds payable, due 2000	200,000	200,000
Common stock, $5 par	500,000	500,000
Retained earnings	305,000	220,000
Total liabilities and stockholders' equity	$1,340,000	$1,235,000

STAR TRACK COMPANY
Income Statement
For the Years Ended December 31

	1999	1998
Sales	$1,000,000	$ 940,000
Cost of goods sold	650,000	635,000
Gross profit	350,000	305,000
Operating expenses	235,000	215,000
Net income	$ 115,000	$ 90,000

Additional information:
1. Inventory at the beginning of 1998 was $350,000
2. Receivables at the beginning of 1998 were $80,000.
3. Total assets at the beginning of 1998 were $1,175,000.
4. No common stock transactions occurred during 1998 or 1999.
5. All sales were on account.

Instructions
(a) Indicate, by using ratios, the change in liquidity and profitability of Star Track Company from 1998 to 1999. [*Note:* Not all profitability ratios can be computed nor can cash-basis ratios be computed.]
(b) Given below are three independent situations and a ratio that may be affected. For each situation, compute the affected ratio (1) as of December 31, 1998, and (2) as of December 31, 1999, after giving effect to the situation. Net income for 1999 was $125,000. Total assets on December 31, 1999, were $1,500,000.

Situation	Ratio
1. 65,000 shares of common stock were sold at par on July 1, 1999.	Returns on common stockholders' equity
2. All of the notes payable were paid in 1999.	Debt to total assets
3. The market price of common stock on December 31, 1999, was $6.25. The market price on December 31, 1998, was $5.	Price-earnings

P12-5B   Selected financial data of two intense competitors in a recent year are presented here (in millions):

Compute selected ratios, and compare liquidity, profitability, and solvency for two companies.

(SO 5)

	Bethlehem Steel Corporation	Inland Steel Company
	Income Statement Data for Year	
Net sales	$4,819	$4,497
Cost of goods sold	4,548	3,991
Selling and administrative expenses	137	265
Interest expense	46	72
Other income (net)	7	0
Income tax expense	14	62
Net income	$ 81	$ 107

	Bethlehem Steel Corporation	Inland Steel Company
	Balance Sheet Data (End of Year)	
Current assets	$1,569	$1,081
Property, plant, and equipment (net)	2,759	1,610
Other assets	1,454	662
Total assets	$5,782	$3,353
Current liabilities	$1,011	$ 565
Long-term debt	3,615	2,056
Total stockholders' equity	1,156	732
Total liabilities and stockholders' equity	$5,782	$3,353

	Bethlehem Steel Corporation	Inland Steel Company
	Beginning-of-Year Balances	
Total assets	$5,877	$3,436
Total stockholders' equity	697	623

	Bethlehem Steel Corporation	Inland Steel Company
	Other Data	
Average net receivables	$ 511	$ 515
Average inventory	868	403
Net cash provided by operating activities	90	160

Instructions

(a) For each company, compute the following ratios:

(1) Current	(8) Return on assets
(2) Receivables turnover	(9) Return on common stockholders' equity
(3) Average collection period	(10) Debt to total assets
(4) Inventory turnover	(11) Times interest earned
(5) Average days in inventory	(12) Current cash debt coverage
(6) Profit margin	(13) Cash return on sales
(7) Asset turnover	(14) Cash debt coverage

(b) Compare the liquidity, solvency, and profitability of the two companies.

FINANCIAL REPORTING PROBLEM

STARBUCKS CORPORATION

BYP12-1 Your parents are considering investing in Starbucks Corporation common stock. They ask you, as an accounting expert, to make an analysis of the company for them. Fortunately, excerpts from a current annual report of Starbucks are presented in Appendix A of this textbook. Note that all dollar amounts are in thousands.

Instructions
(a) Make a 5-year trend analysis, using 1992 as the base year, of (1) net revenues and (2) operating income. Comment on the significance of the trend results.
(b) Compute for 1996 and 1995 the (1) debt to total assets ratio and (2) times interest earned ratio. How would you evaluate Starbucks' long-term solvency?
(c) Compute for 1996 and 1995 the (1) profit margin ratio, (2) asset turnover ratio, (3) return on assets ratio, and (4) return on common stockholders' equity ratio. How would you evaluate Starbucks' profitability? Total assets at October 2, 1994, were $231,421, and total stockholders' equity at October 2, 1994, was $109,898.
(d) What information outside the annual report may also be useful to your parents in making a decision about Starbucks?

COMPARATIVE ANALYSIS PROBLEM

STARBUCKS VS. GREEN MOUNTAIN COFFEE

BYP12-2 The financial statements of Green Mountain Coffee are presented in Appendix B, following the financial statements for Starbucks in Appendix A.

Instructions
(a) Based on the information in the financial statements, determine each of the following for each company:
  (1) The percentage increase in net sales and in net income from 1995 to 1996.
  (2) The percentage increase in total assets and in total stockholders' equity from 1995 to 1996.
  (3) The earnings per share for 1996.
(b) What conclusions concerning the two companies can be drawn from these data?

INTERPRETING FINANCIAL STATEMENTS

MANITOWOC COMPANY VS. CATERPILLAR CORP.

BYP12-3 Manitowoc Company and Caterpillar Corporation are both producers and sellers of large fixed assets. Caterpillar is substantially larger than Manitowoc. Financial information taken from each company's financial statements is provided here:

Financial Highlights	Caterpillar (in millions)		Manitowoc (in thousands)	
	1995	**1994**	**1995**	**1994**
Cash and short-term investments	$ 638	$ 419	$ 16,635	$ 16,163
Accounts receivable	4,285	4,290	51,011	29,500
Inventory	1,921	1,835	52,928	36,793
Other current assets	803	865	14,571	14,082
Current assets	7,647	7,409	135,145	96,538
Total assets	16,830	16,250	324,915	159,465

Current liabilities	$ 6,049	$ 5,498	$110,923	$54,064
Total liabilities	13,442	13,339	243,254	84,408
Total stockholders' equity	3,388	2,911	81,661	75,057
Sales	15,451		313,149	
Cost of goods sold	12,000		237,679	
Interest expense	191		1,865	
Income tax expense	501		8,551	
Net income	1,136		14,569	
Cash provided from operations	2,190		16,367	

Instructions

(a) Calculate the following liquidity ratios and discuss the relative liquidity of the two companies:
    (1) Current
    (2) Acid-test
    (3) Current cash debt coverage
    (4) Receivables turnover
    (5) Inventory turnover
(b) Calculate the following solvency ratios and discuss the relative solvency of the two companies:
    (1) Debt to total assets
    (2) Times interest earned
(c) Calculate the following profitability ratios and discuss the relative profitability of the two companies:
    (1) Asset turnover
    (2) Profit margin
    (3) Return on assets
    (4) Return on common stockholders' equity

SEARS, ROEBUCK AND CO.

BYP12-4 The income statements, selected balance sheet information, and selected note disclosures from the annual report of Sears, Roebuck and Co. for 1993 are presented below and on the following pages.

SEARS, ROEBUCK AND CO.			
Consolidated Statements of Income			
Years Ended December 31			
(in millions except per common share data)			
	1993	1992	1991
Revenues	$50,837.5	$52,344.6	$50,982.9
Expenses			
Costs and expenses	47,233.7	52,478.3	48,568.2
Restructuring (note 4)		3,108.4	
Interest	1,498.1	1,510.9	1,680.5
Total expenses	48,731.8	57,097.6	50,248.7
Operating income (loss)	2,105.7	(4,753.0)	734.2
Other income (loss)	206.0	(27.2)	129.6
Gain on the sale of subsidiaries stock	635.1	91.4	
Income (loss) before income taxes (benefit, minority interest, and equity income)	2,946.8	(4,688.8)	863.8
Income taxes (benefit)	400.9	(2,114.0)	(38.5)

Minority interest and equity in net income of unconsolidated companies	(136.9)	8.0	13.3
Income (loss) from continuing operations	2,409.1	(2,566.8)	915.6
Discontinued operations (note 3)			
Operating income, less income tax expense of $167.7, $299.2, and $231.0	240.1	507.9	363.3
Loss on disposal including income tax expense of $22.0	(64.0)		
Income (loss) before extraordinary loss and cumulative effect of accounting changes	2,585.2	(2,058.9)	1,278.9
Extraordinary loss related to the early extinguishment of debt	(210.8)		
Cumulative effect of accounting changes (note 2)		(1,873.4)	
Net income (loss)	$ 2,374.4	($ 3,932.3)	$ 1,278.9
Earnings (loss) per common share, after allowing for dividends on preferred shares			
Income (loss) from continuing operations	$6.22	($ 7.02)	$2.65
Discontinued operations	.46	1.37	1.06
Income (loss) before extraordinary loss and cumulative effect of accounting changes	6.68	(5.65)	3.71
Extraordinary loss	(.55)		
Cumulative effect of accounting changes		(5.07)	
Net income (loss)	$6.13	($10.72)	$3.71

SEARS, ROEBUCK AND CO.
Partial Balance Sheets
Years Ended December 31
(selected figures, in millions)

	1993	1992
Total assets	$90,807.8	$85,490.6
Retail customer receivables	15,905.6	13,877.6
Inventories	3,518.0	4,047.9
Total liabilities	76,809.7	74,423.2
Common shareholders' equity		
Common shares ($.75 par)	$ 293.8	$ 290.6
Capital in excess of par	2,353.8	2,194.6
Retained earnings	8,162.8	8,772.2
Less: Treasury stock (at cost)	(1,703.5)	(1,734.3)
Adjustments	995.9	(311.2)
Total common shareholders' equity	$10,102.8	$ 9,211.9

SEARS, ROEBUCK AND CO.
Notes to Financial Statements
(selected information)

Note 1. Summary of significant accounting policies
Inventories: Inventories . . . are valued primarily at the lower of cost (using the last-in, first-out or LIFO method) or market by application of internally developed price indices to estimate the effects of inflation on inventories. . . . If the first-in,

first-out (FIFO) method of inventory valuation has been used instead of the LIFO method, inventories would have been $743.7 million and $738.4 million higher at December 31, 1993 and 1992, respectively.

Property and equipment: Property and equipment is stated at cost less accumulated depreciation. Depreciation is provided principally by the straight-line method over the estimated useful lives of the related assets.

Note 2. Accounting changes
Effective Jan. 1, 1992, the Company adopted SFAS No. 106, "Employers' Accounting for Postretirement Benefits Other than Pensions," and SFAS No. 112, "Employers' Accounting for Postemployment Benefits," for all domestic and foreign postretirement and postemployment benefit plans by immediately recognizing the transition amounts. The Company previously expensed the cost of these benefits, which consist of health care and life insurance, as claims were incurred.

Note 3. Discontinued operations
In May 1993, the Company entered into separate agreements to sell the Coldwell-Banker Residential business and Sears Mortgage Banking operations. A $64.0 million after-tax loss was recorded in the second quarter of 1993, primarily due to adverse income tax effects related to the sale of Sears Savings Bank. These sales were completed in the fourth quarter of 1993.

Note 4. Restructuring
The Merchandise Group recorded a pretax charge in the fourth quarter of 1992 of $2.65 billion related to discontinuing its domestic catalog operations, offering a voluntary early retirement program to certain salaried associates, closing unprofitable retail department and specialty stores, streamlining or discontinuing various unprofitable merchandise lines, and the writedown of underutilized assets to market value. Corporate also recorded a $23.8 million pretax charge related to offering termination and early retirement programs to certain associates. Additionally, Homart recorded a $326.6 million pretax write-down of land previously held for office development and selected office properties that were to be sold.

During the first quarter of 1992, the Merchandise Group recorded a $106.0 million pretax charge for severance costs related to cost reduction programs for commision sales and headquarters staff in domestic merchandising.

The Merchandise Group and Corporate restructuring charges and Homart [consolidated subsidiary] property write-downs amounted to a combined after-tax expense of $1.95 billion in 1992.

Instructions
(a) Calculate the following ratios for 1993 and then evaluate Sears' profitability:
   (1) Profit margin for both income from continuing operations and net income
   (2) Return on common stockholders' equity
   (3) Return on assets
   (4) Times interest earned
(b) Sears showed a loss of $1.65 billion from Hurricane Andrew in 1992. In what category does the loss appear in Sears' 1992 income statement?
(c) Sears' revenues from its merchandising operations were $26.29 billion, and its cost of sales was $18.76 billion in 1993.
   (1) Calculate Sears' inventory turnover ratio for 1993.
   (2) Suppose you wanted to compare Sears' inventory turnover ratio with that of a Canadian company, which under Canadian accounting standards must use FIFO. Would you be able to make such a comparison? If so, how?
   (3) Calculate Sears' receivables turnover ratio for 1993.
   (4) Unlike most retailers, whose fiscal year ends a month into the following year, Sear's year-end is December 31. What effect does Sears' year-end have on the inventory turnover and receivables turnover ratios?
   (5) What effect does Sears' nonstandard year-end (for a retailer) have on the comparability of Sears' ratios with those of other large retailers?

(d) Sears sold two business segments in 1993.
   (1) What did it sell and in what quarter were these sales completed?
   (2) Where does the income or loss from these sales appear on Sears' income statement?

GROUP DECISION CASE

BYP12-5 You are a loan officer for Second State Bank of Port Washington. Ted Worth, President of T. Worth Corporation, has just left your office. He is interested in an 8-year loan to expand the company's operations. The borrowed funds would be used to purchase new equipment. As evidence of the company's debt-worthiness, Worth provided you with the following facts:

	1999	1998
Current ratio	3.1	2.1
Acid-test ratio	.8	1.4
Asset turnover ratio	2.8	2.2
Cash debt coverage ratio	.1	.2
Net income	Up 32%	Down 8%
Earnings per share	$3.30	$2.50

Ted Worth is a very insistent (some would say pushy) man. When you told him that you would need additional information before making your decision, he acted offended, and said, "What more could you possibly want to know?" You responded that, at a minimum, you would need complete, audited financial statements.

Instructions
With the class divided into groups, answer the following:
(a) Explain why you would want the financial statements to be audited.
(b) Discuss the implications of the ratios provided for the lending decision you are to make. That is, does the information paint a favorable picture? Are these ratios relevant to the decision?
(c) List three other ratios that you would want to calculate for this company, and explain why you would use each.
(d) What are the limitations of ratio analysis for credit and investing decisions?

MANAGERIAL ANALYSIS

BYP12-6 Coralville Corporation has excess cash that it wishes to invest in the common stock of Nathan Company, a small, family-owned business. Maureen Clever, treasurer of Coralville, has a copy of Nathan Company's most recent financial statements and the schedule of ratios shown below:

	1999	1998	1997
Current ratio	2.5:1	2.0:1	1.3:1
Acid-test ratio	0.5:1	0.9:1	1.4:1
Accounts receivable turnover	7.2 times	8.4 times	10.7 times
Inventory turnover	6.1 times	7.3 times	8.4 times
Sales as a % of 1997	142%	121%	100%
Dividends per share	$3.00	$3.00	$3.00
Dividend payout ratio	50%	60%	70%
Return on total assets	14.0%	12.6%	11.1%
Return on equity	19%	13%	8%
(No issues or retirements of shares 1997–99)			

Instructions
To make this investment decision, Maureen would like answers to questions about the financial trends at Nathan Company during the past three years. As Maureen's assistant,

you are asked to answer each of the following questions using the data above. Provide support for your answers.

(a) Are customers of Nathan Company paying their bills faster or slower now than they did in 1997?

(b) Is it becoming easier or harder for Nathan Company to pay its bills as they come due?

(c) Is the balance in Nathan Company's accounts receivable increasing, decreasing, or staying constant?

(d) Is the amount carried in Nathan Company's inventory increasing, decreasing, or staying constant?

(e) Is the amount of earnings per share increasing or decreasing?

(f) Is Nathan Company's stock price going up or down?

(g) Is the price-earnings ratio of Nathan's going up or down?

(h) Is Nathan Company financially leveraging to the advantage of its common stockholders?

REAL-WORLD FOCUS

THE COCA-COLA COMPANY VS. PEPSICO, INC.

BYP12-7 *The Coca-Cola Company and PepsiCo, Inc.* provide refreshments to every corner of the world. Selected data from the consolidated financial statements for The Coca-Cola Company and for PepsiCo, Inc., are presented here:

	Coca-Cola	PepsiCo
Total current assets (including cash, accounts receivable, and marketable securities totaling $3,056 and $3,539, respectively)	$ 5,205	$ 5,546
Total current liabilities	6,177	5,230
Net sales	16,172	30,421
Cost of goods sold	6,167	14,886
Net income	2,554	1,606
Average receivables for the year	1,384	2,229
Average inventories for the year	1,048	1,011
Average total assets	12,947	25,112
Average common stockholders' equity	4,910	7,085
Net cash provided by operating activities	3,115	3,742
Average current liabilities	6,763	5,250
Total assets	13,873	25,432
Total liabilities	8,638	18,119
Income before income taxes	3,728	2,432
Interest expense	199	682
Cash provided by operating activities	3,115	3,742

Instructions

(a) Compute the following liquidity ratios for Coca-Cola and for PepsiCo and comment on the relative liquidity of the two competitors:

(1) Current

(2) Acid-test

(3) Receivables turnover

(4) Average collection period

(5) Inventory turnover

(6) Average days in inventory

(7) Current cash debt coverage

(b) Compute the following solvency ratios for the two companies and comment on the relative solvency of the two competitors:

(1) Debt to total assets ratio

(2) Times interest earned

(3) Cash debt coverage ratio

(c) Compute the following profitability ratios for the two companies and comment on the relative profitability of the two competitors:

(1) Profit margin

(2) Cash return on sales

(3) Asset turnover

(4) Return on assets

(5) Return on common stockholders' equity

COMMUNICATION ACTIVITY

BYP12-8 L. R. Stanton is the chief executive officer of Hi-Tech Electronics. Stanton is an expert engineer but a novice in accounting. Stanton asks you, as an accounting major, to explain (a) the basis for comparison in analyzing Hi-Tech's financial statements and (b) the limitations, if any, in financial statement analysis.

Instructions
Write a memo to L. R. Stanton that explains the basis for comparison and the limitations of financial statement analysis.

RESEARCH ASSIGNMENT

BYP12-9 The chapter stresses the importance of comparing an individual company's financial ratios to industry norms. Robert Morris Associates (RMA), a national association of bank loan and credit officers, publishes industry-specific financial data in its *Annual Statement Studies*. This publication includes vertical analysis financial statements and various ratios classified by four-digit SIC code. [*Note:* An alternative source is Dun & Bradstreet's *Industry Norms and Key Business Ratios.*]

Obtain the 1996 edition of *Annual Statement Studies* (covering fiscal years ended April 1, 1995, through March 31, 1996) and the 1996 or 1997 annual report of Wal-Mart Stores, Inc.

Instructions
(a) Prepare a 1996 vertical analysis balance sheet and income statement for Wal-Mart.
(b) Calculate those 1996 ratios for Wal-Mart that are covered by RMA. [*Note:* The specific ratio definitions used by RMA are described in the beginning of the book. Use ending values for balance sheet items.]
(c) What is Wal-Mart's SIC code? Use your answers from parts (a) and (b) to compare Wal-Mart to the appropriate current industry data. How does Wal-Mart compare to its competitors? [*Note:* RMA sorts current-year data by firm assets and sales, while 5 years of historical data are presented on an aggregate basis.]
(d) How many sets of financial statements did RMA use in compiling the current industry data sorted by sales?

ETHICS CASE

BYP12-10 Vern Fairly, president of Fairly Industries, wishes to issue a press release to bolster his company's image and maybe even its stock price, which has been gradually falling. As controller, you have been asked to provide a list of 20 financial ratios along with some other operating statistics relative to Fairly Industries' first-quarter financials and operations.

Two days after you provide the ratios and data requested, you are asked by Roberta Sanchez, the public relations director of Fairly, to prove the accuracy of the financial and operating data contained in the press release written by the president and edited by Roberta. In the news release, the president highlights the sales increase of 25% over last year's first quarter and the positive change in the current ratio from 1.5:1 last year to 3:1 this year. He also emphasizes that production was up 50% over the prior year's first quarter. You note that the release contains only positive or improved ratios and none of the negative or deteriorated ratios. For instance, no mention is made that the debt to total assets ratio has increased from 35% to 55%, that inventories are up 89%, and that although the current ratio improved, the acid-test ratio fell from 1:1 to .5:1. Nor is there any mention that the reported profit for the quarter would have been a loss had not the estimated lives of Fairly's plant and machinery been increased by 30%. Roberta emphasized, "The Pres wants this release by early this afternoon."

Instructions
(a) Who are the stakeholders in this situation?
(b) Is there anything unethical in President Fairly's actions?
(c) Should you as controller remain silent? Does Roberta have any responsibility?

Surfing the Net

BYP12-11 *Purpose:* Financial statements communicate to investors, creditors, and management the financial health of the organization. Companies are aware that financial statements are read by individuals who have varying degrees of understanding of financial matters. IBM's "Guide to Understanding Financials," which is located on its homepage, is one company's effort to provide online information for novice users. This guide takes an investor's approach to understanding the different financial statements.

Address: http://www.ibm.com/financialguide

Steps: Go to the above address.

Instructions
Answer the following questions:
(a) List two required elements in an annual report. List one optional element.
(b) What is the auditors' report?
(c) What financial statements are required in an annual report? What is included in the notes to the financial statements?
(d) From an investor's perspective, list two general suggestions for an approach to reviewing financial statements.

BYP12-12 *Purpose:* To understand the Management Discussion and Analysis (MD&A) section of an annual report.

Addresses: http://www.ibm.com/financialguide
               http://www.yahoo.com

Steps:
1. From IBM's Financial Guide, choose **Guides Contents.**
2. Choose **Anatomy of an Annual Report.**
3. Follow instruction (a).
4. From Yahoo Homepage, choose **Stock Quotes.**
5. Enter **GE.**
6. Choose **Get Quotes.**
7. Under "more info" choose **SEC** (this will take you to Yahoo-Edgar Online).
8. Choose **Mar. 1998 Annual Report.**
9. Follow instructions (b)–(e).

Instructions
(a) Using IBM's Financial Guide, describe the content of the Management Discussion and Analysis.
(b) In the overview section, GE's management discusses the company's performance. What were the net 1998 corporate earnings?
(c) Compare 1998 earnings with 1997 earnings.
(d) What were management's reasons for the change in net earnings?
(e) The second part of the MD&A addresses the company's capital resources and liquidity. What was GE's debt to equity ratio in 1998?

Answers to Self-Study Questions
1. d   2. d   3. b   4. d   5. a   6. c   7. c   8. c   9. c   10. b
11. a   12. a

 Remember to go back to the Navigator box on the chapter-opening page and check off your completed work.

APPENDIX A

Specimen Financial Statements: Starbucks Corporation

*T*HE ANNUAL REPORT

Once each year a corporation communicates to its stockholders and other interested parties by issuing a complete set of audited financial statements. The **annual report,** as this communication is called, summarizes the financial results of its operations for the year and its plans for the future. Many such annual reports have become attractive, multicolored, glossy public relations ad pieces containing pictures of corporate officers and directors as well as photos and descriptions of new products and new buildings. Yet the basic function of every annual report is to report financial information, almost all of which is a product of the corporation's accounting system.

The content and organization of corporate annual reports has become fairly standardized. Excluding the public relations part of the report (pictures, products, and propaganda), the following items are the traditional financial portions of the annual report:

Financial Highlights
Letter to the Stockholders
Management's Report
Auditor's Report
Financial Statements (and Management's Analysis)
Notes to the Financial Statements
Supplementary Financial Information

In this appendix we illustrate current financial reporting with a comprehensive set of corporate financial statements that are prepared in accordance with generally accepted accounting principles and audited by an international independent certified public accounting firm. We are grateful for permission to use the actual financial statements and other accompanying financial information from the annual report of a large, publicly held company, Starbucks Corporation.

FINANCIAL HIGHLIGHTS

The financial highlights section, called **Selected Financial Data** by Starbucks, is usually presented inside the front cover or on the first two pages of the annual report. This section generally reports the total or per share amounts for five to ten financial items for the current year and one or more previous years. Financial items from the income statement and the balance sheet that typically are presented are sales, income from continuing operations, net income, net income per share, dividends per common share, and the amount of capital expenditures. The financial highlights section from Starbucks' **Annual Report** is shown below.

Selected Financial Data

(IN THOUSANDS, EXCEPT EARNINGS PER SHARE)

The following selected financial data have been derived from the consolidated financial statements of the Company. The data set forth below should be read in conjunction with "Management's Discussion and Analysis of Financial Condition and Results of Operations" and the Company's consolidated financial statements and notes thereto.

As of and for the fiscal year ended:	Sept 29, 1996 (52 Wks)	Oct 1, 1995 (52 Wks)	Oct 2, 1994 (52 Wks)	Oct 3, 1993 (53 Wks)	Sept 27, 1992 (52 Wks)
Results of Operations Data:					
Net revenues					
Retail	$600,067	$402,655	$248,495	$153,610	$ 89,669
Specialty Sales	78,655	48,143	26,543	15,952	10,143
Direct Response	17,759	14,415	9,885	6,979	3,385
Total net revenues	696,481	465,213	284,923	176,541	103,197
Operating income	56,993	40,116	23,298	12,618	7,113
Provision for merger costs[1]	—	—	3,867	—	—
Gain on sale of investment in Noah's[2]	9,218	—	—	—	—
Net earnings	$ 42,128	$ 26,102	$ 10,206	$ 8,282	$ 4,454
Net earnings per common and common equivalent share—fully-diluted[3]	$ 0.54	$ 0.36	$ 0.17	$ 0.14	$ 0.09
Cash dividends per share	—	—	—	—	—
Balance Sheet Data:					
Working capital	$238,450	$134,304	$ 44,162	$ 42,092	$ 40,142
Total assets	726,613	468,178	231,421	201,712	91,547
Long-term debt (including current portion)	167,980	81,773	80,500	82,100	1,359
Redeemable preferred stock	—	—	—	4,944	—
Shareholders' equity	451,660	312,231	109,898	88,686	76,923

(1) Provision for merger costs reflects expenses related to the merger with The Coffee Connection, Inc. in fiscal 1994.

(2) Gain on sale of investment in Noah's of $9,218 ($5,669 after tax) results from the sale of Noah's New York Bagel, Inc. ("Noah's") stock in fiscal 1996.

(3) Earnings per share is based on the weighted average shares outstanding during the period plus, when their effect is dilutive, common stock equivalents consisting of certain shares subject to stock options. Fully-diluted earnings per share assumes conversion of the Company's convertible subordinated debentures using the "if converted" method, when such securities are dilutive, with net income adjusted for the after-tax interest expense and amortization applicable to these debentures.

LETTER TO THE STOCKHOLDERS

Nearly every annual report contains a letter to the stockholders from the Chairman of the Board or the President (or both). This letter typically discusses the company's accomplishments during the past year and highlights significant events such as mergers and acquisitions, new products, operating achievements, business philosophy, changes in officers or directors, financing commitments, expansion plans, and future prospects. The letter to the stockholders signed by Howard Schultz, Chairman of the Board and Chief Executive Officer, and Orin Smith, President and Chief Operating Officer, of Starbucks is shown below.

When we look back on the past 25 years, we are filled with a great sense of pride and gratitude for all that we have been able to accomplish. As we stand this year on the threshold of becoming a truly global brand, we want to express our enthusiasm for all that is to come.

At the end of fiscal 1993, we became the leading roaster and retailer of specialty coffee in North America, with more than 250 stores in 10 markets. Now, little more than three years later, we have firmly established our leadership position, ending fiscal 1996 with more than 1,000 retail locations in 32 markets throughout North America, and two new stores in Tokyo, Japan.

With more than 20,000 dedicated partners (employees), we are creating opportunities every day for millions of customers around the world to enjoy the Starbucks Experience. From selecting the finest arabica beans to hiring the most talented people, we are committed to applying the highest standards of quality in everything we do.

You can see it in our new store designs, which will appear this year in stores throughout North America. You can taste it in our new drinks, such as Rhumba™ Frappuccino®. You can hear it in our exclusive CDs, ranging from rhythm and blues to sounds from the '70s.

We have created an environment of constant discovery and self-renewal throughout our organization. We are gratified by the way our partners have transformed their passion for our products into a brand with depth and soul. When you walk into a Starbucks store, when you open a mail order package, when you drink our coffee on United Airlines, it is our goal to offer more than just a great cup of coffee—we want to offer a memorable experience.

Which is why we are pleased to say that with the help of our Japanese joint venture partners at SAZABY, Inc., our first stores in Tokyo, Japan opened this summer with lines around the block. We are excited about the global possibilities as more new customers embrace our business, and we know that we have many brand-building opportunities ahead of us.

In 1994, when we entered into a joint venture agreement with Pepsi-Cola to develop ready-to-drink coffee products, we knew that we wanted to redefine the category. In the spring of 1996, we launched our bottled Frappuccino™ coffee drink. After a very short testing period, we realized the enormous potential of this beverage, and we knew that we had to build new production facilities to prepare for the future of this product. We look forward to the positive reception of bottled Frappuccino when we expand the distribution nationwide in the summer of 1997. But most importantly, we knew that we had developed a platform for bigger product innovations.

Using the most sophisticated research and development technology available, we have created a coffee extract that is changing the way people think about everyday products. Early in 1996, we introduced our super-premium coffee-flavored ice creams, developed through our joint venture with Dreyer's Grand Ice Cream, Inc., which have since become the number one selling super-premium coffee-flavored ice creams in the nation.

During fiscal 1996, we installed proprietary, state-of-the-art roasting and manufacturing equipment to create a world-class manufacturing and logistics organization. We expanded our research and development efforts, building new coffee extract plants and new product development facilities. Our specialty sales and marketing team has continued to develop new channels of distribution, forming a new alliance with U.S. Office Products to sell Starbucks coffee to offices throughout the United States. And early in the first quarter of fiscal 1997, our direct response group launched a new America Online Caffè Starbucks store, which, in its previous format, had more than 600,000 visits last year.

This is not to say we haven't had our challenges, or taken risks. We had a holiday season in the first quarter that did not have the impact we had anticipated. We put our management team to the test and they demonstrated how well we can manage the company through difficult times. This team, utilizing their diverse experience, overcame significant green coffee price increases resulting from Brazilian frosts to give us a year with outstanding earnings, all the while paving the way for future growth.

With fiscal 1996 revenues of more than $696.4 million, we continue to work towards our long-term goal of becoming the most recognized and respected brand of coffee in the world. We entered several new markets this year, including Toronto, Rhode Island, North Carolina, and the overseas market of Tokyo, Japan. In fiscal 1997, we look forward to entering the new markets of Phoenix and Miami, as well as Hawaii and Singapore. At this time, we are also pleased to announce that we anticipate that cash from operations, combined with current cash and investments, will fund our core business growth in fiscal 1997.

We believe more strongly than ever that at the heart of our continuing success lie the company's two cornerstones: our coffee and our people. We were pleased to be able to grant eligible full and part-time partners stock options under our Bean Stock program again this year, which affords all partners a financial stake in our company's success. We will also be introducing a flexible benefits program in fiscal 1997, which has been created to meet the needs of our growing and diverse workforce.

Just as we tailor our benefits to our people, we design our stores to enhance our neighborhoods, and we encourage our partners to participate in events that support our communities. For the fifth consecutive year, Starbucks was also the largest corporate contributor to CARE, the international aid and development organization, whose work helps us to give back on a global level to those countries in which we do business.

Moving forward, we will continue to explore new opportunities and build value at all levels of our organization. Twenty-five years from now, when we look back again, if we can say that we grew our company with the same values and guiding principles that we embrace today, then we will know we have succeeded.

To all of you who touch Starbucks in any way, we would like to thank you for your ongoing support.

Warm regards,

Howard Schultz
chairman and chief executive officer

Orin Smith
president and chief operating officer

MANAGEMENT'S REPORT

A relatively recent addition to corporate annual reports is the statement made by management about its role in and responsibility for the accuracy and integrity of the financial statements. Starbucks' management letter is entitled **Management's Responsibility for Financial Reporting.** In it the Chairman of the Board and Chief Executive Officer along with the Chief Financial Officer and the Chief Operating Officer, on behalf of management: (1) assume primary responsibility for the financial statements and the related notes, (2) outline and assess the company's internal control system, (3) declare the financial statements in conformity with generally accepted accounting principles, and (4) comment on the audit by the certified public accountant and the composition and role of the Audit Committee of the Board of Directors. Starbucks' management report is presented below.

Management's Responsibility for Financial Reporting

(STARBUCKS CORPORATION)

The management of Starbucks Corporation is responsible for the preparation and integrity of the financial statements included in this Annual Report to Shareholders. The financial statements have been prepared in conformity with generally accepted accounting principles and include amounts based on management's best judgment where necessary. Financial information included elsewhere in this Annual Report is consistent with these financial statements.

Management maintains a system of internal controls and procedures designed to provide reasonable assurance that transactions are executed in accordance with proper authorization, that transactions are properly recorded in the Company's records, that assets are safeguarded, and that accountability for assets is maintained. The concept of reasonable assurance is based on the recognition that the cost of maintaining our system of internal accounting controls should not exceed benefits expected to be derived from the system. Internal controls and procedures are periodically reviewed and revised, when appropriate, due to changing circumstances and requirements.

Independent auditors are appointed by the Company's Board of Directors and ratified by the Company's shareholders to audit the financial statements in accordance with generally accepted auditing standards and to independently assess the fair presentation of the Company's financial position, results of operations, and cash flows. Their report appears in this Annual Report.

The Audit Committee of the Board of Directors, a majority of whom are outside directors, is responsible for monitoring the Company's accounting and reporting practices. The Audit Committee meets periodically with management and the independent auditors to ensure that each is properly discharging its responsibilities. The independent auditors have full and free access to the Committee without the presence of management to discuss the results of their audits, the adequacy of internal accounting controls, and the quality of financial reporting.

Howard Schultz
chairman and
chief executive officer

Orin Smith
president and
chief operating officer

Michael Casey
senior vice president and
chief financial officer

AUDITOR'S REPORT

All publicly held corporations, as well as many other enterprises and organizations (both profit and not-for-profit, large and small) engage the services of independent certified public accountants for the purpose of obtaining an objective, expert report on their financial statements. Based on a comprehensive examination of the company's accounting system and records, and the financial statements, the outside CPA issues the auditor's report.

The standard auditor's report consists of three paragraphs: (1) an introductory paragraph, (2) a scope paragraph, and (3) the opinion paragraph. In the introductory paragraph, the auditor identifies who and what was audited and indicates the responsibilities of management and the auditor relative to the financial statements. In the scope paragraph the auditor states that the audit was conducted in accordance with generally accepted auditing standards and discusses the nature and limitations of the audit. In the opinion paragraph, the auditor expresses an informed opinion as to (1) the fairness of the financial statements and (2) their conformity with generally accepted accounting principles. The Report of Deloitte & Touche LLP appearing in Starbucks' Annual Report is shown below.

Starbucks Corporation

(SEATTLE, WASHINGTON)

We have audited the accompanying consolidated balance sheets of Starbucks Corporation and subsidiaries (the Company) as of September 29, 1996, and October 1, 1995, and the related consolidated statements of earnings, shareholders' equity, and cash flows for each of the three years in the period ended September 29, 1996. These financial statements are the responsibility of the Company's management. Our responsibility is to express an opinion on these financial statements based on our audits.

We conducted our audits in accordance with generally accepted auditing standards. Those standards require that we plan and perform the audit to obtain reasonable assurance about whether the financial statements are free of material misstatement. An audit includes examining, on a test basis, evidence supporting the amounts and disclosures in the financial statements. An audit also includes assessing the accounting principles used and significant estimates made by management, as well as evaluating the overall financial statement presentation. We believe that our audits provide a reasonable basis for our opinion.

In our opinion, such consolidated financial statements present fairly, in all material respects, the financial position of Starbucks Corporation and subsidiaries as of September 29, 1996, and October 1, 1995, and the results of their operations and their cash flows for each of the three years in the period ended September 29, 1996, in conformity with generally accepted accounting principles.

Deloitte & Touche LLP

Deloitte & Touche LLP
Seattle, Washington
November 22, 1996

The auditor's report issued on Starbucks' financial statements is "unqualified" or "clean"; that is, it contains no qualifications or exceptions. In other words, the auditor conformed completely with generally accepted auditing standards in performing the audit, and the financial statements conformed in all material respects with generally accepted accounting principles.

When the financial statements do not conform with generally accepted accounting principles, the auditor must issue a "qualified" opinion and describe the exception. If the lack of conformity with GAAP is sufficiently material, the auditor is compelled to issue an "adverse" or negative opinion. An adverse opinion means that the financial statements do not present fairly the company's financial condition and/or the results of the company's operations at the dates and for the periods reported.

In circumstances where the auditor is unable to perform all the auditing procedures necessary to reach a conclusion as to the fairness of the financial statements, a "disclaimer" must be issued. In these rare instances, the auditor must report the reason for failure to reach a conclusion on the fairness of the financial statements.

Companies strive to obtain an unqualified auditor's report. Hence, only infrequently are you likely to encounter anything other than this type of opinion on the financial statements.

*F*INANCIAL STATEMENTS AND ACCOMPANYING NOTES

The standard set of financial statements consists of: (1) a comparative income statement for three years, (2) a comparative balance sheet for two years, (3) a comparative statement of cash flows for three years, (4) a statement of retained earnings (or stockholders' equity) for three years, and (5) a set of accompanying notes that are considered an integral part of the financial statements. The auditor's report, unless stated otherwise, covers the financial statements and the accompanying notes. The financial statements and accompanying notes plus some supplementary data and analyses for Starbucks follow.

Consolidated Balance Sheets

(IN THOUSANDS, EXCEPT SHARE DATA)

	Sept 29, 1996	Oct 1, 1995
Assets		
Current Assets:		
Cash and cash equivalents	$126,215	$ 20,944
Short-term investments	103,221	41,507
Accounts and notes receivable	17,621	9,852
Inventories	83,370	123,657
Prepaid expenses and other current assets	6,534	4,768
Deferred income taxes, net	2,580	4,622
Total current assets	339,541	205,350
Joint ventures and equity investments	4,401	11,628
Property, plant, and equipment, net	369,477	244,728
Deposits and other assets	13,194	6,472
Total	$726,613	$468,178
Liabilities and Shareholders' Equity		
Current Liabilities:		
Accounts payable	$38,034	$28,668
Checks drawn in excess of bank balances	16,241	13,138
Accrued compensation and related costs	15,001	12,786
Accrued interest payable	3,004	650
Other accrued expenses	28,811	15,804
Total current liabilities	101,091	71,046
Deferred income taxes, net	7,114	3,490
Capital lease obligations	1,728	1,013
Convertible subordinated debentures	165,020	80,398
Commitments and contingencies (notes 4, 5, 8, and 12)		
Shareholders' Equity:		
Common stock–Authorized, 150,000,000 shares; issued and outstanding, 77,583,868 and 70,956,990 shares	361,309	265,679
Retained earnings, including cumulative translation adjustment of $(776) and $(435) respectively, and net unrealized holding gain on investments of $2,046 and $34, respectively	90,351	46,552
Total shareholders' equity	451,660	312,231
Total	$726,613	$468,178

Consolidated Statements of Earnings

(IN THOUSANDS, EXCEPT EARNINGS PER SHARE)

Fiscal year ended:	Sept 29, 1996	Oct 1, 1995	Oct 2, 1994
Net revenues	$696,481	$465,213	$284,923
Cost of sales and related occupancy costs	335,800	211,279	130,324
Store operating expenses	210,693	148,757	90,087
Other operating expenses	19,787	13,932	8,698
Depreciation and amortization	35,950	22,486	12,535
General and administrative expenses	37,258	28,643	19,981
Operating income	56,993	40,116	23,298
Interest income	11,029	6,792	2,130
Interest expense	(8,739)	(3,765)	(3,807)
Gain on sale of investment in Noah's	9,218	—	—
Provision for merger costs	—	—	(3,867)
Earnings before income taxes	68,501	43,143	17,754
Income taxes	26,373	17,041	7,548
Net earnings	42,128	26,102	10,206
Preferred stock dividends	—	—	270
Net earnings available to common shareholders	$ 42,128	$ 26,102	$ 9,936
Net earnings per common and common equivalent share—primary	$ 0.55	$ 0.37	$ 0.17
Net earnings per common and common equivalent share—fully-diluted	$ 0.54	$ 0.36	$ 0.17
Weighted average shares outstanding:			
Primary	76,964	71,309	59,718
Fully-diluted	80,831	71,909	59,757

Consolidated Statement of Cash Flows

(IN THOUSANDS)

Fiscal year ended:	Sept 29, 1996	Oct 1, 1995	Oct 2, 1994
Operating Activities:			
Net earnings	$ 42,128	$ 26,102	$ 10,206
Adjustments to reconcile net earnings to net cash provided (used) by operating activities:			
Depreciation and amortization	39,370	24,827	14,266
Provision for store remodels and asset disposals	412	2,745	1,333
Deferred income taxes, net	4,407	84	214
Equity in losses of investees	1,935	1,156	—
Gain on sale of investment in Noah's	(9,218)	—	—
Cash (used) provided by changes in operating assets and liabilities			
Accounts and notes receivable	(7,771)	(4,456)	(2,297)
Inventories	40,274	(67,579)	(30,079)
Prepaid expenses and other current assets	(1,769)	519	(1,813)
Accounts payable	9,291	19,590	2,389
Accrued compensation and related costs	2,208	3,717	2,944
Accrued interest payable	3,207	24	7
Other accrued expenses	12,205	5,822	3,403
Net cash provided by operating activities	136,679	12,551	573
Investing Activities:			
Purchase of short-term investments	(178,643)	(136,256)	(106,118)
Sale of short-term investments	17,144	27,702	73,701
Maturity of short-term investments	103,056	74,808	100,103
Investments in joint ventures and equity securities	(6,040)	(12,484)	(300)
Proceeds from sale of equity investments	20,550	—	—
Additions to property, plant, and equipment	(161,814)	(129,386)	(85,288)
Additions to deposits and other assets	(5,432)	(1,154)	(1,804)
Net cash used by investing activities	(211,179)	(176,770)	(19,706)
Financing Activities:			
Increase in cash provided by checks drawn in excess of bank balances	3,096	1,180	5,736
Proceeds from sale of convertible debentures	165,020	—	—
Debt issuance costs	(4,045)	—	—
Proceeds from notes payable	—	19,000	—
Principal repayments of notes payable	—	(19,000)	(1,600)
Net proceeds from sale of common stock	—	163,873	—
Proceeds from sale of common stock under employee stock purchase plan	1,735	263	—
Exercise of stock options and warrants	8,032	3,157	2,571
Tax benefit from exercise of nonqualified stock options	6,808	4,754	3,719
Payments received on subscription notes receivable	—	3,671	—
Payments on capital lease obligations	(575)	(147)	—
Debt conversion costs	(290)	—	—
Net cash provided by financing activities	179,781	176,751	10,426
Effect of exchange rate changes on cash and cash equivalents	(10)	18	(5)
Increase (decrease) in cash and cash equivalents	105,271	12,550	(8,712)
Cash and Cash Equivalents:			
Beginning of year	20,944	8,394	17,106
End of year	$126,215	$20,944	$8,394

Supplemental Disclosure of Cash Flow Information:
Cash paid during the year for:

Interest	$ 5,630	$ 3,738	$ 3,612
Income taxes	12,127	10,761	4,565

Noncash Financing and Investing Transactions:

Capital lease obligation incurred	$ 2,089	$ 1,522	$ —
Net unrealized holding gains (losses) on investments	2,012	141	(116)
Conversion of convertible debt into common stock, net of unamortized issue costs	79,345	100	—
Conversion of preferred stock into common stock	—	—	5,214
Preferred dividends accrued	—	—	270
Retirement of treasury stock	—	—	396

See Notes to Consolidated Financial Statements.

Consolidated Statements of Shareholders' Equity

(IN THOUSANDS, EXCEPT SHARE DATA)

	Common stock		Retained earnings	Treasury stock		Total
	Shares	Amount		Shares	Amount	
Balance, October 4, 1993	55,887,734	$ 78,753	$10,329	161,328	$(396)	$88,686
Exercise of stock options and warrants, including tax benefit of $3,719	1,608,548	6,290	—	—	—	6,290
Preferred dividends accrued	—	—	(270)	—	—	(270)
Conversion of redeemable preferred stock into common stock	602,034	5,214	—	—	—	5,214
Retirement of treasury stock	(161,328)	(396)	—	(161,328)	396	—
Net earnings	—	—	10,206	—	—	10,206
Unrealized holding losses, net	—	—	(116)	—	—	(116)
Translation adjustment	—	—	(112)	—	—	(112)
Balance, October 2, 1994	57,936,988	89,861	20,037	—	—	109,898
Exercise of stock options including tax benefit of $4,754	945,780	7,911	—	—	—	7,911
Sale of common stock	12,050,000	163,873	—	—	—	163,873
Payments received on stock subscription notes	—	3,671	—	—	—	3,671
Conversion of convertible debt into common stock	6,798	100	—	—	—	100
Sale of common stock under employee stock purchase plan	17,424	263	—	—	—	263
Net earnings	—	—	26,102	—	—	26,102
Unrealized holding gains, net	—	—	141	—	—	141
Translation adjustment	—	—	272	—	—	272
Balance, October 1, 1995	70,956,990	265,679	46,552	—	—	312,231
Exercise of stock options including tax benefit of $6,808	1,177,736	14,840	—	—	—	14,840
Conversions of convertible debt into common stock	5,359,769	79,055	—	—	—	79,055
Sale of common stock under employee stock purchase plan	89,373	1,735	—	—	—	1,735
Net earnings	—	—	42,128	—	—	42,128
Unrealized holding gains, net	—	—	2,012	—	—	2,012
Translation adjustment	—	—	(341)	—	—	(341)
Balance, September 29, 1996	77,583,868	$361,309	$90,351	—	$ —	$451,660

Management's Discussion and Analysis of Financial Condition and Results of Operations

General Starbucks presently derives approximately 86% of net revenues from its Company-operated retail stores. The Company's specialty sales operations, which include sales to wholesale customers, licensees, and joint ventures, accounted for approximately 11% of net revenues in fiscal 1996. Direct response operations account for the remainder of net revenues.

The Company's net revenues have increased from $284.9 million in fiscal 1994 to $696.5 million in fiscal 1996, due primarily to the Company's store expansion program and comparable store sales increases. Comparable store sales increased by 9% and 7% in fiscal 1995 and 1996, respectively. As part of its expansion strategy of clustering stores in existing markets, Starbucks has experienced a certain level of cannibalization of existing stores by new stores as the store concentration has increased, but management believes such cannibalization has been justified by the incremental sales and return on new store investment. The Company anticipates that this cannibalization, as well as increased competition and other factors, may continue to put downward pressure on its comparable store sales growth in future periods.

The Company's fiscal year ends on the Sunday closest to September 30. Fiscal years 1996, 1995, and 1994 each had 52 weeks.

The following table sets forth the percentage relationship to total net revenues, unless otherwise indicated, of certain items included in the Company's consolidated statements of earnings:

Fiscal year ended:	Sept 29, 1996 (52 Wks)	Oct 1, 1995 (52 Wks)	Oct 2, 1994 (52 Wks)
Statements of Earnings Data:			
Net revenues:			
Retail	86.2%	86.6%	87.2%
Specialty Sales	11.3	10.3	9.3
Direct Response	2.5	3.1	3.5
Total net revenues	100.0	100.0	100.0
Cost of sales and related occupancy costs	48.2	45.4	45.7
Store operating expenses[1]	35.1	36.9	36.3
Other operating expenses	2.8	3.0	3.1
Depreciation and amortization	5.2	4.8	4.4
General and administrative expenses	5.3	6.2	7.0
Operating income	8.2	8.6	8.2
Interest income	1.6	1.5	0.7
Interest expense	(1.3)	(0.8)	(1.3)
Gain on sale of investment in Noah's	1.3	0.0	0.0
Provision for merger costs	0.0	0.0	(1.4)
Earnings before income taxes	9.8	9.3	6.2
Income taxes	3.8	3.7	2.6
Net earnings	6.0%	5.6%	3.6%

(1) Shown as a percentage of retail sales.

(Results of Operations—Fiscal 1996 Compared to Fiscal 1995)

Revenues   Net revenues increased 50% to $696.5 million for fiscal 1996, compared to $465.2 million for fiscal 1995. Retail sales increased 49% to $600.1 million from $402.7 million. The increase in retail sales was due primarily to the addition of new Company-operated stores. In addition, comparable store sales increased 7% for the 52 weeks ended September 29, 1996 compared to the same 52-week period in fiscal 1995. Comparable store sales increases resulted from an increase in the number of transactions combined with an increase in the average dollar value per transaction.

During fiscal 1996, the Company opened 307 Starbucks stores (including four replacement stores), converted 19 Coffee Connection stores to Starbucks stores, and closed one store. Licensees opened 26 stores. The company opened stores in several new markets including North Carolina, Rhode Island, and Ontario, Canada. The Company ended the fiscal year with 929 Company-operated stores and 75 licensed stores in North America.

Specialty Sales revenues increased 63% to $78.7 million for fiscal 1996 from $48.1 million for fiscal 1995. The increase was due primarily to the Company signing an agreement with a major U.S. airline as well as increased revenues from several hotels, a chain of wholesale clubs, office coffee distributors, and restaurants. Direct Response sales increased 23% to $17.8 million for fiscal 1996 from $14.4 million for fiscal 1995.

Costs and Expenses   Cost of sales and related occupancy costs as a percentage of net revenues increased to 48.2% for fiscal 1996 compared to 45.4% for fiscal 1995. This increase was primarily the result of higher green coffee costs as a percentage of net revenues, partially offset by a shift in retail sales mix towards higher-margin products. By the end of the first quarter of fiscal 1997, the Company expects to have sold most of the higher-cost green coffees acquired subsequent to the 1994 frost in Brazil. Therefore, management expects cost of sales in fiscal 1997 to show improvement relative to fiscal 1996.

Store operating expenses as a percentage of retail sales decreased to 35.1% for fiscal 1996 from 36.9% for fiscal 1995. This improvement reflected lower retail advertising expense, store remodel expense, and preopening expense as a percentage of retail sales.

Other operating expenses (those associated with the Company's specialty sales and direct response operations as well as the Company's joint ventures) decreased to 2.8% of net revenues for fiscal 1996 from 3.0% for fiscal 1995 primarily from operational leverage on the Company's net revenue increase. Depreciation and amortization as a percentage of net revenues increased to 5.2% for fiscal 1996 from 4.8% for fiscal 1995. This increase was primarily the result of increased per-store buildout costs in recent years relative to earlier history. After several years of increased per-store buildout costs, average store buildout costs declined in fiscal 1996 relative to fiscal 1995.

General and administrative expenses as a percentage of net revenues were 5.3% for fiscal 1996 compared to 6.2% for fiscal 1995. This decrease as a percentage of revenues was due primarily to lower payroll-related costs and professional fees as a percentage of net revenues.

Operating Income   Operating income for fiscal 1996 increased to $57.0 million (8.2% of net revenues) from $40.1 million (8.6% of net revenues) for fiscal 1995. Operating income as a percentage of net revenues decreased due to higher cost of sales and an increase in depreciation and amortization, partially offset by lower store operating expenses, general and administrative expenses, and other operating expenses as a percentage of revenues.

Interest Income   Interest income for fiscal 1996 was $11.0 million compared to $6.8 million for fiscal 1995. Average investment balances were higher during fiscal 1996 as a result of proceeds from the Company's October 1995 offering of $4\frac{1}{4}$% Convertible Subordinated Debentures due 2002, which generated $161.0 million, net of issuance costs.

Gain on Sale of Investment in Noah's   In March 1995, the Company invested $11.3 million in cash for shares of Noah's New York Bagel, Inc. ("Noah's") Series B Preferred Stock. On February 1, 1996, Noah's was merged with Einstein Brothers Bagels, Inc., a retailer operating primarily in the Eastern United States. In exchange for its investment in Noah's, the Company received $20.6 million in cash and recognized a $9.2 million pre-tax gain ($5.7 million, net of tax) on the transaction.

Interest Expense   Interest expense for fiscal 1996 was $8.7 million compared to $3.8 million for fiscal 1995. The increase in interest expense is due to the Company's convertible subordinated debentures issued in October 1995.

Income Taxes   The Company's effective tax rate for fiscal 1996 was 38.5% compared to 39.5% for fiscal 1995. The Company's fiscal 1996 effective tax rate was lower than in fiscal 1995 due primarily to changes in state tax allocations and apportionment factors as well as the implementation of tax-saving strategies. Management expects the effective tax rate may increase as the Company expands activities in higher tax jurisdictions.

(Results of Operations—Fiscal 1995 Compared to Fiscal 1994)

Revenues   Net revenues increased 63% to $465.2 million for fiscal 1995, compared to $284.9 million for fiscal 1994. Retail sales increased 62% to $402.7 million from $248.5 million. The increase in retail sales was due primarily to the addition of new Company-operated stores. In addition, comparable store sales increased 9% for the 52 weeks ended October 1, 1995 compared to the same 52-week period in fiscal 1994. Comparable store sales increases resulted from an increase in the number of transactions combined with an increase in the average dollar value per transaction. The increase in average dollar value per transaction included an increase in coffee beverage and whole bean prices which took place in July 1994.

During fiscal 1995, the Company opened 230 Starbucks stores (including two replacement stores), and converted four Coffee Connection stores to Starbucks stores. Licensees opened 23 new stores. The Company opened stores in several new markets including Baltimore, Maryland; Las Vegas, Nevada; Cincinnati, Ohio; Philadelphia and Pittsburgh, Pennsylvania; and Austin, Dallas, Houston, and San Antonio, Texas. The Company ended the fiscal year with 627 Company-operated stores and 49 licensed stores. Of the Company-operated stores, 19 were operated in the Northeast as Coffee Connection stores.

Specialty Sales revenues increased 81% to $48.1 million for fiscal 1995 from $26.5 million for fiscal 1994. Increased sales to several multi-unit retailers, hotels, airlines, and a chain of wholesale clubs as well as sales to a greater number of restaurants and institutions accounted for the increase in revenues. Direct Response sales increased 46% to $14.4 million for fiscal 1995 from $9.9 million for fiscal 1994.

Costs and Expenses   Cost of sales and related occupancy costs as a percentage of net revenues decreased to 45.4% for fiscal 1995 compared to 45.7% for fiscal 1994. This decrease was primarily the result of higher prices on coffee beverages and whole bean coffees, and lower packaging costs as a percentage of net revenues, partially offset by higher green coffee costs.

Store operating expenses as a percentage of retail sales increased to 36.9% for fiscal 1995 from 36.3% for fiscal 1994. This increase was primarily a result of higher retail advertising expense. Other operating expenses decreased to 3.0% of net revenues for fiscal 1995 from 3.1% for fiscal 1994. The decrease was due primarily to lower direct response promotional costs as a percentage of revenues, partially offset by start-up costs related to the Company's joint venture with Pepsi-Cola. Depreciation and amortization as a percentage of net revenues increased to 4.8% from 4.4% for fiscal 1994. This increase was primarily the result of higher store buildout and equipment costs.

General and administrative expenses as a percentage of net revenues were 6.2% for fiscal 1995 compared to 7.0% for fiscal 1994. This decrease as a percentage of revenues was due to the Company's ability to increase revenues without proportionally increasing overhead expenses.

Operating Income   Operating income for fiscal 1995 increased to $40.1 million (8.6% of net revenues) from $23.3 million (8.2% of net revenues) for fiscal 1994. Operating income as a percentage of net revenues improved due to higher gross margin and lower general and administrative expenses as a percentage of revenues, partially offset by an increase in store operating expenses and depreciation and amortization as a percentage of revenues.

Interest Income   Interest income for fiscal 1995 was $6.8 million compared to $2.1 million for fiscal 1994. The increase in interest income was due to higher average investment balances resulting from the Company's public offering of common stock in November 1994.

Interest Expense   Interest expense for fiscal 1995 was $3.8 million, unchanged from fiscal 1994.

Income Taxes The Company's effective tax rate for fiscal 1995 was 39.5% compared to 42.5% for fiscal 1994. The Company's fiscal 1994 effective tax rate was higher than in fiscal 1995 due to one-time, non-deductible merger costs related to the Coffee Connection merger in June 1994.

(Liquidity and Capital Resources)

The Company ended fiscal 1996 with $229.4 million in total cash and short-term investments. Working capital as of September 29, 1996 totaled $238.5 million compared to $134.3 million at October 1, 1995. Cash provided by operating activities totaled $136.7 million and resulted primarily from net income before non-cash charges of $79.0 million, a $40.3 million reduction in inventories, and a $26.9 million increase in accrued liabilities and expenses.

Cash provided from financing activities for fiscal 1996 totaled $179.8 million and included net proceeds of $161.0 million from the Company's October 1995 offering of convertible subordinated debentures. Cash provided from financing activities also included cash generated from the Company's employee stock purchase plan and from the exercise of employee stock options and the related income tax benefit available to the Company upon exercise of such options. As options granted under the Company's stock option plans vest, the Company will continue to receive proceeds and a tax deduction as a result of option exercises; however, neither the amounts nor the timing thereof can be predicted.

Cash used by investing activities for fiscal 1996 totaled $211.2 million. This included capital additions to property, plant, and equipment of $161.8 million which was used to open 307 new Company-operated retail stores, remodel certain existing stores, purchase roasting and packaging equipment for the Company's roasting and distribution facilities, enhance information systems, and expand existing office space.

The Company also invested in its joint ventures. During fiscal 1996, the Company made equity investments of $2.4 million in its joint venture with SAZABY, Inc. and $2.7 million in its joint venture with Pepsi-Cola Company. The Company also made investments in and advances to its joint venture with Dreyer's Grand Ice Cream, Inc. totaling $0.9 million. The Company sold its investment in Noah's and received $20.6 million in proceeds. The Company invested excess cash in short-term investment-grade marketable debt securities.

Future cash requirements, other than normal operating expenses, are expected to consist primarily of capital expenditures related to the addition of new Company-operated retail stores. The Company also anticipates remodeling certain existing stores and incurring additional expenditures for enhancing its production capacity and information systems. While there can be no assurance that current expectations will be realized, and plans are subject to change upon further review, management expects capital expenditures for fiscal 1997 to be approximately $170 million.

The Company currently anticipates additional cash requirements of approximately $20 million for its domestic joint ventures and international expansion during fiscal 1997. In addition, under the terms of the Company's corporate office lease, the Company has agreed to provide financing to the building owner to be used exclusively for facilities and leasehold development costs to accommodate the Company. During fiscal 1996, the Company provided approximately $4.3 million under this agreement, bringing the total amount provided to date to $4.6 million as of September 29, 1996. During fiscal 1997, the Company intends to provide additional funds of approximately $3.8 million under this agreement. The maximum amount available under the agreement is $17 million. Any funds advanced by the Company will be repaid with interest over a term not to exceed 20 years.

Management believes that existing cash and investments plus cash generated from operations should be sufficient to finance capital requirements for its core businesses through fiscal 1997. Any new joint ventures, other new business opportunities, or store expansion rates substantially in excess of that presently planned may require outside funding.

(Coffee Prices, Availability, and General Risk Conditions)

Some of the information in this Annual Report, including anticipated store openings, planned capital expenditures, and trends in the Company's operations, are forward-looking statements which are subject to risks and uncertainties. Actual future results and trends may differ materially depending on a variety of factors, including, but not limited to, coffee and other raw materials prices and availability, successful execution of internal performance and expansion plans, impact of competition, availability of financing, legal proceedings, and other risks detailed in the Company's Securities and Exchange Commission filings, including the Company's Annual Report on Form 10-K for the year ended September 29, 1996.

Green coffee commodity prices are subject to substantial price fluctuations, generally a result of reports of adverse growing conditions in certain coffee-producing countries. Due to green coffee commodity price increases, the Company effected sales price increases during fiscal 1994 and 1995 to mitigate the effects of anticipated increases in its cost of goods sold. Because the Company had established fixed purchase prices for some of its supply of green coffees, the Company's margins were favorably impacted by such sales price increases during much of fiscal 1995. During the latter part of fiscal 1995 and throughout fiscal 1996, gross margins were negatively impacted relative to the prior year by the sell-through of higher-cost coffee inventories. The Company expects to have sold most of these higher-cost coffees by the end of the first quarter of fiscal 1997.

The Company enters into fixed price purchase commitments in order to secure an adequate supply of quality green coffee and fix costs for future periods. As of September 29, 1996 the Company had approximately $47 million in fixed price purchase commitments which, together with existing inventory, is expected to provide an adequate supply of green coffee well into fiscal 1997. The Company believes, based on relationships established with its suppliers in the past, that the risk of non-delivery on such purchase commitments is remote.

In addition to fluctuating coffee prices, management believes that the Company's future results of operations and earnings could be significantly impacted by other factors such as increased competition within the specialty coffee industry, the Company's ability to find optimal store locations at favorable lease rates, the increased costs associated with opening and operating retail stores in new markets, the Company's continued ability to hire, train and retain qualified personnel, and the Company's ability to obtain adequate capital to finance its planned expansion.

Due to the factors noted above, the Company's future earnings and the prices of the Company's securities may be subject to volatility. There can be no assurance that the Company will continue to generate increases in net revenues and net earnings, or growth in comparable store sales. Any variance in the factors noted above, or other areas, from what is expected by investors could have an immediate and adverse effect on the trading prices of the Company's securities.

(Seasonality and Quarterly Results)

The Company's business is subject to seasonal fluctuations. Significant portions of the Company's net revenues and profits are realized during the first quarter of the Company's fiscal year, which includes the December holiday season. In addition, quarterly results are affected by the timing of the opening of new stores, and the Company's rapid growth may conceal the impact of other seasonal influences. Because of the seasonality of the Company's business, results for any quarter are not necessarily indicative of the results that may be achieved for the full fiscal year.

(New Accounting Standard)

In October 1995, the Financial Accounting Standards Board issued Statement No. 123, "Accounting for Stock-Based Compensation". This pronouncement establishes the accounting and reporting requirements using a fair value-based method of accounting for stock-based employee compensation plans. Under the new standard, the Company may either adopt the new fair value-based measurement method or continue using the intrinsic value-based method for employee stock-based compensation and provide pro forma disclosures of net income and earnings per share as if the measurement pro-visions of SFAS No. 123 had been adopted. The Company plans to adopt only the disclosure requirements of SFAS No. 123; therefore the adoption will have no effect on the Company's consolidated net earnings or cash flows.

Notes to Consolidated Financial Statements

(YEARS ENDED SEPTEMBER 29, 1996, OCTOBER 1, 1995, AND OCTOBER 2, 1994)

Note 1: Summary of Significant Accounting Policies

Description of Business   Starbucks Corporation and its subsidiaries ("Starbucks" or the "Company") purchases and roasts high-quality whole bean coffees and sells them, along with a variety of coffee beverages, pastries, confections, and coffee-related accessories and equipment, primarily through Company-operated and licensed retail stores located throughout the United States and in parts of Canada. In addition to its retail operations, the Company sells primarily whole bean coffees through a specialty sales group and a direct response operation.

Basis of Presentation   The consolidated financial statements include the accounts of Starbucks Corporation and its wholly owned subsidiaries. Investments in unconsolidated joint ventures are accounted for under the equity method. Material intercompany transactions during the periods covered by these consolidated financial statements have been eliminated.

Fiscal Year End   The Company's fiscal year ends on the Sunday closest to September 30. Fiscal years 1996, 1995 and 1994 each had 52 weeks.

Estimates and Assumptions   The preparation of financial statements in conformity with generally accepted accounting principles requires management to make estimates and assumptions that affect the reported amounts of assets, liabilities, revenues, and expenses. Actual results may differ from these estimates.

The Coffee Connection Merger   On June 2, 1994, the Company acquired all of the outstanding capital stock of The Coffee Connection, Inc., a roaster/retailer of specialty coffee on the East Coast, in exchange for newly-issued shares of the Company's common stock. The merger was accounted for as a pooling of interests for accounting and financial reporting purposes. All fees and expenses related to the merger and the consolidation of the combined companies were expensed as required under the pooling-of-interests accounting method. Such fees and expenses were approximately $3.9 million ($2.9 million after tax).

Cash and Cash Equivalents   The Company considers all highly liquid instruments with a maturity of three months or less at the time of purchase to be cash equivalents.

Cash Management   The Company's cash management system provides for the reimbursement of all major bank disbursement accounts on a daily basis. Checks issued but not presented for payment to the bank are reflected as "Checks drawn in excess of bank balances" in the accompanying financial statements.

Investments   The Company's investments consist primarily of investment-grade marketable debt securities, all of which are classified as available-for-sale and recorded at fair value as defined below. Unrealized holding gains and losses are recorded, net of any tax effect, as a component of shareholders' equity.

Fair Value of Financial Instruments   The carrying value of cash and cash equivalents approximates fair value because of the short-term maturity of those instruments. The fair value of the Company's short-term investments in marketable debt and equity securities is based upon the quoted market price on the last business day of the fiscal year plus accrued interest, if any. The fair value and amortized cost of the Company's short-term investments at September 29, 1996, were $103.2 million and $99.9 million, respectively. The fair value and amortized cost of the Company's short-term investments at October 1, 1995, were both $41.5 million. For further detail on short-term investments, see Note 3. The fair value of the Company's $4\frac{1}{4}$% Convertible Subordinated Debentures due 2002 (see Note 7) is based on the quoted NASDAQ market price on the last business day of the fiscal year. As of September 29, 1996, the fair value and principal amount of the $4\frac{1}{4}$% Convertible Subordinated Debentures due 2002 were $248.0 million and $165.0 million, respectively.

Inventories   Inventories are stated at the lower of cost (primarily first-in, first-out) or market.

Property, Plant, and Equipment   Property, plant, and equipment are carried at cost less accumulated depreciation and amortization. Depreciation of property, plant, and equipment, which includes amortization of assets under capital leases, is provided on the straight-line method over estimated useful lives, generally ranging from three to seven years for equipment and 40 years for buildings. Leasehold improvements are amortized over the shorter of their estimated useful lives or the related lease life, generally ten years. The portion of depreciation expense related to production and distribution facilities is included in "Cost of sales and related occupancy costs". When facts and circumstances indicate that the cost of long-lived assets may be impaired, an evaluation of recoverability is performed by comparing the carrying value of the asset to projected future cash flows. Upon indication that the carrying value of such assets may not be recoverable, the Company recognizes an impairment loss by a charge against current operations.

Hedging and Futures Contracts   The Company may, from time to time, enter into futures contracts to hedge price-to-be-established coffee purchase commitments with the objective of minimizing cost risk due to market fluctuations. Any gains or losses from hedging transactions are included as part of the inventory cost. The Company did not engage in any hedging activities or futures contracts during fiscal 1996 or 1995. Hedging activities entered into during fiscal 1994 were immaterial.

Advertising   The Company expenses costs of advertising the first time the advertising campaign takes place, except for direct response advertising, which is capitalized and amortized over its expected period of future benefit. Direct response advertising consists primarily of mail order catalog costs and customer retention program costs. Catalog costs are amortized over the period from the catalog mailing until the issuance of the next catalog, typically three months. Customer retention program costs are amortized over six months.

Store Preopening Expenses   Costs incurred in connection with start-up and promotion of new store openings are expensed as incurred.

Rent Expense   Certain of the Company's lease agreements provide for scheduled rent increases during the lease terms, or for rental payments commencing at a date other than the date of initial occupancy. Rent expenses are recognized on a straight-line basis over the terms of the leases.

Income Taxes   The Company computes income taxes using the asset and liability method, under which deferred income taxes are provided for the temporary differences between the financial reporting basis and the tax basis of the Company's assets and liabilities.

Earnings per Share   The computation of primary earnings per share is based on the weighted average number of shares outstanding during the period plus dilutive common stock equivalents consisting primarily of certain shares subject to stock options. The number of shares resulting from this computation for fiscal 1996, 1995, and 1994 were 76,964,000, 71,309,000, and 59,718,000, respectively.

The computation of fully-diluted earnings per share assumes conversion of the Company's convertible subordinated debentures using the "if converted" method, when such securities are dilutive, with net income adjusted for the after-tax interest expense and amortization applicable to these debentures. The number of shares resulting from this computation for fiscal 1996, 1995, and 1994 were 80,831,000, 71,909,000, and 59,757,000, respectively.

Reclassifications   Certain reclassifications of prior years' balances have been made to conform to the fiscal 1996 presentation.

Note 2: Cash and Cash Equivalents

Cash and cash equivalents consist of the following (in thousands):

	Sept 29, 1996	Oct 1, 1995
Operating funds and interest-bearing deposits	$ 11,069	$10,960
Commercial paper	93,306	—
Money market funds	14,590	9,984
Local government obligations	7,060	—
U.S. government obligations	190	—
	$126,215	$20,944

Note 3: Short-term Investments

The Company's short-term investments, including aggregate fair values, cost, gross unrealized holding gains, and gross unrealized holding losses, consist of the following (in thousands):

	Fair value	Amortized cost	Gross unrealized holding gains	Gross unrealized holding losses
September 29, 1996				
Corporate debt securities	$ 33,112	$33,118	$ 11	$(17)
U.S. Government obligations	45,041	45,017	36	(12)
Commercial paper	19,958	19,959	—	(1)
Marketable equity securities	5,110	1,800	3,310	—
	$103,221	$99,894	$3,357	$(30)

	Fair value	Amortized cost	Gross unrealized holding gains	Gross unrealized holding losses
October 1, 1995				
Corporate debt securities	$19,703	$19,655	$58	$(10)
U.S. Government obligations	14,832	14,824	8	—
Commercial paper	6,972	6,972	—	—
	$41,507	$41,451	$66	$(10)

All short-term investments are classified as available-for-sale as of September 29, 1996. Marketable debt securities have remaining maturities of one year or less. The specific identification method is used to determine a cost basis for computing realized gains and losses.

On March 31, 1995, the Company invested $11.3 million in cash for shares of Noah's New York Bagel, Inc. ("Noah's") Series B Preferred Stock. On February 1, 1996, Noah's was merged with Einstein Brothers Bagels, Inc. ("Einstein"), a retailer operating primarily in the Eastern United States. In exchange for its investment in Noah's, the Company received $20.6 million in cash and recognized a $9.2 million pre-tax gain ($5.7 million net of tax) on the transaction. Concurrently, the Company purchased $1.8 million of Einstein/Noah Bagel Corporation common stock.

In fiscal 1996, 1995, and 1994, proceeds from the sale of investment securities were $17.1 million, $27.7 million, and $73.7 million, respectively. During fiscal 1996, 1995, and 1994, gross realized gains totaled $13,000, $30,000, and $167,000, respectively, and gross realized losses totaled $11,000, $62,000, and $437,000, respectively.

Note 4: Inventories

Inventories consist of the following (in thousands):

	Sept 29, 1996	Oct 1, 1995
Coffee		
Unroasted	$37,127	$ 75,975
Roasted	9,753	11,612
Other merchandise held for sale	29,518	32,731
Packaging and other supplies	6,972	3,339
	$83,370	$123,657

As of September 29, 1996, the Company had fixed price inventory purchase commitments for green coffee totaling approximately $47 million. The Company believes, based on relationships established with its suppliers in the past, that the risk of non-delivery on such purchase commitments is remote.

Note 5: Joint Ventures and Equity Investments

Joint Ventures Starbucks accounts for its joint ventures using the equity method. The Company's share of joint venture income or losses is included in "Other operating expenses."

On August 10, 1994, the Company entered into a 50/50 joint venture and partnership agreement (the "Partnership Agreement") with Pepsi-Cola Company, a division of PepsiCo, Inc., to develop ready-to-drink coffee-based beverages. During fiscal 1996, the Company modified the Partnership Agreement to revise the allocation of start-up risks and expenses between partners. The Company's investment in the joint venture was $2.6 million and $0.3 million as of September 29, 1996, and October 1, 1995, respectively. During fiscal 1996 and 1995, the Company's share of the joint venture's losses totaled $0.4 million and $1.2 million, respectively. The Company made capital contributions totaling $2.7 million and $1.2 million to the joint venture in fiscal 1996 and fiscal 1995, respectively.

On October 25, 1995, the Company signed an agreement with SAZABY Inc., a Japanese retailer and restaurateur, to form a joint venture partnership to develop Starbucks retail stores in Japan. The first two stores opened in Tokyo during the fourth quarter of fiscal 1996. The Company's investment in the joint venture was $1.7 million as of September 29, 1996. During fiscal 1996, the Company's share of the joint venture's losses totaled $0.8 million. The Company made capital contributions totaling $2.4 million to the joint venture in fiscal 1996. The Company has guaranteed loans made to the joint venture totaling 190.0 million yen ($1.8 million) as of September 29, 1996.

On October 31, 1995, the Company entered into a joint venture agreement with Dreyer's Grand Ice Cream, Inc. to develop and distribute premium coffee ice creams. The Company's investment in the joint venture was $0.1 million as of September 29, 1996. During fiscal 1996, the Company's share of the joint venture's losses totaled $0.7 million. The Company made capital contributions and advances totaling $0.9 million to the joint venture in fiscal 1996.

Equity Investments As of October 1, 1995, the Company owned a $11.3 million investment in shares of Noah's Series B Preferred Stock which was accounted for under the equity method. As discussed in Note 3, Noah's was merged with Einstein at which time the investment was sold.

Note 6: Property, Plant, and Equipment

Property, plant, and equipment are recorded at cost and consist of the following (in thousands):

	Sept 29, 1996	Oct 1, 1995
Land	$ 3,602	$ 3,602
Building	8,338	8,338
Leasehold improvements	255,567	162,948
Roasting and store equipment	120,575	82,490
Furniture, fixtures, and other	38,794	24,602
	426,876	281,980
Less accumulated depreciation and amortization	(88,003)	(52,215)
	338,873	229,765
Work in progress	30,604	14,963
	$369,477	$244,728

Note 7: Convertible Subordinated Debentures

On August 3, 1993, the Company issued $80.5 million in principal amount of $4\frac{1}{2}$% Convertible Subordinated Debentures Due 2003. During fiscal 1995, $0.1 million in principal amount of the debentures was converted into common stock. On April 12, 1996, the Company called these debentures for redemption. The total principal amount converted, net of unamortized issue costs, accrued but unpaid interest, and costs of conversion, was credited to common stock.

During the first quarter of fiscal 1996, the Company issued approximately $165.0 million in principal amount of $4\frac{1}{4}$% Convertible Subordinated Debentures Due 2002 (the "Debentures"). Net proceeds to the Company were approximately $161.0 million. Interest is payable semiannually on May 1 and November 1 of each year. The Debentures are convertible into common stock of the Company at a price of $23.25, subject to adjustment under certain conditions. The Debentures are redeemable after November 10, 1997 at the option of the Company, at specified redemption prices and subject to certain conditions. The Debentures are subordinate to all future senior indebtedness. Costs incurred in connection with the issuance of the Debentures are included in "Deposits and other assets" and are being amortized on a straight line basis over the seven-year period to maturity.

Note 8: Leases

The Company leases retail stores, roasting and distribution facilities, and office space under operating leases expiring through 2015. Most lease agreements contain renewal options and rent escalation clauses. Certain leases provide for contingent rentals based upon gross sales. The Company also leases certain computer equipment and software under agreements classified as capital leases with original lease terms ranging from two to four years.

Rental expense under these lease agreements was as follows (in thousands):

Fiscal year ended:	Sept 29, 1996	Oct 1, 1995	Oct 2, 1994
Minimum rentals	$37,527	$21,590	$11,928
Contingent rentals	1,190	1,088	1,191
	$38,717	$22,678	$13,119

Minimum future rental payments under non-cancelable lease obligations as of September 29, 1996, are as follows (in thousands):

Fiscal year ended:	Capital leases	Operating leases
1997	$1,490	$ 38,819
1998	1,173	39,013
1999	561	39,095
2000	368	38,976
2001	—	39,129
Thereafter	—	169,708
Total minimum lease payments	$3,592	$364,740
Less: Amounts representing interest and other expenses	(652)	
Present value of net minimum lease payments	2,940	
Less: Current portion	(1,212)	
Long-term capital lease obligations	$1,728	

Assets recorded under capital leases are included in "Property, plant, and equipment" within the "Furniture, fixtures, and other" category. Assets recorded under capital leases, net of accumulated amortization, totaled $3.6 million and $1.5 million at September 29, 1996, and October 1, 1995, respectively.

The Company opened a roasting and distribution facility in Pennsylvania in September 1995 (the "East Coast Plant"). Under the terms of this lease agreement, the Company has an option to purchase the land and building comprising the East Coast Plant for approximately $14 million within five years of the date of occupancy. Such option to purchase also provides that the Company may purchase, within seven years of occupancy, additional land adjacent to the East Coast Plant.

Note 9: Shareholders' Equity

In November 1994, the Company completed a public offering of 12,050,000 shares of newly-issued common stock for proceeds of approximately $163.9 million, net of expenses.

On February 28, 1996, the Company's shareholders approved an amendment to the Company's articles of incorporation increasing the number of authorized common shares from 100,000,000 to 150,000,000.

The Company has authorized 7,500,000 shares of its preferred stock, none of which is outstanding at September 29, 1996.

Note 10: Stock Options

The Company maintains several stock option plans which provide for granting incentive stock options and nonqualified stock options to employees and nonemployee directors. Stock options have been granted at prices at or above the fair market value as of the date of grant. Options vest and expire according to terms established at the grant date.

The following summarizes all stock option transactions from October 4, 1993, through September 29, 1996.

	Shares	Range of prices per share
Outstanding, October 4, 1993	6,308,646	$ 0.75–12.56
Granted	1,546,426	3.45–16.72
Exercised	(1,547,528)	0.75– 8.50
Cancelled	(189,578)	0.75–13.25
Outstanding, October 2, 1994	6,117,966	0.75–16.72
Granted	2,853,476	11.47–20.06
Exercised	(945,780)	0.75–15.00
Cancelled	(1,151,006)	1.50–13.25
Outstanding, October 1, 1995	6,874,656	0.75–20.06
Granted	2,394,617	12.81–26.94
Exercised	(1,177,736)	0.75–16.88
Cancelled	(449,158)	1.50–20.06
Outstanding, September 29, 1996	7,642,379	$ 0.75–26.94
Exercisable, September 29, 1996	3,316,967	$ 0.75–20.06

There were 5,875,009 shares of common stock reserved for future stock option grants at September 29, 1996.

In October 1995, the Financial Accounting Standards Board issued Statement No. 123, "Accounting for Stock-Based Compensation". This pronouncement establishes the accounting and reporting requirements using a fair value-based method of accounting for stock-based employee compensation plans. Under the new standard, the Company may either adopt the new fair value-based measurement method or continue using the intrinsic value-based method for employee stock-based compensation and provide pro forma disclosures of net income and earnings per share as if the measurement provi-

sions of SFAS No. 123 had been adopted. The Company plans to adopt only the disclosure requirements of SFAS No. 123; therefore the adoption will have no effect on the Company's consolidated net earnings or cash flows.

Note 11: Income Taxes

A reconciliation of the statutory federal income tax rate with the Company's effective income tax rate is as follows:

Fiscal year ended:	Sept 29, 1996	Oct 1, 1995	Oct 2, 1994
Statutory rate	35.0%	35.0%	35.0%
State income taxes, net of federal income tax benefit	3.1	3.6	3.3
Non-deductible merger costs	—	—	3.3
Other	0.4	0.9	0.9
Effective tax rate	38.5%	39.5%	42.5%

The provision for income taxes consists of the following (in thousands):

Fiscal year ended:	Sept 29, 1996	Oct 1, 1995	Oct 2, 1994
Currently payable:			
Federal	$19,568	$14,672	$6,424
State	2,398	2,285	910
Deferred liability	4,407	84	214
	$26,373	$17,041	$7,548

Deferred income taxes (benefits) reflect the tax effect of temporary differences between the amounts of assets and liabilities for financial reporting purposes and amounts as measured for tax purposes. The tax effect of temporary differences and carryforwards that cause significant portions of deferred tax assets and liabilities are as follows (in thousands):

	Sept 29, 1996	Oct 1, 1995
Depreciation	$10,699	$ 5,779
Accrued rent	(2,839)	(1,687)
Accrued compensation and related costs	(1,219)	(927)
Inventory valuation	(832)	(1,254)
Capitalized inventory costs	(699)	(707)
Coffee Connection NOL carryforwards	(629)	(645)
Reserve for store remodels	(184)	(953)
Unrealized holding gain on investments, net	1,281	22
Other, net	(1,044)	(760)
	$ 4,534	$(1,132)

Taxes payable of $2.7 million are included in "Other accrued expenses" as of September 29, 1996, and taxes refundable of $0.5 million are included in "Prepaid expenses and other current assets" as of October 1, 1995. The Company has net operating loss carryforwards of approximately $1.6 million expiring in 2007 and 2008.

Note 12: Commitments and Contingencies

Under the amended terms of the Company's corporate office lease, the Company has agreed to provide financing to the building owner to be used exclusively for facilities and leasehold development costs to accommodate the Company. Under this agreement, the Company provided approximately $4.3 million and $0.3 million during fiscal 1996 and fiscal 1995, respectively. As of September 29, 1996, and October 1, 1995, the amounts outstanding under the agreement totaled $4.6 million and $0.3 million, respectively. These amounts are included in "Deposits and other assets" on the balance sheet. The maximum amount available under the agreement is $17.0 million. Any funds advanced by the Company will be repaid with interest at 9.5% over a term not to exceed 20 years.

In the normal course of business, the Company has various legal claims and other contingent matters outstanding. Management believes that any ultimate liability arising from these actions would not have a material adverse effect on the Company's results of operations or financial condition at September 29, 1996.

Note 13: Employee Benefit Plans

Defined Contribution Plans   Starbucks maintains voluntary defined contribution profit sharing plans covering all eligible employees as defined in the plan documents. Participating employees may elect to defer and contribute a stated percentage of their compensation to the plan, not to exceed the dollar amount set by law. The Company matches 25% of each employee's contribution up to a maximum of the first 4% of each employee's compensation.

The Company's matching contributions to the plans were approximately $0.3 million, $0.3 million, and $0.1 million for fiscal 1996, 1995, and 1994, respectively.

Employee Stock Purchase Plan   During fiscal 1995, the Company implemented an employee stock purchase plan. The Company's plan provides that eligible employees may contribute up to 10% of their base earnings toward the quarterly purchase of the Company's common stock. The employee's purchase price is 85% of the lesser of the fair market value of the stock on the first business day or the last business day of the quarterly offering period. No compensation expense is recorded in connection with the plan. The total number of shares issuable under the plan is 4,000,000. There were 89,373 shares issued under the plan during fiscal 1996 at prices ranging from $15.99 to $24.65. There were 17,424 shares issued under the plan during fiscal 1995 at a price of $15.09. Of the 7,944 employees eligible to participate, 1,601 were participants in the plan as of September 29, 1996.

Note 14: Related Party Transactions

An employee director of the Company serves as chairman of a wholesale customer of the Company. Sales to this customer were $22.7 million, $18.5 million, and $10.5 million for fiscal 1996, 1995, and 1994, respectively. Amounts receivable from this customer totaled $2.7 million and $1.9 million as of September 29, 1996, and October 1, 1995, respectively.

A director of the Company serves as a co-chairman and chief executive of a company which provides insurance brokerage and employee benefit consulting services to the Company. Amounts paid for those services (primarily premiums) totaled $3.8 million, $3.5 million, and $1.1 million for fiscal 1996, 1995, and 1994, respectively.

SUPPLEMENTARY FINANCIAL INFORMATION

In addition to the financial statements and the accompanying notes, three items of supplementary financial information typically are presented: business segment information, quarterly financial data, and stock performance information.

BUSINESS SEGMENT INFORMATION

To help financial statement users assess the performance of diversified companies that operate in several different industries and lines of business, segmented financial information is required. The required information for each significant segment includes: revenues, income from operations, capital expenditures, identifiable assets, and depreciation and amortization. This information is generally included in the form of notes and schedules in the notes accompanying the financial statements. Since Starbucks operates primarily in one line of business, it is not required to present business segment data.

QUARTERLY FINANCIAL DATA AND CAPITAL STOCK INFORMATION

Nearly all publicly held companies and many nonpublic companies issue financial information on a quarterly basis to stockholders, regulatory agencies, and others. These quarterly reports are referred to as **interim financial reports,** for which there are prescribed accounting standards. Quarterly financial data along with capital stock information are frequently summarized in the Annual Report. Starbucks summarizes its quarterly data and capital stock information as shown below.

Note 15: Quarterly Financial Information (Unaudited)

Summarized quarterly financial information for fiscal years 1996 and 1995 is as follows (in thousands, except earnings per share):

	First	Second	Third	Fourth
1996 quarter:				
Net revenues	$169,537	$153,609	$176,950	$196,385
Gross margin	83,019	76,671	93,786	107,205
Net earnings	9,566	10,391	9,446	12,725
Net earnings per common & common equivalent share— fully-diluted	$ 0.13	$ 0.14	$ 0.12	$ 0.16
1995 quarter:				
Net revenues	$115,545	$101,113	$119,174	$129,381
Gross margin	63,562	55,474	65,451	69,447
Net earnings	8,620	5,130	6,845	5,507
Net earnings per common & common equivalent share— fully-diluted	$ 0.13	$ 0.07	$ 0.09	$ 0.07

Shareholder Information

(STARBUCKS CORPORATION)

Market Information and Dividend Policy   The Company's Common Stock is traded on the NASDAQ National Market System under the symbol "SBUX". The following table sets forth the quarterly high and low sale prices per share of the Common Stock as reported on the NASDAQ National Market System for each quarter during the last two fiscal years, retroactively adjusted for the two-for-one stock split on December 1, 1995.

Fiscal year ended	High	Low
September 29, 1996		
First Quarter	$23\frac{1}{2}$	$16\frac{15}{16}$
Second Quarter	$23\frac{5}{8}$	$14\frac{1}{2}$
Third Quarter	$29\frac{5}{8}$	$24\frac{1}{8}$
Fourth Quarter	$35\frac{7}{8}$	23
October 1, 1995		
First Quarter	$14\frac{5}{8}$	$10\frac{3}{4}$
Second Quarter	$13\frac{11}{16}$	$11\frac{1}{8}$
Third Quarter	$18\frac{5}{8}$	$11\frac{5}{8}$
Fourth Quarter	$22\frac{1}{8}$	$17\frac{7}{16}$

As of November 18, 1996, the approximate number of common shareholders of record was 6,710. The Company has never paid any dividends on its Common Stock. The Company presently intends to retain earnings for use in its business and therefore does not anticipate declaring a cash dividend in the near future.

Annual Meeting   The Company's Annual Meeting of Shareholders will be held at 10 am (Pacific time), on Thursday, March 6, 1997 at:

Starbucks Roasting Plant
18411—77th Place South
Kent, WA 98032

Form 10-K and Quarterly Shareholder Information   The Company's annual report on Form 10-K for the fiscal year ended September 29, 1996 may be obtained without charge by sending a written request to the address below.

Beginning in fiscal 1997, we will discontinue printing and mailing quarterly reports to all shareholders. Quarterly information will be available to all shareholders immediately upon its release, free of charge, via fax, by calling (800) 758-5804 extension 810887 or through access on the Internet at www.prnewswire.com. To receive a copy by mail, please send your written request to:

Investor Relations
Starbucks Corporation
P.O. Box 34067
Seattle, WA 98124-1067

We believe communicating our quarterly results in this manner will be more timely and cost-effective for our shareholders.

APPENDIX B

Specimen Financial Statements: Green Mountain Coffee

MANAGEMENT'S DISCUSSION AND ANALYSIS OF FINANCIAL CONDITION AND RESULTS OF OPERATIONS

GENERAL

For the year ended September 28, 1996, Green Mountain derived approximately 79.1% of its net sales from its wholesale operation. Green Mountain's wholesale operation sells coffee to retailers and food service concerns including supermarkets, restaurants, convenience stores, specialty food stores, hotels, universities and business offices. The Company also operated twelve retail stores and a direct mail operation, which accounted for approximately 13.0% and 7.9% of net sales, respectively, in fiscal 1996.

Cost of sales consists of the cost of raw materials including green coffee, flavorings and packaging materials, the salaries and related expenses of production and distribution personnel, depreciation on production equipment and freight and delivery expenses. Selling and operating expenses consist of expenses that directly support the sales of the Company's wholesale, retail or direct mail distribution channels, including marketing and advertising expenses, a portion of the Company's rental expense and the salaries and related expenses of employees directly supporting sales. General and administrative expenses consist of expenses incurred for corporate support and administration, including the salaries and related expenses of personnel not elsewhere categorized.

The Company's fiscal year ends on the last Saturday in September. The Company's fiscal year normally consists of 13 four-week periods with the first, second and third "quarters" ending 16 weeks, 28 weeks and 40 weeks, respectively, into the fiscal year. Fiscal 1996 and fiscal 1994 represent the years ended September 28, 1996 and September 24, 1994, respectively, and consisted of 52 weeks. Fiscal 1995 represents the year ended September 30, 1995 and consisted of 53 weeks with the fiscal fourth quarter having 13 weeks instead of the normal 12 weeks.

This document may include forward-looking statements about the Company's sales and earnings and future plans and objectives. Any such statements are subject to risks and uncertainties that could cause the actual results to vary materially. These risks include, but are not limited to, business conditions in the coffee industry and food industry in general, fluctuations in availability and cost of green coffee, economic conditions, competition, variances from budgeted sales mix and growth rates, weather and special or unusual events.

The following table sets forth certain financial data of the Company expressed as a percentage of net sales for the periods denoted below:

Statement of Operations Data:	Year Ended		
	September 28, 1996	*September 30, 1995*	*September 24, 1994*
Net sales:			
Wholesale	79.1 %	74.9 %	68.7 %
Retail	13.0 %	15.0 %	18.2 %
Catalog Sales	7.9 %	10.1 %	13.1 %
Net sales	100.0 %	100.0 %	100.0 %
Cost of sales	59.5 %	63.9 %	61.2 %
Gross profit	40.5 %	36.1 %	38.8 %
Selling and operating expenses	27.3 %	28.0 %	39.5 %
General and administrative expenses	8.2 %	7.6 %	11.8 %
Income (loss) from operations	5.0 %	0.5 %	(12.5) %
Other income (expense)	- %	- %	0.3 %
Interest expense	(1.1) %	(1.2) %	(1.0) %
Income (loss) before income taxes	3.9 %	(0.7) %	(13.2) %
Income tax benefit (expense)	(0.6) %	0.1 %	2.5 %
Net income (loss)	3.3 %	(0.6) %	(10.7) %

FISCAL 1996
VERSUS FISCAL 1995

Net sales increased by $4,323,000 or 12.7% from $34,024,000 in fiscal 1995 (a 53-week period) to $38,347,000 in fiscal 1996 (a 52-week period). On a 52-week to 52-week comparative basis, sales are estimated to have increased by 15.0% in fiscal 1996. Coffee pounds sold, excluding those sold as beverages through the Company's retail stores, increased by approximately 864,000 pounds or 19.6% from 4,408,000 pounds in fiscal 1995 to 5,272,000 pounds in fiscal 1996. On a 52-week to 52-week comparative basis, coffee pounds sold are estimated to have increased 22.0% in fiscal 1996. The difference between the percentage increase in net sales and the percentage increase in coffee pounds sold primarily relates to reductions in Green Mountain's selling prices for coffee during fiscal 1996 as a result of lower green coffee costs.

The year-to-year increase in net sales occurred primarily in the wholesale area in which net sales increased by $4,856,000 or 19.1% from $25,484,000 in fiscal 1995 to $30,340,000 in fiscal 1996. This increase resulted primarily from the year-over-year growth in the number of wholesale accounts.

Net retail sales decreased by $136,000 or 2.7% from $5,106,000 in fiscal 1995 to $4,970,000 in fiscal 1996, principally due to the closing of three espresso carts located at supermarkets during the second quarter of fiscal 1995, and the closing of an espresso cart located in Albany, New York in the first quarter of fiscal 1996. The three supermarket espresso cart locations were converted to wholesale supermarket accounts with pre-bagged, bulk and/or self-service coffee beverage displays. On a 52-week to 52-week comparative basis, retail same-store sales are estimated to have increased 3.3% in fiscal 1996.

Net direct mail sales decreased by $397,000 or 11.6% from $3,434,000 in fiscal 1995 to $3,037,000 in fiscal 1996. This decrease resulted primarily from a shift in strategy whereby the Company focused its mail order solicitations on catalog customers who more regularly buy from the Company, and decreased the number of low-margin product promotions.

Green Mountain's gross profit increased by $3,244,000 or 26.4% from $12,286,000 in fiscal 1995 to $15,530,000 in fiscal 1996. Gross profit increased by 4.4 percentage points as a percentage of net sales from 36.1% in fiscal 1995 to 40.5% in fiscal 1996. These increases were primarily attributable to the impact of lower green coffee costs.

Selling and operating expenses increased by $942,000 or 9.9% from $9,529,000 in fiscal 1995 to $10,471,000 in fiscal 1996, but decreased .7 percentage points as a percentage of net sales from 28.0% in fiscal 1995 to 27.3% in fiscal 1996. The increase in selling and operating expense includes approximately $420,000 in expenses related to the addition in fiscal 1996 of a national supermarket sales manager, a national food service and office coffee services sales manager, and eight people to the Company's direct sales force in the Boston, Connecticut and Florida markets, as well as the addition of an advertising manager and designer to the Company's corporate marketing department.

General and administrative expenses increased by $554,000 or 21.5% from $2,578,000 in fiscal 1995 to $3,132,000 in fiscal 1996 and increased .6 percentage points as a percentage of net sales from 7.6% in fiscal 1995 to 8.2% in fiscal 1996. Significant general and administrative expense increases during fiscal 1996 include: increased MIS personnel and other computer-related expenses of approximately $130,000; increased training and human resource department costs of approximately $75,000; and increased investor relations related expenses of approximately $67,000.

As a result of the foregoing, income from operations increased by $1,748,000 or 976.5% from $179,000 in fiscal 1995 to $1,927,000 in fiscal 1996, and increased 4.5 percentage points as a percentage of net sales from 0.5% in fiscal 1995 to 5.0% in fiscal 1996. The income tax benefit recognized under SFAS 109 was $26,000 in fiscal 1995 compared to income tax expense of $222,000 in fiscal 1996. The Company's effective tax rate increased from 11% in fiscal 1995 to 15% in fiscal 1996, primarily as a result of non-deductible items being a greater percentage of the net loss in fiscal 1995 compared to the percentage of net income in fiscal 1996. Net income increased by $1,480,000 from a net loss of $218,000 in fiscal 1995 to net income of $1,262,000 in fiscal 1996.

FISCAL 1995 VERSUS
FISCAL 1994

Net sales increased by $11,942,000 or 54.1% from $22,082,000 in fiscal 1994 (a 52-week period) to $34,024,000 in fiscal 1995 (a 53-week period). Approximately 22 percentage points of the 54.1% full-year growth rate, or about 41% of the sales growth was due to price increases. Coffee pounds sold, excluding those sold as beverages through the Company's retail stores, increased by approximately 874,000 pounds or 24.7% from 3,534,000 pounds in fiscal 1994 to 4,408,000 pounds in fiscal 1995. On a 52-week to 52-week comparative basis, coffee pounds sold are estimated to have increased 24.7%.

The year-to-year net sales increase occurred mainly in the wholesale area in which net sales increased by $10,321,000 or 68.1% from $15,163,000 in fiscal 1994 to $25,484,000 in fiscal 1995. The wholesale net sales increase resulted primarily from increases in coffee prices to customers (approximately 44% of the 68.1% increase) related to the increased cost of green coffee, and from growth in the number of wholesale customer accounts (approximately 45% of the 68.1% increase).

Net retail sales increased $1,084,000 or 27.0% from $4,022,000 in fiscal 1994 to $5,106,000 in fiscal 1995, principally due to the opening of two new stores near the end of fiscal 1994. Net sales in the direct mail area increased $537,000 or 18.5%

from $2,897,000 in fiscal 1994 to $3,434,000 in fiscal 1995. The increase in direct mail sales resulted primarily from increases in coffee selling prices to customers, related to the increased cost of green coffee.

Gross profit increased by $3,717,000 or 43.4% from $8,569,000 in fiscal 1994 to $12,286,000 in fiscal 1995. As a percentage of net sales, gross profit decreased by 2.7 percentage points from 38.8% in fiscal 1994 to 36.1% in fiscal 1995. This decrease was due primarily to the increased cost of green coffee as a percentage of sales (i.e. Green Mountain passed on the dollar increase in green coffee, not the percentage increase) offset, in part, by lower production, distribution and delivery costs as a percentage of sales.

Selling and operating expenses increased by $807,000 or 9.3% from $8,722,000 in fiscal 1994 to $9,529,000 in fiscal 1995, primarily due to increased personnel and facility costs in fiscal 1995 related to the opening of new wholesale sales territories and retail stores during and following fiscal 1994, offset, in part, by decreased direct mail advertising expenditures. However, selling and operating expenses as a percentage of sales decreased by 11.5 percentage points from 39.5% in fiscal 1994 to 28.0% in fiscal 1995.

General and administrative expenses decreased by $27,000 or 1.0% from $2,605,000 in fiscal 1994 to $2,578,000 in fiscal 1995, and decreased by 4.2 percentage points as a percentage of net sales from 11.8% in fiscal 1994 to 7.6% in fiscal 1995. This decrease in general and administrative expenses reflects management's efforts to redeploy general and administrative personnel to more directly support the selling effort. However, general and administrative expenses as a percentage of sales increased by 3.0 percentage points for the fiscal fourth quarter from 4.5% in fiscal 1994 to 7.5% in fiscal 1995. The fiscal 1994 fourth quarter includes the impact of several short-term cost containment programs and a favorable year-end adjustment of $69,000 related to the Company's self-insured medical plan due to favorable loss experience.

As a result of the foregoing, income from operations for fiscal 1995 was $179,000 compared to a loss from operations of $2,758,000 for fiscal 1994, a $2,937,000 or 106.5% improvement. The income tax benefit recognized under SFAS 109 decreased by $531,000 or 95.3% from $557,000 in fiscal 1994 to $26,000 in fiscal 1995. The net loss decreased by $2,140,000 or 90.8% from $2,358,000 in fiscal 1994 to $218,000 in fiscal 1995.

LIQUIDITY AND CAPITAL RESOURCES

Working capital amounted to $2,433,000 and $745,000 at September 28, 1996 and September 30, 1995, respectively.

Cash used for capital expenditures aggregated $2,519,000 during fiscal 1996, and included $884,000 for equipment loaned to wholesale customers, $633,000 for production equipment, and $499,000 for computer hardware and software. During fiscal 1995, Green Mountain had capital expenditures of $1,602,000, including $961,000 for equipment on loan to wholesale customers, $333,000 for production equipment and $173,000 for computer hardware and software.

Cash used to fund the capital expenditures in fiscal 1996 was obtained from the $3,134,000 of net cash provided by operating activities. Net cash provided by operating activities reflects a $2,839,000 increase as compared to fiscal 1995, which resulted primarily from the Company's improved profitability together with the Company's efforts to control growth in accounts receivable.

The Company currently plans to make capital expenditures in fiscal 1997 of approximately $4,200,000, primarily to fund the purchase of equipment for loan to wholesale customers (approximately $2,000,000) and computer hardware and software (approximately $1,200,000). Assuming a stable mix in packaging types and sizes, management believes that it will operate at approximately 60-70% of capacity in fiscal 1997 and does not foresee significant production equipment expenditures during the year. However, management continuously reviews capital expenditure needs and actual amounts expended may differ from these estimates.

On April 12, 1996, the Company amended its credit facility with Fleet Bank - NH (Fleet). Under the revised facility, the Company borrowed $1,500,000 under a five-year term promissory note to be repaid in equal monthly principal installments. The interest rate on all term debt under the credit facility was reduced, subject to the election of the Company, to the lesser of the variable Fleet base rate (8.25% at September 28, 1996) plus 25 basis points or 275 basis points above the LIBOR rate for maturities of up to one year. The interest rate on this debt approximated 8.2% at September 28, 1996.

The interest rate of the Company's revolving line of credit under the amended Fleet credit facility was also reduced, subject to the election of the Company, to the lesser of the Fleet base rate or 250 basis points above the LIBOR rate for maturities of up to one year. The term of the revolving line of credit was also extended by one year to February 28, 1998. The outstanding balance on the revolving line of credit at September 28, 1996 was $508,000, with a total availability under the amended borrowing base formula capped at $3,000,000.

Management believes that cash flow from operations, existing cash and available borrowings under its credit facility and other sources will provide sufficient liquidity to pay all liabilities in the normal course of business, fund capital expenditures and service debt requirements for the next twelve months.

The average cost of the high quality arabica coffees the Company purchases decreased during fiscal 1996 as compared to fiscal 1995, and the Company's overall gross profit margin has improved. The Company passed the majority of such savings on to its customers through price reductions, and such price reductions had a negative impact on the Company's year-to-year percentage net sales growth rate.

The Company believes that the cost of green coffee will continue to be volatile in fiscal 1997, but expects that its average cost of green coffee in fiscal 1997 will be equivalent to, or less than, that experienced in fiscal 1996, although there can be no assurance that this will be the case. The Company believes that increases in the cost of green coffee can generally be passed on to customers or absorbed through more efficient operations, although there can be no assurance that the Company will be successful in doing so. Similarly, rapid sharp decreases in the cost of green coffee could also force the Company to lower sales prices before realizing cost reductions in its green coffee inventory. Because Green Mountain roasts over 25 different types of green coffee beans to produce its more than 70 different varieties of coffee, if one type of green coffee bean were to become unavailable or prohibitively expensive, management believes Green Mountain could substitute another type of coffee in a blend or temporarily remove that particular coffee from its product line.

DEFERRED INCOME TAXES

The Company had net deferred tax assets of $902,000 at September 28, 1996. These assets are reported net of a deferred tax asset valuation allowance at that date of $3,503,000 (including $2,681,000 primarily related to a Vermont investment tax credit

which is fully reserved). The Company had income before taxes of $1,484,000 in fiscal 1996 and has been profitable in seven of its last nine fiscal quarters including the last five consecutive fiscal quarters. Presently, the Company believes that the deferred tax assets, net of deferred tax liabilities and the valuation allowance, are realizable and represent management's best estimate, based on the weight of available evidence as prescribed in SFAS 109, of the amount of deferred tax assets which most likely will be realized. However, management will continue to evaluate the amount of the valuation allowance based on near-term operating results and longer-term projections.

SEASONALITY

Historically, the Company has experienced lower net sales levels in its second fiscal quarter following high holiday-related levels in its first fiscal quarter, especially in its retail and direct mail operations. This has historically resulted in less favorable operating results during the second fiscal quarter. In addition, quarterly results may be affected by a variety of other factors, including, but not limited to, general economic trends, competition, marketing programs, weather, and special or unusual events. Because of the seasonality of the Company's business, results for any quarter are not necessarily indicative of the results that may be achieved for the full fiscal year.

REPORT OF INDEPENDENT ACCOUNTANTS

Price Waterhouse LLP

To the Board of Directors and
Stockholders of Green Mountain Coffee, Inc.

In our opinion, the accompanying consolidated balance sheet and the related consolidated statements of operations, of changes in stockholders' equity and of cash flows present fairly, in all material respects, the financial position of Green Mountain Coffee, Inc. and its subsidiary at September 28, 1996 and September 30, 1995, and the results of their operations and their cash flows for each of the three years in the period ended September 28, 1996, in conformity with generally accepted accounting principles. These financial statements are the responsibility of the Company's management; our responsibility is to express an opinion on these financial statements based on our audits. We conducted our audits of these statements in accordance with generally accepted auditing standards which require that we plan and perform the audit to obtain reasonable assurance about whether the financial statements are free of material mis-statement. An audit includes examining, on a test basis, evidence supporting the amounts and disclosures in the financial statements, assessing the accounting principles used and significant estimates made by management, and evaluating the overall financial statement presentation. We believe that our audits provide a reasonable basis for the opinion expressed above.

Price Waterhouse LLP

Boston, Massachusetts
November 11, 1996

CONSOLIDATED BALANCE SHEET

(Dollars in thousands except share data)

	September 28, 1996	September 30, 1995
ASSETS		
Current assets:		
Cash and cash equivalents	$ 551	$ 310
Receivables, less allowances of $80 at September 28, 1996 and $63 at September 30, 1995	2,778	2,660
Inventories	3,276	2,766
Other current assets	627	377
Deferred income taxes, net	516	115
Total current assets	7,748	6,228
Fixed assets, net	8,715	8,127
Other long-term assets, net	394	235
Deferred income taxes, net	386	975
	$ 17,243	$ 15,565
LIABILITIES AND STOCKHOLDERS' EQUITY		
Current liabilities:		
Current portion of long-term debt	$ 947	$ 618
Current portion of obligation under capital lease	114	68
Revolving line of credit	508	1,720
Accounts payable	3,002	2,751
Accrued payroll	480	170
Accrued expenses	264	156
Total current liabilities	5,315	5,483
Long-term debt	2,911	2,351
Obligation under capital lease	144	209
Commitments (Notes 8 and 12)		
Stockholders' equity:		
Common stock, $0.10 par value: Authorized - 10,000,000 shares; issued and outstanding - 3,417,306 shares at September 28, 1996 and 3,399,795 shares at September 30, 1995	342	340
Additional paid-in capital	12,508	12,421
Accumulated deficit	(3,977)	(5,239)
Total stockholders' equity	8,873	7,522
	$ 17,243	$ 15,565

The accompanying Notes to Consolidated Financial Statements are an integral part of these financial statements.

CONSOLIDATED STATEMENT OF OPERATIONS

(Dollars in thousands except share data)

	Year ended		
	September 28, 1996	September 30, 1995	September 24, 1994
Net sales	$ 38,347	$ 34,024	$ 22,082
Cost of sales	22,817	21,738	13,513
Gross profit	15,530	12,286	8,569
Selling and operating expenses	10,471	9,529	8,722
General and administrative expenses	3,132	2,578	2,605
Income (loss) from operations	1,927	179	(2,758)
Other income (expense)	(21)	(24)	75
Interest expense	(422)	(399)	(232)
Income (loss) before income taxes	1,484	(244)	(2,915)
Income tax benefit (expense)	(222)	26	557
Net income (loss)	$ 1,262	$ (218)	$ (2,358)
Net income (loss) per share	$ 0.37	$ (0.06)	$ (0.70)
Weighted average shares outstanding	3,427,610	3,383,529	3,377,682

The accompanying Notes to Consolidated Financial Statements are an integral part of these financial statements.

C O N S O L I D A T E D   S T A T E M E N T   O F   C H A N G E S
I N   S T O C K H O L D E R S '   E Q U I T Y

For the years ended September 28, 1996,
September 30, 1995 and September 24, 1994
(Dollars in thousands except share data)

	Shares	*Common stock*	*Additional paid-in capital*	*Accumulated deficit*	*Total stockholders' equity*
Balance at September 25, 1993	3,376,286	$ 338	$ 12,353	$ (2,663)	$ 10,028
Additional issuance costs from initial public offering	-	-	(46)	-	(46)
Issuance of common stock under stock award plan	2,442	-	22	-	22
Issuance of common stock under employee stock purchase plan	4,757	-	21	-	21
Net loss	-	-	-	(2,358)	(2,358)
Balance at September 24, 1994	3,383,485	338	12,350	(5,021)	7,667
Issuance of common stock under employee stock purchase plan	16,310	2	71	-	73
Net loss	-	-	-	(218)	(218)
Balance at September 30, 1995	3,399,795	340	12,421	(5,239)	7,522
Issuance of common stock under employee stock purchase plan	17,511	2	87	-	89
Net income	-	-	-	1,262	1,262
Balance at September 28, 1996	3,417,306	$ 342	$ 12,508	$ (3,977)	$ 8,873

The accompanying Notes to Consolidated Financial Statements are an integral part of these financial statements

CONSOLIDATED STATEMENT OF CASH FLOWS

(Dollars in thousands)

	Year ended		
	September 28, 1996	September 30, 1995	September 24, 1994
Cash flows from operating activities:			
Net income (loss)	$ 1,262	$ (218)	$ (2,358)
Adjustments to reconcile net income (loss) to net cash provided by (used for) operating activities:			
Depreciation and amortization	2,026	1,624	1,239
Loss on disposal of fixed assets	47	15	6
Provision for (recovery of) doubtful accounts	156	157	(9)
Deferred income taxes	188	(26)	(557)
Changes in assets and liabilities:			
Receivables	(274)	(1,324)	(607)
Inventories	(510)	(359)	(981)
Other current assets	(250)	(57)	(96)
Other long-term assets, net	(180)	(97)	(103)
Accounts payable	251	758	(235)
Accrued payroll	310	(131)	70
Accrued expenses	108	(47)	(366)
Net cash provided by (used for) operating activities	3,134	295	(3,997)
Cash flows from investing activities:			
Expenditures for fixed assets	(2,519)	(1,602)	(4,323)
Proceeds from disposals of fixed assets	59	–	24
Net cash used for investing activities	(2,460)	(1,602)	(4,299)
Cash flows from financing activities:			
Proceeds from issuance of long-term debt	1,509	286	2,482
Repayment of long-term debt	(729)	(594)	(2,438)
Principal payments under capital lease obligation	(90)	(5)	–
Net change in revolving line of credit	(1,212)	1,720	(1,108)
Repayment of note payable to stockholder	–	(416)	(125)
Issuance of common stock, net of issuance costs	89	73	9,760
Net cash provided by (used for) financing activities	(433)	1,064	8,571
Net increase (decrease) in cash and cash equivalents	241	(243)	275
Cash and cash equivalents at beginning of year	310	553	278
Cash and cash equivalents at end of year	$ 551	$ 310	$ 553
Supplemental disclosures of cash flow information:			
Cash paid for interest	$ 401	$ 382	$ 224
Cash paid for income taxes	$ 5	$ 8	$ 9

The accompanying Notes to Consolidated Financial Statements are an integral part of these financial statements

1. *Nature of Business and Organization*

The accompanying consolidated financial statements include the accounts of Green Mountain Coffee, Inc. (the "Company") and its wholly-owned subsidiary, Green Mountain Coffee Roasters, Inc. All significant intercompany transactions and balances have been eliminated.

The Company purchases high-quality arabica coffee beans for roasting, then packages and distributes the roasted coffee primarily in the northeastern United States. The majority of the Company's revenue is derived from its wholesale operation which serves fine dining, supermarket, specialty food store, convenience store, food service, hotel, university, travel and office coffee service customers. The Company also has a direct mail operation servicing customers nationwide and currently operates twelve company-owned retail stores in Vermont, Connecticut, Illinois, Maine, Massachusetts, New Hampshire and New York.

The Company's fiscal year ends on the last Saturday in September. Fiscal 1996 and fiscal 1994 represent the years ended September 28, 1996 and September 24, 1994, respectively, and consist of 52 weeks. Fiscal 1995 represents the year ended September 30, 1995 and consists of 53 weeks.

2. *Significant Accounting Policies*

CASH AND CASH EQUIVALENTS

The Company considers all highly liquid investments purchased with a maturity of three months or less to be cash equivalents. Cash and cash equivalents include money market funds which are carried at cost, plus accrued interest, which approximates market. The Company does not believe that it is subject to any unusual credit and market risk.

INVENTORIES

Inventories are stated at the lower of cost or market with cost being determined by the first-in, first-out method.

OPTIONS ON FUTURES CONTRACTS

The Company enters into options contracts on coffee futures to hedge against potential increases in the price of green coffee beans. The resulting gain or loss from the sale of an option is applied to reduce or increase cost of goods sold, as applicable. For the years ended September 28, 1996, September 30, 1995 and September 24, 1994, the Company recognized gains (losses) of $(37,000), $(9,000) and $76,000, respectively, on hedging-related transactions. There were no open future contracts at September 28, 1996. Cash flows from the option transactions are classified with the related inventory.

ADVERTISING

The Company expenses the costs of advertising the first time the advertising takes place. Advertising expense totaled $1,427,000, $1,385,000 and $1,769,000 for the years ended September 28, 1996, September 30, 1995 and September 24, 1994, respectively.

FIXED ASSETS

Fixed assets are recorded at cost. Expenditures for maintenance, repairs and renewals of minor items are charged to expense as incurred. Depreciation of fixed assets is provided using the straight-line method.

Equipment under capital leases is amortized on the straight-line method over the shorter of the lease term or the estimated useful life of the equipment.

In order to facilitate sales, the Company follows an industry-wide practice of purchasing and loaning coffee brewing and related equipment to wholesale customers.

REVENUE RECOGNITION

Revenue from wholesale and mail order sales is recognized upon product shipment. Revenue from retail sales is recognized upon sale to customers.

INCOME TAXES

The Company utilizes the asset and liability method of accounting for income taxes, as set forth in Statement of Financial Accounting Standards ("SFAS") No. 109, "Accounting for Income Taxes." SFAS 109 requires the recognition of deferred tax assets and liabilities for the expected future tax consequences of temporary differences between the financial statement carrying amounts of existing assets and liabilities and their respective tax bases. Deferred tax assets and liabilities are measured using enacted tax rates in effect for the year in which those temporary differences are expected to be recovered or settled.

INCOME (LOSS) PER SHARE

Income (loss) per share is computed based upon the weighted average number of common and dilutive common equivalent shares outstanding during the year. Common equivalent shares represent the net additional shares resulting from the assumed exercise of outstanding stock options calculated using the "treasury stock" method.

STATEMENT OF CASH FLOWS

Following is a summary of noncash investing and financing activities:

During fiscal 1996, the Company financed approximately $109,000 for the purchase of five service vehicles.

During fiscal years 1996 and 1995, capital lease obligations of approximately $71,000 and $282,000 respectively, were incurred when the Company entered into leases for office and loaner equipment.

During fiscal 1995, approximately $61,000 of accrued use tax on production machinery, which had been capitalized in fiscal 1994, was reversed as a result of the State of Vermont determining that the Company qualified as a manufacturer.

FINANCIAL INSTRUMENTS

The Company enters into various types of financial instruments in the normal course of business. Fair values are estimated based on assumptions concerning the amount and timing of estimated future cash flows and assumed discount rates reflecting varying degrees of perceived risk. The fair values of cash, cash equivalents, accounts receivable, accounts payable, accrued expenses and debt approximate their carrying value at September 28, 1996.

USE OF ESTIMATES

The preparation of financial statements in conformity with generally accepted accounting principles requires management to make estimates and assumptions that affect the reported amount of assets and liabilities and disclosure of contingencies at September 28, 1996 and September 30, 1995, and the reported amounts of revenues and expenses during the three years in the period ended September 28, 1996. Actual results could differ from these estimates.

SIGNIFICANT CUSTOMER AND SUPPLY RISK

The Company has one customer which accounted for 12.1% and 10.4% of net sales in the years ended September 28, 1996 and September 30, 1995, respectively. During the year ended September 24, 1994, no customer accounted for more than 10% of the Company's net sales. Concentration of credit risk with respect to accounts receivable is limited due to the large number of customers in various industries comprising the Company's customer base. Ongoing credit evaluations of customers' payment history are performed, and collateral is not required. The Company maintains reserves for potential credit losses and such losses, in the aggregate, have not exceeded management's expectations.

The high-quality arabica coffees the Company purchases as its primary raw material are subject to supply and cost volatility caused by natural, political and other factors which typically affect agricultural products.

NEW ACCOUNTING PRONOUNCEMENT

In October 1995, the Financial Accounting Standards Board issued SFAS 123 ,"Accounting for Stock-Based Compensation." SFAS 123 establishes financial accounting and reporting standards for stock-based employee compensation plans. The statement defines a fair value based method of accounting for stock-based compensation which requires the recording of compensation expense in the financial statements. Companies electing not to adopt this fair value approach are required to disclose the effect on results of operations and earnings per share had the Company adopted the fair value approach. SFAS 123 will apply to the Company for fiscal year 1997, however, the disclosure requirement will include the effects of all awards granted in fiscal year 1996. The Company expects to retain its current method of accounting for stock-based compensation plans, and therefore, the adoption of SFAS 123 will have no impact on the Company's financial position or results of operations.

RECLASSIFICATIONS

Certain reclassifications of prior year balances have been made to conform to the current presentation.

3. Inventories

Inventories consist of the following:

	September 28, 1996	September 30, 1995
Raw materials and supplies	$ 1,291,000	$ 1,025,000
Finished goods	1,985,000	1,741,000
	$ 3,276,000	$ 2,766,000

4. Fixed Assets

Fixed assets consist of the following:

	Useful Life in Years	September 28, 1996	September 30, 1995
Leasehold improvements	5 - 10	$ 2,389,000	$ 2,150,000
Production equipment	5 - 10	4,456,000	4,095,000
Office equipment	4 - 10	3,774,000	3,186,000
Equipment on loan to wholesale customers	3 - 5	4,503,000	3,808,000
Vehicles	2 - 4	230,000	132,000
Construction-in-progress		499,000	102,000
Total fixed assets		15,851,000	13,473,000
Accumulated depreciation		(7,136,000)	(5,346,000)
		$ 8,715,000	$ 8,127,000

Included in office equipment and equipment on loan to wholesale customers at September 28, 1996 and September 30, 1995 are items recorded under a capital lease of $353,000 and $282,000 respectively. Amortization of these items is included in depreciation expense.

Depreciation expense totaled $2,005,000, $1,607,000, and $1,229,000 for the years ended September 28, 1996, September 30, 1995 and September 24, 1994, respectively.

5. Related Parties

NOTE PAYABLE TO STOCKHOLDER

At September 24, 1994, the Company had outstanding a note payable to the Company's majority stockholder totaling $416,000. The note was payable in quarterly installments of $25,000 and bore interest at 7.91%, payable monthly. The note was paid in full in April 1995. Interest paid by the Company to the majority stockholder for the years ended September 30, 1995 and September 24, 1994 was $15,000 and $36,000, respectively.

6. Income Taxes

The provision (benefit) for income taxes consists of:

	September 28, 1996	September 30, 1995	September 24, 1994
Current tax expense:			
U.S. federal	$ 447,000	$ -	$ -
State	120,000	10,000	-
Benefit of net operating loss carryforwards	(533,000)	(10,000)	-
Total current	34,000	-	-
Deferred tax expense (benefit)			
U.S. federal	515,000	(52,000)	(1,029,000)
State	(2,605,000)	(4,000)	(217,000)
Total deferred	(2,090,000)	(56,000)	(1,246,000)
Tax asset valuation allowance	2,278,000	30,000	689,000
Total tax expense (benefit)	$ 222,000	$ (26,000)	$ (557,000)

SFAS 109 is an asset and liability approach that requires the recognition of deferred tax assets and liabilities for the expected future tax consequences of events that have been recognized in the Company's financial statements or tax returns.

In estimating future tax consequences, SFAS 109 generally considers all expected future events other than enactments of changes in the tax law or rates.

Deferred tax assets (liabilities) consist of the following:

	September 28, 1996	September 30, 1995
Deferred tax assets:		
Net operating loss carryforwards	$ 1,744,000	$ 2,101,000
Investment tax credits	54,000	54,000
Vermont manufacturers investment tax credit	2,627,000	-
Section 263A adjustment	91,000	214,000
Other reserves and temporary differences	107,000	71,000
Gross deferred tax assets	4,623,000	2,440,000
Deferred tax asset valuation allowance	(3,503,000)	(1,225,000)
Deferred tax liability:		
Depreciation	(218,000)	(125,000)
Net deferred tax assets	$ 902,000	$ 1,090,000

At September 28, 1996, the Company had net operating loss carryforwards and investment tax credits for federal income tax reporting purposes of $3,599,000 and $54,000, respectively, which will expire between 1997 and 2009. In addition, in November 1996, the Company received notification from the State of Vermont that it had approved a $4,041,000 manufacturers investment tax credit pertaining to certain fixed assets purchased between July 1, 1993 and June 30, 1996, which will expire in 2005. The resulting deferred tax asset, which is fully offset by a valuation allowance, is reflected in the above table net of the federal tax effect.

Realization of the net deferred tax assets is dependent on generating sufficient taxable income prior to the expiration of the loss carryforwards. Although realization is not assured, management believes that the net deferred tax asset represents management's best estimate, based upon the weight of available evidence as prescribed in SFAS 109, of the amount which is more likely than not to be realized. If such evidence were to change, based upon near-term operating results and longer-term projections, the amount of the valuation allowance recorded against the gross deferred tax asset may be decreased or increased. Also, if certain substantial changes in the Company's ownership should occur, there would be an annual limitation on the amount of loss carryforwards which could be utilized, and restrictions on the utilization of investment tax credit carryforwards.

A reconciliation between the amount of reported income tax expense (benefit) and the amount computed using the U.S. Federal Statutory rate of 35% is as follows:

	September 28, 1996	September 30, 1995	September 24, 1994
Tax at U.S. Federal Statutory rate	$ 519,000	$ (85,000)	$(1,020,000)
Increase (decrease) in rates resulting from:			
Other nondeductible items	22,000	33,000	6,000
State taxes, net of federal benefit	(2,597,000)	(4,000)	(232,000)
Deferred tax asset valuation allowance	2,278,000	30,000	689,000
Tax at effective rates	$ 222,000	$ (26,000)	$ (557,000)

7. Revolving Line of Credit

The Company maintains a revolving line of credit agreement under a comprehensive credit facility ("credit facility") with Fleet Bank - NH ("Fleet"). Borrowings under the agreement are limited to $3,000,000 under a borrowing base formula and are secured by substantially all of the Company's assets. In April 1996, the Company amended the credit facility which extended the availability of the line of credit through February 28, 1998, and reduced the interest rate on the revolving line of credit, subject to the election of the Company, to the lesser of Fleet's variable base lending rate (8.25% at September 28, 1996) or 250 basis points above the LIBOR rate up to 30 days. The terms of the credit facility also provide for the maintenance of specified financial ratios and restrict certain transactions, including a prohibition from paying any dividends without prior bank approval. The Company was in compliance with these covenants at September 28, 1996.

The principal amount outstanding on the revolving line of credit at September 28, 1996 and September 30, 1995 was $508,000 and $1,720,000, respectively.

8. *Long-Term Debt*

	September 28, 1996	September 30, 1995
Facility and Equipment Term Loan	$ 2,827,000	$ 1,839,000
Central Vermont Economic Development Corporation Debenture	600,000	665,000
Vermont Economic Development Authority Promissory Note	182,000	222,000
Computer Equipment Installment Loans	153,000	219,000
Service Vehicle Installment Loans	96,000	24,000
	3,858,000	2,969,000
Less-current portion	947,000	618,000
	$ 2,911,000	$ 2,351,000

FACILITY AND EQUIPMENT TERM LOANS

As part of the credit facility, the Company has financed fixed asset purchases under five term loans which are secured by a senior lien on substantially all of the Company's assets and by a security interest in the fixed assets for which the borrowings are made. Under the amended credit facility, the existing equipment line of credit was eliminated and the Company borrowed an additional $1,500,000 under a new five-year promissory note to be repaid in equal monthly principal installments. The interest rate on all term loans under the credit facility was reduced to the lesser of 25 basis points above the variable Fleet base rate or 275 basis points above the LIBOR rate for maturities of up to one year (8.2% at September 28, 1996). The original terms of the loans range from 56 to 84 months and are being repaid in equal monthly payments totaling approximately $60,600 plus interest.

CENTRAL VERMONT ECONOMIC DEVELOPMENT CORPORATION DEBENTURE

The debenture from the Central Vermont Economic Development Corporation (CVEDC) is guaranteed by the U.S. Small Business Administration. The debenture term is ten years and requires equal monthly principal and interest payments of approximately $8,500 and carries a fixed interest rate of 5.812%. The debenture is secured by a secondary security interest in the related fixed assets and is guaranteed by the majority stockholder of the Company. Additional guarantees will be required of any stockholder obtaining more than 20% ownership of the Company.

VERMONT ECONOMIC DEVELOPMENT AUTHORITY PROMISSORY NOTE

The Vermont Economic Development Authority promissory note is payable in monthly principal and interest installments of approximately $4,300 over seven years, with an interest rate of 5.5%. The note is secured by a secondary security interest in the related fixed assets and contains covenants related to restrictions on prepayments of certain portions of the Company's remaining outstanding debt as defined in the underlying agreement. The Company was in compliance with these covenants at September 28, 1996.

COMPUTER EQUIPMENT INSTALLMENT LOANS

The computer equipment installment loans bear interest at 8.69%, and require monthly installments of principal and interest totaling approximately $7,600 through September 1998.

SERVICE VEHICLE INSTALLMENT LOANS

The service vehicle installment loans represent several loans to financing institutions for the purchase of service vehicles. The notes bear interest at rates between 4.8% and 7.4% and require monthly installments of principal and interest totaling approximately $3,500 through February 2000.

MATURITIES

Maturities of long-term debt for years subsequent to September 28, 1996 are as follows:

Fiscal Year	
1997	$ 947,000
1998	943,000
1999	835,000
2000	581,000
2001	314,000
Thereafter	238,000
	$ 3,858,000

9. *Employee Compensation Plans*

STOCK OPTION PLANS

Prior to the establishment on September 21, 1993 of the employee stock option plan (the "1993 Plan"), the Company granted to certain key management employees, individual non-qualified stock option agreements to purchase shares of the Company's common stock. All such options presently outstanding are fully vested and had an original expiration date after the fifth anniversary following the date of grant or earlier if employment terminates. Effective July 26, 1996, the term of 141,440 of such options was extended for an additional five years. The exercise price of these options exceeded the fair market value of the common stock at the date of the extension. At September 28, 1996, 212,166 options were outstanding under these individual agreements.

The 1993 Plan provides for the granting of both incentive and non-qualified stock options, with an aggregate number of 75,000 shares of common stock to be made available under the 1993 Plan. Effective July 26, 1996, and subject to approval by a majority of stockholders at the next Annual Stockholders' Meeting, the total number of shares of authorized common stock to be made available under the 1993 Plan was increased to 275,000. The option price for each incentive stock option shall not be less than the fair market value per share of common stock on the date of grant, with certain provisions which increase the option price to 110% of the fair market value of the common stock if the grantee owns in excess of 10% of the Company's common stock at the date of grant. The option price for each nonqualified stock option shall not be less than 85% of the fair market value of the common stock at the date of grant. Options under the Plan become exercisable over periods determined by the Board of Directors at a rate generally not to exceed 25% per year beginning with the first anniversary of the date of grant. At September 28, 1996 and September 30, 1995, options for 196,005 and 9,565 shares of common stock were available for grant under the plan, respectively.

On April 21, 1994, the Company entered into a marketing consulting agreement (the "Agreement") and granted 50,000 nonqualified options (separate from the 1993 Plan) to the consultant. The exercise price of the options is equal to the market value of the Company's common stock determined on the date of vesting and has an expiration date of two years following the earlier of the termination or expiration of the Agreement. Upon execution of the agreement, 20,000 of the options vested at an exercise price of $6.88 each, and 5,000 additional options were to vest at the end of each 6 month period over the term of the Agreement up to a maximum of 50,000 options in the aggregate. On October 21, 1994, 5,000 additional options vested under the Agreement at an exercise price of $6.50. The remaining 25,000 options were cancelled prior to the next scheduled vesting date as a result of the termination of the Agreement.

Option activity is summarized as follows:

	Number of shares	Option price per share
Outstanding at September 25, 1993	271,101	$ 2.55-8.02
Granted	65,000	$ 6.00-6.88
Exercised	-	-
Cancelled	(47,148)	$ 2.55
Outstanding at September 24, 1994	288,953	$ 2.55-8.02
Granted	59,684	$ 8.50
Exercised	-	-
Cancelled	(34,248)	$ 8.50
Outstanding at September 30, 1995	314,389	$ 2.55-8.50
Granted	18,400	$ 6.25-8.50
Exercised	-	-
Cancelled	(16,627)	$ 8.02-8.50
Outstanding at September 28, 1996	316,162	$ 2.55-8.50

At September 28, 1996, 60,022 of these options were not exercisable.

EMPLOYEE STOCK PURCHASE PLAN

On September 21, 1993, the Company approved the adoption of an Employee Stock Purchase Plan (the "Purchase Plan"). Under the Purchase Plan, the Company reserved 75,000 shares of common stock for purchase by eligible employees. The Purchase Plan provides for five annual offerings of 15,000 shares of common stock per offering, plus any unissued shares from prior fiscal years. Each participating employee has the option to purchase a maximum number of shares equal to 10% of the participant's base pay, divided by 85% of the market value of the common stock at such time, subject to a pro rata reduction of shares if the annual aggregate maximum number of shares offered by the Company would otherwise be exceeded. On September 24, 1994, 4,757 options were exercised under the fiscal 1994 offering, generating proceeds to the Company of $21,000. On September 30, 1995, 16,310 options were exercised under the fiscal 1995 offering, generating proceeds to the Company of $73,000. On September 28, 1996, 17,511 options were exercised under the fiscal 1996 offering, generating proceeds to the Company of $89,000.

For the fiscal 1997 offering there are outstanding options to purchase 20,273 shares under the Purchase Plan at a maximum exercise price of $6.06. The ultimate purchase price of the underlying shares of common stock is 85% of the fair market value of the common stock at the beginning or end of the fiscal year, whichever is less.

10. Defined Contribution Plan

The Company has a defined contribution plan which meets the requirements of Section 401(k) of the Internal Revenue Code. All employees of the Company with one year or more of service who are at least twenty-one years of age are eligible to participate in the plan. The plan allows employees to defer a portion of their salary on a pre-tax basis and the Company contributes 50% of amounts contributed by employees up to 5% of their salary. Company contributions to the plan amounted to $73,000, $52,000 and $29,000 for the years ended September 28, 1996, September 30, 1995 and September 24, 1994, respectively.

11. Warrants

The Company issued warrants for 100,000 shares of the Company's common stock on September 21, 1993 to its underwriter in conjunction with the Company's initial public offering. The warrants carry an exercise price of $12 per share and expire on September 21, 1998. The Company has reserved 100,000 shares of common stock in connection with these warrants.

12. Commitments

LEASES

The Company leases office and retail space, production, distribution and service facilities and certain equipment under various noncancelable operating leases, ranging from one to ten years. Property leases normally require payment of a minimum annual rental plus a pro-rata share of certain landlord operating expenses. In addition, a number of the Company's retail space leases require payment of contingent rentals based upon a percentage of sales in excess of a specified amount.

The Company has entered into a capital lease, primarily for loaner and office equipment.

Minimum future lease payments (net of committed sublease rental receipts of $33,000 for the fiscal years 1997 through 2001, and $43,000 thereafter) under noncancelable operating leases and capital leases, for years subsequent to September 28, 1996 are as follows:

Fiscal Year	Operating Leases	Capital Lease
1997	$ 1,053,000	$ 145,000
1998	941,000	145,000
1999	839,000	12,000
2000	729,000	-
2001	665,000	-
Thereafter	870,000	-
Total minimum lease payments	$ 5,097,000	302,000
Less - amount representing interest		44,000
Present value of obligations under capital lease (including current portion of $114,000)		$ 258,000

Rent expense (net of sublease income of $33,000, $30,000 and $35,000 for the years ended September 28, 1996, September 30, 1995 and September 24, 1994, respectively), under these operating leases was $991,000, $887,000 and $753,000 for the years ended September 28, 1996, September 30, 1995 and September 24, 1994, respectively.

APPENDIX C

Time Value of Money

STUDY OBJECTIVES

After studying this appendix, you should be able to:

1. Distinguish between simple and compound interest.
2. Solve for future value of a single amount.
3. Solve for future value of an annuity.
4. Identify the variables fundamental to solving present value problems.
5. Solve for present value of a single amount.
6. Solve for present value of an annuity.
7. Compute the present values in capital budgeting situations.

Would you rather receive $1,000 today or a year from now? You should prefer to receive the $1,000 today because you can invest the $1,000 and earn interest on it. As a result, you will have more than $1,000 a year from now. What this example illustrates is the concept of the **time value of money.** Everyone prefers to receive money today rather than in the future because of the interest factor.

NATURE OF INTEREST

Interest is payment for the use of another person's money. It is the difference between the amount borrowed or invested (called the **principal**) and the amount repaid or collected. The amount of interest to be paid or collected is usually stated as a rate over a specific period of time. The rate of interest is generally stated as an annual rate.

The amount of interest involved in any financing transaction is based on three elements:

1. **Principal (p):** The original amount borrowed or invested.
2. **Interest Rate (i):** An annual percentage of the principal.
3. **Time (n):** The number of years that the principal is borrowed or invested.

SIMPLE INTEREST

Simple interest is computed on the principal amount only. It is the return on the principal for one period. Simple interest is usually expressed as shown in Illustration C-1.

Illustration C-1 Interest computation

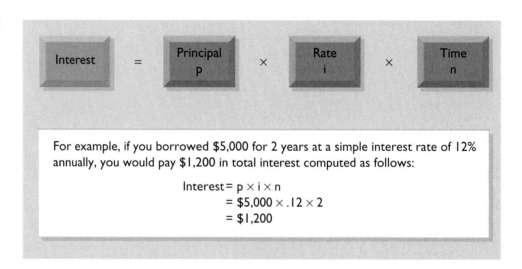

For example, if you borrowed $5,000 for 2 years at a simple interest rate of 12% annually, you would pay $1,200 in total interest computed as follows:

$$\text{Interest} = p \times i \times n$$
$$= \$5,000 \times .12 \times 2$$
$$= \$1,200$$

COMPOUND INTEREST

Compound interest is computed on principal **and** on any interest earned that has not been paid or withdrawn. It is the return on (or growth of) the principal for two or more time periods. Compounding computes interest not only on the principal but also on the interest earned to date on that principal, assuming the interest is left on deposit.

To illustrate the difference between simple and compound interest, assume that you deposit $1,000 in Bank One, where it will earn simple interest of 9% per year, and you deposit another $1,000 in CityCorp, where it will earn compound interest of 9% per year compounded annually. Also assume that in both cases you will not withdraw any interest until 3 years from the date of deposit. The computation of interest to be received and the accumulated year-end balances are indicated in Illustration C-2.

Illustration C-2 Simple vs. compound interest

Bank One				City Corp.		
Simple Interest Calculation	Simple Interest	Accumulated Year-end Balance		Compound Interest Calculation	Compound Interest	Accumulated Year-end Balance
Year 1 $1,000.00 × 9%	$ 90.00	$1,090.00		Year 1 $1,000.00 × 9%	$ 90.00	$1,090.00
Year 2 $1,000.00 × 9%	90.00	$1,180.00		Year 2 $1,090.00 × 9%	98.10	$1,188.10
Year 3 $1,000.00 × 9%	90.00	$1,270.00		Year 3 $1,188.10 × 9%	106.93	$1,295.03
	$ 270.00		$25.03 Difference		$ 295.03	

Note in the illustration above that simple interest uses the initial principal of $1,000 to compute the interest in all 3 years. Compound interest uses the accumulated balance (principal plus interest to date) at each year-end to compute interest in the succeeding year—which explains why your compound interest account is larger.

Obviously if you had a choice between investing your money at simple interest or at compound interest, you would choose compound interest, all other things—especially risk—being equal. In the example, compounding provides $25.03 of additional interest income. For practical purposes compounding assumes that unpaid interest earned becomes a part of the principal, and the accumulated balance at the end of each year becomes the new principal on which interest is earned during the next year.

As can be seen in Illustration C-2, you should invest your money at CityCorp which compounds interest annually. Compound interest is used in most business situations. Simple interest is generally applicable only to short-term situations of one year or less.

SECTION 1
FUTURE VALUE CONCEPTS

FUTURE VALUE OF A SINGLE AMOUNT

The future value of a single amount is the value at a future date of a given amount invested assuming compound interest. For example, in Illustration C-2, $1,295.03 is the future value of the $1,000 at the end of 3 years. The $1,295.03 could be determined more easily by using the following formula:

$$FV = p \times (1 + i)^n$$

where:

> FV = future value of a single amount
> p = principal (or present value)
> i = interest rate for one period
> n = number of periods

STUDY OBJECTIVE

2

Solve for future value of a single amount.

The $1,295.03 is computed as follows:

$$FV = p \times (1 + i)^n$$
$$= \$1,000 \times (1 + i)^3$$
$$= \$1,000 \times 1.29503$$
$$= \$1,295.03$$

The 1.29503 is computed by multiplying (1.09 × 1.09 × 1.09). The amounts in this example can be depicted in the following time diagram:

Illustration C-3 Time diagram

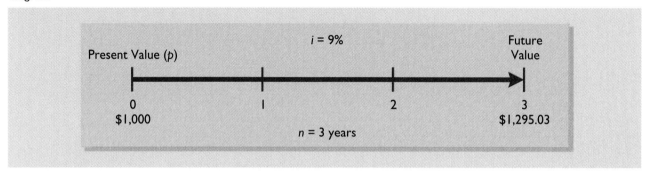

Another method that may be used to compute the future value of a single amount involves the use of a compound interest table. This table shows the future value of 1 for n periods. Table 1, shown below, is such a table.

TABLE 1 Future Value of 1

(n) Periods	4%	5%	6%	8%	9%	10%	11%	12%	15%
1	1.04000	1.05000	1.06000	1.08000	1.09000	1.10000	1.11000	1.12000	1.15000
2	1.08160	1.10250	1.12360	1.16640	1.18810	1.21000	1.23210	1.25440	1.32250
3	1.12486	1.15763	1.19102	1.25971	1.29503	1.33100	1.36763	1.40493	1.52088
4	1.16986	1.21551	1.26248	1.36049	1.41158	1.46410	1.51807	1.57352	1.74901
5	1.21665	1.27628	1.33823	1.46933	1.53862	1.61051	1.68506	1.76234	2.01136
6	1.26532	1.34010	1.41852	1.58687	1.67710	1.77156	1.87041	1.97382	2.31306
7	1.31593	1.40710	1.50363	1.71382	1.82804	1.94872	2.07616	2.21068	2.66002
8	1.36857	1.47746	1.59385	1.85093	1.99256	2.14359	2.30454	2.47596	3.05902
9	1.42331	1.55133	1.68948	1.99900	2.17189	2.35795	2.55803	2.77308	3.51788
10	1.48024	1.62889	1.79085	2.15892	2.36736	2.59374	2.83942	3.10585	4.04556
11	1.53945	1.71034	1.89830	2.33164	2.58043	2.85312	3.15176	3.47855	4.65239
12	1.60103	1.79586	2.01220	2.51817	2.81267	3.13843	3.49845	3.89598	5.35025
13	1.66507	1.88565	2.13293	2.71962	3.06581	3.45227	3.88328	4.36349	6.15279
14	1.73168	1.97993	2.26090	2.93719	3.34173	3.79750	4.31044	4.88711	7.07571
15	1.80094	2.07893	2.39656	3.17217	3.64248	4.17725	4.78459	5.47357	8.13706
16	1.87298	2.18287	2.54035	3.42594	3.97031	4.59497	5.31089	6.13039	9.35762
17	1.94790	2.29202	2.69277	3.70002	4.32763	5.05447	5.89509	6.86604	10.76126
18	2.02582	2.40662	2.85434	3.99602	4.71712	5.55992	6.54355	7.68997	12.37545
19	2.10685	2.52695	3.02560	4.31570	5.14166	6.11591	7.26334	8.61276	14.23177
20	2.19112	2.65330	3.20714	4.66096	5.60441	6.72750	8.06231	9.64629	16.36654

In Table 1, n is the number of compounding periods, the percentages are the periodic interest rates, and the 5-digit decimal numbers in the respective columns are the future value of 1 factors. In using Table 1, the principal amount is multiplied by the future value factor for the specified number of periods and interest rate. For example, the future value factor for 2 periods at 9% is 1.18810. Multiplying this factor by $1,000 equals $1,188.10, which is the accumulated balance at the end of year 2 in the CityCorp example in Illustration C-2. The $1,295.03 accumulated balance at the end of the third year can be calculated from Table 1 by multiplying the future value factor for 3 periods (1.29503) by the $1,000.

The following demonstration problem illustrates how to use Table 1.

Illustration C-4
Demonstration Problem—Using Table 1 for FV of 1

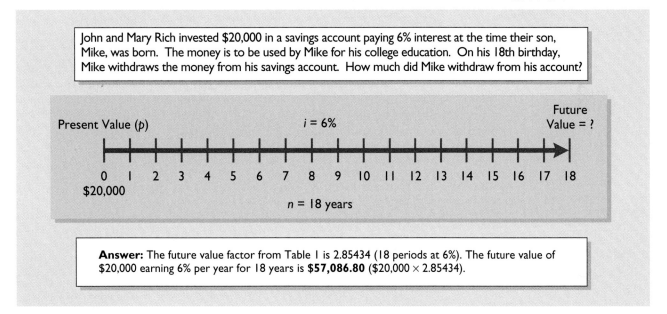

John and Mary Rich invested $20,000 in a savings account paying 6% interest at the time their son, Mike, was born. The money is to be used by Mike for his college education. On his 18th birthday, Mike withdraws the money from his savings account. How much did Mike withdraw from his account?

Present Value (p)   i = 6%   Future Value = ?

0 1 2 3 4 5 6 7 8 9 10 11 12 13 14 15 16 17 18
$20,000

n = 18 years

Answer: The future value factor from Table 1 is 2.85434 (18 periods at 6%). The future value of $20,000 earning 6% per year for 18 years is **$57,086.80** ($20,000 × 2.85434).

*F*UTURE *V*ALUE OF AN *A*NNUITY

The preceding discussion involved the accumulation of only a single principal sum. Individuals and businesses frequently encounter situations in which a series of equal dollar amounts are to be paid or received periodically, such as loans or lease (rental) contracts. Such payments or receipts of equal dollar amounts are referred to as annuities. The future value of an annuity is the sum of all the payments (receipts) plus the accumulated compound interest on them. In computing the future value of an annuity, it is necessary to know (1) the interest rate, (2) the number of compounding periods, and (3) the amount of the periodic payments or receipts.

To illustrate the computation of the future value of an annuity, assume that you invest $2,000 at the end of each year for 3 years at 5% interest compounded annually. This situation is depicted in the time diagram in Illustration C-5.

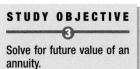

STUDY OBJECTIVE
3
Solve for future value of an annuity.

Illustration C-5   Time diagram for a 3-year annuity

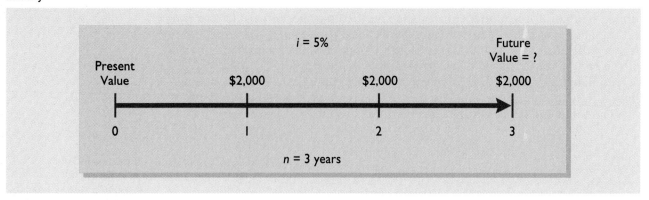

As can be seen in Illustration C-5, the $2,000 invested at the end of year 1 will earn interest for 2 years (year 2 & 3) and the $2,000 invested at the end of year 2 will earn interest for 1 year (year 3). However, the last $2,000 investment (made at the end of year 3) will not earn any interest. The future value of these periodic payments could be computed using the future value factors from Table 1 as shown in Illustration C-6:

Illustration C-6
Future value of periodic payments

Year Invested	Amount Invested	×	Future Value of 1 Factor at 5%	=	Future Value
1	$2,000	×	1.10250		$2,205
2	$2,000	×	1.05000		2,100
3	$2,000	×	1.00000		2,000
			3.15250		$6,305

The first $2,000 investment is multiplied by the future value factor for 2 periods (1.1025) because 2 years' interest will accumulate on it (in years 2 & 3). The second $2,000 investment will earn only 1 year's interest (in year 3) and therefore is multiplied by the future value factor for 1 year (1.0500). The final $2,000 investment is made at the end of the third year and will not earn any interest. Consequently, the future value of the last $2,000 invested is only $2,000 since it does not accumulate any interest.

This method of calculation is required when the periodic payments or receipts are not equal in each period. However, when the periodic payments (receipts) are the same in each period, the future value can be computed by using a future value of an annuity of 1 table. Table 2, shown below, is such a table.

TABLE 2   Future Value of an Annuity of 1

(n) Periods	4%	5%	6%	8%	9%	10%	11%	12%	15%
1	1.00000	1.00000	1.00000	1.00000	1.00000	1.00000	1.00000	1.00000	1.00000
2	2.04000	2.05000	2.06000	2.08000	2.09000	2.10000	2.11000	2.12000	2.15000
3	3.12160	3.15250	3.18360	3.24640	3.27810	3.31000	3.34210	3.37440	3.47250
4	4.24646	4.31013	4.37462	4.50611	4.57313	4.64100	4.70973	4.77933	4.99338
5	5.41632	5.52563	5.63709	5.86660	5.98471	6.10510	6.22780	6.35285	6.74238
6	6.63298	6.80191	6.97532	7.33592	7.52334	7.71561	7.91286	8.11519	8.75374
7	7.89829	8.14201	8.39384	8.92280	9.20044	9.48717	9.78327	10.08901	11.06680
8	9.21423	9.54911	9.89747	10.63663	11.02847	11.43589	11.85943	12.29969	13.72682
9	10.58280	11.02656	11.49132	12.48756	13.02104	13.57984	14.16397	14.77566	16.78584
10	12.00611	12.57789	13.18079	14.48656	15.19293	15.93743	16.72201	17.54874	20.30372
11	13.48635	14.20679	14.97164	16.64549	17.56029	18.53117	19.56143	20.65458	24.34928
12	15.02581	15.91713	16.86994	18.97713	20.14072	21.38428	22.71319	24.13313	29.00167
13	16.62684	17.71298	18.88214	21.49530	22.95339	24.52271	26.21164	28.02911	34.35192
14	18.29191	19.59863	21.01507	24.21492	26.01919	27.97498	30.09492	32.39260	40.50471
15	20.02359	21.57856	23.27597	27.15211	29.36092	31.77248	34.40536	37.27972	47.58041
16	21.82453	23.65749	25.67253	30.32428	33.00340	35.94973	39.18995	42.75328	55.71747
17	23.69751	25.84037	28.21288	33.75023	36.97351	40.54470	44.50084	48.88367	65.07509
18	25.64541	28.13238	30.90565	37.45024	41.30134	45.59917	50.39593	55.74972	75.83636
19	27.67123	30.53900	33.75999	41.44626	46.01846	51.15909	56.93949	63.43968	88.21181
20	29.77808	33.06595	36.78559	45.76196	51.16012	57.27500	64.20283	72.05244	102.44358

Table 2 shows the future value of 1 to be received periodically for a given number of periods. From Table 2 it can be seen that the future value of an annuity of 1 factor for 3 periods at 5% is 3.15250. The future value factor is the total of the three individual future value factors as shown in Illustration C-6. Multiplying this amount by the annual investment of $2,000 produces a future value of $6,305.

The demonstration problem in Illustration C-7 illustrates how to use Table 2.

Illustration C-7
Demonstration
Problem—Using Table 2
for FV of an annuity of 1

Henning Printing Company knows that in four years it must replace one of its existing printing presses with a new one. To insure that some funds are available to replace the machine in four years, the company is depositing $25,000 in a savings account at the end of each of the next four years (4 deposits in total). The savings account will earn 6% interest compounded annually. How much will be in the savings account at the end of four years when the new printing press is to be purchased?

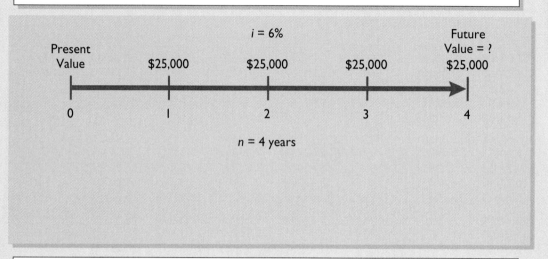

Answer: The future value factor from Table 2 is 4.37462 (4 periods at 6%). The future value of $25,000 invested at the end of each year for 4 years at 6% interest is **$109,365.50** ($25,000 × 4.37462).

SECTION 2
PRESENT VALUE CONCEPTS

PRESENT VALUE VARIABLES

STUDY OBJECTIVE
— 4 —
Identify the variables fundamental to solving present value problems.

The **present value,** like the future value, is based on three variables: (1) the dollar amount to be received (future amount), (2) the length of time until the amount is received (number of periods), and (3) the interest rate (the discount rate). The process of determining the present value is referred to as **discounting the future amount.**

In this textbook, present value computations are used in measuring several items. For example, capital budgeting and other investment proposals are evaluated using present value computations. All rate of return and internal rate of return computations involve present value techniques.

PRESENT VALUE OF A SINGLE AMOUNT

To illustrate present value concepts, assume that you are willing to invest a sum of money that will yield $1,000 at the end of one year. In other words, what amount would you need to invest today to have $1,000 one year from now? If you want a 10% rate of return, the investment or present value is $909.09 ($1,000 ÷ 1.10). The computation of this amount is shown in Illustration C-8.

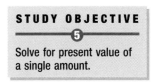

STUDY OBJECTIVE
⑤
Solve for present value of a single amount.

$$\text{Present Value} = \text{Future Value} \div (1 + i)^1$$
$$PV = FV \div (1 + 10\%)^1$$
$$PV = \$1,000 \div 1.10$$
$$\mathbf{PV = \$909.09}$$

Illustration C-8 Present value computation—$1,000 discounted at 10% for 1 year

The future amount ($1,000), the discount rate (10%), and the number of periods (1) are known. The variables in this situation can be depicted in the following time diagram:

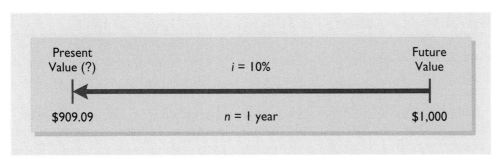

Illustration C-9 Finding present value if discounted for one period

If the single amount of $1,000 is to be received **in 2 years** and discounted at 10% [PV = $1,000 ÷ (1 + 10%)^2], its present value is $826.45 [($1,000 ÷ 1.10) ÷ 1.10], depicted as follows:

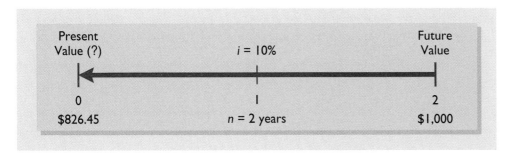

Illustration C-10 Finding present value if discounted for two periods

The present value of 1 may also be determined through tables that show the present value of 1 for n periods. In Table 3, n is the number of discounting periods involved. The percentages are the periodic interest rates or discount rates, and the 5-digit decimal numbers in the respective columns are the present value of 1 factors.

TABLE 3   Present Value of 1

(*n*) Periods	4%	5%	6%	8%	9%	10%	11%	12%	15%
1	.96154	.95238	.94340	.92593	.91743	.90909	.90090	.89286	.86957
2	.92456	.90703	.89000	.85734	.84168	.82645	.81162	.79719	.75614
3	.88900	.86384	.83962	.79383	.77218	.75132	.73119	.71178	.65752
4	.85480	.82270	.79209	.73503	.70843	.68301	.65873	.63552	.57175
5	.82193	.78353	.74726	.68058	.64993	.62092	.59345	.56743	.49718
6	.79031	.74622	.70496	.63017	.59627	.56447	.53464	.50663	.43233
7	.75992	.71068	.66506	.58349	.54703	.51316	.48166	.45235	.37594
8	.73069	.67684	.62741	.54027	.50187	.46651	.43393	.40388	.32690
9	.70259	.64461	.59190	.50025	.46043	.42410	.39092	.36061	.28426
10	.67556	.61391	.55839	.46319	.42241	.38554	.35218	.32197	.24719
11	.64958	.58468	.52679	.42888	.38753	.35049	.31728	.28748	.21494
12	.62460	.55684	.49697	.39711	.35554	.31863	.28584	.25668	.18691
13	.60057	.53032	.46884	.36770	.32618	.28966	.25751	.22917	.16253
14	.57748	.50507	.44230	.34046	.29925	.26333	.23199	.20462	.14133
15	.55526	.48102	.41727	.31524	.27454	.23939	.20900	.18270	.12289
16	.53391	.45811	.39365	.29189	.25187	.21763	.18829	.16312	.10687
17	.51337	.43630	.37136	.27027	.23107	.19785	.16963	.14564	.09293
18	.49363	.41552	.35034	.25025	.21199	.17986	.15282	.13004	.08081
19	.47464	.39573	.33051	.23171	.19449	.16351	.13768	.11611	.07027
20	.45639	.37689	.31180	.21455	.17843	.14864	.12403	.10367	.06110

When Table 3 is used, the future value is multiplied by the present value factor specified at the intersection of the number of periods and the discount rate. For example, the present value factor for 1 period at a discount rate of 10% is .90909, which equals the $909.09 ($1,000 × .90909) computed in Illustration C-8. For 2 periods at a discount rate of 10%, the present value factor is .82645, which equals the $826.45 ($1,000 × .82645) computed previously.

Note that a higher discount rate produces a smaller present value. For example, using a 15% discount rate, the present value of $1,000 due one year from now is $869.57 versus $909.09 at 10%. It should also be recognized that the further removed from the present the future value is, the smaller the present value. For example, using the same discount rate of 10%, the present value of $1,000 due in **five** years is $620.92 versus $1,000 due in **one** year is $909.09.

The following two demonstration problems (Illustrations C-11, C-12) illustrate how to use Table 3.

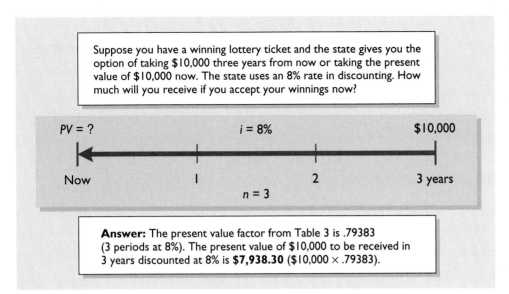

Illustration C-11
**Demonstration
Problem**—Using Table 3
for PV of 1

Suppose you have a winning lottery ticket and the state gives you the option of taking $10,000 three years from now or taking the present value of $10,000 now. The state uses an 8% rate in discounting. How much will you receive if you accept your winnings now?

PV = ?   i = 8% $10,000

Now   1   2   3 years
              n = 3

Answer: The present value factor from Table 3 is .79383 (3 periods at 8%). The present value of $10,000 to be received in 3 years discounted at 8% is **$7,938.30** ($10,000 × .79383).

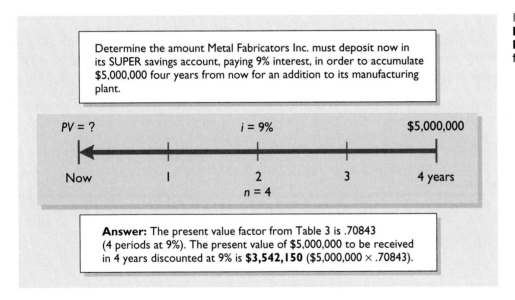

Illustration C-12
**Demonstration
Problem**—Using Table 3
for PV of 1

Determine the amount Metal Fabricators Inc. must deposit now in its SUPER savings account, paying 9% interest, in order to accumulate $5,000,000 four years from now for an addition to its manufacturing plant.

PV = ?   i = 9% $5,000,000

Now   1   2   3   4 years
                        n = 4

Answer: The present value factor from Table 3 is .70843 (4 periods at 9%). The present value of $5,000,000 to be received in 4 years discounted at 9% is **$3,542,150** ($5,000,000 × .70843).

PRESENT VALUE OF AN ANNUITY

The preceding discussion involved the discounting of only a single future amount. Businesses and individuals frequently engage in transactions in which a series of equal dollar amounts are to be received or paid periodically. Examples of a series of periodic receipts or payments are loan agreements, installment sales, mortgage notes, lease (rental) contracts, and pension obligations. These series of periodic receipts or payments are called **annuities.** In computing the present value of an annuity, it is necessary to know (1) the discount rate, (2) the number of discount periods, and (3) the amount of the periodic receipts or payments. To illustrate the computation of the present value of an annuity, assume that you will receive $1,000 cash annually for three years at a time when the discount rate is 10%. This situation is depicted in the time diagram in Illustration C-13.

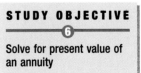

STUDY OBJECTIVE
⑥
Solve for present value of an annuity

Illustration C-13 Time diagram for a 3-year annuity

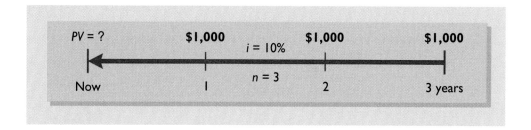

The present value in this situation may be computed as follows:

Illustration C-14
Present value of a series of future amounts computation

Future Amount	×	Present Value of 1 Factor at 10%	=	Present Value
$1,000 (One year away)		.90909		$ 909.09
1,000 (Two years away)		.82645		826.45
1,000 (Three years away)		.75132		751.32
		2.48686		**$2,486.86**

This method of calculation is required when the periodic cash flows are not uniform in each period. However, when the future receipts are the same in each period, there are two other ways to compute present value. First, the annual cash flow can be multiplied by the sum of the three present value factors. In the previous example, $1,000 × 2.48686 equals $2,486.86. Second, annuity tables may be used. As illustrated in Table 4 below, these tables show the present value of 1 to be received periodically for a given number of periods.

TABLE 4   Present Value of an Annuity of 1

(n) Periods	4%	5%	6%	8%	9%	10%	11%	12%	15%
1	.96154	.95238	.94340	.92593	.91743	.90909	.90090	.89286	.86957
2	1.88609	1.85941	1.83339	1.78326	1.75911	1.73554	1.71252	1.69005	1.62571
3	2.77509	2.72325	2.67301	2.57710	2.53130	2.48685	2.44371	2.40183	2.28323
4	3.62990	3.54595	3.46511	3.31213	3.23972	3.16986	3.10245	3.03735	2.85498
5	4.45182	4.32948	4.21236	3.99271	3.88965	3.79079	3.69590	3.60478	3.35216
6	5.24214	5.07569	4.91732	4.62288	4.48592	4.35526	4.23054	4.11141	3.78448
7	6.00205	5.78637	5.58238	5.20637	5.03295	4.86842	4.71220	4.56376	4.16042
8	6.73274	6.46321	6.20979	5.74664	5.53482	5.33493	5.14612	4.96764	4.48732
9	7.43533	7.10782	6.80169	6.24689	5.99525	5.75902	5.53705	5.32825	4.77158
10	8.11090	7.72173	7.36009	6.71008	6.41766	6.14457	5.88923	5.65022	5.01877
11	8.76048	8.30641	7.88687	7.13896	6.80519	6.49506	6.20652	5.93770	5.23371
12	9.38507	8.86325	8.38384	7.53608	7.16073	6.81369	6.49236	6.19437	5.42062
13	9.98565	9.39357	8.85268	7.90378	7.48690	7.10336	6.74987	6.42355	5.58315
14	10.56312	9.89864	9.29498	8.24424	7.78615	7.36669	6.98187	6.62817	5.72448
15	11.11839	10.37966	9.71225	8.55948	8.06069	7.60608	7.19087	6.81086	5.84737
16	11.65230	10.83777	10.10590	8.85137	8.31256	7.82371	7.37916	6.97399	5.95424
17	12.16567	11.27407	10.47726	9.12164	8.54363	8.02155	7.54879	7.11963	6.04716
18	12.65930	11.68959	10.82760	9.37189	8.75563	8.20141	7.70162	7.24967	6.12797
19	13.13394	12.08532	11.15812	9.60360	8.95012	8.36492	7.83929	7.36578	6.19823
20	13.59033	12.46221	11.46992	9.81815	9.12855	8.51356	7.96333	7.46944	6.25933

From Table 4 it can be seen that the present value of an annuity of 1 factor for three periods at 10% is 2.48685.[1] This present value factor is the total of the three individual present value factors as shown in Illustration C-14. Applying this amount to the annual cash flow of $1,000 produces a present value of $2,486.85.

The following demonstration problem (Illustration C-15) illustrates how to use Table 4.

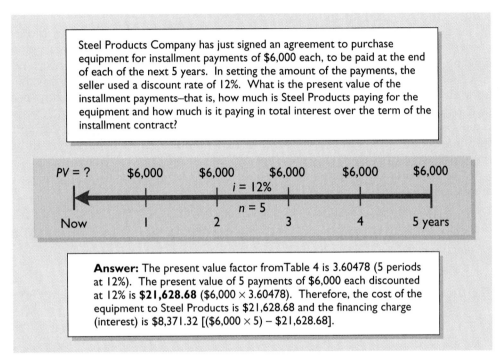

Illustration C-15
Demonstration Problem—
Using Table 4 for PV of an annuity of 1

TIME PERIODS AND DISCOUNTING

In the preceding calculations, the discounting has been done on an annual basis using an annual interest rate. Discounting may also be done over shorter periods of time such as monthly, quarterly, or semiannually. When the time frame is less than one year, it is necessary to convert the annual interest rate to the applicable time frame. Assume, for example, that the investor in Illustration C-14 received $500 **semiannually** for three years instead of $1,000 annually. In this case, the number of periods becomes 6 (3 × 2), the discount rate is 5% (10% ÷ 2), the present value factor from Table 4 is 5.07569, and the present value of the future cash flows is $2,537.86 (5.07569 × $500). This amount is slightly higher than the $2,486.86 computed in Illustration C-14 because interest is computed twice during the same year; therefore interest is earned on the first half year's interest.

---

[1]The difference of .00001 between 2.48686 and 2.48685 is due to rounding.

COMPUTING THE PRESENT VALUES IN A CAPITAL BUDGETING DECISION

STUDY OBJECTIVE

⑦

Compute the present values in capital budgeting situations.

The decision to make long-term capital investments is best evaluated using discounting techniques that recognize the time value of money, that is, the present value of the cash flows involved in a capital investment. The evaluation must reduce all cash inflows and outflows to a common comparable amount. That can be accomplished by either future valuing to some future date all the cash flows, or present valuing (discounting) to the present date all cash flows. While both are useful for evaluating the investment, the present value (discounting) technique is more appealing and universally used.

Nagel-Siebert Trucking Company, a cross-country freight carrier in Montgomery, Illinois, is considering adding another truck to its fleet because of a purchasing opportunity. Navistar Inc., Nagel-Siebert's primary supplier of overland rigs, is overstocked and offers to sell its biggest rig for $154,000 cash payable upon delivery. Nagel-Siebert knows that the rig will produce a net cash flow per year of $40,000 for five years (received at the end of each year), at which time it will be sold for an estimated salvage value of $35,000. Nagel-Siebert's discount rate in evaluating capital expenditures is 10%. Should Nagel-Siebert commit to the purchase of this rig?

The cash flows that must be discounted to present value by Nagel-Siebert are as follows:

Cash payable on delivery (now): $154,000.

Net cash flow from operating the rig: $40,000 for five years (at the end of each year).

Cash received from sale of rig at the end of five years: $35,000.

Illustration C-16 Time diagrams for Nagel-Siebert Trucking Company

The time diagrams for the latter two cash flows are shown in Illustration C-16.

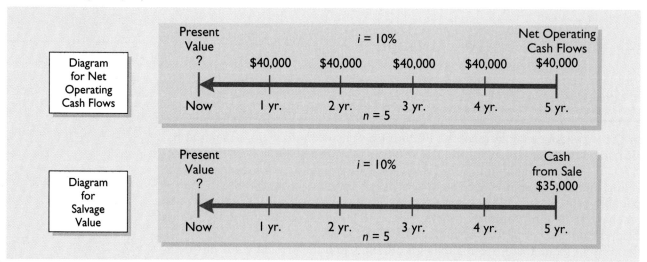

Notice from the diagrams that computing the present value of the net operating cash flows ($40,000 at the end of each year) is **discounting an annuity** (Table 4) while computing the present value of the $35,000 salvage value is **discounting a single sum** (Table 3).

The computation of these present values is shown in Illustration C-17.

Illustration C-17
Present value
computations at 10%

Present Values Using a 10% Discount Rate

Present value of net operating cash flows received annually
over five years:
  $40,000 × PV of 1 received annually for five years at 10%
  $40,000 × 3.79079 = $151,631.60
Present value of salvage value (cash) to be received in five years
  $35,000 × PV of 1 received in five years at 10%
  $35,000 × .62092 =   21,732.20
Present value of cash **inflows**   173,363.80
Present value cash **outflows** (purchase price due now at 10%):
  $154,000 × PV of 1 due now
  $154,000 × 1.00000 =   154,000.00
Net present value $ 19,363.80

Because the present value of the cash receipts (inflows) of $173,383.80
($151,631.60 + $21,732.20) exceeds the present value of the cash payments (outflows) of $154,000.00, the net present value of $19,363.80 is positive and **the decision to invest should be accepted.**

Now assume that Nagel-Siebert uses a discount rate of 15% not 10% because
it wants a greater return on its investments in capital assets. The cash receipts
and cash payments by Nagel-Siebert are the same. The present values of these
receipts and cash payments discounted at 15% are shown in Illustration C-18.

Illustration C-18
Present value
computations at 15%

Present Values Using a 15% Discount Rate

Present value of net operating cash flows received annually
over five years at 15%:
  $40,000 × 3.35216 $134,086.40
Present value of salvage value (cash) to be received in five years
at 15%
  $35,000 × .49718   17,401.30
Present value of cash **inflows**   151,487.70
Present value of cash **outflows** (purchase price due now at 15%):
  $154,000 × 1.00000   154,000.00
Net present value $ (2,512.30)

Because the present value of the cash payments (outflows) of $154,000 ex-
ceeds the present value of the cash receipts (inflows) of $151,487.70
($134,086.40 + $17,401.30), the net present value of $2,512.30 is negative and
the investment should be rejected.

The above discussion relied on present value tables in solving present value
problems. Electronic hand-held calculators may also be used to compute present values without the use of these tables. Some calculators, especially the "business" or "MBA" type calculators, have present value (PV) functions that allow
you to calculate present values by merely identifying the proper amount, discount rate, periods, and pressing the PV key.

SUMMARY OF STUDY OBJECTIVES

❶ Distinguish between simple and compound interest. Simple interest is computed on the principal only while compound interest is computed on the principal and any interest earned that has not been withdrawn.

❷ Solve for future value of a single amount. Prepare a time diagram of the problem. Identify the principal amount, the number of compounding periods, and the interest rate. Using the future value of 1 table, multiply the principal amount by the future value factor specified at the intersection of the number of periods and the interest rate.

❸ Solve for future value of an annuity. Prepare a time diagram of the problem. Identify the amount of the periodic payments, the number of compounding periods, and the interest rate. Using the future value of an annuity of 1 table, multiply the amount of the payments by the future value factor specified at the intersection of the number of periods and the interest rate.

❹ Identify the variables fundamental to solving present value problems. The following three variables are fundamental to solving present value problems: (1) the future amount, (2) the number of periods, and (3) the interest rate (the discount rate).

❺ Solve for present value of a single amount. Prepare a time diagram of the problem. Identify the future amount, the number of discounting periods, and the discount (interest) rate. Using the present value of 1 table, multiply the future amount by the present value factor specified at the intersection of the number of periods and the discount rate.

❻ Solve for present value of an annuity. Prepare a time diagram of the problem. Identify the future amounts (annuities), the number of discounting periods, and the discount (interest) rate. Using the present value of an annuity of 1 table, multiply the amount of the annuity by the present value factor specified at the intersection of the number of periods and the interest rate.

❼ Compute the present values in capital budgeting situations. Compute the present values of all cash inflows and all cash outflows related to the capital budgeting proposal (an investment-type decision). If the **net** present value is positive, accept the proposal (make the investment). If the **net** present value is negative, reject the proposal (do not make the investment).

GLOSSARY

Annuity   A series of equal dollar amounts to be paid or received periodically. (p. C-5)

Compound interest   The interest computed on the principal and any interest earned that has not been paid or received. (p. C-2)

Discounting the future amount(s)   The process of determining present value. (p. C-8)

Future value of a single amount   The value at a future date of a given amount invested assuming compound interest. (p. C-3)

Future value of an annuity   The sum of all the payments or receipts plus the accumulated compound interest on them. (p. C-5)

Interest   Payment for the use of another's money. (p. C-2)

Present value   The value now of a given amount to be invested or received in the future assuming compound interest. (p. C-8)

Present value of an annuity   A series of future receipts or payments discounted to their value now assuming compound interest. (p. C-11)

Principal   The amount borrowed or invested. (p. C-2).

Simple interest   The interest computed on the principal only. (p. C-2)

BRIEF EXERCISES
(USE TABLES TO SOLVE EXERCISES)

Compute the future value of a single amount.

(SO 2)

BEC-1   Don Smith invested $5,000 at 6% annual interest, and left the money invested without withdrawing any of the interest for 10 years. At the end of the 10 years, Don withdrew the accumulated amount of money. (a) What amount did Don withdraw assuming the investment earns simple interest? (b) What amount did Don withdraw assuming the investment earns interest compounded annually?

BEC-2 For each of the following cases, indicate (a) to what interest rate columns and (b) to what number of periods you would refer in looking up the future value factor.

1. In Table 1 (future value of 1):

	Annual Rate	Number of Years Invested	Compounded
(a)	6%	5	Annually
(b)	5%	3	Semiannually

2. In Table 2 (future value of an annuity of 1):

	Annual Rate	Number of Years Invested	Compounded
(a)	5%	10	Annually
(b)	4%	6	Semiannually

BEC-3 Porter Company signed a lease for an office building for a period of 10 years. Under the lease agreement, a security deposit of $10,000 is made. The deposit will be returned at the expiration of the lease with interest compounded at 5% per year. What amount will Porter receive at the time the lease expires?

BEC-4 Gordon Company issued $1,000,000, 10-year bonds and agreed to make annual sinking fund deposits of $80,000. The deposits are made at the end of each year into an account paying 5% annual interest. What amount will be in the sinking fund at the end of 10 years?

BEC-5 David and Kathy Hatcher invested $5,000 in a savings account paying 6% annual interest when their daughter, Sue, was born. They also deposited $1,000 on each of her birthdays until she was 18 (including her 18th birthday). How much will be in the savings account on her 18th birthday (after the last deposit)?

BEC-6 Ron Watson borrowed $20,000 on July 1, 1996. This amount plus accrued interest at 6% compounded annually is to be repaid on July 1, 2001. How much will Ron have to repay on July 1, 2001?

BEC-7 For each of the following cases, indicate (a) to what interest rate columns and (b) to what number of periods you would refer in looking up the discount rate.

1. In Table 3 (present value of 1):

	Annual Rate	Number of Years Involved	Discounts Per Year
(a)	12%	6	Annually
(b)	10%	15	Annually
(c)	8%	8	Semiannually

2. In Table 4 (present value of an annuity of 1):

	Annual Rate	Number of Years Involved	Number of Payments Involved	Frequency of Payments
(a)	12%	20	20	Annually
(b)	10%	5	5	Annually
(c)	8%	4	8	Semiannually

BEC-8 (a) What is the present value of $10,000 due 8 periods from now, discounted at 8%? (b) What is the present value of $10,000 to be received at the end of each of 6 periods, discounted at 9%?

BEC-9 Smolinski Company is considering an investment which will return a lump sum of $500,000 five years from now. What amount should Smolinski Company pay for this investment to earn a 15% return?

BEC-10 Pizzeria Company earns 11% on an investment that will return $875,000 eight years from now. What is the amount Pizzeria should invest now to earn this rate of return?

Compute the present value of an annuity investment.

(SO 6)

BEC-11 Kilarny Company is considering investing in an annuity contract that will return $20,000 annually at the end of each year for 15 years. What amount should Kilarny Company pay for this investment if it earns a 6% return?

Compute the present value of an annuity investment.

(SO 6)

BEC-12 Zarita Enterprises earns 11% on an investment that pays back $110,000 at the end of each of the next four years. What is the amount Zarita Enterprises invested to earn the 11% rate of return?

Compute the present value of bonds.

(SO 5, 6)

BEC-13 Hernandez Railroad Co. is about to issue $100,000 of 10-year bonds paying a 12% interest rate, with interest payable semiannually. The discount rate for such securities is 10%. How much can Hernandez expect to receive for the sale of these bonds?

Compute the present value of bonds.

(SO 5, 6)

BEC-14 Assume the same information as BEC-13 except that the discount rate was 12% instead of 10%. In this case, how much can Hernandez expect to receive from the sale of these bonds?

Compute the present value of a note.

(SO 5, 6)

BEC-15 Caledonian Taco Company receives a $50,000, 6-year note bearing interest of 11% (paid annually) from a customer at a time when the discount rate is 12%. What is the present value of the note received by Caledonian?

Compute the present value of bonds.

(SO 5, 6)

BEC-16 Galway Bay Enterprises issued 10%, 8-year, $2,000,000 par value bonds that pay interest semiannually on October 1 and April 1. The bonds are dated April 1, 1998, and are issued on that date. The discount rate of interest for such bonds on April 1, 1998, is 12%. What cash proceeds did Galway Bay receive from issuance of the bonds?

Compute the present value of a machine for purposes of making a purchase decision.

(SO 7)

BEC-17 Barney Googal owns a garage and is contemplating purchasing a tire retreading machine for $16,280. After estimating costs and revenues, Barney projects a net cash flow from the retreading machine of $2,790 annually for 8 years. Barney hopes to earn a return of 11% on such investments. What is the present value of the retreading operation? Should Barney Googal purchase the retreading machine?

Compute the present value of a note.

(SO 5, 6)

BEC-18 Hung-Chao Yu Company issues a 10%, 6-year mortgage note on January 1, 1998 to obtain financing for new equipment. Land is used as collateral for the note. The terms provide for semiannual installment payments of $112,825. What were the cash proceeds received from the issuance of the note?

Compute the maximum price to pay for a machine.

(SO 7)

BEC-19 Ramos Company is considering purchasing equipment. The equipment will produce the following cash flows: Year 1, $30,000; Year 2, $40,000; Year 3, $50,000. Ramos requires a minimum rate of return of 15%. What is the maximum price Ramos should pay for this eqipment?

Compute the interest rate on a single amount.

(SO 5)

BEC-20 Kerry Rodriquez invests $1,827 now and will receive $10,000 at the end of 15 years. What annual rate of interest will Kerry earn on her investment? (Hint: Use Table 3.)

Compute the number of periods of a single amount.

(SO 5)

BEC-21 Maloney Cork has been offered the opportunity of investing $24,719 now. The investment will earn 15% per year and will at the end of that time return Maloney $100,000. How many years must Maloney wait to receive $100,000? (Hint: Use Table 3.)

Compute the interest rate on an annuity.

(SO 6)

BEC-22 Annie Dublin purchased an investment for $11,469.92. From this investment, she will receive $1,000 annually for the next 20 years starting one year from now. What rate of interest will Annie's investment be earning for her? (Hint: Use Table 4.)

Compute the number of periods of an annuity.

(SO 6)

BEC-23 Andy Sanchez invests $8,851.37 now for a series of $1,000 annual returns beginning one year from now. Andy will earn a return of 8% on the initial investment. How many annual payments of $1,000 will Andy receive? (Hint: Use Table 4.)

Standards of Ethical Conduct for Management Accountants

Management accountants have an obligation to the organizations they serve, their profession, the public, and themselves to maintain the highest standards of ethical conduct. In recognition of this obligation, the Institute of Management Accountants, formerly the National Association of Accountants, has published and promoted the following standards of ethical conduct for management accountants. Adherence to these standards is integral to achieving the *Objectives of Management Accounting.*[1] Management accountants shall not commit acts contrary to these standards nor shall they condone the commission of such acts by others within their organizations.

COMPETENCE

Management accountants have a responsibility to:

- Maintain an appropriate level of professional competence by ongoing development of their knowledge and skills.
- Perform their professional duties in accordance with relevant laws, regulations, and technical standards.
- Prepare complete and clear reports and recommendations after appropriate analyses of relevant and reliable information.

CONFIDENTIALITY

Management accountants have a responsibility to:

- Refrain from disclosing confidential information acquired in the course of their work except when authorized, unless legally obligated to do so.
- Inform subordinates as appropriate regarding the confidentiality of information acquired in the course of their work and monitor their activities to assure the maintenance of that confidentiality.

---

[1]Institute of Management Accountants, formerly National Association of Accountants, *Statements on Management Accounting: Objectives of Management Accounting*, Statement No. 1B, June 17, 1982.

- Refrain from using or appearing to use confidential information acquired in the course of their work for unethical or illegal advantage either personally or through third parties.

*I*NTEGRITY

Management accountants have a responsibility to:

- Avoid actual or apparent conflicts of interest and advise all appropriate parties of any potential conflict.
- Refrain from engaging in any activity that would prejudice their ability to carry out their duties ethically.
- Refuse any gift, favor, or hospitality that would influence or would appear to influence their actions.
- Refrain from either actively or passively subverting the attainment of the organization's legitimate and ethical objectives.
- Recognize and communicate professional limitations or other constraints that would preclude responsible judgment or successful performance of an activity.
- Communicate unfavorable as well as favorable information and professional judgments or opinions.
- Refrain from engaging in or supporting any activity that would discredit the profession.

*O*BJECTIVITY

Management accountants have a responsibility to:

- Communicate information fairly and objectively.
- Disclose fully all relevant information that could reasonably be expected to influence an intended user's understanding of the reports, comments, and recommendations presented.

On the World Wide Web
Institute of Management Accountants:
www.rutgers.edu/Accounting/raw/ima

COMPANY INDEX

SUBJECT INDEX

Chapter 1
Page 3: David Epperson/Tony Stone Images/New York, Inc. Page 6: Jorgen Vogt/The Image Bank. Page 9: Brownie Harris/The Stock Market. Page 9: Steve Dunwell/The Image Bank. Page 17: Will McIntyre/Photo Researchers. Page 18: Eric Kamp/Index Stock. Page 41: Courtesy Anchor Glass Container Corp.

Chapter 2
Page 45: Kathi Lamm/Tony Stone Images/New York, Inc. Page 48: David Plowden/Photo Researchers. Page 52: Courtesy Federal Express Corporation. Reproduced with permission. Page 56: Andy Zito/The Image Bank. Page 64: Bob Daemmrich/The Image Works. Page 83: Courtesy Parlex Corporation.

Chapter 3
Page 87: Peter McArthur/Tony Stone Images/New York, Inc. Page 93: Rick Altman/The Stock Market. Page 120: Courtesy General Microwave.

Chapter 4
Page 125: Courtesy Super Donut. Page 133: Jeff Zaruba/The Stock Market. Page 136: ©PhotoDisc. Page 142: Nick Vedros, Vedros & Associates/Tony Stone Images/New York, Inc.

Chapter 5
Page 171: Simon Norfolk/Tony Stone Images/New York, Inc. Page 181: Reza Estakhrian/Tony Stone Images/New York, Inc. Page 186: Yael/Retna.

Chapter 6
Page 211: Courtesy University of Nebraska. Page 213: Gary Conner/Index Stock. Page 219: Peter Zeray/Photonica. Page 220: Peter Vadnai/The Stock Market. Page 224: Larry Gilpin/Tony Stone Images/New York, Inc. Page 228: Rosanne Olson/Tony Stone Images/New York, Inc. Page 230: David Blum/Pixel Studios/The Stock Market. Page 247: Courtesy Network Computing Devices, Inc.

Chapter 7
Pages 253 and 266: ©Comstock, Inc.

Chapter 8
Page 299: Dick Luria/FPG International. Page 302: SUPERSTOCK. Page 305: Naideau/The Stock Market. Page 310: Michel Tchervkoff/The Image Bank. Page 313: Courtesy United Parcel Service. Page 339: Courtesy Glassmaster Company.

Chapter 9
Page 343: Gary Gladstone/The Image Bank. Page 349: Bob Thomason/Tony Stone Images/New York, Inc. Page 352: William Tautic/The Stock Market. Page 356: ©PhotoDisc. Page 357: Mitch Kezar/Tony Stone Images/New York, Inc.

Chapter 10
Page 375: Pat Lacroix/The Image Bank. Page 377: Chris Thomaidis/Tony Stone Images/New York, Inc. Page 389: Tim Jonke/The Image Bank.

Chapter 11
Page 411: Wolfgang Kaehler/Corbis. Page 415: Lance Nelson/The Stock Market. Page 418: Dick Luria/FPG International. Page 447: Rob Atkins/The Image Bank. Page 452: Index Stock. Pages 453 and 454: Courtesy Intel. Page 474: Courtesy Vermont Teddy Bear Co. Page 476: Courtesy PraxAir, Inc.

Chapter 12
Page 481: Jeanne Strongin. Page 486: Rob Nelson/Black Star. Pages 491, 493, 506, and 511: Courtesy Kellogg Company. Page 496: Nora Good/Masterfile. Page 498: Courtesy J.C. Penney. Page 508: Eric Sander/Gamma Liaison. Pages 537 and 538: Courtesy Sears, Roebuck and Co.